Backward Areas in Advanced Countries

Other International Economic Association symposia

Backward Areas in Advanced Countries

Proceedings of a Conference held by
the International Economic Association

EDITED BY E. A. G. ROBINSON

MACMILLAN · London · Melbourne · Toronto
ST MARTIN'S PRESS · New York
1969

© *The International Economic Association 1969*

Published by
MACMILLAN AND CO LTD
Little Essex Street London WC2
and also at Bombay Calcutta and Madras
Macmillan South Africa (Publishers) Pty Ltd Johannesburg
The Macmillan Company of Australia Pty Ltd Melbourne
The Macmillan Company of Canada Ltd Toronto
St Martin's Press Inc New York
Gill and Macmillan Ltd Dublin

Library of Congress catalog card no. 69–13691

Printed in Great Britain by
R. & R. CLARK LTD
Edinburgh

Contents

Acknowledgements

The International Economic Association wishes to express once again its gratitude to the two bodies without which the work of this conference and all its other activities would be impossible – UNESCO as its earliest sponsor and the Ford Foundation as a major source of its income. Their help and moral support goes far beyond assistance in meeting its budgetary needs. On this occasion, as is explained in the Introduction, the conference reported in this volume was held jointly with the European Centre for the Co-ordination of Research and Documentation in Vienna – itself a protégé of UNESCO's International Social Science Council. The Centre, through M. Raynaud and Professor Turčan, played a large part in the initial planning of the conference and we were conscious of benefiting by earlier work which the Centre had initiated. The conference was held in most beautiful surroundings at the Villa Monastero on the shore of Lake Como. We enjoyed the hospitality of the Royal Victoria Hotel. To the authorities of both we owe many happy memories.

List of Participants

Professor A. A. Arakelyan, Institute of Economics, Armenian Soviet Socialist Republic, U.S.S.R.

Professor Edwin von Böventer, University of Heidelberg, Federal German Republic.

Professor Erik Bylund, Umeå University, Sweden.

Mr G. C. Cameron, University of Glasgow, U.K.

Professor Louis E. Davin, Université de Liège, Belgium.

Professor D. Delivanis, University of Thessalonika, Greece.

Mr Olof Ersson, Umeå University, Sweden.

Professor Luc Fauvel, Université de Paris, France.

Professor S. Groenman, Sociologisch Instituut van de Rijksuniversiteit, Utrecht, Netherlands.

Professor D. C. Hague, University of Manchester, U.K.

Professor E. M. Hoover, University of Pittsburgh, Pa., U.S.A.

Professor E. James, Université de Paris, France.

Dr L. Köszegi, Central Planning Office, Budapest, Hungary.

Professor J. Lajugie, Université de Bordeaux, France.

Professor Erik Lundberg, University of Stockholm, Sweden.

Dr R. G. L. McCrone, Brasenose College, Oxford, U.K.

Mr M. C. MacLennan, University of Glasgow, U.K.

Professor Jean Marchal, Université de Paris, France.

Dr V. A. Marsan, Istituto per la Ricostruzione Industriale, Rome.

Professor K. Mihailović, Institut Économique de la République Fédérale de Serbie, Belgrade, Yugoslavia.

Professor A. Nussbaumer, University of Vienna, Austria.

Professor F. Oelssner, Nationalkomitee für Wirtschaftswissenschaften bei der Deutschen Akademie der Wissenschaften, Berlin, German Democratic Republic.

Professor G. U. Papi, University of Rome, Italy.

Professor D. Patinkin, The Hebrew University, Jerusalem, Israel.

Professor M. Penouil, Université de Bordeaux, France.

Mr R. Petrella-Tirone, European Centre for the Coordination of Research and Documentation in Social Sciences, Vienna, Austria.

Professor K. N. Plotnikov, Association of Soviet Economic Scientific Institutions, Moscow, U.S.S.R.

Mr Edgar Raynaud, European Centre for the Coordination of Research and Documentation in Social Sciences, Vienna, Austria.

Professor D. J. Robertson, University of Glasgow, U.K.

Professor E. A. G. Robinson, University of Cambridge, U.K.

Professor Paul A. Samuelson, Massachusetts Institute of Technology, Cambridge, Mass., U.S.A.

Dr K. Schmidt-Lüders, O.E.C.D., Paris.

Professor O. Šik, Institute of Economics of the Czechoslovak Academy of Sciences, Prague, Czechoslovakia.

Mr M. D. Smyslov, European Centre for the Coordination of Research and Documentation in Social Sciences, Vienna, Austria.

Professor N. V. Sovani, U.N. Research Institute for Social Development, Palais des Nations, Geneva, Switzerland.

Professor Pavel Turčan, Economic Institute, Bratislava, Czechoslovakia.

Professor Imre Vajda, Hungarian Economic Association, Budapest, Hungary.

Professor Jean Valarché, University of Fribourg, Switzerland.

Professor Francesco Vito, Università Cattolica del S. Cuore, Milan, Italy.

Professor B. Winiarski, Wyższa Szkoła Ekonomiczna, Wrocław, Poland.

Mr Gösta Weissglas, Umeå University, Sweden.

Introduction

When some few years back the European Centre for the Co-ordination of Research and Documentation in the Social Sciences was being planned in Vienna under the aegis of UNESCO and its International Social Science Council, those of us who were then made responsible for its administration reached the conclusion that it could make its best contribution to work in the social sciences by identifying from time to time major problems on which research is taking place in a number of institutes in a variety of European countries, and providing facilities for the co-ordination of the research and the exchange of ideas and material between the different institutes concerned. Among the first group of topics that we selected for such work was that of the 'Backward Areas' in the various European countries – a subject proposed initially by Professor Groenman, of the Sociological Institute of the University of Utrecht, and myself and enthusiastically supported by Dr Arzumanian of the Moscow Institute of World Economics.

From 1963 onwards a group of institutes from almost a dozen European countries have been working in touch with each other on different aspects of the problems of backward areas, and representatives have met on several occasions, with the help of the Vienna Centre, for the exchange of ideas. By 1967 the work had reached a stage at which there was obvious benefit to be derived from a wider discussion of the issues involved with economists who have studied these problems in some of the other countries of Europe and in other parts of the world. To make this possible, the Vienna Centre agreed with the International Economic Association to hold a joint conference, taking the form of one of the annual conferences of the latter body. Thus at the Varenna Conference we had the advantage of all the earlier work of the Vienna Centre, which had included Austria, Belgium, Bulgaria, Czechoslovakia, France, Italy, the Netherlands, Poland, Sweden, the United Kingdom and Yugoslavia; we were able at the same time to benefit from being able to draw on experience of the U.S.A., the U.S.S.R., and West Germany in papers prepared for the conference, and more generally in our discussions on knowledge of still other countries possessed by participants.

The first thing that impressed itself on all of us was the universality of this problem. There was no country represented in our conference and none known to any of us which could claim that it had no backward area. The Appalachian region of the United States, the Uzbek Republic of the U.S.S.R., the Mezzogiorno of Italy, the Slovak region of Czechoslovakia, the Montenegran region of Yugoslavia, the south-west of France present

A 2

problems as difficult and recalcitrant as those of the Scottish Highlands, of Northern Ireland or Wales that are so familiar to all my own countrymen. These problem areas exist in every type of country from the richest to the poorest, from the most perfectly socialist to the most *laissez-faire*. There are naturally differences of opinion as to what type of economy is most likely to help best to solve these problems and as to the best policies for doing it. But many of the basic problems transcend economic systems.

One must begin inevitably by trying to define a backward area. Different countries have used slightly different definitions. Typical definitions would fasten on the ratio of regional unemployment to average national unemployment, of regional income per head to average income per head, and regional equipment with the infrastructure of a modern economy to the average for the country as a whole. It was possible – one realised – to produce paradoxical results from a too logical application of a rigid system of definition; the conference did not take very seriously the problems of California which, as the result of an excessive inflow of migrants, could from time to time qualify as a 'backward area' by the definition of unemployment. Without being unduly pragmatic, we were satisfied that 'backwardness' was a real and identifiable phenomenon.

How then had 'backwardness' come about? In some cases it was a backwardness of a basically agricultural region. As population had grown during earlier centuries, extensive small-scale agriculture, with low productivity per head, had spread progressively over the whole area of a country, covering inferior as well as good land, and had yielded incomes which, by the standards of the time, were marginally acceptable. In this century, with growing agricultural population, but still more with the growth of industrial productivity and increasing standards of life, the levels of real income yielded by such methods on marginal land had ceased to be acceptable. At the same time the improvements of productivity in agriculture had principally benefited the high-yielding inframarginal lands; the growth of their productivity, and the growth also of international trade in agricultural products, had meant that agricultural prices generally had not risen sufficiently to bring to these marginal areas the rise of incomes that was being enjoyed by the rest of the population. The incomes yielded by such an agricultural life had ceased to be those which would satisfy the aspirations of the younger generation of inhabitants of the area or the conscience of the government of the country.

Quite apart from the effects of progress on the areas of marginal agriculture, however, the movement of population out of agriculture and into industry, as the result of technical progress in both, often meant a geographical movement also, towards industrial natural resources and locations suitable for industrial processes, but more remote from much of agriculture. These movements had their repercussions on all the other activities of the community. The towns of any mature European country

had grown up primarily in relation to the needs of predominantly agricultural populations. As these agricultural populations declined in number and purchasing power, so also the town populations that provided
services to them declined in relative income and prosperity. This multiplier effect was most noticeable in the areas of marginal agriculture. But
it existed also in the areas of comparatively prosperous agriculture, if
little local industrial development was taking place.

Apart from the problems of these areas of economic backwardness –
areas which, as Professor Vito reminded us, had never been industrially
developed – there were also backward areas of another sort: the areas
which had been developed in the early phases of the industrial revolution
and which had subsequently declined. In some instances the early
development had been based – as in many cases in the United Kingdom –
on mining of coal or ores which had now been exhausted. In other
instances the industries which had formed the basis of the early development have, during the subsequent one or two centuries, so greatly changed
in character, as the result of technical progress, or in geographical location – often as the result of the growing industrial capacities of other
developing nations – that the basic industry of a region has declined.
Examples of such declines can be discovered in relation to almost all the
main industries which developed early in the industrial revolution. In my
own country, the areas of early exploitation of the coal industry, of the
iron and steel industry, of the textile industries spring readily to mind. In
France, in Belgium, in Germany, in Italy, in the United States there are
numerous other examples. The problems of these areas, if they are to
survive, are problems of revitalisation. In one sense these areas are already
more than half developed; they possess many of the resources of infrastructure that are necessary for any new activity – the housing and city
services, the power supplies, the transport facilities and the like. In
another sense they suffer from grave handicaps: the wreckage of obsolete
industries; the clutter of valuable sites by derelict buildings which it is
costly to acquire, clear and remove; urban layouts which are suitable to
Victorian small-scale industries and ill-suited either to modern large-scale
industry or to modern ideas of housing development: their whole image
needs to be changed and modernised.

How then do we tackle these problems of initial development of a
region in the first case, of revitalisation in the second case? Is this a
matter that should at all concern a government and require specific action
by it? Is it a matter in which a government should do no more than promote a general environment of activity and expansion on a national scale
but do nothing more specific on a regional scale? There were those at the
conference, particularly among our American participants, who would
argue for the latter policy.

If others among us were inclined to support a more active policy and to seek to justify it on economic grounds, it was for one or other of three reasons. First, it is by no means clear in a capitalist country that an entrepreneur, in making his decision about the location of a new activity, will take into account all the considerations which from a national point of view are relevant to the optimum resource use. It will be a matter of no direct concern to him, in the capacity of a person maximising his own private profit, whether his action will minimise investment in social capital and make the best use of existing, and still potentially usable, social capital.

In advancing this argument, it is necessary to be scrupulously careful not to push it too far. At any time new social capital has to be constructed to meet the needs of a growing population; old social capital has to be replaced as it becomes worn out. There is no case for replacing it where it happens to have been in the past rather than in some other place where it can better serve the future. The argument is valid only if it permits continued use of social capital which is not time-expired and which would otherwise be underutilised. It is sometimes for debate whether a nation would or would not have in any case to be rehousing large numbers of people and rebuilding large proportions of its older cities; if it is necessary to rehouse them, they should be rehoused where their services can most economically be employed.

Second, and in part as a consequence of the same difference of attitude to costs other than those directly borne by the decision-making undertaking, there may be excessive concentration in a few poles of growth, beyond the point where there are increasing costs from over-concentration imposed on other undertakings and other residents in the overgrown urban area concerned, by a decision to locate another enterprise in it. In terms of European problems, some disquiet was expressed about the recent trends of development which seemed to be emerging from the Common Market: increased concentration of activity in a small number of poles of growth which seemed to be in danger of growing to excessive size, when the implications for social standards and social capital requirements were taken into account; and at the same time increased difficulty in maintaining activity and employment in other regions.

The third justification for a more active policy raises issues beyond the limits of economics narrowly defined, but issues which are germane to economics and which require to be discussed in economic terms. The problems of the optimum resource-use of a nation can best be solved by mobility. There may be exceptions, such as have been discussed in the last few paragraphs, to the proposition that the perfectly free choice of the entrepreneur will always achieve optimum resource-use, as measured from a national standpoint. But, apart from such exceptions, the greater the mobility, the better the resource-use and the higher the real income per head.

When we came to look at the actual problems of backward areas, however, we became more than ever conscious of the difficulties of assuming categorically that all problems should be solved by mobility. The chief reason for this is that scarcely a single one of the nations that we were considering was a single homogeneous nation, in which people were indifferent to which region they lived in. It was interesting that the advocacy for solving problems by free mobility was most vigorous among our American colleagues, who clearly regarded the United States as a single unitary system, cultural and social as well as economic. In almost all other cases, the reasons for reluctance to accept a solution based on mobility were cultural and political as well as economic. Few or none of the European nations are truly homogeneous; almost all are in fact, if not in political structure, federations of nations that have at some time been separate. It is not completely a matter of indifference to the Welshman or the Scot or the Northern Irish whether their problems of unemployment are solved in their own countries or in England. It is not a matter of indifference to the inhabitants of Southern Italy or Sicily whether jobs are created in Milan and Turin or in Naples and Catania. It is not a matter of indifference to the people of the Slovak areas of Czechoslovakia or the Montenegran or Macedonian areas of Yugoslavia where employment is created. The same is equally true of regions in France, in Belgium, in Germany. In all these cases there is some mobility; in a few cases much mobility. But there is a large minority which is extremely reluctant to move and to leave the cultural environment which it loves and values. Nor is such an attitude wholly unknown in the United States; the problems of the Appalachian area or of Northern Michigan spring in large measure from a very similar reluctance to move from an area, however impoverished.

If this is indeed the case, three economic implications are obvious. First, on the basis of diminished mobility, the productivity of the nation will be less than it could have been with greater mobility. Second, if the mobility will not in fact take place, optimum resource-use will only be achieved if some way is found of creating employment for people where they will in fact be living. Third, and most important, if one is not able to assume mobility, the model of thought that one must apply to the problems of economic analysis of a region is that of international trade theory rather than that of the analysis of a single economy. If Welshmen employed in Wales, or Slovaks employed in Slovakia, are less productive than their compatriots employed in Birmingham or Prague, they must, if a balance of payments is to be secured between Wales or Slovakia and the rest of the world, accept a level of regional real incomes which will enable Wales or Slovakia to attract those industries in which they may have the greatest comparative advantage.

While it is proper, as it seems to me, for an economist to emphasise the loss of national productivity which may come from reluctance to accept perfect mobility, it is also proper that, having done so, he should be prepared to analyse the problems of a world of imperfect mobility, in which, confronted by the choice between higher incomes outside a congenial cultural community and lower incomes inside it, people have deliberately chosen to accept the less affluent but more congenial solution.

I know of no quantitative study of the differences to national productivity which may be made by good and bad location decisions, though from evidence of transport costs one may guess at them. There are some activities, particularly in relation to the metallurgical industries, in which the differences are so great that reasonable differences of regional incomes could almost certainly not offset them. For a good many other activities, differences of transport costs are not so great that an appropriate wage differential could not make them economic.

If a solution of the regional problem is to be found otherwise than on the basis of perfect mobility, one precondition, I am convinced, is that which is implicit in what I have just argued: that relative regional real incomes must be able to vary from time to time, as may be necessary in the light of the rise or decay of regional activities and the need to attract new activities. One of the most serious obstacles to the implementation of regional policies in many European countries has been the recent tendency to negotiate national rather than regional wage agreements. To take only a single case, the recent standardisation of coal-miners' wages by the British National Coal Board has aggravated the problems of maintaining employment in the more depressed areas of South Wales, Durham and Scotland.

If an attempt is to be made to solve the regional problems of employment partly, at least, on the basis of bringing work to the workers, there is one interesting and important lesson from Italian experience which has to be borne in mind. One can have too much mobility as well as too little. There has been so much mobility from Southern to Northern Italy that the age-mix of the remaining population, as well as the proportion of persons with technical and administrative skills, has become such that it is far from easy to set up a new and adequately staffed enterprise. This phenomenon has been encountered on earlier occasions in a more limited context in decaying mining areas in other countries. The moral that the Italian experts derive from their experience is that one should make up one's mind comparatively early whether one intends to deal with a problem partly by revitalisation of the area. If one does, one should bring in the new activities before the decay of a region has gone so far that it is irreversible and the region condemned to a lingering death.

But even on the basis of a willingness to accept a lower real income rather than move, not all problems of the regeneration of a backward region are soluble. There are areas so remote and so ill-endowed with any resources other than those of a primitive and marginal agriculture that, save at formidable and unacceptable cost in subsidy, they cannot be made to provide employment. Among such areas, one fears, are not only parts of the Scottish Highlands, but also parts of the Italian Mezzogiorno, parts of Uzbekistan, and parts of Sweden remote from coastal transport.

One of the clearest lessons of the experience of attempts to regenerate backward areas in the past twenty years has been the failure of such attempts where they have been directed to small-scale projects, intended to help local communities. Not only the Italian, but also the Belgian, the Swedish and the Russian experience had been so clear in this respect that, to use Professor Davin's colourful expression, the 'peppering' of a backward area with large numbers of small projects has come to be regarded as a recipe for failure. It is interesting but sad that British as well as American practice is notably backward in this respect.

The implications have been two. First, if one is to define a backward area for purposes of redevelopment it should be defined widely enough to include within the area of permissible special action the places that can reasonably be regarded as potential growth points. If, reverting to an earlier discussion, it is one's objective to redevelop an area which belongs, and wishes to continue to belong, to a given cultural community, one should seek to find the best potential growth points within that cultural area. In too many cases, development areas have, for penny-wise fiscal reasons, been drawn too narrowly to include some of the best potential growth points.

Second, one must try to get clear what constitutes the minimum practical size of an effective growth point. Our concern with this issue took us, as the papers and record of the discussions will show, into a series of fascinating problems concerned with the success or failure of growth points and the relation of complementarity of activities to such success. Professor Penouil, in one of the most interesting papers presented to the conference, helped us to look at the effects of the French natural gas discoveries at Lacq in South-Western France and their repercussions on the economy of Aquitaine. While high hopes had initially been held out, they were in fact largely disappointed, and the reason is not far to seek. The investment in very sophisticated plant had only a small local component. The local operating costs were small as compared with total operating costs. The highly paid expert staff spent their incomes largely on goods imported from Paris and the industrial regions of Northern France. At every stage the 'leaks' of the investment expenditure and the operating expenditure were high, the local expenditure low and the local multiplier low. The same problems had occurred, in rather different degree, in relation to the development of the Italian Mezzogiorno, where again the 'leaks' of expenditure into Northern Italy had been inflationary there rather than successful in curing unemployment in the South.

If one tries to think analytically about these issues, it is at once clear that, in order to create a successful growth point, one needs to think in terms of threshold scale-effects. One needs also to think in terms of a 'big-push', on a scale large enough for the local multiplier to be high, and in terms, in respect of activities, such that it can continue to be high. If one creates a new activity, such as better educational services or better medical services for the local population, which increases local incomes and local expenditures on imports into the region without increasing the exports of the region to the rest of the world, one creates an increased deficit in the regional balance of payments and one does little or nothing directly to help self-sustained future growth, even if one is doing something indirectly.

It is one of the basic difficulties of most declining areas that the industries which have been decaying in them have in the past been 'exporting' industries – exporting in many cases to world markets, in other cases to the rest of a national market. On the basis of these 'exporting' industries, the region has built up a dependence on imports from the rest of the economy. But with this structure, and without these exporting industries, local expenditures do not generate enough local income, cycle by cycle, to maintain local activity. Without them the local level of activity declines to a point where the gap in the balance of payments is covered by capital movements and by the net excess of national government expenditures in the region over government revenues from the region. The first necessity is to find new 'exporting' activities for the region, which will permit self-sustained growth. A successful growth point will almost certainly include a substantial element of 'exporting' activity.

How large must a successful growth point be? An I.E.A. Conference is not a body concerned with reaching international agreements and administrative decisions, but I think the general sense of our discussions was that the minimum size of growth point that experience had shown to be successful was nearer to a population of 100,000 than to one of 10,000, and that even 100,000 was more likely to be an underestimate than an over-estimate. It must be large enough to provide efficiently the main services of education, medical facilities, banking, shopping facilities. With the region that it is to serve, it must be large enough to provide a market for small-scale industries, for market-garden produce. Above all, it must be large enough both to provide an efficient infrastructure of public utility services, and to permit the early and progressive growth of external economies for its local industries. If, once again, we looked at the experience of Italy, it was in Naples, Taranto, Bari, Catania, Palermo, rather than in the smaller towns that something that might be regarded as self-sustained growth had been established. In the United Kingdom, the larger of the overspill towns around London – Harlow, Stevenage, Crawley – had been more successful in attracting a wide variety of industries than had some of the smaller experiments in other parts of the country.

We did not attempt to generalise or to reach specific conclusions regarding the character of the activities which should form a growth point. Apart from the importance of a sufficient component of 'exporting' activity to which I have referred in an earlier paragraph, there is not much that can be said by way of generalisation. It is interesting, none the less, to draw attention to the rather different approach of the authorities of the U.S.S.R.; it is the more interesting since it reflects the application to regional problems of the principles of international trade theory that I have emphasised above.

If a backward area, such as Uzbekistan, is to be developed, they first organise a resource survey, covering the geological, physical – soil and rainfall – and human resources of the region. In the light of that survey they aim to discover the comparative advantages of the region. They plan to develop the activities in which comparative advantage is to be found at the most suitable sites in the region. They provide for this purpose the necessary capital equipment and the necessary infrastructure. While this is being created, they develop an educational and training system designed to provide trained manpower for the new activities. I am not aware of any attempt to apply a similar system of analysis in a capitalist country. But if one has decided that a region must be developed or regenerated in part by bringing work to the workers, such a system of analysis is the logical way in which to plan it.

We came back at the end, with the help of a paper by Professor Hoover,[1] to the question with which we had started: the present stage of economic theory in relation to regional and spatial economics. There were many of us – I was certainly one – who felt that elementary non-spatial economics, as it is ordinarily taught, leaves out dangerously too much of the complications of a real spatial economy, in which the size of markets to be served is related to transport costs from alternative geographically-located places of production; in which, if transport costs are high or access to the individual consumer is necessary, an industry with many producers may yet be essentially monopolistic in each local market; in which regions must have a balance of payments; in which the geographical distribution of population and the geographical distribution of markets are determined by the facts of physical geography as well as by economic factors – by soils, rainfall, rivers, mountains, mineral distributions. Professor Samuelson had reminded us in an early session of the formidable difficulties of the formulation of a mathematical model of a spatial economy, in which the location of demand is at the same time the consequence of the

---

[1] We used Professor Hoover's paper deliberately as a means of collecting our thoughts and summing up our work after looking at the varied experience of many countries, and since the discussion of it took the form of a summing up of the conference, it has been printed at the end of the volume. But in substance it belongs with the papers in Part I on the theoretical background, and a reader may prefer to read it with these.

location of supply, with – as I would want to argue – a large element of lag both in the geography of supply and in that of demand.   But the difficulties of a perfectly tight mathematical formulation should not blind us to the factors that we are assuming away.   We should not go on behaving as if there are no problems of the effects of spatial economics on the achievement of optimum sizes in particular industries, on the character of competition, and above all on the achievement of optimum resource-use in a technically progressing economy.   From time to time – I am convinced – economics makes progress first by recognising qualitatively the character of some of the unsolved problems or the unstated assumptions before it is ready for quantitative precision in their solution.   The whole of spatial economics is, in my view, currently very much in that situation.   Those of us who argued the issues of the practical solution of the problems of 'backward areas' in Varenna would like to feel that our discussions did something to bring to the surface not only the practical experience of a wide variety of countries and some of the economic considerations which should go into interpreting experience and framing policy, but also some rather serious limitations in the analytical armoury of the majority of working economists today when confronted by the sort of issues that are relevant to spatial and regional economics.

Part 1   The Theoretical Background

1 Location Theory, Regional Economics and Backward Areas

E. A. G. Robinson
UNIVERSITY OF CAMBRIDGE

1 LOCATION THEORY AND REGIONAL ECONOMICS

Location theory, in its earlier forms, had very little to contribute to the understanding of regional differences of economic activity. In the hands of Weber, and of those whose thinking primarily derived from Weber, the theory was essentially micro-economic. The problem that Weber and his followers set themselves was that of explaining the geographical location of the individual firm, assuming given physical locations of the necessary materials for production, assuming, if relevant, the existence of possible external economies in some locations, and assuming also – and most important – the location of the market to be served. The theory was micro-economic in the sense that the decision-making unit was by implication small enough for supply and demand to be treated as wholly independent of each other.

The problems of regional economics, in the sense that we shall be discussing them in this conference, are essentially macro-economic. We shall be primarily concerned with the effects of the aggregate of location-decisions, private and public, not only on the immediate profitability of a single small productive unit but also on the aggregates of income and expenditure generated in an area. We shall be concerned with the tendencies of expanding areas to create expanding expenditures and to attract new production activities and of contracting areas to lead to declining expenditures and to discourage new activities.

Any expansion or contraction goes beyond the direct effects on the industry directly concerned. On the one hand, there is a positive multiplier when new investment in an expanding area results not only in increased incomes in that area, but also movement of individuals into the area and a cycle of increased expenditures in the area, creating still further incentives to further investment in the area. On the other hand, there is a negative multiplier when the reduction of activities in an area leads to contracting incomes and expenditures, to less business for shops and services, to less incentive to replace capital that becomes worn out, to increased movement out of the area, thus propagating a further cycle of contraction and depression.

The theoretical analysis underlying regional policy-making needs in this sense to be macro-economic. But it needs, inside a country in which movement of resources is without constraints, to be micro-economic at the same time and to take account of the factors which determine the location-decision of the individual firm. One must, however, beware of importing into the theory of the location-decisions of the individual firm some of the assumptions that are ordinarily regarded as appropriate to micro-economics on a national scale. It may be appropriate on a national scale to assume, as one does in the analysis of perfect competition, that the individual firm is so small in relation to the national market that it neglects the repercussions of its own decisions on the national price of its products or its inputs. That cannot always be assumed on a local scale in a widely distributed industry. A building concern or an automobile service station, very small in relation to the total national market, may have a near monopoly on a local scale. An entrepreneur, considering the establishment of a new unit to serve some region, will necessarily take account, in much the same terms as would a monopolist or a duopolist, of whether or not there already exists in that region a single fairly large and fairly efficient unit, measured in terms of the demand of the region, and of the probable competitive outcome of entering the market.

For purposes of analysis it is convenient to distinguish three categories of economic operation. In the first, the costs of transport and the economies of scale are such that a national or international market can be created and served from a single centre with a high location quotient. In the second, the costs of transport and the economies of scale are such that a wide region can be served, but the marginal economies of scale are insufficient to continue to offset increasing costs of transport over wider distances. In the third, the increasing costs of transport with distance are so high, the marginal economies of scale are so small, and the geographical distribution of necessary inputs is so widespread, that the activity is normally conducted on a purely local basis, each town as well as each region having a location quotient of about unity. This covers the majority of services that need to be provided directly to the consumer and which form an increasing part of all activity. Clearly the divisions between these three, which are in any case ill-defined at any moment, will be affected over a period of time either by changes in the marginal economies of scale or in the marginal costs of transport. There is reason to think that, for many products, possible economies of scale and the scales up to which further economies of size may be secured are increasing. At the same time absolute costs of transport and, as speed and efficiency of transport increases, the marginal costs of transport at a given distance are falling. Thus the area that can be served efficiently from a given centre (which under the familiar law increases as the square of the distance from the centre) grows and more products move from the third into the second and from the second into the first of my categories.

Weber and his followers worked out the analysis of the location-decision of the individual firm, showing how it would be influenced by the attractive force of a weight-losing material or materials and uninfluenced by ubiquitous materials. He brought into his analysis also the economies of aggregation, where the pulls of external economies were significant – and by implication were non-mobile and available only within a certain limit of locations.

Lösch and others, developing Weber's ideas, showed how, in a perfectly homogeneous system of population and income distribution and with perfectly appropriate transport facilities, different categories of activity might so distribute themselves that each producer would be at the centre of a regular hexagon and the market area as a whole would be distributed between the system of regular hexagons represented by these individual markets. Such a system is, however, difficult to visualise in the usually assumed conditions of perfectly homogeneous distribution of population and income. For the whole variety of economic activities cannot reasonably be assumed all to fall neatly into one or other of the categories of national, regional and purely local markets; more important, the desirable size of the resulting hexagons for the regional and local markets will depend upon the specific marginal economies of scale and specific marginal costs of transport of the particular product, so that for each product the hexagon size is likely to be different. This, in turn, implies that the production centres will be scattered and will create non-homogeneous distribution of demand for other products. Thus as one attempts to release the hypothetical constraints and to move towards reality, the implications of an assumed perfectly homogeneous distribution of population and income become more and more unreal and inconsistent with one's analysis.

In practice, local services are normally rendered in a town, which itself represents in a sense a market centre of a small surrounding region, visited by the inhabitants of the region, which, with given means of transport, have access to it. The town systems of the world have grown up initially on the basis of the distances that could be covered on foot or with animal transport and are now being modified and superseded by distances of assumed movement dictated by automobile transport on the one hand and the scale-efficiencies of shops, services and the like on the other hand.

What is more important is that most of the problems of regional economics cannot be seen in terms of a perfect adjustment to a homogeneous distribution of population and income for a second reason also. One has to begin by explaining the existing population and expenditure distributions. These are, admittedly, being progressively modified and adapted towards the currently appropriate national-scale and international-scale use of resources and distribution of population. But that process is itself affected in the interim by the fact that there is an existing pattern of population distribution, which determines the existing location of demand. One cannot start from a *tabula rasa* and place the counters on the board at the places which might best suit today's knowledge of techniques, desired pattern of use of resources, and alternative geographical availabilities of natural resources. There is a constant procession of compromise between the past and the present.

2 THE HISTORICAL GROWTH OF POPULATION DISTRIBUTION

In such circumstances, there is, I suggest, advantage in going back and trying to explain historically the existing distributions of populations which we are now, in different conditions, progressively modifying. One can start, as did von Thünen, from the agricultural problem of a world in which, as in the case of the less developed countries today, agriculture represented something like four-fifths of all economic activity and that agricultural activity was primarily self-subsistent, with the market as a relatively unimportant factor. It was, moreover, an agriculture of low yields per hectare, so that each holding covered several hectares. In any country with a fairly considerable population, that population in such circumstances spread itself progressively over the whole land surface. Holdings tended to be larger in areas of poorer soils and smaller in areas of better soils, if only because the easier of these to work were in most cases settled early, suffered first from overpopulation and, where any system of land ownership existed, imposed higher rents per hectare in some form on the tiller of the soil.

It is to such a primarily agricultural system that the village and town systems of most of Europe and even of large parts of America are related. The villages and towns were fairly evenly distributed over the land surface because agriculture was widely distributed. They provided the centres for certain services, for petty administration, for religious activities. The somewhat larger towns were centres, in most cases, of larger-scale administrative activities and the market centres at which the agricultural surpluses required for the consumption of those engaged in town activities were sold, either in exchange for products or to meet the obligations of land-use payments in some form.

The agricultural and industrial revolutions required a modification of this geographical pattern. On the agricultural side, the proportions of those actually engaged in agriculture have been drastically reduced. For England and Wales, Gregory King estimated in the last decade of the seventeenth century the proportion of population engaged in agricultural occupations to be near to 60 per cent and the proportion of national income generated in agriculture to be about 40 per cent. By the end of the nineteenth century, the share of agriculture in total employment was around

9 per cent and in income around 6 per cent. Today the comparable figures are 5 per cent and 3 per cent. Yet the British population remains distributed not so very differently. In other European countries, while the movement out of agriculture and into other activities has not been quite so great, the change has been similar in character; thus in these countries the present distribution of population remains even more evidently a compromise between that which was initially appropriate to a primarily agricultural distribution and that which is appropriate to the activities of today.

Writing in the 1820s, in the early phases of the industrial revolution, von Thünen was naturally interested in the repercussions of the growth of activity in the towns on the patterns of activity of the agricultural populations. He stressed the effects of the growing demands in the towns in the form of the specialisation of near-town agriculture on market garden produce and the rings of different activities at widening distances from the centre of consumption. But his discussion of these problems was almost wholly in terms of the pattern of activities within a region which was predominantly self-sufficient and in which the relations with other regions were relatively secondary.

The relations of region with region inside a country and internationally developed more slowly. It is, of course, true that Athens, Rome and other great cities of earlier history had been fed by imports and had depended on international trade for their existence. London in the same way had depended not only for food but also for fuel on long-distance transport – in the latter case first of fire-wood, and later of coal. But even in 1801 the population of Greater London was no more than about 9 per cent that of the United Kingdom, excluding Eire, as compared with 17 per cent in 1951. The total population of all other towns exceeding 10,000 in 1801 (and including all of smaller size at that date which exceeded 100,000 in 1951) represented no more than 11 per cent of total population in 1801 but 28 per cent in 1951. In total, about 20 per cent of the population of 1801 lived in these larger towns; in 1951 as much as 45 per cent. At the beginning of the nineteenth century in England and Wales – and I believe the same to be true of most European countries – the population was still distributed primarily on the basis of agricultural activities.

During the nineteenth century, this primarily agricultural distribution of population was modified and adapted to the needs and technologies of that century. In the United Kingdom that inevitably meant in the first stages adaptation to the economic requirements of the textile industries, and to their locational needs – for as late as 1901, textile manufacture represented 26 per cent of all manufacturing employment. These needs, as anyone versed in the theories of location will immediately observe, were in any European country abnormal. The raw materials were, in the case of cotton, wholly imported; in the case of wool, from the 1850s the materials were, in the United Kingdom, about half imported, and by the 1880s four-fifths imported. Within any European country the pull both of the materials and of the export markets was towards the ports. In cotton this helped to influence the predominant location in Lancashire. In wool this force was less powerful, for this was from the first an industry in which external economies were important and the pulls of these towards the new concentration in the West Riding of Yorkshire were stronger than minor economies of transport, the costs of which for the finished product were relatively low and for the raw materials lower in Yorkshire than in most of the other locations in which the industry had earlier flourished.

The second major force in the nineteenth century was the development, stimulated by technical progress in general and the steam engine in particular, of the engineering and metallurgical industries. The metallurgical industries, based on weight-losing and by no means ubiquitous materials (in terms of Weber's analysis), were attracted to specific geographical areas where minerals and fuels have been available or to locations near to ports of entry. The engineering industries were themselves in the earlier phase energy-intensive as well as dependent on heavy materials and attracted also in turn towards the metallurgical industries.

Taking once again the United Kingdom as an example, the main areas of development were in Durham, Northumberland and the North Riding of Yorkshire; in Scotland, principally in Lanarkshire; in South Wales, principally in Glamorgan; in Warwickshire and Staffordshire, in the neighbourhood of Birmingham. There were metallurgical and engineering developments also in the textile areas of Lancashire and the West Riding of Yorkshire.

These redistributional forces of the nineteenth century have been continued into the twentieth century, again creating pressures on the distributions of population in the advanced countries; in this century they have predominantly taken two forms. First, we have seen a second agricultural revolution. Second, we have had increases of income per head and consequent modifications of patterns of consumption in the light of income elasticities which have put a new emphasis on engineering and metallurgy.

This second agricultural revolution, seen from the point of view of national population distributions, has had four main elements: first, the greatly increased yields per hectare, consequent on the use of artificial fertilisers; second, rapidly increasing mechanisation, so that an increased proportion of the effective inputs are in the machinery factories and not on the farms; third, the consequent greatly increased productivity per head in agriculture proper; fourth, the cheapening and speeding up of transport, so that today agriculture is an industry of regional specialities and long-distance exchange through the market.

The increases of yields per hectare since the turn of the century in many European countries have been such that, despite growth of population and such increases of food consumption per head as result from income elasticities, the pressures on agricultural land are reduced and marginal lands, which could provide the levels of farm incomes expected in 1900, are now falling out of agricultural use or are continued in it only by subventions. These trends can be illustrated again from the United Kingdom:

TABLE ONE
CHANGES IN PRODUCTIVITY IN AGRICULTURE IN UNITED KINGDOM 1900–64

	1900–2	*1962–4*
Area of agricultural land	100	87
Output of agriculture	100	256
Output of agriculture per hectare	100	294
Output of cereal crops	100	248
Area under cereal crops	100	111
Output of cereal crops per hectare	100	223
Population	100	142
Supply of food (including imports)	100	212
Supply of food per head	100	151
Output per worker in agriculture	100	370
Proportion of working population involved in agriculture	8·9%	3·8%

Source: Based on figures published in *The British Economy: Key Statistics* 1900–1966 (London & Cambridge Economic Service, 1967).

It can be seen that yield per hectare has, in the case of the United Kingdom, increased nearly 3 times. This has been largely the result of increased yields of the given crops; it can be seen that for cereal crops output per hectare has increased about $2\frac{1}{4}$ times. It is partly also the result of a shift of marginal demand towards types of agricultural products which are less land-intensive and give higher yields of value of output per hectare. The total of agricultural output required to be met from British agriculture has grown a little more than $2\frac{1}{2}$ times. Thus, as has been said, incentives to farm on marginal land are less and certain types of marginal-land farming are currently under heavy economic pressure to contract.

Much of this marginal-land farming – particularly hill farms – is almost by definition more remote from alternative forms of occupation, and occupational mobility is the more difficult. The process of adjustment is made the more complex because the better land and better farming conditions are in many cases to be found in parts of a country where industrial developments and the resulting demands for labour make transfer out of agriculture easy and push up agricultural wages, while the types of agricultural output which can be met from the more distant marginal lands, which can retain labour or family farmers at existing income levels, are not, in many cases, those for which demand is strong.

If I may put the same problem in a slightly different way, one may say that many European countries still retain a distribution of population deriving not very distantly from an agriculture which can no longer provide in the marginal areas a standard of life that a mid-twentieth-century worker has come to expect.

Apart from agriculture, the important forces redistributing production and employment in the twentieth century have been associated with the relative and sometimes the absolute decline of some of the industries and occupations which grew up first in the industrial revolution and with the emergence of new activities, based on new technologies and the income-elasticities corresponding to mid-twentieth-century incomes. Predominant among the declines have been some of the early nineteenth-century developments of coal and other minerals and of the textile industries.

If again I may illustrate from the United Kingdom, in 1851 mining (principally coal-mining) gave employment to 4·2 per cent of the working population; by 1901 the figure had risen to 5·3 per cent; by 1951 it had fallen to 3·6 per cent and has fallen further to about 2 per cent in the past few years. Thus even apart from the working out of the minerals in particular locations, there has been a proportionate shift away from mining activities, resulting from the long-term decline in the raw material content of output. But the main factor in the United Kingdom case has been the exhaustion of the minerals in the areas first developed in the industrial revolution combined with the much reduced value of many of the types of coal which commanded a premium in the period when coal was the main source of energy for shipping and railway transport.

At the same time there has been – taking again the United Kingdom as an example – the decline in the relative importance of textiles. In 1901, as was said earlier, the textile industries employed about 26 per cent of all occupied persons. In 1966 the figure was a little over 3 per cent. The cities in Lancashire built up on the cotton industry and its external economies, today are in some cases centres of light engineering and machine-building. In other cases they have become typical of one aspect of twentieth-century economic maladjustment. Their physical locations are not in most cases those that would be selected with a *tabula rasa* for their present activities. The pull of large local markets and of potential sources of skilled labour have sufficed in some cases to overcome the possible geographical disadvantages of relations to sources of materials and energy and to markets other than those of the locality itself. In other cases, remoteness from markets, from main transport routes, and from the materials of growing industries has made it difficult to replace the declining activities with new ones.

The new developments in the modern growth industries have largely taken place in the Midlands and South of England. In total, the residential populations of the Birmingham–Coventry conurbation and Greater London have grown between 1901 and 1951 by 30 per cent while the

TABLE TWO

POPULATION CHANGES IN CERTAIN PREDOMINANTLY AGRICULTURAL REGIONS OF GREAT BRITAIN 1801–1951

	1801		1851		1871		1901		1931		1951		1961	
	000s	%	000s	%	000s	%	000s	%	000s	%	000s	%	000s	%
West of England *	1,104	10·5	1,805	8·7	1,879	7·2	1,888	5·1	2,063	4·6	2,372	4·9	2,496	4·9
East Anglia and Eastern Midlands †	823	7·8	1,436	6·9	1,476	5·7	1,589	4·3	1,804	4·0	2,022	4·1	2,137	4·2
Central Wales and Welsh Marches ‡	398	3·8	546	2·6	591	2·3	542	1·5	523	1·2	577	1·2	583	1·1
North-East Scotland §	518	4·9	777	3·7	850	3·3	956	2·6	918	2·0	950	1·9	939	1·8
South-West Scotland ‖	191	1·8	328	1·6	357	1·4	399	1·1	426	1·0	470	1·0	489	1·0
Total of above	3,034	28·8	4,892	23·5	5,153	19·8	5,374	14·6	5,734	12·8	6,391	13·1	7,104	13·9
1801=100	100		161		170		177		189		211		234	
Total of Great Britain	10,501	100·0	26,072	100·0	26,072	100·0	37,000	100·0	44,795	100·0	48,854	100·0	51,250	100·0
1801=100	100		198		248		352		427		465		488	

* West of England here represents the counties of Wiltshire, Dorsetshire, Somerset, Devonshire and Cornwall.
† East Anglia and Eastern Midlands here represents the counties of Norfolk, Suffolk, Cambridgeshire and the Isle of Ely, Huntingdonshire and Lincolnshire.
‡ The counties of Herefordshire, Shropshire, Merionethshire, Montgomeryshire, Radnorshire and Cardiganshire.
§ The counties of Perthshire, Angus, Aberdeenshire, Banffshire, Morayshire, Nairnshire, Kincardineshire, Inverness-shire.
‖ The counties of Dumfriesshire, Kirkudbrightshire, Wigtownshire, Ayrshire.

Source: All figures taken from B. R. Mitchell and P. Deane, *Abstract of British Historical Statistics* (Cambridge, 1962).

population of the country as a whole has grown by almost exactly the same. But in both cases the extent of daily commuting to work has very greatly increased and the working populations of both areas greatly exceed their residential populations.

Tables 2 and 3 summarise the history of the past century and a half in the United Kingdom. The extent to which the pre-industrial revolution distribution still in part survives can be seen in Table 2, which shows the trends of population in five areas which have remained predominantly agricultural. All of these areas inevitably contain, it will be appreciated, pockets of modern industry, some of them of considerable importance. It will be seen that in aggregate the population of these areas has slightly more than doubled. None of the areas taken as a whole had less population in 1951 than 1801. Over each half-century the population of each of these regions (though not that of some of the individual counties composing them) has increased, with the two exceptions of the area in Central Wales and the Welsh Marches, where there has been decline since 1871 only partly alleviated by a recent increase in the population of Shropshire, and that of North-East Scotland where a decline between 1901 and 1931 has been almost offset by subsequent growth. A second point that is evident is the relatively small change since 1901; the greater part of the relative decline of these regions had already taken place before the end of the century, and the further change in this century has been surprisingly small.

Table 3 records the population changes in the areas first to benefit from the industrial revolution. The increases of population in the textile areas of Lancashire and the West Riding came earlier and to a significant extent before the first population census in 1801 (production of woollens and worsted had increased about $2\frac{1}{2}$ times during the eighteenth century). By 1801 the two main textile areas contained 12 per cent of the population of Great Britain. Their share of the population grew progressively up to 19·5 per cent in 1901. Since then it has slowly declined. The traditional group of predominantly metallurgical and engineering regions, including the textile regions again, contained 23 per cent of the population in 1801; they contained 38 per cent in 1901. But again their relative growth ceased from about that date. Once again it is of great interest to see the small redistribution since 1901 and the extent to which the present pattern of population distribution had already been reached by then.

3 PRIVATE AND PUBLIC INTEREST IN LOCATION-DECISIONS

May I attempt to summarise this part of my argument? One cannot, as it seems to me, begin an analysis of the location of economic activity at any moment of time from a *tabula rasa* and explain all the current locations of

TABLE THREE

POPULATION CHANGES IN CERTAIN EARLY INDUSTRIAL REGIONS 1801–1951

	1801		1851		1871		1901		1931		1951		1961	
	000s	%	000s	%	000s	%	000s	%	000s	%	000s	%	000s	%
(i) Durham	149	1·4	391	1·9	685	2·6	1,187	3·2	1,486	3·3	1,464	3·0	1,517	3·0
(ii) Northumberland	168	1·6	304	1·5	387	1·5	603	1·6	757	1·7	798	1·6	819	1·6
(iii) North Riding of Yorks.	158	1·5	213	1·0	290	1·1	377	1·0	467	1·0	525	1·1	554	1·1
(iv) Lanarkshire	148	1·4	530	2·5	765	2·9	1,339	3·6	1,586	3·5	1,614	3·3	1,626	3·2
(v) Glamorgan	71	0·7	232	1·1	398	1·5	1,122	3·0	1,229	2·7	1,203	2·5	1,228	2·4
(vi) Warwickshire and Staffs.	450	4·3	1,084	5·2	1,492	5·7	2,271	6·1	2,967	6·6	3,483	7·1	3,757	7·3
Total (i)–(vi)	1,152	10·9	2,754	13·2	4,017	15·3	6,899	18·5	8,492	18·8	9,087	18·6	9,501	18·5
1801=100	100		239		348		599		737		788		824	
1901=100							100		123		132		138	
(vii) Lancashire	673	6·4	2,031	9·7	2,819	10·8	4,373	11·8	5,040	11·3	5,118	10·5	5,132	10·0
(viii) West Riding of Yorks.	591	5·6	1,366	6·6	1,882	7·2	2,843	7·7	3,446	7·7	3,586	7·3	3,641	7·1
Total (vii)–(viii)	1,264	12·0	3,397	16·3	4,701	18·0	7,216	19·5	8,486	19·0	8,704	17·8	8,773	17·1
1801=100	100		269		372		571		671		699		694	
1901=100							100		118		121		122	
Total (i)–(viii)	2,416	22·9	6,151	29·5	8,718	33·3	14,115	38·0	16,987	37·8	17,791	36·4	18,274	35·7
1801=100	100		255		361		584		703		736		765	
1901=100							100		120		126		129	
Total of Great Britain	10,501	100·0	20,817	100·0	26,072	100·0	37,000	100·0	44,795	100·0	48,854	100·0	51,250	100·0
1801=100	100		198		248		352		427		465		488	
1901=100							100		121		132		139	

Source: All figures except those for 1961 taken from Mitchell and Deane, *Abstract of British Historical Statistics.*

economic activities in terms of a set of simultaneous equations relating only to current technical considerations. One of the principal factors in determining the location of capacity in any activity is the location of the market for that activity and in particular the location of that part of the market which is currently least well served by existing capacity. The present location of the market is in part the result of past activities of all kinds; it is being modified progressively all the time by the developments of new activities. Those areas of market which may be expected to be least well served by existing capacity are those in which new demand is being generated by new activities in other industries. There is thus likely to be a polarisation of growth.

The extent to which such polarisation may be expected to operate will depend on the extent to which transport costs may or may not be expected to offset economies either of an external or of an internal character or the economies of a more hybrid, internal-external character that emerge when the expansion of production in a main centre of an industry permits more standardisation and specialisation of plants in the industry. On the one hand there is some reason to think that, with increasingly capital-intensive production, the absolute outputs at which economies of scale become minimal will in future be larger. At the same time there is some reason to think that transport costs are likely to continue to fall relatively to other costs and permit wider areas to be served economically from a given centre; with increased speed and availability of transport and better communications generally, the conveniences of local production of services, as well as of goods, are also likely to be reduced.

On the other hand increasing income and consumption expenditure per head may be expected to result in more than proportionate increases of expenditure on most consumer durables and this, combined with population growth, will imply that substantially larger local markets will in some cases give greater opportunity to achieve full or nearly full economies of scale with more widely dispersed production or assembly.

But while in some respects these factors are providing incentives to greater centralisation of production, the diseconomies of over-centralisation and excessively large concentrations of industry are beginning to become evident. An industrial entrepreneur, in deciding where to establish a new plant, will take account of economies external to the plant but internal to the industry so far as they may be expected to affect his own costs and efficiency. He will not ordinarily – unless forced to do so by government – take account of the marginal diseconomies which his presence may be expected to impose on others through his decision to locate in the overcrowded region, except to the extent that they may be expected to fall on his own enterprise. If the economies internal to the industry but external to the plant are considerable, he may choose to locate in the overcrowded area even though from a national point of view and from that of the efficiency of the area as a whole, both in the particular industry and outside it, there is a net disadvantage in his doing so.

Equally, an individual entrepreneur, in making his location decision, will not ordinarily take account of benefits he might confer on a backward or depressed area by locating there. If a decision is made to locate a new activity in a depressed area and thus replace some older activity that is ending, it will diminish any negative multiplier in the area; it may maintain the activities of already existing public utility services, shops, schools, hospitals and local services generally. To the extent that the equipment of these has not reached the end of its normal working life, it will save in the amount of induced capital formation as compared with a decision to locate in a place in which the social and economic infrastructure is already so fully used as to require additional investment.

Thus it is not legitimate to assume that private advantage in a location-decision is always and everywhere identical with the national advantage. If polarisation and overcentralisation of development has reached a critical point, so that there are significant diseconomies of further development in the overcrowded area, it may be of national advantage to apply the same principles that have been justified in the case of infant industries and take measures to create or assist the creation of suitably located new centres which, when external economies have grown up, may be as economic in respect of the particular industry as have been existing centres before overcrowding and at the same time serve to mitigate the diseconomies of overcentralisation.

These arguments must be used with great care. If population is growing and infrastructure of all kinds will be fully used in the depressed area, or if the infrastructure will in any case need to be replaced, it will make little or no difference whether it is built in the depressed area or the developing area. It is only to the extent that the decline of an area results in pre-mature abandonment or less than full utilisation of already existing resources that these arguments are valid.

If all location-decisions were entirely rational and based on careful consideration of economic advantage, it would not be easy to justify interference with the location-decision to a greater extent than this. If on balance it is more economic to move the worker to a new place of work than to bring the work to potentially available workers, justification is needed for choosing the less-economic location. There is evidence, however, that many location-decisions are influenced by rather minor considerations of personal preference or convenience, rather than by major differences of cost. There are many industries in which transport costs of materials and of the finished product are small in total and the additional cost of a non-optimal location is small. If the personal convenience and preferences of a substantial body of workers would favour the bringing of work to the workers, this can properly be weighed in the balance. In a perfectly

B

working competitive economy one would expect the reluctance of workers to move and their preference to stay where they are to express itself in a willingness to accept lower real incomes in the preferred location. In practice, where wages are nationally negotiated, they are often not in a position to express this preference. If, for family or other reasons, they cannot move, their only alternative, if work is not brought to them, may be to remain unemployed. Thus, in practice, with wages determined as they are, there may be this further justification for putting pressure on entrepreneurs to bring work to available workers and thus to add to national production.

4 THE ESSENTIALS OF A THEORY OF REGIONAL ECONOMICS

May I turn next to the ways in which are determined the relations of a city or conurbation and the immediately associated region to the rest of the economy of which it forms a part, and examine the problem first considered by von Thünen along the lines subsequently developed by Isard and others? Let us assume (in accordance with what appears to be the normal situation today) that about 50 per cent of the expenditures are on goods and services from outside the region and the immediately associated agricultural area. If the city and its associated region (which in the following discussion will be described as 'the region') are to be in equilibrium with the remainder of the economy and the world outside the economy, there must be exports of goods or services from the city and its associated region equivalent to the imports, save to the extent that

(1) there are net receipts of national government expenditures in the region in excess of tax payments made by the region;
(2) there are net receipts of income from investments outside the region owned by residents in the region in excess of similar payments made by the region to residents in the rest of the economy;
(3) there is a net sale of existing assets in the rest of the economy by the residents in the regional economy; this includes the case of the region or city of elderly retired persons living on pensions received from outside the region (e.g. Bournemouth);
(4) there is a net inflow of investment into the region by investors living outside the region, in excess of investment outside by residents in the region.

If there are insufficient net receipts or inflows, there may in the short term be a temporary and involuntary shift of banking funds to offset the inward flow of goods and services, but in a longer period the local expenditures of the region, together with the exports of the region, will not generate local incomes on a sufficient scale to maintain existing levels of expenditure; activity and incomes will decline; there will be an incentive to outward migration; the decline of the region will proceed until

(a) its outside earnings are increased by the attraction of new export activities to the region (possibly resulting from lower real wages in the region for a given efficiency), or

(b) its incomes and expenditures are reduced to the point where the net receipts from government expenditures and the other relevant items (1–4 above) offset the excess of imports over exports of goods and services, or

(c) there is a reduction in the ratio of expenditures on imports of goods and services to total expenditures.

Conversely, where a region is tending to have a surplus on its balance of payments with the rest of the economy it will

(a) generate expenditures on locally produced goods and services in excess of existing capacity to supply them; while the gap is likely to be filled temporarily by added imports, in a longer run there will be an incentive to expand production, to create new jobs and to attract immigration into the area;

(b) there may be an accumulation, temporary or more permanent, of assets in the rest of the economy and a tendency to invest funds outside the region itself;

(c) there is likely to be a relative rise in efficiency-wages and the cost of imports in the region and an adjustment of the flow of imports and exports as a consequence;

(d) there is likely to be an excess of outward tax payments over receipts from government expenditures.

The speed and ease of the adjustment process will depend upon circumstances. If the region is large and the decline of exports is confined to a single relatively small industry, the net loss of local incomes will be relatively small in proportion to total income, the possibilities of absorption of those displaced into other occupations exporting from the region will be high, the ratio of imports to all expenditures will be lower. If the region is small, undiversified and greatly dependent on a single activity, the possibilities of absorption into other exporting activities will be low, the proportionate decline of all incomes will be greater, and, since the region is small and specialised, the ratio of imports to all expenditures is likely to be greater; thus the speed and ease of adjustment are likely to be less.

There is a great deal of evidence that in practice in an advanced country industrial workers move towards jobs and away from unemployment; in Europe and North America the rate of growth of certain cities, such as Detroit or Birmingham, has obviously been related to cyclical variations in the rate of growth of their principal industries. Within industry, there is evidence that occupational mobility is fairly high and geographical mobility, though less than occupational, is greater than the geographical *plus* occupational mobility of persons who need to be transferred from agriculture or mining to new industrial occupations in a new area. It is the latter problem – that of depressed agricultural and mining areas – which usually represents the core of the problem of backward areas.

5 SOME CONCLUSIONS

If one is to tackle the problems of a depressed agricultural area, or a depressed mining area in which mineral activities are declining, or an industrial area in which employment is not growing so fast as is the local population, there are a number of propositions which seem to emerge from my preceding argument:

(1) If it is desired to solve the problems of the backward areas and to raise income per head towards the levels of the rest of the economy, one cannot do this merely by measures to provide infrastructure, social amenities and capital equipment, unless the consequences of these will be to remedy the long-term underlying balance of payments problems of the region. If incomes in the region are raised but regional expenditures 'leak' out of the region without increased exports, they will be maintained at the higher level only so long as there is a net capital inflow or a net inflow of government expenditure to maintain the incomes.

(2) It is difficult for any backward area to make progress towards the fuller use of its manpower resources within the area (i.e. without migration) purely from its own resources and without a net inflow of funds from the rest of the economy, either in the form of government assistance or as the result of private investment content with long-term rather than short-term gain.

(3) The balance of payments problems of a region may be remedied by measures which make the region more self-sufficient – i.e. by creating a level of demand in the region which justifies the establishment of industrial units to meet it, thus reducing the import ratio and the 'leak'. This can be done (as in the case of a developing country) by import-saving investment if it is possible to find means of making import-saving products at prices that will compete with imports.

(4) They may alternatively be met by creating in the region an infrastructure and facilities which, taken in conjunction with labour resources and real wages for given efficiency, now justify the establishment in the region of industrial units to meet the demands of the national market.

(5) Infrastructure investment is likely to be most effective where it has

the result of diminishing any handicap of the region as compared with the rest of the economy, e.g. by reducing transport costs for outward movements of goods produced in the region relatively to those for inward movements (this may happen if the region produces heavy or bulky primary products and imports lighter consumption goods).

(6) There is no *a priori* reason for thinking that a solution can always be found to the problem of creating in an unfavourable location a comparative advantage for the production of some new product on the basis of the payment of the same efficiency-wages to labour as are paid in other more favourable locations. There is, on the contrary, a likelihood that the problem cannot be solved in these terms.

(7) There is *a priori* reason for thinking that, if the constraint of equal efficiency-wages is removed, a solution can be found at some difference of efficiency-wages. But where a present community exists in a very unfavourable location, dictated by past activities in primitive agriculture or in mining, the level of efficiency-wages which would permit the community to attract new activity may be so low as to make it unacceptable.

(8) If, for political or social reasons, there is a strong preference of local communities to retain their identity and achieve development within their own regions, there can be no economic objection to this, provided that it is recognised that the consequence may be the earning of lower efficiency-wages than could possibly be earned in an alternative more favourable location.

(9) Whether a particular location may prove to be favourable or unfavourable to new deveolpment will depend upon the comparative availability of raw materials and the comparative accessibility of the location to new markets for new products or upon a competitive advantage over existing locations for existing markets. A location which is particularly unfavourable in both these respects may be almost incapable of salvation or redevelopment except on the basis of daily travel to work at some distance.

(10) Any policy of wage determination which involves the payment of equal money wages in all regions of an economy is likely to make more difficult the attraction of new industry to backward areas; this difficulty will be increased if the efficiency of the labour of backward areas is below the efficiency of the labour in other areas or requires more expenditure on training before it reaches equivalent efficiency.

(11) If a nation chooses to pay equal efficiency-wages and other rewards to workers working in an unfavourable location, selected not for its present economic advantage but for the existence of a present body of employable workers, this represents in effect the acceptance of a

non-optimal economic solution of its location problems. It is, however, legitimate to take into account in such calculations the economic effects of the location-decision on the full use of all national and social capital and not merely the consequences to the efficiency of the production unit itself.

(12) Any measures are desirable which may remove handicaps in the backward area; it is desirable that capital supplies shall be available at least as cheaply, for a given risk, as in other regions, that land and buildings be at least as cheaply available, that competent and experienced management be available, and that institutions shall exist to ensure that no impediments to development shall exist from imperfection of the markets for such inputs.

FOR REFERENCE

J. H. von Thünen, *Isolated State* (English translation) Oxford, 1966.

A. Weber, *Theory of the Location of Industries* (English translation, 2nd edition) Chicago, 1957.

A. Lösch, *The Economics of Location* (English translation) New Haven, 1954.

W. Isard, *Location and Space Economy*, Cambridge, Mass., 1956.

W. Isard and others, *Methods of Regional Analysis*, Cambridge, Mass., 1960.

J. R. Meyer, 'Regional Economics: A Survey' in *Surveys of Economic Theory*, Vol. 11, London and New York, 1967. (This has a detailed bibliography.)

2 Social Aspects of Backwardness in Developed Countries[1]

S. Groenman

DIRECTOR, SOCIOLOGISCH INSTITUUT VAN DE RIJKSUNIVERSITEIT, UTRECHT

1 INTRODUCTORY

In his foreword to Kusum Nair's *Blossoms in the Dust* [2] Gunnar Myrdal describes the human factor in development as of paramount importance: 'People's attitudes to work and life, hardened by stagnation, isolation and poverty, and underpinned by tradition and often by religion, are frequently found to be inimical to change of any kind.' In addition to this general statement may I make a few carefully chosen quotations from *Blossoms in the Dust*? Writing about the Madras farmers the author tells us that 'five acres on lease is the limit of their aspiration. . . . Their demands are calculated solely on the basis of the family's consumption requirements of rice at two meals a day . . .' (p. 31). About Kerala she remarks that 'an average Malayalee . . . would prefer the security of a small job than take any risk whatever' (p. 40). Caste also is a drawback to development. 'Not one of these Brahmin farmers [in Bihar] ploughs, or is permitted by caste custom to plough and work on the land' (p. 90). In West Bengal 'many communities among the peasants consider it below their dignity to take their farm produce to the market for sale' (p. 141). And one more quotation: '[a landlord's] reaction to land reforms – proposed imposition of a ceiling on land holdings and the fixing of a minimum wage for agricultural labour – is perfectly logical and natural. He feels that they will affect the landlords adversely. And, of course, all this encouragement being given to labour is absolutely disastrous' (p. 43). The author concludes that 'development will not become a self-generating process with its own momentum unless the value system of the community, and the social structure containing it, are first altered and adjusted to be in harmony with the socio-economic objectives of planning' (p. 194).

The purpose of this short introduction to development problems in India is no other than to jump *in medias res* by means of illustrations from an underdeveloped country where the social aspects of backwardness are manifest. The Indian example shows these aspects much more vividly

---

[1] The author is deeply indebted to Mr H. Vincent, who has made a special study of underdeveloped areas within Europe.

[2] Kusum Nair, *Blossoms in the Dust*, with a foreword by Gunnar Myrdal (1964).

than most backward areas within Europe and other developed countries. The social drawbacks to development in the latter regions are doubtlessly different, but sometimes only different in degree. Reading Kusum Nair's description more closely, we may distinguish between cultural and structural elements opposing modernisation or change in general. Attitudes, norms, values, aspirations and goals belong to the realm of culture. By structure we mean the network of social relations. Castes, power distribution, familism and nepotism, social stratification on the basis of prestige, income, education or birth, and women's position in society are important elements in social structure. Culture and structure of course are interconnected. Social layers ranking highly in the power and prestige structure may foster specific values hampering development. The example of the caste structure in India illustrates very clearly the extent to which structure and culture are interwoven. It is somewhat difficult to find similar phenomena in Europe to those found in India. It is, however, possible to quote an example within a country such as the Netherlands of a well-known rural village where a religious caste-like élite (a 'conventivulum' of chosen people) is in the position to impede the development of a small industrial plant by opposing the employment of girls on religious grounds.[1]

It is possible to analyse the social aspects of backwardness with the help of the concepts of structure and culture to a high extent. They are however internal elements only. The picture will be more complete if we pay attention also to the possibilities of communication with the outer world. Here we meet geographical location and the influence of mass media of communication. The conservative forces rooted in structure and culture, striving often at social isolation, are tested as soon as the attack from outside has been launched by means of all sorts of communication. At that moment we will know whether *tradition* is really effective to maintain a static situation or whether it may only seem to be so because there are no dynamising forces to disturb the existing order. In other words: is it true that tradition causes a static order or is it the other way around, in the sense that a static order gives a chance to tradition to be effective?[2] Tradition is the instrument of the internal transfer of culture from generation to generation. Thus it can be considered under the heading of culture. It has its counterpart in the transfer of culture from outside by means of communication.

In the following pages we will pay attention to culture, structure and communication in relation to the process of development.

[1] E. Konijnenberg, 'Research on the Possibilities of Employment for Young People in Agricultural Areas' (1962). Unpublished research study conducted by the Sociological Institute of Utrecht University. See also S. Groenman, *Staphorst* (Meppel, 1947).

[2] S. Groenman, 'External and Internal Causality in Cultural Change', *International Journal of Comparative Sociology,* vol. I, no. i (Mar 1960) p. 103 ff.

2 CULTURE

Culture has been defined by M. Herskovits as 'man-made environment'. In this paper we are principally interested in attitudes, values, norms, beliefs, aspirations, as the underlying phenomena leading to a mental climate. The value-laden attitudes and patterns of behaviour are effective in different fields of people's existence. With respect to underdevelopment, economic life and education seem to be most important.

In developed countries the principle of achievement has acquired a strong emphasis. Moreover, economic goals now have priority over other values. Achievement in economic life has therefore a basic meaning. In underdeveloped areas, and also in areas within developed countries, the achievement-principle is far less effective and other than economic goals come to the forefront. Ossowski[1] gives an interesting example of the rank-order of values in a Polish mountain village. The Tatra farmers are suffering from serious fragmentation of holdings and from an infertile soil – so the planning bodies maintain. The farmers, however, prefer to toil in an irrational way and are satisfied with their existence. They even join the socialist party in order to prevent the execution of reforms. The incentive of greater wealth does not work with them because their value-system is different.

The attitude described by Ossowski has parallels in other under-developed parts of Europe, in the Mezzogiorno and the Italian islands, in Spain and Portugal, even in parts of France. This attitude is the opposite to that of the ideal-typical *homo economicus*. It has the implication that the population feels an aversion against risk-taking production.[2] This has considerable implications for its economic behaviour. Investment for long-term benefits is not very attractive. New industries of the usual kind cannot readily be started. Only the traditional industries with which people are familiar, most of them derived from the traditions of crafts-manship, are acceptable – such industries as weaving-mills, potteries, brass-shops and certain types of food-processing. Metallurgy and electro-technical operations remain beyond the horizon. In the expanded and still expanding world of today the traditional small-scale industries have to cope with serious difficulties. These difficulties are structural in character. It is interesting to read what Moscovici[3] has to say about the reactions of entrepreneurs and of the population of a French problem-area in face of the phenomenon of unemployment. They have known this

[1] S. Ossowski, 'Social Conditions and Consequences of Social Planning'. Paper for I.S.A. Congress, Stresa, 1956.
[2] J. Meyriat *et al.*, *La Calabrie, une région sous-développée de l'Europe méditerranéenne* (1960) p. 201 ff.
[3] S. Moscovici, *Réconversion industrielle et changements sociaux. Un exemple: la chapellerie dans l'Aude* (1961) p. 161 ff.

B 2

phenomenon from old times, but merely as seasonal unemployment. Today they still regard the unemployment as seasonal, thus adopting an unrealistic attitude to it.[1]

The strong reluctance to look for new means of existence outside agriculture or traditional industry is not rooted in a lack of capital to be invested. The 'power élite' often has at its disposal considerable financial resources, but they prefer investment in real estate. The unwillingness of the upper layers of the social hierarchy to start new industries for the remainder of the group has other motives also than the desire to stick to tradition. Industrialisation might, or certainly would, undermine their power.

Thus far we have dealt with attitudes in economic life. In the realm of education we can observe similar phenomena. Modernisation and development would imply an emphasis on training in technical science and on commerce. The emphasis is, however, on the *humaniora* (law, literature and arts).[2] This preference is favourable also to the maintenance of the existing social order, strongly supported by the upper strata. This orientation existing in Sicily and in Greece derives also from national pride. When the Greek state came into existence in the 1820s, instead of concentrating the educational system on technology, medicine, agriculture and other practical fields, badly needed in a poor and economically underdeveloped country, the highest status was given to studies of classical antiquities or Justinian law.[3]

In fact the cultural outlook of the population in a number of underdeveloped areas in Europe is such that the very idea that their regions are underdeveloped and that there is a strong need for modern economic development, especially in the form of industrialisation, has had to be stimulated from outside. Of course, in these regions large numbers of people suffer from poverty; but the concept of poverty differs from the concept of backwardness in principle in the way it is regarded subjectively by the population. Backwardness is a relative concept and it comes to the fore only when there is intensive communication with other regions. The basis for backwardness is communication facilitating comparisons. Now communication means a link between different milieus. The comparison leading to the feeling that a region is backward may arise either within this region itself or with the outside world. I have the strong impression that the problem-areas, or backward-areas as they are now called, are so labelled initially by the central government and by the 'developed' parts

[1] B. Hoselitz, 'Tradition and Economic Growth', in *Tradition, Values and Socio-Economic Development*, eds R. Braibanti and J. Spengler (Duke University Commonwealth Studies Center, Durham, U.S.A., 1961) pp. 94–5. He describes for nineteenth-century France a traditional orientation in entrepreneurship, somewhat narrow-minded and paternalistic, and believing in state support.

[2] R. Rochefort, *Le Travail en Sicile* (1961) p. 284 ff.

[3] B. Hoselitz, *Tradition and Economic Growth*, p. 106: 'The predominance of Greek traditionalism had disastrous results'. See also pp. 100, 108.

of a country. It is often the surrounding society that evokes feelings of dissatisfaction. In this surrounding society the *principium medium* of the welfare state (a principle not to be monopolised by the non-socialist countries) motivates the responsible authorities to take action in the poorer parts of the country: at that stage poverty has been transformed into backwardness.

Ossowski's example of the mountain village population opposing development is a good illustration of the attitude of ingroup versus out-group and vice versa in matters of development. His example demon-strates also the feature, especially manifest in the 'backward' Mediter-ranean areas, of unwillingness until recently to leave the native soil. Most people stick to their village and to their family. Effective communication is needed to make them mobile and to broaden their horizon. On the other hand the experience of recent years has proved that the psychological drawbacks to mobility can certainly be overcome. There is no reason to exaggerate the depth of these parochial and familistic feelings. They are fostered by relative isolation and as soon as isolation is broken down they go through a process of weakening. The doubt we expressed above concerning tradition is strengthened by the fact that so many Italians, Greeks and others now are employed in West European industry.

There is no need to solve here the problem raised earlier as to how far tradition is a real conservative force. I confine myself to some suggestions. Hoselitz [1] elaborating Max Weber's thinking on traditional societies gives the following classification:

habits	non-normative	not self-conscious	not formalised
usages	normative	not self-conscious	not formalised
norms	normative	self-conscious	not formalised
ideologies	normative	self-conscious	formalised

On the one extreme we find habits, on the other ideologies. Hoselitz quotes Edward Shils ('Tradition and Liberty: Antinomy and Inter-dependence', *Ethics*, vol. XLVIII (1958) no. 3 pp. 160–1) for a distinction between tradition and traditionalism. Where the traditional transmission derives from a sacred orientation he speaks of 'traditionalism'. Tra-ditionalism implies an ideology. 'It is the exaltation of tradition for the sake of tradition' (p. 100). There is however an important difference between traditional norms and ideologies (see above). 'If traditional norms are self-consciously held, without necessarily being attached to sacred origin, and without being justified and "rationalised" as deriving their validity from their connection with those sacred origins, they will be more easily subject to alteration and even rejection, than if a set of norms is considered to derive their authority because they are transmitted from a sacred source in the past' (p. 86). Our conclusion might be that in the

[1] B. Hoselitz, *Tradition and Economic Growth*, p. 87.

Mediterranean area ideology is only partly involved. Habits, usages and even norms can be overcome.

3 STRUCTURE

My remarks concerning the cultural pattern of people in backward areas have touched already on the two other phenomena to be dealt with: structure and communication. It is only for purposes of analysis that culture has been separated from them. In my opinion structural phenomena are of more importance than cultural features. Under the heading of social hierarchy we can bring together a whole cluster of considerations. Social hierarchy is the expression of the distribution of wealth, power and prestige. In a number of backward areas of the Mediterranean area – not in Ireland, Finland and other countries – the wealthy rural upper class is a small minority in quantitative terms. At the other end of the social ladder we find the mass of have-nots: small tenants, share-croppers and farmhands. In between a small middle-class category is to be found, for whom the upper layer is the reference-group. Wealth and power are concentrated with the upper class. The interest of this upper class is in the maintenance of the *status quo*. They are opposed to social change, especially to change of a mobilisation character, because it would endanger their position. The weak middle class depends on them. Individuals from this middle class who might be prepared to take new initiative are frustrated from doing so, and their only chance is to emigrate to developed regions. This phenomenon is well known in Italy and its counter-selective effect is clear. The illiteracy of the lower class may be considered as a condition for the position of the power élite.

If Spengler's thesis is true 'that the state of a people's politico-economic development . . . depends largely upon what is in the minds of its members, and above all upon the content of the mind of its elites',[1] there is a strong argument for emphasising the position of the élite in under-developed areas. In this context I may mention the phenomenon of the Mafia in Sicily. The power of this small élite has not been reduced by the process of formal political demonstration. It makes use of the political party system to make its power effective. Max Weber has called this structure the clientele-system. G. Brenan [2] has described the *caciquismo* in Spain, the cacique being an Indian tribal chieftain. In an ECOSOC report [3] the

[1] J. Spengler, 'Theory, Ideology, Non-Economic Values and Politico-Economic Development' in *Tradition, Values and Socio-Economic Development*, p. 4.

[2] G. Brenan, *Spanish Labyrinth* (1943) pp. 7, 94, 268. A. H. H. van Lier, *Spanje, land van tegenstellingen* (*Spain, Country of Contrasts*) (Meppel, 1952) pp. 64–5.

[3] ECOSOC Economic Commission for Latin America, Mar del Plata, Argentina, May 1963, 'Social Development of Latin America in the Post-War Period', document of 15 Apr 1964, pp. 45, 33, 38, 49. See also S. N. Eisenstadt, *Modernisation: Protest and Change* (N.Y., 1966), p. 85 ff.

clientele or caciquismo-system of Latin America has been described. Only the small upper class exercise their civil rights such as voting. The rest of the population depends on them. This large lower class takes part in the life of the country only indirectly. They live, as it were, in a pre-nationalist period. Their bonds of dependence are not formal but on an informal family basis. The upper class functions as a buffer between the central government and the local rural population. In a way there is much resemblance to the former indirect rule system in the former British and Dutch colonies where certain local princes who were granted powers of self-rule insulated the mass of the people from the central government. 'Since [the colonial powers and] indigenous rulers were interested in maintaining the political loyalty of the population they aimed at maintaining a relatively passive type of obedience and identification and were whenever possible ready to utilize the existing traditional loyalties or to transfer them to the new setting without much change in their basic social and cultural orientations.' [1]

In modern times the caciquismo-system (or patronage) has been transformed and has been channelled into the party-structure and other modern media of control.[2] The effect however is similar. We may use the term 'caciquismo' as a *terminus technicus* for the phenomenon of the political dependence of the mass of the population on a small élite. Relics of the system, albeit in modern disguise, could be discovered in such a well-developed country as the Netherlands only a few decades ago, long after the universal right to vote had been laid down in law.

It is obvious that the power structure described above can be disastrous to efforts at modernisation. Vested interests may be able to obstruct government policies designed to increase technical output or to execute land reforms. What Eisenstadt has described in relation to Latin America, where rural improvement agencies were taken over and swallowed, as it were, by these vested interests without the Government being able to control them effectively, has parallels in the Mediterranean area.[3] Eisenstadt makes the surmise that a certain lack of flexibility in the French political system since the Revolution and the politico-diplomatic manœuvres of certain sections of the bureaucracy in Italy have had the effect that the nation state has been established only with relative difficulty in those countries. Thus in France the Revolution created 'continuous rifts between the traditional and modern (revolutionary), aristocratic and republican, religious and secular orientation. . . . In Italy several regions never became fully integrated into the new national frameworks set up around the House of Savoy. These rifts were to no small extent articulated and borne by different regional and professional élites, which tended also to perpetuate them through the establishment of special institutional

---

[1] Eisenstadt, *Modernisation: Protest and Change*, p. 111.
[2] Eisenstadt, ibid., p. 91 for Latin America.   [3] Ibid., p. 92.

frameworks, such as distinct schools and different family, educational and professional traditions.'[1] He speaks of pockets of resistance to change and to modernisation.

Not only has the position of the power élite been dysfunctional for modern economic development; the entire social hierarchy has often been equally so. This hierarchy is rigid. Opportunities for upward social mobility are rare. It cannot be assumed that social mobility is highly valued. In a society directed towards achievement this may be true; where ascriptive role-positions are dominant, mobility is not a thing to be encouraged. Social mobility will become easy, moreover, only when there is a more evenly graduated distribution of wealth. The absence of a wide middle-class stratum is a well-known obstacle to social mobility and to economic development. By means of a mechanism which some authors call penalisation,[2] the population may focus their aspirations on family and village life. In the backward areas of Southern Europe strong emphasis is laid on the (extended) family. The social climate does not favour individual initiative. A relatively high birth-rate, leading to rapid population increase, reduces economic standards of life. In many underdeveloped areas, the young of school-age – to use this term because the degree of actual scolarisation may be low – are relatively numerous. This is a burden for the labour-force, made still more serious because the economically active population is restricted by the fact that married women are seldom gainfully employed. All these facts have been described in terms of Brazil by Jacques Lambert[3] who uses the term *dualistic society*, because some parts of the country are highly developed. The position of the woman is crucial in these backward areas. Alfred Sauvy stresses, among other phenomena, the low position of the woman as one of the criteria for underdevelopment.[4]

Another structural element that requires mention here is the dependence of entrepreneurs on the State. The attitude of seeking to find economic opportunities independently of state support has been developed only slowly in the now developed countries. Talcott Parsons[5] has written an outstanding essay dealing *inter alia* with the origin of entrepreneurial initiative in Western Europe. In the pre-industrial stage, economic productivity was not yet highly appreciated. The political and religious

[1] Eisenstadt, ibid., p. 65.

[2] A. J. Toynbee quoted by F. van Heek in *Het geboorteniveau der Nederlandse Rooms-Katholieken* (*The Birth-Rate of the Dutch Roman Catholics*) (Leyden, 1954) p. 122. [Toynbee, *A Study of History*, vol. II (1935) p. 209.]

[3] 'Resistências à mudença' (Rio, 1960) pp. 27–50. This is a seminar report on 'Fatôres que impedem ou difficultam o desenvolvimento'. See also J. Lambert, 'Croissance démographique et instruction dans les pays en voie de développement', *Population* (1960) p. 655 ff.

[4] A. Sauvy, *Théorie générale de la population*, tome I (1952) pp. 241–2.

[5] T. Parsons, *Structure and Process in Modern Society* (Chicago, 1959) ch. iii.

system was not favourable to rapid economic development. Religion is in general opposed to economic development. It fears secular values as luxury and it favours a traditional behaviour moulded into fixed forms. The Christian religion has however distinguished itself from others by a more secular orientation. Max Weber's famous thesis of the role of Calvinism need not be repeated here. Catholicism has, however, remained not very favourable to economic development. The State (the Prince) has been interested only in short-term goals, in fact in confirming the existing order. Dynamics might endanger the institutional structure. Important for the economic future of Europe has been the balance of power between State and Church. This balance, especially in Northern Europe where the possibility of a theocracy was remote, created opportunity for the cities to become centres of economic development. Over a period of centuries these centres became the nuclei of capitalist economic growth and of emancipation from the powers of State and Church. This led to the emergence of wide differences within Europe and even within single countries. Even in contemporary France such differences are still discernible. The transition from dependence to independence has not been completed. We might speak of a *Fernwirkung*[1] of the traditional situation of the past under which initiative in the economic field was limited to a number of urban centres, even though the actual restrictions are in fact no longer operative. It is the climate of the past that is still prevalent. It is remarkable that so many of the underdeveloped areas of Europe are to be found in countries where Protestantism is absent. In other parts of Europe, on the other hand, Protestantism is the dominant religion or there is the stimulating conflict which operates functionally on less tradition-bound minds.

4 COMMUNICATION

Reference has been made above to the importance of communication for the process of economic development. Lack of communication creates differences in wealth. Communication makes poverty manifest and transforms it into backwardness and may lead on to the beginnings of economic progress. As soon as communication is effective, vague hopes of alleviating of poverty may be replaced by an essentially different type of action to promote a take-off in economic development. Where there is lack of communication, a change in the economic situation implies a comparison with the past. Communication, however, replaces this temporal comparison by a spatial or lateral comparison with other regions. Underdevelopment in one region then is relative to development elsewhere.

Communication not only leads to a new kind of comparison, the lateral one, but also implies a challenge, either for one or both of the regions

[1] F. Löwenthal in *Das kommunistische Experiment* (Köln, 1957) p. 12, coins this expression.

concerned in the comparison. There are many descriptions of partly developed, partly underdeveloped, countries, or 'dualist' countries.[1] Lambert [2] compares Brazil with France in the beginning of the nineteenth century. In France north of the Loire the economic development was more rapid than in the South. Wide differences did not last long, however, because of the opportunities for communication. Where population is less dense and the means of communication are poor, the process of economic and cultural diffusion takes longer. The dualist society as such is not the result of a rapid economic development having its take-off in some centres while others lag behind; it is the result of difficulty of culture diffusion. This culture diffusion, moreover, is not only hampered by geographical isolation but also, as Lambert points out, by social isolation wherever the social hierarchy or power structure (feudalism or large rural estates) resists diffusion. Diffusion, moreover, is a selective process. Some elements are easily overcome, others very slowly. In the field of demography, the death-rate can be lowered within a couple of years; a high birth-rate, on the other hand, will decrease with long delays. Where communication between social categories is not intensive, in the sense that they form social sub-systems of their own, the decrease of the birth-rate has been less. This may be one of the explanations of the relatively high birth-rate in the Netherlands, where until recently Catholics and members of other denominations did not have frequent and intimate social relations and there was a low degree of intermarriage.[3]

Communication has a number of consequences for regions that are relatively little developed in the economic sense of the word. E. F. Schumacher,[4] during a symposium on development policy recently held in Germany, raised the question whether communication may not lead to still greater differences. He underlined the meaning of 'the law of breaking the balance'. The richer regions get richer by communication, the poorer lag behind more and more. He pointed this out not only in relation to parts of India but also to Europe, contrasting Switzerland and parts of Italy. Lack of communication protected the leading economic centres in earlier periods from outside competition. These centres grew proportionately to the increase of communication. Communication worked at that time in their favour; it was disadvantageous to the centres and regions that did not enjoy an early start.

This argument of Schumacher is valid in so far as economic development

[1] See the ECOSOC report, footnote 3, p. 28. Cf. P. González Casanova, 'México desarrollo y subdesarrollo', *Desarrollo económico*, vol. 3 (Apr–Sep 1963) nos 1–2. For Brazil see Lambert, 'Croissance démographique et instruction dans les pays en voie de développement'. [2] Lambert, ibid.

[3] S. Groenman, 'Befolkningsproblemer i Holland og Danmark', *Økonomi og Politik* (Copenhagen, 1951).

[4] E. F. Schumacher, Bergedorfer Gesprächskreis, Protokoll 15: 'Entwicklungshilfe– Mittel des Aufstiegs oder des Verfalls?' (1964).

is left to the free interplay of forces. As soon as State intervention has become the rule, communication will have the counter-effect that the poorer or backward areas will be integrated into development plans for the whole country. The position of the élite in the backward areas in other circumstances is crucial, because they are the first among the local population to have contacts with the wealthier parts of the country concerned. A conservative stand when confronted with the possibility of economic change may postpone the effects of a policy of development. On the other hand if the local élite were to insist on rapid economic growth of an ultra-modern character there might arise problems of a quite different nature. As W. E. Moore [1] has put it clearly: 'The attempt to compress time, to jump a period of decades or a century, may be exceptionally costly or in some instances impossible. The most advanced productive technology is likely to be capital-intensive but labor saving. Yet capital is acutely scarce and labor is generally abundant in underdeveloped areas.'

These comments are relevant, however, more to the new nations outside Europe than to areas in a developed country. In the regions with which we are here dealing there is little evidence that the élite will insist on very modern plants, whereas cheaper and more labour-intensive equipment would seem to be a more economically justifiable policy. In developed countries, moreover, objections to ultra-modern development would have less relevance because the economic diversity is not as great as it is if we compare developed with underdeveloped countries. Furthermore, experience has shown that the local population is often prepared to migrate to other places with greater opportunities of employment. Schumacher's plea for an 'intermediate technology' for underdeveloped areas does not seem appropriate to most underdeveloped areas within developed countries. For these regions we must reject also his proposal that we should avoid making communication with developed areas too intensive, so as to create thus sorts of islands protected from the effect of the 'law of breaking the balance'. In developed countries communication is a reality that simply cannot be denied. Either the population of a backward area will take the situation in other parts of the country as a frame of reference; or these other parts – or, more likely, the central government – will try to start a development programme. Possibly there are regions where it is not physically possible to raise the economic level up to the national standard, as may be the case in some Alpine Valleys.[2] In that case the only solution may be migration.

[1] W. E. Moore, *Man, Time and Society* (N.Y., 1963) p. 143.
[2] Giuseppe Carone, 'The Alpine Economy and its Present Problems', in *Regional Rural Development Programmes: with Special Emphasis on Depressed Agricultural Areas Including Mountain Areas*, O.E.C.D. Documentation in Agriculture and Food, no. 66 (1964) p. 61 ff.

A development policy may make use of the effects of communication by creating centres for development, rather than attempting a uniform distribution of the new economic facilities. I do not propose to deal here with the economic effects of the creation of poles of growth as analysed by François Perroux and others. I shall confine myself to some of the sociological effects of such an unequal distribution. C. Arnold Anderson [1] has suggested that one should work out a strategy for educational development such that development is started in nuclei attached to a hierarchy of centres, having it in mind that the surrounding areas, deprived of the benefits of this policy, will be stimulated to higher aspirations. To quote him: 'I maintain that effective elementary and middle education should be sustained in the dynamic centres – even at the expense of remote villages' (p. 267). What he proposes is precisely the exploitation of the effectiveness of 'the law of breaking the balance', in this case with the hope that communication and diffusion will arouse aspirations for economic development. In the United States in the nineteenth century, education (closely linked to economic development in ecological clusters) spread from an (unplanned) hierarchical system of centres to the countryside where education was first on a very primitive basis. Anderson shows that the earlier inequality has been replaced by an impressive outlevelling. The diversities had the desired effect. An important precondition, however, was that the population outside the centres was receptive of this stimulus of inequality and had come to the U.S.A. already possessed of aspirations for a better life.

My impression of the situation, in Europe at least, is that communication plays a very important role in the problem of backwardness. It will impose a severe strain on conservative cultural attitudes and will also weaken the position of the local or regional élite. It creates feelings of dissatisfaction and frustration in the mass of the population. It stimulates migration and makes individuals with initiative aware of new possibilities, either at home or elsewhere.

The importance of communication in development may be inferred also from the fact that most backward areas are remote from the economic centres of the country. This is true not only of the larger areas in the Mediterranean region but also for the smaller problem-areas in other countries. The latter are backward indeed, but in reality they are not poor in the real sense of the word. They do not suffer from such non-economic criteria of underdevelopment as low standards of medical care or illiteracy. In Germany, Belgium, the Netherlands or France these problem areas are close to the national frontiers. So where frontiers have a real social meaning, this location implied relative isolation. Notwithstanding the close

[1] C. Arnold Anderson, 'The Impact of the Educational System in Technological Change and Modernization', in *Industrialization and Society*, eds B. F. Hoselitz and W. E. Moore (1963) p. 259 ff.

economic relations existing nowadays between countries in Western Europe, we may say that the social importance of frontiers is more powerful than in the nineteenth century. The much greater number of the legal measures of individual states concerning prices, wages, social security, education, taxes, military service has created differences on the two sides of the existing frontiers. Newspapers bring the national news precisely up to the boundaries of national territories; the foreign news is far less detailed. The frontier in fact brings about a big difference in scale concerning the spread of news. *Connubium* and *convivium* across the borderlines are less frequent than in the nineteenth century. The distant large centres within the national territory seem much nearer than the nearby centres of the neighbouring country. Social distance and geographical distance have become different since the borderlines have acquired a more social meaning. It is true that radio and television are not hampered by national frontiers and it is true also that in recent times a start has been made in lowering the barriers between the different countries. Nevertheless the population living inside the frontiers of a country is still overwhelmingly oriented to national interests. It is quite understandable that they are far more interested in the national policy of their own government than in the national policy of the government on the other side of the frontier. In fact radio and television, and not only the press, intensify the concern about national affairs. That there is an increased concern also about international affairs does not make this less true. The point that matters here is that there is no detailed concern about the neighbouring foreign country as such and its policy in different spheres of life.

I re-emphasise therefore that it is in our generation that location of an area near the frontier has come to mean partial isolation. Such an area is marginal; it looks, as it were, in one direction, the direction where the political, economic and social centre of the home country is lying. Hitherto it has been a rarity to find a development plan prepared for a region containing parts of more than one country.[1]

5 SOME CONCLUSIONS

Value systems remain of importance in the backward areas of developed countries. They are especially so in the case of cultural values rooted in a sacred origin. On the other hand there is no reason to lay too much emphasis on cultural obstacles in general. The strength of cultural traits may often be ascribed to the power of an élite, whose social, political and economic position is likely to be endangered by social change. Structural

[1] International Planning, *Regio basiliensis*, Bulletin, International Federation for Housing and Planning (1967). Soziologisches Seminar des Instituts für Sozialwissenschaften der Universität Basel, Soziologische Regio Untersuchung (1965).

factors seem to be of more importance than cultural traditions. Those structural factors include not only the presence of a conservative élite, but also the lack of a middle class, and the position of the family and of the woman in society.

Communication is the dynamising factor in backward areas. It creates awareness of differences in comparison with other areas, and it will make these differences more significant. It functions on the other hand as an incentive to level out the differences. Communication thus brings about an attack on regional value systems and on the position of the social élite. In developed countries communication is an indispensable instrument in a policy of programme implementation in backward areas. Communication activates the population, leads to a change of values and attitudes. It stimulates migration. It weakens vested interests and paves the way for new initiative with the support of the government. Better means of communication improve the industrial climate and form an essential part of the infrastructure of economic development.

Part 2 The Experience of Western Europe and the United States

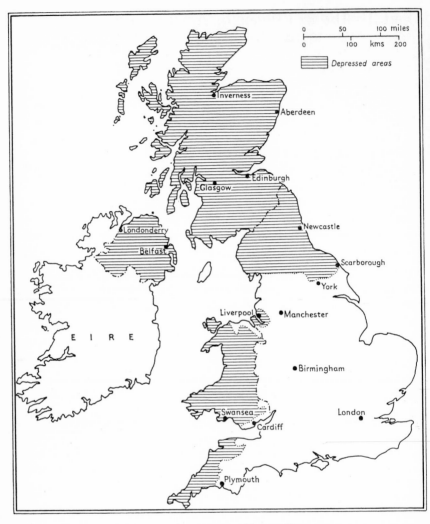

DEVELOPMENT AREAS IN THE UNITED KINGDOM

3 Regional Policy in the United Kingdom

M. C. MacLennan and D. J. Robertson

DEPARTMENT OF SOCIAL AND ECONOMIC RESEARCH,
UNIVERSITY OF GLASGOW

1 INTRODUCTORY

It is not possible, nor indeed desirable, to attempt a full factual description
of the history and operation of regional policy in Britain in this paper.
The paper begins with statements of the main problems which have
necessitated regional policy. It then moves on to an analysis of the
objectives and some of the main issues of regional policy in the United
Kingdom and concludes with a discussion of the relationship between
national and regional economic planning. This subject is treated at some
length because the organisers of the conference wished us to do so, and
because it is an issue which is central to both national and regional
economic policies in the United Kingdom at the present time.

2 THE MAIN PROBLEMS

The United Kingdom is largely urbanised: over four-fifths of the population lives in towns and 35 per cent lives in 7 conurbations; 6 of these are
of more than a million people and 5 are of more than $1\frac{1}{2}$ million. The
London conurbation has a population of around 8 millions or about 15
per cent of the total population of around 54 millions. Employment in
agriculture is small (3 per cent of insured employees). The total land area
of the United Kingdom is small (about 94 thousand square miles, which is
only about 2 per cent of that of the continental U.S.A. excluding Alaska,
and a little less than that of New England). Over 30 per cent of the total
area is in Scotland which has less than 10 per cent of the population. The
only really substantial undeveloped areas, not closely attached to cities,
are in the Scottish Highlands, where the seven 'crofting counties' in the
North and West account for about 15 per cent of the area of the United
Kingdom and only 0·5 per cent of the population. There are lesser
'empty' areas in the South-West of England, down the central spine of the
Pennines, in Central and Northern Wales, and to the West of Northern
Ireland. By and large the areas which are thinly urbanised are also
mountainous or moorland – notably the Scottish Highlands.

It follows from this brief description of the geography of Britain that its
regional problems are scarcely at all concerned with opening up new areas

for development, but are urban and industrial in character and centred on the distinctions between two sets of areas – those to the North and West of the country which may be termed 'underemployed' and the South-Eastern and Midlands regions which are the most fully employed and most rapidly growing parts of the country. As a matter of perspective, however, it should be recorded that the average level of unemployment in Britain since the war has rarely been much over 2 per cent, and that the average level of unemployment in the 'underemployed' regions is usually less than twice the national average. Only in the case of Northern Ireland, with unemployment rates of 6 or 7 per cent or more, do the unemployment figures indicate any substantial departure from full employment on conventional definition.

The problems of the 'underemployed' regions of the United Kingdom are those of areas which were industrialised and urbanised in the nineteenth century. Their large cities are in need of redevelopment and have more than their share of bad housing and urban decay. Their industrial structure is hampered by an above-average share of slow-growing or declining industries, reflecting their early industrialisation and the subsequent shift of emphasis from the older capital goods (such as shipbuilding) and export industries (such as cotton textiles and South Wales coal) towards the consumer goods and technologically more advanced industries of the twentieth century. During the 1930s, and more particularly as the rest of the economy began to recover from the depression of the earlier part of that decade, the industrial regions in the North and West of Britain were seen to have below-average incomes, above-average unemployment, and generally to suffer from the kind of social obsolescence which goes with high unemployment and lagging or declining industrial sectors. The war changed the picture somewhat since the older heavy industries enjoyed a boom period during the war years.

At the same time, however, the debate about regional policy which had begun in the thirties continued and at the end of war, with the Distribution of Industry Act 1945, serious attempts to try to rebuild the prosperity of such regions commenced. The list of 'backward' regions which then emerged has continued relatively unchanged since that date – Northern Ireland, the central industrial belt of Scotland, the North-East Coast of England, some parts of the North-West of England and South Wales. Their below-average wage earnings are usually accompanied by an unsatisfactory occupational spread, with a tendency to be short of administrative and professional salaried groups, while their above-average unemployment is accompanied by a tendency to low activity rates. They tend to lose population by emigration, and the net emigrant flow results in a loss of younger people and of skilled rather than unskilled workers. They have more problems of outdated social capital, and perhaps especially housing obsolescence, than is customary in the expanding areas, though housing in London for different reasons has also been a problem. Urban improvement requires a change in the pattern of land use to take account of the higher space standards now customary and also generally to improve the environment, and this requires physical planning involving some degree of relocation of industry, of housing and of social facilities, and planning of the distribution of activity within the regions, and especially of the relationships between their older cities and newer locations where further growth can be achieved.

In recent years there has been a growing realisation in Britain that the problems of regional development are not in fact confined solely to the 'backward' regions and that a number of problems now face the rapidly expanding areas. Most of these are not at all concerned with industrial structure, but rather with the increasing social costs of congestion deriving from prosperity. The internal replanning of the South and East of England has become a subject of increasing attention and the view has grown that it will be necessary to find some means of spreading the growth of these prosperous regions somewhat more widely over the ground than at present.

Problems of the regional development of societies which have a substantially agricultural or rural tradition, while they are typical of many countries, do not have a large place in the British scene. The only example which receives any emphasis is that of the development of the Highlands of Scotland. In this case, however, the natural resource endowment is poor and, apart from a few locations, the labour is scattered. The main claim of this area to attention on the ground of resources is its ample supply of land for recreation and for possible urban development should the rest of Britain become over-congested. However, since it is very much a special case, this particular aspect of the British regional problem will be set aside in the remainder of this paper.

3 THE OBJECTIVES OF REGIONAL POLICY

Three possible statements of the objectives of regional policy are appropriate to the British situation. Heavy unemployment and depressed living standards naturally and properly generate political pressures for their amelioration. It is reasonable to contend that measures adopted up until the late fifties had a strong flavour of a social welfare policy simply designed to improve the lot of the less fortunate parts of British society. The main measures were designed to improve social infrastructure and to diversify the industrial structure of the backward regions so as to offset the unemployment problems of the heavy industries. The policy was not intended to be highly selective in terms of the areas and industries that should be induced to expand in the regions and it was motivated by social and political concern rather than a desire to promote economic growth in the regions. It will be obvious that this type of policy is difficult to justify on economic grounds and does not depend on an economic assessment of particular proposals for development. At its worst it simply means taking jobs to workers wherever they may be found and looking for bad social conditions and trying to improve them by expenditure on infrastructure. It is perhaps not surprising that the policy did not work quite in this way and that its successes derived from selection by administrators and industrialists from the areas and opportunities offered to their attention of those in which they thought they saw some prospect of growth.

The second possible objective of policy is that of aligning regional development to the growth of the economy as a whole. This view, which began to develop strongly only in the present decade, is now the one which holds the field in Britain. It is exemplified by the inclusion of regional policy in the National Economic Development Council's publication *Conditions Favourable to Faster Growth*, and subsequently in the National Plan, where a positive regional policy is seen as one of the means of obtaining the Plan's overall growth target. Viewed in this way, regional policy is concerned to utilise available resources. The argument is that the resources of labour available in particular regions cannot readily be transported to other regions without some surplus capacity remaining in the underemployed regions since a low activity rate can only be improved in the region where it occurs, and emigration on a sizable scale has the effect of diminishing the chances of growth in the region supplying the emigrants because of its qualitative effects on the labour force. It can also be argued that regional development is a means of using social capital which, though in many cases inadequate and obsolescent, exists in the underemployed regions, and a means of ensuring that new social capital established in underemployed regions as a result of national policies can be put to the most effective use. In Britain, at least, social investment policies on matters like hospitals, schools and housing are determined by the inadequacy of the existing stock of such capital and thus the underemployed regions are likely to receive a share of such investment at least equal to their share of total population.

A further argument for regional development which is particularly important in the British context is the opportunity which the underemployed regions offer for running the economy at a higher level of capacity utilisation without creating inflationary pressures and weakening the balance of payments. On several occasions since the war, restraints have had to be imposed on national economic expansion because of the existence of inflationary pressures while some regions of the economy have not been under these pressures and indeed have been operating below full employment. A more even pattern of utilisation of resources is therefore seen as one way of avoiding the need to halt growth before the economy as a whole is fully employed. A policy of regional development aimed at obtaining growth in the regions as part of a policy to achieve a faster rate of national growth must be highly selective as regards the locations within the region to be favoured and the nature of development and the types of investment by public authorities to be promoted within the region.

A third objective of regional policy concerns urban development and redevelopment. Urban development policy in Britain is concerned chiefly with the problems of redevelopment of older urban centres and the relief of congestion in certain urban areas. These problems are particularly acute in the expanding areas of the South-East but are present in all urbanised regions. Essentially the argument is that the social costs of continuing to redevelop and extend existing cities are high and increasing. There is, therefore, a case for choosing new locations for urban development, and for planning them on a scale which will allow economies of scale to be obtained and which will enable them to attract and sustain industrial, commercial and service expansion. Such a policy creates a mobile population which is being relocated for urban reasons, and makes it more feasible to think of an interregional redistribution of population, or at the least a changing of the pattern of migrant flows so as to obtain more even growth as between regions. This is an objective of regional policy for the underemployed regions but it is also a strategy which may be employed in all regions.

4 THE MEASURES EMPLOYED

It is possible to regard the regional policy measures currently employed in Britain as an attempt to meet the second and third of the above objectives – the promotion of faster national and regional growth and urban redevelopment and avoidance of congestion. It is now accepted that the most effective way to improve social conditions in a region is to create a healthy regional economy. Such a regional policy must include improvements to social capital and give attention to physical planning just as much as industrial policy. This section will discuss briefly three of the more interesting aspects of the policies actually employed over the last few years – the use of controls on development, direct assistance to industrial enterprise in the regions, the link between infrastructure planning and regional development, including the concept of growth areas.

CONTROLS ON DEVELOPMENT

Ever since 1947 entrepreneurs wishing to expand their premises or create new premises have been required to obtain an Industrial Development Certificate. Originally, Certificates were required for developments of more than 5,000 square feet but are now needed for developments of more than 1,000 square feet, and some controls have also been put on office development in the London area. Is such a policy essential to the successful operation of regional policy and is it efficient and effective?

The evidence of pressure by employers to expand in the South and East of England since the war suggests that without this control there would have been an even more rapid expansion of demand for labour and facilities than has actually taken place there. The expansion that has actually occurred has been sufficient to create higher levels of demand for labour, higher activity rates, lower unemployment and generally greater shortages of manpower in that part of Britain than elsewhere. This imbalance has posed problems for the management of the British economy since it has meant that the economy has had to be regulated to avoid demand inflation in those areas while surplus labour supplies have been available elsewhere, thus creating a social cost of wasted resources in other regions. At the same time immigration and natural increase in the South and East have been sufficient to create demands for new infrastructure at costs per unit which are generally considered to be above those obtaining in other parts of the country, while there has also been an increase in the social costs created by congestion and distance between work, home and facilities. These factors have led physical planners to recommend a substantial relocation of population. To some extent, therefore, the controls on industrial development have harmonised with the intended pattern of controls of the physical planners.

If, then, the Industrial Development Certificates have been necessary, have they been efficient? There are three possible tests of efficiency. First, efficiency can be defined in terms of obtaining a fuller use of national resources; secondly, efficiency may be taken to mean securing a certain level of productivity from the relocated enterprise; thirdly, efficiency may be the ability to distinguish between those investments which are able to prosper in alternative locations and those which cannot. The third type of efficiency depends largely on the finesse with which I.D.C. policy is administered. Whatever else is needed in regional policy an experienced and flexible group of administrators is required, and here the high quality of the British Civil Service is an important asset. As to the first point, the effect of the controls has been to make available for location in underemployed regions employment opportunities thus shifting demand for labour which, even taking account of migration flows, would otherwise have increased the unsatisfied demand for labour in the overemployed regions, and also to improve the utilisation of social capital in a number of parts of the country while avoiding some part of the need to provide more social capital in high-cost areas. For this argument to have any validity in the longer term, however, it is also necessary to ensure that the productivity of labour in the underemployed regions will not be significantly below that in other regions for an extended period of time. Thus the first two criteria of efficiency are linked. This point leads naturally to a consideration of the more positive inducements to industrial development in the regions and the type of new employment and other economic effects which they create there and the need to provide appropriate infrastructure investment and external economies in the regions. These issues are discussed in turn below.

DIRECT ASSISTANCE TO INDUSTRY IN THE REGIONS

The simplest theoretical explanation of disparities in the economic development of different regions is that factor costs in the underemployed regions are higher than in other regions. If it is decided to promote the development of such regions, the most effective policy is to reduce the factor costs incurred by industries expanding in the regions. In the British context, however, the disparities in regional development are in large measure due to changes in the structure of industry and the pattern of domestic demand. These changes have left the underemployed regions with industrial structures dominated by industries whose products are facing a secular decline in demand. Such structural disadvantages may be regarded as removable by the attraction of newer, growing industries to the regions. In this case, therefore, policy measures should be made self-terminating as injections of new employment and income into the regions correct the adverse condition and should be expressly designed to promote new growth which is self-sustaining. To achieve this objective, special efforts must be made in the training and retraining of labour to meet the requirements of the newer industries, the development of managerial expertise, the promotion of research and development, the provision of modern factory buildings, and in improving financial and related institutions as well as improving the infrastructure and physical planning of the regions.

British regional policy has contained all the above elements but in recent years the main form of direct aid to industry has been that of building and investment grants. Such grants have the advantage of giving a start to new enterprise which must then become self-sustaining. If they are to be effective they must be sufficiently certain in incidence and clear in conception to be firmly and safely included in a firm's decision-taking on the location of new operations. In the past this was not true of the British system of grants, loans, and favourable tax provisions. But although the recent switch to clearly defined grants has simplified and clarified the system of inducements it is still inadequate in certain respects. One major limitation of grants towards initial capital cost is that the firm is left to meet the costs of the first few settling-in years in its new location unaided, and settling-in problems can affect management, labour productivity and training, component supplies and transport and communications generally.

The Government's decision to introduce, in September 1967, the controversial regional employment premium (REP) amounting to $7\frac{1}{2}$ per cent of labour costs for a period of seven years will, for the first time in the history of British regional policy, give firms in manufacturing industry a subsidy on *current* costs which will help to offset the additional operating costs incurred during the settling-in period. It can be argued that such a subsidy given unselectively to all manufacturing industry may prop up inefficient firms and attract to the underemployed regions firms which are labour-intensive and therefore less able to achieve high levels of productivity. On the other hand, investment grants are still in operation and continue to offer considerable attractions to the capital-intensive industries required by the regions. It is also debatable whether REP will for any length of time shore up an uncompetitive firm faced with a declining demand for its products or whether it can offer greater benefits to a potentially efficient firm than could be obtained by the introduction of new equipment with the subsequent raising of productivity. Moreover, if REP is successful as an additional inducement to new development it will necessarily speed up the reduction of employment in declining firms and quicken the desired structural changes in industry in the regions.

It is difficult to be precise about the productivity of firms in the underemployed regions. It can be said, however, that (*a*) the kind of grants and other aids available to help industry in the regions have in the past tended to favour capital-intensive operations, (*b*) all aid is temporary and, therefore, has required firms to become competitive with those in other regions to survive, and (*c*) the underemployed regions have industrial experience and past successes so that the problem can be regarded as one of structural adjustment rather than the launching of completely new development. The only element of cost that is likely to be greater is that of transport, and here as much or more stress is laid by industrialists on convenience as on the cost of transport narrowly defined. Much of the success of regional policy, therefore, depends on the way in which social infrastructure is developed to provide a proper environment for growth and the creation of external economies in the regions which will offset the disadvantage of an inconvenient location.

INFRASTRUCTURE PLANNING AND REGIONAL DEVELOPMENT

Any comment on this large and complex topic must necessarily be extremely brief, but there are four main points that should be made.

(1) Modern industry needs an efficient transport system for the movement of goods and people. People require air as well as land services and goods require satisfactory access to the ports. It is obvious that a conjunction of such facilities requires both prior planning and the selection of locations for development.

(2) It is important to provide a large and varied labour market. This again requires well-developed communications and the choice of locations for development which can pull together the labour reserves of a wide area.

(3) Environment and facilities are important both because the facilities are a source of varied employment and because of the need to have the

type of community that can attract and retain managerial and professional workers. Some of the facilities required such as hospitals and educational institutions depend on timely government investment. The provision of commercial facilities is related to the scale of existing development and new growth. A varied range of housing is an essential need in regional policy (and is the Achilles heel of much of British regional planning).

(4) All this implies selection and concentration of effort. An area which is selected and is being developed in line with the above criteria, whether development consists of a large expansion of an existing community, the pulling together and refocusing of a number of older communities, or (less desirably) large-scale expansion on a new site, can be regarded as a growth area. With some aberrations and occasional forgetfulness, British regional policy has a growth area outlook.

5   RECENT CHANGES IN THE MACHINERY OF REGIONAL PLANNING

The machinery of regional planning in Britain has been changing in recent years as well as the policies. Up to five years or so ago location of industry policy was the responsibility of the Board of Trade, labour policy was administered by the Ministry of Labour, town planning was guided by the Ministry of Housing and Local Government, and so on. Only in Scotland and Northern Ireland could it be said that there was anything in the way of a single coherent unit of administration of a number of aspects of regional policy and only the Government of Northern Ireland, which is a very special case, had powers in matters relating to labour and trade.

It is generally unwise for an underemployed region to seek too much autonomy in economic affairs since it is usually dependent on the national government for some assistance with its development. On the other hand, a coherent policy for a region requires detailed application and for this co-ordination is most important. Some degree of co-ordination has been achieved in the last few years by the creation of regional planning Boards and Councils for 'regions' in every part of the United Kingdom. The planning Boards (for which the Scottish Development Group based on the Scottish Office and set up by the Conservative Government was the original model) are staffed by civil servants from all the relevant departments of government – except the Treasury. These Boards have achieved a greater degree of coherence in policies within their regions by forcing comparison and reconciliation of the policies of the separate agencies of government. The effectiveness of their efforts has, however, been related both to the strength of the regional offices of the Ministries which are represented (and here the Scottish region has benefited from its tradition of regional civil servants), and to the coherence of the regions with which they are concerned (and some of the 'regions' in the southern half of

England seem disturbed by finding themselves classified as regions at all). The political aspect of regional interests in planning has been represented by the creation of appointed Councils. These Councils, though experience varies with personalities and with the strength or weakness of the Boards, have as yet not appeared to have a clear and separate function. They are neither obviously representative nor obviously expert and have occasionally appeared to have rather little to do.

The need for co-ordination in administration also arises, of course, in the application of policies in areas within the regions themselves, especially since physical plans and the location of infrastructure are at issue. Sub-regional administration in Britain has been seriously hampered by the competing jurisdictions of local authorities, which are usually too small to give simple administration to areas which form any part of a satisfactory unit of analysis for employment, residential, transport or other economic or physical planning purposes. Royal Commissions on Local Government in England and Wales and in Scotland are presently sitting and have received recommendations in favour of many fewer and much larger jurisdictions from those interested in regional planning.

It was to be expected that the growth of interest in national planning and the division of the whole country into regions by the creation of the Boards and Councils would increase interest in the reconciliation of regional plans with each other and with national planning. The task of doing this is now entrusted to the Department of Economic Affairs. It cannot be said that the process of reconciliation is fully operative. It is possible to argue that regional plans are to be regarded as target-setters, and that all that is needed is a process of rough averaging of aspirations and plans rather than precise accounting. Precise figures have, of course, to be put on regional social investment and the task here appears to be still largely with the traditional conciliator and adjuster of British governmental expenditure – the Treasury. The emphasis on economic planning imparted to the process by the Department of Economic Affairs may perhaps be thought to have left too much to one side the physical planning processes which, in England, are still related rather to the Ministry of Housing and Local Government while the precise divisions of guidance on broad transport planning between Economic Affairs and Transport are not clear. The essential question to ask, however, is how closely national and regional planning should be related, and this is the topic of our next and last section.

6　THE RELATIONS BETWEEN NATIONAL AND REGIONAL PLANNING

A national economic plan for the British economy can be said to contain three main features.

　(1)　It is likely to state a limited number of general objectives, all of them related to a particular rate or rates of growth of G.N.P. which it is considered the economy can achieve over a given period of time. The objectives might, for example, include an increase in social expenditure, an increase in productivity in one or more broad sectors, an increase in defence expenditure. Such a statement may lay emphasis on available resources within existing constraints and begin from there, or begin with objectives and consider the resulting problems of resource availability and allocation.

(2) These objectives are then stated in the form of a consistent, quantified programme of expansion for the economy, indicating the probable state of the economy in the terminal year of the plan, possibly including alternative limiting assumptions and related performances. This programme is likely to be disaggregated to the industry or sector level.

(3) A plan to be operational must contain an amalgam of policies and measures which are consistent with each other and directed towards promoting the objectives set out in the programme.

The contribution of such a plan to the management of the national economy may take several forms:

(1) It may reduce uncertainty about future developments in the economy by presenting a detailed, coherent forecast of the potential increase in resources available, taking account of probable changes in technical progress and other factors. It is hoped that this will help to raise expectations and thus stimulate investment and growth.

(2) It will enable each sector of the economy, whether publicly or privately controlled, to be better informed about the plans and policies of the others and, therefore, about the future movement of demand for its products. This will allow a more rational and accurate view to be taken of investment opportunities. It is likely, however, that the direct association between the planning process and decisions on expenditure will be closer for government investment programmes than in the private sector.

(3) It will act as a co-ordinating framework for economic policy measures affecting production and costs, i.e. the supply rather than the demand side.

(4) The attainment of the plan's objectives must be a major factor to be taken into account in every economic policy decision about the management of demand in the short term.

A national plan for growth must inevitably involve different assumptions about the degree of utilisation of the resources of the regions in the economy. In this sense regional development is bound to be integrated with national development. The working out of a national plan tends, however, to compel a more detailed and comprehensive analysis of the different contributions which different regions can make to the desired increase in national resources, and of the pattern of government expenditure in the

C

regions. Some kind of regional planning is needed, therefore, to complement the national plan. The question then arises whether the regional plans ought to be different in form from the national plan, as defined above, or the same model on a smaller scale.

The argument that a national plan will have a favourable 'expectations' effect assumes that the productive machine is flexible and that the growth of output can be brought about by creating an optimistic view of the future growth of demand. This is the main justification for a 'target plan' at the sector or industrial level. The assumption of flexibility is a large one, as the short-lived British experience has eloquently shown, particularly in an economy with a high degree of dependence on international trade which has difficulty in competing with other nations. No coherent forecasts of domestic demand can, by themselves, widen these constraints. In the case of a regional economy, especially that of an underemployed region dominated by declining industries, the same constraints apply *a fortiori*. A system of regional industry targets, conceived as a method of promoting growth, has several serious disadvantages. First, if the region is dominated by uncompetitive, declining industries, the stimulating effect of the plan is likely to be either ineffective or undesirable. Secondly, the job of preparing a regional target plan is very much more costly and difficult than the national exercise. For what ideally is required for a coherent forecast of a region's economy disaggregated to the industry level is not just an *intraregional* input-output table dealing only with output and demand within the region with columns for all regional exports and imports, but an *interregional* input-output table which would allow the location and forecast performance of client and supplier industries in other regions to be identified. Finally, any forecast of the demand for the output of a region's industries must involve assumptions about the competitiveness of the industries and, in the case of a declining region, the changes in the industrial structure of the region which are necessary to enable it to expand.

Regional industry forecasts can be got much more easily, and with as much hope of accuracy, by splicing extrapolations of past performance with modifications to the national industry forecasts to take account, as far as is at all possible, of the consequences of a change in the industrial structure of the region. The most important job of regional planners must be to use the weapons provided by regional policy to organise such changes – in effect, to alter the technical coefficients of the input-output table and not simply assume them. The industry targets can be no more than benchmarks. Like the industry figures in a national plan they cannot, by themselves, affect the constraint of uncompetitiveness. It may well be, of course, that the regional planners may wish to examine the interindustry and interregional links between important new firms induced to establish in their region and their suppliers and outlets. But this kind of partial analysis of a specific complex of industries is a much less ambitious undertaking than a general industry level forecast for the region. It is, moreover, essentially an aid to other policy actions and does not make any claims to self-fulfilling powers.

The various policy measures referred to above as the supply side actions of a plan are, therefore, of crucial importance for regional planning. They must be aimed at promoting development in the regions in a way and at a pace which is compatible with the objectives of the national plan. This condition distinguishes policies aimed at achieving the objectives of the regional 'section' of a national plan from regional development policies pursued on an *ad hoc* basis in response to regional needs at any given time. Furthermore, the policies required to stimulate regional development have several specific characteristics which make a regional plan different from a national plan.

(1) To be compatible with a national plan for growth a regional plan must be directed towards producing the maximum possible growth in the region. This will require a selective policy concentrating on those areas within the region where growth can most successfully be promoted. It may also require a selective policy as between industries but, in any event, a decision must be made about the future distribution of industry and population within the region. This means that a regional plan must examine the land-use pattern of the region, the communications system and the nature and size of communities, and the relation of all these to industrial growth in the region. A regional plan must, therefore, pay much more attention to the *physical planning* aspects of economic growth than the national plan, and this requires a quite different type of expertise.

(2) To create self-sustaining growth, regional policy must create economies of scale and external economies in the declining regions, similar to those which exist in the more prosperous regions, which will offset any geographical disadvantages which the regions may have. Such a strategy requires large-scale public infrastructure investment in the regions, concentrated particularly in pre-selected areas where it is physically and economically possible for industries to expand. This, in turn, means that the amount of public investment allowed for in the national plan must take into account not only the need for each category of investment but the complexes of public investment required to stimulate regional growth. It must be a primary function of a regional plan to spell out such requirements and the task of regional planners to argue for them. Substantial infra-structure investment laid down in advance of demand for it may not yield returns, either financially or in terms of increased output, within the period of a five-year plan, but be essential for long-term regional expansion. Regional planning agencies must, therefore, have a voice in discussions about the volume and pattern of public investment in both the plan and the annual budget if the basis of the regional plans is to be assured.

(3) Since regional planning requires the selection of areas where

conditions are favourable to growth, and since the promotion of this growth requires large-scale public investment over a more or less long period, the Government must form a view about the long-term distribution of population and industry which it wishes to promote and which will be written into the various regional plans. A strategy to achieve a certain distribution of population and industry is a much longer-term operation than a medium-term national plan. The total costs and benefits to the economy of various regional settlement patterns cannot, therefore, be calculated in terms of accretions of resources within the period of the national plan. The promotion of regional development may, in these circumstances, appear to the Government to yield low or negative returns if it looks only at the period of the plan, particularly if an additional requirement of regional development is the expansion of fast-growing, high-productivity industries away from their original or preferred locations to others where their rate of expansion may be temporarily slowed down and the expenditure of public funds to encourage them to do so. A long-term view of the prospects of all the regions in the economy must, therefore, be worked out and held as an eventual aim of regional policy.

(4) The pace of regional development and the future of regional planning will depend to a large extent on whether the Government considers regional policy as unproductive expenditure, at least in the short-term, and therefore liable to postponement and restriction if the economy runs against the balance of payments constraint, or whether it sees the development of the underemployed regions as a way of breaking this constraint. In the former case, if the balance of payments position should cause the national plan to be interrupted or revised, public expenditure on infrastructure may be one of the first items to be cut back. Moreover, if increased productivity is emphasised as a way of breaking the balance of payments limitation, the central government may be more than usually reluctant to operate a policy of controls and incentives which encourages the movement of growth industries to locations where they will take some years to reach full efficiency. On the other hand, it may be argued, as it was for the regional employment premium in the United Kingdom, that the development of the underemployed regions may be a useful and, in terms of national output, an immediately profitable way of maintaining expansion in the face of inflationary pressures since the pressure on resources in these regions is lowest. This presupposes, however, that there will be no large leakage of demand from these regions, that it is possible to stimulate such expansion by financial incentives alone, and that national productivity growth will not suffer for any significant time. There are, therefore, real possibilities of conflict between the national plan and regional plans. This fact underlines the importance of having some long-term strategy for the growth and distribution of industry and population. This cannot be arrived at by a summation of regional plans but must be decided after

consultation and argument between regional and national interests. Such a strategy may be interrupted and distorted but it will go some way towards preventing the regional balance of the economy being determined simply as a by-product of the exigencies of successive medium-term national plans.

In summary, regional planning is more detailed in its attention to physical planning and to infrastructure than national planning. It requires different expertise and, while there is a regional ingredient in the quantitative presentation of a national plan, regional plans must be more statements of related policies, and less simply numerical, and be longer-term in their application. In the light of recent experience, perhaps the same might be accepted for national planning in the United Kingdom as well.

4 The Regional Problem in the U.S.A.

Benjamin Chinitz

BROWN UNIVERSITY, PROVIDENCE, RHODE ISLAND

1 INTRODUCTION

Since 1961 when the late President Kennedy signed the Area Redevelopment Act, the federal government has extended financial and technical assistance to depressed areas and regions. The assistance comes in three forms: grants and loans to communities to help cover the cost of public facilities such as access roads and sewer systems which are deemed to be essential for industrial development; long-term low interest loans to new or expanding private enterprises locating in these areas; grants and direct staff assistance in support of planning and research within the community or on behalf of the community.

In strictly formal terms there are in the current legislation (Public Works and Economic Development Act of 1965) seven independent criteria for area eligibility, as follows:

(1) substantial unemployment,
(2) persistent unemployment,
(3) low median family income,
(4) high out-migration,
(5) Indian reservations,
(6) prospect of sudden rise in unemployment,
(7) at least one eligible area in every state.

With the exception of the last provision – an excellent example of how economics is tempered by politics in our form of government – all of the criteria can be subsumed under one of two indicators of economic distress: high unemployment, low income. High unemployment is a phenomenon which occurs in almost all sections of the nation and is found in growing (California) as well as declining regions, and in prosperous as well as in poor regions. Reflecting the vigorous growth of the national economy in the last five years, the number of high unemployment areas is now smaller than it was in 1961 but there is no doubt that the malady persists and will not be cured by prosperity alone.

Low-income counties, on the other hand, are almost entirely concentrated in the rural South but not just the deep South. Eastern Kentucky counties in the Appalachian Region and counties in the neighbouring states are part of this group. If this runs counter to one's impression of the location of poverty, two factors should be kept in mind. One is that the criterion here is median family income; the second is that the standard is 40 per cent or less of the national average. It is perhaps not surprising, therefore, that there are no low-income counties, by this definition, in the growing and prosperous sections of the nation.

Most economists would regard high unemployment and low income as distinct problems, arising out of different sets of causes and requiring different policies and programmes for their solution. Low income is the classic problem of economic development as seen in the context of the underdeveloped nation: low levels of education, inadequate social overheads, anaemic entrepreneurship, too many resources in agriculture and

BLE ONE

)ME SOCIO-ECONOMIC CHARACTERISTICS OF DISTRESSED AREAS
 THE UNITED STATES

Socio-Economic	Models							
Attribute 1960	I	II	III	IIIA	IV	V	VII	Total
imber of areas	38	37	492	105	441	253	126	1,492
pulation: 000s	11,416	17,073	12,548	3,911	6,391	4,205	367	55,911
an population: 000s	300	461	26	37	14	17	—	—
an unemployment: %	6·85	7·6	8·58	7·64	3·98	8·66	43·0	—
an 1959 median amily income: $	6,014	5,602	4,437	5,037	2,322	2,392	1,500 (approx.)	—
an % population hange 1950–1960	+44·7	+7·16	−1·12	+44·8	−10·78	−10·7	—	—
an population)er square mile	282	3,728	68	131	27	31	—	—
an % non-white)opulation	8·6	7·2	7·8	11·9	27·9	21·6	—	—
an median school ears completed:)opn. over 25	10·9	10·4	9·6	10·2	8·0	7·9	—	—
an % labour force mployed in manu- acturing	25·0	30·0	19·0	8·8	16·9	15·9	—	—
an % labour force mployed in agriculture	4·8	3·7	12·8	9·3	30·1	21·3	—	—
population participating n labour force	36·4	38·0	34·8	33·8	32·8	29·6	—	—

not enough in industry. By contrast, high unemployment is typically associated with technological and taste changes which result in a sharp reduction in the demand for labour in specific industries without compensating changes elsewhere in the labour market, either on the supply side or on the demand side. Senator Douglas, who pioneered federal legislation in this field, apparently intended that it should be addressed exclusively to this kind of problem.

The common denominator of high unemployment and low income is the

Areas with Districts primarily of Model I
"   "   "   " II
"   "   "   " III
"   "   "   " IIIa
"   "   "   " IV

0   500 Miles
0   400   800 Kms

DEVELOPMENT AREAS IN THE UNITED STATES

potential for greater output, in the one case, through the fuller utilisation of resources, and in the other, through higher levels of productivity. Granted that the mix of remedies might be different, it remains for the administrators of the legislation to apply the various forms of assistance authorised by the legislation in their proper proportions. Investment in social overheads may be more appropriate for the low-income areas and the provision of technical assistance to facilitate adjustment in the high unemployment industrial areas.

In this paper I should like to examine the variety of area distress in the United States in greater detail. There are today close to 900 eligible areas. (An area is defined as a county, a labour market, or a municipality with a population in excess of 250,000.) While it is true that every area, with few exceptions, manifests *either* high unemployment *or* low income, or *both*, these simple categories hardly convey the range of problems encountered in America's distressed areas. My approach will be to describe a series of distinct 'models'. First, however, I will give some indication of the relative numerical significance, socio-economic characteristics and location of each of these distressed area models (Table 1 and map). These figures relate to 1960 when a very much larger number of areas than at present would have qualified to receive Federal assistance.

2 MODEL I: THE 'RICH' AND RAPIDLY GROWING DISTRESS AREA (38 Areas)

I thought I would begin with perhaps the most paradoxical case which (to borrow the title of a popular book) could happen 'Only in America'. Nothing illustrates more dramatically the tremendous range of 'distress' which is embraced by our legislation than the inclusion of areas in California where *per capita* income is very high, growth very rapid, but the rate of unemployment is also high, thus providing a basis for eligibility. The average citizen would probably be shocked to learn that the benefits of a programme which is directed at areas in Appalachia are also available to the richest areas in the nation. On the other hand, the sophisticated student of our particular brand of democracy would have no trouble in recognising a familiar process at work.

Why is there large-scale unemployment in California? In the simplest terms, the rate of in-migration has been more rapid than the rate of growth of job opportunities in some parts of the state. The phenomenon is an interesting one because it suggests that the sluggish response of migration to economic opportunity operates at both ends of the spectrum.

The difficulty in California stems from the retardation of the defence oriented manufacturing industries. Employment in these industries had been growing at a very rapid rate up to recent years. Our overall defence-budget is still growing, of course, but not in terms of the demand for the output of California's defence industries. Employment has actually declined in some sectors, but the people keep pouring into the state. There is evidence, however, that the rate of in-migration has declined in recent years.

Politics notwithstanding, one can seriously question the applicability of depressed area policies to Model I areas.

3 MODEL II: THE WELL-TO-DO MATURE DISTRESSED AREA (37 Areas)

This is the case which Senator Douglas really had in mind when he first designed the legislation in the mid-fifties. A classic example is Pittsburgh about which I have written and spoken on numerous occasions. This model is one of average or slightly above average *per capita* income combined with very slow growth or absolute decline, and generally, in a highly urbanised setting. This secular trend is intensified and leads to serious unemployment during national downturns.

The basic cause is one of secular decline in the historically important industries with only moderate compensation in other sectors of the economy. Steel employment in Pittsburgh has declined for two reasons: first, employment in the whole industry has declined, and second, Pittsburgh has lost out competitively to other regions of the country. When the national economy is booming, unemployment in Pittsburgh is very low because the nation needs every bit of capacity, however high the cost; when demand is sluggish, Pittsburgh is the first to feel the pinch and the unemployment rate soars.

A large part of the problem is corrected through out-migration. Pittsburgh is unique among the larger metropolitan areas in this respect. The 1970 census will probably show an absolute decline in the population of the metropolitan area.

Lesser metropolitan areas in Pennsylvania and the New England states (e.g. my own city of Providence, Rhode Island) have experienced the same kind of difficulty in recent decades. The migration of textile mills from North to South left many New England towns with sharply curtailed levels of job opportunity. True, there are some important differences between steel and textiles in terms of their influence on regional growth.[1] The emergence of Boston as a major centre for the electronics industry has no parallel in the Pittsburgh case. But for many textile-oriented communities, these differences have not been critical.

The Model II area is depressed, but not underdeveloped in the ordinary sense of the term. The basic problem is one of specialisation in declining industries and a poor capacity to adapt its resources to alternative uses.

[1] 'Contrasts in Agglomeration', *Papers and Proceedings of the American Economic Association* (New York and Pittsburgh, May 1961).

Such an area *is* underdeveloped in the sense that a retired professional boxer is often underdeveloped. The area's assets are geared to a narrow range of functions. Labour is trained for specific tasks. The experience of local entrepreneurs, bankers, and other economic agents is severely limited. The plants which have been abandoned are not easily adapted to other industries. The 'public' plant – housing, community facilities, streets and highways – has deteriorated.

The tools of federal policy, it would appear, are rather well suited for these circumstances. The combination of technical assistance, long-term low interest financing, and grants for public facilities 'ought' to be effective in creating new opportunities for industrial expansion. Undoubtedly there are areas where such assistance is redundant and other areas where it will do no good. But, in principle, at least, it should be possible to find Model II areas where the natural forces of adjustment are just powerful enough to work with and not without this assistance.

4 MODEL III AND MODEL III(A): THE NOT-SO-POOR DEPRESSED RURAL AREA (492 and 105 areas)

Here I have in mind the upper reaches of the Great Lakes region, the Pacific Northwest, and Northern New England where unemployment is high, income is moderately below national averages, and the setting is basically rural, although there are small towns dispersed throughout these regions. The difficulty is caused by a decline in employment opportunities in extractive industries: agriculture, mining, fishing, timber. In the Model III areas population is declining, with heavy migration from rural to urban areas. However, in the III(A) areas the large natural increase in population is not offset by a net migration loss.

In contrast to Model I and Model II areas, Model III and Model III(A) areas lack the scale and the experience to nourish the growth of industrial activities on a broad front, but attempts are made to encourage resource-oriented industries which need to be close to their material sources. Technical assistance often proves to be very useful in identifying new processes and new markets and grants and loans come into play to encourage a particular expansion. Even the grant for public capital is likely to be addressed to the needs of a particular enterprise.

The *Development District* approach is likely to offer more for this type of region than for others. Current legislation encourages the formation of districts which comprise a number of counties, at least two of which meet the normal criteria of distress, and a 'growth centre' which is taken to be a reasonably large town with definite growth prospects. When such a district is formed, the growth centre becomes eligible for assistance on the theory that projects undertaken there will stimulate the whole district.

The theory is as yet without empirical validation, but the strategy seems to make sense in Model III and Model III(A) areas in terms of the need to take advantage of scale factors in promoting industrial development.

5 MODEL IV: THE POOR DEPRESSED RURAL AREAS (441 Areas)

Models I, II, III and III(A) earn their membership in the club by their high rates of unemployment. Model IV is the low income area which meets the very rigorous standard of a median level of family income less than 40 per cent (in some cases 50 per cent) of the national average. This model, as we suggested earlier, is confined to the southern sections of the United States where the classic characteristics of underdevelopment still prevail. Agriculture is a declining source of employment, but offers low returns to large numbers of workers, in any case. Industrialisation is very limited. Community facilities are often primitive. The population is relatively unskilled and uneducated. On top of all this, there is the very acute problem of racial discrimination against a very large, often majority, Negro population. But the white population is also relatively poor. Out-migration is very heavy.

The capacity of such areas to absorb grants, loans, and technical assistance for economic development can be seriously questioned. The growth-centre approach offers some hope, but even so, the combination of racial discrimination and the great gap in human resource development may be very difficult to overcome.

6 MODEL V: THE SPECIAL CASE OF MODEL IV: APPALACHIA (253 Areas)

Model IV areas generally do not suffer from high unemployment as it is normally defined. And, as we said, they generally have large Negro populations. The core of the Appalachian region – East Kentucky and neighbouring areas in Virginia, West Virginia, North Carolina, and Tennessee – is white, poor, and unemployed. Here you have compounded the liabilities of Model II and Model IV areas. The earlier exploitation of the region's mineral resources has left a heritage of liabilities and no assets. The land is ravaged, the waters are being poisoned by acid mine drainage, the miners are unemployed and unsuited for alternative occupations, there is no indigenous entrepreneurship, and public capital is almost totally lacking. I do not know of any other episode in American history which offers a better example of exploitation in its most derogatory sense.

The futility of area policy in this setting led to the creation by the Congress, in 1965, of a new vehicle, the Appalachian Regional Planning Commission. The area embraced by the Commission is much larger than the one just described. It was felt that the salvation of this area, or more accurately, of its population, depended upon the stimulation provided by closer ties with neighbouring areas which had far greater growth potential. The Act which authorised the Commission, a federal-state body, specifically calls for the pursuit of the growth point strategy. The emphasis is on improving infrastructure and most of the funds initially authorised are devoted to highway improvements in some of the least accessible portions of the region.

7 MODEL VI: THE LARGE CITY GHETTO

Under the present rules, the smallest unit which can be designated for financial assistance is a county or a municipality of 250,000 people. Increasingly, however, the locus of high unemployment is shifting to the core areas of our major cities in the North, the Midwest, and the Far West. The non-white population of these areas has been increasing rapidly as a result of heavy in-migration from the rural South (and in the 1950s from Puerto Rico). A recent projection done by the staff of the Economic Development Administration suggests that the labour surplus in large central cities will be even greater by 1975.

The 'ghetto' problem, as we call it, is a composite of many forces. The rural migrant is typically unskilled and uneducated and inexperienced in urban living. At the same time, the location of many jobs which would be suitable for such workers is shifting towards the suburbs. Discrimination in housing constrains the residential adaptation of the Negro to employment opportunities. Automobile ownership is low because income is low, hence access to suburban locations is limited. Discrimination in employment also does not help.

Economists and other social scientists are in sharp disagreement on strategies to cope with this problem. There is a natural tendency to assume that the key lever is integration. But this largely begs the question. Where should pressure be applied, in education, in housing, or in employment? Which variable leads and which lags?

For our purposes, the important aspect of the debate is whether an effort should be made to increase and otherwise improve employment opportunities in the ghetto. The 'hard' line is that such a policy is doomed to failure because of overwhelming market forces working towards decentralisation of industrial location in the metropolis. The other view is that we must realistically accept the ghetto for the next few decades and we must therefore exert every effort to stimulate Negro entrepreneurship in the ghetto and otherwise induce the location of industry there through subsidy. Legislation to this effect has been introduced in Congress, prompted in part by the civil disorders of the summer of 1967.

The Economic Development Administration has in the past lobbied unsuccessfully for congressional authority to designate ghettos as distressed areas. Unless budgets were substantially increased, such a broadening of E.D.A.'s authority would further dilute E.D.A.'s potential effectiveness in dealing with its traditional clientele. But even with additional funds there is considerable scepticism as to whether E.D.A.'s tools are powerful enough to deal with the problem.

8 MODEL VII: THE INDIAN RESERVATION (126 Areas)

This is also a special case of Model IV with the obvious unique characteristics. As an example, take the Navajo Indian Reservation. The personal income of the Navajos is based on the use of tribal land, mainly for sheep and goat grazing. Besides grazing, in order of importance, their livelihood depends on commercial timber exploitation, primitive farming, and recreation and tourism. Most of the Navajo land is inaccessible and barren. Fifty-five per cent is desert with temperatures ranging from the extremes of 110° F in the summer to 11° F in the winter. Rainfall is scarce.

Life on the reservation is still primitive and inadequate by any standard. The housing comprises a wide range of dwellings from tents to multi-roomed buildings of modern construction with modern conveniences. The vast majority, however, dwell in one room, log or frame hogans, with dirt floor and no sanitary facilities.

There is a scarcity of skilled Navajo workers qualified for jobs existing in areas immediately surrounding the reservation. Because of their isolation from the outside world, Navajos in general are unfamiliar with trade terms and are often unable to follow instructions. Also contributing to the high levels of unemployment is the birth-rate, which is considerably above the national average.

9 CONCLUSION

One of the principal tasks for the federal agency charged with promoting regional development, the Economic Development Agency, is to determine an appropriate policy response to each of these types of distressed area problem. This task will demand not only considerable technical sophistication in delineating the correct policy weapons but a political strategy which is strong enough to prevent federal funds from being allocated to areas which have no potential for economic development.

5 An Appraisal of Regional Development Policy in the Aquitaine Region

M. Penouil

UNIVERSITÉ DE BORDEAUX

1 THE BACKGROUND

French economic policy has always paid considerable attention to the subject of regional development. The field of action has even been considerably extended in recent years, with separate projects for crisis areas giving way to a more general policy aiming to eliminate imbalances in the growth pattern of the country's major economic regions. The present trend is towards measures to improve the geographical distribution of economic activity and budgetary expenditures. Today, the requirements of European integration (profitability, increasing productivity, concentration and the like), the industrial readaptation necessitated by the depressed conditions in such sectors as textiles, the progress in techniques and marketing, the slowdown of growth in a climate of recession, and the need to satisfy collective needs in economically active regions whose infrastructures (roads, recreational facilities and so on) have reached saturation point, are all factors promoting intervention by the public authorities which tends to benefit highly developed regions as much as, or more than, backward ones. It may well be that equality of development opportunities for all regions has always been an illusion; but it appears ever more true that the mechanisms of economic growth and the logic governing changes in economic structures operate to prevent any reduction of existing imbalances.

After twelve years of experience, it seems of interest to assess the results of the measures taken in the Aquitaine region, to try to specify the causes of what has been at least a partial failure of policy, and more particularly to identify the mechanisms which produced this result. The Aquitaine region, moreover, is of interest from a number of standpoints. In the first instance (as will be discussed in more detail below), Aquitania presents the features characteristic of an underdeveloped region, underdeveloped in the sense that its economic development lags behind the average for France as a whole. Secondly, it has received sustained and diversified development assistance from the public authorities. Finally, it had the good luck, following the discovery of the gas deposits at Lacq, to experience the development of a new industrial complex which has been regarded by many as a 'growth point'. At first glance, it might seem that

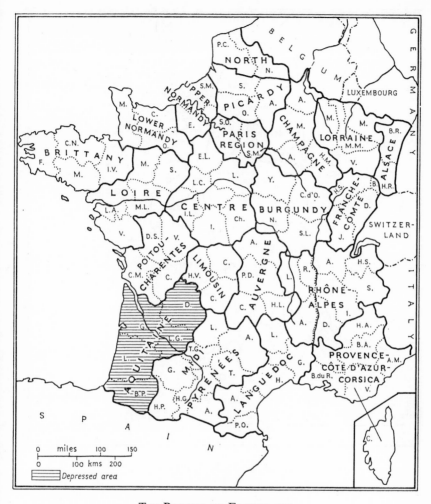

THE REGIONS OF FRANCE AND
THE DEPRESSED REGION OF AQUITAINE

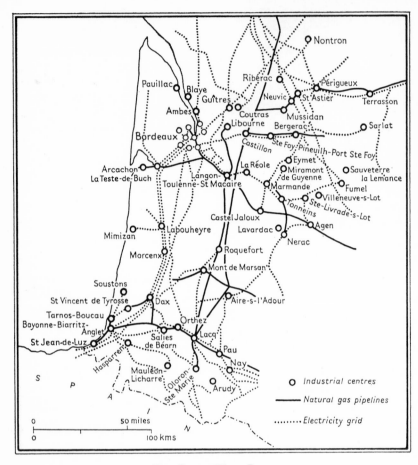

Nontron

Ribérac
Pauillac
Blaye
Guîtres
Périgueux
Neuvic
St Astier
Terrasson
Ambès
Coutras
Mussidan
Libourne
Bergerac
Sarlat
Bordeaux
Ste Foy-Pineuilh-Port Ste Foy
Castillon
Arcachon
La Réole
Eymet
Sauveterre-
La Teste-de-Buch
Miramont
la Lemance
Langon-
de Guyenne
Toulenne-St Macaire
Marmande
Fumel
Villeneuve-s-Lot
Ste-Livrade-s-Lot
Tonneins
Castel Jaloux
Agen
Mimizan
Labouheyre
Lavardac
Morcenx
Nerac
Roquefort
Mont de Marsan
Soustons
St Vincent de Tyrosse
Dax
Aire-s-l'Adour
Tarnos-Boucau
Bayonne-Biarritz-
Orthez
Anglet
Lacq
St Jean-de-Luz
Salies
de Béarn
Pau
Nay
Hasparren
Mauléon-
Licharre
Oloron-
Ste Marie
Arudy

S
P
A
I
N

	○ Industrial centres
	— Natural gas pipelines
	.... Electricity grid

0   50 miles
0   100 kms

The South-West Region
of France

the future growth of the region was secure, through the combined influence of new resources, the operation of the development mechanism and the impact of regional development policy.

In the writer's view, much of the blame for the failure to achieve this result can be placed on an often presented, but only partially accurate, analysis of the situation. The phrase 'growth point' has proved to be an illusion, for everything was based on an incomplete and false view of the operation of such a growth point. There is no doubt that Aquitania's experience can be used to derive further material for the theoretical analysis of the process of regional development and for the formulation of policy measures. An attempt to do this will be made in the present paper.

2 THE LONG-TERM CHARACTER OF AQUITANIAN UNDERDEVELOPMENT

Measured by the principal criteria used in assessing regional under-development, the relative position of the region *vis-à-vis* the French economy as a whole can easily be shown to have changed little if at all, and in some fields, it is possible to hold that the situation has actually deteriorated.

(i) DEMOGRAPHIC FACTORS

Demographic trends are one of the most characteristic indicators of the region's economic difficulties. The signs of a human environment which has reached its limits are numerous. They include a rate of population growth below the average for France, an ageing population structure, and perhaps most important of all, a high net emigration of persons of working age, associated with high net immigration of persons aged above fifty-five. To make the analysis more specific, the regional data presented below will be rounded out at appropriate points with data for the Basses-Pyrénées Department of the region, where the installation of the Lacq-based industrial complex might have been expected to generate a rather special growth pattern.

The recent trends of the growth of population are shown in Table 1[1] and compared with those of other regions of France. Four figures from this table will serve to indicate its main conclusions. In the last decade, the population of France has risen by 11 per cent. The population of the Parisian region has risen by 19 per cent while the average for the rest of the country is 9 per cent. For the Aquitaine region, the corresponding figure is no more than 7 per cent.

[1] Unless otherwise stated, the statistical material presented has been taken from the Budget Proposals for 1967 (projet de la loi de finance 1967). It is in general based on the statistics prepared by the Institut national de la Statistique et des Études économiques (I.N.S.E.E.).

TABLE ONE

FRANCE: POPULATION BY REGION 1955–1964

(In 000s)

Regions	1955	1956	1957	1958	1959	1960	1961	1962	1963	1964 (Provisional)
Paris Region	7,527·1	7,656·4	7,801·0	7,946·1	8,084·1	8,225·3	8,376·2	8,607·7	8,835·4	9,022·4
Champagne	1,148·8	1,156·8	1,165·6	1,174·8	1,183·5	1,192·2	1,201·7	1,215·0	1,229·3	1,241·2
Picardy	1,407·7	1,419·1	1,430·9	1,442·6	1,454·2	1,465·6	1,477·5	1,493·3	1,510·5	1,524·6
Upper Normandy	1,297·8	1,311·6	1,326·0	1,340·8	1,355·5	1,370·0	1,385·0	1,408·6	1,427·0	1,443·6
Centre	1,779·9	1,790·9	1,803·5	1,816·4	1,828·6	1,840·2	1,852·0	1,873·5	1,895·1	1,909·5
North	3,437·9	3,468·0	3,499·5	3,531·5	3,562·8	3,594·0	3,627·2	3,681·8	3,723·2	3,763·3
Lorraine	1,995·5	2,022·4	2,056·5	2,092·0	2,123·6	2,154·1	2,188·8	2,212·6	2,252·7	2,285·5
Alsace	1,236·1	1,246·8	1,259·0	1,271·7	1,283·8	1,295·4	1,308·2	1,329·5	1,349·7	1,365·5
Franche-Comté	870·5	878·7	887·7	897·1	906·2	915·3	925·2	938·6	954·7	966·5
Lower Normandy	1,176·4	1,181·1	1,185·7	1,190·5	1,195·3	1,199·7	1,203·8	1,213·4	1,219·4	1,223·6
Loire	2,349·4	2,364·2	2,379·8	2,396·6	2,377·6	2,430·0	2,446·3	2,475·7	2,496·7	2,513·7
Brittany	2,359·9	2,360·9	2,365·4	2,371·3	2,413·8	2,383·3	2,389·0	2,404·7	2,410·5	2,414·0
Limousin	743·3	742·0	741·0	740·3	739·2	738·0	737·0	737·5	738·8	737·4
Auvergne	1,256·9	1,259·2	1,262·2	1,265·7	1,269·1	1,272·1	1,275·6	1,282·4	1,292·6	1,298·1
Poitou-Charentes	1,408·1	1,414·0	1,421·0	1,428·7	1,435·9	1,442·0	1,448·2	1,461·5	1,472·5	1,477·2
Midi-Pyrénées	1,995·4	2,004·4	2,015·2	2,026·5	2,036·3	2,044·8	2,054·8	2,102·9	2,150·9	2,164·9
Burgundy	1,389·8	1,396·4	1,404·0	1,412·0	1,419·3	1,425·9	1,433·2	1,450·4	1,464·6	1,473·3
Rhône-Alps	3,698·3	3,741·1	3,789·2	3,839·1	3,887·6	3,937·2	3,991·1	4,081·7	4,180·1	4,247·4
Languedoc	1,467·4	1,478·7	1,493·6	1,508·8	1,581·6	1,533·2	1,546·9	1,593·2	1,641·5	1,658·9
Provence-Côte-d'Azur-Corsica	2,650·3	2,703·6	2,762·8	2,820·4	2,872·6	2,924·7	2,980·6	3,091·5	3,227·7	3,289·3
Aquitania	2,234·2	2,246·8	2,261·3	2,276·0	2,289·1	2,301·2	2,314·5	2,342·2	2,380·1	2,397·0
Total	43,427·7	43,843·4	44,310·9	44,788·9	45,239·7	45,684·2	46,162·8	46,997·7	47,853·9	48,416·9

The situation in the Basses-Pyrénées Department is appreciably better. While population growth in this Department earlier tended to match that of the region generally (it accounted for approximately 19 per cent of the region's total population), it has recently speeded up and the Department now accounts for 20·5 per cent of population. Growth in the Department has in fact been faster than for France as a whole, but given the lag that developed in the 1950s, its share of total French population is still below what it was in 1946.

The low birth-rates of the region are shown in Table 2. The Aquitaine region, it can be seen, takes sixteenth place in the birth-rate ranking, 2·1 per thousand below the average rate for France, and 5·1 per thousand below the rate in Lorraine.

The Basses-Pyrénées Department is in a more favourable position than the Aquitaine region as a whole, with a birth-rate of 17·2 per thousand. But it too lies well below the French average. This is important; it shows that although a degree of economic development has modified the population picture, the operative mechanism has been migration of labour, rather than a profound transformation of the demographic structure.

The ageing population structure is another feature betraying the region's backwardness. The median age in the Aquitaine region is 35·7 years against a national median of 32·8. The median is lowest in Lorraine: 29·1 years. Aquitania is eighteenth in this particular ranking table.

Here again, the position in the Basses-Pyrénées has improved, although there is no evidence to suggest any real structural change. The age group 20–44 has maintained its percentage share of total (31·4 per cent in 1954, and 31·3 per cent in 1962). The same is true of the 65-plus group (13·9 per cent and 13·8 per cent) whose share of the regional population as a whole, however, rose from 14·3 per cent to 14·7 per cent. The median age in the Basses-Pyrénées is 35, compared with 35·1 for the region, whereas in 1955 the corresponding figures were 34·9 in each case. It can again readily be seen that the situation has hardly changed over the decade.

The extent of net outward migration provides marked evidence of the depressed nature of the Aquitanian economy. But it is somewhat difficult to interpret and analyse, since most regions of France experience net out-migration because of the attraction of population to the Parisian region. Migrational balances, further, are not always meaningful, inasmuch as an outflow of young persons may be offset by a reflux of those who, by reason of age, are no longer economically active. It is striking that on this last point, the Aquitaine region has one of the highest positive in-migration balances for the age bracket 55 and over (see Table 3).

Although demographic criteria are far from being determinant, they already signpost the fact that structural changes in the South-West have been very slight.

TABLE TWO
BIRTH AND FERTILITY RATES

Regions	Birth-Rate										Fertility Rate	
	1955	1956	1957	1958	1959	1960	1961	1962	1963	1964	Average 1953 to 1955	Average 1963–1964–1965
Paris Region	16·7	16·7	16·9	16·8	17·3	17·1	17·3	16·8	17·2	17·2	6·55	7·14
Champagne	21·2	20·7	20·7	20·5	20·6	20·3	20·2	19·7	20·5	20·1	9·63	9·63
Picardy	21·8	21·2	20·9	20·5	20·6	19·9	20·3	19·8	20·6	20·3	9·98	9·80
Upper Normandy	22·0	21·5	21·6	21·1	21·5	20·7	20·8	20·0	20·8	20·4	9·41	9·45
Centre	18·4	18·5	18·3	17·8	18·1	17·4	17·3	17·0	17·7	17·7	8·57	8·31
North	22·7	22·2	21·7	21·5	21·6	21·2	21·4	20·4	20·9	20·5	9·68	9·65
Lorraine	22·6	22·5	22·4	22·3	22·2	21·7	22·1	21·4	21·6	21·1	9·65	9·94
Alsace	19·5	19·4	19·5	19·3	19·2	19·1	19·5	19·0	19·5	19·7	8·05	8·91
Franche-Comté	20·2	20·0	20·1	19·8	19·8	19·3	20·0	19·0	20·0	19·9	8·95	9·19
Lower Normandy	22·0	21·5	21·5	20·8	21·0	20·2	20·3	19·6	20·1	19·8	9·48	9·15
Loire	21·3	21·0	21·1	20·6	20·8	20·1	20·4	19·8	20·0	20·3	9·22	9·22
Brittany	18·7	18·9	18·9	18·7	18·5	18·2	18·3	17·9	18·2	18·3	7·88	8·23
Limousin	14·2	14·1	13·8	13·6	13·5	13·2	13·3	12·8	13·1	13·5	6·54	6·61
Auvergne	16·3	16·3	16·0	15·4	15·9	15·5	15·6	15·1	15·5	15·6	7·31	7·48
Poitou-Charentes	19·8	19·7	19·7	19·0	18·8	18·2	18·3	17·8	17·9	17·8	8·95	8·65
Midi-Pyrénées	15·8	15·7	15·4	15·0	15·1	15·1	15·3	15·2	15·3	15·3	7·14	7·27
Burgundy	17·7	17·4	17·3	17·1	17·1	16·7	16·9	16·7	17·0	17·1	8·42	8·37
Rhône-Alps	17·1	17·0	17·3	17·1	17·6	17·2	17·6	17·4	18·1	18·2	7·47	8·01
Languedoc	14·6	14·4	14·3	14·4	14·6	14·5	14·7	14·7	15·4	15·3	6·78	7·13
Provence-Côte-d'Azur-Corsica	15·8	15·8	16·3	16·1	16·3	15·9	16·4	15·5	15·8	16·2	6·39*	7·00*
Aquitania	16·6	16·4	16·4	15·9	16·0	15·6	15·7	15·6	16·0	16·0	7·40	7·44
France*	18·5	18·3	18·3	18·1	18·2	17·9	18·1	17·6	18·1	18·1	7·98	8·19

* Excluding Corsica.

TABLE THREE
INTERREGIONAL MIGRATION, BY AGE-GROUP 1954–1962

Regions	Out-Migration			In-Migration			Net Migrational Balance			
	Below 25 years	25–54	55 years and over	Below 25 years	25–54	55 years and over	Below 25 years	25–54	55 years and over	Total
Paris Region	202·0	215·4	151·1	411·0	415·7	68·1	+209·0	+200·3	−83·0	+326·3
Champagne	55·1	48·8	10·6	40·7	36·5	11·4	−14·4	−12·3	+0·8	−25·9
Picardy	72·5	62·9	16·7	60·4	52·3	19·9	−12·1	−10·6	+3·2	−19·5
Upper Normandy	52·1	47·4	12·3	44·9	44·0	12·7	−7·2	−3·4	+0·4	−10·2
Centre	83·7	74·4	19·1	76·3	71·5	33·0	−7·4	−2·9	+13·9	+3·6
North	70·1	67·1	16·4	49·8	45·6	12·3	−20·3	−21·5	−4·1	−45·9
Lorraine	62·9	59·0	12·4	62·3	55·7	8·7	−0·6	−3·3	−3·7	−7·6
Alsace	24·9	23·2	4·8	27·0	25·6	5·2	+2·1	+2·4	+0·4	+4·9
Franche-Comté	31·7	29·7	6·1	30·3	28·2	7·6	−1·4	−1·5	+1·5	−1·4
Lower Normandy	67·1	58·7	11·8	37·7	35·7	12·0	−29·4	−23·0	−0·2	−52·2
Loire	92·5	82·7	16·5	63·5	56·7	19·9	−29·0	−22·0	+3·4	−52·6
Brittany	98·0	91·7	12·6	47·9	43·8	17·6	−50·1	−42·9	+5·0	−93·0
Limousin	31·9	32·0	7·1	22·2	19·6	8·9	−9·7	−12·4	+1·8	−20·3
Auvergne	41·1	42·1	10·4	33·5	32·0	13·1	−7·6	−10·1	+2·7	−15·0
Poitou-Charentes	65·5	58·9	12·4	44·0	39·1	16·6	−21·5	−19·8	+4·2	−37·1
Midi-Pyrénées	63·6	65·3	16·6	48·2	46·9	18·5	−15·4	−18·4	+1·9	−31·9
Burgundy	62·9	56·9	15·0	51·9	49·1	28·7	−11·0	−7·8	+13·7	−5·1
Rhône-Alps	72·5	75·5	21·4	95·2	100·5	22·8	+22·7	+25·0	+1·4	+49·1
Languedoc	58·1	61·3	13·0	39·0	41·1	17·2	−19·1	−20·2	+4·2	−35·1
Provence-Côte-d'Azur-Corsica	69·9	75·3	20·0	95·7	101·7	46·1	+25·8	+26·4	+26·1	+78·3
Aquitania	68·2	70·4	18·0	64·3	58·7	24·2	−3·9	−11·7	+6·2	−9·4
France	1,445·8	1,399·0	424·5	1,445·8	1,399·0	424·5	0	0	0	0

AVERAGE HOUSEHOLD INCOMES (1962)

(Francs 000s)

Region	Agricultural Self-Employed	Agricultural Hired Labour	Business Owner-Managers	Upper Management and Liberal Professions	Middle Management and Technician
Paris Region	*	11·0	25·0	40·5	29·1
Champagne	6·1	9·0	18·9	31·4	17·0
Picardy	9·1	7·2	20·0	28·4	17·9
Upper Normandy	5·7	3·8	19·0	34·1	20·3
Centre	4·8	5·1	14·5	24·3	17·4
North	5·8	5·7	16·2	32·6	20·0
Lorraine	4·0	5·0	24·1	31·1	19·6
Alsace	5·1	(11·2)	16·5	38·2	13·6
Franche-Comté	4·1	(8·0)	17·4	38·0	25·1
Lower Normandy	5·8	4·3	12·8	41·6	16·5
Loire	2·7	5·2	12·2	33·8	16·4
Brittany	2·7	4·5	14·6	22·2	16·0
Limousin	2·8	5·1	14·5	(32·4)	15·6
Auvergne	2·4	4·3	16·4	32·4	18·1
Poitou-Charentes	3·5	4·0	11·8	28·8	15·7
Midi-Pyrénées	2·6	4·1	12·8	32·0	21·7
Burgundy	4·6	4·7	14·2	30·9	16·6
Rhône-Alps	2·7	5·8	17·2	36·5	18·4
Languedoc	4·0	5·0	13·5	25·7	20·6
Provence-Côte-d'Azur	3·8	5·7	16·8	32·9	17·7
Aquitania	2·6	4·3	12·3	32·9	18·7
France	4·0	5·8	17·1	35·7	20·1

Socio-Professional Categor

* Numbers too small for the figure to be significant.

(ii) TRENDS IN INCOME AND THE STANDARD OF LIVING

An initial indication of relative income levels in the region is available from an examination of the statistics of the yield of personal taxation. Aquitania accounts for some 5 per cent of the French economically active population, but for only 3·3 per cent of total personal taxes paid. The discrepancy is confirmed by I.N.S.E.E. statistics of average household incomes: the regional index stands at 82 (taking the national average as 100); it represents only 55 per cent of the average income of households in the Parisian region (see Table 4).

The data presented in Tables 5–8 relate more particularly to wage-earners. But for the various categories studied, they provide ample *of Head of Household*

Salaried Employees	Production Workers	Service Occupations	Other Categories	Not Economically Active	Total
13·5	13·4	7·8	14·9	9·1	16·4
9·5	9·7	(8·1)	7·7	6·2	10·0
9·7	9·7	9·0	8·5	4·3	11·3
14·3	10·6	6·3	12·4	4·9	10·8
10·7	9·2	7·3	10·2	4·9	8·5
12·5	9·7	4·8	12·8	5·8	10·2
12·7	10·3	8·6	13·4	6·5	11·3
10·5	10·4	6·6	11·6	6·1	10·8
10·5	10·0	(7·1)	10·6	6·3	10·7
10·9	9·1	(9·6)	9·5	7·4	9·3
9·4	8·3	3·9	7·8	4·7	7·5
10·5	8·0	6·4	11·7	5·0	7·3
8·7	8·4	(1·3)	(12·1)	4·8	7·4
9·9	9·1	(8·7)	(12·3)	4·9	8·3
10·4	8·0	(4·8)	9·8	4·0	7·1
10·7	9·2	9·0	12·0	5·7	8·5
9·9	8·9	9·5	10·8	4·4	8·3
11·3	9·7	7·5	13·3	5·9	10·4
10·6	8·0	5·6	13·6	5·4	9·5
12·5	9·3	8·8	12·3	7·6	11·0
10·6	9·3	8·9	10·4	7·0	8·9
11·9	10·2	7·5	12·4	6·3	10·8

confirmation of the region's backwardness. It should be borne in mind that the income differences disclosed are not solely due to lower rates of earnings in a given occupation but also reflect the lower proportions of highly paid executives and expert technicians. Productivity differences have their impact on employment and earnings in the same way as differences in scale of production (Tables 5–8).

It is again illuminating to examine the position of the Basses-Pyrénées, which has in fact shown some improvement. The annual average rate of increase of earnings between 1959 and 1963 was 5 per cent in Aquitania, 6·2 per cent in France, and 6·8 per cent in the Basses-Pyrénées Department. As a result, earnings in the Department, which were 94·6 per cent of the average figure for the region in general in 1959, stood at 101·2 per cent in

TABLE FIVE

AVERAGE ANNUAL EARNINGS BY SOCIO-PROFESSIONAL CATEGORY

(Francs 000s)

Region	Upper Management						Middle and Lower Management					
	1963			1964			1963			1964		
	Men	Women	Total	Men	Women	Total	Men	Women	Total	Men	Women	Total
Paris Region	39·5	24·2	37·9	42·0	26·9	40·6	19·9	14·1	18·6	21·9	15·2	20·5
Champagne	29·1	18·6	28·3	34·5	18·8	33·4	15·2	9·7	14·3	15·5	10·8	14·8
Picardy	29·8	16·6	28·7	31·5	22·4	31·0	15·2	10·5	14·4	15·8	10·6	15·0
Upper Normandy	29·7	15·4	29·0	32·4	21·9	31·9	16·9	10·6	15·9	17·5	10·9	16·6
Centre	33·1	18·5	31·7	34·0	20·1	32·8	16·5	9·8	15·3	16·2	10·4	15·2
North	32·1	20·3	31·4	36·4	19·2	35·9	16·2	9·4	15·3	16·4	10·6	15·8
Lorraine	29·9	14·7	29·0	36·0	23·0	35·3	15·2	9·6	14·5	17·5	10·4	16·6
Alsace	35·1	23·0	34·4	40·9	28·2	39·7	16·2	10·6	15·4	17·2	12·8	16·8
Franche-Comté	24·3	16·2	24·1	37·5	19·4	36·7	14·4	9·3	13·6	16·8	11·6	16·0
Lower Normandy	27·6	19·1	26·9	31·9	24·9	31·5	14·6	9·3	13·6	14·9	9·4	13·8
Loire	29·3	18·7	28·6	33·5	17·6	32·3	15·5	9·1	14·1	16·6	9·9	15·2
Brittany	26·6	17·6	25·9	30·3	17·5	29·4	15·0	9·7	14·0	15·4	10·2	14·5
Limousin	30·6	26·8	30·4	31·1	27·1	30·9	18·9	9·9	13·1	14·7	11·1	14·4
Auvergne	28·8	14·8	27·7	31·7	18·3	30·1	16·6	9·4	15·0	16·7	10·3	15·7
Poitou-Charentes	29·1	11·5	26·7	32·5	13·0	30·9	14·3	9·1	13·2	15·8	9·9	14·5
Midi-Pyrénées	27·5	18·7	27·0	31·4	18·8	30·7	14·5	8·8	13·4	16·1	9·9	15·0
Burgundy	28·4	15·9	27·4	32·3	15·3	31·4	15·1	9·3	14·2	16·1	10·3	15·2
Rhône-Alps	31·3	16·1	29·9	34·4	21·3	33·5	16·1	9·6	14·7	17·3	10·9	16·4
Languedoc	26·8	16·4	26·0	26·6	15·4	25·6	13·9	8·4	12·8	14·7	9·0	13·6
Provence-Côte-d'Azur-Corsica	27·5	16·4	26·5	29·3	16·1	28·4	16·3	10·5	15·2	17·3	11·4	16·2
Aquitania	29·7	15·5	28·2	33·8	21·6	33·1	15·9	9·8	14·8	16·3	10·6	15·1
France	33·6	20·4	33·3	37·0	23·5	36·0	17·3	11·8	16·7	18·7	12·8	17·6

TABLE SIX
AVERAGE ANNUAL EARNINGS BY SOCIO-PROFESSIONAL CATEGORY

(N.F. 000s)

Region	Salaried Employees						Production Workers					
	1963			1964			1963			1964		
	Men	Women	Total	Men	Women	Total	Men	Women	Total	Men	Women	Total
Paris Region	11·5	8·9	9·7	11·6	9·6	10·4	10·3	6·9	9·6	11·1	7·4	10·3
Champagne	9·0	6·3	7·6	9·6	6·7	8·1	7·6	5·2	7·1	8·2	5·4	7·6
Picardy	8·9	6·4	7·6	10·1	6·8	8·3	7·9	4·9	7·3	8·5	5·1	7·8
Upper Normandy	9·2	6·5	7·6	9·7	6·8	8·0	8·8	5·1	8·1	8·1	5·2	8·3
Centre	9·6	6·1	7·8	9·5	6·5	7·8	7·1	4·8	6·6	7·7	5·0	7·1
North	9·2	6·4	7·8	10·1	6·7	8·5	8·1	4·8	7·5	8·5	4·8	7·8
Lorraine	10·1	6·0	8·2	10·7	6·3	8·6	8·2	4·7	7·7	8·7	4·9	8·2
Alsace	8·3	6·0	7·0	9·3	6·5	7·8	7·8	4·9	7·2	8·3	5·2	7·7
Franche-Comté	9·6	6·3	8·1	9·9	6·6	8·0	7·8	5·3	7·3	8·6	5·6	7·9
Lower Normandy	8·0	5·9	6·9	8·9	6·3	7·6	7·1	4·6	6·7	7·6	4·9	7·2
Loire	8·2	6·1	7·0	9·1	6·7	7·8	7·0	4·6	6·6	7·5	4·8	6·9
Brittany	8·1	5·9	6·8	9·0	6·4	7·5	7·0	4·8	6·7	7·4	5·0	7·1
Limousin	7·8	6·1	7·0	8·4	6·7	7·6	6·6	4·7	6·2	6·9	4·7	6·4
Auvergne	10·1	6·7	8·4	9·7	6·8	8·2	7·1	5·1	6·7	7·8	5·8	7·8
Poitou-Charentes	7·2	5·5	6·5	8·8	6·0	7·4	7·1	5·0	6·7	6·9	4·6	6·5
Midi-Pyrénées	8·7	6·1	7·4	9·1	6·7	7·9	6·8	4·6	6·4	7·4	4·7	7·0
Burgundy	8·8	6·0	7·4	9·1	6·3	7·6	7·2	4·8	6·8	7·8	5·0	7·3
Rhône-Alps	10·1	7·0	8·3	10·8	7·7	9·0	8·6	5·5	7·9	8·9	5·7	8·2
Languedoc	8·6	6·2	7·4	9·2	6·3	7·8	7·0	4·4	6·6	7·5	4·3	7·1
Provence-Côte-d'Azur-Corsica	10·3	6·9	8·6	10·3	7·1	8·6	8·3	4·8	7·9	8·7	5·0	8·2
Aquitania	8·4	6·4	7·3	9·2	6·7	7·8	7·1	4·6	6·7	7·6	4·7	7·1
France	9·6	7·3	8·1	10·4	7·9	9·0	8·2	5·6	7·6	8·8	5·7	8·2

TABLE SEVEN
INDICES OF HOURLY WAGES (1 APRIL 1962 = 100)

Region	Manufacturing and Construction		Manufacturing Only		Textiles		Construction and Public Works		Electrical and Engineering Industries		Chemicals and Rubber	
	1965	1966	1965	1966	1965	1966	1965	1966	1965	1966	1965	1966
Paris Region	122·8	130·2	122·4	129·6	125·3	132·5	125·3	134·1	121·8	128·3	122·0	129·9
Champagne	123·0	129·5	122·3	128·7	128·3	130·2	128·3	136·7	121·4	127·2	122·8	128·7
Picardy	123·0	130·2	122·7	130·0	125·1	129·5	125·1	131·9	121·8	129·5	122·4	129·5
Upper Normandy	123·7	130·5	122·5	129·6	128·5	128·5	128·5	134·6	124·2	130·7	121·9	128·8
Centre	125·8	133·3	124·3	131·7	130·4	133·7	130·4	138·6	124·0	130·8	122·9	130·0
North	121·6	128·5	120·7	127·6	126·7	128·9	126·7	133·2	119·4	125·2	118·5	125·0
Lorraine	122·1	128·2	122·1	128·1	122·3	126·9	122·3	128·7	120·4	126·9	123·4	127·2
Alsace	127·1	134·9	125·7	133·6	132·7	133·0	132·7	139·8	124·5	132·2	121·4	129·4
Franche-Comté	124·3	131·2	123·7	130·6	128·3	128·0	128·3	135·9	122·8	130·2	114·1	121·3
Lower Normandy	128·8	136·0	125·8	132·7	133·9	135·1	133·9	142·0	125·2	131·2	121·9	125·9
Loire	124·0	130·7	123·6	130·3	124·7	128·1	124·7	131·4	122·8	129·6	119·1	123·0
Brittany	129·1	137·1	127·7	135·2	131·6	131·9	131·6	140·7	128·5	137·9	121·3	131·3
Limousin	124·0	130·3	122·9	129·3	127·4	128·4	127·4	133·3	123·4	129·7	129·0	132·2
Auvergne	123·6	131·0	122·2	129·2	127·0	133·3	128·8	137·4	122·6	129·7	121·8	128·8
Poitou-Charentes	124·7	132·5	123·4	131·7	128·7	120·6	128·7	135·2	122·7	132·2	126·1	130·5
Midi-Pyrénées	123·4	131·1	121·7	129·1	129·2	128·4	129·2	137·5	124·3	131·6	116·0	123·3
Burgundy	125·1	133·5	124·6	132·7	124·7	131·5	127·0	136·5	125·1	133·5	126·2	134·3
Rhône-Alps	122·4	129·5	121·7	128·6	121·5	128·3	126·8	134·9	121·2	127·4	120·9	127·4
Languedoc	122·5	130·1	123·3	130·2	118·4	128·8	125·9	132·8	122·6	130·2	118·7	125·9
Provence-Côte-d'Azur-Corsica	124·6	132·6	122·9	130·3	130·2	143·1	129·2	138·5	122·6	129·0	122·3	129·0
Aquitania	122·8	129·4	121·8	128·9	126·7	128·5	126·7	132·1	122·1	129·7	125·5	129·8
France	123·3	130·5	122·2	129·3	121·3	129·0	127·3	134·8	121·6	128·2	121·9	128·9

TABLE EIGHT

CUMULATIVE FREQUENCY DISTRIBUTIONS, BY REGION, OF ANNUAL EARNINGS

Region	Below F. 3,000		Below F. 4,000		Below F. 5,000		Below F. 6,000		Below F. 8,000		Below F. 10,000		Below F. 15,000		Below F. 20,000	
	1963	1964	1963	1964	1963	1964	1963	1964	1963	1964	1963	1964	1963	1964	1963	1964
Paris Region	2·42	2·41	4·49	4·14	8·64	7·24	15·88	12·23	33·99	28·10	53·91	47·15	80·88	77·47	89·66	88·14
Champagne	6·52	6·44	12·53	11·32	23·05	19·80	36·31	30·92	62·36	55·84	79·98	76·47	93·28	92·01	96·59	96·03
Picardy	6·84	6·33	13·38	11·63	23·94	20·14	36·06	31·05	59·82	54·26	77·36	73·37	92·79	91·87	96·43	95·91
Upper Normandy	6·63	5·70	12·46	10·49	22·22	18·43	34·02	28·70	55·75	49·58	73·34	68·67	90·93	88·97	95·80	94·87
Centre	9·94	8·77	17·21	14·04	29·14	22·92	43·34	35·36	69·08	61·43	83·75	79·13	94·34	92·79	97·08	96·40
North	6·16	5·40	12·15	10·32	21·77	18·54	34·32	28·98	61·34	52·08	79·87	72·91	93·66	92·06	96·08	96·03
Lorraine	7·18	6·86	12·54	11·20	21·79	19·11	32·55	28·27	54·16	48·29	73·64	67·93	92·72	91·01	96·66	95·86
Alsace	8·18	7·50	12·73	11·13	22·07	18·56	34·85	29·54	55·99	52·70	77·73	73·15	92·38	90·59	96·20	95·43
Franche-Comté	5·16	4·52	10·86	8·58	21·35	17·26	34·45	28·66	57·98	51·63	76·67	73·66	92·44	92·13	96·46	96·28
Lower Normandy	8·86	7·32	15·51	12·51	28·47	21·98	49·04	35·16	68·58	62·16	83·45	79·43	94·57	92·74	97·47	96·28
Loire	9·32	8·14	16·13	13·02	28·89	22·99	40·83	36·46	67·90	63·10	83·04	80·39	93·76	92·54	96·89	96·36
Brittany	7·05	6·16	16·46	11·45	28·15	21·36	58·88	35·37	71·79	64·65	84·82	81·49	94·63	93·91	97·20	96·92
Limousin	7·11	6·55	17·50	13·59	35·70	28·18	42·82	43·80	74·88	69·15	85·83	82·66	94·49	91·76	97·01	96·40
Auvergne	7·31	5·51	15·31	11·03	27·07	20·26	40·48	32·07	67·20	57·90	82·99	76·82	93·82	91·76	97·01	95·95
Poitou-Charentes	8·93	8·97	18·27	15·90	33·86	27·98	50·82	42·68	73·41	68·32	85·68	82·90	94·84	93·68	97·37	96·44
Midi-Pyrénées	7·04	6·23	16·71	13·44	31·63	25·69	47·01	39·61	69·04	62·70	82·03	77·55	93·30	92·18	96·58	96·00
Burgundy	8·91	7·90	15·27	12·51	26·27	20·92	39·75	32·71	66·44	58·52	82·60	78·45	93·95	93·13	97·03	96·34
Rhône-Alps	6·30	4·77	11·90	8·50	22·29	15·96	34·46	26·45	57·56	49·04	75·33	68·90	91·17	89·29	95·42	94·52
Languedoc	7·87	6·76	17·22	13·69	31·04	25·58	45·32	38·82	68·60	62·35	82·14	77·97	93·54	92·09	96·82	96·12
Provence-Côte-d'Azur-Corsica	6·09	4·70	13·17	9·78	23·92	18·30	35·52	29·92	56·67	49·88	73·22	67·86	89·87	87·75	94·89	93·74
Aquitania	6·53	5·32	15·82	12·64	38·30	25·57	47·03	39·36	68·07	62·08	81·24	77·44	92·97	91·51	96·22	95·46
France	5·83	5·13	11·30	9·26	20·71	16·68	32·12	26·47	54·67	47·91	72·09	66·60	89·54	87·50	94·55	93·12

1963; but they were still no more than 83·8 per cent of the national average earnings figure. Bearing in mind that the Lacq-based industries use highly advanced techniques and that their manning correspondingly calls for a high proportion of specialised personnel, it may be concluded that wage progress in other sectors has been roughly at the average rate recorded in the region.

Living standards depend partly on income levels, but they may also be increased as the result of various measures taken by the public authorities. From this point of view, the available data have some rather surprising features. In the first place, the region's lag in consumer durables seems to be small. In April 1965, 52·4 per cent of households in the South-West had a refrigerator, as against a national average of 54 per cent and 68·3 per cent for the Parisian region. The corresponding figures for April 1959 were: 14·2 per cent for the South-West, 20·5 per cent for France and 35·6 per cent for the Parisian region. The gap, in other words, has largely been overtaken. This performance is all the more noteworthy in that in the investigation quoted, the 'South-West' includes the Poitou-Charentes and Midi-Pyrénées regions, both of which lag slightly behind the Aquitaine region. The same situation obtains with television receivers: in 1959 there was one set for 78 persons in Aquitania, one for 33 in France, one for 15 in Paris. In 1964, the respective ratios had risen to 1:13, 1:9 and 1:7, and in 1965, Aquitania reached the national average of one set for 8 persons. Passenger car statistics show the region in an extremely good position, with one car for 13 persons, compared with a national average of one for 15, and a figure of 1:21 for the Parisian region. It seems possible to conclude that consumption behaviour in the region has been influenced greatly by emulative considerations, though this cannot be taken as a sign of development.

A very different state of affairs rules in other sectors of private consumption, such as housing: one dwelling completed per 147 inhabitants of the Aquitaine region against a nationwide figure of one per 131, and one per 113 inhabitants in the Parisian region. Given that the region started with a housing infrastructure that was about as unsatisfactory as it could be, and (especially in rural areas) about as dilapidated, this situation can be interpreted as one of the consequences of low income levels. But it is rendered all the more serious in that the imbalance is most marked in construction of fair-rental housing projects (Habitation à Loyer Modéré). In 1964 one new H.L.M. dwelling unit was constructed per 630 inhabitants of the Aquitaine region. The comparative figures for France (average) and the Parisian region are 1:384 and 1:216. This inequality, it is only fair to observe, has become less apparent, in that the situation has been partially rectified by state intervention: in 1959 the ratio of new H.L.M. units *per capita* of population was 1:2,637 for Aquitania, compared with 1:349 for the Parisian region. The comparison of these figures is instructive. It

TABLE NINE
REGROUPING OF AGRICULTURAL HOLDINGS

(000 hectares)

Region	1962 Operations Completed	1963 Operations Completed	1964 Operations Completed	1965 Operations: Completed	In Progress	Total	Still to be Regrouped	To be Regrouped (%)
Paris Region	417	433	439	448	43	490	70	12·5
Champagne	441	491	542	588	152	740	640	46·5
Picardy	556	583	626	659	109	760	590	43·5
Upper Normandy	220	232	243	251	21	272	150	35·5
Centre	588	636	663	697	127	824	950	53·5
North	48	59	75	91	44	134	410	75·5
Lorraine	264	294	326	353	82	435	670	60·5
Alsace	55	70	78	90	48	138	340	71·0
Franche-Comté	55	67	89	109	97	206	690	77·0
Lower Normandy	85	99	107	110	48	159	760	82·5
Loire	60	75	90	131	143	274	1,470	84·5
Brittany	103	136	147	139	326	515	1,340	72·5
Limousin	16	24	28	31	93	125	700	85·0
Auvergne	79	91	100	114	101	214	920	81·0
Poitou-Charentes	189	216	246	277	106	383	660	63·5
Midi-Pyrénées	7	10	25	38	119	157	1,520	90·5
Burgundy	282	309	332	358	114	471	870	65·0
Rhône-Alps	68	70	83	98	104	202	690	77·5
Languedoc	6	9	10	14	23	37	260	87·5
Provence-Côte-d'Azur-Corsica	12	13	13	14	30	44	230	84·0
Aquitania	14	20	28	38	101	139	1,360	90·5
France	3,565	3,937	4,290	4,690	2,028	6,718	15,290	69·5

shows that governmental policy has played an appreciable corrective role. But population and development pressures are such that the most urgent problems are those met in connection with the economically most advanced regions, and for political and social reasons, they must be given attention in the short term. Thus it is only natural that state intervention should be oriented in the first place to these regions. Activity can be more widely spread geographically in a second phase. But even so, the high figures achieved in more advanced regions are far from being equalled, and the overtaking of existing arrears becomes still more of a pipedream.

(iii) THE GROWTH OF ECONOMIC ACTIVITY

This paper is not the place to undertake a comparative analysis of the growth, as compared with that of the economy as a whole, of the various activities conducted in the region. It is of greater interest to look for indications of structural change likely to lead to more rapid economic growth. The indicators examined here are open to criticism on the score that by reason of their generality, they conceal profound sectoral disparities. This does not make the picture that they give of the overall situation of the region any less significant.

(a) *The Agricultural Sector.* Three types of indicators have been selected to illustrate the scope for structural readaptation: regrouping of holdings, the growth of stocks of producer's equipment, and the recourse to credit financing.

Table 9 presents data on regrouping operations; this is of the utmost importance for the region.

Aquitania, together with the Midi-Pyrénées, has the dubious privilege of being the region with the lowest ratio of regrouping operations actually undertaken to operations required – 9·5 per cent for Aquitania against 30·5 per cent for France and 64·5 per cent for the Normandy region. The persistence of agrarian structures which, in many sub-regions, prevent mechanisation and stultify progress, is clear proof that state intervention has not succeeded in modifying the existing situation to any significant extent.

It can thus easily be seen why it has been impossible for a more capitalistic structure to take root. The ratio of new agricultural equipment purchased to land area provides useful evidence here; in this respect Aquitania stands very slightly above the national average, but lags considerably behind regions organised on more capitalistic lines, such as Picardy. As the South-West continues to be predominantly agricultural, its under-equipment is particularly serious, and also revealing, in the sense that no trend of change can be observed. Worse, if the data presented in Table 10 are taken in conjunction with those given in an earlier section, it can be seen that despite its poorly adapted and rigid agrarian structure, the region is over-equipped so far as profitable utilisation is concerned; the emulation effect has been operating here also.

TABLE TEN

PURCHASES OF NEW AGRICULTURAL EQUIPMENT

(Francs per hectare of usable agricultural area)

Region	1959	1963	1964
Paris Region	107·93	75·86	149·38
Champagne	64·32	80·36	120·91
Picardy	99·63	117·72	132·17
Upper Normandy	77·91	92·68	103·51
Centre	74·64	80·14	101·98
North	93·20	106·37	135·28
Lorraine	71·91	59·34	83·39
Alsace	133·72	127·86	250·77
Franche-Comté	62·28	72·05	110·60
Lower Normandy	57·08	58·49	79·36
Loire	58·48	56·75	70·71
Brittany	90·55	92·85	115·11
Limousin	54·72	38·10	53·94
Auvergne	46·16	47·32	56·61
Poitou-Charentes	65·90	66·59	78·36
Midi-Pyrénées	58·02	62·16	78·56
Burgundy	50·95	63·48	77·08
Rhône-Alps	69·37	60·42	88·93
Languedoc	74·49	66·27	76·66
Provence-Côte-d'Azur	46·10	53·67	85·98
Aquitania	82·27	82·07	95·21
France	69·13	72·02	92·93

This inadequate use of modern agricultural techniques is also reflected in the statistics of fertiliser use, as is shown in Table 11. Average fertiliser consumption per hectare is 80 kg. in the Aquitaine region, against a national average of 94 kg., and above 200 kg. in a modern agricultural area such as the Picardy region.

Finally, it is worth examining the trends in the demand for credit as an indicator of agricultural progress. These are set out in Table 12.

The data relating borrowing to useful area show that the region is tending to increase its indebtedness faster than other regions. It is to be hoped that the counterpart of these higher long- and medium-term debts will be a degree of modernisation; to this extent indebtedness is a favourable sign. If, however, the acquisition of new financial resources is to be neutralised by structural rigidities, this policy of indebtedness could turn out to have grave consequences. For the time being, it is a source of

D

worry for many leading agricultural operators, who are only too well aware of the danger.

TABLE ELEVEN
FERTILISER DELIVERIES

(Kilograms per hectare of usable agricultural area)

Region	1959	1963	1964
Paris Region	143·47	202·87	248·45
Champagne	85·85	88·57	143·05
Picardy	138·62	183·38	203·25
Upper Normandy	103·99	144·82	159·82
Centre	74·04	111·59	134·25
North	143·64	167·24	194·82
Lorraine	25·73	99·69	48·78
Alsace	41·44	50·70	84·15
Franche-Comté	17·81	29·65	39·85
Lower Normandy	60·51	81·13	89·00
Loire	63·07	84·92	92·36
Brittany	74·26	105·53	110·04
Limousin	16·02	51·18	33·35
Auvergne	14·03	20·51	24·22
Poitou-Charentes	44·03	64·23	71·82
Midi-Pyrénées	27·19	48·68	50·16
Burgundy	35·90	57·34	63·60
Rhône-Alps	27·43	41·32	46·09
Languedoc	39·96	45·66	42·73
Provence-Côte-d'Azur	38·89	44·22	74·31
Aquitania	49·30	72·69	77·29
France	55·89	79·69	90·16

(b) *Industrial Development.* An attempt will be made in this sector also to concentrate attention on a limited number of general indicators providing an overall picture of development.

An appropriate first approach is to use fiscal statistics to provide some information on turnover. While the gross data are of debatable accuracy, interregional ratios and changes over time may reasonably be used as evidence. The relevant data are presented in Tables 13 and 14.

It can be seen from these tables that Aquitanian enterprises have a turnover representing only 2·6 per cent of that of the nation as a whole (49 per cent of the total is accounted for by the Parisian region). The figures are, of course, only of limited significance since many firms have head offices in Paris, while most of their business lies in the provinces. But while the comparison with the Parisian region is of debatable value, the regional turnover figure is manifestly a low percentage of total. Even

TABLE TWELVE

LONG- AND MEDIUM-TERM LENDING
BY THE AGRICULTURAL CREDIT FUND
(CRÉDIT AGRICOLE)

(Francs per hectare of usable agricultural area)

Region	Long-Term Loans 1963	Medium-Term Loans 1963	Long-Term Loans 1964	Medium-Term Loans 1964
Paris Region	109·14	324·28	138·23	532·50
Champagne	103·12	301·54	117·41	407·34
Picardy	93·50	280·65	110·38	426·66
Upper Normandy	131·38	131·02	151·89	315·50
Centre	93·73	253·31	109·87	365·55
North	129·61	327·78	153·64	450·28
Lorraine	15·74	248·44	109·27	334·18
Alsace	191·57	219·79	289·74	397·06
Franche-Comté	109·54	179·36	152·86	293·56
Lower Normandy	128·07	234·93	153·13	280·04
Loire	122·16	250·19	265·58	316·87
Brittany	178·37	359·44	171·43	443·38
Limousin	97·72	150·89	60·05	218·50
Auvergne	89·63	179·16	106·89	248·92
Poitou-Charentes	129·69	205·25	149·26	276·62
Midi-Pyrénées	153·95	223·80	145·18	375·02
Burgundy	93·91	211·49	10·43	268·78
Rhône-Alps	164·83	283·79	192·94	417·77
Languedoc	187·04	368·86	200·19	667·60
Provence-Côte-d'Azur	143·82	318·48	220·62	800·19
Aquitania	236·82	369·31	199·17	482·88
France	132·51	263·85	151·40	386·97

more serious, this percentage has not risen over the ten-year period. In 1955, the turnover of Aquitanian firms assessed on actual profits represented 2·5 per cent of the figure for France; in 1964 it stood at 2·4 per cent.

The features of Aquitanian underdevelopment emerge even more clearly from an examination of the structural changes in industry than they do from the overall data just presented. The trend to greater concentration, for example, is less marked here than it is for the country in general, as can be seen from Table 15.

More than half of the firms in the Aquitaine region have no paid staff,

TABLE THIRTEEN

TURNOVER OF FIRMS ASSESSED TO TAX ON ACTUAL PROFITS

(m. francs)

Region	1955	1956	1957	1958	1959	1960	1961	1962	1963	1964
Paris Region	134·4	155·0	180·3	203·4	221·6	254·6	284·3	311·3	356·2	394·2
Champagne	4·9	5·6	6·4	7·1	7·5	8·4	9·2	10·4	12·0	13·5
Picardy	4·4	4·9	5·5	6·0	6·5	7·1	8·2	9·1	10·4	11·9
Upper Normandy	5·6	6·4	7·2	8·0	8·4	9·2	10·1	11·0	12·5	14·3
Centre	4·8	5·5	6·3	7·0	7·3	8·0	8·9	10·3	11·6	14·0
North	21·3	23·6	26·8	27·9	30·0	33·0	35·5	38·0	42·0	45·8
Lorraine	9·6	10·9	12·6	13·6	15·3	17·1	18·8	20·2	21·8	23·9
Alsace	7·3	8·3	9·4	10·5	11·2	12·1	13·4	14·8	16·4	18·3
Franche-Comté	3·4	3·8	4·3	4·7	5·0	5·6	6·2	6·9	8·1	8·8
Lower Normandy	2·7	3·0	3·4	3·7	3·9	4·6	5·0	5·8	6·6	7·7
Loire	5·8	6·6	7·5	8·4	8·8	10·6	11·0	12·4	14·7	16·8
Brittany	4·2	4·9	5·7	6·3	6·8	7·4	8·5	9·9	11·6	13·4
Limousin	1·7	1·9	2·2	2·4	2·6	2·8	3·7	3·5	3·9	4·4
Auvergne	3·4	3·9	4·3	4·8	5·3	5·8	6·5	7·3	8·0	9·1
Poitou-Charentes	3·2	3·7	4·3	4·8	4·9	5·6	6·2	7·1	8·3	9·5
Midi-Pyrénées	4·9	5·6	6·4	7·1	7·7	8·5	9·4	10·3	12·8	14·1
Burgundy	3·9	4·4	5·0	5·5	5·8	6·5	7·3	8·0	9·3	10·6
Rhône-Alps	18·9	21·7	24·9	28·0	30·2	33·9	37·9	42·6	49·2	55·5
Languedoc	4·0	4·7	5·6	6·5	6·6	7·1	7·8	8·8	10·0	11·3
Provence-Côte-d'Azur-Corsica	10·5	12·1	13·7	15·7	17·3	18·5	20·8	23·9	27·9	31·6
Aquitania	6·7	7·5	8·5	9·6	10·1	11·2	12·3	14·1	16·1	18·1
France	265·7	304·1	350·4	391·0	422·9	477·7	531·0	585·4	669·5	746·8

and the relative importance of this kind of business actually increased between 1958 and 1962, the share of large- and medium-scale enterprises remaining stable or varying only slightly. From data on the distribution of the economically active population in industry as between specific

TABLE FOURTEEN

TURNOVER OF FIRMS ASSESSED TO TAX UNDER AGREED DECLARATIONS

(Régime fiscal du forfait)
(m. francs)

Region	1955– 1956	1957– 1958	1959– 1960	1961– 1962	1963– 1964
Paris Region	4·7	6·3	9·1	10·9	12·5
Champagne	0·7	0·9	1·2	1·5	1·8
Picardy	0·9	1·1	1·6	2·0	2·3
Upper Normandy	0·9	1·1	1·5	2·0	2·4
Centre	1·2	1·5	2·1	2·6	3·2
North	2·2	2·8	3·8	4·7	5·5
Lorraine	1·1	1·4	2·0	2·4	2·9
Alsace	0·6	0·7	1·0	1·2	1·4
Franche-Comté	0·5	0·6	0·8	1·0	1·2
Lower Normandy	0·9	1·1	1·6	1·9	2·3
Loire	1·4	1·9	2·6	3·2	3·9
Brittany	1·3	1·7	2·3	2·9	3·6
Limousin	0·5	0·6	0·8	0·9	1·1
Auvergne	0·8	1·0	1·3	1·6	1·9
Poitou-Charentes	0·9	1·2	1·6	1·9	2·4
Midi-Pyrénées	1·1	1·5	2·1	2·6	3·3
Burgundy	0·9	1·1	1·5	1·9	2·3
Rhône-Alps	2·5	3·4	4·6	5·6	6·9
Languedoc	0·8	1·1	1·5	1·9	2·4
Provence-Côte d'Azur-Corsica	1·6	2·2	3·2	3·9	4·8
Aquitania	1·2	1·6	2·2	2·7	3·4
France	26·6	34·9	48·4	59·3	71·8

branches of activity, the industries accounting for above-average shares of total employment turn out to be sectors without any great prospects of development. They include the food and agricultural product processing industries, woodworking, leather, paper, cardboard, water, electricity, construction, aircraft and shipbuilding (the last named is experiencing a full-scale recession), oil and natural gas. Apart from the last two, none of these industries is particularly dynamic. Oil and natural gas, which will be considered at greater length in the third part of this paper, are directly connected with the Lacq complex or are affected by decisions by the public authorities; but it may reasonably be doubted whether these activities (whose relative importance, none the less, has grown considerably since 1962) are sufficiently integrated into the region's economy to constitute an appreciable stimulus to growth. Major manufacturing industries supplying the market with consumption goods for which demand is rising are absent, as are the basic industries.

TABLE FIFTEEN

SIZE OF INDUSTRIAL ESTABLISHMENTS IN FRANCE
AND IN AQUITANIA

			Total Number of Establishments *Employing Different Numbers of Persons*				
	No *Employees*	*1 to* *10*	*11 to* *200*	*201 to* *1,000*	*Over* *1,000*	*No* *Return* *Made*	*Total*
			1962				
France	339,717	354,518	70,991	4,255	530	1,305	771,316
Aquitania	23,643	17,766	2,805	140	12	116	44,366
			1958				
France	407,765	378,736	67,387	3,760	479	6,953	865,080
Aquitania	25,159	20,953	2,940	123	12	251	49,438
			Percentages of all Establishments				
			1962				
France	44	45	9·2	0·55	0·07	0·17	
Aquitania	53	40	6·0	0·30	0·03	0·26	
			1958				
France	47	43	7·0	0·43	0·05	0·80	
Aquitania	50	42	6·0	0·25	0·02	0·50	

Source: I.N.S.E.E.

A study of Tables 16 and 17 will show that, apart from the two new sectors referred to above, the growth pattern between 1954 and 1962 has not been very favourable, since the Aquitanian share of the French total has risen only in less dynamic sectors. So far as major industrial activities are concerned, the region still accounts for less than 1 per cent of total French employment, and the figures are not very significant. In such crucial sectors as mechanical and electrical equipment or chemicals, the region has lost further ground and the principal sectors whose shares are increasing, the leather and construction industries, do not have particularly good growth prospects.

3LE SIXTEEN

TERPRISES RANKED IN DECLINING ORDER OF SIZE, 1962

ployment in (a) Aquitanian industries; (f) the same industries, France; (A) total industrial nomically active population, Aquitania; (F) total industrial economically active population, nce.

Sector	Rank-ing	Employment in Aquitania (a)	Proportion of all Employment in Aquitania (a/A)	Proportion of all Employment in France (f/F)	Relative Significance Factor Ratio of a/A:f/F	Ranking of Significance Factor
astruction	1	80,240	29·0	22·0	1·3	8
od and processing of agricultural roduce	2	33,300	12·0	8·5	1·4	7
aber and furniture	3	27,740	10·0	3·8	2·6	3
ther	4	22,760	8·0	2·6	3·1	1
thing	5	11,860	4·3	5·1	0·8	12
chines and mechanical equip-ent (except metal structures)	6	10,980	4·0	8·4	0·4	16
craft fabrication, shipbuilding nd repairing	7	10,840	3·9	2·4	1·6	5
micals and rubber	8	10,380	3·8	0·5	0·7	13
n-ferrous semi-finished products, rst processing of steel, foundries nd metal-working	9	8,640	3·1	5·7	0·54	15
lding materials (including eramics)	10	7,900	2·9	2·6	1·1	9
er and cardboard	11	7,820	2·8	1·6	1·7	4
lic utilities	12	7,340	2·7	1·7	1·5	6
natural gas and petroleum roducts	13	6,140	2·2	0·8	2·7	2
lication, printing and ublication	14	5,880	2·1	2·7	0·7	13
tiles	15	5,860	2·1	7·2	0·29	19
ore and steel manufacture	16	2,740	1·0	3·4	0·29	19
tic manufacture and other dustries	17	2,580	0·9	2·3	0·39	18
omobiles (except repair)	18	2,280	0·8	4·0	0·2	21
tric and electronic equipment or household or professional se, electrically-powered con-mer durables)	19	2,220	0·8	4·0	0·2	21
ss	20	2,120	0·7	0·8	0·87	11
-ferrous ores and metals	21	760	0·3	0·4	0·4	16
d mineral fuels and coking oducts	22	380	0·1	2·7	0·05	23
	23	300	0·1	0·2	0·9	10
		271,060	100·0	100·0		

Source: I.N.S.E.E.

Finally, the statistics of industrial building permits for sites exceeding 500 square metres may be used to provide further relevant information. These are presented in Table 18. This table suggests that there has been some degree of improvement in the region's position.

TABLE SEVENTEEN

CHANGES IN EMPLOYMENT PATTERNS 1954–1962

Nature of Employment	Changes in Employment per cent		Employment in Aquitania as Percentage of Employment in France	
	France	*Aquitania*	*1954*	*1962*
Food and processing of agricultural produce	+ 2·4	– 5·0	5·7	5·3
Solid mineral fuels and coking products	– 22·0	—	0·13	0·18
Gas	– 26·5	—	1·2	1·7
Public utilities	+ 12·6	+ 26·8	5	5·7
Oil, natural gas and petroleum products	+ 32·5	+ 104·1	6·5	9·7
Building materials (including ceramics)	+ 0·7	– 1·4	4·0	3·9
Glass	+ 23·5	+ 16·2	3·8	3·6
Iron ore and steel manufacture	+ 12·9	– 24·0	1·6	1·1
Non-ferrous ores and metals	+ 22·5	—	0·3	2·3
Ferrous and non-ferrous semi-finished products	+ 16·5	+ 22·0	1·9	2·0
Machines and mechanical equipment	+ 25·1	+ 11·9	1·9	1·7
Electric and electronic equipment	+ 50·2	+ 68·7	0·6	0·6
Aircraft fabrication, ship-building and repairing	+ 13·7	+ 28·5	5·2	6·0
Chemicals and rubber	+ 19·9	+ 14·4	2·9	2·8
Textiles	– 17·0	– 21·5	1·1	1·1
Clothing	– 19·7	– 31·5	3·6	3·1
Leather	– 16·5	+ 8·3	9·2	11·9
Timber and furniture	– 9·0	– 31·5	12·5	9·8
Paper and cardboard	+ 15·0	+ 20·3	6·1	6·4
Duplication, printing and publication	+ 19·2	+ 5·2	3·2	2·8
Plastic manufacture and other industries	+ 10·3	– 2·1	1·6	1·5
Construction	+ 23·8	+ 47·06	4·3	5·2

Source: I.N.S.E.E.

(*c*) *The Relative Stagnation of Trade and Commerce* must also be emphasised. The importance of commercial activity in the economic life of the Bordeaux area is such that this point on its own would normally warrant

TABLE EIGHTEEN

INDUSTRIAL BUILDING PERMITS AWARDED

(Floor Area 500 sq. m. or more)

(000 sq. metres)

Region	1956	1957	1958	1959	1960	1961	1962	1963	1964	1965 Provisional
Paris Region	632	448	594	411	622	502	432	381	572	589
Champagne	123	97	48	78	119	157	168	182	236	155
Picardy	81	126	133	121	269	248	284	283	279	311
Upper Normandy	70	96	158	211	131	141	176	221	226	308
Centre	144	123	203	130	273	286	359	353	372	319
North	151	176	142	132	224	307	296	293	466	303
Lorraine	139	153	115	143	167	139	289	152	203	194
Alsace	111	104	152	160	182	239	237	224	209	225
Franche-Comté	53	64	63	55	64	116	149	130	148	148
Lower Normandy	38	32	57	39	44	114	101	236	183	177
Loire	145	103	97	76	191	283	224	225	350	346
Brittany	21	23	37	204	78	121	123	205	256	306
Limousin	19	20	33	14	33	26	53	58	43	48
Auvergne	48	52	93	48	106	122	98	107	135	74
Poitou-Charentes	33	32	27	39	87	185	98	120	187	148
Midi-Pyrénées	25	86	75	67	84	115	74	109	175	235
Burgundy	27	68	125	90	138	120	236	203	231	300
Rhône-Alps	358	305	365	257	389	454	509	495	699	752
Languedoc	21	31	25	26	43	41	64	59	97	114
Provence-Côte-d'Azur–Corsica	85	115	75	67	161	125	193	120	229	233
Aquitania	92	62	222	89	107	209	155	153	257	331
Total	2,416	2,316	2,839	2,457	3,512	4,050	4,318	4,309	5,553	5,616

Source: Ministère de l'Équipement. Direction de l'Aménagement foncier et de l'Urbanisme.

D 2

TABLE NINETEEN

GENERAL MERCHANDISE TRANSITED THROUGH MARITIME PORTS

(000 tons)

	1956	1957	1958	1959	1960	1961	1962	1963	1964	1965
Dunkirk	7,793	7,663	8,133	7,135	8,321	8,596	8,648	12,228	13,860	15,887
Calais	1,052	1,013	1,058	1 201	1 595	1 728	1,789	1,378	1,360	1,114
Boulogne	806	861	750	834	1,066	1,967	1,195	1,484	1,614	1,317
Dieppe	808	888	733	739	654	622	620	644	703	563
Le Havre	16,078	15,690	6,267	16,261	16,627	20,075	21,243	25,136	27,137	26,938
Rouen	9,244	9,489	7,913	6,599	6,894	8,328	7,837	10,469	11,091	10,369
Caen	2,287	2,417	2,000	2,040	2,251	2,168	2,130	2,393	2,486	2,115
Cherbourg	289	409	357	270	244	279	219	293	225	217
St-Malo	267	307	254	260	296	351	470	556	552	537
Brest	634	1,000	885	1,092	1,241	1,348	1,657	2,466	1,594	1,271
Lorient	516	516	508	493	516	582	683	801	901	768
Nantes-St-Nazaire	4,964	5,455	5,988	5,945	6,451	7,298	8,618	9,446	9,727	10,400
La Rochelle	1,370	1,558	1,340	1,306	1,405	1,620	1,799	2,357	2,300	2,270
Rochefort	94	87	95	—	132	131	1,620	207	160	164
Bordeaux	5,705	5,331	4,778	4,895	5,509	5,751	6,011	7,024	7,086	7,004
Bayonne	727	779	726	988	1,351	1,799	1,539	2,123	2,300	1,961
Port-Vendres	140	138	167	—	123	124	112	123	74	42
Sète	3,107	3,239	3,917	3,594	3,623	4,047	4,211	4,071	4,048	3,521
Marseilles	21,053	19,777	23,373	23,748	23,936	27,507	27,757	36,005	47,188	54,959
Toulon	386	316	373	359	401	448	373	538	542	496
Cannes	—	—	—	—	—	—	—	—	—	—
Nice	359	353	343	312	332	240	254	268	277	254
Bastia	—	—	—	—	—	—	—	—	—	292
Ajaccio	—	—	—	—	—	—	—	—	—	304
Other ports	3,432	3,875	3,722	3,994	4,143	4,502	4,634	5,566	6,263	5,035

Source: Ministère de l'Équipement. Direction des ports maritimes et des voies navigables.

thorough analysis. Consideration will, however, be limited to the data relating to the activity of Bordeaux port presented in Table 19.

These figures provide another example of a situation which, while improving in absolute terms, is deteriorating relatively to that of the country as a whole. The merchandise tonnage handled at Bordeaux rose by 22 per cent between 1956 and 1965, but over the same period, traffic at Le Havre rose by 67 per cent, at Nantes by 109 per cent and at Marseilles by 161 per cent. Rouen was the only port to register less progress, with an increase of 12 per cent, but there were special factors there in the form of closer and more severe competition.

This general survey has inevitably been somewhat superficial. But it has presented a wide range of evidence, the unanimity of which can consequently be taken as significant. The diagnosis appears to be inescapable: the Aquitaine region has unquestionably shown considerable progress in recent years. There is no question of actual contraction of the region's economy (there never has been). But although noteworthy improvements are to be found, there is no evidence that the region has recovered any of the existing gap as compared with the rest of the country, or even that its growth is equivalent to the average rate recorded for the economy as a whole. First and foremost, however, it is certain that in all essentials the indispensable modernisation of industrial and agricultural structure has not been achieved, despite the fact that it is a precondition for the take-off of economic growth in the region. It may of course be objected that the figures used do not fully reflect the full effects of the Lacq 'growth point' or the development of the new aerospace industries. The data for 1965, however, are significant with respect to Lacq, and this problem will be further considered below. The fact is that since then new industrial projects have been scarce, while neither the aerospace industry nor the Ambès petroleum complex is capable, for good reasons, of exercising any immediate effect on the development of the region generally.

But the balance sheet of the decade is on the whole a disappointing one, and it remains to discover why, and to draw the relevant conclusions for the future. The first possibility that strikes one is that there may have been an insufficient degree of public-authority intervention. As will be seen, this explanation is by no means sufficient, and another, more in terms of economic mechanisms, has to be sought.

3 A SHORT SURVEY OF STATE INTERVENTION IN THE AQUITAINE REGION

No attempt will be made in the limited space available to draw up an exhaustive catalogue of government action in the Aquitaine region designed to promote its growth, directly or indirectly. A large number of studies has been devoted to the specific forms of regional action by the State, and the reader is referred for a description of this to the articles by Doyen Lajugie in the *Revue d'économie politique* or the *Revue juridique et économique du Sud-Ouest*, and also to the various reports of the Social and Economic Council.

The Aquitanian region, like other French regions, has unquestionably derived benefit from the introduction of the new administrative arrangements designed to facilitate the operations of the public authorities. The arrangements so created include the regions themselves, headed by a regional prefect who is assisted by an economic mission; the formation of the C.O.D.E.R. to secure improved participation of the local persons in authority in the regionalisation of the Plan; and the system of *tranches opératoires* – the operating programmes by which the Plan is implemented in successive segments. These reforms, however, are of general scope, and specify neither the extent of public authority aid to Aquitania, nor its limits.

(i) THE SCOPE OF PUBLIC AUTHORITY DEVELOPMENT
    ASSISTANCE

Development aid can be considered at two levels, the first by examining the prospects envisaged in development plans, and more particularly the Fifth Plan, the second by undertaking an analysis of the volume of aid granted by various public financial agencies to the region.

(*a*) The Aquitaine region has benefited in the past, and continues to benefit, from large-scale regional development projects more or less closely linked to one of the successive Plans. Two examples will serve to illustrate past actions of this kind: the Gascony Landes and Cotaux development schemes, the latter mainly to the benefit of the Midi-Pyrénées region. The Compagnie des Landes de Gascogne was created to secure improved agricultural equilibrium in the Landes area by promoting the cultivation of various crops (especially maize) alongside the traditional forestry activities. Considerable efforts were deployed to this end, including the specification of standard operating units which were put at the disposal of local or immigrant cultivators. The economic, social and human returns obtained were, it must be admitted, rather slight, and the company failed to lay the foundations of the regional revolution in agricultural methods it had been hoped to generate.

New projects are taking shape at present. One of the most important relates to the improvement of the tourist facilities offered by the Aquitaine coast, the aim being to use the attractive powers of some 150 miles of beaches and the many lakes in the coastal zone to lure French and foreign tourists to the region in greater numbers. Tourism could in fact be an important makeweight in the region's economy, and secure better utilisation of the capital represented by land resources which are only too often left unexploited. It is debatable, however, whether an activity which by

TABLE TWENTY

SUMS SUPPLIED TO ASSIST REGIONAL INDUSTRIAL EXPANSION BY THE ECONOMIC AND SOCIAL DEVELOPMENT FUND (F.D.E.S.)

(Francs 000s)

Region	Gross Amount of Investments in Connection with which Funds made Available					Premiums Paid		F.D.E.S. Loans		S.D.R. – Guaranteed Borrowing*	
	1962	1963	1964	1965	Total 1962–1965	1964	1965	1964	1965	1964	1965
Paris Region	—	—	—	—	—	—	—	—	—	—	—
Champagne	57,165	37,802	15,313	68,516	178,796	889	—	—	—	—	18,670
Picardy	48,171	53,621	84,919	—	186,711	1,116	—	—	—	16,850	—
Upper Normandy	39,710	88,190	38,950	66,072	232,922	88	815	—	8,200	13,750	10,790
Centre	47,467	43,600	121,818	26,314	239,199	3,358	50	—	—	19,450	8,450
North	7,595	224,215	115,785	5,007	352,602	627	506	—	—	26,500	—
Lorraine	12,268	64,522	79,179	119,341	275,310	3,838	11,202	—	—	16,055	—
Alsace	83,443	118,109	32,583	154,305	388,440	1,978	32	—	—	—	30,520
Franche-Comté	17,285	37,697	17,319	37,159	109,460	85	289	745	—	8,890	9,500
Lower Normandy	54,273	29,762	21,486	29,207	134,728	219	597	103	2,273	4,550	3,930
Loire	59,034	273,194	162,021	233,316	727,565	6,898	24,149	—	35,000	33,080	38,050
Brittany	89,697	167,455	206,104	147,183	620,439	9,771	8,679	778	25,385	11,230	15,850
Limousin	73,799	28,385	13,940	29,906	146,030	1,228	3,145	—	—	1,670	—
Auvergne	46,912	14,708	62,540	72,463	196,623	2,104	3,495	2,000	—	7,690	—
Poitou-Charentes	20,448	82,577	60,147	90,105	253,277	2,415	4,854	1,764	3,400	11,050	3,550
Aquitania	74,654	270,369	336,245	244,195	925,463	22,323	20,004	3,000	14,800	27,010	15,530
Midi-Pyrénées	32,460	18,734	120,715	58,797	230,706	5,378	4,206	1,900	—	11,100	—
Burgundy	34,829	32,575	35,474	28,295	131,173	346	506	—	—	10,460	—
Rhône-Alps	145,094	100,644	174,459	20,191	440,388	2,866	208	4,970	4,310	16,755	8,825
Languedoc	45,786	40,383	36,126	77,773	200,068	3,023	2,122	585	—	4,180	—
Provence-Côte-d'Azur-Corsica	47,517	36,522	84,126	45,138	213,303	930	4,541	518	15,451	22,270	12,545
France	1,047,607	1,763,064	1,819,249	1,553,283	6,183,203	80,180	89,400	16,363	108,819	264,540	176,210

Source: F.D.E.S. Rapport annuel.

* Société de Développement Régional and regional development companies.

necessity is seasonal can be expected to have a major impact in terms of the structural change of the region as a whole.

Hence, greater significance will be attached by many to the decisions to introduce new economic activities. The two projects involved are the petrol refining complex at Ambès, and the Landes Testing Centre (Centre d'Essais des Landes), to be used as a station for launching rockets which will be fabricated, at least in part, by aerospace industry firms in the Bordeaux region.

Lastly, state intervention has taken the form of the implementation of major local infrastructural projects, and continues to do so. Among the many that could be cited in this context are the construction of two new bridges over the Garonne, the equipment and/or creation of university and hospital centres, the improvement of communication channels (roads, telephone, telegraph networks) and the decentralisation of research and occupational training centres. All this suggests that an attempt is being made to make good at least a part of the region's lag in this field. These schemes, however, do not exhaust the development assistance provided, and it is therefore of value to attempt to draw up a balance sheet of the financial aid made available to the region.

(b) It is very difficult to draw up the full list of financial development assistance, but significant information can be garnered from an examination of the activity of the main financial agencies. France is divided into five Zones, and the Aquitaine region is in Zone I, 'the Industrial Development Zone'. Among the facilities applying in Zone I are the grant of lump-sum industrial development premiums, accelerated tax depreciation of buildings, relief from payment of the licence register fee (patente) and reduction of the duties levied in connection with transfers of ownership. Businesses in the Parisian region which decentralise may be awarded 'decentralisation subsidies' amounting to up to 60 per cent of their removal expenditures. As many of these advantages cannot be directly quantified, the examination can most appropriately be focused on financial aid only.

Table 20 makes it clear that F.D.E.S. aid to the Aquitaine region has been very considerable, for the region has received almost one-sixth of the total funds supplied to all the twenty-one French regions. Payments of premiums account for a very large proportion of this aid, and in fact represent one-quarter of the total of premiums paid in 1964 and 1965. By contrast, as may be seen in Table 21, borrowing guaranteed by the Regional Development Companies is much less substantial, which explains why the EXPANSO Company's operations have been relatively less extensive than those of other companies of this type. The privileged status of Aquitania in respect to state intervention at this level is again visible in the accounts of the FIAT (Fonds d'Intervention pour l'Aménagement du Territoire: Regional Development Fund), the principal operations of which are listed in Table 22.

While the Aquitaine region received only 7·4 per cent of the credits made available between May 1963 and July 1966, this is nevertheless the highest percentage registered for any region except Brittany. The amounts granted, however, are too small to have an appreciable effect on regional development.

TABLE TWENTY-ONE

REGIONAL DEVELOPMENT COMPANIES

(Francs 000s)

		Total of Funds Invested since 1965	
	Loans 1965	Grand Total	Of which against Borrowed Funds
Alsace (S.A.D.E.)	30,520	149,237	123,800
Nord and Pas-de-Calais	—	146,000	133,275
Lorraine (LORDEX)	—	73,683	64,240
Centre and Centre-West (SODECCO)	—	89,587	82,715
Mediterranean Region	—	81,155	73,670
South-West Industrial and Financing Company of Toulouse (TOFINSO)	—	94,185	89,830
South-West (EXPANSO S.D.R.)	19,080	97,258	89,110
South-East	—	101,530	91,675
Brittany	15,850	70,201	62,980
Normandy	14,720	103,708	95,850
West (SODERO)	46,500	202,877	195,850
Centre and East (CENTREST)	18,325	103,805	97,580
Champagne (CHAMPEX)	18,670	68,322	63,575
Languedoc-Roussillon (SODLER)	12,545	42,616	37,970
Picardy	—	49,352	45,250
Total	176,210	1,473,516	1,347,370

A last indicator of the volume of financial assistance is given by the table of loans accorded to local authorities by three agencies, the Caisse des Dépôts, the Crédit Foncier and the Crédit Agricole, shown in Table 23. Although the Paris region clearly benefits from the considerable facilities put at its disposal, this reflects the extent of its needs, and it will be observed that the Aquitaine region is better placed here than many active areas of the country – a fact which can, moreover, be explained by inadequacy of the proceeds of local taxation. This Table, while it focuses attention on the financial needs of Paris, also provides evidence of the limits of the policy applied.

REGIONAL DISTRIBUTION OF INVESTMENTS BY
THE F.I.A.T. REGIONAL INVESTMENT FUND *

Region	*Cumulative Funds Supplied May 1963 through July 1966*		*Fresh Operations (Funds Allocated between August 1965 and July 1966)*	
	Frs (000)	%	*Value Frs* (000)	*Principal Projects*
Champagne-Ardennes	15,200	3·16	5,000	Construction of an express road linking Mézières, Charleville and Sedan
Picardy	955	0·20	255	Construction of an urban link road at Ham (Somme)
Upper Normandy	1,370	0·29	—	
Centre	920	0·19	—	
North	34,047	7·08	12,663	Forestry operations in connection with creation of a national park at Saint-Amand; construction of premises at Lille for extension of Telex services; flood protection works on the Liane river to safeguard the town of Boulogne; the regional 'economic observatory' at Lille
Lorraine	23,526	4·89	10,110	Construction of a lock at Blénod, on the Moselle; installation of an automatic telephone exchange at Remiremont
Alsace	24,865	5·17	8,750	Site acquisition for the Rhine–Rhône canal project
Franche-Comté	4,865	1·01	3,140	Site acquisition for the Rhine–Rhône canal project; improvement of the RN83 highway between Besançon and Lons-Le-Saunier; outer-circular road at Lons-Le-Saunier; automatic telephone exchange at the winter sports station, Rousses (Jura)
Lower Normandy	11,917†	2·48	2,500	Provision of fresh water supply for the Auge and Normandy bocage districts
Loire	37,834	7·87	9,102	Bypass of Oudon on the road RN23; provision of fresh water supply for certain Olonne and Vendée districts; oyster beds in the Vendée; laying the Nantes-St-Nazaire coastal cable; drainage work in the Bauloise region

* No allowance is made in this table for credits made available for preliminary design studies, even where these are localised, as is the case for certain town planning schemes.

† An allocation of 440,000 francs for improvement of telephone services in Z.U.P.s (preferential urban development areas), decided by the Interministerial Committee in 1963, was transferred to the Aquitaine region from Lower Normandy.

TABLE TWENTY-TWO (*continued*)

Region	Cumulative Funds Supplied May 1963 through July 1966		Fresh Operations (*Funds Allocated between August 1965 and July 1966*)	
	Frs (000)	%	Value Frs (000)	Principal Projects
Brittany	78,396	16·32	12,090	Harbour installations for pleasure navigation; day-school premises for the new technical study centre at Brest; household garbage incineration plant at Rennes; installation of telephonic facilities in the industrial zone of Kerpont-en-Caudran; rural electrification schemes in the coastal areas of the Finistère peninsula; town planning projects in the north-eastern quarter of Dinan (road improvements and sundry networks)
Limousin	9,885	2·06	1,700	Improvement of the RN89 highway in the Corrèze Department
Auvergne	22,983	4·78	628	Drainage works at the Super–Lioran tourist resort; purification treatment plant at Cusset-Bellerive
Poitou-Charentes	20,072	4·17	3,018	Poitiers East access highway; road improvements on Oleron Island
Aquitania	35,629†	7·41	13,425	Bridge over the Adour at Bayonne and a second bridge at Pau; access roads to the Saint-Jean bridge at Bordeaux; harbours for pleasure navigation at Arcachon and Cap-Breton, improvement of the RN10 highway in the Landes; urban bypass road at Dax; access roads in the Basque country; improvement works to the Caudéran at Bordeaux
Midi-Pyrénées	55,272	11·50	20,090	Rodez airport; E.N.S.A. Laboratory at Toulouse, extension of the downtown district of Toulouse; stabilisation of the bed of the Garonne
Burgundy	5,795	1·21	—	
Rhône-Alps	21,010	4·37	4,060	Roadworks to facilitate traffic leaving Grenoble; access road to the Vanoise national park; reinforcement of the fresh water supply network at Chamonix; access road to the Villarembert resort (Savoy)
Languedoc-Roussillon	25,721	5·35	10,437	Extension of Sète harbour; improvement scheme for the tract of water at Villefort

TABLE TWENTY-TWO (*continued*)

Region	Cumulative Funds Supplied May 1963 through July 1966		Fresh Operations (*Funds Allocated between August 1965 and July 1966*)	
	Frs (000)	%	Value Frs (000)	Principal Projects
Provence-Côte-d'Azur (excluding Corsica)	33,923	7·06	6,538	(Lozère); equipment of irrigation networks in the Bas-Rhône-Languedoc area; harnessing the Agly basin (Eastern Pyrénées) Water supply for the Toulon region; equipment for airborne forest fire-fighting; flood protection of the Fréjus-Saint-Raphaël urban areas; protection of the Saintes-Maries against incursion by the sea; anti-mosquito campaign in the Marseilles region; regional 'economic observatory' at Marseilles
Corsica	16,460	3·43	1,500	Improvement of the CD55 road in Ajaccio bay
Total‡	480,645	100·00	125,006	

‡ The fact that the figures in this table are lower than in the table showing the distribution of investment by sector follows from the fact that some projects cannot be allocated on a regional basis. This is true of preliminary studies, but in the case of a number of overall schemes covering several regions, the proportion of the total accounted for by any one of them cannot be determined with sufficient accuracy.

(ii) THE LIMITS OF STATE INTERVENTION

These limits can be summarised in very few words: the means available to the State for correcting regional disequilibria are considerably limited by the very size of the needs of the developing regions. As often as not its actions are wholly insufficient to set in motion the essential structural modernisation.

The economic growth actually taking place in the more dynamic regions and the necessary requirements of European integration both force the State to concentrate its expenditure so as to achieve the most rapid possible improvement of the infrastructures of these already prosperous areas. Some examples of this may be cited: of the 462 million francs spent in 1966 by the Land Development Fund (F.N.A.F.U.), no less than 135 million went to the major beneficiary, the Paris region. Again, with the exception of some urban access freeways, the principal motorways already built or under construction serve economically advanced areas. The full implications of this may be seen in Table 24.

It may, again, be noted that more than one-third of the credits devoted to improvement of the national road system go to the Parisian region, as do almost one-quarter of investments in educational facilities (535 million

TABLE TWENTY-THREE

TOTAL LOANS TO LOCAL AUTHORITIES IN 1965 BY LENDING AGENCIES

(m. francs)

Region	Caisse des Dépôts	Crédit Foncier	Crédit Agricole *	Grand Total
Paris Region	1,542	11	—	1,554
Champagne	165	4	1	169
Picardy	164	6	2	172
Upper Normandy	214	7	—	221
Centre	258	13	2	272
North	323	10	—	333
Lorraine	191	4	1	196
Alsace	127	3	1	132
Franche-Comté	126	5	2	133
Lower Normandy	171	10	1	183
Loire	334	14	4	351
Brittany	351	5	9	364
Limousin	82	1	3	86
Auvergne	165	4	3	172
Poitou-Charentes	172	6	4	182
Midi-Pyrénées	266	5	3	274
Burgundy	189	7	1	198
Rhône-Alps	721	10	5	736
Languedoc	209	8	7	224
Provence-Côte-d'Azur-Corsica	457	6	6	469
Aquitania	302	7	4	313
France	6,528	147	59	6,733

* — = less than 0·5 million francs.

out of 2,195 in 1967), more than half of the sums expended on scientific and technical research (996 out of 1,517 million), above one-third of the equipment credits allocated for postal and telegraphic networks, and so on. Clearly, such investments are essential for the Paris region to function properly, but it can easily be seen that in percentage terms, they far exceed the region's share of the country's total population. Investment concentration is governed by economic activity, not by population factors. The structure of the State's operating and capital expenditure budget is such that outlays are predominantly undertaken in the most well-developed part of the country. Set against this, the corrective activities of special funds with only limited financial means at their disposal must necessarily be of little more than symbolic significance.

At the same time, it may be questioned whether the various projects implemented do in fact constitute a direct frontal attack on the major problems. The backwardness of the Aquitaine region is associated in

TABLE TWENTY-FOUR

MOTORWAYS: PROJECT AUTHORISATIONS
UNDER 1965 BUDGET APPROPRIATIONS

(Francs 000s)

| | Siting | | | | |
| | *Open Country* | *Major Urban Centres* | *Other Towns* | *Borrowed Funds* | *Total Value of Projects* |
Region					
Upper Normandy	2,830	—	—	—	2,830
Centre	—	—	9,000	—	9,000
North	—	18,500	33,000	—	51,500
Lorraine	—	21,400	5,481	—	26,881
Alsace	900	—	—	—	900
Aquitania	—	2,500	3,000	—	5,500
Rhône-Alps	40,851	31,586	1,900	—	74,336
Languedoc	10,550	—	58,131	—	68,682
Provence-Côte-d'Azur-Corsica	535	775	40	—	1,350
Total provincial	55,666	74,761	110,552	—	240,979
Paris region	1,353	128,515	—	—	129,868
Total above	57,019	203,276	110,552	—	370,847
Turnpikes					
Northern Motorway	37,750	—	—	146,450	184,200
Paris–Normandy Motorway	17,100	—	—	—	17,100
Paris–Lyons Motorway	23,900	—	—	82,350	106,250
Rhône Valley Motorway	60,300	—	—	112,000	172,300
Total	139,050	—	—	340,800	479,850
Other projects not listed above	—	—	—	—	62,639
Grand total	196,069	203,276	110,552	340,800	913,337

large measure with the region's isolation from the major national and European arteries. Separated from the Rhine–Rhône artery by the Central Plateau, bordered to the south by Spain, both underdeveloped and hardly integrated into the European economy, the region is a kind of island at the edge of the continent. Vital prerequisites for Aquitania are to ease the difficulties of road and rail transport, to lower transportation costs, and for the region to become a part of a continental or intercontinental development axis. Nothing has been done in any of these directions. Yet it is clear that the precondition of growth is the creation of dynamic activities which can provide a new impetus to growth. Earlier hopes have been disappointed. The region is, in a sense, in quest of its growth point.

4 THE CONDITIONS OF DEVELOPMENT AND THE PROBLEMS OF GROWTH POINTS

The discovery of the Lacq gasfield raised great hopes in the region. At long last, a raw-material source, the only one of its kind in France, was going to enable new industries to be set up. As a raw material and a source of energy, the new industries to be brought in by this gas would transform the outlook for existing enterprises. Industrial expansion would, it was believed, generate new income and the well-known multiplier effect would see to it that production rose, and would hence increase the level of regional income. It must be admitted that these hopes have not been borne out. Does this mean that the mechanisms related to the existence of a growth point failed to emerge, and that the theory is false? It is more likely that the conditions of existence of growth points were themselves inadequately analysed. The belief that any large industry constitutes a growth point is as widespread in advanced as in underdeveloped countries. But to render this analysis more accurate, the terminology employed must first be specified accurately. The term 'growth focus' will be used to designate an activity or set of activities whose presence involves certain changes in the structure of the surrounding economic environment and leads to an increase in production. 'Growth point' will be used [1] to refer to a complex of activities whose presence determines the structural re-organisation of an entire geographic zone and lays the foundations for a rapid and cumulative increase in its total output. The author's view is that Lacq played the role of a local growth focus, and as such had an impact on part of the Basses-Pyrénées Department, but that it is not, in the wider sense, a growth point. The reason for this is to be found in the nature of the economic activity undertaken at Lacq, the surrounding environment and the specific characteristics of the region's backwardness.

(i) THE INFLUENCE OF THE NATURE OF THE ECONOMIC ACTIVITY

An economic activity must fulfil three conditions simultaneously if it is to perform satisfactorily as a growth point. These are as follows:

(*a*) Its technical content must be within the reach of the surrounding

---

[1] Following O.E.C.D. terminology. The French terminology is *pôle de croissance* (growth pole) and *pôle de développement* (development pole). (Translator's note.)

economic and human environment. If the activity is too complex, neither the sub-contracting industries nor the technical staff required will be available locally. Most of the investment will consequently be undertaken by using outside resources. Underdeveloped regions constitute a typical case. Most often what one finds are pseudo-growth points whose actual effect on the local economy is negligible, and experience proves that the impetus to growth produced by a multiplicity of small manufacturing industries is greater than that produced by a large, but non-integrated, activity. And certainly, in the case of Lacq (as in the case of the aerospace industries), the necessary equipment and technical staff had to be brought in from outside.

(*b*) The more the processing of a product can be undertaken locally, the greater will be the development impact. Once provided that the raw material can be exported as such, it is a matter of chance whether complementary 'induced' activities appear or not. Again the experience of less developed countries confirms this conclusion. If the processing industries and the producers of finished goods locate near their markets rather than near their sources of raw materials, in other words, if transport costs do not operate as a determinant factor, and in the absence of bulk diminution in the course of manufacture, the processing units and finished goods producers will not locate near the source. This happened at Lacq, where it was found more efficient to take the gas to the user than to create new industries centred on the source of energy production.

(*c*) Lastly, allowance must be made for the repercussion of activity on employment and the distribution of incomes. One of the important aspects of the process engendered by a growth point is the income-multiplication effect, whereby outlays made are translated into the local distribution of incomes, which in turn swell the volume of demand to be met by local firms. The greater the recourse to local manpower, the greater the wage bill distributed and the stronger the induced effects. The labour costs of petroleum-based gas and electricity industries, however, like most of the other industries in the complex, are only a small component of their total cost structure. A full-scale accounting calculation for the whole complex made in 1964 by the Société d'Économie et de Mathématique Appliquée showed that of the total value added of 857 million francs, the wage bill, including employer contributions to social security, amounted to only 112 million francs. Gross profits were 626 million francs, with taxes making up the remainder. It may be remembered that the gross profit figure corresponds to amortisation of capital. On this basis, it is likely that some 75 per cent of the value added by the complex leaves the region, and so generates income distributed in other regions. The global turnover of the complex in 1964 amounted to 1,190 million francs, of which 337 million francs represented purchases of goods and services, mainly, as has been seen, from outside the region. It is no surprise, then, to find that the impact on regional growth has been slight. This was all the more so because the items produced by the complex could easily be exported without much on-the-spot processing, or without involving any local marketing operations. The local market, in fact, is too small, and the products – the gas itself (for which an immense supply network has been built), aluminium (87,000 tons in 1964), fertilisers, and such chemicals as methanol, butanol or monomer vinyl chloride – are all shipped to the traditional industrial areas. Sulphur is, indeed, available in such vast quantities that outlets are required on an international rather than a national scale.

All in all, the nature of the activity at Lacq is such that it does not constitute a growth point in either a French or a regional context. This is all the more so in that the local environment at the outset was not particularly propitious for the establishment of a growth point.

(ii) THE INFLUENCE OF THE ENVIRONMENT

A growth point's existence does not necessarily or exclusively depend on the presence of a major industry. The mechanism of growth implies the establishment of a close interrelationship between the growth-generating activity and the environment. If this relationship does not occur and there is a failure of the environment to adapt, the expected effects will either not be generated, or will only be slight. It can be taken that the growth-promoting influence of a growth point is based on three factors, namely, the 'forward and backward' effect of complementary relationships arising between the growth point and earlier and later stages of production; the existence of a multiplier mechanism resulting from the distribution of incomes by the growth point and linked to the development of local activities intended to satisfy rising levels of demand; and a psychological impact on behaviour which tends to modify traditional patterns in favour of a more productive organisation of output. The economic environment of the Basses-Pyrénées and Aquitania has not turned out to be sufficiently flexible.

This must be attributed in the first instance to the local economy's lack of internal coherence. In this connection it is of interest to examine the regional input-output table compiled by the Institut d'Économie Régional du Sud-Ouest that is presented as Table 25. Despite the imperfections inherent in such estimates, it can be seen that intersectoral relationships in the region are not at a very advanced stage. This means that enterprises purchase the best part of their inputs outside the region, and that their sales are made in part to final consumers in the region but in large part also to enterprises outside it.

A more detailed examination of these relations can be made on the basis of the SEMA report cited earlier. Three of the most significant tables will be given and commented on here. The first, Table 26, concerns the

TABLE TWENTY-FIVE
INPUT–OUTPUT TABLE FOR THE GIRONDE DEPARTMENT, 1960

Enterprises

PRODUCTS \ *SECTORS*	1. Agriculture and forestry	2. Food and processing of agricultural products	3. Solid mineral fuels	4. Coke oven gas	5. Public utilities	6. Oil, natural gas and fuel	7. Construction materials	8. Glass	9. Iron ore and steel products	10. Non-ferrous ores and metals	11. Metal production	12. Machinery and mechanical equipment	13. Electrical machinery and equipment
1. Agriculture and forestry	12,306	266,532											
2. Food and processing of agricultural products	8,217	179,634											
3. Solid mineral fuels		3,334	8,700			29	586			26		1,030	85
4. Coke oven gas													
5. Public utilities	2,030	3,897	79		135	1,675	4,544	817		1		2,306	251
6. Oil, natural gas and fuel	14,645	19,104			22,945	276,862	13,020	2,799				1,708	179
7. Construction materials	297	297					29,470	302				431	288
8. Glass		1,659						4,395					205
9. Iron ore and steel products					1,452		801			4,145		82,776	8,698
10. Non-ferrous ores and metals					148	124						30,370	
11. Metal production	79	1,639			440	7,254						38,106	2,027
12. Machinery and mechanical equipment													
13. Electrical machinery and equipment												4,787	5,975
14-15. Shipbuilding, aircraft, automobile and bicycle fabrication													

Row									
16. Chemicals and rubber	30,629	1,204	1,237	2,579	1,055	1,718		3,041	913
17. Textiles	853	3,436		441					257
18. Clothing									
19. Leather									273
20. Timber and furniture	1,495			124				66	
21. Pulp, paper and cardboard	5,944				3,354			367	
22. Printing and publishing									
23. Other manufacturing				124				452	
24. Building and public works									
25. Transport	20,297		350	53,716	6,304	1,617	35	8,719	247
26. Postal services and communications	1,879		30	400	542			450	154
27. Housing services									
28. Other services	49,946		300	4,185	3,528	764	1	4,172	1,029
29. Unallocated	16,986		208	316	2,315	1,718		8,293	
Intermediate consumption of industries (gross)	123,963	566,521	10,905	347,829	65,524	14,133	4,219	187,680	20,586
Value-added	542,363	544,526	7,094	942,162	109,069	26,866	707	152,055	32,693
Real cost of production (gross) of industries' output	666,326	1,111,047	18,000	1,290,000	174,593	41,000	4,927	339,736	53,280

Geographical Origin of Purchased Inputs

Gironde	NA	18·20	1·00 (100)	2·25	39·90	26·28	22·02	16·23	34·25
Rest of Aquitania	NA	4·98		54·00	2·96	1·31	0·67	4·83	
Paris region	NA	1·51		1·10	5·67	14·43	18·68	18·92	17·18
Rest of France	NA	30·17		0·80	18·44	55·83	26·08	52·50	48·57
Rest of franc zone	NA	32·46		15·27	0·31	2·11		0·03	
Rest of world	NA	12·68		26·58	32·72		32·55	3·48	

Geographical Distribution of Sales

Gironde	NA	17·40	86·50	28·74	46·14	31·44	16·15	24·66	6·58
Rest of Aquitania	NA	11·29	13·50	15·02	13·38	3·33	1·66	18·74	5·28
Paris region	NA	9·02		11·42		11·78	3·46	16·73	8·33
Rest of France	NA	44·05		44·81	34·56	34·25	54·40	33·20	59·24
Rest of franc zone	NA	11·24			5·32	12·45		4·26	
Rest of world	NA	7·00			0·60	6·75	24·35	2·41	20·57

TABLE TWENTY-FIVE (continued)
INPUT–OUTPUT TABLE FOR THE GIRONDE DEPARTMENT, 1960

Enterprises (continued)

PRODUCTS / SECTORS	14–15. Shipbuilding, aircraft, automobile and bicycle fabrication	16. Chemicals and rubber	17. Textiles	18. Clothing	19. Leather	20. Timber and furniture	21. Pulp, paper and cardboard	22. Printing and publishing	23. Other manufacturing	24. Building and public works	25. Transport	26. Postal services and communications
1. Agriculture and forestry		17,475				25,856	151	4	566		1,390	300
2. Food and processing of agricultural products		3,147				180						
3. Solid mineral fuels	69	291		95	50	59	2,125		61	192	11,728	
4. Coke oven gas												
5. Public utilities	1,454	3,305		369	813	1,672	6,042	437	195	912	4,919	400
6. Oil, natural gas and fuel	609	5,500		290	141	437	5,787	1,505	15	7,367	43,035	700
7. Construction materials							197			53,616	1,500	400
8. Glass		1,100				289				4,068		
9. Iron ore and steel products	30,877									31,658	1,500	
10. Non-ferrous ores and metals	3,146				66	387		89	76	54		
11. Metal production	85,291	15,280				2,772			209	25,534	7,104	100
12. Machinery and mechanical equipment												
13. Electrical machinery and equipment	3,012									1,982		900
14–15. Shipbuilding, aircraft, automobile and bicycle fabrication												

16. Chemicals and rubber	386	80,787	151	17,422	5,088	12,465	1,057	2,398	5,911	10,908	733
17. Textiles		2,070	92,985	9,148	1,243		32	937		975	
18. Clothing											400
19. Leather				3,677							
20. Timber and furniture	3,548	1,538		126	48,014	40,839		319	7,581	2,400	333
21. Pulp, paper and cardboard		505	562		2,884	35,653	27,870		176	652	
22. Printing and publishing		84					80			1,688	800
23. Other manufacturing					119					1,289	500
24. Building and public works		91	457	5,703				937	711		
25. Transport	2,136	26,526	1,894	1,609	3,720	11,115	2,319	206	6,222		3,400
26. Postal services and communications	68	994	476	297		532	2,221	39	1,468	652	
27. Housing services											
28. Other services	4,000	4,919	1,923	2,534	3,341	4,522	2,396	371	20,948	22,294	600
29. Unallocated	2,360	16,974	2,115	2,201	2,888	548	17	1,363	11,408	9,477	300
Intermediate consumption of industries (gross)	137,759	180,392	101,322	79,918	88,949	119,981	38,952	7,691	174,630	121,381	9,896
Value-added	84,740	140,179	83,660	97,088	104,570	134,622	71,047	7,308	345,369	381,619	56,164
Real cost of production (gross) of industries' output	222,500	320,725	184,983	177,009	203,520	254,603	109,919	15,000	520,000	503,000	66,060
Geographical Origin of Purchased Inputs											
Gironde	11·75	13·90	1·80	9·81	36·05	45·72	3·79	4·79	48·36	NA	100
Rest of Aquitania	6·35	2·28	0·24	3·87	19·27	12·52	1·04	5·37	14·24	NA	
Paris region	28·87	12·11	7·86	15·42	5·65	2·10	5·70	16·44	12·77	NA	
Rest of France	34·15	50·07	90·10	69·40	13·19	29·04	84·15	69·77	24·58	NA	
Rest of franc zone	13·88	10·82		1·50	25·84	5·12	0·08	3·69	0·05	NA	
Rest of world	5·00	10·82				5·44	5·24			NA	
Geographical Distribution of Sales											
Gironde	11·20	10·30	16·43	3·13	22·91	14·44	41·52	16·57	60·00	NA	1·00
Rest of Aquitania	4·98	12·37	27·15	2·28	8·02	10·60	22·24	12·44	18·88	NA	
Paris region	3·68	8·13	8·99	19·84	12·72	13·75	11·12	41·68	8·13	NA	
Rest of France	37·76	61·31	33·92	57·08	37·86	56·56	23·27	16·68	12·29	NA	
Rest of franc zone	39·37	3·22	6·36	10·47	8·64	2·93	1·29	5·44		NA	
Rest of world	3·09	4·67	7·15	7·20	9·85	1·70	0·64	7·19		NA	

INPUT–OUTPUT TABLE FOR THE GIRONDE DEPARTMENT, 1960

PRODUCTS / SECTORS	Enterprises (continued)						Households		Administration		Trade Balance	
	27. Housing services	28. Other services	29. Unallocated	Immediate consumption	Consumption	Investment	Consumption	Investment	Consumption	Investment	Imports	Exports
1. Agriculture and forestry		34,055		358,331			863,693		1,163		554,535	
2. Food and processing of agricultural products		93,225		289,403			663,363		8,811			154,470
3. Solid mineral fuels		4,018		32,782	3,522		48,398		3,902		70,604	
4. Coke oven gas												
5. Public utilities		4,924		41,177	5,291		45,170		341			4,108
6. Oil, natural gas and fuel		15,239		431,887	21,120		72,709		7,847			756,577
7. Construction materials				86,797					4,696			83,100
8. Glass				11,716					142			29,142
9. Iron ore and steel products				157,762					832		156,939	
10. Non-ferrous ores and metals				53,898							48,971	
11. Metal production		5,120		176,562	1,763	284,360	39,505		10,158	1,888	174,501	
12. Machinery and mechanical equipment											115,500	
13. Electrical machinery and equipment				13,644		84,660	59,279		10,655	564	34,380	
14-15. Shipbuilding, aircraft, automobile and bicycle fabrication				3,012		116,400	90,727		46,011	730	159,301	

	C1	C2	C3	C4	C5	C6	C7	C8
16. Chemicals and rubber	11,931	192,128	2,645	50,054	3,277		59,197	81,489
17. Textiles	2,058	114,435	3,527	39,111	2,228			31,746
18. Clothing	2,082	2,482	1,763	237,480	2,455			145,008
19. Leather		41,195		53,245	1,078			77,538
20. Timber and furniture	1,886	107,509	7,045	53,657	2,554	1,000		165,005
21. Pulp, paper and cardboard	2,180	79,746	8,050		1,802			77,536
22. Printing and publishing	16,635	19,327	8,800		4,256			
23. Other manufacturing	2,989	13,248	3,529		2,412	4,187		
24. Building and public works		223,868		210,000				5,165
25. Transport	6,272	156,929	47,500	28,058	26,546	54,421		258,425
26. Postal services and communications	2,764	10,966	10,058		12,088			40,725
27. Housing services				228,797	4,313			
28. Other services	17,467	167,499	29,800	703,888	9,180			76,633
29. Unallocated	10,055	127,317	154,954	68,268	20,899	2,736		
Intermediate consumption of industries (gross)	234,233	2,686,083	154,954	3,344,932	141,880	61,340		503,000
Value-added	752,500	4,718,050	647,502	210,000				
Real cost of production (gross) of industries' output	987,000	7,404,303	802,456					

Geographical Origin of Purchased Inputs

Gironde	100	14·70	NA
Rest of Aquitania	NA	20·00	NA
Paris region	NA	6·10	NA
Rest of France	NA	27·60	NA
Rest of franc zone	NA	16·90	NA
Rest of world	NA	14·70	NA

Geographical Distribution of Sales

Gironde	78·00	26·00	NA
Rest of Aquitania	17·00	12·30	NA
Paris region	5·00	10·80	NA
Rest of France	NA	40·00	NA
Rest of franc zone	NA	7·10	NA
Rest of world	NA	3·80	NA

accounts of enterprises. Table 26 depicts the movement of the Department's enterprise account between 1959 and 1964. It shows a considerable increase in value-added, which rose by some 1,721 million francs during the period, mainly the result of the rising activity of the Lacq complex, which contributed 708 million francs of this figure. Table 27 provides useful complementary information; it shows the increase in value-added to

TABLE TWENTY-SIX

ACCOUNTS OF ENTERPRISES

	Value-Added			Wages		
Sector	1959 (1964 Francs)	1964	Average Annual Increase	1959 (1964 Francs)	1964	Average Annual Increase
Agriculture	302,000	328,600	1·7%	21,050	29,887	7 %
Energy	97,500	69,800	—	21,600	27,400	4·9%
Lacq complex	149,300	857,130	41 %	35,950	80,660	17·1%
Metals and engineering	270,000	378,000	6·7	80,200	108,000	6 %
Building and public works	216,000	353,000	9·8%	73,00	96,000	5·6%
Textiles and leather	159,000	218,000	6·1%	51,500	70,600	6·2%
Other industries	222,000	320,500	7·2%	49,500	79,700	9·5%
Transport and communications	93,000	137,410	7·5%	48,500	61,057	4·6%
Commercial and service	501,000	1,069,000	16·1%	118,000	210,500	12·4%
Total	2,009,800	3,731,440	13·2%	499,300	763,804	8·9%

TABLE TWENTY-SEVEN

BUSINESS DONE BY DEPARTMENTAL FIRMS WITH THE LACQ COMPLEX AND OUTSIDE SUPPLIERS OF THE COMPLEX: TURNOVER, VALUE-ADDED AND WAGES

(Francs 000s)

	Sales Turnover				
Sector	To the Complex	To Outside Suppliers of the Complex	Total	Corresponding Value-Added	Corresponding Wages
Agriculture	—	—	—	—	—
Energy	829	400	1,229	1,070	420
Complex	—	3,000	3,000	2,320	220
Engineering	20,783	3,500	24,283	16,450	4,700
Building, public works	17,385	12,500	29,885	20,500	5,570
Textiles, leather	181	—	181	100	30
Other industries	3,828	1,000	4,828	2,280	560
Transport	12,913	3,500	16,413	11,500 *	5,100
Commercial and service	9,357	800	10,157	2,830	560
Total	65,276	24,700	89,976	57,050	17,160

* Estimated at 70% of turnover.

be imputed to the purchases from sources within the department made by the enterprises in the complex. This increase of 57 million francs, seen in the perspective of the general increase in activity (excluding the complex) of 1,013 million francs, provides a perfect picture of the limited effects of complementarity in the case of a poorly integrated environment unprepared for the incorporation of a new activity within its structure. This table relates – it is true – to value-added in 1964, when it must be admitted that, with construction and installation work on the complex at an end, purchases from regional sources were lower (especially those from the building industry). But even assuming that purchases in earlier years were much higher (perhaps twice as high in the years 1958 and 1959), they still account for only a limited share of the total, and the decline in that share is a very significant indicator of the limited nature of the influence under examination.

Table 28 makes possible an assessment of the induced effects generated by the complex resulting from the distribution of incomes in the region

TABLE TWENTY-EIGHT
ESTIMATE OF INDUCED EFFECTS

Sector	% of Total Turnover	Increase in Turnover	Increase in Value-Added	Increase in Wages
Agriculture	—	—	—	—
Energy	4	8,500	7,400	2,900
Complex	—	—	—	—
Engineering	5	10,600	7,200	2,100
Building, public works	6	12,700	8,700	2,400
Textiles, leather	—	—	—	—
Other industries	—	—	—	—
Transport	3	6,400	4,500 *	2,000
Commercial and service	82	173,800	48,500	9,800
Total	100	212,000	76,300	19,200

* Estimated at 70% of turnover.

by enterprises directly or indirectly related to the complex. The increase in value-added of these regional enterprises resulting from purchases made out of these new incomes was no more than 76 million francs. This induced effect, while not totally negligible, is certainly much lower than might have been expected.

All in all, the situation can be summarised as follows: between 1959 and 1964, the Department's value-added rose by 1,700 million francs, of which the direct production activities of the Lacq industries accounted for 700 million francs (or 41 per cent), those of the growth-generating industries for 900 million francs (or 54 per cent).

It can be seen that the inadequate diversification of local economic activity has operated as a brake on the growth mechanism. As often happens in less developed areas there is a tendency for the region to develop a dualistic economy characterised by the presence of two unintegrated types of activity which have only very slight repercussions on one another. So long as this isolation is not breached, the growth point cannot fulfil its role.

This is all the more so in that the multiplier effects are registered in the regions in which the incomes are in fact distributed and towards which the outlays are directed. A backward region, like a backward country, is characterised by a marked degree of leakage; and the impact of expenditure is felt in the most advanced regions where the goods utilised or consumed locally are produced. The fact that local labour is not fully capable of supplying the high level of technical skills involved in these activities, as has been noted, only aggravates matters still further.

Lastly, it may be remarked that the take-off effect will be the more limited the lower the absorptive capacity of the local market. What matters here is less the nature of the growth-generating industry than the relations it is likely and able to establish with the rest of the economic environment. Development results from the integration of the growth point with its surroundings, and not from the sole fact of existence of a growth-generating activity. The danger of an insufficiently precise economic vocabulary can be seen here. Use of the terms 'growth point' or 'growth-generating activities' induces the belief that it is only necessary to introduce such activities, and development will occur spontaneously. In point of fact, the development mechanism is based on the establishment of a system of complementary relationships between the principal industry and its supplying and client industries, and between local production and the induced demand of local consumers. Development policy, therefore, must not be limited to the mere introduction of major economic activities (which will of course have a favourable effect, for example on employment); but it must seek to prepare the ground by creating an environment which can subsequently harbour strong, growth-triggering activities. This is a field in which there is, of course, no set order of priorities, but an imperative need simultaneously to organise the environment and to install growth-generating activities. Unfortunately, an overall policy of this kind comes up against particular obstacles in an underdeveloped region.

(iii) THE SPECIFIC NATURE OF REGIONAL UNDERDEVELOPMENT

It is probably more difficult to implement a regional development policy than a policy at national level. The region is integrated in the national economic continuum. Its supplies are furnished by national industries which exist already, and which will take the necessary steps to control the establishment of new capacity as demand rises. There is thus little likelihood that major induced industries can be developed. This is the classical problem of restriction of access to the market by existing firms, an action which is made possible by the fact that the national market is a unified and comparatively integrated one. By contrast, the market in a less developed country tends to a fair degree of independence, whether through natural factors or artificially (for example, through customs barriers). The introduction of complementary activities therefore can be facilitated even if at the price of costs of production higher than those of foreign firms. But in a regional context, such a type of policy is difficult to accept. This implies that while no doubt it is possible in a backward region of an economically advanced country to introduce particular new activities, the other side of the medal is the difficulty met in attempting to install an integrated and coherent set of such activities; for they will tend to integrate directly at national level, skipping the stage of integration into the regional economic continuum. The danger inherent in certain types of historical comparison can be seen here. In the past, the development of new industries (textiles, engineering, chemicals, and the like) has been the starting point for the formation of high-growth economic regions. These industries operated as growth points because the existing industries had not yet, in general, expanded to the point of serving a national market, or as yet grown in size so far as to have disproportionate weight *vis-à-vis* the new activity. Hence, secondary industries located within the ambit of the growth point benefited from its presence and grew rapidly. Integration was achieved through parallel development of the growth point and its environment. This happens even today in certain developing economies where the take-off threshold has been crossed. But it can no longer happen easily at a regional level because the 'secondary' industries have already grown up in other regions, where they have become of national scale, and are therefore able to meet any increase in demand levels. This position is further reinforced by the operation of the demonstration effect. Whereas in a less developed country, much of the specifically local consumption pattern persists during the early stages of development, the consumption structure of backward areas of an advanced country is very close to that of the nation in general. Rising local incomes, in consequence, are spent on products (such as consumer durables) which are not, and cannot be, manufactured in the region.

It may further be observed that the greater the gap between the under-developed area and the country at large, the more difficult it will be to create a growth-generating ensemble. At the same time, the lower the region's weight in the economy in general, the more limited will tend to be the scope of corrective policy. This raises the problem of the effects of European integration. The creation of a single market raises the number of potential suppliers interested in satisfying the region's growing demand, but without introducing new industries there; and at the same time, the more intense competition at national level gives firms an incentive to concentrate and rationalise rather than to set up new production units. Restrictions on entry into the various industries are strengthened, while the markets outside the region for the products of the new activity are growing. The weaker the competition within a given area, the brighter will be the prospects for development of the complementary relationships needed to induce economic development, and the more time there will be available for their implementation. The stronger the degree of internal and external competition, the lower become the chances of diversification of local economic activity.

5 SOME CONCLUSIONS

The conclusions to be drawn from the complete study seem tinged with pessimism. The basic aim has been to show that no development policy for a backward area is possible or efficient unless a radical overall structural transformation can be carried through. It is doubtful whether such a transformation has been achieved – or even begun – in the case of Aquitania. The experience of the past can be used to derive a number of lessons which some of those responsible for development policy do not yet appear to have learnt. Launching a few French-made rockets will probably not have a greater impact on the overall economic development of the region than did the installation of the Lacq complex at the same time; a lower impact is a fairly safe guess. At best, the effect will be to limit the seriousness of the employment problems which may be met as certain traditional industries contract. But if the local economic environment deteriorates, the introduction of a new, poorly integrated activity can have no effect. A contrast has often been made between two alternative approaches to development policy, namely, the 'growth point' and the 'dispersal of activity'. If the analysis in this study has been solidly founded, the conclusion for policy is that the distinction is to a large extent a specious one. Clearly, a totally unco-ordinated distribution of credits is not going to trigger a regional take-off. But the creation of a large-scale but non-integrated industry (whatever its advantages at the national level) does not imply the automatic existence of optimally dynamic structures. The real problem is that of finding a way so to combine the two types of action as to create the greatest possible number of the complementary relationships which form the only possible basis for causing the region's take-off into growth. Thus it is not out of the question that some degree of 'diversification of activity' may in fact be a precondition of growth. But this is subject to the absolute condition that the measures adopted are in accordance with the possibilities for internally consistent development of the region as a unit, and permit the subsequent dissemination of the take-off impact of a genuine growth point.

6 The Structural Crisis of a Regional Economy. A Case-Study: The Walloon Area[1]

Louis E. Davin
UNIVERSITÉ DE LIÈGE

1 INTRODUCTION

Like other areas where industrialisation started early, the Walloon area suffers from a structural maladjustment due, on the one hand, to the high cost of the energy used (in this case, Belgian coal) and on the other hand to trade deficiencies in certain industrial sectors, even when technical progress is most advanced, as it is in metal industries or in chemicals. These particular sectors, including iron and steel industries, have specialised in branches of production the demand for which increases very slowly or even declines.

The future of the French-speaking part of the country depends upon both the establishment of new industrial concerns and a transformation of the existing industries, which must undergo a complete change towards mass-production and the meeting of basic and increasing demands. While endowed with substantial assets, such as a first-rate labour force and an excellent geographical location since it lies in the centre of the Common Market region, the Walloon area will only stop dropping behind in economic and demographic respects if it starts attracting concerns which can in their turn attract related industries likely to promote a functional intersectoral or intrasectoral integration, regardless of any national, administrative or linguistic boundaries. Depressed areas, or areas lagging in one way or another, cannot now make any economic recovery through short-term and limited measures aiming at self-sufficiency, such as a policy of 'industrial peppering' would have them do. In small-sized areas such as the Walloon area, no attempt at economic transformation will prove realistic unless it is conceived, programmed and implemented as part of an overall policy, taking into account all the facts of life, regionally, interregionally and internationally.

2 THE FUTURE OF THE WALLOON INDUSTRIES

(A) THE EXTENT OF THE COAL CRISIS AND THE PROBLEM OF ENERGY SUPPLIES

The decline of the coal-mining industry in the Walloon area, as in any other mining area of the so-called 'Little Europe', is the last stage of a

[1] Translated from the French by Mrs N. Perlstein.

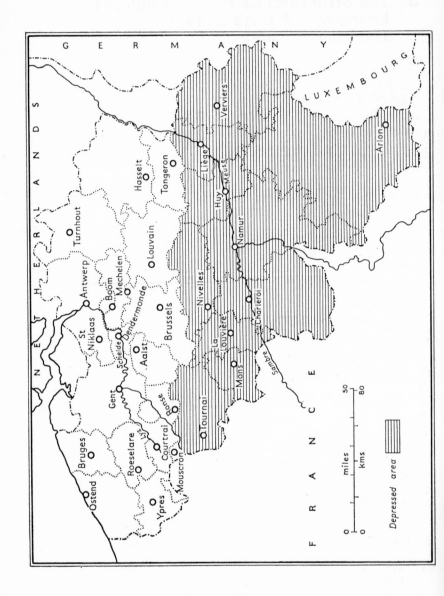

structural deterioration which has called in question the future of coal as a source of energy and as a raw material, particularly for the chemical industry. Table 1 overleaf shows, first, that the members of the European Coal and Steel Community (E.C.S.C.) have all been affected by this coal crisis and, second, that the decline in output has varied from one country to another, and also from one area to another within each country.

Belgium appears to be the country where the decline has been most pronounced if considered from its relative position among the members of E.C.S.C. When comparing 1966 to 1956, which was the peak output year for E.C.S.C., the following percentages are to be noted: with a decline of 12,054,000 tons, Belgium's contribution to the total decrease of output of E.C.S.C. members was 31 per cent. This decline is all the more substantial when it is observed that Belgium's share in the entire community output was only 12 per cent in 1956. It can be seen that West Germany's absolute share in the community reductions is larger than Belgium's, as West Germany is responsible for half the decline in output of the six countries. Proportionately speaking, however, the implications are not as significant as they are for Belgium since West Germany's share in the community output is 61 per cent. In the last ten years, the German output fell by 13 per cent only. Nationally speaking, Italy is the country where the decline was the most spectacular, reaching 60 per cent. Still, the impact, however damaging to the areas concerned, is not as serious as the closure of the Belgian pits has been. In 1955 the Italian mining industries [1] accounted for 1·9 per cent of the gross national product at market prices; in 1965, that percentage was down to 0·7 per cent. For Belgium, however, the share of the mining industries [1] in the gross national product at market prices declined from 3·9 per cent in 1955 to 1·9 per cent in 1965. The coal mines' share was 3·5 per cent in 1955 and 1·4 per cent in 1965 respectively.[2]

In Belgium, the decline in output, from 29,555,000 tons in 1956 to 17,501,000 tons in 1966 – a fall of 41 per cent – has not been equally distributed among the various Belgian coalfields. While in the southern area the output fell by 56 per cent (i.e. in the Borinage, Centre, Charleroi and Liège areas, all in the Walloon region), it was down by only 14 per cent in the Campine area (i.e. in Limburg, which is a Flemish province). In the longer run, the Walloon output came down by 59 per cent from 1952 to 1966, whereas the Limburg pits maintained their output at practically the same level during the same period (9,712,000 tons in 1952 and 9,011,000 tons in 1966 respectively).

A decline in output normally results in a fall of employment. In the Walloon coal mines over 70,000 people have been laid off since the crisis

---

[1] I.e. coal along with the other mining industries.

[2] *Les Comptes nationaux 1955–1965*, Office Statistique des Communautés Européennes, Luxemburg (1966) (*National Accounts 1955–1965*, Statistical Office of the European Communities).

TABLE ONE
TRENDS IN COAL OUTPUT BY COUNTRY

(Tonnes 000s)

Country	1952	1956	1966	Share of Each Country in the Total Community Output			Rate of Decline		Share of Each Country in the Total Community Decline
				1952	1956	1966	1966/1952	1966/1956	
E.C.S.C.	238,883	249,092	210,155	100·00	100·00	100·00	−12·03	−15·63	−100·00
West Germany	139,513	151,497	131,581	58·44	60·78	62·12	−5·62	−13·14	−51·15
France	55,365	55,129	50,337	23·18	22·14	23·46	−9·08	−8·69	−12·31
Italy	1,089	1,076	418	0·45	0·43	1·68	−61·61	−60·42	−1·69
Netherlands	12,538	11,836	10,319	5·23	4·78	4·61	−17·65	−12·81	−3·90
Belgium	30,384	29,555	17,501	12·70	11·87	8·03	−42·40	−40·78	−30·95
Campine	9,712	10,468	9,011	4·05	4·21	4·09	−7·22	−13·91	−3·74
Southern Belgium	20,672	19,085	8,490	8·65	7·66	3·94	−58·98	−55·52	−27·21

Source: From the annual *General Report of the High Authority*, published by the E.C.S.C., Luxemburg.

started. Employed labour was reduced from 119,000 people in 1952 to 43,931 in 1965. It is expected [1] that between 1965–70 a further 20,000 persons will have to be dismissed in the coal mines in the South. [2]

The steady down-trend of the coal output may be explained by quite a number of reasons, but there are two main ones: the high extraction costs and active competition from other sources of energy.

The supply of alternative sources of energy is steadily increasing so that coal must sell for lower prices while its production cost constantly reaches new highs. The reason for this is the low yield of the Belgian coal mines, due to the layout and the depth of the Belgian deposits. This is why Belgium and the other members of the E.C.S.C. cannot compete with some other major world producers such as the United States, where advantage is taken of open-cast mines, or hillside ones, coupled with extremely advanced techniques. Naturally the high costs of the Belgian coal have a direct impact on all other industries, particularly as these are duty-bound to get their coal supplies, in part at least, from domestic mines.

Among the various coal substitutes, the most active are oil products, natural gas, and, in the very near future, nuclear power. In Belgium and in the Community as a whole, the pattern of the primary energy consumption has changed to the extent shown in Table 2 (p. 118). That table shows that while the share of coal in the total energy consumption has been reduced, the increase of that of oil products has been substantial. In eight years only, oil consumption has more than doubled.

Apart from its value as a source of energy, oil provides the raw materials for the chemical industries. The major processing industries (plastic

---

[1] J. Delode, 'Pour une reconversion effective de nos bassins miniers', *Revue du Conseil Économique Wallon*, Liège, no. 78 (juin 1966) p. 4 ('How to Accomplish an Effective Economic Conversion in our Mining Areas?', *Review of the Walloon Economic Council*).

[2] It is somewhat more difficult to assess the quantitative effects of the closing down of the coal mines upon the other industrial sectors. Mr E. Nols has calculated the rates to be applied to ascertain the losses in income and employment in these other sectors. The financial losses suffered by all the other industries considered as a whole (iron and steel, non-ferrous metals, metal manufacturing, coking, electric-power production, chemicals, rubber industries, textiles, clothing and hides and leather, construction, transport and trade) accounted for 23 % of the income losses due to the decline in output taking into account the indirect effects only, and 130 % when adding the indirect and the secondary effects. The rates to apply in order to ascertain the employment losses in these other industries are 39 % and 160 % of the laying off in the coal mines respectively. The 'indirect effects' are the reduction in the orders passed by the coal mines to their suppliers (which are mostly located in the Walloon area). The 'secondary effects' are defined as the reductions in the retail sales due to the gradual decline of the personal incomes; as these apply directly to the end demand, their impact is not exclusively felt locally and gets diluted into the whole economy.

See E. Nols, 'La Reconversion des régions minières de Wallonie', *Revue du Conseil Économique Wallon*, no. 72–3 (janvier–avril 1965) pp. 19–25 ('The Economic Conversion of the Walloon Mining Areas').

materials, synthetic fibres, synthetic rubbers, resins, dyes and detergents, etc.) all derive from the oil chemical industry. In order, however, that the Walloon area may take advantage of such new industries as are prime-movers for economic growth, a reappraisal of the distribution of oil refineries in Belgium is absolutely necessary. At present, most of the refining or distilling plants are located in the North, in and around

TABLE TWO

TRENDS OF PRIMARY ENERGY CONSUMPTION IN BELGIUM AND IN THE COMMUNITY

Source of Energy	1957		1965	
	Belgium	*E.C.S.C.*	*Belgium*	*E.C.S.C.*
Coal	79·6	65·0	53·0	38·2
Lignite	0·3	8·0	0·2	6·0
Oil	20·1	18·3	46·5	44·9
Natural gas	—	1·9	0·3	3·8
Primary source electricity	—	6·8	—	7·1
Total	100·0	100·0	100·0	100·0

Source: *Le Problème charbonnier – données de base.* Published by the Brussels coal industry (1966) p. 9 (*The Coal Problem – Basic Data*).

Antwerp or along the Gent–Terneuzen canal. To send petrol and fuels from these plants all the way would not only be far too expensive for the Walloon area, as the increased cost of transportation from Antwerp would be charged to it, but it would still remain deprived of all the related oil-based industries whose presence is a prerequisite for a fresh economic start. Moreover, it has been found that it is less expensive to send crude oil through pipelines down to consumers, to process it there, than to distribute it locally within the consuming area.

The coal consumption, which has declined both in absolute figures and in relation to the total energy consumption, has been further impaired since Belgium has started importing Dutch natural gas. In December 1965 Belgium and the Netherlands signed a twenty-year contract for the supply to Belgium of 5 billion cubic metres per year, including 3 billion cubic metres for public utilities and 2 billion cubic metres for industrial needs. Those new imports naturally have implications for the coal mines. The price the Netherlands can sell its natural gas to Belgium may be only half that of the gas supplied by Belgian coking plants. This new competition implies that the gas-consuming industries will insist on lower prices, which will entail new difficulties for some of the coking plants. As a result, as soon as the coal gas sells for less, coal-production costs will rise again. Hard coal is now bought mainly by the iron and steel industries, and, since these are dependent on exports and are also experiencing some structural difficulties of their own, whenever the coal price is up, their situation must deteriorate further.

Dutch gas will be used mainly for industries such as glassmaking, ceramics, chinaware, insulators, which all require absolutely pure fuels and special furnaces where the temperature can be easily regulated. It will also be used as a reducing agent in iron and steel industries and in non-ferrous metal manufacturing. For chemical industries, the natural gas from Groningen is more useful than the French gas from the Lacq area, because it lacks the latter's high sulphur and unsaturated hydro-carbons content.

In the longer term, coal, oil products and natural gas will no doubt be gradually replaced by nuclear power which proves successful in a wide range of applications, particularly for the production of electricity [1] and heating through nuclear fission, for the use of radioisotopes in the medical, agricultural and industrial fields in general, for ship propelling, for freshening sea or salt waters, etc. It will be up to Belgium, and to the Walloon area in particular, not to remain dependent on its neighbouring countries for the utilisation and industrialisation of this new source of energy which is already past the experimental stage and will very shortly be part of the competition proper.

(B) THE IRON AND STEEL INDUSTRIES

In Belgium, the iron and steel industries are experiencing a number of structural difficulties which are due on the one hand to an increase in the output of all traditional products which is higher than what the current and paid-for demand would require, and, on the other hand, to the successful competition of some substitutes such as concrete, synthetic chemicals and non-ferrous metals.

Western countries have often tended to turn to the developing countries market, because the demand there was both varied and substantial. Most of these countries unfortunately face serious balance-of-payment difficulties while others, aiming at self-sufficiency, are building up their own production units. Other countries still, such as Japan, have resolutely changed

---

[1] Nuclear power will primarily be used for electricity production. It is anticipated that the electricity consumed by the E.C.S.C. members will increase from 400 billion kWh in 1965 to 3,450 billion kWh by the year 2000, including 2,400 billion produced by nuclear reactors, in particular fast-breeders. Estimated production costs in the nuclear power generators to be set up between now and the end of the century are to reach 7,500 billion Belgian francs, but savings will nevertheless be in the neighbourhood of some 7,000 billion compared to what the final cost would be if this amount of electricity were still to be supplied by conventional methods. See *Premier Programme indicatif pour la Communauté Européenne de l'Énergie Atomique*, Publication de la Communauté Européenne de l'Énergie Atomique (juin 1965) (*First Indicative Programme for the European Atomic Energy Community*, EURATOM).

E 2

TABLE THREE
THE TRENDS OF CRUDE STEEL PRODUCTION
IN THE E.C.S.C. AND IN THE WORLD

(Tonnes 000s)

Country	1952	1956	1966 *	Share in World Production			Rate of Growth	
				1952	1956	1966	1966/52	1966/56
E.C.S.C.	41,996	56,961	85,157	19·6	20·2	18·6	102·77	49·54
West Germany	18,629	26,563	35,316	8·7	9·4	7·7	89·57	70·59
France	10,867	13,441	19,591	5·1	4·8	4·3	80·28	45·75
Italy	3,635	6,076	13,635	1·6	2·1	3·0	275·10	124·40
Netherlands	693	1,051	3,309	0·3	0·4	0·7	377·49	214·84
Belgium	5,170	6,376	8,916	2·4	2·3	1·9	72·41	39·87
Luxemburg	3,002	3,456	4,390	1·4	1·2	1·0	46·23	27·02
U.K.	16,681	20,978	24,704	7·8	7·4	5·4	48·09	17·76
U.S.A.	87,766	105,575	124,700	41·1	38·1	27·1	42·08	18·09
Soviet Union	34,492	48,698	96,900	16·1	17·2	21·1	180·93	98·98
Japan	6,988	11,106	47,769	3·3	3·9	10·4	583·78	330·12
World †	213,750	282,500	459,500	100·0	100·0	100·0	114·97	62·65

* Provisional data.
† Estimates only (and the Democratic Republic of China is not included).

Source: *Sidérurgie*, Office Statistique des Communautés Européennes (1967) no. 1, p. xxx (*Steel Data*).

the structural basis of their economy and created modern iron and steel plants and facilities.

In 1952, Belgium was producing 5,170,000 tons of crude steel, which accounted for 2·4 per cent of world production. In 1966, however, this percentage was down to 1·9 per cent. During the same period the Japanese share of world production rose from 3·3 per cent to 10·4 per cent. In the ten years from 1956 to 1966 Belgian production rose by 39·87 per cent while it doubled in Italy, tripled in the Netherlands and quadrupled in Japan. Japan, which ranked sixth in world steel production in 1956 with 11·1 million tons output, is now the third world producer, with 47·8 million tons, overtaking Germany, the United Kingdom and France, and is now immediately behind the United States and the Soviet Union.

In order to remain competitive the Belgian steel industry, and especially the Walloon one, must adjust to, and make use of, all technical advances so as to achieve greater efficiency and lower production costs. The industry must achieve this technical rejuvenation from top to bottom, from the mere pig iron or cast steel production stage (by installing large-sized blast furnaces [1]) up to converting pig iron into steel by oxygen-blasting and processing ingot-steel rolled products.

Moreover, these concerns can only be profitable if they gradually turn themselves into large industrial groupings or 'complexes' from both the viewpoint of integration and specialisation at each and every production or processing stage. They must specialise for instance in manufacturing specific products such as fine sheets or plates (hot or cold-rolled), or special steels, or stainless steels, which are still imported at present. As the demand for such products is increasing, it becomes therefore possible to diversify the production, at lower costs, while doing away with Walloon products whose demand is receding (as is the case of the rails, in the Liège area, and in particular around Charleroi and the centre) or barely steady (as is the case for merchant steels or steel sections in the Charleroi and Central Areas).

It must lastly be noted that an economic modernisation of the iron and steel units cannot be completely successful unless the basic three transportation systems are adequate, i.e. the inland waterways – the Meuse River waterway must be properly equipped, the Albert Canal must be widened for the benefit of the Liège area, the Meuse–Escaut connection must be improved for the benefit of the Borinage – as well as the road and railway systems which are used for less heavy materials. The improvement of the Albert Canal would make it possible to lower the transportation cost of one ton of ore (which is approximately 30–35 Belgian francs at present) by about ten Belgian francs from Antwerp to Liège.

---

[1] Most of the larger European concerns now use 9-metre-wide blast furnaces, the capacity of which averages 1,500 to 2,000 tons, but Belgium has only 4 of those, 2 in Sidmar (Gent) and 2 in the Liège area.

(C) METAL MANUFACTURES

The metal manufacturing industries, which constitute the driving force of industrial growth, find themselves in quite favourable circumstances: in this sector, growth seems certain, thanks to constant innovations and technical progress in all the various fields concerned. Moreover, the frequent appearance on the market of new and better products, with a high value added, helps keep up the prices.

From 1955 to 1964, despite the decline in coal production, the high cost of all power supplies and the slowdown in the steel industries, the output in metal industries rose by 6·9 per cent. Employment in these branches, which numbered 187,728 workers and employees in 1955, rose to 250,612 people in 1965,[1] that is by 33·5 per cent in ten years.

This rate of growth, however, both in production and in employment, does not reflect the same picture of development in the whole of the country. There are marked differences in economic rates of growth between the Flemish and the Walloon areas. As far as production is concerned, the average rate of growth in the Flemish area was 9·8 per cent from 1955 to 1964 as compared to 4·3 per cent in the Walloon area. As to employment, the figures point to an increase of 72·1 per cent in Flanders between 1955 to 1965, as compared with 8·3 per cent in the Walloon area.[2]

The low rate of expansion in the Walloon area is due to the fact that the production is quite specific, favouring preferably articles for which the demand is declining or increasing very slowly. In fact, quite a number of the articles manufactured in the South are mainly intended for the home market, either because of their very nature (steel bridges and structures, iron works), or because of the relatively simple manufacturing process still used. Other articles, such as arms and ammunitions, have already attained a very slow rate of growth which is not likely to change drastically over the next few years. Finally, there are a number of items (such as bolts) which are already condemned by technical progress to disappear sooner or later.

On the other hand, those sectors where expansion is generally quite fast in all industrialised countries are not abundantly represented in the Walloon area. In the motor-car industry field, for instance, there would be room in the Walloon area for assembly lines, or even for the manufacturing of some mass-produced parts. More important still, because this is more basic, efforts should be made to set up electrical and electronic

---

[1] From *Rapport annuel de l'Office National de Sécurité Sociale*, Brussels (*Yearly Report of the National Social Security Office*).

[2] The figures relating to output are quoted from the *Bulletin de statistique*, l'Institut national de statistique (*Statistical Bulletin*, National Statistical Institute) nos. 11–12 (novembre–décembre 1966) p. 2,271. The figures relating to employment are quoted from *Rapport annuel de l'Office National de Sécurité Sociale*.

construction firms. The Walloon area ought to specialise in the production of a limited number of specific articles where it would not be submitted to any direct competition from the giant concerns which can afford to be pioneering or mass-producing.

(D) THE CHEMICAL INDUSTRIES

So far as these industries are concerned, statistics show that Belgium as a whole is expanding – the national output rose by 5·3 per cent from 1955 to 1964 – but the Walloon area is very definitely lagging behind Flanders: its rate of growth is 2·3 per cent only compared to 8·3 per cent in Flanders.

Because the Belgian chemical industries, especially in the Walloon area, are far from diversified, and because any chemical concern would have to meet unduly expensive requirements to set up a new plant in the River Meuse Basin, this industry, which is so progressive, must nevertheless at present give up any hope of expansion in the south of the country. As it is, on the one hand, the industries which have settled in the Walloon area deal mainly with sodium and fertilisers, whereas carbon chemistry and oil chemistry are still almost ignored; all the more the pity, because research in these fields can yet be very rewarding, and production could be highly diversified on a wide range of elaborate and remunerative articles, such as plastic materials, which still have to be imported. While coal and, even more, oil open up vast opportunities for chemical industries, natural gas, with which the Walloon area will shortly be supplied, is also ideal for the establishment of competitive chemical industrial groupings.

On the other hand, all Walloon chemical concerns, present or future, unlike those in Flanders, also face special difficulties which make it more expensive for them to run their existing plants and more risky to set up new ones. This is because these concerns are bound to settle along the Meuse River or one of its tributaries and are required to devote a large share of their operating resources to equip used-water purification plants. As the Meuse River with its tributaries penetrates the whole Walloon area, it is classified, under official regulations, as a source of supply of drinking and industrial water. This means that all chemical concerns, however little pollution they might be likely to cause, will prefer to settle in the north of the country, where they would not be submitted to such financial obligations.

3 SOCIO-ECONOMIC IMPLICATIONS

(A) THE DEMOGRAPHIC BACKGROUND

An examination of the Walloon population data relating both to its past trends and to its medium-term prospects shows that this population is one of the most aged in the world. The total number of the population has practically kept steady since 1930 (see Table 4 below), while the corresponding figure rose by 800,000 people in Flanders and by over 200,000 in Brussels.

The most definite sign that a population is ageing is the growing proportion of aged people in the total population. The position would

TABLE FOUR

BELGIAN POPULATION BY LINGUISTIC AREA
AS SHOWN BY THE LAST THREE POPULATION CENSUSES

	1930		1947		1961	
	Absolute Figures	%	*Absolute Figures*	%	*Absolute Figures*	%
Walloon area	3,001,479	37·1	2,940,085	34·5	3,038,796	33·1
Flanders	3,885,935	48·0	4,272,185	50·2	4,711,409	51·3
Brussels	1,204,590	14·9	1,299,925	15·3	1,439,536	15·6
Belgium	8,092,004	100·0	8,512,195	100·0	9,189,741	100·0

Source: *Recensements généraux de la population*, l'Institut National de Statistique (*National Population Census*).

TABLE FIVE

POPULATION TRENDS IN THE WALLOON AREA
1960 TO 1975 BY AGE-GROUPS

	1960		1975		
	Absolute Figures	%	*Absolute Figures*	%	*Increase in % from 1960 to 1975*
Young (under 20)	825,000	27·5	921,000	29·5	+ 11·5
Adults (from 20 to 65)	1,779,000	59·3	1,692,000	54·1	− 4·9
Aged (over 65)	396,000	13·2	512,000	16·4	+ 29·0
Total	3,000,000	100·0	3,125,000	100·0	+ 4·1

Source: A. Sauvy, 'Conditions du développement économique et mesures à prendre en vue d'un renouveau général', *Revue de Conseil Économique Wallon* (janvier 1962) no. 54–5 p. 33 ('The Prerequisites for Economic Development and Measures for a General Overhaul').

appear to have been normal in 1960, as the percentage of aged people was only 13 per cent (Table 5 above). But it is anticipated that, taking into account the low birth-rate and the declining mortality rate, the number of aged people will increase by 29 per cent in 1975 as compared to the 1960 figures. The increase in the number of young people is explained mainly by the fact that the smallest age-groups, those born between 1941 and 1945, were fifteen to twenty years old in 1960.

The extent of this ageing process appears even more plainly when comparing the 1975 estimates for the Walloon area and those for Flanders and neighbouring countries.

For the Walloon population not to be in an even more serious position than the German or English populations which are already quite aged, the percentage of its aged persons should always remain below 24 per cent.

TABLE SIX

POPULATION DISTRIBUTIONS FOR 1975, BY AGE GROUPS, IN THE WALLOON AREA, FLANDERS AND CERTAIN NEIGHBOURING COUNTRIES

	Young	*Adults*	*Aged*	*Total*
Walloon area (as anticipated under normal circumstances)	29·5	54·1	16·4	100·0
Flanders	32·7	54·3	13·0	100·0
France	32·6	54·7	12·7	100·0
Netherlands	33·2	54·8	12·0	100·0
Germany	30·3	55·8	13·9	100·0
U.K.	30·2	55·9	13·9	100·0

Source: A. Sauvy, 'Conditions du développement économique et mesures à prendre en vue d'un renouveau général', p. 36.

This rejuvenating process of the population implies on the one hand that the present birth-rate (15 per 1,000) must increase to the level reached in Flanders (18 per 1,000) and, on the other hand – for this increase in birth-rate would still not be enough to ensure that the aged people group would not constitute more than 14 per cent of the total Walloon population – that immigration must fill in part of the population deficit, at least by an inflow of approximately 32,000 persons a year.[1]

More recent population statistical data show that the birth rate was up in 1963 and 1964 in the Walloon area (Table 7 overleaf). Is this the first sign of a new rejuvenating trend, or must it be explained by other factors? It would be premature to answer one way or the other, especially as there was a slowdown in 1965, even a dropback. The same statistical data, moreover, show that for any one birth in the Walloon area, in any given year, two babies are born in Flanders.

Even if during the next few years fecundity rates were to be identical in both the Walloon and Flemish areas [2] (in 1961, fecundity rates [3] were 8·5

[1] A. Sauvy, 'Conditions du développement économique et mesures à prendre en vue d'un renouveau général', *Revue du Conseil Économique Wallon*, nos 54–5 (janvier–avril 1962) p. 36 ('The Prerequisites for Economic Development and Measures for a General Overhaul').

[2] An increase in the number of births could be ensured through a series of 'pronatalistic' measures, such as substantial family allowances, birth grants, pre-natal allowances, wedding savings incentives, etc. Such measures might prove successful in the Walloon area, as the results achieved have been quite satisfactory in France where such policies have been implemented since 1939.

[3] The fecundity rate is defined as the ratio of the number of births to the number of women within procreative age limits, i.e. between 15 and 45 years old.

per cent and 9·5 per cent in the Walloon and the Flemish areas respectively), the Walloon birth-rate would still not reach the required 18 per cent because of the unfavourable basic distribution of the population by age groups:

TABLE SEVEN

COMPARISONS OF NATURAL INCREASES OF POPULATION IN THE WALLOON AND FLEMISH AREAS

	Walloon Area				Flemish Area			
	Births				*Births*			
	Absolute Figures	*%*	*Deaths*	*Natural Increase*	*Absolute Figures*	*%*	*Deaths*	*Natural Increase*
1962	46,191	15·15	42,575	3,616	87,931	18·51	50,738	37,173
1963	48,386	15·47	44,975	3,411	95,471	18·50	56,503	38,968
1964	49,604	15·73	42,421	7,183	96,047	18·41	53,381	42,666
1965	48,225	15·21	44,238	3,987	91,790	17·44	56,047	35,743

Source: *Annuaire statistique de la Belgique*, l'Institut National de Statistique (*Statistical Yearbook of Belgium*).

the ratio of the number of women within procreative age limits to the total female population in each region is lower in the Walloon area than it is in Flanders. (In 1961, these ratio were 36·53 and 39·64 respectively.)

While its birth-rate must go up, the Walloon area should also take steps to stimulate and speed up *immigration*. At the national level, such a policy has undoubtedly achieved positive results, as can be seen from the numbers of working permits granted to foreign workers who came to Belgium (1959: 3,610; 1960: 3,526; 1961: 5,200; 1962: 15,414; 1963: 26,397; 1964: 33,158; and over 35,000 in 1965).[1] Among those foreign workers, large numbers settled in the Walloon area. In the Hainaut province, for example, foreign workers exceeded 20 per cent of the entire labour force in some localities. In the Liège province, the corresponding figure is about 15 per cent and it is approximately 10 per cent in the Greater Brussels area.[2]

Taking into account the number of immigrating women and children, and also the number of emigrating persons, the net balance of foreigners immigrating and settling in the Walloon area was 11,677 in 1963, 17,635 in 1964 and 18,338 in 1965. In the city of Brussels, the similar figures were: 13,155 in 1963; 19,190 in 1964; 15,192 in 1965. These are substantial achievements, even if still a far cry from the yearly target of 32,000 entrants as set by Mr Sauvy in his report.

[1] Figures obtained from the Walloon Economic Council.

[2] G. Demaître, 'Pour un meilleur accueil', *Revue du Conseil Économique Wallon*, no. 80 (octobre 1966) p. 14 ('For a Better Welcome').

While a specific immigration policy has been developed and implemented in Belgium, to the extent that welcome centres have been established in some cities, there is practically no information service in the various countries where this emigration movement originates, where would-be emigrants can discover what kind of occupations are at the moment available on the Belgian labour market, or what social and fringe benefits may be offered to local and foreign labour. It is clearly necessary to establish such information centres if an advance selection is to be made among emigrating candidates so as to get the required skilled and semi-skilled labour.[1]

(B) EMPLOYMENT AND UNEMPLOYMENT

Even though the coal crisis and the decline in output in some of the metal manufacturing industries have caused the employers to lay off approximately 100,000 occupational units,[2] unemployment rates are still comparatively low (they were 2·9 per cent for the whole of Belgium, 3·7 per cent in the Walloon area and 2·8 in Flanders in 1966). This significant absence of unemployment is mainly due to the fact that many of the dismissed workers have managed to find another occupation, either in the remaining collieries or in various other forms of business. Among those who are thus no longer unemployed, some have succeeded in staying in the same area, but most of them have had to move, either to other provinces or abroad. As an example, of the total of 7,944 persons affected by the closure of four pits in 1966 (three of them in the Walloon area), 6,794 either were laid off or have left of their own will. The remaining 1,150 remained registered in the same collieries. Out of those 6,794 people, 2,309, or 43 per cent of the total laid-off workers, found work in other pits; 1,902, or 28 per cent, in other industries; 278, or 4 per cent, at their own request registered in a training institute;[3] 676, or 10 per cent, were considered as no longer available for work, that is they retired with full pensions some time in advance, and the last group, that is 1,051 persons, or 15 per cent, were still registered at the end of the year as 'totally unemployed', with full compensation.[4]

[1] It is amazing to note that 43 % of the foreign workers entering Belgium in 1964 have applied for a working permit in the coal-mines, precisely where the coal crisis had started already 10 years before.

[2] R. Paquet, 'Essai d'évaluation du coût de la reconversion des régions minières du Sud', *Revue du Conseil Économique Wallon*, no. 76 (septembre–octobre 1965) pp. 1–7 ('An Evaluation of the Cost of the Economic Conversion of the Southern Mining Area'.)

[3] In 1966, only 4 % of the laid-off workers took advantage of national training facilities. It would seem that most of the industrial firms do not know that the European Economic Community and the E.C.S.C. have a grants-in-aid programme for finding new jobs for former miners and retraining them (Article 56 of E.C.S.C. and Article 125 of the Rome Treaty relating to the European Social Fund).

[4] *Informations statistiques*, Ministère de l'Emploi et du Travail, Brussels, no. IX and X (1966) p. 6 (*Statistical Data.* Ministry of Labour, Brussels).

This emigration which was partly due to the lack of alternative occupations,[1] has resulted in a regional decline in employment in the Walloon area, whereas employment rose by 23·6 per cent in Flanders during the same period.

TABLE EIGHT

CHANGES IN TOTAL EMPLOYMENT IN THE DIFFERENT LINGUISTIC REGIONS

(at 30 June in each year)

	1957	1965	Percentage Change from 1957 to 1965
Walloon area	632,398	622,215	−1·6
Flanders	830,352	1,026,524	+ 23·6
Belgium	1,938,214	2,128,806	+ 9·8

Source: *Annuaire statistique de la Belgique.*

TABLE NINE

COMPARISONS OF TOTAL UNEMPLOYMENT IN BELGIUM AND THE WALLOON AREA

	Belgium	Walloon Area	Walloon Unemployed as Percentage of Belgian Unemployed
1956	94,523	17,248	18·3
1957	81,444	15,564	19·1
1958	116,354	21,865	18·8
1959	132,292	27,717	21·0
1960	114,274	28,382	24·8
1961	89,130	21,985	24·7
1962	70,943	18,572	26·2
1963	59,075	16,791	28·4
1964	50,363	15,589	31·0
1965	55,375	18,930	34·2
1966	61,498	24,780	40·3

Source: Office National de l'Emploi (National Labour Office).

Table 9 shows the changes in unemployment for Walloon and Flemish 'totally unemployed' from 1956 to 1965. From 1959 to 1964, Belgian unemployment tended to diminish because the overall economic situation proved favourable. The expansion phase has made it possible not only to eliminate unemployment but to include almost all the labour laid off

[1] This, despite official statements such as this pronouncement by J. van der Schueren who said on 17 December 1959 before the Senate: 'The Government will do everything possible to create new jobs, to attract and subsidize new investment. Our target must be that 50,000 new posts will have been offered by the end of 1963.'

from the closed pits into the general economic activity. The present higher rate of unemployment, however (from 2·5 for the wholeof Belgium in 1964 to 2·7 and 2·9 in 1965 and 1966 respectively), shows that the labour market is getting overloaded, and the economy has reached a standstill, which might be the beginning of a general down-trend phase.

The number of Walloon unemployed is seriously important only when compared to the total number of Belgian unemployed (Table 9, col. 4), that is when it is noted that 17,248 unemployed in 1956 accounted for 18·3 per cent of the total unemployment but that 25,000 unemployed in 1966 account for 40·3 per cent of the same total. Moreover, all the areas of the country are not equally affected by this increase in unemployment. In 1966, a further 6,123 'totally employed' were registered in addition to those already counted in 1965. Of these, 80 per cent came from four specific regional offices (out of a total of twenty-nine such offices in Belgium): Liège (2,753 workers), Charleroi (850), Mons (666) and La Louvrière (638).[1] It is worth observing that these areas are the very spots where pits had to close down and where metal and steel industries are facing the serious problems mentioned above. This renewed emphasis on the basic structural problems to be solved is due to the now obvious change in the overall economic picture, after these problems have been more or less ignored while the country as a whole was still thriving.

(C) PSYCHOLOGICAL OBSOLESCENCE [2]

When all is said, the problem which still proves most difficult in the areas which have long been industrialised is that these areas are psychologically old, which has nothing to do with physical age, social categories, or economic categories.

It is too facile to say that this is only a matter of entrepreneurship (or lack of it). It is always easy to blame the obvious scapegoat. No one can help it, but no one is aware of it.

Of course, the responsible economic authorities cannot easily break through the old patterns. In quite a number of sub-regions, current investment has an emergency life-saving character and very often is only expected to safeguard vested interests from a dead past. At the most, it makes it possible merely to go on for some time, barely coping with competition. This position may be kept up throughout a favourable economic phase. But as soon as the boom is over and a general down-trend sets in, all this holding-the-fort attitude breaks down. Daily habits of thought and action, management techniques, on-the-job staff training,

---

[1] *Situation du marché de l'emploi en 1966*, Office National de l'Emploi, pp. 5–6 (*The Labour Market in 1966*).
[2] Our readers will readily understand that we have felt compelled to skip the factual details and only spell out a few general conclusions easy to draw from so many painful, appalling and hopeless stories.

marketing and financial policies, research directing, everything is regulated by self-defence reflexes instead of creative aggressiveness. Locally, there is absolutely no desire to invest anything in new production or manufacture. Here, one will find groups of modern plants engaged in types of production for which the world supplies are by definition already too large as against a steadily declining effective demand. There, inside brand-new buildings, one finds old-fashioned plants, still manufacturing products of yesterday despite ever-shrinking marketing prospects. Investments, however, are spectacular. What is wrong after all with suddenly cutting off access to the few hundred available acres which might have attracted new industries of the kind that breed industrialisation? And have we not heard countless business top executives, after reluctantly admitting that the economic indicators are more favourable anywhere rather than in Liège, complacently protest that after all, Liège cannot be in such a tight spot, since they have spent a whole month in Majorca where they could indulge themselves with the whole family?

The unions are as bad. They also are unable to break through the old pattern of claims that do not make sense any more since the entire concept of capitalist enterprise has changed. But power came to them after such a long and brave struggle that the union leaders fear they would lose their privileges and their own position if they now gave up those very same claims. The revolution, however, does not mean a clash of opposite interests any more; it should prompt them to speak the language of truth to the rank and file, which must know of the forthcoming efforts and sacrifices required of them: occupational and/or geographical mobility, the giving up of quick satisfactions, the recovery of creative and saving habits which have been forgotten. Poorly assimilated modern economic literature has given rise to immature slogans: too often the keyword is 'full employment' even if this must be ensured by dying concerns or sectors, or pointless navvying works while the thing to do would be to transfer as much labour as possible to industries that have a future, both in themselves and in relation to other industries, industries with a drive. It proves so easy for prosperous union leaders to inflame their own troops with forceful and empty speeches, with negative claims. The unfortunate young unionists who would try to denounce these worn-out patterns, and base a new revolutionary start on modern technological progress, are thrown to the wolves by their own leaders, *beati possidentes*.

As to the intellectual élite, administrative or political, if any, they would leave anyone speechless ! As if isolated in 'ivory towers', they acquire a distorted view of the entire world, as if through a prism: the distorting prism of the Belgian linguistic problems – the distorting prism of an education still based on excessively traditional subjects – the distorting prism of personal petty jealousies against those who have a more realistic approach to current problems and dare to prove it. This is the springboard for a whole series of nihilistic measures, always in rosy hues, of course. An intraregional solution of local economic problems is admittedly inevitable, but common action with other regions is not to be endured. Interdisciplinary co-operation is admittedly of primary importance, but research or action centres are still tightly partitioned, clinging to their own sphere of authority. Economic problems must admittedly be solved first, but it is useless to look around for well-conceived, organised, programmed institutes: there are none; if there ever was one, it would have been eliminated. It is recognised that more contacts with the foreign world are necessary, but they still cannot bring themselves to learn a foreign language. It is recognised that training is important at all levels, but in practice there is no attempt at training for fear that young people, once trained, might leave to look for a job in Brussels or Antwerp. It is not clear to them yet that occupational and geographical mobility is healthy. Neither is it clear to them that the future of any region, and especially a new economic start for it, cannot depend merely upon tricks. Glib and easy talk glossing over problems can never replace a factual solution.

How, against this background of obsolescence, the psychological old age adding to the demographic and structural problems, can one help feeling that this land is dying? When the élite itself has to leave and find in some other place the full range of opportunities that its own land can no longer provide, how can one help feeling that history, once more, proves inescapable and that civilisations are ultimately bound to fail where they once succeeded?

(D) REGIONAL INCOME

According to the various output, employment and unemployment indicators, the Walloon regional income is expected to rise slightly.

TABLE TEN

PER CAPITA GROSS NATIONAL PRODUCT AT FACTOR COST

(Belgian francs 000s)

	1955	1962	1963	1964	*Classification of the Provinces Based on the* 1964 G.N.P.
Brabant	58·1	79·8	85·1	91·5	1
Liège	52·7	67·5	70·9	78·8	3
Antwerp	47·9	66·8	71·7	80·1	2
Hainaut	45·9	55·1	58·4	63·6	6
Namur	42·8	56·2	59·6	65·9	5
West Flanders	39·0	56·2	61·1	68·3	4
Luxemburg	37·6	46·2	48·6	52·6	8
East Flanders	37·1	49·5	53·6	58·5	7
Limburg	36·1	42·2	45·6	52·6	8

Source: *Bulletin de statistique* (novembre–décembre 1966) nos. 11–12, p. 2289.

Table 10 shows the *per capita* production for the last three available years, compared to 1955 as a base.

If classified by their relative importance, the various provinces are not in 1964 in the same order as they were in 1965: on the whole, the Walloon provinces, except Namur which has kept its rank, lose to Flemish provinces. This regression of the Walloon area is even more obvious in Table 11, which shows the annual rate of growth of production.

TABLE ELEVEN

AVERAGE ANNUAL GROWTH OF PRODUCTION

(at Constant Prices of 1953)

	1955–1960	1955–1964
West Flanders	3·4	4·4
Antwerp	2·5	3·8
East Flanders	2·6	3·2
Limburg	−0·4	2·4
Namur	2·3	3·0
Liège	1·2	2·5
Hainaut	−0·1	2·0
Luxemburg	1·0	1·7
Brabant	2·2	3·2
Belgique	1·8	3·1

Source: *Bulletin de statistique* (novembre–décembre 1966) nos. 11–12, p. 2290.

From Table 11 it is easy to see how far the two linguistic communities respectively show evidence of being dynamic. From 1955 to 1964, the average yearly rate of growth in the Walloon area never reached the national average, whereas in Flanders there is only one single province which has been consistently below the national average.

4 AN INTERREGIONAL ECONOMIC MODERNISATION POLICY

(A) THE FIRST ATTEMPTS AT SOME REGIONAL POLICIES IN BELGIUM

From the very beginning of the coal crisis, the Walloon economic modernisation required political measures of an exceptional character – hence two special Bills, passed on 17 and 18 July 1959, which were supplemented by a third on 14 July 1966.

Under the 18 July 1959 Bill, designed to 'implement and co-ordinate measures towards the promotion of economic growth and the establishment of new industries', a royal order of 27 November 1959 defined some fifteen 'development areas' which would receive special help and call for specific intervention. Almost all the official government measures proposed represented broadly one of the following incentives: rebates of interest, government guarantees, tax privileges, capital grants, construction and purchase of industrial buildings. Moreover, under the same Bill, certain semi-public regional bodies were to be given official recognition and status: new regional capital-investment bodies were to be established with possible joint contributions from both local government and the private sector. Even before that Bill there had been a ministerial order on 13 July 1959 providing that advisory economic expansion committees could be set up. Following these measures, several 'inter-communal' bodies were set up in the Hainaut province, together with the 'Provincial Industrialisation Society' in the Liège province. Lastly, a Bill of 2 April 1959 provided for the simultaneous establishment of a national investment body and several regional ones, which legally would be public institutions, designed to promote the setting up or expansion of large industrial or merely local craft firms, through temporary share-holding in private companies.

Despite this, the Walloon economy continued to decline as a whole, which brought home the fact that the regional policies implemented under the 18 July 1959 Bill were not in fact being successful. In particular, the economic modernisation of the Central and Borinage areas which had been most affected by the crisis, has not yet caught on. Why, then, this failure?

The government authorities responsible for the 1959 Bill had approached the concept of a 'development area' through a whole series of criteria: there must be some substantial permanent unemployment, or a substantial fraction of the population must have been migrating permanently, or a substantial part of the available labour must have submitted to daily or seasonal migrations, or there must be, or likely to be shortly, a decline in economic activities such as would be bound to result in a sharp decline of the regional income. It was enough for a given region to suffer from any one of these conditions to be within the scope of the Bill. The critical areas that have been thus defined however were not proper development areas.[1] The basic factors for expansion were lacking to such an extent that only artificial intervention could have saved or mobilised whatever potentialities were left. On the other hand, a development area is, by definition, an area where economic growth may concentrate if desired, in terms of functional integration on some larger scale, which does not necessarily have to be the national scale, provided the basic prerequisites

---

[1] The definition in Article 4.1 was as follows: 'A development area constitutes a consistent whole, whose population is confronted with common problems as regards economic growth which may be solved in the long run by regular expansion based on adequate infrastructure.'

of consistency and common interests are met. But 'you cannot reverse a declining trend through a steady sprinkle of loans and subsidies. Only the emergence of one or several growth-attracting centres can have a lasting effect and turn regional decline into renewed expansion'.[1]

In the industrial Liège area for instance, the Lower Meuse region, that is a group of five 'communes' (the smallest territorial division) devoted mainly to metal industries, had been the only one to be retained as a 'development region'. In fact this is a depressed area and not a development region, and the responsible authorities were ignoring the fact that the actual growth centre – the entire industrial area of Liège – has been noticeably decelerating, this process being partially due to insufficient industrial diversification.

So by confusing the two different concepts of 'development' and 'critical' areas, the authorities had seriously impaired the 1959 economic incentive Bill even before it was implemented and, in a complementary Bill of 14 July 1966, had to select larger development areas according to different criteria. This new Bill has set the 31 December 1968 for its deadline and is designed to ensure 'exceptional help to coal mining areas and to any area confronted with urgent and pressing problems'. From the amount of financial and fiscal resources to be devoted to the economic modernisation and development of some of these areas it is obvious that the Government really intends to remedy the structural crisis which threatens the country. It is however to be deplored that, bowing to certain pressures, the Government, which at first had only intended to try to save the coal mining areas, saw fit to extend the advantages of this new Bill to the 'areas confronted with pressing and urgent problems'. Jointly with the coal mining areas which are in any case easier to define – the Limburg coal area in the Southern Campine and Hageland regions which comprise 179 'communes', the Hainaut province which covers the Borinage, Centre and Charleroi areas and comprises 156 'communes', and lastly, the Liège–Verviers area which comprises 83 'communes' – the authorities have now also included the Flanders Westhoek area (which covers the Furnes, Dixmude and Ypres districts with 111 'communes')[2] and the

---

[1] J. Milhau, 'La Théorie de la croissance et l'expansion régionale', *Économie appliquée*, no. 3 (Paris 1956) p. 354 ('A Theory of Regional Growth and Expansion', *Applied Economics*).

[2] The difficulties confronting the Westhoek region for instance are certainly not to be questioned but they cannot compare with the kind of problems experienced in the coal-mining areas. In all its three districts, the Westhoek area registers a rate of activity and development such as have never been equalled in the Walloon area. Taking as a reference factor the trend of the rate of activity – or the ratio of the 1959 employment index to the 1964 population index brought back to 1959, Dixmude is ranking first, with an exceptional activity rate of 147·4, Ypres ranks third (129·9), Furnes is fourteenth (114·4), whereas in all the districts affected by the coal mining crisis, the activity is pointedly stagnant, as it is in Liège (101·3) and Charleroi (100·2) or significantly declining as it is in Mons (93·0), Soignies (89·8) and Thuin (83·9). For this, see Pertinax, 'Quelles

southern part of West Flanders (73 'communes'), and, in the Walloon area, the southern region and the Luxemburg province. These six areas include 621 'communes' as a whole, together with certain 'groups of "communes"' and some 'isolated spots' (fifty-seven 'communes' in all) which are widely distributed over the whole country. As a whole, therefore, 678 'communes' come within the scope of the 14 July 1966 Bill, including 380 in the Flemish area and 298 in the Walloon area.[1]

In fact, even though 'exceptional help' is still granted to areas which do not equally qualify for it, even though once again the authorities have not been able to resist giving in to policies of broadcasting their investments, the new Bill has certainly improved upon the former one because it emphasises the necessity for qualitative changes and innovations instead of merely extending the capacity of existing industries.[2] The permissive role which the government can play may, however, considerably restrict the effects of the new Bill, particularly as the Walloon area is structurally behind the times.

The first question is whether the measures advocated by the government will prove stimulating enough for the Walloon area to regain the dynamic and creative industrial atmosphere of the last century. At present the whole area bewails its loss of prestige, the absence of the rapid progress experienced in new industries throughout the rest of the country, the full-scale emigration of concerns, trained personnel, young graduates, but does nothing to stop this process of decline. Not only has economic modernisation not started; though foreign investors are so badly needed in the area because of their technological input, because of the dynamic impulse that may result from the orders that they give, or simply because they breed imitation, very few of the foreign investors in Belgium have so far located in the Walloon area. While foreign investments totalled 42 billion B.fr.

---

sont, en Belgique, les régions confrontées à des problèmes aigus et urgents?' *Revue du Conseil Économique Wallon*, no. 79 (août 1966) pp. 1–10 ('Which are the Areas Confronted with Pressing and Urgent Problems in Belgium?').

[1] By 30 June 1966, out of the 'totally unemployed' registered in all the 678 'communes' concerned, 61·6% belonged to the Walloon area, 38·4% to the Flemish ones.

[2] From a sectoral viewpoint, the first economic promotion Bill did not produce the desired structural changes. From 1959 to 1965, investments totalled 125·9 billion B.fr., but, out of this total amount, 51 billions only were granted under the so-called regional Bill (18 July 1959) – 41% of such investments went into the steel industries (21 billion B.fr. helped setting up the complex Sidmar plant in Gent and the Liège steel industries were granted 9 billions), 25% into metal manufactures and 10% only to chemicals. This assistance has been distributed as and when required, and was not submitted to any overall programming or even any strict selection rules so that it mainly contributed to capacity increases instead of qualitative structural changes, and, consequently, it contributed to maintain industries whose efficiency was in any case bound to remain sub-level. In this respect, see A. Camu, 'Pourquoi une nouvelle loi d'aide régionale', *Le Monde, Courrier de Belgique* (21 octobre 1966) p. 17 ('Why is a New Regional Assistance Bill Necessary').

from 1959 to 1965 (including any Belgian participation) less than 10 per cent went into the Walloon area.[1]

Will the new or more general assistance granted to both national and foreign investors be able to turn Walloon producers into real 'entrepreneurs', so that they show a taste for innovation and attract foreign investors by choice into the Walloon area? A few comments on the overall economic situation may be in order at this point.

All the Western countries are at the time of writing (the summer of 1967) undergoing economic tensions, even a definite slowdown in some industrial sectors, which means that very few private investors would try to meet a final demand which is already doubtful, and therefore has a regressive effect on intermediate demand. The setting up of new industries or the modernisation of old ones, if justified, and especially because this reflects the policy of the central government, implies a stepping-up of all the supplying industries and in some cases structural adjustments on their part. This is likely of course to be very advantageous for the regional economy when a new general upturn comes, because there will then suddenly be a larger and more diversified demand to be met.

In some cases, therefore, the estimated cost as modified by the provisions of the 14 July 1966 Bill, can even now stimulate investments; but even in such cases, foreign investors will continue to prefer Flanders where under present legislation they are better off. The two Flemish areas, the Westhoek and Campine regions, which have been defined as 'confronted with pressing and urgent problems', offer in fact real advantages over the Walloon areas. The Westhoek Province, which is very forward-minded, lies half-way between the Escaut River and the North Sea, near Lille; the Campine area is adjacent to the Antwerp province, the most dynamic industrial growth centre in Belgium, and in addition it already possesses a good basic communication system provided by the Albert Canal and Ruhr–Antwerp speedway. Thus the Walloon area is likely in any case to be less profitable than Flanders, particularly because of the lack of a real 'infrastructure' in the full sense of the word, but also because all industrial concerns in the Walloon area are legally bound to purify all water taken from the Meuse River Basin.

To sum up, the Government should be in a position to offset any deficiency of the private sector as regards investment while ensuring equal profitability in the whole country. To this end, they should immediately assist the Walloon area to build for itself a modern basic infrastructure both as regards the transportation system, including inland waterways, roads and railways, and as regards basic modern industrial resources. They should also be able to ensure decent housing in pleasant surroundings, and technical training suited to the objectives of an economic modernisation to all interested Belgian nationals or foreigners, young or more

[1] From the yearly report issued by the Ministry of Economic Affairs.

mature. Such a comprehensive plan of action, which must inevitably be complex because it has to cover many widely different fields, cannot be fully effective unless it is guided in practice by an overall co-ordinating policy which will have regard not only to the technico-economic pre-requisites of the production factors and processes, but also to the inter-regional and international forces which make themselves felt as soon as national frontiers are opened and trade opportunities expand.

(B) THE SELECTION OF DYNAMIC INDUSTRIES

The economic modernisation of any given region such as the Walloon area depends upon the presence of a few vital industries which serve as poles of growth. It would be useless to encourage the establishment of small- or medium-sized concerns totally unrelated to each other, for the sole purpose of reducing unemployment. All that these new economic units would achieve would be to preserve an already deteriorated situation. On the other hand, a number of large industrial concerns, radiating action around themselves, can alone breathe new creative force into a region and increase the regional income to an extent substantially greater than the investment outlay. This is because the repercussions of such concerns contribute to the prosperity of all the surrounding firms through increased flows between suppliers and customers, and contribute also to an increase of activity in the tertiary sector because of the new incomes they generate. They also attract new enterprises to take advantage of the new marketing and production facilities.

The industries best suited to such a basic role as poles of growth are those in which the value added per production unit is highest. Such is the case with some of the metal manufactures, such as electrical and elec-tronic appliances of all kinds. The high productivity in these sectors is explained by the easy adjustment of the production processes to subsequent innovations or increases of capacity. These are made possible on the international level by an ever increasing demand for diversified products not met by any other concern either in Belgium or the Community.

Any area affected can derive the maximum internal advantage from the presence of such a dynamic industry when it possesses capital goods industries likely to be of assistance to the dynamic industry as it settles down and wants to expand, and if it can provide that industry with various related and complementary enterprises, specialising in a range of manu-factures or processing the appropriate semi-manufactures at some inter-mediate stage. These supplementary units thus specialising in sub-contracts can remain independent but will be assured of a market. On the other hand, they can take advantage of technical advice, research services and experience of the central industry. The latter can on the other hand depend on these related industries for further expansion, applying any investment saved either to applied research or personnel training.

One of the most illuminating examples of a pole of growth is presented by the building and operation of a nuclear power station. These, equipped with reactors of proved types, advanced converters, or fast breeders, require an astonishing number of contributions from the other industries which are needed to supply them with all kinds of equipment, metal, electrical, electronic manufactures and special steels. While giving an impulse to chemical industries and advanced research centres, they also depend upon the establishment of a wide range of more or less directly related industries (ore-processing, refining and conversion facilities, isotope separation, manufacture of uranium, natural or slightly enriched, re-processing of irradiated fuels, manufacture of heavy water), which are all independent activities. The same could equally be said of the industries related to the conquest of space.

(C) TRANS-REGIONAL DEVELOPMENT ZONES

One of the nuclear power stations which will soon be needed in Europe could very well be set up in the Walloon area and serve a vast industrial region with electric power, over a circle of some 300 kms radius with Liège as its centre, covering the North of France, the Lorraine, Alsace, and Rhine area regions together with Amsterdam and Rotterdam. These areas, which are major consumers, could in turn supply to the nuclear power stations all that they would need. The Walloon site, especially the Ardennes, offers a double advantage: first, it lies in the centre of this industrialised region, and secondly, it can draw upon a large water reserve which extends throughout the Belgian Ardennes and the German and Luxemburg Eiffel area.

Apart from any such particular solution for the long-term future, in the shorter term the choice of various regions for development must depend upon the extent of areas of homogeneous economic demographic characteristics which in many cases do not coincide with local administrative or even national boundaries.

We would be heading for a waste of the available resources, a dilution of investment capital and possibly for the failure of the attempt to achieve economic modernisation in the longer term if we were to regard the Hainaut Province as an independent development area and ignore the larger economic unit of which it forms a part, including Hainaut, the two French North and Pas-de-Calais 'départements' (territorial districts) and the West Flanders Province. Since the political split between Belgium and France in 1668, and more recently the linguistic split between the Belgian Flanders and Hainaut Provinces, resulting from their two independent cultures, both the French and Belgian sub-regions, which still had coal as their main resources ten years ago, have diversified their economic activities along the same lines. Parallel industries have settled along both sides of the political frontier, especially textile industries (in the area of Lille–

Roubaix–Tourcoing in France; along the Lys River valley up to Gent in Belgium) and metal industries (along the Sambre and Haine rivers in Belgium and around Valenciennes in France). The coal crisis, which has hit the Hainaut Province harder than Northern France, has resulted in a mass emigration of Belgian labour into France, where industrial activities are more diversified and the equipment in many plants is better. In 1964, 32,000 workers were commuting daily to France, 60·6 per cent going to textile plants, 17·2 per cent to metal industries, and 8·7 per cent to public construction works. Under these circumstances, any modernisation should be carried out within the limits of this homogeneous region, so that, on both sides of the boundary line, all the subsidiaries now engaged in identical activities within a few miles of each other can be replaced by complementary sub-contracting industries. The North of France area may be better equipped to be the location of one or other of the vital growth-attracting concerns, but the Hainaut Province has plenty of trained labour to offer in addition to a large water reserve fed by underground river or water supplies extending from the Tournai area to the Eupen region.

In the same way it would be pointless to try to devise a redevelopment of the Liège area while ignoring the economic potentialities of the neighbouring political sub-divisions, mainly the Zuid Limburg (Maastricht) and the Rhine area (Aachen, Cologne, Düsseldorf). Since they have been politically separated (in 1815 as between Germany and Belgium, and the Netherlands) these three areas have diversified their production independently from each other but again on the same lines because coal has been their common source of energy. Within this vast region, the Zuid Limburg area has specialised in woodworking industries, the Rhine area has made a name for itself in chemicals, textiles, metal manufactures, while Liège has tended mainly to specialise in food, drink, and tobacco industries, as well as woodworking, leather, non-ferrous metal and the steel industries.[1] While the economy of the Liège area is also based on metal manufactures this sector is not diversified, which makes it impossible to treat it as the sole motive force. With carefully planned modernisation, in which all the structural assets of the three sub-regions would be employed and integrated in a carefully prepared community development, this already homogeneous region could become one of the major growth poles of the new Europe.

A development area based upon one particular industry must not be designed to maximise only the local or interregional flow of industrial products. A co-ordinated development of all the three sectors, primary, secondary and tertiary defined by Colin Clark, given some geographical

[1] L. E. Davin, 'La Vocation transnationale de la région liégeoise', *Revue du Conseil Économique Wallon* (décembre 1966) no. 81, pp. 8–29 ('The Trans-National Vocation of the Liège area').

specialisation, can contribute to the vitality of a region. A good illustration of this is to be found in the Lorraine area [1] which includes the Arlon and Virton sub-districts in Belgium and the Longwy, Longwyon and Montmédy sub-districts in France. The monolithic mining and steel industries along the French section of the Chiers River, the only industrialised area, have precipitated the whole Lorraine region into a rapid process of decline. While 60 per cent of the steel output in the Ruhr area is processed on the spot, only 15 per cent of the Lorraine steel output goes to local manufacturing industries, since the Lorraine steel industries are owned by powerful groups which have their headquarters elsewhere. A few related industries, however, specialising in the processing and the manufacture of final products, would nevertheless be enough to restore the area to its former level of activity and to increase its regional income.

Most of the labour employed in these plants is Belgian. In Southern Luxemburg, only 25 per cent of the labour employed in the secondary sector is in construction. During the next few years, additional Belgian labour will be needed even more. The reason is that what space remains available in France is filled with a maze of old and often insanitary private houses, interlocked with groups of industrial buildings; the few unbuilt patches cannot be used because of physical obstacles or surrounding iron mines. In the near future, the French industrial population could settle in the Belgian area where the landscape is still attractively green within a few miles of the industrial zone [2] and near the tourist country that extends from Virton to Florenville. Arlon, the main city of the province, can provide a number of tertiary services, both administrative and commercial, which are almost entirely lacking in this part of the North of France. It would still remain to provide this proposed major centre with the necessary educational, cultural and social facilities. In the educational field, the Longwy technical training institute could cater for Belgian students and at the same time the Izel agricultural institute could be available to French students. In the agricultural field the Belgian area could become a source of supply to the Lorraine region, and even the entire

---

[1] This definition of the Lorraine area only covers the northern part of a larger area, the Moselle area, which includes the French Lorraine, the German Saarland, the Luxemburg Gutland and the Belgian Southern Luxemburg. The basis of the economic unity of the entire area is the ferrous ore body, the largest in Europe.

[2] This particular Belgian region used to be comparatively wealthy but is now plagued with mass emigration for various reasons: there are no cultural centres, the Canadian military personnel and their families have left Marville, their French base, and also (the major reason in fact) there is a nearby paper mill (which, by the way, is the only Belgian firm which was granted some assistance from the European Investment Bank under the economic conversion projects) which has not installed any deodorisation plant. For all these reasons the Virton sub-district has lost a good deal of its population, and for the area to be turned into residential districts implies that welfare measures would first be taken against this paper pulp concern whose profitability moreover can certainly be questioned.

Moselle region, especially for dairy and cheese products, meat and meat preserves. It still remains true, however, that the complementary development of the two areas depends on the creation of an adequate infrastructure. In particular, it would imply electrifying the railway line between Arlon and Longwy, a distance of no more than 23 kms, to bridge the gap between the French and Belgian systems.

(D) MAIN LINES OF DEVELOPMENT

For all new industries, the right location is where profits can be maximised rather than where production costs are minimised; an adequate infrastructure is therefore a determining factor for profitability and thus the expansion of the growth poles. A policy based on main lines of development must include a number of features: the building of highways and speedways; the electrification of the railways, the widening of the inland waterways to accommodate the larger barges, the construction of airports, telecommunications and other utilities (water, gas, electricity services, etc.), the construction of pipelines, the improvement of urban and industrial centres.

The selection of the main lines of communication depends not only upon the objectives of the modernisation policy but also upon the direction of interregional trade and must therefore be guided by the different infrastructure policies of the neighbouring countries so as to be consistent with these (for instance, France has chosen to modernise its railway system, the Netherlands have concentrated on their waterways, while Germany is famous for its highway system).

While no traditional system should be neglected, the form of transport to be developed in any particular region should be that which best meets the specific needs of the activities selected for special promotion. The inland waterways, which in future are likely to be devoted almost exclusively to heavy primary products, remain vital to the carrying of raw materials such as coal and minerals from the mines to the processing plants. Railways and highways can rapidly carry less heavy products and also carry workers to their work and back. Apart from these main connections secondary transport systems also have considerable importance for the distribution of goods and supplies within more limited areas. As national boundaries are progressively opened within the framework of the European Economic Community, international lines of development must now be taken into account and the old national concepts of transportation systems radiating from the capital in the shape of a 'star' must be abandoned.

For example, the economic expansion of the Hainaut Province depends upon the modernisation of the north–south (Amsterdam–Brussels–Mons–Paris) and east–west (Cologne–Liège–Mons–Lille) main lines of communication of the railway system; only the north–south line is electrified at present. It was decided as early as 1947 that the Tournai–Liège line should be electrified but the Charleroi–Liège section, regarding which the E.E.C. approved a similar recommendation in 1960, is not to be electrified until 1968. The Charleroi–Lille section is not yet included in any of the development projects. The two European highways mentioned in the programme included in the 1950 Geneva Declaration – the E.10 from Amsterdam to Paris via Brussels and the E.41 from Valenciennes to Liège via Mons known as the Walloon highway, will not be completed until 1971. Modernising the inland waterways requires that the Sambre River, the Charleroi Canal, the Nimy–Péronnes canal and the upper Escaut River for the east–west main route, on the one hand, and the Brussels–Clabecq–Charleroi for the north–south main route on the other, be improved to accommodate barges of up to 1,350 tons measurement.[1]

While Liège is at present directly connected to Antwerp by a highway and a canal, its economic growth depends upon highway connections to Brussels,[2] to Paris (via the Walloon highway) and to Amsterdam via Maastricht. Moreover, when the Albert Canal is modernised, the Upper-Meuse River is widened and a canal linking the Meuse and Rhine rivers is constructed, Liège will become a semi-maritime port, a basic pre-requisite of its economic development. As for the railway system, apart from the delays in the electrification of the Namur–Liège section it is very regrettable that the electrification of the Liège–Maastricht section, which is part of the international main line from Amsterdam to Basle, should not yet be included in any scheme, despite recommendations of both the E.E.C. and the Dutch Government to that effect.

While following their general policy of main lines of development the government authorities should at the same time make certain that industrial zonings are wisely distributed. This term includes any unitary site provided with all the necessary facilities in the form of 'infrastructure' to be offered to a new industry. Such zonings must be included in some overall physical planning programme together with the creation of residential zones, public gardens and parks, economic activity zones, so that the confused overlapping of industrial building and private housing may at last come to an end.

---

[1] Under the 1957 Bill (called the '1350 measurement tons bill') it has been decided to widen the Sambre River and the Charleroi, Nimy–Péronnes and Upper-Escaut River canals. At present only the Nimy–Péronnes canal has been completed – its modernisation works took 6 years – but it still is not put to full use as it can offer no exit for 1,350 measurement-tons barges so long as the Upper-Escaut and the Charleroi canal are not widened, which will not be until 1970 and 1975 respectively. The widening of the Charleroi–Clabecq–Brussels canal was decided as early as 1938 but the works will not be completed until 1968.

[2] The creation of this particular highway as well as of the Walloon highway is included in the public construction programme for 1967–71. As to the E.10 highway, only its general alignment is known, though its building was decided as far back as 1950.

5 CONCLUSIONS

The economic modernisation of the Walloon area depends upon the implementation of a number of new policies. Internally these must, with the problems of demography and with the structural adaptation of industry, be based on a sectoral approach (as opposed to any policy of 'industrial peppering'). In its external relations, a policy must deal with the problems of attaching the Walloon area to the neighbouring dynamic regions, through the setting up of an appropriate 'infrastructure' based mainly on the highway and railway systems.

A modernisation of the traditional industries of the area has its part to play, provided that it is accompanied by a complete change in the methods of management.

The establishment of new and more modern industries is absolutely vital: the manufacture of more sophisticated products, whose value added is greater and whose demand is basically expanding, will improve through joint-production contracts and sub-contracts, and greater trade co-operation.

The measures of government assistance to be taken must be directed to those development areas which meet certain basic conditions as to their homogeneity. If the government authorities of the six member states of the Community are prepared to replace the existing political, administrative and linguistic concept of a territorial unit by an economic concept of the 'region', the co-ordinated and planned development of some areas which overlap the Belgian–French and Belgian–German boundaries could help those areas found to be 'cumulatively declining and generally obsolescent in every respect' to make a new dynamic start. For this they would get the continuing impulse of the vigorously advancing regions which lie close to them in the areas of Paris, the Rhine and the Schelde.

F

7 The Backward Region of Fribourg in Switzerland[1]

Jean Valarché
UNIVERSITY OF FRIBOURG

1 INTRODUCTORY

Switzerland has one of the most highly developed economies in the world, but there are appreciable differences in the level of development as between one canton and another. This may seem astonishing in so small a country; the explanation lies in natural and human divisions. Factors of production do not easily move between cantons, and there is no large-scale federal expenditure to equalise opportunities between unequally well-endowed regions. Yet a poor canton does not compare with a rich canton in the same terms that a depressed area compares with an advanced one, and this is one reason why the case of backward regions in Switzerland is of special interest.

Another reason is that Switzerland has a preponderantly liberal economy. While partial planning is the rule in all neighbouring countries, Switzerland remains as faithful to economic decentralisation as to political federalism. Consequently, regional development is left to the precarious interplay of local authorities and large national firms. The Swiss example may serve to bring to light the common features of regional development, with or without central planning, and also to show what part large firms play in establishing a link between regional development and its national setting by trying to mobilise unutilised resources and to make good the labour shortage – just as, incidentally, an Economic Ministry might do or a Planning Board.

The canton of Fribourg (with an area of 1,670 square km. and 164,000 inhabitants, situated right in the middle of the Swiss plateau) is a region in the economic meaning of the word, for we find in it both homogeneity and polarisation. In all the canton's districts, agriculture and agricultural processing industries occupy a place which they no longer hold in the rich cantons. The city of Fribourg is the political and the economic capital of the region, the locus of its intellectual infrastructure, its leading industries and the bulk of the tertiary sector. The region's economy is developed, but on a level lower than the Swiss average. Geography and history explain why this is so. Unlike Basel or Lausanne, Fribourg does not lie on any of the great European railway routes. Its political and religious choices brought it into conflict with more powerful neighbours. Having

---

[1] Translated from the French by Elizabeth Henderson.

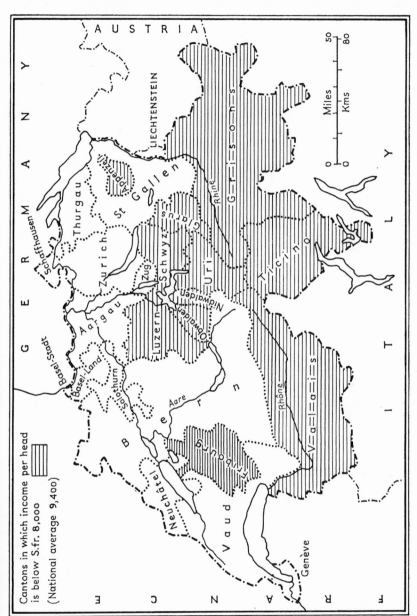

BACKWARD AREAS OF SWITZERLAND

Cantons in which income per head
is below S.fr. 8,000
(National average 9,400)

missed the first industrial revolution, the region settled down to being a supporting economy for the other more fortunate cantons. A first spurt at the end of the nineteenth century created an infrastructure of power supply and universities, and brought with it a beginning of industrialisation. But subsequently the region indulged in the dream of slow but sure progress on the basis of federal subsidies to agriculture and of the propagation of prosperity from beyond its borders. In the middle of the current century, there came a rude awakening in the form of a crisis in agriculture and a steady population drain. At that stage the authorities took action to induce Swiss industrial firms to decentralise and move plant into Fribourg, and also to co-ordinate development on a sectoral and geographical basis. And in fact the growth rate was higher in Fribourg in the years 1955 to 1965 than elsewhere in the country. But the initial lag was so great that progress would have to continue for some time yet before one could speak of the region's having 'caught up'.

The first section of this paper measures the region's backwardness at present in relation to the Swiss average. The second section analyses regional development promotion. The last two sections deal with the positive and the negative aspects of the region's growth potential. The former outweigh the latter – but this might well be due as much to the boom which Switzerland has enjoyed since the war as to the wisdom of cantonal and federal policies, or indeed to the efficiency of large firms.

2   THE EXTENT OF THE REGION'S BACKWARDNESS

There are three main signs of backwardness in Fribourg: low incomes, the prominence of the agricultural sector, and inadequate secondary schooling.

(A)   RELATIVELY LOW PER CAPITA INCOMES

In comparing incomes in Fribourg with Swiss average incomes, we shall use the direct method and the method of outward signs. The first looks at the amount of income accruing to the individual; the second deduces income from spending.

(1)   Direct estimation. In Switzerland as elsewhere incomes are known from tax registers. An economist from Basel has measured incomes with the help of post-office accounts. Here we shall add a separate investigation of agricultural incomes, because of the special place which agriculture occupies in the canton's economy.

(*a*)   Income comparison on the basis of fiscal statistics. There is in Switzerland only one direct federal tax which allows of comparison on the national scale, and that is the national defence tax. Its average yield per taxpayer in Fribourg was S.fr. 38·42 during the fiscal period 1961-62, compared with an average of S.fr. 83·47 for the whole of Switzerland. But the disparity of tax yields is not really a good reflection of the income gap, because the assessment is different. The proportion of farmers is much higher than average in the canton of Fribourg (30 as against 10 per cent) and, in Switzerland as everywhere else, farmers are less heavily taxed than others.

(*b*) Income comparison on the basis of post-office accounts. M. J. Rosen has worked out a novel method for comparing income in the different cantons. Noting the close correlation between national income and the sum of payments as shown in the movements of post-office current accounts, he deduced the regional distribution of Switzerland's social product from the turnover figures of twenty-three postal cheque offices. He corrected his results to take account of the fact that postal cheque districts do not in all cases coincide with cantonal boundaries, and also to make allowance for payments pertaining to a district other than that of the postal cheque office at which they are made. In this way Rosen arrived at a figure of S.fr. 8,740. for average income per inhabitant in Switzerland in 1963, and a corresponding S.fr. 4,510 for the canton of Fribourg.

The two methods of calculation lead to the same conclusion: that *per capita* income in Fribourg is half of what it is in Switzerland as a whole. Similar below-average incomes are found in other cantons, like Valais, Schwyz and Appenzell, which share with Fribourg the preponderance of agriculture. It is thus reasonable to assume that the low cantonal income figure is due to low agricultural incomes. This has indeed proved to be so.

(*c*) Agricultural *per capita* income. We can get approximate figures of agricultural incomes from the accounts of farm enterprises. Incomes vary within a wide range on either side of the average, according to the farm's situation in mountain country or the plains, its size and its products. Average farm income in Fribourg is 14 per cent below the Swiss average, and works out at S.fr. 300 per month for each person whose livelihood is in agriculture. Average monthly income in Fribourg is somewhat higher, to wit, S.fr. 350. Like nearly everywhere else in the world, therefore, average farm incomes are lower in Fribourg than non-farm incomes.[1]

(2) Outward signs. Income spending may serve as a cross-check on the relatively low income figures.

(*a*) Housing has a lower amenity rate, a higher occupancy rate and a higher average age in Fribourg than in Switzerland as a whole.

	Fribourg	*Switzerland*
Dwellings built before 1947 (per cent)	79·8	73·2
Dwellings without running water (per cent)	6·7	2·1
Dwellings without bath or shower (per cent)	58·6	36·9
Average number of occupants per room	1·01	0·85
Telephone instruments per 1,000 inhabitants	165	244 [2]

[1] See J. Valarché, 'Le Problème de la parité des revenus', *Rivista internazionale di scienze economiche e commerciali*, no. 11 (1963).

[2] Federal population census, 1963.

(*b*)   There are relatively fewer motor vehicles in Fribourg than would correspond to the Swiss average.

	Fribourg	Switzerland
Motor cars per 1,000 inhabitants	66·8	90
Any kind of motor vehicles per 1,000 inhabitants	77·5	106 [1]

(*c*)   Medical services are less dense in Fribourg.

	Fribourg	Switzerland
Number of inhabitants per physician	1,665	1,102
Number of inhabitants per dentist	4,082	2,472 [1]

Outward signs confirm our direct income estimates; there can be no doubt that *per capita* incomes are less than average in Fribourg.

(B)   A LARGE PRIMARY SECTOR IN A DUAL ECONOMY

(1)   The size of the primary sector. Agriculture and forestry occupy a very high place in the economy of Fribourg. Persons at work in farming accounted for 31·4 per cent of the working population in 1960 (11·6 per cent on the average in Switzerland). From this point of view, the canton is now at the stage at which Switzerland was in 1900. The industries which developed out of the primary sector are still the most prevalent; the food industry today employs more labour than any other, and the timber industry ranks third in this respect.

In absolute figures, too, the size of the agricultural population is striking. In 1960, there were 12 persons at work in farming for every square kilometre of agricultural land; this was the average figure for Switzerland in 1941.

(2)   Characteristics of a dual economy. The extent of the service sector in Fribourg differs widely from the rest of Switzerland.

SECTORAL COMPOSITION OF THE POPULATION, 1960

	Agriculture %	Industry %	Services %
Fribourg	31·4	42·0	26·6
Switzerland	11·6	49·5	38·9

The Fribourg figures are below average in all service activities, including administration, free professions, trade, and the hotel business. The cantons of Bern and Vaud, on the other hand, Fribourg's major neighbours, are notably rich in tertiary activities. Here we have clear evidence of a dualism of geographical origin. Fribourg is prevented from developing the most profitable activities by the very size of its nearest neighbours. This applies particularly at the outer edges of the canton; the industrial

[1] Federal population census, 1963.

micro-region of Flamatt is economically linked to Bern and the Veveyse district depends economically upon Lausanne.

The location of the large firms' decision-making power equally points to a harmful dualism. Half of Fribourg's twelve largest firms have their head office outside the canton – two at Bern, two at Zürich, one at Basel and one at Vevey. Not only are their branches in the canton of Fribourg subject to outside policy decisions, but most of the key staff are 'imported'. So are a number of Italian and Spanish workers, whose temporary presence underscores the marginal character of industrialisation in Fribourg.

(c) INADEQUATE SCHOOLING

While the schooling rate is no lower in Fribourg than elsewhere in Switzerland or, for that matter, in Europe, schooling is ill-adapted to the needs of economic expansion. Here are two examples.

(1) Apprenticeship training. Fewer than average people take the final apprenticeship examinations in Fribourg; in 1965, the figures were one for every 191 inhabitants in Fribourg, and one for every 142 in Switzerland as a whole.

(2) Secondary schooling. Lower secondary schools, which turn out skilled workmen and technicians, take in only a small proportion of the children who have completed their primary education. Too few girls, especially, go to these schools; the education of girls is more or less left to religious orders, which receive little public subsidy and consequently ask fees which most Fribourg families cannot afford. Yet it is common knowledge that large-scale participation of women workers is a condition of economic development.

To sum up, backwardness in Fribourg is attributable to two factors, one proportional and the other differential. In the first place, the proportion of the least productive activity is particularly high. Secondly, the sectoral growth rates are lower than the national average (except for a few years between 1955 and 1965). Fribourg's main industry, the food industry, has below-average linkage effects[1] and pays lower wages than the others. Similarly, trade and the hotel business yield lower returns in Fribourg than elsewhere in Switzerland.

3 REGIONAL DEVELOPMENT POLICY

The Swiss federal constitution upholds freedom of trade and industry just as it upholds the cantons' self-government. It follows that the federal government is not concerned either with economic expansion in general or with helping any backward canton to 'catch up'. It is up to the cantons to develop as best they may, subject, of course, to an equally detached

[1] See H. B. Chenery and T. Watanabe, 'International Comparisons of the Structure of Production', *Econometrica*, Oct 1958.

attitude towards private enterprise. Yet a spirit of mutual aid in the Confederation and national solidarity would surely justify some intervention in the interests of balanced growth.

(A) MEASURES AT FEDERAL LEVEL

(1) Financial equalisation payments to cantons. Federal subsidies for national highway construction and maintenance are paid to cantons according to their financial capacity. These highways help to pry the mountainous, and for this very reason less developed, regions out of their isolation; the subsidies may therefore rightly be considered as regional development aid.

(2) Subsidies to mountain areas. Federal subsidies for a number of activities connected with agriculture, the crafts and transport are paid at different rates according as these activities are located in the plains or the mountains. Other subsidies are paid only to people who live in the mountains. The range of these subsidies is very broad. In agriculture, there are some for the protection of cattle herds, for the improvement of mountain pastures (including buildings), for cheese-making, for growing wheat and potatoes, for vocational training and agricultural extension. The crafts are encouraged to the extent that they provide the underemployed with work they can do at home. All forms of mountain transport are exempt from taxes; this applies to local passenger travel, to livestock transhuming to mountain pastures, and to freight for food and bread-grain seeds.

It will be clear from this catalogue of measures that they are all concerned with protection rather than guidance. The beneficiaries are the less-developed cantons, which lie mostly in the Alpine range. Fribourg benefits from them in so far as part of the canton is situated in the pre-Alpine zone.

(B) MEASURES AT CANTONAL LEVEL

The Fribourg authorities take the same view of economic development as do the federal authorities. Development is the responsibility of the parishes, but these in turn do receive equalisation payments. The function of government is merely to create an environment propitious for industry and to publicise it.

(1) Financial measures. The cantonal authorities grant tax reliefs to new firms for a certain period, and help them to obtain credit. It is thanks to such measures, for instance, that a textile mill was set up in a small mountain town (Neirivue).

Company profits are taxed at a low rate, one of the lowest in Switzerland. In fact, the tax rate is lower only in cantons which for reasons of size and location cannot compete with Fribourg.

There are government subsidies for vocational training in agricultural schools, apprenticeship centres, etc.

(2)   Public relations.   Since 1956, when a new Director of Industry and Trade took office, the government of Fribourg has been contacting industrial producers whose location choice was undecided as between Fribourg and neighbouring cantons.   Timely intervention of this kind led to the establishment of a metallurgical factory (Polytype, 355 employees) and to the replacement of a small photochemical research laboratory by a larger one.   It also encouraged the establishment of two factories (one for meat products and one cannery) which are subsidiaries of the famous co-operative federation MIGROS.

(C) MEASURES AT PARISH LEVEL

A certain number of parishes own land which they make available either free or cheaply.   Some build premises for industrial use and let them at cost.   Sometimes, finally, a local dignitary puts himself out to attract industry to his parish; thus the chairman of the farmers' association at Estavayer was personally responsible for the presence of factories employing several hundreds of people.

Side by side with official action of this kind, there is also action at professional level.   The Alpine Economy Society of Fribourg, for example, concerns itself with the improvement of mountain pastures.   To this end, the Society conducts research into their technical, economic and social aspects (number of animals per unit of land, incomes of owners, tenants and workers), and organises conferences and visits to model pastures. Finally, the Society brings influence to bear on the government with a view to reforms; one of its successes so far was to get some work done on the paths which lead to mountain pastures and have to be used to transport materials for building summer chalets.

All these measures go to make up what might be called regional development policy, except that the word policy implies some sort of planning or at least a measure of co-ordination, of which there is none.   Financially much the most sizeable aid is the one that comes from furthest away, from the Confederation.   At cantonal level, there is no investment choice according to returns, nor any attempt to concentrate aid on any given point so as to make sure of complete success.   Every village thinks it can become a development pole.   It is true that forty-eight factories have been set up in the canton since 1958, but precious few of them owe anything to public initiative.   The most spectacular ventures in recent years, such as the establishment of a CIBA factory employing 575 people at the outskirts of Fribourg, are explained simply by the large firms' need to decentralise beyond the borders of the traditionally industrial cantons.   It is largely thanks to big capitalist enterprise that the Fribourg economy has known rapid progress in the last ten years.   Progress was striking, especially, in the sectoral distribution of the population.   Between 1955 and 1965 the number of jobs rose from 19,801 to 29,768 in industry, and in the tertiary

F 2

sector from 13,843 to 16,458. Some standard-of-living indicators in Fribourg are now close to the national average; in 1964, there were 228 motor vehicles per 1,000 inhabitants in Fribourg, and 235 per 1,000 in Switzerland as a whole.

May we conclude, then, that the forces of progress have lifted the economy of Fribourg up to the Swiss average? Experts estimate that if progress went on at the same rate for another ten years, the manpower distribution in Fribourg would be close to the pattern of Switzerland in 1960. But Switzerland herself made rapid progress between 1960 and 1965, and continues to do so, though at a slower pace. Thus Fribourg's progress in absolute terms still meant relative stagnation. The question whether this is likely to change in the future can only be answered by analysis.

4 PROGRESS IN ABSOLUTE TERMS

(A) FACTORS CONTRIBUTING TO PROGRESS

The canton of Fribourg possesses two valuable assets of paramount importance for economic expansion, namely, reserves of manpower and of natural resources.

(i) *Manpower.* In Switzerland, one wage-earner out of four is a foreigner, and the proportion is still higher in industry. Labour shortage is a limiting factor for expansion. Fribourg is in a good position in this respect, at least to the extent that its manpower is skilled.

The labour supply originates, as is usual, in a natural population surplus and in a shift of farmers to other occupations. The birth-rate is high and generates an annual population surplus of 1 per cent. The outflow of people from the land began after the Second World War and is still increasing; on present estimates, 2·5 per cent of the rural population leave the land every year. Between 1950 and 1960 half of the available labour supply had to take jobs outside the canton, for lack of sufficiently fast development in the secondary and tertiary sectors. To be sure, it was not a one-way flow, for foreigners came to Fribourg in large numbers – so much so that in 1965 they accounted for 11 per cent of the labour force. Nor is Fribourg now the only canton from which people emigrate; all others are losing some of their highly qualified young. But while the entry of foreign, mostly unskilled, workers certainly is a good thing, in that they replace Swiss workers in necessary, but hard and not very productive jobs, emigration from Fribourg was a sign of bad occupational circulation. The canton turned out too many people with administrative training, and too few with technical training as skilled workers. This was normal enough at a time when industry was scarce. It is no longer so.

Today the canton has a pool of skilled workers ready for a new wave of industrialisation. This is evident from an extrapolation of the figures for the last ten years, 1955–65. New job opportunities per year numbered 1,000 in industry, and 260 in the tertiary sector. As against that, 670 new jobs were wanted annually for persons having left agriculture, and 700 for surplus young entrants to the labour force. The shortfall of new vacancies compared with new labour supply is a measure of emigration from Fribourg. Emigration may well increase somewhat in the near future, given that the outflow from the land is gathering speed. But there are two unknowns which make it hard to arrive at a precise estimate.

(1) Is former agricultural labour going to be suitable for work in industry and the services? The answer is probably in the affirmative, thanks to the creation of a new vocational training and commercial school at Fribourg.

(2) Will those who are capable of performing jobs in industry and the services take up employment in the canton itself? They may be tempted away by the higher wages paid in the high-productivity industries and services located in German Switzerland or on the shores of the Lake of Geneva.[1] To prevent this, the industrial range of Fribourg would have to become rather more like that of Switzerland as a whole.

(ii) *Natural Resources.* Industry needs water and space, and industrial countries are often short of them. The region of Fribourg is relatively rich in both. A certain number of towns, such as Bulle and Romont, for example, have bought building plots to make available to firms, and similarly the water and sand of the Lake of Neuchâtel have attracted producers of cellular concrete (for prefabricates). The purity of the Alpine water is a valuable asset for dye-works and chemical factories. Electricity is cheaper than in neighbouring cantons, and the series of pre-Alpine dams which has been built leaves a considerable margin of power still awaiting use.

(B) FORMS OF PROGRESS

A regional economy can progress by becoming either more extensive or more intensive. In the first case it takes in space hitherto not used for economic purposes, and the key to this is an extension of infrastructures. In the second case diversification raises productivity in an already developed environment, which means discovering complementarities.

(i) *Extension of infrastructures.* The canton of Fribourg has two development axes, along the permanent ways that run from Bern to Fribourg and from Fribourg to Morat. Extending infrastructures has therefore meant

---

[1] It is difficult to know what a top-ranking employee actually earns, but definitely a good deal less in Fribourg than he could earn elsewhere in Switzerland for the same job. Civil service salaries may be taken as an example. A university professor in Fribourg earns 15 % less than the Swiss average.

spreading into two peripheral areas; the borders of the Lake of Neuchâtel and the Gruyère mountains.

(1) Estavayer-le-Lac – industrial newcomers. Estavayer, a small fishing and yachting port, has the combined efforts of leading local personalities and of public authorities to thank for the fact that in recent years four industrial establishments have been set up there, of which three employ more than 100 people. The biggest is a cannery with a personnel of 329; the others make cellular concrete, metal blinds and electrical machinery, which fit in well enough with the pattern of modern industrial expansion.

(2) Moléson – a new tourist resort. At an investment cost of S.fr. 14 million, tourist amenities have been created on the Moléson mountain, a peak of 2,000 metres altitude, to take advantage of its splendid natural position (plenty of snow and sun) and to give new life to an isolated mountain area. The company which runs the skiing resort registered a turnover of S.fr. 700,000 during its first year, a figure which must be multiplied by $3\frac{1}{2}$ to evaluate its regional impulse effect.[1]

(3) Romont – commercial facilities. The town of Romont is the geographical centre both of the canton of Fribourg and of the whole of French-speaking Switzerland. An international cold-storage firm has chosen this town as the turntable of food transports throughout Europe. Europe's largest cold-storage warehouses are to built there, together with a whole lot of related plant and facilities, such as a liquid-nitrogen factory, a refrigeration research laboratory, a food supermarket and a produce exchange.

(ii) *Complementarities.* Although new centres of activity have thus made their appearance, industry is still densest where it started up originally. It is there that most new firms chose to settle, either because they wanted to take advantage of the existing economic and social infrastructure, or by virtue of an agglomeration effect.

(1) *Infrastructure and directly productive activities.* A certain number of firms settled along the Morat–Fribourg axis and at Bulle, because of the existence of adequate infrastructures.

(*a*) Public services, especially of the educational kind, are concentrated mainly at Fribourg (University, Technicum, vocational training and commercial school), but are available also at Morat and Bulle.

(*b*) Transport has the benefit of cantonal roads, a future motorway now under construction, two railway lines and a canal.

(*c*) There is a supply of the basic elements needed for industrial production, such as water supply, purification plant for the waste waters of industry, a ready power supply.

[1] According to the Swiss Tourist Federation, $3\frac{1}{2}$ is the multiplier for the tourist industry.

(*d*) There are good leisure-time facilities, such as concerts, theatres, museums, sports grounds.

Wherever these services and facilities are available, there is a possibility for the establishment of big firms whose raw materials may come from far away and whose products in turn may be sold far afield. A case in point is Stephan, an engineering company at Fribourg, which sells its boilers as far away as South Africa. Another example is Photochimie, a firm at the outskirts of Fribourg, which employs 650 people and sells films and photographic paper throughout Switzerland. Finally, one might mention S.A.I.A., makers of electrical machinery at Morat; this firm has a personnel of 782 and exports the bulk of its output. Except for the last-named, all these factories were set up during the last ten years. They might well have settled elsewhere, for the above-mentioned advantages are to be had anywhere on the Swiss plateau. What attracted them to Fribourg was the availability of manpower and sites, and the inducement of financial and fiscal facilities.

(2) *The agglomeration effect.* Unlike the preceding cases, those now to be mentioned are the result of a natural location choice. In any agricultural canton, food-processing industries develop. For these industries, it is of advantage to be near their raw materials, for transport cost is lower for the processed than for the crude product, which is heavier. While, therefore, these are traditional activities, they feel the impact of general economic change via the concentration of firms and the centralisation of decision-making power.

(*a*) Concentration of firms may take two forms, in Fribourg as elsewhere. First, firms expand so as to be able to broaden the range of their products; thus the Cardinal brewery now produces not only beer but soft drinks, and the Nestlé factory has added dietary milk products to its chocolate production. Secondly, firms grow by vertical integration; the same brewery controls a firm which uses brewer's yeast for canned foods.

(*b*) Centralisation of decision-making power is evident in the relationship between agriculture and the firms which process and market agricultural products. Some of the farmers agree to sell their vegetables and poultry [1] through an 'integrator'. The source of integration is the MIGROS co-operative federation, which has set up a factory canning vegetables at Estavayer-le-Lac, and another at Courtepin, 15 km. from Fribourg, which makes the Micarna brand of meat products. The Estavayer cannery is one unit, though no doubt a major one, but still only one unit in an industrial area. Micarna, by contrast, completely dominates Courtepin, a small village which in 1955 employed 110 people and ten

[1] J. Valarché, 'Innovation in Stock Farming: Information Flow from the Agricultural and Animal Food Industries'. Paper prepared for the International Economic Association's Conference on Economic Problems of Agriculture in Industrial Societies and Repercussions in Developing Countries, Rome, 1–8 September 1965.

years later employed 834, of whom 630 work for Micarna. The establishment itself is an integrated one, since besides the factory for meat products it comprises a poultry abattoir, a test laboratory for all the food products sold by the co-operative federation, a school for its sales staff and a retail butcher's shop. With this kind of organisation, decision-making power is centralised, in so far as part of the meat supply is now offered on new terms. Poultry supply is in the hands of a few large firms which control production, while the farmer himself becomes a sort of cottage-industry piece-worker with no responsibilities whatever for marketing; and the supply of pork products (charcuterie) and butcher's meat is divided between the MIGROS co-operative outlets and ordinary delicatessen and butcher's shops.

Micarna's supply range extends to 50 km. for slaughtering animals and to 70 km. for fattened chickens. Its sales market, on the other hand, covers more than half of Switzerland, wherever there are MIGROS co-operative shops. The firm's central location and its large-scale cold-storage facilities enable it to adjust its supply to demand fluctuations.

Micarna's influence in the region has many aspects. The firm is a major customer for the packaging and cardboard manufacturers of Fribourg, for builders (it has been expanding steadily since 1960, when it started up with a personnel of 150) and electricity companies. It uses a local railway line, and employs some Fribourg labour, both a number of people from certain trades, like butchers, and also a few skilled workers. Lastly, it is of course taxed on its declared profits.

Yet what the example of Micarna shows most clearly is how much less a firm under outside control counts for a region than a firm which has its roots in the local environment and grows with it. Investment comes from Zürich, the unskilled workers are Italians or Spaniards, the skilled workers are in part from Fribourg and in part German Swiss, with a preponderance of outsiders in the top jobs. The firm uses its own refrigerated trucks much more than Fribourg railway wagons. It gets its orders from Zürich; every day, the head office gives instructions as to what proportion of killed chickens is to be marketed and what proportion to be put in cold storage, depending on demand in Switzerland and on foreign orders. Fribourg is completely by-passed by all this. In any event, the food industry does not have enough intersectoral links to qualify as an impulse industry.

Nevertheless, animal husbandry in Fribourg does have the advantage of secure outlets, the public finances of Fribourg have the benefit of big new taxpayers after the first few years of special exemptions, and there is of course the multiplying effect of 600 wage packets spent to some extent in the canton.

All this adds up to a sum of progress which explains the rapid growth of the secondary sector and of total employment among a population barely more numerous than in the past. The canton has definitely gained. New bank branches have been set up (by the Société de Banque Suisse in 1965, and Crédit Suisse in 1966). The region is beginning to stand on its own feet economically and ceasing to be a mere manpower reservoir for its richer neighbours. But there is no doubt that its neighbours still are richer. Their economic progress has been even faster; while the number of farm enterprises diminished by 20 per cent in Fribourg, it declined by 28 per cent in Vaud.

As regards incomes, estimates based on post-office accounts suggest a higher rate of increase in Fribourg than in the richer cantons, but the initial lag was so great that the gap is still growing in absolute terms. Between 1948 and 1963, social product per inhabitant rose from S.fr. 1,360 to 4,510 in Fribourg, while for Zürich the corresponding figures are S.fr. 6,140 and 12,680; in other words, it trebled in the first case and doubled in the second. Yet in absolute terms the gap widened from S.fr. 4,780 to 8,150. The regional economy of Fribourg has made progress in comparison with its own past and its present growth rate is that of a developed country, but to reduce its relative backwardness and to catch up with the average would seem a difficult thing to do, for reasons which it now remains for us to discuss.

5 RELATIVE STAGNATION

(A) ABSENCE OF EXTERNAL ECONOMIES

The most propitious setting for economic activity is one where all the different social and occupational groups support each other, so that any firm can be sure of the suppliers, the manpower, the savers and the customers it needs. Such a setting exists in North Switzerland. There is a broad range of industries, agriculture is intensive, the banks of Basel are at the junction of three rich countries, tourist resorts are a mere hour by car from the big cities. Technological progress then involves no hardship; people set free by any declining branch easily find new employment because new entrepreneurs obtain finance funds from the banks. The key men without whom there can be no economic expansion will stay on their homeground and others will join them there, because an environment of this kind possesses the social infrastructure (public services, entertainments) which makes life pleasant.

The region of Fribourg has no such environment; worse still it is handicapped by the proximity of the rich parts of Switzerland. (1) *Commercially* speaking, it is polarised by its neighbours; people from Fribourg shop as much at Bern and Lausanne as they do in their own canton. The demonstration effects works to the detriment of the region; the people of Fribourg are no less anxious to own a car or a motorcycle, but their vehicles are assembled in the cantons of Bern or Geneva. (2) In respect of *industry*, the region is too close to Switzerland's industrial areas to attract many complementary industries; to date, the canton has only one industrial centre with factories employing more than 100 workers, and although decentralisation in the neighbouring large cantons sends branches and subsidiaries into Fribourg, these do not add up to a true industrial environment as in North-East Switzerland. (3) Much the same applies to *tourism*; the canton lies in between two railway lines, to the Lötschberg and the Simplon, which end to the east and west of the canton, respectively. (4) And finally, this applies also to *agriculture*, which, with its 30 per cent of the working population, is the mainstay of the canton's prosperity. But agricultural productivity is not high enough, as is only too obvious. According to the calculations of the cantonal agricultural school, a farm, to be viable, would need to be of a size of 17–20 hectares. The average size of farm is 8 hectares. The annual upkeep of one large head of livestock requires 20–25 working days; in certain districts, the actual figure is now 75. Perhaps nature is more to blame than men, for a good part of the region lies in the sort of medium-altitude hill or mountain country whose ills are decried today; 'In these broken and uneven landscapes, the modern farmer finds neither the large areas, nor a chance of homogeneous farming, nor the easy and rapid means of communication which he needs.'[1] Thus the location of Fribourg has prevented the emergence of a development pole like those in the north and east of the country.

(B) SHORTAGE OF REGIONAL INVESTMENT FUNDS

In Fribourg, as everywhere else, economic expansion is financed either by private investment, that is, saving, or by public investment, that is, taxation. Both sources of finance are insufficient.

(i) *Private Investment.* Compared with their income, people save as much in Fribourg as elsewhere in Switzerland. A striking example is the small mountain village of Lessoc, with 209 inhabitants; in 1965, deposits at the local Raiffeisen savings bank amounted to no less than 433,000 francs, and in one single year, 1960, they rose by 249,000 francs. But in Fribourg, saving does not necessarily equal investment in the region, because of two leaks.

(1) Leakage of agricultural capital. Among owner farmers, there is always the risk of a capital drain through the division of inherited estates. The individualist mentality of the twentieth century does not easily take to joint ownership. When a farmer leaves several children, the estate is divided, either in kind or in money. If it is divided in kind, the farm is broken up and each portion is too small. If brothers and sisters have to be

[1] R. Livet, *L'Avenir des régions agricoles*, Ed. Économie et Humanisme (Paris 1965) p. 28.

paid out in money, the heir who actually takes over the farm is bled of his liquid assets.

(2)   Leakage of company earnings. The fact that many Fribourg firms are simply branches or subsidiaries depending upon an outside decision centre, has two adverse consequences for the distribution of company earnings.

Few really high salaries are paid to local recipients, for the top-ranking commercial, financial and administrative staff are usually not resident in Fribourg. A striking example is Micarna, which, among its personnel of 630, has no more than twenty-eight white collar workers.

Similarly, profits are usually not distributed in Fribourg but transferred to headquarters; they find their way back to Fribourg only to the extent that there are any shareholders in the canton.

(ii)   *Public Investment.* In Switzerland, economic expansion is financed not only by local authorities, at the level of the parish and canton, but also by the federal government. The result is nothing like a big push of public origin.

(1)   Parishes. Parish budgets can set little aside for investment, because in Fribourg parishes are very small (284 of them for 164,000 inhabitants) and current administrative expenses therefore disproportionately high.

(2)   Cantons. The cantonal budget is not as large as the canton's social product would warrant, because farmers are under-taxed. The 31 per cent portion of farmers contributes very little to the coverage of public expenditure. This is a widespread phenomenon, because farmers are nearly always taxed on an agreed lump sum basis rather than on tax returns, but in Fribourg this has assumed particularly large proportions. The farmers' associations actually have obtained the right to discuss with the tax authorities what the tax schedules shall be. The result is tax evasion with all its ill effects. There is no doubt at all that the declared figures fall short of the real ones; we know of a rural parish in which none of the 300 taxpayers allegedly earns more than S.fr. 6,000 a year.

(3)   Federal government. The federal equalisation payments to the cantons sometimes boomerang. The principle is that even the poorest cantons should contribute some portion of the expenditure involved (which is legitimate enough; the same principle is applied to small wage earners). But it may happen that the difficulty of contributing deters a canton from requesting federal aid for an investment which would yet be of advantage to the canton.

6   CONCLUSIONS

The region of Fribourg is an economically backward region, but not in the same sense as either an underdeveloped country or a depressed (or critical) area.

(1)   Fribourg differs from underdeveloped countries

    (*a*) by the amount of *per capita* income, which is as high as in Austria;

    (*b*) by the extent of infrastructures, especially in the field of education – a population of 164,000 has at its disposal a University (with 3,000 students, of whom 12 per cent belong to Fribourg families), the Technicum with 500 students, and a vocational training and commercial school with 3,000 students.

(2)   Fribourg differs from depressed (or critical) areas, in that

    (*a*) it has never in modern history been at the level of the advanced regions of Switzerland (Basel, Zürich, etc.);

    (*b*) the economy of Fribourg displays no structural maladjustment to contemporary patterns of development – on the contrary, we have seen that its new firms belong to leading industries (engineering, chemicals) or at least apply the most rational methods (integration, specialisation).

(3)   Fribourg is a typical case of retarded development.

In the light of this example we may identify the following characteristics of a backward region in an industrial country.

(*a*) The economic distortions which growth always brings with it are particularly marked (for example, the special obsolescence of mountain farming).

(*b*) The social inequalities which always accompany growth are also particularly marked – witness the inequalities in income distribution, with 38·5 per cent of Fribourg taxpayers assessed on less than S.fr. 350 per month, compared with an average of S.fr. 654.

(*c*) The vicious circle of poverty inherent in any state of underdevelopment is a typical feature of backward regions. Social and cultural conditions are not propitious for rapid expansion (the political weight of farmers). Nor are demographic conditions. Emigration constitutes a pure loss, since it is not simply a case of temporary absence economically compensated by remittances to the family at home. But the example of Fribourg also demonstrates just how far this vicious circle goes. The canton got off to an industrial spurt during the last ten years in spite of the 'backwash effect' of its developed neighbours and partly because of the 'spread effect' which emanates from them at the same time. To be sure, regional expansion did require some local initiative, but it was assisted by the Swiss environment. The country's political structure implies the existence of numerous cantons which would lose their individuality without a minimum material base. This political federalism prevented the Swiss economy from hurting the weakest by domination effects and at the same time justified equalisation payments which ultimately work to the benefit of the weakest.

These characteristics are of the essence in any backward region without a developed economy, regardless of the ruling economic order. The private firms which largely dominate the course of Fribourg's economy do not appear to be acting otherwise than an cantonal planning board would be expected to act. What rules out any idea of setting up a steel or petrochemical complex in Fribourg is simply the nature of things economic. The two overriding reasons are:

(*a*) that the region's location is not particularly favourable, so that it would be costly for the factories to bring in their supplies of raw material and to transport their finished products away;

(*b*) that the highest productivity can be obtained from Fribourg's resources by using them in nearby and better endowed regions. The alleged barrier implied by political self-government in the cantons is no hindrance to economic unity under the leadership of the north and east of Switzerland.

8 The Role of the Tertiary Sector in the Economic Development of Switzerland [1]

Jean Valarché
UNIVERSITY OF FRIBOURG

1 INTRODUCTORY

In Switzerland the tertiary sector possesses the same features as the secondary sector:

(1) Firstly, a large degree of economic concentration offsets the geographical dispersion of the country. Banking and commercial establishments are numerous but most of the business of the country is conducted by the large organisations (five large banks, a union of consumption co-operatives and a Federation of MIGROS Co-operatives).

(2) Secondly, the sphere of business activity goes beyond the national border. Switzerland is the world's leading exporter of reinsurance policies; Swiss bankers work on an international scale; her transport industry represents a quarter of her world traffic in goods. [2]

We can thus assume that the role of the tertiary sector in the growth of the Swiss economy is comparable with that of the secondary sector. This is in relative terms; for the part played by the tertiary sector is smaller than that of the secondary sector. The Swiss economy is still predominantly industrial, even though the country is one of the richest in the world (the second richest measured by gross national product *per capita* in 1962). In the last fifty years the tertiary resources of the country have increased hardly any faster than secondary resources and the former remain distinctly lower. [3] Nevertheless, there are certain signs which indicate that the tertiary sector of the Swiss economy will soon reach the same standards as those already set by other wealthy countries.

[1] Translated from the French by J. E. Sugden.
[2] V. J. P. Baumgarten, 'The Transport Industry', *Swiss Review of Politics and Statistics* (1964) nos. 1–2.
[3] V. R. Zollinger, 'On the Structure of Population and Society', *Swiss Review*, nos. 1–2 (1964).

2 TERTIARY RESOURCES IN SWITZERLAND

(A) THE EVOLUTION OF ITS AGGREGATE STRENGTH [1]

According to the O.E.C.D.,[2] the tertiary sector included, in 1950, 32·9 per cent of the working population, and according to the Federal Office of Statistics, 39 per cent. In 1960 it was 33·3 per cent, according to the O.E.C.D., but still 39 per cent according to the Federal Office. This difference is due to a different definition: transport workers are not included by the O.E.C.D.

For 1965 the secretariat of the O.E.C.D., in another article in *The O.E.C.D. Observer* which came out at the same time (February 1967), gives the figure as 39·2 per cent. As regards a figure of Swiss source, we have at our disposal an estimate made by the Union of Swiss Banks (the U.B.S.) of 40·3 per cent. The second of these figures includes transport workers. The first did not include them if we suppose that the second article in *The Observer* used the same statistical source as the first. It is more likely, however, that the classification which was used this time was the Swiss classification. In fact the divergences between the figures of 1962 on pages 4–5 of *The Observer* and those of 1965 on page 22 are large in the case of all countries concerned and a difference of definition explains why the figure as given by the O.E.C.D. is in the second case much nearer to that of the U.B.S.

Whatever classification is adopted, it is clear that the tertiary sector in Switzerland is smaller in comparison with other countries on the same economic level (in 1965 39·2 per cent as against 49 per cent in England).[3] And this is despite a considerable increase in the national income of the country. Between 1950 and 1960 the number of people employed in the tertiary sector went from 823,000 to 986,000 – an increase of 20 per cent.

(B) THE REASONS FOR THE SMALL AGGREGATE STRENGTH OF THE SECTOR

(1) Demographic concentration. Switzerland is a very densely populated country. This, where there is equality of service, results in an economy based on transport costs, and administrative overheads.

(2) The small strength of her public services. A country like Switzerland, decentralised and divided into departments, has few professional administrators. The public-service functions are partly divided between the various grades of the federal, cantonnal and communal organisations, and partly taken over by ordinary citizens. The most

---

[1] Statistics are derived from the *Swiss Statistical Year Book*.
[2] From 'From the Industrial Economy to the Service Economy', *The O.E.C.D. Observer* (Feb 1967).
[3] 'The Member Countries of the O.E.C.D.', *The O.E.C.D. Observer* (Feb 1967).

striking example is that of the national defence which in Switzerland is represented almost entirely by men performing military service whereas in other countries the similar functions are performed by professional soldiers who are counted as belonging to the tertiary sector. It is only recently that this low level of tertiary activity has begun to change. From 1963 to 1966 the strength of the central administration increased by 7 per cent, while the working population increased by only 3 per cent.

Two other less important reasons can also be used to explain the relatively small strength of the tertiary sector.

(1) The seasonal elements in the tertiary sector. The occupational censuses are carried out on 1 December and therefore do not include foreigners who stay for only a season, and who are numerous in certain branches of the tertiary sector (e.g. the hotel trade).

(2) The technical advance in railway transport. Switzerland electrified her railways before other countries, and was continually rationalising the system and conditions of transport. The result is that the number of railway personnel is small compared to the volume of traffic. Between 1920 and 1950 goods carried by the railways doubled, the number of passengers carried more than quadrupled – while the number of railwaymen dropped slightly – from 38,100 to 37,100. It is important to realise here that the proportion of traffic carried by the railway is higher in Switzerland than in any other country (62 per cent of all goods in 1961).

(C) THE COMPOSITION OF ITS TOTAL

Swiss statistics include in the tertiary sector:

PERCENTAGES OF TOTAL WORKING POPULATION

	1950	*1960*
(1) Commerce	10	10·5
(2) Transport	5	5
(3) Hotels and restaurant trade	4	5
(4) Banks and insurance companies	1	1·5
(5) Public services	2	2·5
(6) Various (theatres, welfare, health services)	17	14·5
	39	39·0

To the theorist, these different categories fall under two headings. Firstly, the tertiary sector includes those services which need to be used to make effective other processes of production – such services as the transport of goods or wholesale trade. Their expansion is the corollary of that of the sectors which produce these goods and the results of the employment of these services will show themselves directly in the tables of national accounts. But the activities of the tertiary sector also include services rendered directly to final buyers,[1] which, as far as their influence on the growth of the economy is concerned, seem to fall into two categories: the first covers personal services, which are purely a reflection (as in the case of domestic service) of the growth of the economy, or are even completely independent of it (as in the case of religion); the second represents the infrastructure of the country and determines the productivity of the whole of the national economy, and may thus be regarded as a genuine factor in causing the growth of the economy.

This distinction is not of course absolute. It is quite feasible that such and such a business in the tertiary sector may simultaneously be both a consequence of growth and a factor in causing growth. It is even possible that a given activity may at one moment be the former, and at the next time the latter (there is a lesson here for John Vaizey). Nevertheless the distinction fits in with two ideas which are widely held:

(1) The value added to the national product by a nurse is not as great as that added by a bank employee.
(2) Some activities in the tertiary sector are independent in character; others are directly related to the general circumstances of the economy; religious activity is not linked to industrial expansion in the same sense as is trading activity.

If, in another sense, we connect the tertiary sector to industrial development, it is because industry is the driving force behind the Swiss economy. The post-war prosperity is for the most part due to the success of metallurgic and chemical exports. Between 1950 and 1960 the value of exports from the metallurgical industries doubled (it represents 40 per cent of total Swiss exports) and the value of exports from the chemical industry tripled (18 per cent of total exports). Their total strength has increased by half, a figure which is only obtainable by working out by how much the number of employees has increased. The preponderance of industry is best indicated by the relative growth of the production goods industries as compared with the consumer goods industries (58 per cent of total industrial employment in 1960 as against 50 per cent in 1950).

3 THE TERTIARY SECTOR AS A REFLECTION OF INDUSTRIAL DEVELOPMENT

There are certain activities which reflect the industrial development of the country, in the sense that they benefit from it without their being the

[1] C. Clark, *The Conditions of Economic Progress*, French translation, p. 311

necessary or sufficient condition for it. This is the case, in particular, of domestic service: the progressive increase of wealth of the country increases it at the onset and then diminishes it. As J. Rowastie has said, 'We are all rich enough to want to have servants, and also rich enough to refuse to be servants'.[1] In Switzerland the number of people employed in domestic service has been declining in absolute terms since 1930 and has been declining even faster as a percentage of the working population. This is exactly the same in the case of religion, art and sport: the relations of all these with the state of the economy of a country are only remote. The case of the professions is perhaps not dissimilar. Undoubtedly, the setting up of companies and the sale of stocks and shares are not independent of the general economic situation. But the repercussions on the activities of the liberal professions are complex. The legal activities, which form an important element in the total of professional services, are partly related to the general economic situation (the sale of goods) and are partly independent (the legal problems of the individual citizen, criminal and other non-financial matters). The medical profession likewise depends initially on the general economic situation; its progress is more a consequence than a precondition of industrial development. Nevertheless, the bond is not so weak: in Switzerland there is a lag between the increase in net national product and that of the expenditure and employment on hygiene and health. As we are concerned with services supplied directly to final purchasers, we cannot identify a pattern of growth of productivity translatable into external economies available for industrial enterprises; it is seen as a mere slowing down in the production of services.

4 THE TERTIARY SECTOR AS A COROLLARY OF INDUSTRIAL DEVELOPMENT

There are certain activities in the tertiary sector which are partly, or even completely, dependent on the development of the nation's industry. For example, the goods transport industry develops necessarily side by side with industrial production. It is a corollary of it. The passenger transport industry, on the other hand, is dependent on leisure, and thus for its part reflects the overall wealth of the country. Trade also develops as a corollary of industrial activities, and so does the branch of service activities which provides industry with advisory services. They are influenced by industrial development, but on the other hand, they influence it themselves. For example, progress in trading methods has reduced the distributive margin by rationalising through bulk buying. Rising prices have thus been checked and monetary stability has been ensured, which in its turn facilitates the pursuit of the long-term planning so indispensable

[1] *Les 40,000 heures*, p. 44.

to growth. This is particularly true in the case of Switzerland. Colin Clark noticed even in 1951 that the distributive margin for milk was particularly low in Switzerland. The distributive margin for fruit – the most sensitive of all distribution industries – is lower in Switzerland than in neighbouring countries. If we treat such facets of progress as a corollary of growth and not as a factor of growth, it is because commercial services for the most part are concerned with final buyers.[1] Certain trading services, however, can be regarded as factors contributing to growth, because they open up outlets for goods produced, and thus permit economies of scale to be achieved. This is the case with those 'abstract' markets, which keep brokers, commission agents and wholesalers active.

Public services may be classed as corollaries or as factors working for growth, depending firstly on whether their productivity progresses, and secondly on whether the progress of their productivity affects private enterprise or not. The postal service may be considered as a factor of growth in Switzerland in the period from 1955 to 1965. During this period, postal operations concerned with postal cheque accounts increased by 58 per cent; postal orders issued increased by 78 per cent; sending of parcels and periodicals by 48 per cent; all this was done with a total staff increase of only 35 per cent. This is a case of definite progress in the productivity of work which directly affects private businesses, the main customers of the service. Such progress can, therefore, be looked on as an external economy, a factor in growth.

An analysis of the public teaching service might lead us to a similar conclusion. The conditional is used here because one cannot measure the growth of productivity in this case as one can in the postal service. The best way to judge it, according to John Vaizey, 'is to look outside the formal education system to the development of systems of training in industry and agriculture, and the subsequent incorporation of these systems and of their techniques, practices and curriculum in the formal education system.' [2] There is also the other side to the matter. We are concerned with a service which is directed generally at final buyers. If therefore the correlation between the increase in gross national product and that of the education system is high, the nature of the relationship is not evident. John Vaizey seems to suppose that it is some kind of race, where sometimes one, sometimes the other, is leading. In a country where wealth is growing, educational expenditures grow more rapidly than national income, and yet in the longer term they accelerate the rate of growth of the economy. This

[1] Connections between sectors of commerce are weak. The relationship between purchases made by various sectors and total production – 16%. The relationship between sales made by sectors to total demand – 17%. Calculations by Chenery and Watanabe, 'International Comparisons of the Structure of Production'.

[2] 'The Role of Education in Economic Development' – in *Planning Education for Economic and Social Development: Mediterranean Regional Project*, O.E.C.D., 1962, p. 41.

is the issue in general. What happens in Switzerland? The role of education is given priority. The ratio of university places [1] to the eligible age-group is 3·51 per cent (in 1962) – i.e. relatively low compared to the ratio in other countries on a similar economic level. On the other hand, secondary commercial and technical education was developed earlier in Switzerland than anywhere else. Similarly apprentice schemes still retain an important place, which is the more noteworthy in that the shortage of labour gives young workers a chance to earn good wages from the first.

5   THE TERTIARY SECTOR AS A FACTOR IN INDUSTRIAL DEVELOPMENT

There are certain tertiary activities which contribute more than others to capital formation. This is primarily the case of banking and insurance companies. The growth of productivity of these organisations means that they have acquired external economies. Thus the figure for the business conducted by Swiss banks has been multiplied by two and a half times between 1950 and 1958, but the number of bank employees by only twice.

The role of insurance in the growth of the economy is even more marked. The concentration of individual security measures allows money saved to be used as a means of financing projects and lessening the risks of production; insurance thus encourages and economises capital formation.[2] It facilitates the direction of investment into those industries which by their very nature involve serious risks (e.g. aircraft construction) but which pay a larger dividend in the long run. Swiss insurance contributes to growth in another way. The business which it conducts abroad is a source of large amounts of foreign currency – 198 N.F. million net in 1965.

We are here obviously concerned with a two-way repercussion: that of the tertiary activities on the general economy, and that of the general economy on the tertiary activities. The former is more important than the latter.

It is the tourist trade which features largest in the Swiss income account as a factor contributing to growth. The difference between what foreign tourists spend in Switzerland and what Swiss tourists spend abroad was estimated at 1·580 million Swiss francs in 1965. Added to this there is the amount spent by the Swiss themselves on tourism within their own country. The multiplier effect of the expenditure deserves particular attention. Tourist expenditure is widely diversified in Switzerland. A study made in 1948 and quoted by Colin Clark [3] indicates that the average foreign tourist spent 20 per cent more in Switzerland than in France,

---

[1] The relationship between the number of Swiss students and the number of Swiss aged between 20 and 27.

[2] Dangibeaud, *L'Assurance et la croissance économique*.

[3] *The Conditions of Economic Progress*, pp. 38–45.

although the amount he spent on food was 5 per cent lower. This is of special importance in the growth of the economy.

The Swiss Association for Tourism has tried to estimate the 'multiplier effect' of tourist expenditure. Their estimate is based on the work of Dr Clement,[1] using the same time limit (the spreading effect of the expenditure is traced over the period of one year) and the same variables (number of tourists involved, regional trade, the sources of regional supply of provisions). The Association's estimate has modified Clement's calculations by taking account of

(1) the high percentage of local goods which the tourist demands, whether they be products of agriculture, such as dried meats, or industrial products such as watches;
(2) the limited effect of 'leaks' from reinvestment of capital outside the country due to the fact that Swiss hotel and restaurant owners are under pressure to be self-financing.

The first calculation is concerned with the distribution of the initial expenditure – that of the tourist. The Swiss Association for tourism estimates that one-half goes to the hotel/restaurant trade, and the other half mainly to the retail trade. This is about the same proportionate breakdown as that estimated by Dr Clement. (Lodging 25 per cent, meals and drink 32 per cent, purchases 25 per cent, visits and amusements 10 per cent, local transport 5 per cent, sundries 3 per cent.)

The second item of expenditure – hotel expenditure – is analysed in the same way. 4·2 per cent goes in wages; 10 per cent in administrative expenses; 5 per cent in agency commissions; 7 per cent in maintenance and repairs; 5 per cent in interest fees; 5 per cent in paying off debts.

Dr Clement estimates the multiplier effect at 3·27, the Swiss Association for Tourism estimates it at 3·5, and certain cantons at 4.

6 CONCLUSION

The role of the tertiary sector in the development of the Swiss economy can be summed up as follows:

(i) It minimises the general expenses of the country and especially those which are the responsibility of the Government. State current expenditures and revenues are much lower in relation to gross national product in Switzerland than in other similar federal countries of the same economic standard, such as Canada or Federal Germany. This does not imply an unfavourable social judgement. 'If international comparisons with regard to welfare and social security show Switzerland as seeming to occupy a very

[1] *The Future of Tourism in the Pacific and the Far East*, Washington, 1961.

low position, this is because none of the services in kind provided by private industry and most of the services in kind which derive from the workings of the Cantons and Communes are nowhere included in the relevant statistics.' [1]

(ii) It paves the way admirably for the economic future of the country. In Switzerland gross fixed capital formation is higher *per capita* than in any other country in the world.[2] The overriding cause of this is undoubtedly industrial prosperity, which gives rise to massive investment, and if one traces back the causes step by step, one would find the economic outlook of the people as the basic cause: there is a whole psycho-sociological environment conducive to growth. Nevertheless one can hardly overestimate the role played by certain tertiary services, such as scientific research both at the public and private level. Switzerland is in the top world rank of Nobel Prize Winners (based on the number of prize winners per million of population) and the number of inventions which the country produces puts her in this rank too. The Swiss national fund for scientific research received 50 million Swiss francs from the Federal Council in 1967 in order to expand applied and theoretical research. The logistic expansion of such services is to be contrasted with the efforts made to reduce expenditure on other tertiary services. There are some writers who put this effort down to the survival of a healthy scorn of the State, others to anxiety to widen the base of national production at the expense of the satisfactions of present consumers.

(iii) The most recent tendency is for Switzerland to approximate more closely to the norms of other rich countries. It has been estimated that between 1965 and 1974 the strength of the federal administrative body will increase by 40 per cent, and that of the canton and commune administrations by 60 per cent. The latest figures regarding the distribution of socio-professional jobs indicate that the manpower released from the agricultural sector moves into the tertiary sector. The role of this sector in the general economy will thus be modified. Productivity per worker will be lower, but the purchasing power represented by the overall strength of the sector will count for more in the vitalisation of the country's economy.

[1] 'The Member Countries of the O.E.C.D.' in *The O.E.C.D. Observer* (Feb 1967).
[2] R. Deonna, *New Memorandum of the Swiss Economy*, p. 131.

9 Regional Economic Problems in West Germany[1]

Edwin von Böventer
UNIVERSITY OF HEIDELBERG

1 INTRODUCTION

In West Germany, interest in promoting a balanced regional economic development and in aiding its problem areas by an active regional policy is as old as the Federal Republic. This preoccupation with regional problems does not merely have its roots in a long tradition of locational studies. It has been necessitated by problems of the regional distribution of the population influx after the war and has more recently been based to a growing extent on a desire to improve the educational and employment opportunities in all low-income areas through industrialisation and accelerated economic growth – so as to offer people in all parts of the country 'equal chances', whatever that may mean. According to a recent definition,[2] 144 out of 566 county districts and cities were backward in 1964, with 34 per cent of the area of West Germany, 12 per cent of the population, 5 per cent of industrial employment and 7·6 per cent of gross domestic product. These districts were mainly located (see Map 1) as follows: in Schleswig-Holstein (Area I); in Lower Saxony: Emsland (Area II) and part of the Luneburg Heath (Area III); in Rhineland–Palatinate; the Eifel region (Area IV); in Hessen and Northern Bavaria, the Rhön–Vogelsberg mountains (Area V); and in Eastern Bavaria, the Forest region (Area VI).

The West German regional policies of the federal and the state (Länder) governments have attempted

(i) to improve the infrastructure in backward areas,
(ii) to offer special (cheaper) loans for industrial enterprises that settle in these areas,
(iii) to help by placing government orders in those regions,
(iv) to grant freight subsidies,

[1] I am much indebted to Messrs G. Keil and B. Lachmann for their help in collecting material and for many fruitful discussions.
[2] All county districts and cities in which in 1964 at least 3 out of the following criteria were fulfilled: (i) population density below 95 per square km. (about 42 % of the West German average of 226); (ii) industrial employment per 1,000 inhabitants less than 78 (52 % of West German average of 150); (iii) per capita tax bases adjusted to regionally uniform rates (Realsteuerkraft) below 62 % of West German average; (iv) gross domestic product *per capita* below D.M. 4,180 (59 % of the West German average of D.M. 7,150 in 1964).

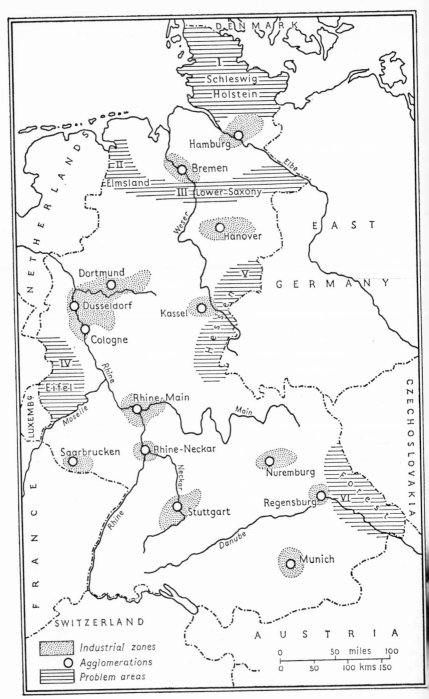

WEST GERMAN INDUSTRIAL AND PROBLEM AREAS

(v) tax exemptions or tax relief,
(vi) to foster structural improvements in agriculture,
(vii) to train labour (or help in retraining labour) and, in general,
(viii) to promote the mobility of labour.

It is difficult to judge the separate effects of the various area development programmes of the federal and state governments. In the first place, only rather limited good statistics on area economic development exist; on a county district (Kreis) basis, gross domestic product figures are only available for three different years – 1951, 1961, 1964 (*per capita* gross product figures have also been estimated for the working population of the districts). In the second place, the various regional programmes have not only been relatively little co-ordinated (either as to the selection of areas to be assisted or as to the specific means of spending money) but, above all, it is impossible to get satisfactory data on how much help has been given to a particular area in a given year. The total sums have been provided under almost a hundred different programmes or headings both by federal and by state ministries of the interior, of agriculture, of housing, of defence, of labour, and of family affairs (to name just the most important ones) and many important expenditures are not sufficiently broken down on a regional basis. Matters are even worse for someone who, as a naïve economist, makes his first effort to study regional problems and policy effects in West Germany or any country. For such a newcomer it is much easier to formulate a few questions with regard to regional economics that he thinks should have been answered in the past than it is to give definite answers. Nor is there much comfort in knowing that experts in the various West German agencies and institutes know very little themselves as to what the exact effects of regional policies have been, or for that matter should have been, and what regional policy should be in the future.

The characteristics of the economic development of West German regions, whether wealthy or backward, are best understood in the light of the overall economic development of the country, since regional problems constitute but a special aspect of the structural problems of adaptation and growth. The overall economic development, in turn, may be described in terms of the interactions of long-term regional trends and certain events which from the point of view of the West German economy represent outside shocks, but which have quite different impacts on different regions.

I shall begin, therefore, by giving a broad, general description of the overall picture of the economic development of the country, with some of the regional facets of this development (Section 2). Subsequently (Section 3) I shall show types of regional structural problems that have arisen in specific parts of West Germany. Leaving out all the healthy areas, I shall distinguish four kinds of areas: (i) low-income areas with a satisfactory agricultural structure but too few industries; (ii) small-farming backward areas; (iii) special-problem areas – areas whose problems derive from the fact that due to a new eastern boundary (between West and East Germany) traditional economic ties have been cut and hinterlands have been lost; and (iv) new problem areas – areas which still belong to the richest parts of the country but whose industrial structure has not adapted fast enough. In Sections 4 and 5 I shall select four areas which may be taken as representing the four above-mentioned types of regions (and combinations of types) and describe their developments in some little detail. In Section 6 I shall discuss what, on the basis of my experience with the West German data, to me seem to be some questions that should be investigated in more detail, and in Section 7 some conclusions on the West German regional situation will follow.

2 OVERALL ECONOMIC DEVELOPMENT AND ITS REGIONAL IMPLICATIONS

The general picture of the overall post-war economic development is one of rapid growth during the reconstruction and development periods after 1948. Substantial unemployment and underemployment (particularly in agriculture) were reduced and wiped out, a heavy influx of population was absorbed, and during an overemployment period (after 1961) foreign labour was attracted. Down to 1966 the postwar economy had only experienced growth cycles, but at the time of writing the first absolute decline in employment and output is to be observed. During these periods the population influx has been uneven from a regional point of view, and the new boundaries in the east as well as the partial (and increasingly more effective) opening of boundaries towards the west and south have affected the West German regions differently. The war destruction, the population influx, and the changed situation in the world economy may be considered as the three external shocks mentioned in an earlier paragraph to which the economy has had to adapt itself within a new political setting. The kinds of shocks that the various regions experienced depended very much on their location within West Germany as well as their previous industrial structure.

For an understanding of the post-war development, a few comments on the pre-war German economy (or more strictly its western sections) and its trends are necessary. Speaking very broadly, the highest incomes have been found towards the north-west, but some of the regions lying further to the south-east have been rapidly catching up. Also very broadly speaking this income gradient reflects a transition from areas with medium-sized farms to poor farming areas with insufficient land per farm, as well as a transition from the Ruhr industrial agglomeration to less industrialised areas. Thus, there have been highly developed agricultural regions with a sound farm size structure and high incomes in the north-west (the best examples being Schleswig-Holstein, and part of Lower Saxony); there have been small-farming areas, some of them just poor and ill-structured (as in Hessen and in parts of Baden–Württemberg and Bavaria), some of them downright backward (as in the western border region of the Eifel as well as in the south-eastern border region of the Bavarian Forest and the Upper Palatine Forest, the earlier mentioned Forest region VI); there have been the old heavy industry agglomerations (with the Ruhr area as the most important example); and, finally there have been newer industrial areas with strongly diversified manufacturing industries, independent local raw material bases, a flexible industry structure and high growth rates (in West Germany most outstandingly in the Rhine–Main area, with Frankfurt also as an important tertiary centre, and the Rhine–Neckar area and in other parts of Württemberg).

Per capita incomes have been around the German average figure in the agricultural areas of the northwest of the country (Schleswig–Holstein and Lower Saxony) and they have also continued to grow at the average German national rate [1] surplus labour being absorbed by such rapidly growing industrial and commercial centres as Kiel, Hamburg, Bremen and Hanover. The large areas of the Rhine Province and Westphalia similarly occupied an average position in the inter-war period, both as to incomes and as to growth rates. Within these large areas, the industrialised regions along the Ruhr and the Rhine were distinctly above, and the small-farming regions in the mountainous areas east of the middle Rhine and in the regions west of the Rhine were somewhat below the average, with the western border area of the Eifel at the tail end. Bavaria, in spite of its industrial centres (such as Munich, Nuremberg, Augsburg) held a steady position about 10 per cent below the average German income level, with its eastern sections worst off. Parts of Hessen, predominantly the mountainous and small-farming areas, were significantly below the national average, while other parts, like the areas around Frankfurt, Wiesbaden and Kassel were either above the national average or were in the process of developing manufacturing and service industries and thus slowly catching up with the German national average. The most rapidly progressing part of the country, from an economic point of view, was the large region that, after the war, became the Land Baden–Württemberg, and here it was the Württemberg section of it that grew fastest. From a position more than 12 per cent below the average in 1913, it reached the average in the late twenties and rose to around 15 per cent above the average in the thirties.

On the basis of these long term trends of the broad regions of West Germany, one might have expected a still further relative improvement in

---

[1] During the great depression, of course, almost all of the agricultural areas were relatively better off than the industrial areas. But such cyclical movements are not relevant to the immediate purposes of this paper.

G

the position of Baden–Württemberg and also more than average growth in the Rhine–Ruhr industrial agglomeration (though, with hindsight, one might have suspected that structural difficulties would eventually appear in the Ruhr area). The long-term trends also suggested more than average growth in Hessen and in Lower Saxony around Hanover. The industrialisation process in Hessen and southern Lower Saxony was in a position to derive great advantages from the central location within the German market of these areas and from excellent railway and road connections with other parts of the country. Schleswig–Holstein and northern Lower Saxony, being predominantly agricultural areas, might have shown slow, relative decline, but without posing any serious economic problems, in particular if the Hamburg–Lübeck, Bremen and Hanover–Brunswick regions had maintained their (relative) pre-war growth rates and absorbed surplus farm labour from the surrounding agricultural areas. But one could have predicted that large areas in Eastern Bavaria, to the left of the Rhine (the Eifel region) and in the border region of the Ems would need help if they were to be developed satisfactorily.

The 'external shocks' mentioned above have made the West German regional economic problems look somewhat different from the broad long-term trends just outlined. For a limited period of time, until reconstruction got well under way, the biggest problems were found in the cities that had been destroyed. Thus, above all, the industrial areas, both in the Rhine–Ruhr and in other parts of the country, were damaged most. Little attention could be paid to the agricultural areas as such since the most urgent needs for food and housing could better be satisfied there than in the industrial areas. As an immediate pressing economic problem, the new eastern border also was less serious in the late forties than in the fifties and sixties.

Taking a broad view of the agricultural and the industrial sectors of the economy and considering their regional aspects, one may generalise on the post-war development as follows. The war damage to industry and the influx of refugees greatly improved the relative position of agriculture in the West German economy. Since industrial export capacities were at first practically non-existent in the immediate post-war period, and since for this reason the capacity to import was severely limited for all kinds of goods, the population increase in West Germany led to an enormous growth in the demand for domestic agricultural products, while, at the same time, the availability of cheap unemployed labour made it possible to expand total agricultural output well above pre-war levels. But what brought profits to the individual farmer and an apparent advantage to agriculture as a whole, also meant, for a long period, a preservation of inefficient, excessively labour-intensive production methods. In the long run it allowed large numbers of inefficient farmers to carry on as independent operators and thus to withhold their land from more efficient competitors who needed larger areas to modernise their operations. This problem dates back to the thirties when a policy of more complete agricultural autarky was initiated and cheap German labour (partly 'Arbeitsdienst') was made available to agriculture at a time when machinery supplies were relatively small. A similar situation continued during the war and down to the mid-fifties with cheap foreign labour, or to some extent with cheap refugee labour. Thus both the ratio of agricultural population to land and the ratio of agricultural employment to land have been higher from the thirties on than they would have been without cheap labour supplies, with more machinery supplies, and with less protection.

3 TYPES OF REGIONAL STRUCTURAL PROBLEMS

These general trends of development were true of West Germany as a whole, but different agricultural regions were affected in different degrees. The regional development depended on the farm structure, on the existence of manufacturing industries ready to absorb surplus labour, and on the accessibility of the area, with industrialisation, in particular, heavily dependent on the accessibility. The problem areas are, in general, those with little industry and a poor accessibility. These may be divided into three categories:

(1) healthy agricultural areas with a heavy population influx;
(2) small-farming areas with a heavy population influx;
(3) small-farming areas with almost no population influx.

Category 1 comprises Schleswig–Holstein and large parts of Lower Saxony, in whose agricultural areas the population increase from 1939 to 1950 has been between 50 and 100 per cent. There has been no particular agricultural development problem: there has been, in particular, a surplus of labour, and unemployment and agricultural underemployment have had to be reduced. People have had to move out of the region and out of agriculture. The principal problem has been to what extent the surplus people should be moved to other, more industrialised regions, and to what extent industries should be introduced so that the surplus people could stay where they were. Obviously both actions were simultaneously called for, but the problem has been the determination of the optimum for each area between the two extremes.

Category 2 regions were to be found, principally, in Hessen and Bavaria. (By 1950 the population had risen to 150 per cent of the pre-war level in Hessen and 130 per cent in Bavaria.) Here people had to be moved into industrial and tertiary occupations, but at the same time an agricultural development problem existed: from a long-term point of view, farms were too small and inefficient.

In all agricultural areas, the population influx substantially reduced the short-run optimum farm size. But both for technological and institutional reasons, the actual farm size could not easily be reduced and in practice has not been reduced to the extent required. Thus, though the refugees have found employment in large numbers, they have not really been absorbed into the West German agricultural areas; only a few of them have obtained farms of their own. By any ethical standards, this has been unjust; for all practical purposes the indigenous farmers have had to make no sacrifices. But from a more long-term economic point of view, there have been definite economic advantages in this constant and unchangeable farm structure since more people have been free to enter other occupations. The mobility of people has been greater than if farm sizes had been adjusted downwards and more people had obtained farms of their own. (That more recently the farm size flexibility upwards has also turned out to be much too small is another question.)

The pressure on the land was alleviated in the fifties as millions of people were resettled or voluntarily migrated, principally to North Rhine–Westphalia, to Baden–Württemberg and to the industrialised regions of the agricultural states. But even in areas where many of the people who had moved in after the War moved out again in the fifties, the temporary population influx had two effects of long-term importance on the possibilities of economic development. Relatively few of the additional people could be employed in agriculture with a reasonable degree of profitability; on the other hand, the resettlement process, directed as it was towards more industrialised areas with better job opportunities, took time; and in any case not all people wanted to move once more into what they thought was too risky a future. Thus, in the first place, new employment possibilities had also to be opened up in the overpopulated agricultural areas. The more industries were already there (offering agglomeration economies from the start), the easier this was. But in many areas new small nuclei for industrial development had to be created which otherwise might never have come into existence and which gave employment opportunities to the indigenous population also. Secondly, this population influx from distant areas served to aid the break-up of traditional village societies, bringing in new attitudes and new ideas; it increased the intersectoral and interregional mobility and it accelerated the rate of social and economic change, no matter whether this intrusion proceeded smoothly or not.

The Category 3 agricultural areas with no population influx, (as in Rhineland–Palatinate) have also had the experience that the demand for their agricultural produce went up after the war; but the rate of social and economic change was smaller than in most other parts of the country.

Only a few words need to be said about the industrialised areas of West Germany. What is relevant here, is above all, the regional aspects. The increased demand for coal and other primary products led, for a long time, to a forced development of the basic industries. This meant that the Rhine area, and initially also the Saar, were in an extremely advantageous position. People were drawn into the Ruhr agglomeration areas. From a long-term point of view and by comparison with other industrialised countries, the ratio of the value of the output of the basic industries to the total G.N.P. was much above 'normal'. In addition, the share of the whole secondary sector of the economy was, and still is, higher than 'normal' for a country with West Germany's level of *per capita* income. Though there is no such meaningful thing as a 'normal share' of a sector, and though these high ratios for West Germany are partly an indicator of a healthy international division of labour (such as an exchange of West German manufactures for Italian landscape and tourist services), another part of the explanation is the head start that the *basic* industries got in West Germany after the war (and the high investment ratio).

But alongside the basic industries, manufacturing industries developed in many regions, above all along the Rhine and in Baden–Württemberg – industries that were not dependent on local raw materials. These could be expected to have, and actually have had, the highest rates of growth, in particular during the past few years. Apart from the Rhine areas and Baden–Württemberg, flexible, diversified industrial regions also developed in Hessen and around Hanover, Nuremberg and Munich. From a regional point of view, the new frontier in the east and the progressive opening of frontiers in the west had the effect that the whole Rhine area obtained a new central location as an important axis of the E.E.C. market. This also meant that North Rhine–Westphalia acquired a new locational advantage, while areas with eastern border locations, whose traditional economic ties were severed, ran into new difficulties as new markets had to be secured for their industrial development at greater distances.

Summarising the overall development, in the first stages there was an increasing degree of concentration of economic activities and population in the old industrialised regions. Capital attracted people and more capital, and the highest rates of growth of gross regional product were to be found in North Rhine–Westphalia and in Baden–Württemberg, while the regional economies of Schleswig–Holstein, Lower Saxony, and Bavaria lost ground, in which process several million people migrated from the latter, mostly agrarian, states to the most highly industrialised states of Baden–Württemberg and North Rhine–Westphalia. This migration turned out to be the most efficient way of achieving a slow progress towards regional equalisation of *per capita* incomes. While in Schleswig-Holstein and Lower Saxony, the regional product grew more slowly than the German average, *per capita* incomes grew distinctly faster than the average – for Schleswig–Holstein from approximately 30 per cent below the German average in 1959 to only 20 per cent below the average in 1957, and for Lower Saxony from 20 per cent to 17 per cent below these averages. By 1964 the figures closely approached the national average. (This equalisation process is even more true of some smaller regional units, as will be shown below.)

After full employment had been reached in the second half of the fifties, the regional picture changed significantly in one important respect. Speaking very broadly, the incentive for labour to migrate into industrialised areas was greatly reduced: it was no longer the need to find *any* job, but only the desire to secure a significantly *better* job that induced people to migrate. Moreover, by the middle of the fifties, workers were better housed than before and for this reason became less mobile.

Consequently, to a considerably higher degree than before, capital went to labour. Industries moved to the less industrialised areas and drew underemployed labour from agricultural and from less efficient handicrafts and local business firms. This has been reflected in the fact that the poorer states began to grow faster than the developed regions. Schleswig–Holstein, Lower Saxony, and Bavaria grew faster than the West German average, while North Rhine–Westphalia's growth rate fell below the average (Baden–Württemberg and Rhineland–Palatinate being exceptions in that the first continued to grow faster, and the second more slowly, than the average). But since the labour force in the rich states was smaller and that in the agrarian states greater than it would have been if the early migration process had continued, the equalisation process for *per capita* incomes between the states has slowed down. But this slowing down also reflects sectoral differences that are never likely to be eliminated completely. If one considers regional units smaller than states, the geographical concentration of population from small villages into larger towns has continued on a large scale.

On the basis of the foregoing analysis, one may group the West German problem areas into four types:

(A)   low-income agricultural areas suffering from overpopulation;
(B)   backward small-farming agricultural areas;
(C)   special-problem areas;
(D)   new problem areas suffering from an inflexible 'backward' industrial structure.

As Type A, Schleswig–Holstein will be discussed in more detail below. For Type B, a part of the Bavarian and Upper Palatine Forest (B1) near the eastern border of Bavaria, and the Eifel region near the western border (B2) shall be taken. Next, a region in eastern Hessen (but actually called Northern Hessen) will be examined as an example of a special problem area C. Only within a wider context, a few words will be said later on the Ruhr area as an example for Type D.

4 EXAMPLES OF PROBLEM AREAS

(A) A LOW-INCOME AGRICULTURAL AREA: SCHLESWIG–HOLSTEIN

An agrarian state with a pre-war population of 1·6 million and a present population (1967) of 2·5 million, Schleswig–Holstein was close to the *average* national income *per capita* before the war, with increasing industrial employment opportunities near Hamburg (which is not part of Schleswig–Holstein), Kiel, Lübeck, and other growing industrial centres. The state suffered after the war a population influx amounting to almost two-thirds of its pre-war population. In 1950, *per capita* incomes were about 70 per cent of the low post-war West German average. In 1950 only 46 per 1,000 of population were employed in industry (the West German average being 111).

In the subsequent years, improvements in the economic situation of the state were attempted in two ways, both of which were supported by the state and the federal government:

(1) people were induced to move out to more industrialised areas;
(2) industrialisation was stimulated.

Thus the population was reduced by about 20 per cent of the pre-war number – from an index of 164 in 1950 to 143 in 1956 (1939 = 100). During the same period, the ratio of industrial employment was raised by more than 50 per cent: from 46 to 73 per thousand population (or, from two-fifths to a little more than one-half of the West German average, which had risen from 111 in 1950 to 143 in 1956). The relatively healthy state of Schleswig–Holstein's agriculture is reflected in the fact that people engaged in agriculture produced in 1959, in output value *per capita*, 55 per cent more than the West German average, and were able to increase this lead to 220 per cent of the average in 1964.

The picture is less rosy, however, as far as industrial development is concerned. Apart from its disadvantageous location within West Germany, and its unsatisfactory highway connections with the rest of the country, the state has come to regard itself increasingly, from the second half of the fifties on, as holding a supra-national frontier position inside the European Economic Community towards both the EFTA and the COMECON countries. This has increased its relative isolation as compared with the other West German states which have profited much more from the opening up of the frontiers to the west.

Since 1957, industrial employment *per capita* for the state as a whole has not risen further, and the new business enterprises that have been eatablished in Schleswig–Holstein have overwhelmingly been concentrated in the region north of Hamburg, towards Lübeck and, to a much smaller extent, around Kiel, while the rest of the state has attracted almost nothing. Between 1959 and 1964, the regional economy grew a little faster than the whole of the West German economy, but its growth was partly due to a population increase by 4·2 per cent. Thus, the level of *per capita* income in Schleswig–Holstein rose only from 80 to 83 per cent of the West German average.

But these relatively satisfactory average figures conceal the fact that in the northern parts of the state *per capita* incomes are only about half those in the Schleswig–Holstein areas around Hamburg, Lübeck and Kiel. *Per capita* industrial employment in the five northernmost areas (Kreise) is only about one-third of the state's average. Similarly, *per capita* income in the poorest Kreis (Flensburg) was only about two-thirds of the state average in 1964.

The difficulties which – in spite of heavy transfer payments to Schleswig–Holstein – have arisen in getting industries to locate in that state are reflected in the fact that the share of the tertiary sector has risen to an exceptionally high level in Schleswig–Holstein (the employment and income shares are higher than the West German average).

Summarising, while the agricultural development of Schleswig–Holstein has been quite satisfactory and the state profits from an increased demand for tourism, the prospects for industrial development have not turned out to be very good, in particular for the northern parts of the state. The population influx after the war and the state and federal development programmes have been an important stimulus to economic development, and the industrial development has probably gone further than if the low pre-war population density had prevailed throughout. In this way, it has been possible to create new small nuclei for economic development and to strengthen old ones. But there has been, and there still continues to be, a significant intra-state migration towards the southern parts which in the long run may jeopardise the existing development in the central and northern parts of the state. Thus it is necessary to improve the bad accessibility of the state as a whole by better road connections to the rest of West Germany – in particular by the construction of an autobahn to run from Lower Saxony, west of Hamburg, to Neumünster and all the way to Flensburg and the Danish border. As a counter-pull to the Hamburg–Lübeck region, it has been suggested that an industrial region shall be created in the centre of the state – a triangular region near Kiel, Neumünster and Rendsburg. As yet far too little information is available as to the overall profitability of such a scheme. 'Growth centres' in all parts of the state are scheduled to be supported by state and federal programmes, but in this case, too, one knows far too little about how large such growth centres should be or what the optimal distance between them should be. (I shall return to these questions below.) In any case, the intra-state concentration of the population may be expected to continue, partly by migration to the southern parts of the state, possibly also through the development of a central industrial area in the Kiel–Neumünster–Rendsburg region, and almost certainly also through a concentration *im kleinen* of the Schleswig-Holstein population.

(B) SMALL-AGRICULTURAL REGIONS: BAVARIAN AND UPPER PALATINE FOREST REGION (B1), EIFEL (B2)

These are two areas of small farming, with inadequate acreage per person in agriculture, and with too few industrial firms and other enterprises to support the rest of the population. The regions are, moreover, mountainous, with a severe climate and poor soil. From an economic point of view, a major difference between the areas is the fact that the Forest region (B1) has had a post-war population influx of about one-third of its pre-war population, while the second has absorbed no refugees but has on the other hand lost 7 per cent of its 1939 population, in spite of a very high birth-rate, through migration. The population of the Forest region declined down to 1965 but is slowly increasing again (with 1939 =100, it was 133 in 1946, 132 in 1950, 119 in 1956, 118 in 1961 but 122 in 1965). The population of the Eifel region has steadily grown since 1946, mostly as a result of natural population increase (with 1939 =100, it was 93 in 1946, 102 in 1950, 110 in 1956, 115 in 1961, 121 in 1965). In both areas, extensive and expensive attempts have been made to set into motion a strong industrialisation process.

In the Forest region a start was made immediately after the war with large numbers of refugee firms. But many of these enterprises collapsed later because they turned out to be inefficient – the result of the isolated location of the region, its poor accessibility and its inadequate infrastructure. Nevertheless, the industrial employment figures per 1,000 of population have steadily gone up, from 44 in 1952 to 69 in 1959 to 75 in 1961, and have continued to do so during the sixties, reaching 84 in 1964. Since 1961 the support programmes have been stepped up. This has helped to retard the population outflow and has, for the first time, raised *per capita* gross domestic product to a level more than half the West German average. But it has to be stressed that the agricultural structure is still very unsatisfactory, in just the same respects as in the other area.

The Eifel region has had the advantage of being somewhat less isolated, but since it experienced no population inflow after the war, traditional attitudes have persisted more than in the rest of the country. *Per capita* incomes are higher than in the Forest region (64 per cent of West German average in 1957, 68 per cent in 1961), but recent changes have been small. Industrial employment per 1,000 of population has also not grown significantly since the middle fifties (it was 41 in 1951, 55 in 1957, 59 in 1961, 60 in 1964). The Federal Government supports an industrial development programme in the region, but it is questionable whether in

G 2

the long run this will be economically successful, in spite of the fact that the Eifel region occupies a central geographical position among the countries of the European Economic Community. Obviously good road connections need to be provided and the educational system needs to be improved; also, a number of cities should be enabled to supply more basic central services to their districts. But as an alternative to an artificial industrialisation programme, the plan to develop the Eifel region into a large recreation area for people from the western stretch of West Germany, from Lorraine and from eastern Belgium seems to be both cheaper and more desirable in the long run. The area's accessibility will be greatly improved when the planned autobahn connections with the adjacent areas in the north, east, and south have been finished. This should also make it easier for additional industries to move into the region. But it will also make it more likely that people will move out, as soon as the interior parts of the region have increased their contacts with the outside world and traditional attitudes have more and more changed. On the basis of the available information, it is in any case impossible to determine with any degree of certainty what the optimal population density for the region and the number of growth centres should be.

5   A SPECIAL PROBLEM AREA

NORTHERN HESSEN

The region of Northern Hessen is an area that has experienced economic difficulties as compared with the rest of West Germany, and for a variety of reasons. Much of the area has small-farming on not very good soil, and a large part of the area has been affected by the new eastern frontier. But even within the Northern Hessen region, these factors have been operative in widely different degrees. At the same time a variety of other factors have contributed to a development that is characterised by great inter-local and regional differences. It is just these differences that make the region as a whole an almost ideal subject for a detailed study of locational factors as they have been at work during the recent past. I began such a study a few months ago in connection with the preparation of this paper. The main objective of this study is to determine how far traditional locational factors have been operating and what the main determinants for the migration of people and of business firms have been. As yet no quantitative results can be offered, but in a qualitative way some preliminary results can be given.

After the reconstruction process in West Germany had started, the region was at first much worse off than most other regions of Germany, partly because of an exceptionally high post-war inflow of people many of whom could not be employed, and partly because traditional hinterlands and supply connections had been cut off and the accessibility of large parts of the region had been severely reduced. This was true above all of the areas close to the eastern frontier. But with the help of the post-war labour influx, and with public support, new industrial firms were established in all parts of the region. Through intensive road construction, including the improvement of connecting roads to the autobahn that crosses Northern Hessen, the accessibility of the region has been progressively improved. Money has been poured into the region both by the Federal Government under its regional improvement programmes and by the State Government of Hessen under its Hessen Plan and its agricultural improvement programmes, which have helped in particular to improve the size structure of the farms (which is, however, still not wholly satisfactory).

Since not all parts of the Northern Hessen region were affected in the same way by all these factors, a very varied picture has persisted. This makes this region much more interesting for a locational analysis than the other regions.

The objective of the study has been to discover in what kinds of places industries have grown and how population figures have changed as a result. Since no separate income data are available for the approximately 1,500 towns and villages of the eighteen Kreise of the region, the study had to proceed on the basis of the population data (a study on the eighteen Kreise and their economic development is to follow; for the individual Kreise, employment and gross product figures are available for three selected years). Instead of investigating, in *two* steps, (i) how industrial sites have been determined and how they have affected employment and incomes and (ii) how employment possibilities and other factors have influenced people's decisions as to their choice of place of residence, these two steps have had to be combined. The hypothesis has been that new choices of residence are determined on the basis of both the industrial growth potentialities and tertiary services that are offered in the neighbourhoods of potential residential sites.

The preliminary results of the study may be summarised as follows. The population changes from 1956 to 1961, as measured by growth rates, for the 1,500 towns and villages have to a significant degree been dependent on the following factors:

(a) To start with a negative result, raw material sites *may* explain the existence of old industrial centres, but they cannot explain current *growth rates* of industry and population any longer. Growth has not been dependent on raw material sites.

(b) An important factor has been the industry structure at the beginning of the investigation period. This structure is measured by the employment shares of broad industrial sectors weighted by past national and state growth rates of these sectors. The share of agriculture is certainly important but its influence is inconclusive;

a large share of agriculture may be a retarding factor, but it may also be beneficial if additional labour can be supplied by agriculture. (On a broad scale, the latter has been true of the past development of Baden-Württemberg.)

(c) Another factor has been the availability of industrial sites measured by the area made available for industrial use divided by the sum of the new industrial areas plus old industrial areas (and multiplied by 100). It is here that aid programmes have played an important role, just as in the construction of new roads.

(d) Development of the towns has also been influenced by their accessibility. This is to be measured by the number of roads crossing at the town, by the road qualities (local road, highway, etc.), and by the distance from the nearest autobahn.

(e) The distance from the frontier, which had been most important, in a negative sense, in the early fifties, has steadily diminished in importance as excellent roads have been built to serve all isolated areas. This is not true, however, for towns quite close to the frontier that have lost important economic connections. For small centres, the effects of the frontier seem to decline rapidly after 10 kilometres and it seems to disappear completely after about 20 kilometres. This does not mean, however, that the Northern Hessen region *as a whole* might not be considerably better-off *vis-à-vis* the Rhine areas if Nordhessen had remained near the centre of a national economy. The accessibility of the region will further improve when the new autobahn, Bad Hersfeld–Fulda–Würzburg, has been completed, which will establish an almost direct autobahn connection from Hamburg–Hanover–Kassel to Nuremberg and Munich.

(f) It also appears that the growth rate of a town has been a function of the size of the town. Towns with a certain minimum size (around 1,000 population) tend to grow much faster than smaller towns. Thus there has been a concentration *im kleinen* of the population. This reflects the fact that people have moved closer to their jobs and/or to places that offered more tertiary functions: either shopping facilities or recreational, cultural and administrative services. Obviously for these services a minimum town and surrounding population is necessary from which customers may be drawn.

(g) Since the attractiveness of a town is not just a function of its size, at least one special feature has to be taken into account also – its importance as an administrative centre. For Kreis (county district) centres an additional variable (K) is introduced which is set equal to zero for all other towns. K will measure the number of people within the administrative area of the Kreis centre (with allowance for population density of the area over which these people are spread).

(*h*) Since the supply sites of central services are not spread evenly over the whole area but are concentrated at certain points in space, one may expect that, at certain distances from each other, somewhat larger agglomerations will develop. Small towns that are very close to growth centres may be expected to profit from spill-over effects of these centres, while towns at certain minimum distances from bigger towns will develop into small growth centres themselves. But towns somewhere in between are worst-off. Such effects can be observed within Northern Hessen. A distance of 5 to 6 kilometres from a small centre seems to be the most advantageous distance, while distances above 10 kilometres from the nearest centre give larger villages a chance to grow into small growth centres of their own. (Thus one factor in the distance variable to be used is the number of kilometres from the nearest larger centre minus 5, and I shall further experiment with these distances.) The relevant distances depend in any case on the population density of the area. On the next three higher levels of centrality, 20–25 kilometres, 40 kilometres and 80 kilometres appear to have been advantageous distances for the development of higher order centres.

(*i*) Furthermore, in a number of cases the available statistics do not contradict the hypothesis that growth has been a positive function of the step-up of Federal aid to the particular county district.

In conclusion, the region of Northern Hessen is an interesting subject of investigation because, starting from a position of disadvantage both as to its location and its agricultural and industrial structure and with a *per capita* income much below the West German average, the region has managed – with outside help – to grow substantially faster than the average, and after an initial outflow of population it has been able to stop this outflow through the incentive of high economic growth rates. At present, the regional population growth rate is roughly equal to the West German average. It was only in 1959 that *per capita* gross regional product of the Regierungsbezirk Kassel had reached a level as high as 75 per cent of the West German average; by 1961 it had risen to 83 per cent and only four years later it was up to 86 per cent of the West German average (on the basis of preliminary figures for 1966, it has maintained its above-average increase and had probably reached a level of 88 per cent in 1966).

Such a regional study is interesting to the extent that it can show us more clearly what kinds of spatial concentrations have occurred, based on what factors, and to what extent raw materials, good accessibility, and the existence of other business firms are necessary for the initial creation and subsequent growth of industrial nuclei. For a thorough understanding of these relationships is a prerequisite for policy decisions on the degree of specialisation or spatial concentration of the secondary and tertiary sectors in centres of various sizes. Only if the results of market forces are better understood, can more exact judgements be made of the effects of aid programmes.

For these reasons, the above study has had to be supplemented with a more detailed analysis of the two aspects mentioned earlier :[1] the chain of causation from basic factors to business decisions, on the one hand, and that from business decisions to residence decisions of private households on the other hand (and then back again from the places of residences to the business decisions).

Furthermore, a similar study is necessary at a higher level, that is to say on the regional distribution and growth of larger cities and agglomerations in West Germany after the war. The important relationships to be studied are those between growth rates and (i) the absolute size of a city including its suburbs, (ii) its central functions (administrative and others) and its supply areas, (iii) its location and its accessibility, in particular the distances to the nearest bigger cities, and (iv) its industry structure.

Investigations have shown that, as far as central functions and agglomeration economies are concerned, there may be certain population or city size threshold values beyond which new kinds of economies become effective. The relevant population figures may be minimum values of around 1,000, around 20,000, around 100,000, and then again beyond 500,000 or 750,000 including the associated hinterland – depending very much, however, on other factors also such as the size and population of the associated hinterland and of competing centres.

6   FURTHER ISSUES

Before an optimal set of regional programmes can be devised, one has to know much more than is known at present, at least in the West German Federal and State Regional Planning offices, about the optimal spatial distribution of population and business activities in a central European country – not just in a static but in a dynamic setting, and on the basis of certain political and welfare aims. The basic problem as it has presented itself in West Germany is how far a further concentration of people and of economic activities is to be encouraged or discouraged – both on a larger scale, as it concerns the states and their large agglomerations, and on a smaller scale, within smaller regions.

The answer depends in part, obviously, on the costs of the various elements of infrastructure as a function of the size and density of the agglomeration, as well as on the ability and willingness of the public authorities to supply them. On the other side of the question much more needs to be known about the 'demand for infrastructure' and the 'demand for agglomeration economies', both from producers' and consumers'

[1] See p. 185.

points of view. To secure more information on this matter, questions to be studied are, apart from the usual questions about the optimal site of a given plant, the following:

(i) The extent to which it is feasible for various activities to be separated (i.e. to delegate parts of the production process to branch plants in less industrialised areas) as against the economies of a vertical integration of the process.

(ii) The extent to which factor input coefficients may be adapted to the particular regional or local factor proportions as reflected in different regional factor price relations (the old Thünen problem of agricultural location theory in so far as it not only determines optimal product choices, but also optimal input coefficients as a function of the distance from a certain reference point).

(iii) The optimal output or activity mix of a producing centre. The problem as distinct from that mentioned under (i) is to what extent big firms which prefer to have their administrative offices in a capital city can move their production sites to smaller cities or towns with little industry. For this, one needs to know to what extent the so-called agglomeration economies are based on product interrelationships as opposed to the advantages of a large labour market. If the importance of the labour market is paramount, then a much greater degree of spatial decentralisation is possible or feasible *wherever workers commute in cars of their own* and thus are mobile over short distances. This is true in particular if instead of, say, a 20-minute ride over 5 miles through the rush-hour traffic of a large city, the same person could reach a decentralised branch plant, maybe 10 miles away, within no more than 12 minutes. The same would hold true for a well-known specialised store, or even a theatre, in a *smaller* city. This all leads to the question of the optimal degree of specialisation of economic activities and is to be seen in the context of the next question.

(iv) The extent that hierarchic or specialised structures should be realised in a spatial setting – or, more technically: with regard to which activities do we need (modified) Christaller structures and where do we need (even more modified) Lösch structures?

Much of the regional planning of West Germany is based on the idea that there has to be a hierarchy of centres in which bigger centres always provide not just a greater variety of services but, in particular, supply at the same time all the goods and services that all smaller centres offer. If the question is formulated in the usual way as: 'What kinds of services should be offered in cities of what size?' then the idea easily follows that all centres, at least as far as the tertiary sector is concerned, should be very much alike, and that there should be a clear-cut hierarchy of centres. This notion is certainly correct as far as schools, movies, dime stores, groceries and the like are concerned. But in my opinion this should not be applied to more specialised services when these require a very high degree of specialisation, or very specialised skills, or which depend on relatively few people of many communities with a particular taste, or with specialised needs. To illustrate, not every city has to have *specialised* fashion stores, or a good theatre, or a good department of theology, or a university with a good economics department.

More specialisation is obviously feasible wherever substantial internal economies accrue to the producer, but the external economies in shopping for the purchases concerned are small. The latter consideration applies if the particular purchase is very important, or if for other reasons a trip will be made in any case even if other activities are not always combined with it. For such activities the Christaller conception of a hierarchy of centres need not be applied. But several questions arise. At what places should groups of elements in a hierarchical spatial set-up be provided? What is our conception of the right degree of spatial specialisation between different cities, as well as between different shopping centres within the same city or metropolitan area? How far are there quite different considerations that need to be added? I hasten to stress that the questions raised above under (i) to (iv) cannot be seen in isolation.

To focus once more on crucial alternatives to be considered in the context of locational choice and optimal spatial structure, let me simplify the problem of a given firm that seeks a new location by considering only the following three dimensions of the problem: (1) size of the town, (2) number of other firms, (3) land rents plus tax rates. If one neglects for the moment differences of wage and capital sites, the important questions to be asked about a location are:

(*a*) How many potential customers, with how much purchasing power, are accessible from the site? Or simplified and reduced to one dimension: what is the city size (neglecting the location of the city relative to other cities)?

(*b*) How many other firms (of what size) exist? That is, (i) competitors, (ii) firms that either supply inputs to this firm, or buy its outputs, or are complementary to this firm from *other* firms' points of view. Or, reduced from as many dimensions as there are different types of 'other firms' to one dimension: what is the possible weighted index of other (competitive or complementary) firms?

(*c*) How much does the potential site cost (rent on the land) and what are the costs of the infrastructure that have to be paid in the forms of taxes (considering only one particular state of the infrastructure for each town, thus leaving important variations in community services and tax rates out of the picture)?

For this purpose, take a 'representative bale' of land and infrastructure and community services and put down hypothetical prices p^* for this bale at which the firm would be equally well off (i.e. making a given level of profits) – hypothetical prices as a function of (1) the number (n) of selected other firms and (2) the size of the town. Wherever for a given town, the curve representing these hypothetical prices – the price-indifference curve for a given profit level – moves up, this implies that the firm expects to reap additional advantages (agglomeration economies) from being close to other firms (and thus would be able to pay higher rents or higher taxes). Fig. 1 gives an example of such a set of curves for four different city sizes.

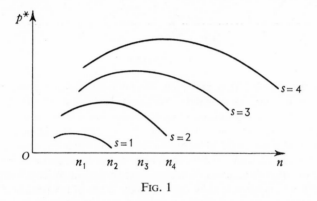

FIG. 1

It is highly significant to know where, for different activities, these curves move upwards and at what number of firms curve maxima ($n_1, \ldots, N_4$) are reached, and, in particular, what prices p^* the firm could pay in alternative environments. If the firms included in n supply complementary goods or produce intermediate goods that this firm uses, the price-indifference curve would rise throughout – unless these other firms would worsen the traffic situation (or the labour market situation) for the firm in question.

Alternatively, instead of the number of firms, one might consider the number of possible local 'contacts' with other firms and with organisations or political agencies and the like, the contacts being somehow weighted in accordance with their importance.

To frame regional policy in regard to the size of new centres, it would be desirable to know these functional relationships in numerical terms for different types of businesses, not only in the simplified terms here discussed, but also with all the complicating considerations from which we have been abstracting in these paragraphs. It would be desirable to know whether the relevant curves are like those in Fig. 2(a), or in 2(b) or 2(c) or 2(d), to give just four examples for two city sizes ($S_1 = 1$, $S_2 = 2$).

In determining its optimal location, the firm would consider the number of other firms and compare the actual prices at alternative sites with the corresponding hypothetical prices for *different profit levels* (for a higher profit level, the price-indifference curve would lie below the initial curve)

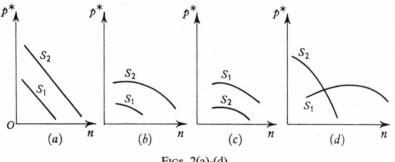

Figs. 2(a)-(d)

and choose that location at which the price-indifference curve with the highest profit index is reached. Within a theoretical model, one could describe static and dynamic equilibrium conditions for prices and locations and study the implications. For actual policy problems knowledge about these relationships could help one in answering such questions as these: How far is it likely that the effect of a low level of local contacts (or a small number of other firms) will be neutralised by certain price advantages of the location? What would be the necessary levels of tax rates and rents to enable a certain town to compete successfully with another, much bigger, town? What interstate transfer payments would this imply? If there are just a few firms that need each other and contacts with all other firms are not significant, then all of them could jointly locate at a greater distance from the centre even though separately they could not do this) and thereby have the advantage of being closer to their employees' places of residence.

Extending the analysis to interregional wage rate differences, the question is how far inadequate agglomeration economies at a location may be offset by lower wage bills. In some cases in West Germany, firms have had difficulties in finding enough labour even in less developed areas which were thought to have underemployment. Was it that they have attempted to absorb too large a proportion of the total local labour force within too short a time?

In qualitative terms at least, a great deal is known about these problems for all kinds of industries, but I would submit that much too little is known (not only by myself but also by many of the policy makers of West Germany) about the quantitative relationships, in particular with regard to inter-firm contacts and interrelationships, which are as important as the pure input-output relationships about which much more is known in quantitative terms.

But since not all firms have very close contacts, direct or indirect, with all or even the majority of other firms in an agglomeration, at least one important qualitative general result follows. Wherever firms do not have to be close to very many other firms – do not have to cluster like stores in a central business district – but need fast road and railroad connections, and wherever distances to places of residence are of great importance, a spatial distribution like that in Fig. 3 would be the result – a combination of nodes and of industrial zones connecting them. This holds in particular if the diseconomies and costs of traffic congestion are taken into account and if deliveries have to be made to and from other more distant areas. I hasten to add that the detailed layout of such a system (60 degree or 90 degree angles, for example) would need to be determined at the basis of geographical features and historical trends. Furthermore, in between big centres large recreation areas might be envisaged (thus the Eifel region would fit in at the left in Fig. 3 at *E*). On a smaller scale, the picture of Fig. 3 might be repeated with suitable adjustments (fewer industrial zones between the centres), and on the smallest scale of the spatial layout more

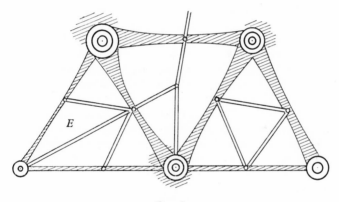

Fig. 3

and more non-economic factors would contribute to the determination of the structure. In any case the relevant question would necessarily be what would be the cost of a given spatial structure in economic as well as in psychic, social and political terms.

7 CONCLUSIONS

Returning to the actual spatial layout of economic activities in West Germany (see Map 1, p. 172), it can be seen that, in spite of the existence of the Ruhr industrial area, the picture looks reasonably balanced, more particularly if recent trends are considered. There is, of course, the heavy agglomeration in the Ruhr but, on the one hand, agglomerations are necessary and, on the other hand, the heart of the Ruhr has grown distinctly less rapidly than the rest of the country as a whole. The existing industrial structure, as embodied, among other things, in the land-use structure and in the residential areas, has been a great handicap to further economic development; people do not wish to live there, and new firms have difficulties in obtaining land because old firms (in particular the coal mining companies) literally sit on it.

Apart from the Ruhr, there are the Rhine–Main (Frankfurt) and the Rhine–Neckar (Mannheim–Ludwigshafen–Heidelberg) agglomerations, the Stuttgart centre which stretches through large parts of Baden-Württemberg, the centres of Munich and Nuremberg in Bavaria, the Saar basin around Saarbrücken, and in the north the big commercial and manufacturing centre of Hamburg, and, somewhat smaller, Bremen and Hanover and Kassel.

Quite significantly, more and more diversified industrial zones have developed (Baden-Württemberg and areas north-west and south-east of the Ruhr) and on the whole the outskirts of the big agglomerations grow most rapidly and develop into industrial zones that tend to link the big agglomerations with each other – Hamburg grows towards Lübeck, Hanover towards Hildesheim and Brunswick and Wolfsburg. The Ruhr grows towards the north-west, south-east and south-west, with Cologne and its surroundings developing into a large centre of its own, the Frankfurt area grows in almost all directions, and similarly there is rapid growth also in other parts of Hessen, in Bavaria, and almost all other parts of the country. Thus on the whole, the regional structure is not a very bad one, with growing new centres and the areas between the agglomerations being built up as industrial zones. Smaller centres have proved their viability, in particular if they had a good location (good accessibility), or an important administrative or political function (as Bonn), or merely good fortune.

Regional policy has subsidised all the problem areas and has picked certain towns and has helped them to develop into lower-order centres. This has been a wise policy. But as yet too little is known about optimum town sizes and service areas, about the optimal degree of centralisation or decentralisation and specialisation, and how adaptation best takes place in a dynamic setting.

Great reserves still exist in the agricultural parts of the country. Agricultural policy has failed on a large scale, partly because of the vested interests of pressure groups. For them, the existence of subsistence farming was a better vehicle for obtaining price subsidies than a healthy farm would have been.

It has to be seen whether new industrial nuclei in agricultural areas prove to be attractive to new firms and whether in the future regional money-wage differences will be great enough to counteract the pull towards the agglomeration areas.

At present, the chances for backward areas to become strongly industrialised and to catch up with the advanced industrial areas are small. Growth in the backward areas depends on growth in the advanced regions, and differences in the economic opportunities of various regions cannot be eliminated by subsidies, and from an economic point of view they ought not to disappear completely. Thus one should never expect a complete equalisation of regional *per capita* incomes.

But apart from the chances of backward areas to become industrialised, much remains to be desired as regards the accessibility of the backward regions and their educational facilities, as well as the co-ordination of regional policies at various administrative levels. Nevertheless, on the whole as much has been achieved as might realistically have been expected with regard to balanced regional development. Only if someone had expected that regional policies would make all regions equally well off, would the past performance have to be called a failure. But if one has in mind that there are no really depressed areas in West Germany, the regional development may, as a whole, be termed satisfactory. This does not however settle the question whether the overall regional development has been the effect of the overall economic development or of regional economic measures. My own view is that in the past ten years it was mainly the overall economic development. Moreover, before one terms a situation unsatisfactory, one has at least to be able to define in a clear-cut way in which direction one should have moved to obtain better results without wasting resources on ill-founded industrialisation programmes (here, of course, sociological and political considerations enter heavily).

I am far from convinced that regional policies as a whole could have done much better, not because I am in any sense against the planning of regional development (which I am not), but because I am not sure that we yet know enough about the relevant facts and interrelationships to give a well-founded judgement and to define clear-cut aims. A number of questions on economic interrelationships may be easier to answer when the regional effects of the current economic recession have become known in detail.

10 Industrial Location Policy and the Problems of Sparsely Populated Areas in Sweden

Erik Bylund
UMEÅ UNIVERSITY

1 PROBLEMS

The concept of underdevelopment is largely relative. The degree of development, economic or cultural, in any one area should always be seen in relation to the level of development in other areas of the same country. Thus an area may appear to be highly developed in relation to one area, but in comparison with another it may seem underdeveloped.

As far as Sweden is concerned it is possible to distinguish areas with varying economic and cultural standards; consequently it would be possible to point to certain areas which are less developed than others. The struggle for human equality brings with it desires and attempts to develop these so-called underdeveloped areas. The object is to achieve, as far as possible, the most equal and just distribution of a country's prosperity.

The so-called location policy which has been introduced in Sweden means that the State, in the form of loans and direct contributions to firms for new location or the expansion of existing firms, will help bring about a removal of those differences in economic levels which can be seen in the country. The aims of Sweden's location policy are as follows:

(1) The policy of location is designed to be an integral part of an active industrial policy and to promote rapid economic progress.
(2) The policy of location is designed to help to provide the population with satisfactory social and cultural services.
(3) The security of the individual is to be safeguarded during the reconstruction of society.
(4) Sweden's defence policy is to be provided for.

These objectives need to be seen against the background of generally accepted conditions for the economic policy in its entirety. These conditions were stated more than a year ago in a government report as follows: free choice of consumption; free economic competition; free choice of employment; and free right to establish an enterprise. These basic principles are recognised as being generally accepted in Sweden; and this is certainly a correct judgement of public opinion.

It can be said that the general attitude in Sweden towards the present structural transformation in commercial and industrial life is clearly favourable. This attitude is due, naturally enough, to the realisation that an effective commercial and industrial structure is a basic necessity for a continued and rapid increase in real income. But this favourable attitude is also based on the belief that the State is prepared to try to overcome the difficulties of the transformation and to alleviate the pressures on individuals which can result from such rapid economic change. It is quite clear that a change of this nature demands that society takes an active part in the event.

It very rarely happens in these days, however, that economic changes occur with any uniformity over a whole country. Industrial and commercial life is not the same everywhere in the country, it is heterogeneously differentiated; different trades are represented in different parts of the country; various branches of industry have different indices of location in different areas. This means that an economic change in one branch of an industry or trade has different regional effects depending on the area where the firm in question is located. One region will be more severely affected by an economic depression than another region. Now that the State is taking various steps to alleviate the effects (chiefly, of course, the adverse effects) of an economic change or a structural rationalisation, the Government must have a definite policy not only in regard to the question of distribution between the various sectors of industrial life, but also in regard to the regional distribution of supplies and resources. There is no doubt in my mind that the central problem of planning here involved is that of the rational distribution of our resources in respect of trades and regions. The debate about the so-called policy of location is first and foremost concerned with the regional distribution of resources and the principles governing this distribution.

The present economic development in Sweden has to a large extent helped to bring this problem within the bounds of the location debate. The actual economic development in the past few years has caused one region in Sweden to suffer more than any other as regards employment as a result of the present structural rationalisation of industry.

This region is Northern Sweden, Norrland as it is called, and especially the interior and northern parts. This is because the old basic industries of Norrland's livelihood, agriculture, forestry, forest industry and mining, are all industries which are in the process of being thoroughly rationalised. For example Sweden's largest firm in the field of forest industry, Sveriges Cellulosa AB, has more than doubled its production of pulp over the last ten years, quadrupled its production of paper, but has at the same time reduced employment from about 17,000 employees to 13,000. The same is true of the other industries. This has meant that Norrland's local activities and its industrial activities, based on the local natural resources, cannot continue to provide employment without the demand for man-power falling more and more rapidly. This has meant that Norrland has been subjected to a very heavy depopulation that began in the first half of the 1960s. The four most northerly counties, with a total of 903,000 inhabitants in 1967, have lost so many people that the net changes represented a reduction in the population of some 5,600 a year for all the four counties in 1961–4. During the last two years, 1965–6, a change has taken place. The losses were considerably less in 1965, and there was actually an increase in population in 1966 in all the four counties with the exception of Jämtland (– 1,000; + 1,800 in the others). A lively argument has now begun as to the reasons for the change during the last few years. Many would like to interpret this favourable trend in 1966 as a result of the so-called policy of location; others point to the diminished attraction of the southern parts of the country because the labour market there has hardened.

2 THE POLICY OF LOCATION

I come now to the policy of location and the actual form it takes. If unlimited resources had been available it is unlikely that the heated discussion about the justification of the policy of location and the form it has taken would have occurred. The debate, however, must be seen against the background of the general trend of economic development in Sweden in the 1960s. The first half of the 1960s was marked by an upward trend seldom before experienced in Sweden. I shall not attempt to examine in further detail the reasons for this. I would merely point out that the gross national product in Sweden showed a yearly increase of 5–6 per cent over the first five years of the 1960s – a considerably higher rate of growth than the average of only 3 per cent for the 1950s. The first half of the 1960s is thus characterised by a growth of the gross national product which has brought Sweden into the group of leading countries as compared with the rest of the world; there are very few European countries which exceed the Swedish figure of income per head. The reason was partly connected with the favourable international economic situation of Sweden and partly with favourable trends in the labour market within the country itself. I would particularly draw attention to the fact that the demand for additional manpower was propitious, in the sense that large numbers of children born during the war years began to enter the labour market. In all activities Sweden was thus able to enjoy a considerable expansion during the first half of the 1960s.

More recently, however, a completely different trend has started. Briefly, we cannot expect the same high growth rate in the future, partly because of less favourable trends in world markets; world market prices for Sweden's chief export products, pulp, timber goods and iron ore, are falling and thus constitute an unfavourable factor. In addition, the supply of manpower will be reduced in future because of the reduction in the birth-rate after the middle of the 1940s. Thus additional manpower available will be considerably less. Price trends are also unfavourable because of the greatly increased demand and the difficulty of meeting it. There are fairly strong inflationary tendencies in Sweden at present. The so-called 'Long Investigation' established the fact that we can only reckon on about a 4 per cent increase of gross national product a year down to the middle 1970s. And even this will not be achieved unless all available productive resources are fully employed. It is in this connection that the policy of location comes into the picture. To what extent is a regional redistribution of our resources going to affect adversely the growth of the national product and our standards of life? We have a given, and rather restricted, framework of resources and it is thus necessary to distribute them both sectorally and regionally in the best possible way within this framework, so as to bring about the greatest possible increase in the national product. There are now many who think that a policy which entails an increase in the resources of the weaker areas, the depopulated areas in Norrland, would be disadvantageous to this effort to achieve the greatest possible productive efficiency. This would be better achieved by encouraging the concentration of our resources at certain points in the middle and south of Sweden.

We have, however, already decided on a policy of location which directs certain of our resources towards Norrland – something which many consider to be a withdrawal of resources from the central and southern parts of the country. The reason for the introduction of this policy of location was to be found in the alarming reports of depopulation in Norrland – the figures which I quoted earlier. With its customary thoroughness the Government carried out a so-called location investigation, the original intention of which was unquestionably to give government assistance to the very weakest areas in the interior of Norrland by means of loans and investments in industrial concerns. One suggestion that emerged from the investigation was that the criteria to be satisfied in order that an area might receive a share of the government subsidy should be these: that this assistance should go chiefly to the interior areas of Norrland; that it should be available to regions with especially high unemployment and a large increase in the employable population; that in addition it should benefit regions which had a small proportion of the occupied population engaged in manufacturing industries and a low average net income per inhabitant. The areas concerned were, for these reasons, chiefly located in the interior of Norrland. The Government did not, however, accept this proposal but held that almost the whole of Norrland, including the coastal areas, should be eligible for the government subsidy. The so-called subsidised areas that were finally determined north of this line can be seen in Map 1. As can be seen, the boundary of the subsidised area cuts diagonally across the country, mainly following the boundary of the so-called Norrland terrain, from the boundary between the provinces of Gästrikland and Hälsingland diagonally across the country to the northern parts of the county of Bohus. The Government took the view that the trends of population showed that the problem was not confined to the interior of Norrland; the whole of Norrland was in danger from heavy depopulation. Thus it would be necessary to strengthen industry in all parts of Norrland where industrial enterprises could be carried on with profit on an economic basis. As can also be seen from Map 1, this has meant that the government subsidy which had up to that time been given to Norrland had been concentrated chiefly in the coastal areas: about 80 per cent of all assistance was given to the coastal areas, while a typical inland county, such as that of Jämtland, had received up to this time only 4 per cent of the location subsidy, made available in the form of loans and direct contributions from the State. In this way the subsidy went to areas in Norrland which already had been and still are expanding areas. But it was considered urgent to speed up this expansion in order to slow down the depopulation of the areas concerned as quickly as possible. To judge from the figures for 1966 quoted earlier, it can perhaps be claimed to have had a certain amount of success. But it is interesting to note that another and more difficult problem arose in consequence. Taking everything into account, the policy of location will not promote industrial life in the vast sparsely populated areas of the interior to any considerable extent; this is because there are few industrial firms there and it is the firms themselves which have to take the initiative in obtaining a government grant; there will not, therefore, be many applications from inland regions and in consequence neither will there be much financial assistance to these areas. The assistance goes to those areas where there are already firms which see here a possibility of a short-cut to quick capital. Many applications come in from expanding areas and location grants are given. On the other hand the stimulation of industrial life along the coast, now undertaken with government aid, will hasten the depopulation of inland areas and will shorten the time available for something to be done for the areas with the greatest problems. People have, in fact, moved more quickly than was expected from the inland areas to the expanding areas on the coast.

3   HISTORICAL CAUSES OF BACKWARDNESS

In these circumstances, it may perhaps be worth while to look back a little at the historical developments which led to this situation in the interior of Norrland. The Government's earlier policy of colonisation was designed by various methods to alleviate difficulties and encourage settlement in Norrland. The most recent widespread attempt by the

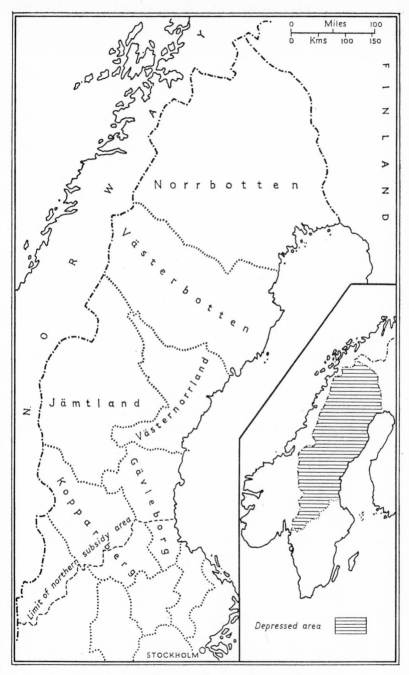

MAP 1: THE NORTHERN SUBSIDY AREA OF SWEDEN

State to increase the cultivated areas and to create a new means of support in Norrland based on agriculture was the so-called colonising policy of the 1920s and 30s; it was then hoped that, by the extensive improvement of swamplands, new agricultural units, so-called colonies, could be established thus stimulating consumer demand at a time of economic depression and unemployment in the country. In parenthesis it must be said that this policy failed – partly because the colonies were wrongly located, and partly because many colonists coming from the south of Sweden were completely unused to the conditions in the interior of Norrland, and were not able to adapt themselves to the life there. Steps were also taken to encourage forestry in an attempt to extend the spread of settlements, especially in the inland parts of northern Norrland. From the 1890s right down to the 1940s, forest and crown smallholdings were set up and subsidised by different forms of grant, in order to ensure a supply of manpower for forestry in the Government's very extensive territories.

All these government actions in the past have contributed greatly to the picture of very isolated settlements that we have everywhere in Norrland, except along the coast and the river valleys where settlements are rather more closely concentrated. Much of what is now happening in respect of land depopulation and decline of settlements must be seen against this background of the colonising policy undertaken by the Government over a long period of time. It is unquestionable that many of the steps that have been taken and are likely to be taken in the future to help the population of these depopulated areas are motivated by the sense of responsibility which the authorities today feel for the effect of earlier measures when settlers were enticed into the interior of Norrland.

Another significant factor is the fact that the natural increase of population in Norrland right down to recent times has been abnormally large and has brought into the labour market a much greater addition to the available manpower than in southern or central Sweden. It is true that the picture is now beginning to change rapidly because of the high emigration rate of people in the child-bearing age-groups and the consequent inversion of the normal age pyramids. As a result of this, conditions will no longer be favourable to a high birth-rate. In earlier years, and over a long period, the interior of the county of Norrbotten had the highest birth-rate in Sweden. The general birth-rate was between 25 and 30 per thousand. But even in Norrbotten, which has had a notoriously high birth-rate, there are now a dozen parishes with fewer births per thousand than the national average, which is no more than about 15 per thousand. The reserves of manpower in the north are declining rapidly but this decline has only begun during the last ten years. Norrland's labour market is still affected by the large increase in the birth-rate which continued right up to the beginning of the 1960s.

A third factor of very great significance in explaining the surplus manpower in Norrland today is the fact that agriculture has provided employment for a very long time for a larger proportion of the population than it has further south. This is still particularly true in the central areas where migration has been greatest. There agriculture, combined with a number of subsidiary industries, was able to provide a livelihood for a considerably larger number of people than if agriculture alone had been the only means of subsistence. There was, as a matter of fact, a dual, or multiple, industrial system with a satisfactory balance between the main industry (agriculture) and the subsidiary industry, creating a certain degree of prosperity in the areas where demands for labour both from agriculture and from subsidiary production were effective.

I should also mention the special characteristics of the agriculture of the area. Carried out in the nineteenth century, the artificial flooding of the swamplands enabled the yield of fodder to be more than doubled. The means of subsistence was thus greatly improved and this, together with the introduction of the potato crop at the beginning of the nineteenth century, is unquestionably the main reason why so many people were able to make a living in the interior of Norrland. In other parts of the country the pressure of population has gradually eased through emigration. In the inland regions of Norrland many discovered their America well into the twentieth century, sometimes by bringing under cultivation land which was previously unused, sometimes by increasing yields by adopting different methods of flooding the swamp meadows. But this intensive agriculture became uneconomic with the decline of self-employment in the 1930s; at the same time specialisation in industrial life brought with it a pressure to abandon the dual-industry system. The severities of the money economy of today and its rigid specialisation have thus been responsible for the fact that very many of the settlements in Norrland, and especially in its interior, today represent relics of a different age with different needs for subsistence. This has had the result that the inland regions of Norrland have become increasingly overpopulated in recent years. In this area, with a greater proportion of employment in agriculture than in other areas of Sweden and still greatly affected by the earlier rise of the birth-rate, it was inevitable that there should be a greater dependence than elsewhere on industrial development to provide openings for employment when in the past decade the decline in the main form of livelihood was greatly accelerated. Despite a very rapid expansion in Norrland industry – for example, the engineering industry has grown twice as fast as in Southern Sweden in the past few years – industry has not been able to absorb the excess manpower, particularly in the past few years.

As has been stated, the decline in the agricultural population has accelerated; in the counties of Västerbotten and Norrbotten for example, it is calculated that not more than one-third of the present farmers will be able to make a living exclusively from agriculture in ten years' time. At the same time the rationalisation which has taken place in the large basic industries – the forest industry and mining – has obviously caused them, for the time being and for quite a number of years ahead, to have reached saturation point as regards the capacity to absorb manpower.

The concomitant of depopulation is urbanisation. Both these phenomena are expressions of the same social process, and regionally the consequences of this are all the more obvious. Hitherto the process of urbanisation in Sweden has had astonishingly few regional effects, if one compares different parts of the country with one another. Thus we can see that the different parts of the country have, to a large extent, been able to maintain their relative shares of the population. This means that the growth of urban centres, seen from the point of view of the country as a whole, has hitherto been a decentralised and decentralising process to a surprisingly high degree. A number of small and medium-sized conurbations have appeared throughout the country and these have absorbed the excess manpower from nearby country areas. As long as the consumer demand from surrounding country districts for the services offered in the conurbations has been sufficient, or more than sufficient, there have been conditions favourable for the appearance of new conurbations and some expansion of those already existing. This development has meant at the same time an improvement in the services offered. The situation now, however, is different. There is a great demand for more differentiated and more professional services, and both private and public services, for reasons of profit, have to aim at securing the economies of large scale. This means that as a result of depopulation the total number of consumers tends to fall in the forest districts and inland regions, and this causes a reduction in service facilities.

Forestry is, of course, the basic and in many places the only form of livelihood in the interior of Norrland. It is now becoming evident, however, that we can hardly expect that this alone will be enough to support adequate and well-differentiated services. Since the present demand of the forestry workers to be allowed to live at home and not in barracks has been widely approved (from a social point of view this has been seen as a step in the right direction), we have the very interesting problem of the extent to which it may be possible in future to localise the forestry workers in a limited number of places, where their families can be provided with really satisfactory services. There could, under these circumstances, be only a few such places – fairly large central communities with at least 3,000 inhabitants. It is obviously impossible – if we accept the demand to live at home during the working week – to assume, with present transport techniques, a commuting distance of more than about 40 km. from home to lumber site. Schematically, on a map, this means a circle of about 30 km. radius with the centre point in the service centre – the living community.

Having regard to regrowth, calculated lumber volume, manpower requirements and continued rationalisation in these lumber regions, the necessary population over the next five to ten years will not exceed 2,000 persons. The demand of this population is completely insufficient to meet the requirements of satisfactory services. This is likely to be the basic factor in deciding on future policy with regard to these sparsely populated areas. Forestry alone cannot generate a sufficient consumer demand for services for the central communities in these lumber regions to be able to offer good quality and sufficient variety in their services. The central communities would be far too small to be able to provide such services, and in these circumstances the network of service communities would be much too thinly spread. One must, therefore, imagine a more widely distributed pattern of service centres so that these may become big enough to be able to offer satisfactory services. How this problem is to be solved it is not easy to say. Either the forestry worker's attitude to daily commuting must be changed – persuading him to accept again living in barracks in lumber camps during the week – or transport techniques must be radically changed. The problem is far from being solved. Indeed it has still not been tackled really seriously.

Apart from the question of what can possibly be done to encourage various forms of activity in sparsely populated areas in Norrland and other parts of the country, and indeed the problem of whether or not there is any possibility at all of increasing industrial activity there, it is necessary in broad terms to regard the problem of those areas as being that of providing services for those who remain there. It is not simply a question of physical services and distribution but also of cultural services and a satisfactory social atmosphere. As the percentage of old people (those over sixty-five) is going to increase very greatly in some areas because of the inversion of the normal age pyramids, the question of the care of the aged in all its various aspects comes to the foreground. An investigation into the demographic trends in twenty-nine sparsely populated administrative areas in so-called commune blocks within the subsidy area shows quite clearly that there tend to be more old people in these areas. In 1960 there were in these regions approximately 45,000 people over the age of sixty-five. According to population forecasts, the total number of people in these areas will fall by about 90,000 by 1975. On the other hand, the number of people over sixty-five will increase over the same period by about 14,000, i.e. from 43,000 to 57,000. It can be seen in Maps 2 and 3 that this trend will be particularly acute in the county of Jämtland. In five to ten years' time many communities there will have an age distribution with between one-quarter and one-third of the population in the age-groups over sixty-five. As things are in Sweden this means that the communes will have the responsibility of providing for them. In addition, the Swedish communes have the responsibility of building schools. This will

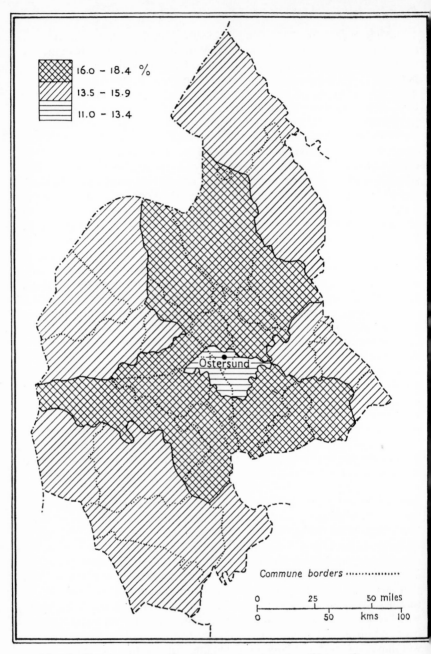

MAP 2: PROPORTIONS OF TOTAL POPULATION OF AGE 65 + IN COMMUNES
OF JÄMTLAND IN 1964

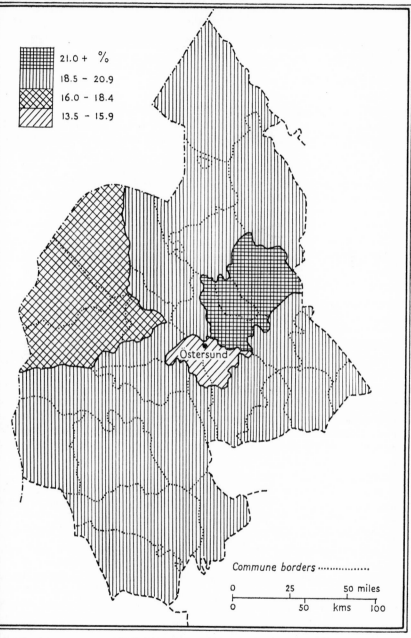

	21.0 + %
	18.5 – 20.9
	16.0 – 18.4
	13.5 – 15.9

Östersund

Commune borders ················

0   25   50 miles

0   50   kms   100

MAP 3: PROPORTIONS OF TOTAL POPULATION OF AGE 65 + IN COMMUNES
OF JÄMTLAND IN 1970

mean that the communities will be under very heavy economic strain. The consumer element in the population will become proportionally larger and larger while the producing element will become smaller and smaller.

4 THE PROBLEMS TO BE SOLVED

This raises a large number of problems which need to be tackled both by politicians and even more by social scientists. The problems to be solved are these: What sort of depopulation are we dealing with? How can the problem be solved? How long can redundant services be maintained in an area? What are the minimum scales on which the services can be provided in terms of consumer demand? How are these affected by structure, income level and the like? How does a population adjust to a more thinly scattered pattern of service centres? What are likely to be the effects of communications and transport on people living in these areas? All these questions can, moreover, be asked on a regional basis. In what areas are these expected or existing phenomena of sparse population to be found? What will be the future regional effects?

Seldom before have the regional consequences of changes in Swedish economic life been more serious than today. The present problems of planning have developed into a question of how to base a regional organisation on the two poles of the same energy field: the large town and the sparse settlement. The new developments will, to all appearances, lead us rapidly, and in contrast to what has happened in the past, to a very considerable shift of the balance between different parts of the country. The effect of the streams of net emigration will be an even clearer shift of the focal point of population in the country to the areas with large population agglomerations. The growth of these is encouraged by the steady expansion of public community services, by the rationalisation of economic structure and by the growth of mass-production and its effects on economies of agglomeration and thus on industrial location, both to secure a market and to benefit from external economies.

It is said that we are in transition to an even higher degree of economic and social efficiency. At the same time we have all the more reason to be aware of the problems of large towns and of sparse population. In fact, one recent study of our social conditions shows that despite a great deal of evidence of social and economic efficiency and good working conditions, conditions for those who do not work – the children, the sick and the aged – are rapidly deteriorating. For example, a city environment makes it very difficult for these categories of people to obtain social care and desirable contacts. These problems, in their human aspects, are frequently much greater in the cities than are the corresponding problems in the extremely isolated areas with little population. An urbanisation that is allowed to proceed without restraint or control would, quite obviously, create greater economic problems than those that arise from the sparsely populated areas which now seem doomed. The great task facing us all, which needs to be tackled with the help of the policy of location is to attempt to create an effective, prosperous and well-balanced society for all classes of people in all parts of Sweden. This is a great and urgent undertaking which is not only a matter of concern for Sweden within her own boundaries, but must be seen as a common duty for all nations for the sake of the future prosperity of us all.

11 Problems of the Underdeveloped Regions of Italy

Francesco Vito [1]

UNIVERSITÀ CATTOLICA DEL S. CUORE, MILAN

1 THE CAUSES OF BACKWARD AREAS

Interregional differences in the standard of living are a common feature of all nations, even the most industrialised. Historical experience shows that in the latter they are less pronounced than in underdeveloped countries. They are at the same time less acutely felt and less likely to arouse political pressures for the obvious reason that the *per capita* income of the backward regions in an advanced economy, though lower as compared with more advanced areas or the national average, is nonetheless sufficient, in absolute terms, to assure a satisfactory standard of living.

If from this obvious starting point we go on to consider what policy should be followed to eliminate as far as possible these differences, it is necessary to make certain fundamental distinctions. The lower level of the *per capita* income may take either of two alternative forms. On the one hand there are areas where it takes the form of a level of unemployment above the national average; in other cases it takes the form of a high rate of net emigration; sometimes it takes both forms.

In an industrial area again, the decline may be a consequence of loss of competitiveness in activities long established there, or of a fall in the demand for the goods produced, or the introduction of new industries producing substitutes for the traditional products. In agricultural areas, on the other hand, particularly in areas of mountains, the decline may be due to the fact that productivity has become too low as compared with the less mountainous areas where modern technical improvements are more easily applicable. Areas of either kind, industrial or agricultural, may be called depressed or declining areas if we think of them in relation to the past. They may be called redevelopment areas if we look at what needs to be done in the future to help them.

Problem areas within industrialised economies may result also from circumstances other than those mentioned. Areas may be found where the tempo of development is considerably slower than in the rest of the country,

---

[1] All the participants at the conference who enjoyed Professor Vito's vigorous and well-argued contributions to its papers and discussions will greatly regret his sudden death in the midst of his work only a few months later, and before this paper – one of the last of his writings on economics – could be published.

reflecting itself in a lower *per capita* income, a higher unemployment rate and a considerable net emigration. The factors leading to this kind of problem area are different from those that lead to depressed or redevelopment areas. In the case of depressed or redevelopment areas the backwardness is a consequence of a halt in development. In the other areas it is the effect of inadequate development at any stage in their history. They are best described as underdeveloped areas.

It needs only a moment's reflection to appreciate that differences of the causes that have led to the emergence of these different kinds of problem areas must be reflected in corresponding differences in methods of handling them in order to reach the common objective of raising the welfare of those who live in these low-income areas.

2 THE DEPRESSED AREAS OF ITALY

The Italian economy includes depressed areas – both agricultural and, though to a less extent, industrial – and also underdeveloped areas. But the last constitute by far the most serious problem of the Italian economy today. And they have peculiar characteristics. There is no industrial country in Europe or elsewhere, where the underdeveloped section of the economy covers so wide an area as in Italy. It forms the southern part of the country, the co-called 'Mezzogiorno'. It is not a region in the ordinary sense of the word. It comprises seven administrative regions covering 41 per cent of the national area, with 38 per cent of its population. It has an area about the size of Greece, with twice its population; or the same as that of Czechoslovakia with five million more inhabitants. Another peculiar feature is the gap in the standard of living and the rate of economic development as compared with the rest of the country. When a policy for the development of the South was started about twenty years ago, the best estimate of *per capita* income as compared with the Centre-North (which from now on I shall call the North) was slightly below 50 per cent.

The concept of income may be taken as an index covering all aspects of underdevelopment: predominance of the agricultural sector; low productivity both in agriculture and in other sectors; inadequate education and shortage of occupational skills; a higher birth-rate; high unemployment; a persistent high level of emigration.

It is not easy to explain fully such a complex phenomenon. If one leaves aside the long-term factors deriving from centuries of history and focuses attention on those that accompanied and followed the industrial revolutions of Europe, the causes of the slow progress of the economy of the South may be reduced to three:

(i) Unfavourable natural conditions: poverty of soil, adverse climate, shortage of water, lack of mineral resources. In addition, account must be taken of the geographical remoteness from the rich markets of Northern Europe at a time when cost of transport was of paramount importance in the location of production. This geographical setting leads us on to the second group of factors.

(ii) The regions in the North of Italy, because of geographical proximity to the countries which had started and continued the industrial revolution, enjoyed a favourable stimulus to industrialisation. The familiar cumulative effect of every development process, operating through external economies, commercial credit, financial organisations, and the like, and invigorating the industry in the North, made it more difficult for other regions to develop competitive activities. The cumulative effect worked also in the human and social field. The higher standard of living offered wider opportunities for general education and occupational training; the latter was also extended within the factories themselves. It created opportunities and incentives for scientific research for industrial purposes. This in turn required the widening of pure research. It made it easier to train executives for industrial management. It improved both the public and private administrative organisation. It encouraged participation in political life, local and national, and strengthened the democratic institutions. A higher intellectual level increased social relations; spread the means of communications; eased relations between town and village and between villages, between different strata of the population; and all these factors, typical of what we commonly call an industrial society, have reduced and even eliminated resistance to change, always present in any pre-industrial society.

From this we can see that the priority of the North in the process of industrialisation helped to increase the gap, not only in the standard of living as compared with the South, but also in the potentiality for industrial development. But it is possible that neither the natural factors nor the chronological factors would have caused such a wide difference, were it not for a third factor, to which the historians of the future will probably attach the greatest importance of all: the economic consequences of the political unification of the country a century ago.

(iii) At that time it was believed or, more precisely, it was never even questioned, that by eliminating obstacles to the movements of goods, capital and people between different economies and by the widening of means of communication, beneficial effects were to be expected not only to the advanced but also to the less-developed area concerned. Today no one advances or accepts this optimistic view except in a much modified form. By increasing communications between communities at a different stage of development there is no certainty that the less-developed will benefit as well as the more advanced. The contrary is very likely to happen: the rich areas will become still richer and the poor will lag even further behind. It is necessary to proceed gradually; and at the same time, to modify the free play of the market by giving some support to areas that are economically weak. As is well known, this is the procedure adopted by the European Economic Community.

It is understandable that the economic policy of the nation, after the political unification, should have been conceived for many decades in accordance with a belief in the principle of the automatic dissemination of the advantages consequent on the liberalisation of movement of goods, services and capital within the unified country. The monetary, credit, fiscal and commercial policies were mainly concerned with the interests of the industrial parts of the country. The South depended rather on occasional programmes of public works and other temporary forms of assistance. All this helps to explain why the economic conditions of the South over a period of 100 years did not improve to the extent that the prevailing ideas of the nineteenth century would have anticipated.

3 REGIONAL DEVELOPMENT POLICIES

The regional policy directed towards raising the *per capita* incomes in the less-developed areas takes a particular form in Italy. Here it is not a question of redeveloping industrial zones that are suffering from stagnation or a slowing down of progress. Nor is it a question of putting a brake on progress in over-congested areas and transferring industries or establishing new industries in areas which, though not offering the same favourable conditions to private enterprise, are none the less adequately provided with infrastructures, have a supply of skilled labour and possess the advantages of an industrial society.

The task to be accomplished in the Italian South is that of accelerating the development of areas which for a number of natural, social and political reasons have been unable to keep up with the rest of the country in its race towards progress. To avoid misunderstanding, it is well to re-emphasise that in Italy there do exist depressed industrial areas which give rise to problems such as may require redevelopment and the transfer of industry. But for the reasons already given, the problem of Southern Italy's underdevelopment stands out because of its scale, its importance and its urgency.

The new theories of economic development, enriched by contributions of the sociology of development as well as by those of cultural anthropology, seem to prescribe for Italy a type of regional policy that differs, in part at least, from those adopted in the various other industrialised countries of Western Europe.

(i) A policy aimed at modifying the consequences of factors which have operated for several decades must necessarily be able to count on an adequate degree of continuity.

(ii) In an area in which agriculture is still the main activity, great efforts must be made to increase productivity in this sector so as to raise the income of the agricultural classes: land reclamation and preservation, irrigation, land transformation.

(iii) The existence of a considerable volume of unemployment and underemployment, of a strong flow of emigration with the usual qualitative effects on the population and the very fact that progress in agriculture tends to create redundancy of manual labourers, all point to the desirability of industrialisation.

(iv) Since the region is not at present suitably equipped for the establishment of industries that may be expected to attain a competitive standard, a vast programme of investment in infrastructures is necessary: material infrastructures such as roads, bridges, electricity, means of transport and communications; social and human infrastructures such as schools for primary education, hospitals, social assistance centres, institutions for occupational training and for the education of a managerial class both in the technical and administrative fields, scientific research, and the like. These measures will of course benefit agriculture as well as industry.

(v) The investments designed to improve agricultural efficiency reduce employment in that sector. Again, the investments in infrastructures do not have an immediate effect on productivity nor do they absorb labour to any considerable extent or on a permanent basis. Inevitably, therefore, emigration will continue until larger incomes in agriculture and in other activities stimulate demand for industrial products, both in the form of consumer goods and capital goods, and thus complete as far as demand is concerned, the creation of the conditions favourable for the establishment of industries, which had been initiated by the programme of infrastructures. As a consequence of the material infrastructures and the resulting external economies, costs of production will be reduced; and at the same time labour costs will be lowered, as the result of social and human infrastructures increasing the productivity of labour.

(vi) It is difficult to believe that it will be possible solely by such measures to create economic conditions in the underdeveloped areas as suitable for industrial investment as those existing in the already industrialised parts of the country, and that as a result entrepreneurs will become indifferent between the developed and the now underdeveloped areas in choosing an industrial location. It is even more difficult to persuade oneself that such infrastructures will in themselves create the necessary incentive – a preference for the underdeveloped areas. To complete the framework necessary for industrialisation, or to accomplish what has been called pre-industrialisation, a system of incentives is also required: fiscal incentives, credit incentives, and others.

(vii) The contributions of sociology and cultural anthropology to the study of development highlight the fact that the main factor retarding industrial progress in the underdeveloped areas is the scarcity of managerial and entrepreneurial expertise. Thus to establish industrial enterprises in such areas, it is necessary to rely on attracting people from economically and socially more advanced areas. But as is well known, for people with high incomes, the amenities the place can offer are of great importance when choosing where to work or live. It is not surprising, therefore, that greater profits or higher salaries are not sufficient in themselves to attract to the underdeveloped areas managers and entrepreneurs who are working elsewhere. Public enterprises which can mobilise technicians, managers and entrepreneurs throughout the country, or are in a position to train new staff, may partly overcome this difficulty. Public enterprises must, however, operate under the same conditions as private concerns. Any special privilege granted to them would upset the whole framework of conditions designed to attract industrial undertakings to the underdeveloped areas, to their advantage but to the disadvantage of private business, and in the long run would discourage the initiative and willingness to bear risks which are the essence of private enterprise.

4 THE 'CASSA PER IL MEZZOGIORNO'

The policy for the development of the South, inaugurated in 1950 by the constitution of the 'Cassa per il Mezzogiorno', a public body entrusted with the administration of State resources for that purpose, is closely in accordance with the above criteria. To measure its results, it is necessary

TABLE ONE

ECONOMIC STRUCTURE OF THE PRIVATE SECTOR *

(Percentages)

	Year 1951			Year 1965		
	South	*North* †	*Italy*	*South*	*North* †	*Italy*
Agriculture, forestry and fishing	45·3	24·9	29·6	27·0	11·9	15·4
Industry	28·3	48·9	44·1	33·1	48·9	45·3
Other activities	26·4	26·2	26·3	33·9	39·2	39·3
Total	100·0	100·0	100·0	100·0	100·0	100·0

* Net product for 1951; gross product for 1965.
† Comprises central and northern regions.

Source: Comitato dei Ministri per il Mezzogiorno, *Il bilancio economico del Mezzogiorno. Studi monografici sul Mezzogiorno* (30 Apr 1966).

to take into account the actions of other institutions in regard to agriculture, public works, and certain other activities. One must moreover bear in mind the relatively short time that has as yet been available for a process involving the total transformation of the social and physical environment of the area. In addition it has been necessary in this case to

H 2

evolve methods of public action which had never ever before been attempted in Italy or elsewhere. Taking account of all this, it is not surprising that the results have been meagre. The *per capita* income, at current prices, which in 1951 was 59·5 per cent of that of the rest of the country increased to 61·2 per cent in 1965. The economic structure has been modified, though slightly, as is shown in Table 1. At the same time the distribution of labour between different sectors has been modified in the same way as shown in Table 2. From Table 3 it can be seen that

TABLE TWO
LABOUR FORCE 1954 AND 1965

(Percentages)

	South		North *		Italy	
	1954	1965	1954	1965	1954	1965
Agriculture	50·9	37·9	32·7	20·3	38·4	25·8
Industries	26·8	30·9	38·0	44·4	33·9	40·2
Other activities	22·3	31·2	29·3	35·3	27·7	34·0
Total	100·0	100·0	100·0	100·0	100·0	100·0

* Comprises Central and Northern regions.

Source: As for Table 1.

TABLE THREE
REGISTERED UNEMPLOYMENT (1952 AND 1965)

	South		North *		Italy	
	1952	1965	1952	1965	1952	1965
Unemployed and persons seeking first employment	820,000	279,000	1,253,000	490,000	2,073,000	769,000

* Comprises Central and Northern regions.

Source: Istituto Centrale di Statistica, *Indagini campionarie sulle forze di lavoro.* Results recently published in *Annuario statistico del lavoro e della emigrazione* (1958, 1965).

Note: Population of Southern Italy as % of all Italy (resident population): 31/12/1951 = 38·8%; 31/12/1965 = 37·7% (same source as above).

evidence of progress, resulting from the development policy, is to be found in the figure of unemployed and persons seeking first employment.

The results could no doubt have been better. In retrospect it is possible to make some criticisms, which should be useful in formulating future policy in relation to the South. The improvements in agriculture might have been pursued more consistently and more vigorously. The gross saleable production of the South was 33·6 per cent of the national production in 1951 and increased only to 36·9 per cent by 1965.[1]   Apart from that, any considerable increases were confined to products, such as cereals, bringing the lowest return.   As is now admitted, the slow progress is to be attributed to a wide dispersal of investment, which has been described, with much truth if with some exaggeration, as a policy of trying to increase the yield of every single lump of soil.   The same criticism can be made of the policies of infrastructures and incentives to industrialisation, as will be seen below.

The lack of sufficiently vigorous action to improve agriculture in the Southern regions will make conditions in that area more difficult in the future.   At present Italy has an unfavourable balance in foodstuffs.   The principal contribution to payment for the necessary imports must come from exports of industrial products.   It will thus be necessary to stimulate the manufacture of industrial products; this must obviously be mainly in the Northern area where industry is more competitive; but it will inevitably diminish the resources available for the industrialisation of the South.   The imperative need to increase the competitiveness of Italian industries so that they can face the complete elimination of trade barriers in the E.E.C. area, operates in the same way.

It needs scarcely be said that the purpose of developing agriculture in the South is to increase productivity and not to retain on the land the whole of the existing agricultural population.   On the contrary, it will free manpower for the non-agricultural sectors. The more advanced countries are characterised by a low percentage of working population in agriculture as compared with underdeveloped countries.   The productivity of labour in advanced countries is, however, substantially higher than in under-developed countries.   In particular they depend on their most advanced industries to maintain and if possible increase their earnings in order to cover their deficits in foodstuffs.

5   GRADUALISM AND DUALISM

A policy of improvements in agriculture, in infrastructures, and in incentives to private businesses represents the type of regional development which has been pursued in Italy over the last twenty years.   It is the method of gradualism which has rightly been preferred to the so-called big push which has been recommended by some of the foreign economists who have studied the Italian case.   The advantage of the gradual method which is generally emphasised in any discussion of development arises chiefly from the fact that it makes it possible to avoid serious mistakes which would result in too heavy losses for any economy which still is relatively weak. In Italy's case, the reason for this choice which appears to be decisive is a

---

[1] Source: Istituto Centrale di Statistica, *Indagini campionarie sulle forze di lavoro.* Results in *Annuario statistico de lavoro e della emigrazione,* 1966.

different one. With the gradual method the rate of injection of capital is commensurate with the absorptive capacity of the areas to be developed, in terms of the natural, economic, social and human factors. In these areas, if the inflow of resources diverted from other regions that are more attractive in terms of profitability exceeds the absorptive capacity, the objective of development will not be achieved.

When discussing absorptive capacity of capital one thinks immediately of the infrastructures which, by definition, are largely lacking in the underdeveloped areas. There is no doubt that this is right. In accordance with this principle the Cassa has earmarked (from 1 July 1950 to 3 December 1965) one-third of its available resources (33·4 per cent), for this purpose.[1] In this case equal importance attaches, however, to social and human investment. The main obstacle to development in regions such as the South, is, as mentioned earlier, the scarcity of managerial and entrepreneurial expertise. Another obstacle is the resistance to the changes imposed by technical progress of a population whose social structure is only slowly escaping from the traditions, customs and mentalities typical of a pre-industrial society.

Some foreign observers have exaggerated this aspect and have thought that one should apply to Italy the model of the dual economy. As is well known, this model was developed some decades back to explain the economies of colonial countries where, in the middle of an archaic community with primitive institutions and an underdeveloped economy, there was to be found an island of economic organisation similar to that existing in western countries and operating through institutions reflecting a quite different civilisation: an invisible barrier in such cases has prevented an actual penetration of the western world by these economic institutions and methods typical of the indigenous milieu of the colonial countries. Because of the gap between the institutional characteristics of the two worlds nothing more than a co-existence of the two ways of life and the two types of economic organisation could establish itself – one of them based on the rationalisation of experience directed towards technological progress and resting on a broad division of functions, the other one bound to the traditional system of the country. The mutual impenetrability of the two systems coexisting in the single political unit, appeared as a dualistic phenomenon, tending to perpetuate itself. In one economy, high productivity made possible the increase of production and thus of consumption and investment. This raised the standard of living; but only a small fraction of the indigenous population shared in the increase of welfare. In the second economy the archaic structure formed a continuing obstacle to the abandonment of traditional methods of organisation and work. This mutual impenetrability was made the greater by the fact that foreign

[1] Source: Comitato dei Ministri per il Mezzogiorno, *Relazione sulla attività di coordinamento* (30 aprile 1966) cap. i.

investment was mainly directed to the exploitation of natural resources and not to the spreading of diversified productive activities in these colonial countries. Using the terminology of modern cultural anthropology, it can be said that the invisible barrier was parallel to the co-existence of two deeply indifferent cultures.

While the dualistic model is thus applicable to economies, it is not applicable in a country in which, while traditions, customs, mentalities and social structures are slightly different in the various regions, there is no fundamental difference in culture. The common language, the common political organisation as well as the common spiritual ideals which unite the various regions make it impossible to speak of a barrier making the different regions mutually impenetrable from either an economic or a social viewpoint. Thus the method of the crash programme or the big push to accelerate progress in the underdeveloped regions is not applicable. For this method rests on a pessimistic, even a contradictory, view of development. There is a general agreement that it is not possible to have a continuing development without the community concerned having the will to develop. But by using the aggressive method that we have been discussing one tries to impose development on people. It is clear that any attempt to do this sooner or later loses its efficacy and becomes sterile.

It is debatable whether the big push method is applicable to economies which have not made even a first step towards development and remain in a state of stagnation where the standard of living, already very low, is likely to deteriorate further because of high population increase. But it should be absolutely clear to all who know how easily workers coming from that region adapt themselves to any kind of activity, however technically advanced, when moving to the North or to other industrial countries in Europe or in other continents, that this model is not applicable to the South. One can see how successfully individuals from the region, entrusted with highly responsible administrative or professional tasks, stand out anywhere in the country or abroad. What appears to be inadequate in the South is the economic, social and human environment required to allow everybody to exploit his own ability without having to move elsewhere. Here we can see the great importance of infrastructures, not only material but also and mainly social and human, if a full exploitation of material and human resources in the region is to be achieved.

This has not hitherto been sufficiently taken into consideration. The Cassa activities began to show amounts earmarked for social and human investments for the first time only eight years after it started to operate. These amounts have been a very low proportion of all investments made or approved. From 1 July 1950 to 31 December 1965 the figure was not more than 5 per cent.[1] It is true that other public and private bodies,

[1] Source: ibid.

particularly the Labour Ministry, made funds available for the same purposes. But even allowing that, there is obviously a disproportion between what is spent on material infrastructures and on social and human.

6 CRITERIA FOR THE APPRAISAL OF THE POLICIES

The policy of creating infrastructures and creating incentives designed to attract private enterprise can be appraised from various aspects. First of all it is useful to ask whether rational criteria have been followed in the geographical distribution of the investment made or approved. Pre-occupation with absorbing unemployment as widely as possible had led to excessive dispersal of investment and the achievement of only uncertain results. Obviously the distribution of investment seldom took account of economic principles governing the location of industry. Those responsible for the economic policy are now convinced of the necessity of changing course in this respect. The present trend is to concentrate effort in areas possessing the essential requirements of a rational location of production. But, as I shall explain below, it is still necessary to examine closely the concept of a growth centre.

The fact that the response of private enterprise to the stimuli of favourable fiscal and credit conditions had not been as great as expected may be attributed to several causes. In the first place, it may be attributed to an insufficient volume of infrastructure to offset the higher costs in the South. This interpretation is supported by the following evidence: public enterprises in 1958 invested in the South 23·6 per cent of the volume of investment made in Italy as a whole; in 1963, in compliance with the law requiring them to contribute to the acceleration of development in the South by devoting to it not less than 40 per cent of their total investments they actually increased the proportion to 46·8 per cent; they maintained it, in 1965, at 42·9 per cent).[1] From these figures it is clear that public enterprises have been able to accept risks in respect of costs which the private sector hesitates to accept. On the other hand the fact that the public enterprises have not increased but have decreased, if only slightly, their investments in the South between 1963 and 1965 seems to suggest that other factors may have had some influence on the low levels of investment in the South despite the improvement of infrastructures.

One such factor is the inadequate number of individuals and enterprises with the necessary ability to plan satisfactory investment projects. This may be inferred from the figures of applications for the financing of industrial projects submitted to credit institutions by enterprises in the South and the numbers that have received approval: from a total of 6,717 applications

---

[1] Source: Ministero del Bilancio, *Relazione generale sulla situazione economica del paese* (1959, 1964, 1966).

amounting to 2,493 million lire only 4,669 have been accepted for a total investment of 1,695 million lire.[1]

Another aspect from which we may examine the policy of pre-industrial and industrial development concerns the volume of inflow of funds from the rest of the country promoted by the State (the inflow of private funds depends, as has been said, on the efficacy of the infrastructures created with funds raised by taxation). So far as concerns the funds provided by the Cassa, the position is as follows: as a proportion of the gross national product the annual average of its investments for the period 1963–5 amounts to 1·8 per cent and to 7·7 per cent as compared to the gross southern product. It amounts to 7·9 per cent of the total gross investment of the country and to 28·8 per cent of the total investment of the South.[2]

It must be remembered that this is not the whole picture of the investment in the South. The Cassa has been created to finance investments of an abnormal character. To these one must add the investments of the ordinary public administration of which from July 1950 to 31 December 1965 38·5 per cent were devoted to the South and 61·5 per cent to the North.[3] Further, we must take into account the investments of public enterprises, whose capital is partly state owned and partly private.[4] In 1964 they represented 54·1 per cent of the industrial investments in the South; we owe to public enterprises the establishment in the South of the large iron and steel mill at Taranto, a conspicuous example of the principle of concentrating investment.

To appreciate this, one must have in mind the difficulty of reconciling the need to accelerate the improvement of underdeveloped areas with the principle of making the best use of resources. If one sticks to the latter principle, one would be led to reject any diversion of resources from areas where they may be used more efficiently. By the most efficient use of resources, the development of the whole economy is maximised and resources for more needy areas are secured. On the other hand, primary consideration of the need to speed up the improvement of the standard of living of the low income population would imply disregarding the principle of the best use of resources and not taking into account the possibilities of securing economies by concentration of production in large undertakings. In practice, as is well known, as the result of political pressures, policy is designed, more or less consciously, to reconcile both objectives. Theoretically, in consequence, the results so far achieved do not appear to be completely satisfactory.

---

[1] Source: Comitato dei Ministri per il Mezzogiorno, *Relazione sulla attività di coordinamento* (30 aprile 1966) cap. iv.

[2] Source: ibid.

[3] Source: ibid.

[4] Source: Ministero del Bilancio, *Relazione generale sulla situazione economica del paese* (31 marzo 1965).

The solution of this problem seems at first glance to be easier when one is dealing with depressed areas in highly industrialised economies. In such a case one is concerned on the one hand with industrial areas which have suffered a slow-down or halt of development as a result of changes of demand or technological innovations, on the other hand with prosperous areas, some of which have reached such a degree of agglomeration as to be on the verge of overcrowding. There is an almost complete homogeneity in respect of infrastructure, the occupational training of labour, the organisation of trade, credit, insurance, and the like between the depressed and the prosperous areas. A calculation of the relative marginal yield of additional investment in the two types of area can therefore be very precise and trustworthy.

In the depressed area, the cost to be borne by the enterprise which wishes to establish itself there is high as compared with that which it would bear in a prosperous area, where it would benefit from greater external economies. In the richer area, on the other hand, the social cost of investment beyond the level of maximum activities is higher. By comparing the sums of the social cost and the private cost (to the individual enterprise) for additional investments in the two different types of areas, a most valuable criterion for decision-making is to be obtained.

This criterion does not seem to be applicable to countries where the differences in regional income levels, in infrastructures, in economic organisation, in training and skills are as wide as those existing between the North and South of Italy. One argument frequently advanced in this connection points to the time-scale of development. It has been emphasised that by diverting resources from places in which they would be more productive to areas lacking infrastructures and adequate conditions for industrial enterprises, the best use of the resources is not achieved. But, it must be added, this is all a question of time. When the efforts to develop such areas have yielded their fruits, the economic level reached by them, through exploiting resources never used before, will benefit the whole national economy. The immediate delay in overall development will be offset by a higher rate of progress for the country as a whole at a later stage.

Another argument is concerned with the distinction between economic and social aims. The eradication of the striking interregional differences in standards of living is a social objective to which economic maximisation must be subordinated.

Undoubtedly there are valid points in both arguments. None the less, they still remain vague and indefinite. As far as the first is concerned, it must be borne in mind that a too prolonged diversion from the best use of resources may lead to a set-back to the whole economy, which will not easily be offset by the beneficial effects to be expected later in the underdeveloped areas. Secondly, it is not easy to define the limitations to be applied to the economic treatment of development if this is to be sub-ordinated to social considerations. It would seem more appropriate to start from the basic economic principle that economics is concerned with the optimum use of scarce means to achieve defined social objectives; and then to proceed to define such objectives. These consist in the advancement, including the material advancement, of man, of all men, and thus of the whole society. These objectives are not to be taken in the utopian sense of equalising economic conditions for everyone, whether that involves the equalisation of economic conditions in all areas or not. What can be achieved, and in fact must be achieved in every human society, is the removal by public action of all obstacles hindering the reaching by everybody of a standard that conforms to human dignity: that these objectives be very actively pursued. With respect to the achievement of this aim, economic principles maintain their validity intact. Economics is an instrument in relation to these social objectives. But once the objectives have been defined, it is the task of economics to indicate the rational measures to be accepted, in accordance with the principle of the optimum use of scarce means.

7 THE PRESENT TREND OF POLICY

The course at present adopted by Italian regional policy is to concentrate investments in a few places instead of spreading them over as great a number of areas as possible. The outstanding example of this new trend is provided by the large iron and steel plant built at Taranto by public enterprise. The benefits are obvious enough. In making the choice of a place for it, the relevant location factors were taken into account. The greatest use of existing external economies is made possible and new facilities have been created.

The multiplier effect of the additional demands for goods and services generated by the higher incomes is obviously greater than it would be if investment to the same total amount had been scattered in a large number of places. The incentives to enlarge existing undertakings producing the required goods and services are also increased. The local external economies and scale economies are thus strengthened and at the same time employment in these other activities is increased.

To make geographically-concentrated investment have a polarising effect in the real sense of the word, requires that another phenomenon shall occur on a very considerable scale. As a result of the more favourable conditions for acquiring capital goods offered by these undertakings which were first to choose to locate in the area, new enterprises must be established and existing ones expanded. If such capital goods are sold at lower prices in other regions of the country or abroad, a genuine polarisation of activities obviously cannot be expected. For this reason it is much more likely that such a polarisation effect will occur in a developed but depressed area than in an underdeveloped one.

In the latter, the choice of industries capable of starting off induced secondary effects of various possible kinds also presents difficulties. It is a common procedure today to think of new industries, such as aeronautics, electronic equipments and the like, as potential accelerators of the development of a region in the belief that the dynamic character of such industries makes them more appropriate for this task. The industries will not, it is hoped, have to meet in the first stages competition with undertakings in other regions because these do not exist. But they cannot long avoid foreign competition. This fact obviously affects underdeveloped areas to a greater extent than depressed areas.

8   THE EFFECTS OF THE EUROPEAN ECONOMIC COMMUNITY

The effect of the supernational economic policy, and in particular that of the European community, on regional differences may be examined under three separate heads. The first concerns the frontier areas between two or more countries of the community which need similar development programmes and require investment which can be reduced in amount and made much more efficient if it is planned and carried out in collaboration by the various nations involved.

In the second place, it is possible to attempt to analyse the effects on the economies of the various regions deriving from the removal of customs barriers between member states.

Thirdly, it is important to have in mind the effects of the activities of the organs of the community designed to benefit those regions that particularly need assistance. These include the loans granted by the European Development Bank as well as the contributions of the European Social Fund and the European Fund for the Guidance and Protection of Agriculture (F.E.O.G.A.).

The first and third of these are dealt with by Professor Davin; here only a brief account will be given of the first results of an enquiry made into the repercussions of European integration on the economic conditions of various Italian regions.

The starting point has been the belief that by reducing the obstacles to trade between one community and another, a rise in exports ensues which, if not offset by corresponding increase in imports, causes income also to rise and that this, in turn, stimulates investment and thus leads to further increases in income. It must be asked whether such favourable repercussions have been limited to a few regions or whether they have extended to many of them, and if so how far they have affected existing regional differences in income.

To answer these questions an investigation has been made to find how the net increment of exports has affected two specific areas (which in this case correspond to two regions in the administrative sense): the first being an underdeveloped region, actually situated in the South (Apulia), and the other being a depressed industrial region (Liguria). The latter region forms part of the so-called industrial triangle of the North: Liguria, Piedmont and Lombardy. It is needless to say that no absolute certainty can be attached to the findings since the regions in question, like almost all others, have been simultaneously exposed also to the influence of the regional policy pursued by the Italian State. In the underdeveloped area favourable effects are apparent under at least three heads. Agricultural activity, which predominates, reacted with a visible attempt to mechanise and rationalise. The industrial undertakings expanded and made an advance towards larger scale. Agriculture and industry derived greater benefits from external economies. This has not however arrested the emigration of young workers or the capital outflow towards other regions.

The repercussions in the depressed area were, as was to be expected, substantially different. The structure of production has undergone a transformation. Here also the emigration of skilled workers continued none the less. On the other hand, the outflow of capital has been substantially reduced.

12 Development Policy in an Over-populated Area: Italy's Experience

Pasquale Saraceno

ISTITUTO PER LA RICOSTRUZIONE INDUSTRIALE, ROME

1 THE CHARACTERISTICS OF ECONOMIC BACKWARDNESS IN THE SOUTH: THE CASSA PER IL MEZZOGIORNO

In the immediate post-war period, the nature of the Mezzogiorno problem did not closely correspond with the problems that are principally to be discussed by this conference. The Mezzogiorno was a large underdeveloped area almost on a national scale, and one which, even if in some places it presented conditions no more backward than those of other parts of the country, taken as a whole was characterised by a low level of economic development in comparison with that of most of Europe, and by special backwardness in economic and social structures. It was therefore legitimate to regard the underdevelopment of the Mezzogiorno as substantially different from the problem of a backward area such as occurs in many highly developed countries. It was rather a problem all of its own, comparable with that of the so-called underdeveloped countries.

It should not be forgotten that the Mezzogiorno at the end of 1950 had 17 million inhabitants in an area of 123,000 square kilometres. The Mezzogiorno, that is to say, with much the same area, had a population twice as large as that of Greece and five million greater than that of Czechoslovakia. The three Benelux countries between them had only two million more inhabitants; the three Scandinavian countries three million fewer. *Per capita* income in the Mezzogiorno was approximately $150, about half that of the north-central regions, a fifth of that of France and a tenth of that of the United States.

It was in this setting that in 1950 government intervention in the southern regions was started, with the creation of a special agency for the development of the South, the 'Cassa per il Mezzogiorno'. The law setting up the Cassa per il Mezzogiorno provided for the preparation of a ten-year plan of 'an organic series of extraordinary works directed specifically at the economic and social progress of Southern Italy', and ensured the necessary finance. This plan was intended to provide for a complex of measures conceived as additional to those of public administration, normally financed on the basis of annual budget allocations. The Cassa assumed the character of a public organ, entrusted with the implementation

BACKWARD AREAS IN ITALY

Boundaries of areas included in Southern Italy as determined by special regulations

of the plan and the formulation of executive programmes. The intention was to make available a body operating outside the traditional apparatus of public administration, so as to inject into public action technical ability and procedures more appropriate to the specific projects to be undertaken. By means of the Cassa's action the essential aim was, on the one hand, to make the investment needed for improving general and environmental conditions, to increase the income and productivity of agriculture, and, on the other hand, to inject into the Mezzogiorno economy a volume of monetary resources capable of initiating a development mechanism affecting the entire system. The creation of the Cassa introduced a number of elements which were substantially new to the country's traditional economic policy. The multiennial life of the plan, the freeing of operational decisions from the normal procedures laid down for out-payments, the intersectoral powers that gave opportunity for a role as co-ordinator of all public intervention in the Mezzogiorno: these were the initial features of planned public action, destined, however, to mature and change over the following years.

Whatever judgement may be passed on the degree to which the Cassa's intervention really matched the planning criteria attributed to it at the time of its creation, there clearly emerged in the following years a number of fundamental limitations in the initial concept laid down.

Studies of the multiplier effects of the Cassa per il Mezzogiorno's expenditure revealed that these effects were being felt to a far greater degree than had been foreseen in the more developed regions of the country, and only to an insufficient extent in the southern regions themselves; while because of the shortcomings of their industrial structure the southern regions were not in a position to benefit from the multiplier effects. The Northern economy had the advantage, furthermore, of a number of general policies, including those in the field of foreign trade, while gave a powerful impulse to the area's exports. The intensification of economic development in the northern regions required, moreover, a growing volume of public investment there. This naturally contributed to the diversion towards those regions of a considerable proportion of the Government's ordinary expenditures to the detriment of the concept of the Cassa as making an addition to the existing expenditures in the South.

2 SETTING THE MEZZOGIORNO PROBLEM IN THE COUNTRY'S GENERAL DEVELOPMENT POLICY: THE VANONI SCHEME

From these experiences it became obvious that the problem of territorial equalisation could not be solved by special measures in the underdeveloped part of the country – measures limited, moreover, to agriculture and infrastructure sectors alone.

It was in this way that the idea of planning the economic development of the Mezzogiorno was turned into a scheme for the development of the Italian economy as a whole, centred on the objective of a substantial reduction, if not elimination, of the gap between the level of economic development of the Mezzogiorno and that of the rest of the country. This idea underlay the preparation, in 1954, of a document which was named the Vanoni Scheme after the then Minister of the Budget.

The Vanoni Scheme is not a plan in the narrow sense of the term. Nor is it, on the other hand, a theoretical exercise, indifferent to questions of economic policy. Essentially the value of the Scheme lies in the attempt made to identify the development mechanism of the Italian economy. And the identification of this mechanism covers a number of general assumptions.

Of these assumptions, that concerning the tasks to be attributed respectively to public enterprise and private enterprise seems particularly important. The development of employment in the productive sectors, the fundamental objective proposed by the Scheme, was to be achieved first and foremost through private capital accumulation. State intervention in the finance market was to be kept within limits so as to permit private initiative to carry out the role entrusted to it.

The sphere of action for public intervention was essentially confined by the Scheme to the so-called propulsive sectors – agriculture, public utilities, public works – in which it was considered able to operate more effectively both for the achievement of the general objectives of expansion of income and employment, and for overcoming territorial imbalances. With what we might describe as a reminiscence of Keynesian ideas, the Scheme was also concerned with the problems of giving continuity to the initial progressive impetus in the system. To this end, cyclical action was, even if only in part, treated as a function of the plan, in the sense that the expansion of certain sectors – denominated 'regulator' sectors – was to be intensified or restrained according to whether the progress made in the system required slowing down or speeding up in view of emergent dangers of inflation or deflation; the two regulator sectors were taken to be residential building and reafforestation.

The Vanoni Scheme, however, rejected the idea that public action should be limited to the cyclical field, leaving to the plan the task of developing particular productive sectors. The central idea of the Scheme is, on the contrary, the concern that the strengths and weaknesses of the economy be identified, with the object of fully utilising the former to set the latter right as quickly as possible.

For this reason the Scheme laid down that the State should take on direct entrepreneurial responsibility in the industrial field also, in all those cases in which private enterprise showed itself to be insufficient, especially so far as concerns the territorial distribution of new productive activities.

In other words, while keeping within the pattern of general assumptions in favour of private initiative, the Scheme attributed also to public initiative an important role for the purpose of overcoming territorial imbalances in directly productive sectors.

The role of public intervention in the years immediately following the presentation of the Scheme was unquestionably far more modest than that indicated in the Scheme. The dynamism of internal demand and the broadening of foreign demand, following the progressive reduction in international trade restrictions both with other member countries of the European Community and with third countries, guaranteed the Italian economic mechanism sufficient stimuli for achieving a pace of development that corresponded overall to that predicted in the Scheme. The rate of increase in income was, indeed, even higher than the 5 per cent indicated by the scheme, high as this was. Italian economic policy thus reflected the conviction that public action should not superimpose new stimuli on those automatically produced by the market, the more so as the pressure towards an increase in current public expenditure was so great that it absorbed a significant proportion of the very considerable additional liquid resources raised by the tax system.

On the other hand, it was not considered advisable to restrain the pace of economic expansion stimulated directly by the market in order to obtain additional resources necessary to intensify investment in the propulsive sectors of the southern regions. Consequently, investments in these sectors of the southern regions could not fulfil the equalising function assigned them in the Scheme.

When we come to pass judgement on policies for the development of backward areas in industrialised countries, it is interesting to recall that the Vanoni Scheme contains a concept of the Italian problem which not only still conserves its full validity today, but seems destined to become the bench-mark for future policies aiming at the elimination of the divergencies existing in the Italian economy. As has been said above, the Scheme stated that 5 per cent a year was the rate of expansion which not only *can* but *must* be pursued in the Italian economy throughout the long period required to overcome the imbalance existing between North and South. Three components go to make up this rate. In the first place there is the need for the productivity of the labour force already in employment to increase at a rate estimated at not less than 3·5 per cent a year, if it is to be hoped that the policies of European integration and the liberalising trade with the rest of the world followed by Italy ever since the last war are to be successful – policies in contrast to the autarkic policy followed during the twenty years between the two wars. In the second place there is the contribution to the annual growth of national income, estimated at about 0·5 per cent, from the annual increase in the labour force. In addition there is an increase of about 1 per cent a year from the gradual absorption of the supply of labour forthcoming from the unemployed and underemployed labour forces of the Mezzogiorno. This absorption can, however, only take place if national income increases at a rate of more than 4 per cent, since the increase in productivity of the existing labour force and the labour force's own growth would be enough to cover any lesser rate. Taking account of the country's potential capital accumulation, the Scheme therefore assessed at 1 per cent the contribution that would have to be made *on a continuing basis* to the increase in income by the systematic utilisation of excess Southern labour.

These ratios still today underlie the economic development process in Italy. Recent studies by SVIMEZ, the Association for the Development of Industry in the Mezzogiorno, and the Centre for Studies in Economic Development, covering the period up to 1981, seem to confirm this. But what is important to emphasise is not so much the fact that the rates indicated above remain valid today as that the criterion of economic policy can be deduced from them and hence from the Scheme. In essence, it seems clear today from Italy's experience that an incomes policy in a country having a dual economy must be carried out in such a way as to guarantee not only monetary stability, but also an appropriate division of new capital between the two fundamental destinations, the increase in the productivity of those already in employment and the creation of new jobs for the unemployed and underemployed. Now, the task of maintaining monetary stability has in the Treasury and in the Central Bank monitors endowed with technical ability and political powers; the other objective of incomes policy, that of reconciling increases in wages with a given rate of investment in the underdeveloped area, has no institutions whatever at its disposal to ensure that it will be efficiently pursued. Within an underdeveloped country there is, therefore, a tendency for the same 'impasse' to be reproduced that exists in the world as a whole in regard to relations between developed and underdeveloped countries. For the entrepreneurial classes, underdevelopment is a non-existent problem, or at least it is a problem only in that it gives rise to waste of capital which could otherwise find fruitful employment in richer areas.

For the industrial working classes, who are obviously concentrated in the richer areas, the upward pressure on rates of pay is not consciously reduced because of the necessity to encourage the capital investment required for creating jobs in the underdeveloped area. Thus a situation tends to arise in which the country's savings have to be employed for investment required to increase the productivity of those already employed, in order to offset the greater cost resulting from the raising of wage levels. The absorption of the labour force of the underdeveloped area thus becomes a fortuitous by-product of the development of the richer area and in any case comes about largely as an effect of migrational movements, inevitably quite unplanned in themselves, towards the richer area.

The interest of the Vanoni Scheme lies precisely in the fact that it underlines the necessity for creating and maintaining the balance that has been described between the two flows of investment: that for sustaining the trend in the increase in the wages of those already employed and that for providing work for the unemployed. The Scheme, provides also the explanation for the gap that still persists after twenty years of intervention in spite of the considerable progress nonetheless achieved. The policy of development has not, in fact, succeeded in being carried out on the basis of the balance described above. In other words, Italy still continues to be a federation of two economies: the developed and the underdeveloped. And if the economically backward part manages from time to time to secure the acceptance of policies and measures which reflect the general interests of the country's economic unification, the richer regions tolerate this as an inevitable price, justified solely by the requirements of social peace.

3   A POLICY OF INDUSTRIALISATION

It is in the framework described above – substantially different from that conceived by the Scheme – that one must judge the inadequate success obtained in these years by Mezzogiorno policy even though a number of interesting legislative innovations have been introduced in the period. As has been said, it was soon realised that the creation of infrastructure alone was not sufficient to bring about a process of development in the Mezzogiorno and, in any case, would have involved a far longer delay than more than a third of the country's population could reasonably endure.

The view then began to make headway that it was not possible to limit special action to the infrastructure sector, but that it should be extended to the industrial sector, the only one from which the Mezzogiorno could be expected to receive the push towards that development which seemed indispensable for the overall development of the country also.

As early as 1953 arrangements were made for reorganising or setting up *ex novo* special medium-term credit banks, with the task of financing, on favourable terms, the location of small and medium industrial ventures in the Mezzogiorno. But it was only with the 1957 law that Mezzogiorno policy received a new impulse towards industrialisation. Besides an increase in the endowment fund of the Cassa per il Mezzogiorno and a number of provisions designed to ensure a greater degree of co-ordination between the ordinary action devolving on the public authorities and the extraordinary action entrusted to the Cassa per il Mezzogiorno, the law provided for more direct action on the part of the public authorities in the field of industrialisation by means of the intervention by the State Share-holding organisations in the Mezzogiorno and the improvement of an environment to meet industrial requirements. Lastly, specific regulations concerning incentive measures were designed to favour both the location of new productive ventures and the development of those already existing in the southern regions.

In the context of the first of these, it was made obligatory on the Ministry for State Shareholding to present each year to the Committee of Ministers for the Mezzogiorno the investment programmes of the agencies and firms falling under its supervision. These programmes had to ensure such a territorial distribution of the investments as would bring about a progressively better economic balance between the various regions. In particular, it was laid down that, with effect from the entry into force of the law, the investments of these agencies and firms should be so arranged that not less than 60 per cent of the total sum be placed in the South. At the same time, total investments for whatever purposes made by the State Shareholding agencies and firms in the South were under no circumstances to represent less than 40 per cent of total investments made by them in the country as a whole.

The law also regulated the creation of Consortia between local authorities (which later became, as the institution evolved, Consortia for the 'Areas of Industrial Development' and for the 'Industrialisation Nuclei'), with the task of executing, developing and running – with the help of money grants from the Cassa – the works necessary for establishing industrial zones, i.e. in specific zones in which it was intended new productive ventures should be concentrated.

Lastly, particular importance attaches to the regulations aimed at encouraging new industrial ventures: among other things, for the first time, there were provisions for making outright grants (20 per cent for buildings and 10 per cent for the purchase of machinery) to small and medium firms.

This second phase of southern policy unquestionably produced a number of by no means unimportant effects: there were important 'episodes' of industrialisation in the early sixties in a number of areas in the South (Syracuse, Taranto, Brindisi, Gela) especially those resulting from the construction of a number of large plants in the steel, chemical and petrochemical sectors by both State Shareholding and private industry. But the rapid economic development of those years continued to be located to by far the greatest extent in the north-central regions of the country and the backwardness of the Mezzogiorno was relatively worsened.

It was clear, then, that the failure to implement the Vanoni Scheme, in as much as it prevented action in favour of the Mezzogiorno from losing its merely regional nature and from becoming action of a 'national' character, was at the root of this backwardness. This point underlies the experiments in national economic planning of recent years.

4 PLANNING POLICY

The Mezzogiorno problem, thanks to the rapid development enjoyed by the Italian economy in the years preceding the recession of 1964–5, has today acquired new features which mean that it can now be quite legitimately defined in terms which match exactly the concept of this conference.

The fact that the Italian economy should have reached relatively advanced levels of development has certainly altered radically the concept of planning policy. The standpoint underlying both the note presented to Parliament in June 1962 by the Minister of the Budget, La Malfa, which initiated the work of planning, and the report with which, at the end of 1963, the activities of the National Economic Planning Commission were concluded, are profoundly different from those which underlay, for example, the Vanoni Scheme.

In the report of the Planning Commission, the problems of individual productive sectors were ignored. At the same time, relatively little attention was paid to the nature of the mechanism operating in the country, except for an energetic insistence at the beginning on monetary stability and on the uselessness of any plan whatsoever in the absence of such stability. The primary concern of the report was rather that of building up a coherent picture of the objectives to be pursued for achieving orderly balanced civil, as well as economic, progress in the country; schools, culture, social welfare, health services, public services, sports, all the fundamental sectors of national life were reviewed not so much to achieve this or that objective, and least of all to maximise the rate of growth in income and employment, as to make possible the orderly progress of national life. This shift in interest from the economic to the civil aspect of development is indicated by the fact that the pursuit of the plan's objectives is linked to the rate of increase of the national income only by way of example.

It is in this shift of attention from the economic to the civil aspect of development that the Mezzogiorno finds a new place in the planning context. More and more attention is, in fact, being paid to the importance of the costs caused by the excessive concentration of industry in a limited number of areas; on this question it is interesting to recall that, according to a recent study by SVIMEZ, with the backing of the National Research Council, the costs of urban infrastructure attributable to new residents (and thus net of metropolitan infrastructure costs and of urban renewal costs) could be reduced by 700–800 thousand million lire (11–12 per cent of the total), if by 1981 there were to be a more balanced distribution of new employment between North and South than in the past.

Regarding the problems of congestion, the fact should not be overlooked that, whereas in the past, unplanned developments in more advanced regions have given rise to conditions of land-use which it would be costly to rationalise, in the less advanced regions, in which development is at the initial stages, this is capable of being planned in the direction of more efficient conditions of land-use.

Industrialisation policy in the Mezzogiorno has recently been rendered more difficult by new factors resulting from technological progress. Technical progress tends, as is known, to increase company size, making large-scale production more advantageous. As a consequence of this, industrial expansion seems to take place more by the processes of expansion of already existing plants, which are located in the North, than by the setting up of new plants which could be located in the South.

Apart from that, technical progress increases the interdependence of firms and the importance of the availability of a wide range of complementary products and services. In other words, the importance of external economies increases relatively to other location factors and hence makes more difficult the continuation, with modern productivity standards, of the process of industrialisation which has been begun in the Mezzogiorno.

The possibilities of further progress have to be judged separately in terms of large plants and in terms of small- and medium-size plants. The location in the South of large new plants, calls for two types of public action: the intervention of State Shareholding companies; agreements with the not very numerous private controlling bodies on which the country's industrial groups depend. In the case of the former, it has to be remembered that it is made easier by the type of public enterprise which has become established in Italy. On the basis of what is now more than thirty years of experience, public enterprise in the manufacturing sector and in some service sectors is not organised through public agencies operating in the specialised sector and endowed with a monopoly position. It has been preferred to form so-called management agencies which operate in several sectors in competition with private business through firms whose legal form is that of a private company with shares; this type of organisation gives the Italian public enterprise freedom of initiative and the opportunity for rapid entry into new sectors to an extent unknown to the traditional nationalised enterprise.

Recent experience seems, however, to show that the location in an underdeveloped area of a large productive unit often remains an isolated incident, which does not give rise to those favourable repercussions on the rest of the economy which many expected from it. If, then, it is borne in mind that the number of *new* large production units that can be foreseen for the future in the Italian industrial system is very limited, it has to be concluded that important developments in the industrialisation of the South must depend principally on a variety of medium and small undertakings. The question that arises today in Italy is whether this objective can be achieved under the conditions that exist at present.

The setting up of a medium- or small-size firm can, in fact, only result from the personal initiative of a private entrepreneur and not from decisions taken by distant executive boards of large groups and implemented through managers. Thus neither the State shareholding firms nor private industrial groups, both of which have already obtained considerable industrial experience in the Mezzogiorno, are in a position to extend their action to the setting up of small- and medium-size units to operate in competition with similar units run directly by entrepreneurs in the North. On the other hand, the Mezzogiorno still does not have a numerous entrepreneurial class; nor is it easy, with the incentives currently available, to induce a larger number of entrepreneurs from the North to move personally to the South to run newly-formed companies of their own.

It has been thought that for the development of medium and small firms it could be possible to utilise an instrument that falls half-way between public enterprise and monetary incentive: the acquisition by public institutions of minority shareholdings in small- and medium-size private firms. The results of this type of intervention have, however, not been very satisfactory hitherto. Probably the best entrepreneurs do not want to have a public agency as partner. The latter may then find itself associated, where it does not wish to remain inactive, with a mediocre enterprise and, moreover, in a very weak position, both because it has little to contribute to the decisions that the other partner makes, and because, in cases of unfavourable results, it has to carry on with its own managers an enterprise which its partner, being short of capital, has been unable to finance. The acquisition by public agencies of minority shareholdings in small- or medium-size firms, control of which remains in the hands of a private entrepreneur, is therefore an instrument whose efficacy, on the basis of experience acquired up to now, is somewhat doubtful. As an instrument it should not, however, be abandoned, since it could be that in a more advanced stage of development it will produce better results.

Another instrument that has been considered is that of introducing disincentives which should fall on investments outside the Mezzogiorno, or at the least in the so-called congested areas. Such disincentives would be so designed that the burden the community has to bear as the result of the consequences of congestion is passed on to the required extent to enterprises that make such investments. But while for large plants a composite system of incentives in underdeveloped zones and of disincentives in the congested zone could bring about the transfer of investment projects from North to South, for medium- and small-size firms it is feared that disincentives might produce the effect of slowing down the development of firms in the congested areas without, however, inducing entrepreneurs to move to the underdeveloped area. In this case the overall development process would slow down in conditions in which this was not required by considerations of inflation, and thus the disincentives would become a deflationary element.

5 CURRENT PROSPECTS FOR THE MEZZOGIORNO

The action taken in the Mezzogiorno over the last twenty years has without question profoundly modified the area's economic conditions, both as regards the standard of life and the stock of productive capital. It is clear, however, from what has been said above that the Mezzogiorno's place in the development process of the Italian economy still retains elements of uncertainty and risks which are even greater than in the past.

To appreciate this, we must turn to the figures in Table 1 below which represent SVIMEZ estimates of the additional labour supply expected over the fifteen years from 1965 to 1980 in Italy.

TABLE ONE

ESTIMATED ADDITIONAL LABOUR SUPPLY IN THE PERIOD 1965–80 IN THE ABSENCE OF INTERNAL MIGRATION

(000s)

Group of Regions	Increase in Labour Force	Outflow from Agriculture	Total
North and Central Italy	450	870	1,320
Mezzogiorno	1,900	930	2,830
Total	2,350	1,800	4,150

It can be seen from the figures given in the table that in the fifteen-year period 1965–80, 68 per cent of the additional supply of labour in the country as a whole is likely to be provided by the Mezzogiorno. Since the Mezzogiorno, in spite of the development action taken in the past, produces only 22 per cent of overall national income produced by the non-agricultural sectors, it seems inevitable that, so long as no new factors intervene, the considerable flow of migration from the South towards other regions and abroad, which has so greatly altered not only the economic but also all other aspects of the life of the region, must continue. This fear is the more justified in that the industrial equipment of the South has been weakened to a greater extent than that of the North by the economic crisis of the past few years. In consequence, its capacity for expansion is thought to be even less than is represented by the Mezzogiorno's present 22 per cent contribution to the country's non-agricultural income.

This prospect is the more worrying because the labour reserves in the Mezzogiorno are being seriously depleted as a result of past emigration. There is no doubt that the younger labour force available in the Mezzogiorno will find employment outside the Mezzogiorno during the next fifteen or twenty years if the rate of development in the area proves to be inadequate. In this case, the quality of the Mezzogiorno population will have been so much weakened that no further policy for eliminating the gap would be possible.

For all these reasons, the Mezzogiorno problem is at the moment being very closely studied in Italy. The National Economic Plan contemplates ample intervention in the fields of infrastructure, education and training and, naturally, industrial development; but it is not so much the detail of such measures that will interest the present conference as the lessons that we can draw from the Italian experience.

6 THE LESSONS OF ITALIAN EXPERIENCE

In the first place it must be said that, in drawing attention to the difficulties encountered in taking action to help the Mezzogiorno, it is in no way intended to suggest that such difficulties could have been entirely avoided and that thus much more rapid progress could have been made. Indeed, the decisions made as Mezzogiorno policy was given practical application must be judged in the light of the possible alternative courses that have been proposed in practice. To be more precise, it is necessary to assess the state of existing development theory and the character of the instruments for development that were historically available at particular times. So long as this is borne in mind, it can be said that the experience of Italy in promoting progress in its underdeveloped region provides, on the one hand, material of very great interest for analysis at the theoretical level and for the possible further development of economic thinking on development problems; on the other hand it provides a very useful object lesson for the choice of intervention measures in areas which are today at a stage of development not dissimilar from that in which the Mezzogiorno found itself some twenty years ago.

Perhaps the most important comment suggested by Italy's experience is that not sufficient attention has been paid to the fact that industry growing up in an underdeveloped area must operate under the shadow of industry already established in other areas of the same country, while benefiting from a degree of protection – provided by so-called incentives – which is inevitably far less than that which infant industries have always enjoyed in all countries at all times. In Italy, for example, industry in the North and Centre, until the entry into force of the Rome Treaty and thus for more than half a century, had benefited from a degree of protection varying between 20 per cent and 40 per cent. Furthermore, the accumulation of industrial capital has been facilitated in those same regions by two great periods of inflation resulting from war; by the profits made on orders entrusted to industry by the State in preparation for those wars, as well as by outright grants made by the State during the great depression to cover the losses suffered by the banks in their dealings with industry.

In contrast to this, the newly developing industry of the Mezzogiorno enjoys a series of incentives equivalent to customs protection varying, according to circumstances, from 5 per cent to 10 per cent. It can be understood then that this makes substantial development by public enterprise inevitable, since it alone can run the heavy risks of an enterprise operating under conditions of great difficulty – risks which are offset only to a small extent by existing incentives. It can also be understood that the special industrial development banks operating in the Mezzogiorno cannot avoid making far larger losses than they would have to bear if they were working in a developed area. The high cost of development policy in the Mezzogiorno and other unfavourable features that are often quoted in criticism of the development action undertaken cannot, therefore, be considered as indicators of the policy's lack of success. With only such protection as is available to Mezzogiorno industry, the north and centre of Italy would still today be a largely agricultural area, subject, as in the first decades of the century, to a massive outflow of emigrants abroad. Indeed, it is to be reckoned a success of the policy adopted that so considerable a change has taken place in the South when allowance is made for the fact that development has been subject to the limitations described above.

None the less, it remains a fact that the incentives applied in the Mezzogiorno have been substantially less than are necessary to create an impetus to progress in the underdeveloped area sufficient to eliminate – perhaps even to reduce – the gap between North and South. New forms of development within the framework of the objectives of the National Plan, have to be adopted for the assistance of the South, if the elimination of the existing differences is to be seriously pursued.

In conclusion, Italy's experience seems to go to show that the central problem of development policy for an underdeveloped area lying within an industrialised country is that of instituting a system of incentives equal in economic effect to that of the customs' tariff protection which would currently be considered necessary to establish and ensure the progress of an industry in a country in which it is absent.

I

Part 3 The Experience of the Socialist Republics of Eastern Europe

BACKWARD AREA OF SLOVAKIA

13 The Development of a Backward Area in Czechoslovakia [1]

Pavel Turčan

1 INTRODUCTORY

The subject will be dealt with in two parts: the first part will be devoted to an analysis of the post-war economic policy whereby Czechoslovakia proposed to solve its basic regional problem and stimulate the development of its less advanced area, namely Slovakia; the second part will contain the more general ideas and conclusions emerging from the lessons and the achievements of this regional policy.

2 POST-WAR POLICIES IN SLOVAKIA

Although there are considerable differences in the economic levels of smaller areas such as the administrative districts, the main regional problem in Czechoslovakia is the backwardness of Slovakia as compared with the Czech area. It is a problem of special significance in that the Czech provinces and Slovakia constitute two ethnical and political regions inhabited by two distinct nations, and the backwardness of Slovakia thus also emerges as the economic basis of a national problem.

For historical reasons, at the beginning of the socialistic development of Czechoslovakia in 1945, Slovakia was a backward agrarian area, with an agricultural sector split up into innumerable smallholdings, with a latent threat of serious overpopulation and a weak industrial sector incapable of providing work for the surplus rural population. The territory of Slovakia represented 38·2 per cent of the whole of Czechoslovakia and its population 30 per cent of the total population of the republic, whilst its share in the industrial production of the country as a whole amounted to about 12 per cent and in agricultural production to about 28 per cent. The national income produced per inhabitant in Slovakia was 45 per cent lower than in Bohemia. In the Czech provinces 37 per cent of the total labour force was employed in industry and less than 30 per cent in agriculture, including forestry. At the same period, in Slovakia the corresponding figures were approximately 16 per cent in industry and 64 per cent in agriculture.

Immediately after the liberation of Czechoslovakia, a programme was drawn up to enable Slovakia to make up its lee-way. Because of the

[1] Translated by M. C. Lemierre.

ethnical and political nature of the problem, the programme was specifically designed to bring Slovakia, as a coherent macro-region, up to the economic level of the Czech provinces and to ensure a uniform social, cultural and economic level for the two areas. The policy was conducted along three main lines: firstly, the accelerated industrialisation of Slovakia; secondly, the development of its agriculture; and thirdly, the stimulation of culture, national education and scientific research. This programme formed part of the overall development plan for the national economy of Czechoslovakia. For its implementation there were two groups of resources on which it could draw – firstly on the resources of Slovakia itself and secondly on the material resources of the richer Czech area.

In respect of Slovakia's own resources, first and foremost there are its resources in manpower. These are being progressively vitalised by the transfer of redundant labour from the agricultural sector to non-agricultural branches, to industry in particular, by the increasing employment of women, and lastly by the reinforcements provided by the expanding population as it reaches the productive age. Owing to the rate of growth of the population in Slovakia, these reinforcements are relatively – and in recent years even absolutely – higher than those of the Czech provinces. As local resources, next come certain raw materials, mainly under the heading of agriculture and forestry. In view of Czechoslovakia's economic relations with Soviet Russia and the other social democracies of Eastern Europe, the geographical situation of Slovakia, with its common frontier with the Soviet Union from which most of the industrial raw materials are received, has become a major element of economic growth for Slovakia.

For the accelerated development of Slovakia, it is the second group of resources, i.e. the transfer of means from the Czech provinces, that is of primary importance. In the setting of a socialist economy with centralised planning, the central administrative machinery, through the intermediary of direct or indirect agencies, can decide on the geographical or the sectoral allocation of the available means of investment, regardless of their place of origin.

The economic policy designed to accelerate the process of bringing Slovakia up to the level of the Czech region thus finds its material support in the effective power of the centre to carry out an interregional redistribution of the means of investment. And in fact, Slovakia's share, both of investments and of non-productive consumption, throughout the post-war period was considerably higher than its contribution to the national income. It is, however, only fair to note that, with the increase in Slovakia's economic potential, the volume of these transfers is decreasing, even though construction is expanding considerably in Slovakia.

During the twenty-year post-war period, Slovakia, which was half a century behind the times, has undergone the accelerated large-scale development corresponding to the phase of industrialisation through which more advanced countries, including the Czech region, had passed many years earlier. It is a phase of development characterised by an expansion in breadth, by the construction of numerous industrial undertakings and by a rapid rise in employment in non-agricultural branches, accompanied by an accelerated fall in the volume of manpower employed in agriculture. Concomitantly with this development in the economic field, the construction of a network of technical training schools and colleges and also of basic and applied scientific research centres is likewise proceeding apace.

As the result of this rapid development there has been a significant increase in Slovakia's economic potential, a progressive reorganisation of the social and vocational structures of its population and a rise in the standard of living. Although the underdevelopment of Slovakia can be said to have been overcome in the absolute, there still remains the problem of lee-way in relation to the Czech region and it will be some time before this situation can be rectified. Moreover the very success that has been achieved in developing the Slovak area conceals problems which are fairly typical of all backward areas of industrialised countries whilst they are engaged in making up for lost time.

With the interregional redistribution of the means of investment, Slovakia has benefited during the 1946–65 period from a 30·6 per cent share in the total investments of the Czechoslovak economy. It has received 28·8 per cent of the investments in the productive sphere and of this total 26·3 per cent were allocated to industry and 33·2 per cent to agriculture. In the investments in the non-productive field, Slovakia's share was higher, amounting to 35·5 per cent because of the relatively high rate of housing construction.

The reorganisation of the Slovak economy as a result of the investment policy is best illustrated in the changing pattern of employment in the different branches.

In the distribution of manpower by branches, it is non-agricultural employment which now comes at the top of the scale. Whereas in 1948 the number of persons employed in agriculture was four times that in industry proper, by 1965 there were more industrial workers than agricultural ones. Even though the growth of the tertiary sector has been spectacular, the proportion of non-productive activities in Slovakia's total work force rose from 10·3 per cent in 1950 to 19·7 per cent in 1965. Whilst the number of persons employed in the productive branches has shown a slight fall in the course of these fifteen years, the number of workers engaged in non-productive activities has more than doubled. The increase has been particularly rapid in the sectors of national education, culture, science and research, and also in the public-health sector.

Special attention has been given to the training of manpower. In the 1948/9 academic year, there were 4 higher educational establishments

in Slovakia, with a total of 15 faculties and 9,000 students. In the 1965/
1966 academic year, there were already 12 higher educational establishments, with 33 faculties and 50,000 students, a third of whom were at the
same time earning their living. Nearly half the number of students were
taking courses of a technical nature. New university centres have been
created and alongside the scientific institutes attached to the Slovak

TABLE ONE

NUMBER OF WORKERS IN THE SLOVAK ECONOMY

(yearly average: 000s)

	1948		1965	
	Absolute Numbers	As %	Absolute Numbers	As %
Economy as a whole	1,526	100·0	1,709	100·0
Industry	231	15·2	497	29·1
Building	93	6·1	163	9·5
Agriculture	918	60·2	462	27·0
Forestry	95	1·6	44	2·6
Transport and post office	65	4·3	119	6·9
Trade	80	5·3	131	7·7
Scientific and technical research	4	0·2	27	1·6
Public services and housing services	14	0·9	43	2·5
Public health	13	0·8	58	3·4
National education and culture	25	1·6	112	6·5
Administration, justice	41	2·7	37	2·2
Finance and insurance	5	0·3	8	0·5
Other sectors	13	0·8	8	0·5

Academy of Science or to the relevant ministries or under the auspices of
certain large industrial firms, they are becoming centres of scientific and
technical progress of vital importance for the modernisation of industry
and of the national economy as a whole. In 1965 27,000 persons were
employed in research and development. In the last ten years, the material
equipment of the research institutes has been increased to 2·2 times the
original quantity.

In addition to the formation of specialists and research workers at
graduate level, the training of technical cadres and skilled workers at
secondary school level has also been developed. There are now six times
more students in the technical training colleges, the total number having
reached 92,000 by 1965. In 1965 alone, nearly 23,000 students passed out
from these establishments. The number of apprentices receiving two to
three years' training, if not more, in the vast network of apprenticeship
centres increased during the 1955–65 period from 33,000 to 88,000.

Slovakia's educational level is gradually approaching that of the Czech region. Already in 1963, 25·6 per cent of Czechoslovakia's total number of graduate specialists were provided by Slovakia and 21·1 per cent of the total number of specialists trained at secondary school level.

In twenty years of industrialisation a modern industry has been built up in Slovakia, with a total of 256 new factories installed and 171 undertakings reconstructed and considerably enlarged. These figures include, in addition to small- or medium-sized plants, a number of large concerns which are providing the necessary dynamic for the region and will gradually influence the structure of the Czechoslovak industry as a whole.

The chief undertaking of this type is the 'Forges of Eastern Slovakia', a powerful iron and steel combine of wide reputation, operating on the basis of coal from Ostrava and ore from the Soviet Union. It is run on the most up-to-date technological lines and, by its production of thin sheet in particular, it will be instrumental in developing and improving the whole pattern of iron and steel production and will make a valuable contribution to the modernisation and expansion of the machine industry. A second achievement of vital importance is the construction of a huge petrochemical combine – Slovnaft – near Bratislava, which refines the petroleum imported by pipe-line from the Soviet Union. With the completion of this undertaking, the centre of gravity of its production is shifting from the production of fuel to production of a petrochemical nature.

Other metal works have also been set up during this development period, in particular for the treatment of non-ferrous metals, and also chemical works which are among the most important in the whole of Czechoslovakia in addition to large factories for the machine industry at Martin, Komárno Tlmače, Trenčin, Kysuché Nové Mesto, Zlaté, Moravce, Krompachy and elsewhere. Factories that were already in existence, in particular at Dubnica and at Považská Bystrica, have been considerably modernised and enlarged.

The volume of industrial production in 1965 was 15 times that of 1937 and 7·5 times that of 1948. With a view to putting Slovakia on the same economic footing as the Czech region and to using Slovakia's potential resources for the development of the Czechoslovak economy as a whole, industrial production was deliberately developed at a swifter rate in Slovakia than in the rest of the country. Whereas in 1937 the Slovak share in the production of the whole of Czechoslovakia was only 7·8 per cent, it had risen to 20·7 per cent by 1965.

Table 2 shows the expansion of industry and its main branches from 1948 to 1965 and also the development of the branch structure of industry, both for Czechoslovakia as a whole and for Slovakia alone.

A peculiarity of Slovakia's development lies in the fact that no use has been made of the possibilities of growth of its agriculture which had at its

I 2

disposal 37 per cent of the agricultural land of Czechoslovakia and 33 per cent of its arable land.

In economic practice, the role of industrialisation has been over-estimated and that of agriculture very much underestimated. Investments have been made in industry partly at the expense of agriculture; for a long time, not even the build-up of stocks was used for the development of this

TABLE TWO

GROWTH OF INDUSTRIAL PRODUCTION IN CZECHOSLOVAKIA AND IN SLOVAKIA

	1965 as Percentage of 1948		*Shares of Different Branches in Industrial Production in 1965*	
Industrial Branches	*Czecho-slovakia*	*Slovakia*	*Czecho-slovakia*	*Slovakia*
Industry as a whole	480	753	100·0	100·0
of which:				
means of production	576	988	61·8	59·7
consumer goods	378	568	38·2	40·3
Branches of production:				
electricity	504	950	3·3	3·2
fuel	315	1,216	7·1	5·3
iron and steel	488	805	9·2	4·7
machinery	909	1,494	32·7	29·7
chemicals	958	1,549	6·8	9·7
building materials	626	774	3·3	5·3
wood industry	400	390	4·0	5·7
glass, porcelain, pottery	351	529	1·5	0·4
textiles	277	490	6·0	4·3
clothing	383	515	2·5	3·7
leather industry	298	451	2·5	3·2
food products	305	481	16·4	19·2

sector. While everything was being done to attract labour to the non-agricultural sectors, little effort was made to compensate for this loss by mechanisation, the use of chemicals or improvement of the land, despite the fact that the income from agriculture was remaining very much lower than that from industry. In these circumstances the loss to agriculture of its most productive manpower meant that the differential effect of migration from one sector to another was not an entirely positive one for the national economy as a whole. The negative effect of this disproportionate reduction in the number of workers was accentuated by a change for the worse in the age-pattern of the manpower remaining in the agricultural sector. By 1965, 45·5 per cent of the persons employed on a permanent basis in agriculture were fifty years old or more.

By 1965 the gross agricultural product in Slovakia had risen by over 40 per cent compared with 1948 and by approximately one-third compared with the last pre-war period. As there has been a sharp fall in the number of workers, the market product of agriculture has more than doubled in relation to the pre-war period. The gross product per full-time worker is 3·2 times higher than before the war but it is only 38 per cent greater per acre. The yield per acre of agricultural land is 27 per cent lower than in the Czech area. Likewise the production per full-time worker is 24 per cent lower. Slovakia's overall share in the gross agricultural production of Czechoslovakia is 30 per cent.

During the rapid development of the Czechoslovak economy over the last twenty years, Slovakia has increased its participation in the production of the national income for the whole country from 19 per cent to nearly 25 per cent. The percentage of the national income used by it was nevertheless considerably higher than its share in the formation of that income.

3 THE LESSONS OF CZECHOSLOVAK EXPERIENCE

Slovakia is now making up for lost time and is going through the process of industrialisation, or more precisely its final phase, at an accelerated pace or perhaps one might say, in a condensed form. This phase is characterised by an intensive build-up of industry, by the substitution of large-scale industrial production for what had hitherto been mostly small family concerns and by a wholesale transfer of the surplus agricultural labour force to the transforming industries. There has been a complete change in the structure of labour, in respect of its distribution among the various sectors, the levels of skill demanded from it and its capital equipment.

Slovakia now has to complete its phase of industrialisation and must at the same time look ahead and plan the foundations for the post-industrialisation period. There must be no dissociation between these two tasks, in terms either of time or, to a certain extent, of equipment. They must be carried out simultaneously and conjointly for two reasons. This necessity stems from the circumstances peculiar to the process of developing the Slovak economy. Another important factor that has to be reckoned with is the pressure exerted by the conditions resulting from the reorganisation of the economy, and by the conversion to a new economic policy in Czechoslovakia. What was previously a strictly centralised and controlled economy is now being replaced by a system in which the market is allowed to play an active role, in which a large share of responsibility for economic matters is decentralised at the level of individual undertakings and in which the pressure of the world market on the activity of the undertakings is increasing progressively. The financing of investments in the business sector is no longer a matter for the national budget. The firms will henceforth cover their investments from their own resources and from loans.

Conditions for the development of the backward areas will be considerably harder, even after the introduction of various measures of assistance, for the competition between firms on both the national and the foreign market will highlight the degree of economic, technical and organisational maturity of the various firms and in the context of the economic structure of the areas will also bring out any differences in respect of their capacity and general aptitude for steady long-term development.

For these reasons, the future development of Slovakia demands that the tasks involved in solving the outstanding problems of the industrialisation phase should not be allowed to relegate to the background the long-term undertaking that lies ahead; in other words, that the tasks of the industrialisation phase should be conceived in terms of the approaching post-industrialisation period. It is therefore important that the methods adopted for the policy of industrialisation, of expansion in breadth, of stimulation of industries employing a great deal of labour, should not be carried over to the next phase when the projected development will have to be patterned on criteria of technical maturity, modernism and dynamism in the various branches that make up the production structure of Slovakia. The urgency of the present day problems cannot of course be disregarded but it is the dynamic development of this backward area that must govern the policy of bringing it up to the level of the rest of the country.

What are these vital problems that reveal the incompleteness of the process of industrialisation and that must be solved simultaneously with the creation of the conditions that will promote steady and dynamic development in the years to come?

The permanent pressure exerted by the surplus labour force throughout Slovakia gave rise during the process of industrialisation to a situation in which the governing factor in the build-up of industry was the need to increase industrial employment. This meant that investments were directed towards branches that had the highest requirements in manpower, whilst the technical level of the new installations was often only a secondary consideration. Moreover, the means of investment were spread out over too many factories all being put up at the same time. The completion of these factories was often delayed, the funds for investment remained immobilised for years because of the large number of plants under construction, and frequently the installations had become economically and technically obsolescent before they were finished. There was considerable delay in making them operational and equipping them with their pre-production services. They often failed to attain their full dimensions and were unable to benefit from the economic advantages of large-scale operation.

The industrial build-up was accompanied by an excessive geographical and sectoral dispersion. Out of 420 industrial branches (listed under the standardised industrial nomenclature of the Council of Mutual Economic

Assistance) the Czechoslovak industry is represented in 408 branches and Slovak production appears in 317 branches.   The industrial production of Slovakia, which constitutes one-fifth of the total production of Czechoslovakia, is thus dispersed among 78 per cent of the total number of industrial branches in Czechoslovakia.   This is a relatively much greater dispersion than in the Czech area where the industrial tradition has established a highly developed production in a range of important branches for which the Czech industry is renowned the world over.

The sectoral dispersion is further accentuated by the geographical dispersion and by the fact that the greater part of the production of the industrial branches is spread out over a vast number of factories.   Only seventy-four branches, i.e. less than a quarter of the total, are concentrated in a single basic unit of production, whereas the production of fifty-four branches is dispersed between more than ten basic units of production. From two to ten basic units are involved in the production of 189 branches.

This dispersed industrial production is reflected in Slovakia by a small volume of production in the basic units and by the multifarious nature of most of these units.   The production programmes of the factories with such a diversified pattern of production for a relatively small volume of production are not conducive to really efficient production since they do too little to encourage technical progress, for which the essential prerequisite is specialisation.

The only important industrial complex was until recently Bratislava and even there the degree of concentration was not very pronounced: the town itself represented 6·1 per cent of the population of Slovakia and 9·5 per cent of the total number of workers in the industry.   A new industrial complex is now being installed at Košice, based on the Forges of Eastern Slovakia.

The conditions needed to give rise to the external economies which would result from a rational territorial integration of production were not forthcoming to an adequate degree.   The geographical and sectoral dispersion of industrial production was accompanied by only a meagre flow of goods and services within the region.   The products of the basic industries had for the most part to be sent for their finishing processes to factories in the Czech region.   This not only involved higher transport costs but it also meant that the potential impetus provided by the new factories in Slovakia did not really serve to stimulate the economic activity of the area that was actually under development.   The effects that might have been obtained were dissipated among the various branches throughout the economy and were thus deprived of their value for the development of the area.   The territorial integration of economic activity made little or no progress and the linking-up of the backward area to the more advanced part of the country remained unilateral in its effect and was of little benefit to Slovakia.

The shortcomings in the sectoral and geographical structure of the industry built up in Slovakia were further aggravated by the delay in providing the necessary infrastructure, without which development cannot proceed at its proper rate.

And it is precisely in the dispersion of the productive and technical basis and in its lack of cohesion that the incompleteness of the industrialisation of Slovakia as a coherent macro-region is most clearly apparent. The essential task of completing the process of industrialisation and at the same time looking ahead and planning the next stage, involves consolidating the industrial set-up from the sectoral and geographical point of view, providing the production capacities with the necessary cohesion and integrating them on a functional basis within the framework of the region, perfecting and modernising the branch structure of industrial production, completing the unfinished infrastructure and placing it effectively at the service of production.

Viewed in the perspective of these structural problems, the problem of the particularly backward micro-areas in Slovakia takes second place, despite the fact it is very much to the forefront at the present time and is the subject of a considerable amount of social and political pressure. The micro-areas in question are finding themselves with a certain amount of surplus labour, particularly female, in agriculture, since the non-agricultural branches in these areas have not provided sufficient possibilities of employment. The solution of this particular problem is essentially a matter for the big firms which could set up a certain number of specialised factories that would co-operate on a sub-contracting basis with the parent firm and benefit from the services of its research and development facilities and the guidance of its directors. Another possibility would be to develop industries of local value and install tourist facilities since these are mostly mountainous areas. Lastly, something must obviously be done, within the ethnical-political area that Slovakia represents, to encourage a certain amount of emigration of labour, particularly from its valleys and scattered hamlets, towards the new industrial townships now being created.

4   DIFFICULTIES OF A LONG-TERM SOLUTION

The lack of cohesion in Slovakia's production, its inability to produce fully finished goods and the overall nature of the co-operation existing between the production of Slovak and Czech factories are all features which reflect one of the peculiarities of a backward area within an advanced industrial country.

The undertakings in the advanced area, with their valuable experience and a long tradition of production behind them, tend to be drawn to the most up-to-date branches which are dynamic and progressive and offer high rewards for a production employing highly skilled labour, and they are in consequence inclined to transfer activities which employ a great number of workers but make little demand on skill, to the backward area.

The apparent logic of this situation nevertheless conceals the perpetuation of interregional inequality and the maintenance of elements of dualism within the country. The area with a forward-looking structure which applies the contribution of modern science and the latest technical achievements to its production and constitutes the intellectual vanguard of production is able, with the assistance of residual factors, to accelerate its economic development and further increase its advance over the backward area which will be more likely to follow the traditional trend of broadening the capabilities of industry and the manpower it employs.

With the revolutionary advances of science and technique in the world of today, a backward area in an industrialised country is faced with the following problem: either it will cling to its out-of-date concepts of industrialisation and concentrate on non-dynamic branches involving no very advanced techniques, in which case it will fall even further behind the more highly developed area; or else it will find its proper place in the division of labour with that area and will direct its effort towards the modern industrial branches and there make use of the intellectual and material forces which it has accumulated and which will act as the driving force for the modernisation of its structure. This second alternative presupposes that the final phase of industrialisation, the build-up and development of industry, will be carried through concomitantly with already some measure of reconversion and modernisation of the structure that has been set up, on the understanding, of course, that the effective assistance of the industry and the research and development facilities of the more advanced area will be forthcoming.

The efficacy of a development policy for the backward area of an advanced country, the effort required to solve the problem and remove its causes is not at the present time proportionate to the mere volume of grants, benefits and subsidies made available by the State or by other public bodies. These benefits – possibly involving the use of unskilled local labour – are only too apt to attract to the area firms in the less prosperous branches of industry that make little demand on infrastructure, on skilled labour or on the general cultural and technical qualifications of the population. Such undertakings may bring a certain amount of economic life to the area but are not capable of instilling the necessary dynamism and may even in the long run leave the backward area with a greater lee-way than before, as a result of its structural deterioration.

A special problem involved in bringing a backward area such as Slovakia up to the level of the rest of the country resides in the fact that, considering the degree of social and economic maturity which the area has already attained, it is not very expedient to follow in the wake of the advanced region and proceed through exactly the same stages transversed by it at an earlier date.

To solve the problem of Slovakia, to ensure that it can stand on its own feet and will not depend on special measures of assistance, that it will have its own driving force, its own dynamism, there must first be an up-to-date regional policy. Planned and implemented from the centre, it will be based on the utilisation of the human and material potential already built up and will be patterned on the latest trends in the scientific and technical world. This means that the future evolution of the economy must be anticipated and that Czechslovakia's long-term expansion planning must allow for the creation of equal conditions for both parts of the country and equal opportunities in the allocation of work. In practice this will involve identifying the specific spheres in which Slovakia will be capable of reaching the standards set by the world's most up-to-date producers. To this end, all the forces of the area must be harnessed and the regional economic policy so designed as to ensure its achievement.

A plan for the Slovak economy in the 1980-1985 period will shortly have to be prepared, with modern centres of development, one for instance round the Forges of Eastern Slovakia, from which a whole complex of auxiliary and sub-contracting industries would branch out, another centre of development round the large petrochemical combine at Bratislava and possibly a third one on the basis of the machine industry factories in Western Slovakia. The undertaking serving as prime-mover would of course have to be a specialised one, so that it could expand to an optimum production capacity, build up its own advanced research and development service and become capable of providing the necessary impetus for the economic activity of the whole area. But complementary productions from other industries would also have to be linked up with it in order to obtain the necessary diversification in the production of the area so as to encourage the multilateral development of its staff and also to lessen the effects of temporary slumps or setbacks. These potential centres of development must therefore be transformed into effective ones.

With an economic structure of this kind as the goal for the years 1980–5, it is also important to give careful thought to the economic policy for the area at the present time and in the intermediate period, without which the final goal cannot be attained.

But a regional policy conceived on these lines is very different from the one followed in the past. Replacing the former system of scattered, isolated investments planned at branch level and of piecemeal measures of assistance, there will be a single state policy directed to the long-term build-up of industrial complexes, based on a modern infrastructure and on adequate road, rail power and water systems and at the same time backed up by the necessary training schools and colleges, scientific research institutes and services, sanitary installations and cultural and spare-time facilities. Under such a policy the factories of the modern industries that will be playing the role of prime-movers will be installed with all the latest technical equipment.

On the basis of our own experience and on that of other countries we may conclude that the solution of the problem of backward areas depends primarily on their progressive industrial and territorial structure. The success of a development policy for such areas is therefore conditioned by their state of readiness for development, by their ability to assimilate the most advanced technique and technology and the up-to-date organisation of production. If a modern undertaking provided not only with technical equipment but also with senior staff from another, more advanced, area, is installed in a milieu where nothing has been done to prepare the social structure that is to receive it, the result may very well be to maintain for long years the elements of a dualist economy within the backward area. The greatest importance must therefore be attached to the formation and training of qualified senior and managerial staff from the ranks of the local population, for it is people of this kind who can be instrumental in changing the mentality and the psychological attitude of the workers who will be employed, and can engender in the area the necessary elements of dynamism and of modern thinking and technique. To succeed in making the prime-mover enterprise and its management into a nucleus of cultural and technical progress that can gradually help to produce the necessary change in the mentality of the population, is of primary importance in eliminating the lack of active psychological motivation that is particularly prevalent among the agricultural population of the area.

The centres of development thus described will not be created by the automatic effect of a market economy but will demand very definite action by the State. In the change-over to the new system of economic administration in Czechoslovakia there will have to be a reconception of the role of the State in the field of investment, particularly in respect of the backward area. There can be no doubt that during the implementation of the regional policy that has been outlined, the State will have to play a decisive role, either directly as an investor or by making state loans available with special terms of repayment. The State will have to intervene to tide over the intermediate period while the centres of development are being created and assist with large-scale investments in infrastructure, and again when the centres are nearing completion but are not sufficiently operational to produce full returns on the investments that have been made.

What at the present time is to be the role of the central plan in the steady long-term development of Slovakia and what will be the role of the market? What is to be taken care of by the state budget and how much can be left to the initiative of undertakings possessing their own resources? What is to be the role of Slovakia's own economic and political agencies? These are the questions which the new situation is bringing to the attention of Czechoslovakia's regional economists.

14 On the Yugoslav Experience in Backward Areas

K. Mihailović
UNIVERSITY OF BELGRADE

1 INTRODUCTORY

Yugoslavia is a country with a dual structure, a multinational structure of her population, a federal system with socialism on a self-management basis and an institutional system which is experiencing deep changes. Intricate conditions had to leave visible traces upon the whole treatment of the development of backward regions. This paper is an attempt to strike at the root of this development, to find out where the bases of some of its sufficiently evident characteristics are to be found. Some of these are: strong evidence of backward areas; contradiction between desires and possibilities; different emphasis placed on distribution and the concept of development; the insufficient conformity between sectoral and territorial structure.

2 DETERMINANTS OF BACKWARD AREAS DEVELOPMENT

There is nothing peculiar about the beginnings of the Yugoslav phenomenon of North and South. As in many countries between the Wars, the free market forces increased the inherited differences between developed and underdeveloped regions in Yugoslavia. Investigations have shown that immediately after World War II the *per capita* income in Slovenia, the most developed region, was three times greater than in Kosmet, the least developed. In this light the inherited state did not look dramatic, especially since the notion of 'developed' under Yugoslav conditions had an altogether relative meaning. Relationships seem to be different if the fact is borne in mind that the two types of regions are separated by a perhaps crucial phase in economic development. While developed regions, in which the necessary preconditions already existed, could start an accelerated industrialisation, the basic preconditions in backward regions had first to be created.

Since backward areas covered in the first phase the major part of the population and territory, it was they that determined the main characteristics of the whole economy: the *per capita* income below 200 dollars, the 75 per cent of rural population, the agrarian overpopulation, and so on; all these characteristics ranked Yugoslavia among underdeveloped countries. It seemed as if existing conditions, especially the great area of the underdeveloped territory and the low rate of accumulation, gave rise to the provocative question whether in the early stage the development of backward areas should at all be fostered, since it might, perhaps, affect adversely the growth of the economy as a whole, or whether such development should be postponed until a higher level, say 300 dollars *per capita*, was reached. In this case the risk of the consequences that might arise from the probable increase of regional disequilibrium would have to be taken. Leaving aside the question whether this frequently debated problem was relevant, one must make it clear that no such alternative was at the time under discussion. The recognition of backward areas had taken place previously, in step with social changes.

If we start from the fact that social tension is the driving force of development, then this tension must be expected, first of all, in backward areas. The constant increase of the population pressure in crowded agricultural areas and the very low rate of industrialisation between the Wars deprived the population of backward regions of almost every hope for the future. As time went by, poverty became all the more unbearable until the wish for radical changes found vent during the War. The liberation movement, inspired by a revolutionary programme, found full support in backward regions. The new society was morally and politically obliged to backward regions both for their moral and material support and their humanitarian and ideological objectives. This obligation was the greater since, for various new reasons, the poverty of backward regions became even more evident.

The socialisation of the means of production was an additional reason why interregional economic relations became important. Nationalisation eliminated the well-known conflict between the desire of the State to achieve a territorial allocation of economic activities in line with social and humanitarian goals and the interest of the private entrepreneur, whose decision-making is governed by his profit goals. It is true that in the recent period of development in Yugoslavia this conflict has reappeared in a somewhat altered form. But from the point of view of the more long-lasting socio-psychological effect, it is important that one factor has disappeared which had made interregional economic relations less immediate and less visible. Without this intervening factor the interests of regional economies were unobscured and directly comparable. Since people were aware of the importance of production, since they knew their own economic position and were conscious of the population pressures, this comparison did not exclude any of the relevant issues.

Even though these factors brought to the surface the interregional economic relations from the very beginning, a major social tension might perhaps not have arisen if Yugoslavia were not a country with several nations and languages, three religions, two alphabets, a heterogenous social structure and numerous local characteristics. The multinational society made regional differences very sensitive, rendering them socially important. Since some nations had a relatively developed and others an underdeveloped economic basis, regional development became a matter of national equality. Of major importance also was the history of the relations between these various nations, which had been critical between the Wars and went through their deepest crises during the War. It was necessary to react immediately to this prehistory. This is why interregional economic relations presented acute problems.

Owing to the existing tension, Yugoslavia had to choose between two extreme alternatives: to accelerate her industrialisation, thereby changing radically all economic and social relations, or to allow the existing conflicts to destroy such equilibrium as there was and to emerge as destructive forces. The social movement is due to refusal to contemplate the second and to a determination to achieve the first alternative. Thus, interregional relations, so closely linked to national problems, were pushed into the centre of social and economic events, while the treatment of backward regions represented a challenge to the proclaimed objectives of the nation.

This new approach to social and economic relations called for the creation of a new programme of ideas, the change of the social system, the development of an adequate form of socialism and the introduction of a new machinery for the functioning of the economy. All these changes bore either directly or indirectly upon the development of backward areas. It is essential to describe some of these impacts.

Equality and solidarity are the two values which bear especially upon the fate of backward areas. These are values which found their affirmation in the ideology. The specificity of the Marxian approach to equality is to be found, first, in the assertion that it is only thanks to the social means of production that this humanitarian objective can be fully achieved and, second, in the fact that economic and social equality depend essentially upon the distribution of conditions of production. As a consequence of nationalisation the first assumption has been fulfilled; the second was the leading idea of regional policy. As to solidarity, this objective was of unquestionable social importance from the point of view of the relations between the various nations composing Yugoslavia. The appeal to solidarity served as a well-tried weapon against opportunist ambitions, such as are to be found at times even in developed regions.

The repercussions of social policy upon the backward areas are strong and often controversial. The six republics and two autonomous regions, of which the Yugoslav Federation consists, represent political and national units with their legislative and executive bodies as well as their planning authorities and professional staffs. The role of actors with such competences was a major one within the region, but it was not at all minor, although not always visible, in interregional relations. With such a system all regional development, and especially that of backward regions, has its political and social aspects. There could be no objection to such an approach if one started from the assumption that the social aims were of predominant importance, while economic aims were subordinate. The trouble is, however, that social and political aspects are overemphasised. This is why the issue of how to reconcile the social and economic criteria, delicate enough already, is becoming constantly more complicated. With the strong emphasis placed on the political and social aspects, regionalisation cannot be handled on a strictly economic basis. The eight territorial and political units functioned in reality as separate regions, and it was by the same political criteria that the main areas were determined which were to be accorded the status of underdeveloped regions.[1]

The fact that regions are politically determined does not mean that the development of backward regions can be pushed into the background. Even if this should happen at times, regional political authorities, which are very well informed and alert to all that happens in their territories, would inevitably react. The local initiative has ample scope and so has any free enterprise aimed at the achievement of structural equilibrium between regions, which cannot be always seen from the centre or which does not seem to be important. The weak side of the politically determined regionalisation is that, owing to rigid borders among republics and regions, the physical territory is being 'banalised', while the mobility of capital and labour force is decreasing. This is the source of serious trouble in any attempt to give priority to the use of indirect methods in the development of backward areas.

Rigid borders between regions are a serious obstacle to the integration of a long-term concept of regional development into a national economic policy which would take account of the whole territorial structure of the economy. Without such a positive concept, a policy of coordination gets bogged down in regional contradictions and an attempt to solve them in detail by compromise. The arbitration of political bodies, which becomes necessary in such circumstances, puts even more stress on political criteria and pushes economic criteria into the background; it creates, on the other hand, an additional source of difficulties, which in a multinational community are already numerous.

The fact that detailed planning and management from the centre have now been abandoned shows in broad terms the extent to which the economic system has now changed. During the transition period to decentralisation and self-management, indicative planning has been adopted, while the market has become very much more important. Such changes

---

[1] Of 8 political and territorial units, there are 4 which are being treated as backward areas: the Republic of Bosnia and Hercegovina, Montenegro, Macedonia and the Autonomous Region of Kosmet. Developed regions used to treat some sub-regions as underdeveloped, either with their own funds or with the assistance of the Federation.

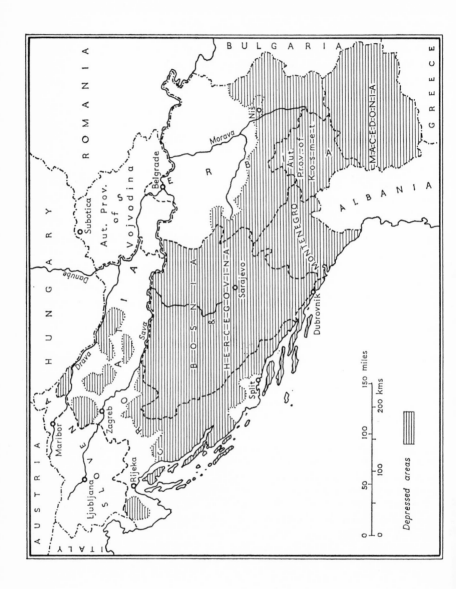

were bound to affect the backward areas also. The repercussions which followed or which might have followed are fascinating and could easily divert a theoretical economist into precedents and logical speculations instead of analysing scrupulously all the relevant factors and thus estimating their real implications. Caution is especially necessary with regard to some permanent characteristic of the federal system, which have provided for the continuity of major objectives and to some extent also of the methods of development of backward areas.

Any comparative investigation makes use of arguments, which, when account is taken of them all, usually give the advantage to centralisation. The concentrated financial resources are perfectly mobile and there is, in consequence, no obstacle to the territorial allocation of economic activities in underdeveloped regions. Thus, a satisfactory treatment of backward areas is possible and they may be integrated into the development of the economy as a whole. Indeed, in this context we cannot discuss the question of initiative on a regional basis. The share of the regions in the elaboration of the overall plans is usually reduced, in practice, to a formality, while courses of action which might be possible within the framework of locally determined economic activities usually do not have the necessary backing.

It would appear that decentralisation and the market-mechanism cannot offer any comparable advantages. The fragmentation of the financial resources, linked to particular territories and thus insufficiently mobile, acts as a brake upon the territorial allocation of economic activities. Indeed, decentralisation, while it gives opportunity for local initiative and a more efficient solution for the structure of the region, impedes co-ordination among regions as well as the regional division of the development of the economy as a whole. By emphasising the role of the market, we can expect nothing but a deeper gap between developed and underdeveloped regions. These arguments are the more cogent since the experience of many countries has confirmed them.

According to this line of thought, it would be natural if the decentralisation of backward regions ran into serious trouble. This has not, however, been the case in Yugoslavia. On the contrary, the effect has been just the opposite. Since 1956 the development of backward regions has been more rapid than in the earlier period. The question is why?

To understand this unexpected change, we must bear in mind that such fundamental questions as the volumes of investment funds and budgetary spending, and later on also terms of trade, have always been associated with some sort of political compromise. Thus, neither centralisation nor decentralisation could affect their nature. Significant changes occurred in the way in which compromises were reached. Throughout the period of centralisation, compromises were reached within the Government, and the public had no insight into them and could take no part in them. Even such a body as the Council of Nations, the function of which is to arbitrate in all disputes between the republics, had no responsibility for this. Compromises reached in such a way were not rigid, and consequently, could be changed without major social repercussions, the more so since changes could be easily justified on the ground that they were necessitated by the development of the economy as a whole, by external factors, or by any other argument which seemed to be reasonable and cogent enough.

One has the impression that the establishment of the Fund for the Development of Backward Regions has negative aspects also. The single accumulation fund is being abolished and problems will be handled separately and independently within the various territories. The importance of these aspects is neither denied nor underestimated, but the primary reason why this fund has been established is to be found in the certainty of the fixed amount of help which will be extended to backward regions. At the same time, further institutional changes will not be able to endanger the availability of these funds. It is typical of the whole process that the position of backward regions became legally and financially more clearly determined, the more it was endangered by institutional changes and the market mechanism. The enactment of the law requiring the obligatory faster rate of growth of backward regions and the guaranteed minimum of the budgetary spending on them reflect this sort of reaction. The rise in prices of agricultural products and raw materials created more favourable terms of trade for backward regions, but since the price scissors have not been completely closed thereby, compensation which is included in the total resources earmarked for underdeveloped regions may be made. The development of the economy as a whole, which was fairly rapid while these changes in the institutional system were taking place, made possible a better treatment of backward regions as well as an efficient settlement of issues associated with decentralisation.

Apart from the volume of resources earmarked for the development of backward regions, the question of the territorial allocation of economic activities remained unsettled. Expectations that enterprises in the developed regions would invest in the underdeveloped regions proved to be over-optimistic in a country where capital is tight and where the institutional influences upon the investment allocation are still strong, though not always visible. Some enterprises from developed republics did, indeed, invest in backward regions, but their contribution was limited, in most cases, to professional help and the establishment of business co-operation. The relatively small number of such cases indicates that they represent a gesture, sometimes with a political background, rather than a method of operation which is playing an important role. The fact that capital is connected to a particular territory bears not only upon territorial, but also upon inter-industry relations. Since the economy does not function any longer as a single unit, direct administrative interference of

the State with the economy has been abolished. But decentralisation calls
for integration through economic links, and this is only now beginning.
All this involves, moreover, the problem of balancing out the movements of
capital through banks and the allocation of it on a territorial basis.

Apart from the processes of political compromise there is another
factor connected with institutional change. Centralisation coincides with
the first and decentralisation with the second stage of a first and very long
investment cycle. The earlier orientation towards basic industries and a
limited number of large projects was inevitably inelastic on a territorial
basis; on the other hand, the later growth of the total volume of investment, largely directed to manufacturing industries, agriculture and services, had offered more possibilities for freedom of location and quick
reallocation. The fact that, throughout the period of centralisation,
Yugoslavia faced complex international political and economic relations,
which changed essentially and were more settled after 1956, was also
important.

3 OBJECTIVES AND RESULTS

All factors mentioned above have found their joint expression in equality,
which appears in all documents and plans as the single objective of regional
development. Equality is in its operative meaning conceived as a process
in which all areas are developing rapidly on the basis of industrialisation,
while underdeveloped republics and areas, with a higher rate of growth, are
gradually to reach the same level as the developed ones. A brief analysis
will illustrate whether and to what extent these norms have hitherto been
achieved.

In Table 1, a few relevant indicators show the changes that have occurred
in the economic and social structure of four regions, which at the level of
federal policy were accorded the treatment of underdeveloped regions. If
one takes these four regions together, during the period of seventeen years
(from 1947–64) the *per capita* income at constant prices rose from
52,901 to 126,307 dinars (as from 100·0 to 238·7). Thanks to such a
growth these regions reached in 1964 the *per capita* income of Slovenia of
1947, which was very considerably higher than the income of the backward
areas at that time, and exceeded the average income of Yugoslavia as a
whole in 1947 by 71 per cent. The real value of fixed capital at constant
prices per inhabitant of the four backward areas together exceeded in 1964
the Yugoslav average of 1947 by 51 per cent. Simultaneously, employment rose rapidly. Table 1 also shows that the development of the backward regions was not limited to economic development but included also
considerable social and cultural development.

What is important in this development is the fact that, except for
Kosmet, an end has been put to the secular rising trend of the absolute

SOME INDICATORS OF THE DEVELOPMENT OF BACKWARD AREAS IN YUGOSLAVIA

	Bosnia and Hercegovina	Montenegro	Macedonia	Kosmet
Geometrical rate of *per capita* income growth 1947–64	4·94	6·10	6·58	3·68
Increment of fixed capital *per capita* 1947–64 (dinars of constant real value) [a]	348,281	612,009	382,944	—
Share of industry in income formation [b]				
1947	25·5	12·5	20·9	28·0
1964	52·9	49·9	33·1	47·5
Share of agriculture in income formation [b]				
1947	32·3	46·8	53·1	51·8
1964	17·8	16·0	24·7	30·8
Number employed in the social sector per 1,000 inhabitants [c]				
1952	95	72	70	46
1963	131	141	149	74
Number of agricultural population [d]				
1953	1,770,332	258,102	818,467	584,803
1961	1,641,638	221,350	718,415	617,679
(difference (– or +))	– 128,694	– 36,752	– 100,052	+ 32,876
Share of agricultural population in total population in per cent [d]				
1953	62·2	61·5	62·7	72·4
1961	49·6	46·4	50·6	63·6
Percentage of illiterates				
1953 [d]	40·2	30·1	35·7	54·8
1961	32·5	21·7	24·5	41·1
Secondary education [d] per 1,000 inhabitants				
1953	101	227	137	72
1961	148	313	225	117
Higher education per 1,000 inhabitants				
1953	21	38	21	10
1961	62	101	78	35
Number of hospital beds per 1,000 inhabitants [e]				
1953	2·4	4·3	3·2	1·8
1961	3·6	6·4	4·5	2·8

Sources: [a] Income – 'Jugoslavija 1945–1964' (constant prices 1960) in Savezni zavod za statistiku (S.Z.Z.S.), *Statističkigodišnjak S.F.R.J.*

[b] Dr Ivo Vinski, *Rast fiksnih fondova po jugoslovenskim republikama 1946–64 po cenama 1962. g* – to be published shortly.

[c] S.Z.Z.S., *Zaposlenost*, Statistički bilten no. 310.

[d] S.Z.Z.S., *Statistički godišnjak S.F.R.J.* – stanje popisa stanovništva.

[e] Saveznog zavoda za zdravštvenu zastitu, *Statistički godišnjaci.*

Note: All values in this paper are expressed in old dinars.

number of the agrarian population. The number of the industrially employed per thousand inhabitants has nearly doubled.

These relevant criteria demonstrate that the backward areas have rapidly passed through a period in which preconditions have been created, through changes of their economic and social structure, under which direct effects upon income and employment have been evident. The question arises whether such a development alone can lessen the differences between the developed and the underdeveloped areas. The relative development of the two types of areas in Yugoslavia offers ample possibilities for arbitrary interpretation. Conclusions depend heavily on how one approaches the choice of criteria, differences of lower and higher levels of economic development, the interrelationship of the development of the economy as a whole and that of the backward areas, the problems of limiting factors, the evaluation of demographic factors, the trends and absolute amounts of *per capita* income, the interpretation of the task of equalising areas in the medium or the longer run, and so on. The discussion of all these various possible approaches lies outside of the framework of this paper. Thus, the comparative development must be presented on the basis of a limited commentary on the facts.

The total and *per capita* incomes have shown different trends in the period 1947–64.[1] While the index of total income in the four backward areas was higher (330·0 versus 326·6 in developed ones), the index of the *per capita* income was lower (238·7 versus 279·5). Such movements indicate the great influence of the different rate of population growth, which acted as a limiting factor on development. During the seventeen years under consideration, population in developed areas rose by 13·7 per cent; in the underdeveloped regions, on the other hand, by 38·2 per cent.

All the backward areas did not develop alike in the post-war period. The geometrical rate of growth of *per capita* income in Yugoslavia as a whole, amounting to 5·91 per cent, was exceeded by two backward regions (Macedonia 6·58 and Montenegro 6·10 per cent), while the other two had a lower rate (Bosnia and Hercegovina 4·94 and Kosmet 3·68 per cent). Owing to the lower starting point, absolute differences in *per capita* income increased also in instances in which the rise in income of underdeveloped regions was relatively higher. The ratio of *per capita* income increment of the four underdeveloped areas to that of the developed ones turned out to be 1 to 2 dinars.

The unequal rate of growth of the various backward areas is due to different combinations of three factors: the rate of population growth, the intensity and the structure of investment. The fact that the rate of *per capita* income growth was inversely related to the rate of population

[1] All income calculations in this paper refer to the period 1947–64 in constant prices of 1960. Throughout 1965 the parity of prices was changed. Series at new prices do not yet exist.

growth points to the conclusion that the demographic factor contributed largely also to the differences of the development of the backward areas. There is no doubt that this influence exists; but it must not be overrated. The relatively most rapid development of Macedonia is due to the structure of investments, with a large share devoted to manufacturing industries,

TABLE TWO

PER CAPITA INCOME

(in old dinars at prices of 1960)

	1947	1964	Increment	Index 1947= 100	Average of S.F.R.J.=100 1947	Average of S.F.R.J.=100 1964
1. Bosnia and Hercegovina	60,575	137,499	76,924	227·0	82·9	70·9
2. Montenegro	51,739	141,559	89,820	273·6	70·8	73·0
3. Macedonia	45,293	133,966	88,673	295·8	62·0	69·1
4. Kosmet	38,437	71,026	32,589	184·8	52·6	36·6
5. Underdeveloped areas as a whole (1–4)	52,901	126,307	73,406	238·7	72·4	65·1
6. Slovenia	127,874	378,303	250,429	295·8	175·0	195·1
7. Croatia	78,430	292,191	153,761	296·0	107·3	119·7
8. Vojvodina	79,538	202,845	123,307	255·0	108·8	104·6
9. Inner Serbia	69,849	186,514	116,665	267·0	95·6	96·2
10. Developed areas as a whole (6–9)	81,857	228,788	146,931	279·5	112·0	121·6
11. Serbia as a whole	68,842	174,950	106,108	254·1	94·2	90·2
12. Socialist Federal Republic of Yugoslavia	73,086	193,917	120,831	265·3	100·0	100·0

Source: For national income and population 'Jugoslavija 1945–1964', S.Z.Z.S. Calculations have been carried out in the Economic Institute in Belgrade.

as well as to the rise in the yield and share of intensive farm products in agriculture. The fact that the rise of the *per capita* income in Montenegro was above the Yugoslav average is due to fixed capital investment, of which the large increase outweighed the rather inefficient investment structure. The relatively slower development of Bosnia and Hercegovina and Kosmet derives from the coincidence of the relatively higher rate of population growth, low investment and the unfavourable investment structure. All these three factors were especially powerful in the case of Kosmet, which has remained the least developed region in Yugoslavia.

As regards the developed areas, these three same factors together brought about an entirely opposite result in Croatia, and primarily in Slovenia. The high rate of the *per capita* income growth, with a relatively higher starting point, distinguished Slovenia and Croatia in terms of the degree of development from other areas. While Kosmet is the extreme of the underdeveloped areas, Slovenia is the other extreme of the developed regions. Inner Serbia, which has always been somewhat below the Yugo-slav average, is the only region whose relative position has not changed, while Vojvodina is a particular case. As the most important agricultural region in Yugoslavia, Vojvodina contributed, through low prices of agri-cultural products, very much to the development of the economy as a whole. The accumulation which has been created on this basis was refunded only in part to the same territory in investment. Apart from that, it was only from Vojvodina that reallocation of industrial enterprises into other areas was carried out. Thus, it is clear why this region not only moved from second to third place in terms of the degree of development, but approached closely the Yugoslav average.

Budgetary spending has been an important corrective of incomes generated on a regional basis, and it acts as an equalising factor of material and social conditions in the various territories. Expenditure on schools, medical care, social and cultural institutions and administration has always been considerable in the backward areas throughout all the post-war period; a rough notion of this may be obtained from Table 1. Differ-ences have been due to the ways in which these services were organised at

TABLE THREE

PER CAPITA BUDGETARY SPENDING IN 1965

(current prices – in 000 dinars)

	Bosnia and Herce-govina	Monte-negro	Mace-donia	Slovenia	Croatia	Serbia Totally	Vojvo-dina	Kosmet
Budgetary spending	37·4	49·9	41·4	71·5	56·7	43·9	42·8	44·6
Grants received *	6·1	17·1	10·4	—	—	—	—	17·7

* This represents direct grants for budgetary spending (schools, medical care, social insurance, administration). Investments out of the Fund for the Development of Backward Regions are not included.

Source: *Statistički godišnjak S.F.R.J.* (1966).

different periods. During the period of centralisation, all services were provided out of a single budget. In the period of decentralisation, how-ever, underdeveloped regions were guaranteed additional budgetary re-sources, approximately on the Yugoslav average.[1] Table 3 above shows how this practice worked out.

[1] The Basic Law on the Financing of Social and Political Communities of July 1964 (Art 38) provides that the Federation is to guarantee additional resources to any republic whose own *per capita* revenue is below the *per capita* revenue in the republic whose revenue equals the Yugoslav average or is closest to it.

Income alone cannot show adequately the achievements in the development of the backward areas. The increment of fixed capital is perhaps a more relevant criterion in the stage in which preconditions are being created. In any case it is relevant to the evaluation of what has been done.[1]

TABLE FOUR

FIXED CAPITAL PER HEAD

real value in 000 dinars at prices of 1962)

	1947	1964	Index 1947= 100	Increment 1947 Over 1964	S.F.R.J.=100 1947	S.F.R.J.=100 1964
1. Bosnia and Hercegovina	259·5	601·8	231·9	342·3	61	74
2. Montenegro	267·1	870·5	325·9	603·4	63	107
3. Macedonia	265·4	643·1	242·3	377·7	62	79
4. Underdeveloped as a whole (1–3)	261·8	643·5	245·8	381·7	61	79
5. Slovenia	759·7	1,404·2	184·8	644·5	178	172
6. Croatia	516·1	973·6	188·6	457·5	121	119
7. Serbia	402·1	734·1	182·5	332·0	94	90
8. Developed as a whole (5–7)	482·8	890·8	184·5	408·0	113	109
9. S.F.R.J.	426·0	815·7	191·5	389·7	100	100

Source: Vinski, *Rast fiksnik fondova po jugoslovenskim republikama 1946–64. Po cenama 1962 g.*

The percentage increment of real fixed capital has been greater in underdeveloped areas, while the absolute increment in both types of areas is almost the same. The increase is 381,000 dinars of *per capita* fixed funds in underdeveloped regions as compared with 408,000 in developed ones (the Yugoslav average being 389,000). On closer examination one can see that Serbia and Bosnia and Hercegovina had the lowest absolute increment, which was below the Yugoslav average. As to underdeveloped regions, the relatively heaviest investments were made in Montenegro and this is why in 1964 this republic was above the Yugoslav average. However, in this case a thinly populated territory had to be activated. Thus the *per capita* criterion was not adequate.

To get a fuller insight into the unequal rate of growth in the backward areas, the dynamics of investment in the post-war period must be borne in mind. Bosnia and Hercegovina was the backward area which started with the highest income and, thanks to her abundant resources of energy and raw materials, absorbed heavy investment during the early years.

---

[1] Unfortunately, the possibilities of statistical analysis are limited by the fact that the figures for fixed capital funds in the Republic of Serbia have not been divided between Kosmet, Inner Serbia and Vojvodina. Those given are, however, sufficiently good to indicate the general trends.

Consequently, this republic for a period made no call upon the fund for the Development of Backward Regions. However, from 1961 on it was again accorded – at first in part and from 1966 in full – the treatment of an underdeveloped region. The shortfall in revenue could not be made up for. Throughout the period in which Bosnia and Hercegovina made no call on the fund, more intense investment was made in Montenegro, Macedonia and Kosmet.

The fact that emphasis was put first on one backward area and then on another one indicates that inadequate accumulation could not continuously keep investment high in all backward areas. With the development of the whole economy, the growth of accumulation and the assistance of foreign resources, there emerged wider possibilities for intervention, and it can be seen that later all areas could be covered at the same time. Thus, while the dilemma of how to conduct policy in a condition of general economic backwardness was not important for the definition of the backward areas, it could not be escaped in practice. The application of the method of successive development reflected it very clearly.

4 RELATIONS BETWEEN SECTORS AND REGIONS

The comparative changes of fixed capital and of incomes bring out very clearly the fact that investments are less effective in backward regions than they are in developed ones. Every analysis will show that in backward regions there has been a longer period of construction, that it took a long time before all was ready for production, that there was a lack of skilled labour, and so on. This group of factors bore only to a limited extent upon investment efficiency, since it turned upon the margin of available absorptive capacities. In any case, this factor was less important than that of the unbalanced early investment structure, in which capital-intensive industries prevailed.

This structure has been made less effective mainly by lower investment in agriculture, which is to be explained by the fact that the northern, developed regions have a greater comparative advantage. Since agriculture occupied the major part of the population, this structural inefficiency had powerful effects upon total income. The second trouble is to be found in the limited development of manufacturing industries, with an emphasis upon traditional industries (the textile and foodstuffs industry) or which, if based upon contemporary technologies, began only in the more recent period. Services have also found but little room in the structure of economic activities. Investment in energy, transportation and the production of raw materials, although considerable in size and share, could not compensate for the insufficient share of other sectors and branches. The fact that the *per capita* income in the industry of backward regions amounted to 70 per cent and at times even to 80 per cent of the

Yugoslav average, would have had an altogether different effect with a more diversified structure.

A few data will show the extent to which the underdeveloped regions were principally oriented towards energy and raw materials. Electrical energy, ferrous metallurgy and the cellulose industry absorbed about 75 per cent of gross investment in industry in Montenegro.[1] (Transportation took 24·3 per cent of total investment in the economy.) In Kosmet, non-ferrous metallurgy and coal absorbed 50 per cent of gross investment in industry. From electrical energy, coal and ferrous metallurgy, which constitutes more than one-half of gross investment in industry in Bosnia and Hercegovina, there has been produced only 37 per cent of all industrial income.

Macedonia is an exception among backward regions. Being rather poor in energy and mineral resources and having relatively favourable conditions for intensive plantation agriculture, both manufacturing industry and agriculture occupy an important place in the structure of economic activities. In comparison with Montenegro, one of the three regions referred to above, Macedonia, as an exception among the underdeveloped regions, shows the effects of its different structure. As may be seen from Tables 2, 4 and 5, both republics started in 1947 with much the same *per capita* income and number of employed per 1,000 inhabitants, while the difference in birth-rate was insignificant. However, while the increment of *per capita* fixed capital funds from 1947 to 1964 was 43·3 per cent lower in Macedonia than in Montenegro, the increment of *per capita* incomes was the same, while the growth of employed per 1,000 inhabitants was even larger.

If one compares the developed and underdeveloped regions, one can see in the main the same relations as follow from the comparison of Macedonia and Montenegro, except that the effects of different structures are even more pronounced. Thanks to their already developed and subsequently completed infrastructure and to their developed natural resources (apart from those in electro-energy) the developed regions achieved a balanced structure with an important share in manufacturing industries, services and intensive agriculture. Such a structure contributed on a larger scale not only to the rise of output and employment but also to personal and family incomes.

It is natural that throughout the post-war development process a division of labour was adopted in Yugoslavia under which backward regions produced for the most part raw materials, while manufacturing activities were normally to be found in developed regions. Some of the consequences of this division of labour, which is not, of course, rigid, are evident firstly, in the terms of trade between primary products and

---

[1] Data refer to cumulative gross investments for the period 1947–64 in constant prices.

K

TABLE FIVE

EMPLOYMENT CHANGES IN THE SOCIAL SECTOR

(per 1,000 Inhabitants)

	Total Employed			Employed in the Economy			Employed in Industry		
	1952	1965	Absolute Growth	1952	1965	Absolute Growth	1952	1965	Absolute Growth
S.F.R.J.	100·2	183·7	83·5	81·2	149·8	68·6	33·5	70·6	37·1
Bosnia and Hercegovina	94·9	137·1	42·2	81·9	112·9	31·0	30·5	55·7	25·2
Montenegro	71·6	140·0	68·4	51·5	106·9	55·4	11·8	49·8	38·0
Croatia	117·7	218·5	100·8	96·2	180·4	84·2	39·7	82·5	42·8
Macedonia	69·9	154·8	84·9	53·8	123·2	69·4	15·6	48·2	32·6
Slovenia	171·2	308·7	137·5	143·9	257·0	113·1	77·1	138·6	61·5
Serbia	84·4	168·4	84·0	65·6	135·5	69·9	26·3	62·2	35·9
of which:									
Inner territory	87·2	168·1	80·9	67·1	133·0	65·9	27·3	66·4	39·1
Vojvodina	95·1	219·3	124·2	76·6	185·7	109·1	28·7	70·6	41·9
Kosmet	46·1	80·9	34·8	33·9	59·6	25·7	15·5	28·8	13·3

Source: S.Z.Z.S., *Zaposlenost, Statistički bilteni* nos 310, 394 and 414.

TABLE SIX

AVERAGE NET PERSONAL INCOMES IN 1965

(000 dinars)

	S.F.R.J.	Bosnia and Hercegovina	Montenegro	Croatia	Macedonia	Slovenia	Total	Kosmet
Total	50·1	48·2	45·0	52·4	41·5	62·3	46·9	41·8
Industry and mining	50·1	50·8	45·9	53·1	41·5	61·1	45·5	44·1

Source: S.Z.Z.S., *Statistički godišnjak S.F.R.J.* (1966) p. 477.

manufactures. These terms of trade were less favourable to producers of raw materials, especially in the period in which accumulation was being enforced through high prices in manufacturing industries. The economic reform adjusted prices approximately to prices in the world market. Disparities have, however, not been altogether averted. This is why part of the Fund for the Development of Backward Regions has served as compensation for unfavourable terms of trade. A second important aspect is the vulnerability of the insufficiently diversified structures of the backward regions. Changes in the pattern of fuel consumption, for example, brought about difficulties in the sale of coal, especially in Bosnia and Hercegovina. Thirdly, manufacturing industries in developed regions, having considerable reserves of capacity, have discouraged underdeveloped regions from expanding the same branches; since this fact was overlooked, manufacturing capacities were often duplicated.

The structure of economic activity in the backward regions derived from a combination of various relevant considerations. The state of development called for considerable investment in infrastructure. The development of the backward regions depended, because of the comparatively limited possibilities of developing agriculture, primarily upon industry. The backward regions possessed considerable unexploited energy and mineral resources, in which the whole economy was interested. Skilled labour was an important limiting factor on the development of more advanced types of manufacture.

Structural disequilibrium provided a guide for the development of the economy in the backward regions. The growth of industrialisation and the more favourable prices for agricultural products encouraged the development of agriculture. Industry no longer depends more upon natural raw materials alone. Manufacturing industries are developing as the result of more advanced techniques of the manufacture of artificial materials. The extraction of lead in Kosmet has stimulated the expansion of the manufacture of accumulators as well as the chemical industry. Spinning-mills are paralleled by weaving mills. In Bosnia and Hercegovina the engineering industry is developing, while timber is being used increasingly for such technical purposes as furniture and cellulose. The beauties of the underdeveloped regions have encouraged the development of tourism, which is growing rapidly. A marked development of such services as hotel-keeping, transportation, maintenance services for durable consumption goods and the like is also to be recorded. Efforts to establish structural equilibrium in this way are significant rather as a marked trend in development than in terms of results already achieved.

This trend does not mean, however, that the emphasis that has been placed hitherto on the creation of an infrastructure and a raw materials basis is likely to be abandoned completely. The solution of some of the vital problems of some of the backward regions is directly conditional on measures to deal with these problems. The expansion of the aluminium industry as well as the construction of the railway line from Beograd to Bar depend, for example, on such vital considerations for the economy of Montenegro as the full incorporation of this region into the Yugoslav economy, the development of the port of Bar, measures to reduce costs of production and sale, the development of tourism, as well as other factors.

The allocation of economic activities to backward regions in Yugoslavia has shown that structural disequilibria are inevitable if sectoral solutions are imposed subsequently on regions. Nor could the difficulties be avoided under conditions in which sectors and branches were divided equally between regions and the economy as a whole. For this reason it is right to ask whether the conventional approach, under which sectors play an active and regions a passive role, is the proper one. In the light of the Yugoslav experience, this is not the best approach, not only because of the effects upon income and employment, but for other reasons also.

A model of development of an economy as a whole under conditions of dual structure brings out best the fact that the basic role of regional considerations cannot be ignored, or else it will entail a whole array of theoretical and practical anomalies. A model that depends on the hypothesis of equally developed regions does not meet the case of some developed and some underdeveloped regions. If one works with the average of all regions, one ignores the specificities of both types of regions. Dilemmas of this kind do exist in the approach to the development of the economy as a whole and in the search for institutional solutions. Divergences of views have been due, for the most part, to the fact that some writers have had in mind the first type of regions and others the second type. Growth of labour productivity through changes in the structure of the economy and its population corresponds to the case of underdeveloped regions; while growth of labour productivity within a constant structure applies to developed ones. This has frequently led writers to rather contradictory attitudes in regard to such questions as employment, concentration of social capital, investment volumes, new investment as against reconstruction, the rise of living standards in the short and long run. There would be fewer divergences of views, if any, if the model took account from the first of the need to include regional conditions and requirements.

The influence of regions upon sectors, and not merely that of sectors upon regions, may be well illustrated by the example of one region. Vojvodina has a well-developed infrastructure, which is, however, insufficiently utilised. Through the allocation of material production to this region considerable savings in unproductive investment might be achieved, while the share of productive investment might be increased. Such a territorial allocation might result in any case in reduced investment in transportation.

Special difficulties arise from an unprecise definition of the sector-region concept. In practice, a single economic activity is meant thereby, whose effects are being observed in a certain region. This inadequate account is far from representing the full and intricate relations between sectors and regions. Sectors represent a highly differentiated structure with branches and sub-branches. On the other hand, the territorial structure does not consist simply of a total of regions, but of a series of structures of smaller and larger units, ranging from those of minor districts to the national stucture as a whole. All these structures and substructures are inter-related. To neglect the differentiated national structure and the existence of such a unit would have important practical consequences, as is illus-trated by the Yugoslav experience.

The starting point has been made the sum of the isolated regions and not the national structure as an aggregate. Thus, regions of development to be given special assistance have not been identified, while owing to the constant conflict of various regions, the border-area between them have remained the least developed parts of the republics and regions. River basins, on which great emphasis is normally placed for obvious reasons, have not been dealt with seriously, simply because the most important rivers represent borders between regions.

The attempt to make regions play as active a role as sectors is inspired by analytical reasoning. It represents only a small step towards the ulti-mate clarification of this intricate relationship. In the background of this relationship is the more fundamental question whether sectors and regions are to be treated as two separate things or as two aspects of the single problem of the development of the national economy as a whole. There are immense theoretical and practical implications in both approaches. In the first case, one starts from assumptions of pluralism. Sectors and regions are to be interrelated as separate elements, usually on the basis of mechanical causality. In this relationship one factor is *a priori* given the advantage, and thus appears as the cause, while the other one is the conse-quence. Interrelationship may be established alternatively on the basis of the interactions of the two. In this case causality gives way to a functional relationship. Causal and functional relations, comprising only some of the forces at work and restricted to non-essential changes, presuppose that the essence of the relations is given and that the determining forces are known.

The thesis that two dimensions of a single development of the economy are involved is based on the simple fact that sectors are fused into regions and regions into sectors. Their existence is mutually interrelated. The logical consequence of such an approach is that in seeking optimum solu-tions for economic development, the spatial composition of the economy must also be taken into account. Thus, the question arises whether and how far an investment efficiency calculus is adequate, if it does not take account of such social costs as those represented by urbanisation costs, the progressive growth of unproductive investment per head in the case of over-concentration, costs of interregional migration, social costs of consumption, and costs involved in the creation of more favourable conditions of life. At the same time not only the direct, but also the indirect effects on production must be kept in mind, which are associated with the spatial combination of economic factors. In addition, the spatial dimension is an important link which integrates the problems of economics with those of other social sciences. This is why, apart from economic efficiency, social efficiency must also be examined.

The unity of treatment of sectors and regions, as they affect the subject matter of social and economic development, does not mean that the separate identity of these two elements is denied, but rather that they have to be integrated within the structure of the whole economy. Their separate identity is to be seen in the differentiation, in the existence of specific substructures in the composition of these elements, whose relations are interdependent. The notion of structure takes account of this differentiation, integrating it through causal and functional relationships into a whole on the basis of dialectical interdependence. To constitute a total of economic relationships without denying this differentiation means to reckon with contradictions within sectors and regions as well as between these two components. The existence of these contradictions is empirically very well known. The explanation of the essence of the relationships between sectors and regions is reduced to demonstrating their internal inconsistencies.

These inconsistencies are the driving forces of development. It is necessary, however, to discover the dominant change with the most powerful creative force. The major trouble lies exactly in the fact that the dominant change in respect of sectors is often not the dominant change in respect of changes in the regional structure. Yugoslav experience has shown that the exploitation of resources of energy and raw materials has opened up new possibilities for the expansion of production and the whole economy, while this exploitation has had a very limited effect upon changes in the regional structure. Contradictions of this kind cannot be overcome by merely disregarding one or the other element. If, on the other hand account is taken of their dynamic interaction, based on the optimum development of the economy as a whole, these contradictions can be overcome.

15 The Programming and Development Policy of Backward Areas in National Economic Planning in Poland

B. Winiarski
WROCLAW SCHOOL OF ECONOMICS [1]

1 INTRODUCTION: THE ORIGINS OF THE REGIONAL ECONOMIC STRUCTURE OF POLAND

In order to present the main problems of the underdeveloped regions and regional development policy in Poland during the past twenty years it is necessary to look first at the sources of the regional economic structure of Polish territories. The evolution of the present structure was influenced by various factors acting differently in three historical periods determined by changes in Poland's political circumstances:

(i) the nineteenth and the beginning of the twentieth century, when Polish territories belonged to Russia, Prussia and Austria, the three powers which had partitioned Poland among themselves;

(ii) the twenty years between the two world wars, after Poland had regained her independence;

(iii) the years after the Second World War and after the essential changes in territory as well as in the social and economic system.

The fact that the three parts of Poland consequent on the partition belonged to the three partitioning powers was highly significant for the different lines of regional development of different Polish territories. The areas were inhabited by Poles who had never given up the hope of independence, often taking the line of political, economical and military resistance. The Polish territories were in a sense peripheral for the partitioning powers. Their development was designedly limited, or directed towards the exploitation of natural resources and manpower; they acted also as a kind of overflow region.

These tendencies were opposed by the patriotic and progressive sections of Polish society, which attempted to keep and strengthen the Polish elements in the economy. At the same time each of the partitioning powers created different economic, political and social conditions. The differences were most evident in the field of industrialisation. At the turn from

[1] The author is Professor of Economic Policy and Planning and a member of the Committee for Regional Economy and Spatial Planning of the Polish Academy of Science.

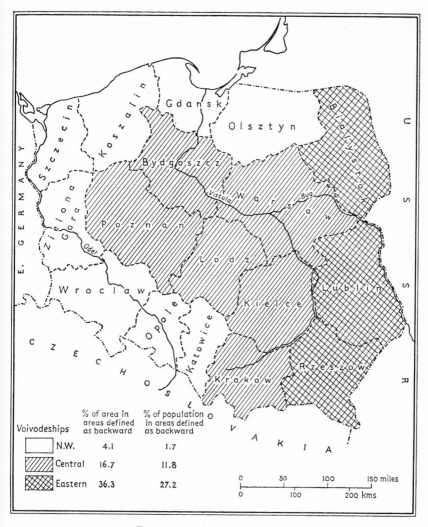

Voivodeships	% of area in areas defined as backward	% of population in areas defined as backward
N.W.	4.1	1.7
Central	16.7	11.8
Eastern	36.3	27.2

BACKWARD AREAS IN POLAND

the nineteenth to the twentieth century the greatest disparities emerged between the regions within each of the three annexed territories.

The industrial development was greatest in the area annexed by Prussia. In the second part of the nineteenth and the beginning of the twentieth century, industrial investment took place in Upper Silesia in coal mining and in Lower Silesia (in the Wroclaw region and south of it). Industrial centres were established in Szczecin, Poznan, Gdansk, Bydgoszcz, Elblad and Torun. Before the First World War the employment in industry in this area reached 710,000 equivalent to 63 employed per 1,000 population.[1]

The Polish territories annexed by Russia were less industrialised. The basis for industry had been built before the partition of Poland at the end of the seventeenth century and also in the time of the Kingdom of Poland, formed after the Vienna Congress and linked with Russia by personal union. When the prospect of the Kingdom's independence disappeared after the 1830 and 1863 uprisings, the Polish intelligentsia and bourgeoisie attempted to introduce industrialisation on a wider scale, the main hindrances being limited capital and certain specific political obstacles. In those territories, cheap manpower contributed to the development of the textile industry, and, to a smaller degree, metallurgy and mining industries. The Lodz industrial district (textiles), the Dabrowa–Sosnowiec mining district, the Warsaw district and smaller industrial centres in Czestochowa, Radomsk, Zyrardow, Wloclawek and Bialystok were established during that time. Before the First World War the employment in industry on the territories annexed by Russia did not exceed the number of 400, equivalent to 34 employed per 1,000 population.

The level of industrialisation was lowest in the territories annexed by Austria. The coal, salt, and oil deposits in the South-East were partly developed. The area lying to the West of Kracow had relatively the highest degree of industrialisation. The total number of employed in industry in the territories annexed by Austria was 70,000, equivalent only to 6 employed per 1,000 population.

When Poland regained her independence after the First World War the State had to face the problems of administration and of administrative and economic integration of regions which had been partitioned for many decades. Between some of these regions – for instance, along the border of the Russian and Prussian occupied territories – there was an economic desert created in particular by the deliberate policy of the Tsarist government. There were no communications. Different laws obtained in each region. War devastation had made the situation still worse. Thus the period of economic reconstruction required great efforts; even so progress was delayed by the fact that the beginning of economic expansion in

[1] S. Lesczycki, 'Changes in Spatial Economic Activity in the Twenty Years of the Polish People's Republic' ('Zmiany w przestrzennym zagospodarowaniu kraju w XX–leciu P.R.I.'), *Nauka Polska*, nr 5–6 (1964) pp. 37–8.

the late twenties was disturbed by the economic crisis. The subsequent revival took place only in 1936–9, the years immediately preceding the Second World War.

Certain essential changes in the structure of the regional economy of Poland during these inter-war years should be emphasised.[1] Great efforts were made to develop the Baltic Coast which Poland had been awarded by the Versailles Treaty. After the port and town Gdynia had been built, this economically undeveloped region was transformed into an important maritime industrial district. It was linked with Silesia, the most important industrial region of the country, by a new railway line. During the years 1936–9 the building of the so-called Central Industrial Area in the region of Kielce, Lublin and Rzeszow 'voivodeships' made notable progress. More than 100,000 new jobs were created in this area which had been mainly agricultural and had had a considerable surplus of manpower. Metallurgy, machinery, chemical and aircraft industries were the main forms of investment in that region.

Wide-scale regional planning was undertaken during the second half of the thirties.[2] During those years ten regional planning offices were established. Their studies and planning covered about 50 per cent of the total area of the country. Studies relating to the development of the Warsaw Sea Coast districts as well as the Central Industrial Area are of special significance in this period. In the last two cases, regional planning supported and accompanied the government investment policy.

The Second World War left Poland in a state of devastation in terms of both human and economic potential.[3] Manpower losses were in the order of six million people, and 38 per cent of the fixed assets were destroyed. Losses in industry were estimated at 35 per cent for buildings, power stations 52 per cent, and technical equipment 45 per cent. The big cities such as Warsaw, Wroclaw, Szczecin, and Gdansk suffered the greatest destruction. In the Wroclaw, Zielona Gora and Szczecin 'voivodeships' the social capital, particularly in the towns, was badly damaged. The Upper Silesian, Lodz and Krakow regions luckily escaped devastation. The industry that had been saved in Upper Silesia, Lodz and other smaller centres was the main element of Poland's economic potential in the first period of reconstruction.

After the Second World War, and as the result of it, a westward territorial shift of Poland took place, With both war losses and territorial changes there resulted a decrease of population of the order of ten million.

---

[1] S. Lesczycki, 'Changes in Spatial Economic Activity in the Twenty Years of the Polish People's Republic' ('Zmiany w przestrzennym zagospodarowaniu kraju w XX-leciu P.R.I.'), *Nauka Polska*, nr 5–6 (1964), pp. 37–8.

[2] J. Zarembe, 'Regional Planning in Poland' ('Planowanie regionalne w Polsce') *Planowanie regionalne – materialy*, Zeszyt 2 (1961).

[3] K. Secomski, 'Wartime Destruction', in collective work: *XX lat Polski Ludowej* (P.W.E. Warszawa, 1964) pp. 51–61. (Bilans zniszczen wojennych.)

K 2

The territories regained in the West made up one-third of the total area of the country within its new borders. Those territories required not only the settlement of Polish population but also large-scale reconstruction, as the degree of destruction here was particularly high. The regional economic structure of the Polish economy after the Second World War presented a very complex picture. This was the result partly of the earlier disparities in development, partly of the recent war devastation, but partly also of the unplanned and hurried post-war reconstruction. Deficiencies in statistical data concerning the early post-war years make it difficult to produce a full picture of the situation in that period.

In general, the starting point for the current regional development policies can be characterised as follows:

(i) The relatively high economic potential in the West had been regained as a result of the war, but its infrastructure, particularly the resources of the urban economies and industries, was devastated. The western regions had been largely abandoned by the German population before the Polish authorities were established in them. These regions required the settlement of Polish population as well as reconstruction.

(ii) The areas lying on the eastern banks of the Vistula were characterised by low economic development, the heritage of the years of partition. The level of industrialisation was strikingly low. The economy was mainly based on small farms.

(iii) The central area was characterised by mosaic layout of regions economically more or less developed. There were areas where the backwardness went back to the years before the First World War. There were others where the industrial equipment was destroyed during the Second World War. Almost in the centre of the country, between the area round Warsaw and Lodz, with industry developed still in the second half of the nineteenth century, and the Wielkopolska region with an advanced economy, there was a belt of underdeveloped areas.

(iv) The main economic potential of the country was in Upper Silesia, the region which escaped war destruction, and in the western part of Krakow region. The town itself and its resources hardly suffered any damage.

This account would not be complete if it did not mention the revolutionary changes which resulted in new political, social and economic conditions. The nationalisation of the basic branches of the national economy was the starting point for the change-over to the socialistic system. These changes enabled the subordination of the reconstruction and the later extension process to the general social interest. They also made it possible to introduce wide-scale economic planning which became the main form of planning and carrying out of the whole of the socio-economic policy. Those changes also made possible the development and appropriate exploitation of all the means required in the process of reconstruction for the gradual transformation of the spatial economic structure.

2   MAIN LINES OF REGIONAL DEVELOPMENT POLICY IN POLAND

The first line of regional development policy in Poland after World War II – so far as both chronology and rank of importance are concerned – was the setting up of the economy in the recovered territories and their integration with the other parts of the country.   The process had begun with the spontaneous and non-organised immigration of Polish population into these western and northern areas.   The first post-war national census in 1946 showed that the recovered territories, with a total population of 5,022,000, were inhabited by over 3,000,000 Poles including over 1,000,000 autochthonous Poles.   Soon the process of immigration of Polish population became organised and co-ordinated, with simultaneous repatriation and re-emigration of Poles from the U.S.S.R. and from the Western countries.   In 1950 the population in the recovered territories amounted to almost 6,000,000, after taking into account the exodus of Germans repatriated from these areas.

The central regions of Poland took the most active part in populating the recovered territories.   Nearly 50 per cent of all immigrants came from there. Of the rest, about 30 per cent of the immigrants came from U.S.S.R. as well as – although in smaller numbers – from France and Germany.   The remaining 20 per cent of the population were autochthonous Poles.[1]

Most of the newcomers settled in the less damaged rural areas.   The predominance of country people in the settling groups (which was characteristic for the former social structure of Poland) resulted in the fact that rural areas in the first stages made a more rapid economic start.   The populating of towns required first their reconstruction.   This has been achieved; the result is that today there are more people in towns in the recovered territories than before the War.   After 1950 migrations continued.   But the foremost factor responsible for the increase of population in the recovered territories appears to have been a high birth-rate.   Over 3,000,000 people have been born in these territories.   At present the population in the Western Territories amounts to a total of nearly 9,000,000.   The past twenty years have seen the integration of that population, who now form a strong and dynamic society and are an important factor in the high economic activity represented by the Western Territories in the present economic potential of Poland.

[1] L. Kosiński, 'Demographic Processes in the Recovered Territories in 1945–1960' ('Procesy ludnosciowe na Ziemiach Odzysanych w latach 1945–1960'), *Prace Geograficzne Instytutu Geografii P.A.N.*, nr 40 (Warszawa, 1963).

In addition to the reconstruction and extension of existing industrial centres and the setting up of completely new branches of industry (particularly such modern ones as the electronics industry), the process of economic expansion affected areas which in the pre-war period were completely undeveloped. For example in the Wroclaw voivodeship, industry was well established only in the southern belt, while the north-west areas, with a predominance of farming and forestry, were economically less active. Two large industrial centres have been built in these areas: a mining and power centre in Turoszow, right on the Czechoslovakian and German borders, and an enormous copper mining centre in the Legnica–Glogow area.[1]

A second line of regional policy in Poland has been the maximum utilisation of the possibilities of expansion of such of the economy as had survived in the already industrialised and urbanised areas, together with a rapid reconstruction of the destroyed sites. This line was started in the first years after the War when it became clear that the reconstruction of the whole country must be based on the potentialities in the areas which had not been destroyed during the War. This approach was continued in the following years. It resulted both from the acceptance of a particular structure of national economic expansion and from the economies of location. At the same time it brought further increase of economic potential to Upper Silesia and to the western part of Krakow voivodeship, as well as the reconstruction and expansion of Warsaw area. The policy of the exploitation of the existing infrastructure with the advantages of an already existing economic setting resulted in the further development of the industrial centres in the districts of Poznan, Bydgoszcz, Gdansk, and Kielce and Rzeszow, the latter two being the former Central Industrial Area.

Extensive exploitation of the possibilities of expansion in existing industrial centres proved to be an important factor in maximising the rate of economic growth. In view of the low level of development of the whole of pre-war Poland, most regions needed to break down the barriers of backwardness. The economic level of more advanced areas did not permit the full mobilisation of potential possibilities. Even in Upper Silesia, the largest agglomeration of industrial plants and towns in the country, there were reserves of both natural resources and manpower. Mobilisation of these reserves and their intensive exploitation made it possible to avoid higher costs in activating backward areas.

Activation of the most backward areas, particularly those in eastern regions, was at the same time a third important line of regional development policy, additional to the policy of location of productive forces. This policy was inaugurated in 1950 when the country was about to embark on the Six-Year Plan for the years 1950 to 1955. Under the Plan a number

---

[1] K. Secomski, 'New Economic Geography of Poland', in collective work: *XX lat Polski Ludowej*, cit. ed. p. 66–7. (Nowa geografia ekonomiczna kraju.)

of industrial plants were located in backward areas with the purpose of achieving a number of effects of a cumulative character. Practice showed that the highly strained norms of the Plan and the full distribution of all means of social accumulation did not produce the expected results. New plants built in remote places without adequate infrastructure found themselves in difficulties so far as operation was concerned. This fact later caused some opposition, among some economic administration authorities, against such 'pioneer' undertakings.

It is true that in most cases these undertakings, considered in terms of the general level of economic development, were premature.[1] They were introduced for the sake of the principle of equal location of productive forces in the whole country; but this imposed additional costs on the national economy in a period of acceleration of the total growth rate. In the second half of the fifties the policy of developing the backward areas was analysed thoroughly. It was proved that the goal of this policy should not simply be equal location of economic units, but the optimum exploitation of the existing conditions and resources of individual regions as well as the steady removal of disparities in the living standards in all regions.[2] Modification of the approach to the backward areas problem was closely bound up with the advance of studies of regional economies on the one hand and with the development of regional planning on the other, the latter associated with perspective planning of national economic growth. Finally, it was established that it was imperative to make an individual approach to each separate backward area and to integrate the development projects into the main development strategy of the whole economy. This question will be discussed in later parts of this paper.

In recent years regional development policy has been subject to the general principle of a rational location of productive forces and optimum use of the spatial economic structure. This principle aims to create those particular economic structures which will assure their most effective functioning from the social point of view. It is bound up both with the need to overcome the backwardness in the undeveloped areas and also with preventing excessive concentration in heavily built-up areas. The policy takes account of definite objectives for the development of backward areas and the dispersal of industry from regions with a high density of investment where obstacles to further development have begun to be apparent.

---

[1] K. Secomski, *Introduction to the Location of Productive Forces* (*Wstep do teorii rozmieszczenia sil wytworczych*) (P.W.G. Warszawa, 1965) p. 47.

[2] K. Secomski, *Theoretical Problem of the Location of Productive Forces* (*Teoretyczne problemy rozmieszczenia sil wytworczych*) (P.W.A. Warszawa, 1965).

B. Winiarski, *Activation of Economically Underdeveloped Regions* (*Aktywizacja regionow gospodarczo nierozwinietych*) (P.W.G. Warszawa, 1961) p. 75 ff. B. Winiarski, 'Factors and Stages in Economic Activation of Backward Areas' ('Czynniki i etapy podnoszenia intensywnosci gospodarki obszarow nierozwinietych'), *Biuletyn K.P.Z.K. P.A.N.*, nr 31 (Warszawa, 1965).

3　THE DEVELOPMENT OF BACKWARD AREAS IN POLAND 1945-65

Unlike those of some other European countries, the underdeveloped areas in Poland are not ethnographically distinct. As regards the administrative division of the country, only the recovered territories, which had a special Ministry, had been separate till 1950. Even that administrative difference disappeared after the full integration of the western and northern regions with the rest of the country. Table 1 shows the rapid economic growth of those territories that has resulted from all these efforts.[1]

TABLE ONE

THE WESTERN AND NORTHERN TERRITORIES

	1946	*1950*	*1960*	$\dfrac{1960}{1946}$ (%)
1. Population in towns (000s)	1,766·4	2,485·9	3,983·0	255·6
2. Employment in industry (000s)	355·0	638·5	949·3	267·4
3. Four cereal crop yields (quintals per hectare)	7·8	12·5*	18·3†	

* 1949　　　† 1961

In industry only the more modern branches were developed in these territories. Employment in manufacturing increased from 14·9 per cent of total employment in 1946 to 23·9 per cent in 1960. The general growth rate of industrial employment in the western regions in the period 1946–1960 was higher than that for the whole country, where the index in 1960 was 252 (1946 = 100).

At present underdeveloped areas in Poland exist in two forms:

(i) as major spatial complexes made up of geographically linked backward areas mainly in the east of Poland;
(ii) as small spatial units of mosaic location mainly in central regions and some units scattered in the west and north.

The backward areas are separated by regions with high or average economy activity. The accepted basis for the definition of a backward area is the analysis of the existing situation in a district as a whole. A district is the smallest administrative unit for which it is possible to collect and compare statistical data.

[1] Collective work: *Economic Development of Recovered Territories in the Twenty Years of People's Poland and their Perspective* (*Rozwoj gospodarczy Ziem Zachodnich w dwdziestoleciu Polski Ludowej i jego perspektywy*) (Instytut Zachodni, Poznan, 1964).

The Central Office of Statistics, in evaluating the rate of economic development of a district, takes into account all the available indices with special emphasis on the following: [1]

(*a*) for estimation of development in production, the employment in industry per 1,000 inhabitants and the population engaged in farming per 100 ha. of arable land;

(*b*) for estimation of infrastructure, the total length of hard-surface roads per 100 sq. km., and the number of hospital beds per 10,000 inhabitants.

The estimation of the development rate is made by comparing the position in individual districts by reference to the appropriate indices for the country as a whole over a given period.

Table 2 presents the average indices regarded as relevant in the definition of backward areas in Poland measured in 1949 and 1965. [2]

TABLE TWO

NATIONAL AVERAGES OF RELEVANT INDICES

Index for Country as a Whole	1949	1965
1. Employment in industry per 1,000 population	75	119
2. Population occupied in farming per 100 ha. of arable land	57 *	55 †
3. The length of hard-surface roads per 100 sq. km.	33·6	37·4
4. The number of hospital beds per 10,000 population	39·9	59·3

* For 1950.   † For 1960.

The districts classed as backward or undeveloped are those in which

(i) the employment in industry per 1,000 inhabitants is below one-fifth of the comparable index figure for the country as a whole, at a given date;

(ii) farming is the main occupation and the number of persons making a living by farming exceeds 90 persons per 100 ha. of arable land. (The latter is regarded as a symptom of the manpower surplus in agriculture for whom there are no other possibilities of employment in these regions at present;

---

[1] 'Economic Development in Districts in 1950–1965' ('Roswoj gospodarczy powiatow w latach 1950–1965'), in Central Office of Statistics, *Year Book* (Glowny Urzad Statystyczny, *Rocznik statystyczny*) (Warszawa, 1967) p. lxxi.

[2] Ibid. p. lxx.

(iii) the length of hard-surface roads is less than one-half of the average figure for the whole country;

(iv) the number of hospital beds in a district is less than one-third of the figure for the country as a whole.

The analysis made by the Central Statistical Office shows that, of a total of 391 districts in Poland in 1950, there were 130 undeveloped districts; in 1965 the number of the backward districts was reduced to fifty-five. The central voivodeships in Table 3 include: Kielce, Krakow, Lodz,

TABLE THREE

THE BACKWARD AREAS OF POLAND

1	*1950* Total *2*	Backward Areas *3*	Percentage Share *4*	*1965* Total *5*	Backward Areas *6*	Percentage Share *7*	*1965 as Percentage of 1950* 6÷3 *8*
Poland as a whole	311·7	137·5	44·2	311·7	52·1	16·1	37·5
Area (1,000 sq. km.)							
Population (m.)	25·0	7·4	29·6	31·6	3·2	9·9	43·2
Number of districts	391	130	34·3	391	55	14·0	42·5
A. *Central voivodeships*							
Area (1,000 sq. km.)	129·9	56·4	43·2	129·9	21·7	16·7	38·3
Population (m.)	12·2	3·9	35·0	15·1	1·8	11·8	46·0
Number of districts	159	56	35·0	159	25	15·7	44·5
B. *Eastern voivodeships*							
Area (1,000 sq. km.)	66·6	44·9	67·8	66·6	24·2	36·3	53·9
Population (m.)	3·9	2·4	61·5	4·8	1·3	27·2	54·0
Number of districts	66	41	62·0	66	24	36·5	58·2
C. *North-west voivodeships*							
Area (1,000 sq. km.)	115·2	36·3	24·8	115·2	6·2	4·1	25·0
Population (m.)	8·5	1·1	13·0	11·7	0·2	1·7	18·2
Number of districts	166	33	20·0	166	6	0·4	18·1

Poznan, Bydgoszcz, and Warsaw voivodeships. In the eastern voivodeships group there are: Bialystok, Lublin and Rzeszow voivodeships. The group of northern and western voivodeships includes: Olsztyn, Gdansk, Koszalin, Szczecin, Zielona, Gora, Opole and Katowice voivodeships.

Special attention should be given to the changes between 1950 and 1965. In the northern and western voivodeships the backward areas have been reduced to 4 per cent of the total area of the country and now comprise only 1·7 per cent of the population, whereas in 1950 the backward areas amounted to about one-quarter of the area of these voivodeships. There was a considerable reduction of backward areas in the central part of

Poland also. Relatively least progress was achieved in the eastern regions, but here also the backward areas were reduced by a half, when comparing with 1950. On a national scale, the progress is quite remarkable. In 1950 the backward areas covered 44 per cent of the country with 30 per cent of the total population. Now only 16 per cent of total area with 10 per cent of the total population is classed as backward. The table shows the rapid economic development of the backward districts which has taken place in the course of those fifteen years.[1]

The regional development in Poland reflects the growth of the whole national economy. This has supplied the necessary resources for regional development and the sectoral structure of national economic growth

TABLE FOUR

CHANGES IN THE LEVEL OF SOCIO-ECONOMIC
DEVELOPMENT OF POLAND 1950 TO 1965 [2]

	1950	1960	1965
1. Population (m.)	25·0	29·8	31·6
of which: in towns	9·6	14·2	15·7
2. Non-farming population (%)	52·0	61·6	..
3. Average employment (000s)	5,104	7,264	8,794
4. National income	100	208	280
(1950=100)			
5. Investment in fixed assets	100	274	410
(1950=100)			
6. Total gross output	100	338	508
(1950=100)			

created conditions and imposed limitations on the more rapid development of the backward regions. Table 4 presents some of the more important data concerning economic growth in Poland between 1950 and 1965.

The rapid growth of the national economy in the post-war decades made it possible to raise the general economic standard of the country, in comparison with the inter-war period. In 1962 the national income in Poland had grown 3·4 times compared with 1937 and investment had grown 8·4 times. That growth made it possible to reduce the gap between Poland and the advanced countries in Western Europe.

Economic development in Poland in the post-war period has been mainly based on intensive industrialisation. In these years about 70 per cent of the total outlay was devoted to production investment and more

[1] Data taken from Central Office of Statistics, *Year Book* (Warszawa, 1967). (Zestawiono na podstawie danych w cytowanym wydawnictwie G.U.S.)
[2] Central Office of Statistics, *Year Book* (*Rocznik statystyczny*) (Warszawa, 1966) pp. 34–6.

than 40 per cent to industry. The outlays for the fuel industries, metallurgy, the machinery industries, electrical industry, transportation, as well as investment in the chemical industry and in the production of electricity and heat, were dominating in the structure of industrial investment. Nonproductive investment such as housing, municipal economy, education,

TABLE FIVE

INDICES OF GROSS NATIONAL INCOME PER HEAD[1]
IN 1937 AND 1960

Country	1937	1960
Poland	100	100
France	420	220
Italy	220	120
Federal German Republic	500	230
Belgium	490	240
Great Britain	560	240

science and culture and health service accompanied the expansion of industry.

The necessary branch structure of national economic growth imposed limitations on regional development policy and planning. The emphasis placed on industrialisation provided first of all made industrial investment the chief instrument of regional development policy. The structure of that investment imposed further limitations: the outlays for the expansion of the fuel industry could be located only in those regions where appropriate raw materials could be found: the basic location factor for the chemical industry was water resources: the outlays for machinery and metallurgy industries had also a locationally-bound character. Moreover the share of total investment that had to be devoted to the expansion and reconstruction of existing plants was fairly considerable and shows a higher return than new building.

The available resources and economic requirements for their exploitation were decisive determinants in the development policy of the backward regions. Priority had to be given to those regions which possessed either raw materials or reserves of infrastructure, or other advantages for industrial investment location. In the following areas new important industrial regions were created: [2]

(1) The Rybnik coal region, in the south-west of Katowice voivodeship with highly valuable coke mines, provided a new fuel basis for industry.

[1] K. Laski and L. Zienkowski, 'National Income', in collective work: *XX lat Polski Ludowej*, cit.ed. p. 272. (Dochod narodowy w pracy zbiorowej.)

[2] Secomski, 'New Economic Geography of Poland', in collective work: *XX lat Polski Ludowej*, pp. 66–7.

(2) The Turosnow mining and power region, in the western part of Wroclaw voivodeship, based on brown coal exploitation and production of electric power.

(3) The Kracow industrial region concentrating on the metallurgy industry, machinery industry and chemical industry.

(4) The Kielce industrial region with machinery and metallurgy industries.

(5) The lower Vistula region, between Wloclawek, Bydgoszcz and Gdansk with machinery industry and chemical and electrotechnical industries.

(6) The Plock industrial region based on petrochemical works in Plock.

(7) The Konin Leczyca industrial region (also called Kujawy region) with brown coal mining, power facilities and chemical industry.

(8) The Tarnobrzeg industrial region based on sulphur extraction and the corresponding processing plants.

(9) The Pufawy industrial region based on new large chemical plants (fertilisers).

(10) The Legnica–Glogow industrial region based on non-ferrous mining (mainly copper).

During those fifteen years it has been the sector structure of the national economic growth together with the natural and economic conditions of these regions that has determined the geography of the backward areas development. The relatively small share in the total structure of the national outlays that is represented by investment that is free of locational ties has limited fundamentally the possibilities of wider regional development in the eastern part of the country.

4 REGIONAL AND NATIONAL ECONOMIC PLANNING

The experience of Poland demonstrates a strong interdependence and interconnection between the structure of national economic growth both in terms of sectors and branches of industry on the one hand and the spatial structure of the growth of economic elements and regional growth on the other. This interdependence and this interconnection make necessary a close integration of regional and national economic planning.[1] Such integration is being introduced in Poland. Present solutions are the outcome of the evolution of economic planning system in Poland. Planning on a regional scale in Poland goes further back in time than national economic planning. It was introduced at the turn of the twenties and

[1] K. Secomski, *Basis of Perspective Planning* (*Podstawy planowania perspektywicznego*) (P.W.E. Warszawa, 1966). B. Winiarski, 'Basis of Programming the Regional Economic Development' ('Podstawy programowania ekonomicznego rozwoju regionów'), *K.P.K.Z. Pan Studia*, t. XII (P.W.N. Warszawa, 1966).

thirties, when the socio-economic structure of the country differed from that of today. The regional planning of the inter-war period to some extent resembled town planning; it consisted in determining the lines of exploitation of a region and in setting spatial limits on the different ways of expanding the areas economically. There was, however, no means of enforcing the implementation of the regional plans worked out. In practice only those regional plans which received state support had any real chance of implementation. Such was the case, for example, with the expansion of the sea-coast area (the building of the port and town of Gdynia) and with the creation of the Central Industrial Area.

The taking over of key branches of the economy by the State after the Second World War made both possible and necessary the co-ordination and subordination of economic units to large-scale social ends. The pre-requisites were created for a uniform plan to govern the overall socio-economic process. The first scheme under the national planning system had been prepared in 1946. It was a dual system: it based its organisational structure upon a two-fold division of planning: economic planning and spatial planning, each having its particular agency and kinds of plans.

The chief governing body for economic planning was the Central Planning Office which was responsible for the co-ordination and the synthetic elaboration of the plans for the ministries, the enterprise unions, and the enterprises. At first the plans were one-year plans. Next a Three-Year Plan determining the direction of and means for the economic reconstruction of the country was devised for 1947–9.

Spatial planning was organised in the form of a three-level structure. The highest place in this hierarchy was given to the spatial plan for the economic expansion of the country, then came the regional plans, and next the local plans for separate towns and settlements. The spatial plans retained the character they had acquired in the inter-war period: they provided the means of location of investment in the territory under long-term programmes, using methods similar to town planning methods. This latter type of planning, on a local basis, constituted a part of the spatial planning system.

A large number of research and outline studies on the planned economic expansion of the country and its regions had been made in 1946–1949. These studies were helpful in the process of reconstruction of the country; they also provided the guiding principles for the future location of the productive forces. The Central Spatial Planning Office, with agencies in all voivodeships, gave leadership to this work. The duality of the planning system, however, caused numerous difficulties. The spatial plans were elaborated mainly with the purpose of creating a rational set-up in the long-term perspective; the economic plans were mainly concerned with the co-ordination of current economic decisions with regard to the kinds of output, employment, costs and investment.

The two-fold organisational structure of the planning system was formally terminated in 1949 both at the national and at the regional level. In place of the two respective bodies one was created – the State Commission of Economic Planning. The local (town) planning survived the organisational change as a separate agency. The reform resulted in fact in an end to progress in regional planning and in the local discontinuance of all activities in spatial planning. In the period of the realisation of the Six-Year Plan (1950–5) the economic expansion of regions was carried on by investment location policy exercised by the central bodies. The location was chosen by individual decision.

The experience of this period proved that the decisions with regard to investments (location included) present a real difficulty when there is a lack of knowledge concerning a long-term growth perspective of the overall economy and of individual regions as well as of sectors and branches. Planning on the long-term scale proved to be insufficient. In 1957 the decision was taken to introduce a new form supplementing the previous: perspective planning for periods of fifteen to twenty years.

This decision opened new possibilities of revival and expansion of regional planning. The defining of the long-term development programmes for the national economy provided a basis for the reconstruction of regional development principles. Accordingly, in 1957, the regional plans – understood as the plans of perspective economic growth and economic expansion of individual voivodeships – were introduced into the new system of national economy planning. This new situation was consolidated in 1961 by a new spatial planning law which secured a link between the regional planning and perspective planning.

The perspective plan of national economic growth in Poland now covers a period of twenty years. Every five years the plan is brought up to date, adjusted and prolonged for the next five years. In this way the successive versions of the plan for the periods of 1961–75, 1961–80 and 1966–85 have been worked out. The perspective plan is worked out from two aspects: according to sectors and branches of economy on the one hand and in spatial set-up on the other. The second aspect of the plan determines the regional proportions in the economic growth of the country, and as a so-called spatial economic expansion plan, at the same time provides the basis for co-ordination and for drawing up the guiding principles with regard to the construction of regional plans. Regional plans are worked out in all voivodeships on a corresponding basis for the same periods as the national plan. In their final versions they must be in complete accordance with the national perspective plan. One of the functions of the regional plans is to define the policy of location of the more important investment undertakings. They also provide the guiding principles for drawing up the local (town) plans. In the sector and branch structure the perspective planning provides the starting assumptions for building up long-term plans determining more precisely the activity of economic units. Finally, the establishment of long-term plans provides a basis for setting up one-year plans.

Regional plans are worked out in highly specialised offices working at and in co-operation with all voivodeship commissions of economic planning. Those commissions are responsible for their methods of working and organisation to the chief planning body in Poland – the Commission of Planning at the Council of Ministers. They also are connected with the state administration bodies on the regional level – Voivodeship People's Council Presidia – which possess authority for the co-ordination of all economic activities in the voivodeships and directs the affairs of the local economy. Today regional studies and plans cover the whole area of the country. The planning is continuous. It is not a sporadic attempt to focus on some particular objective of economic activity but is concerned with the systematic direction of regional growth on a long-term scale.

Although regional planning in organisation has thus been fully integrated into national planning, it has still to face difficult problems of a theoretical and methodological nature. The problem of the consistent determination of both the sectoral and the spatial structure of growth is one of the more essential points. It has also proved difficult to co-ordinate the requirements of regional planning, since it must yield specific figures and trends for the location of production, for the settlement network, for the extension of infrastructure, for employment, all of these consistent with the more general assumptions regarding the directions of national economic growth. It must at the same time take account of the available resources for branch and sector programming.

Great interest has been taken by research centres and by economic executives in the problems of optimising the structure and the rate of growth of national economy in both sectoral and spatial patterns. The problem of regional planning has been the subject of wide scientific discussion and of serious contributions to economic literature. There is a Committee of Regional Economic and Spatial Planning of the Polish Academy of Science which promotes all research work in this respect. Numerous scientific institutions of a regional type co-operate with the Committee. In the course of discussion two theoretically possible approaches to the regional plan structure were indicated.[1] The first approach might rest upon the disaggregation – carried out by the central authorities – of the values fixed in the national plan for individual regions. These values would then constitute the principle guiding lines for working out the regional development plans.

The second approach would be based on working out regional plans in individual regions – independently of central authorities – with the local conditions, possibilities and needs taken into account. The national plan

---

[1] Secomski, *Theoretical Problem of the Location of Productive Forces*, pp. 38–9.

would in this case be a kind of a sum of plans worked out on regional level.

Of course neither the first nor the second approach would be satisfactory in isolation. The plan imposed by the central authorities would, more or less, be an arbitrary solution of spatial growth structure. The plan worked out at the regional level would not be in a position to achieve values representing a balance on the scale of the overall national economy or to take proper account of its foreign links.

At the present stage of study the idea of a multiphase process of perspective plan construction on both the national and regional scales with a broad application of an iterative procedure holds the field. The following stages may be identified:

(i) The first stage is preparatory. The central national planning body works out overall national economy perspective growth concepts and draws initial proposals with regard to distribution of general values among regions.

(ii) The second stage consists of the elaboration of the regional plan drafts in regions, referring to national concepts, taking into account the alternative concepts, and giving emphasis to local conditions, possibilities and needs.

(iii) The next stage consists of the co-ordination and verification of regional plan drafts, and studies of development and reconstruction programmes for sectors and branches of the national economy (regional and sectoral projects of the plan).

(iv) Correction of regional plans on the basis of co-ordination principles worked out at the central level during the third stage.

5 THE PROBLEM OF BACKWARD AREAS IN PLANNING

In the course of the past fifteen years in Poland a transition in the approach to regional development policy has taken place. The initial approach was oversimplified and represented a tendency towards equality in the location of productive forces in the whole country area. According to the new approach, regional development policy should be an integral part of action undertaken to optimise the regional structure of the national economy as it grows. In this connection the term undeveloped does not so much emphasise the deviation below the average economic index figures for the whole country, but rather stresses the fact that there are unused resources and potentialities for the economic process, this fact being a criterion for underdevelopment. These unused resources and potentialities include natural resources, fixed assets, for example of infrastructure, and especially manpower. The latter implies reduced sources of income for the local population and consequently a lower living standard.[1]

The development of regional planning points to a more and more close connection between the strategy of development of backward regions and the strategy of perspective national economic growth.[2] The links may be presented as follows:

(1) The possibility of including the less intensively-used potentialities of a backward area as a growth factor of the national economy (e.g. economic exploitation of raw material resources, exploitation of water and other elements in the natural environment, utilisation of manpower reserves) in other words the use of 'location potentialities'. These possibilities become particularly significant when various limitations to growth appear in regions which had been the earliest to be highly developed.

(2) The other linking element may be the general tendency in socio-economic policy towards equalisation of living standards on a national scale. This task is easier in the field of mass consumption (the equalisation of socio-cultural conditions, housing, communication etc.). It becomes complicated when concerned with individual income: the increase of income requires the raising of professional activation factors (higher employment), a modification of the professional structure of the population (setting up more modern branches of industry) etc.

Undoubtedly a factor that has made the equalising process more difficult has been the concentration of all the efforts of the national economy on the development of industry. Industry, and particularly those branches which have had the largest share in investment, is characterised by strong location requirements, not always to be met by conditions existing in backward regions. Industry also requires concentration, economies of large scale, and external economies. Thus industry cannot be the only factor in the development of backward areas. If, however, the share of the remaining branches in the total of national growth is limited, the economy cannot adequately provide the other means of development.

From this point of view an advantageous concomitant of a rise of the general economic level may be emphasised, The crucial point here is the gradually rising share of services, in which there are large possibilities of

---

[1] Winiarski, *Activation of Economically Underdeveloped Regions.*

[2] B. Winiarski, 'Linking of the Plan of Spatial Economic Activation with Regional Plans of Voivodeships' ('Problemy powiazania planu przestrzennego zagospodarowania kraju z planami regionalnymi wojewodztw'), *Planowanie regionalne – materialy,* Zeszyt 6 (1964).

    B. Winiarski, 'Problems of Backward Areas' ('Problemy regionow opoznionych'), *Gospodarka i administracja terenowa,* nr 1 (1967).

employment. A proper geographic location of economic and social infrastructure may be a factor effectively accelerating the development of backward areas. Services, unlike industry with its indivisible and concentrated installation, can be introduced even in small territorial units. During the post-war decades the number of people employed in services has increased from 18 per cent in 1946 to about 25 per cent in 1965. The assumptions of the 1966–85 Perspective Plan anticipate a growth to 40 per cent.[1] Thus an important new factor appears at the disposal of development policy in backward areas as well as more generally in regional planning.

Following the general growth of the economic standard of the country, a growth of the interregional flow of accumulated and distributed national income can be observed. The spatial redistribution of national income based on differentiation of production and services in the regions will make possible a further removal of disparities.

The characteristic feature of the attempt to introduce regional development planning into the national planning system is the necessity for the complex consideration of all elements and factors in the whole of the socio-economic system. It creates numerous difficulties, because all the various elements are interrelated with each other and there are numerous and multifarious feedbacks. That is also a reason for the limited applicability of some theoretical models well known in the literature of western countries. These models accept a number of parameters of a general economic system as given data which are fixed by prognosis based on extrapolation of trends. The problem of regional analysis amounts to finding the optimum means of adjustment for individual economic units (plants or whole regions) to the general system. In cases where the social economy is determined as a whole by a uniform national plan, this approach is not sufficient because the general system is also subjected to an active directing by the central planning authority.

The national plan could assume a rapid and effective development of backward regions and this process of rapid equalisation could be carried out. But that would require the application of a special sector and branch structure which would prove less efficient from the point of view of the whole socio-economic progress. The development programming of backward areas requires a most careful linking of regional and general criteria as well as the co-ordination of the principle of equality with the principle of efficiency and effectiveness of the whole national economy.

[1] K. Secomski, 'Some Problems of Perspective Planning of Science' ('O niektorych problemach perspektywicznego planowania nauki'), *Nauka Polska*, nr 4 (1966).

16 Development Problems of Backward Areas in Hungary

L. Köszegi

CENTRAL PLANNING OFFICE, BUDAPEST

1 THE UNEVEN GEOGRAPHICAL DISTRIBUTION OF THE HUNGARIAN ECONOMY

In spite of the small area of Hungary (93,000 sq. km., with a greatest width east–west of 528 km. and north–south 268 km.), the geographical distributions of both population and economic activity are characterised by great variations and by a certain measure of concentration. A fundamental feature is the discrepancy between the Budapest agglomeration and the rural areas, and the associated differences in development levels.[1]

About one-quarter of the country's population is concentrated in the capital, Budapest, and its immediate surroundings, and here – in an area amounting to about 3 per cent of the country – is concentrated about 45 per cent of industrial employment and an even greater percentage of industrial production. At present, Budapest is a centre almost without a competitor simultaneously in transport, trade, education, culture, administration, technical research and training.

Another major characteristic feature of this regional variation is the discrepancy that has emerged in the rural areas between underdeveloped, more-developed and highly developed areas.[2] This becomes manifest mainly in the geographical distribution of industry and in the varying industrial development levels of these areas but measurable also by the level of urbanisation and still more by the development of infrastructure and to be seen also in the incomes and cultural conditions of the population. The differences existing in agricultural development in some cases offset these differences but in the majority of cases reinforce them.

Interrelated with these regional variations are variations of the population densities and fundamental differences in development levels between urban and rual arreas. Budapest has a population of almost two millions; in the next category the five major towns have only between 100 and 160 thousand; the population of the other 62 towns is between 10 and 60

---

[1] For more detailed references see: L. Köszegi, 'The Problems of the Budapest Agglomeration of Industry and Population in the Regional Planning of the Economy'. Paper submitted to the Conference of Senior Economic Advisers, U.N. – E.C.E., Geneva, November 1964.

[2] See also I. Bartke and J. Kóródi, 'General Problems of Industrial Development in the Country Areas of the Hungarian People's Republic', Conference of Senior Economic Advisers, Geneva, 1964.

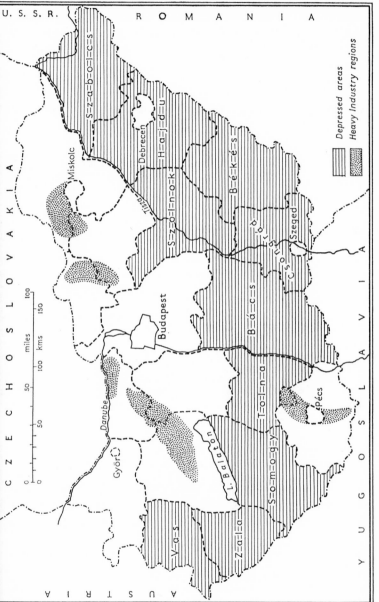

BACKWARD AREAS IN HUNGARY

This map is reproduced from Bartke and Kóródi, *General Problems of Industrial Development in the Country Areas of the Hungarian Republic.*

thousand. There are many places with a population below 1,500, and even tiny ones with 200–600 inhabitants. The infrastructure of these is very poor even today. About 10 per cent of the population still lives in scattered settlements or homesteads at a low level of civilisation.

The major variations in the geographical structure of the economy and the differences in development levels in those of the nineteen counties of

TABLE ONE

DATA RELATING TO INDUSTRY IN THE UNDERDEVELOPED COUNTI OF HUNGARY, 1965

Counties	Proportion of Total				Industrial Employment	Adjusted Net Production Value †	Share o Large-Sco Industry Industric Employm
	Population	Land Area	Industrial Employment	Fixed Industrial Assets *			
	percentages				per 1,000 of population		Employm
Bács-Kiskun	5·6	9·0	3·1	1·3	83	2·04	46·9
Békés	4·5	6·1	2·4	1·7	83	2·33	56·3
Csongrád	4·3	4·6	3·7	1·8	131	3·29	50·7
Hajdu	5·1	6·7	2·4	1·9	73	2·23	48·7
Somogy	3·6	6·5	1·5	1·5	67	2·15	62·0
Szabolcs	5·5	6·4	1·4	1·2	39	1·14	45·4
Szolnok	4·4	6·0	2·5	2·6	87	2·96	63·6
Tolna	2·5	3·9	1·3	0·8	80	2·22	61·3
Vas	2·7	3·6	2·0	1·3	112	3·31	72·7
Zala	2·6	3·5	1·5	2·7	85	3·89	63·7
Underdeveloped counties, total	40·8	56·3	21·8	16·8	82	2·42	60·0
Developed counties, total	31·8	36·2	32·4	47·2	155	7·18	85·7
Budapest and Pest county	27·4	7·5	45·8	36·0	256	12·43	76·4
of which: Budapest	19·1	0·6	40·4	31·6	323	11·26	78·6
Hungary	100·0	100·0	100·0	100·0	153	5·69	76·5

* 1964.

† 1964. The contents of the adjusted net value are the following: wages actually paid *plus* industrial product, calculated by reference partly to the value of fixed assets and partly to wages p For a detailed description of the method see: I. Bartke, 'Determination of Industrial Developr Level of Territorial Units.' *Közgazdasági Szemle* (1967).

Hungary which are treated as underdeveloped, mainly on the basis of industrial development, are shown in the Map and Tables 1–4, as illustrated by the more important indicators.

In appraising these differences it should be borne in mind that the nearly two decades of planned economy – despite certain unfavourable features – have had a fundamentally mitigating effect on the regional variations inherited from the past and have diminished the differences between areas and the conflicts of interest between developed and backward areas.

2 MAJOR RESULTS ACHIEVED IN DEVELOPING THE BACKWARD AREAS

The major results achieved in developing the backward areas are indicated by Tables 5–6 and Charts 1–3. This development has been uneven; it has proceeded by stages; and at times there have even been unfavourable trends or unfavourable factors affecting them.

TABLE TWO

AGRICULTURAL DATA RELATING TO THE UNDERDEVELOPED COUNTIES OF HUNGARY, 1965

(Percentages)

	Proportion of Total			Agricultural Income Level of a Co-operative Family	Gross Production Level in Value per Unit of Area
Counties	Agricultural Area	Area of Vineyards and Fruit Plantations	State Purchase of Agricultural Products		
Bács-Kiskun	9·7	16·6	10·7	105·7	110·1
Békés	7·1	2·5	8·8	125·2	132·2
Csongrád	5·2	4·8	6·2	110·5	120·7
Hajdu	7·4	3·3	6·5	97·9	103·8
Somogy	5·8	4·2	5·4	96·4	100·8
Szabolcs	7·1	10·3	6·2	67·9	103·5
Szolnok	6·9	3·2	7·8	128·8	116·8
Tolna	4·1	3·3	4·3	130·9	124·8
Vas	3·3	2·1	2·9	63·2	88·4
Zala	3·2	4·9	2·6	51·4	90·1
Underdeveloped counties, total	59·8	55·2	61·4	100·1	109·1
Developed counties, total	33·3	30·7	33·1	98·3	101·8
Budapest and Pest county of which:	6·9	14·1	5·5	107·4	123·8
Budapest	6·4	2·1			
Hungary	100·0	100·0	100·0	100·0	100·0

This is not the occasion to survey all the historical causes that led to such a pattern of economic and industrial development in Hungary and brought about these geographical differences. I would only mention that, as a consequence of various natural, economic and politico-social factors, in 1938 more than 52 per cent of industrial employment was concentrated

in Budapest, and an even greater percentage of all the processing industries. Some industries indeed, were entirely located there. Apart from
the smaller industrial centres of less importance in the countryside, which

TABLE THREE

URBANISATION AND PUBLIC UTILITY SUPPLY LEVEL
OF UNDERDEVELOPED COUNTIES, 1964

(Percentages)

Counties	Urban Population as Percentage of Total *	Level of Education †	Public Utilities ‡	Health, Social, Cultural Institutions §	Cultural Level ‖	Retail Turnover per Head of Industrial Goods
			As Percentage of National Supply Level			
Bács-Kiskun	32·1	—	23·5	79·4	73·4	97·5
Békés	24·5	—	7·3	84·7	81·0	94·2
Csongrád	56·8	—	48·7	114·0	100·8	107·4
Hajdu	41·7	—	61·1	93·9	80·2	86·2
Somogy	13·6	—	35·0	80·8	87·8	90·0
Szabolcs	11·1	—	5·1	76·9	62·4	69·5
Szolnok	40·9	—	22·2	88·0	83·6	87·0
Tolna	8·5	—	17·1	91·4	86·4	96·0
Vas	25·3	—	63·6	92·9	93·8	88·4
Zala	25·5	—	43·5	76·3	77·9	84·4
Underdeveloped counties, total	28·7	64	32·0	86·4	80·6	87·5
Developed counties, total			81·6	90·3	88·0	89·9
Budapest and Pest county of which:	53·3	121	229·0	124·0	139·6	122·4
Budapest			313·0	179·6	171·4	141·2
Hungary	43·3	100·0	100·0	100·0	100·0	100·0

　* 1965
　† Population census in 1960.
　‡ Calculated on the basis of flats connected to the water and drainage system.
　§ Calculated on the basis of the major health and education indicators.
　‖ Calculated on the basis of theatre and cinema attendance, library stock of books,
subscribers to daily newspapers, TV. and radio.

produced on a smaller scale, the agricultural regions of the country, representing more than half of the area and almost half of the population, bore
the stamp of feudal estates at one extreme and of tiny holdings and a mass
of agricultural labourers at the other. Industrial and infrastructural
development was minimal in these regions.

Reconstruction after World War II restored, as a rule, the old regional balances or imbalances. After the completion of reconstruction, the transformation and rapid development of the country's economy became the order of the day and the main objective of economic policy was to transform the country from a backward agrarian-industrial one into a

TABLE FOUR

INCOME LEVEL IN UNDERDEVELOPED COUNTIES OF HUNGARY, 1965

(Percentages)

Counties	Average Earnings Per Industrial Worker	Average Income of a Co-operative Member from Agricultural Work	Average Annual Net Income in: Worker– Employee Households	Peasant Households
Bács-Kiskun	79·5	108·8	78·5	100·0
Békés	79·9	122·3	80·1	104·8
Csongrád	82·5	117·6	80·1	104·8
Hajdu	89·4	100·6	69·1	88·9
Somogy	86·9	87·2	74·2	95·4
Szabolcs	82·3	79·7	69·1	88·9
Szolnok	90·1	126·0	69·1	88·9
Tolna	84·1	119·4	74·2	95·4
Vas	88·4	73·7	69·5	89·4
Zala	95·0	63·2	69·5	89·4
Underdeveloped counties, total	85·2	101·8	76·4	94·6
Developed counties, total	111·3	96·0	80·0	94·1
Budapest and Pest county of which:	98·8	102·9	100·0	100·0
Budapest	99·6	—		
Hungary	100·0	100·0		

developed industrial-agrarian country. This affected also the geographical distribution of economic activity.

In the first major phase of development, down to 1957, important new industrial centres were established in the formerly industrially backward areas. But it was primarily the already industrialised rural areas which were further developed on the basis of their existing industries, mainly extractive and raw material producing. However, as the effect of the attractive forces of advantages of agglomeration, the greatest development occurred in the capital and its immediate surroundings both as regards volume and rate of growth.

This much too concentrated industrial development resulted in a considerable movement of population. The lag in infrastructure development and particularly in housing as compared with productive investment

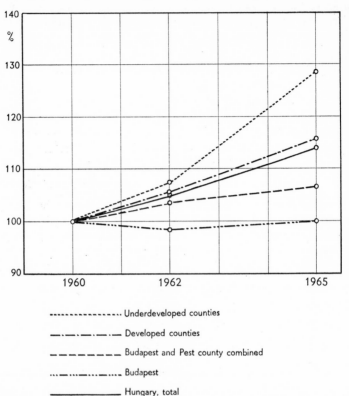

CHART 1. RATE OF GROWTH OF INDUSTRIAL EMPLOYMENT (1960 = 100)

raised grave problems in the new and rapidly growing centres as well as in Budapest itself. Distances between place of work and domicile became great, long-distance and large-scale commuting became the rule and created many problems.

The concentration of industrial development in the already developed areas also absorbed a large proportion of the resources available for infrastructure investment. Thus, there remained very limited resources for similar development in the backward regions.

Towards the end of the 1950s (1957–60) the problem of economically developed and underdeveloped areas in the country became greatly accentuated. Partly as a result of the reconstructive character of industrial development policy, development continued to concentrate principally in

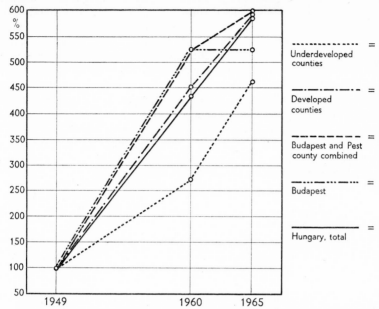

CHART 2. RATE OF GROWTH OF INDUSTRIAL EMPLOYMENT (1949 = 100)

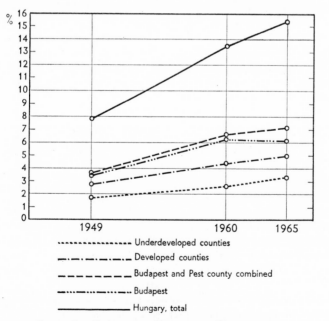

CHART 3. GROWTH OF INDUSTRIAL EMPLOYMENT

L

Budapest and the industrialised rural areas. On the other hand, in the wake of the socialist reorganisation of agriculture, a considerable volume of manpower was released from agriculture and – because of the weak manpower absorptive capacity of the agricultural areas – this manpower migrated mainly to Budapest and some of the developing regions in the rural areas.

Under the pressures of the growing social problems – employment difficulties, demographic ageing, overcrowding and tensions over housing, difficulties of transport, and others – several government measures were

TABLE FIVE

DEVELOPMENT IN THE UNDERDEVELOPED COUNTIES AS
REFLECTED BY SOME MAJOR INDICATORS

Counties	Changes in Population 1949 = 100	Growth of Industrial Employment				Changes in the Degree of Urbanisation	Change Educatic Standa
		1949–1960 (000s)	1960–1965	1965/ 1949 (1949 = 100)	1965/ 1960 (1960 = 100)	1949 = 100	
Bács-Kiskun	95·5	9·3	13·6	196·6	141·2	126·6	—
Békés	94·1	5·0	7·8	152·5	126·5	120·4	—
Csongrád	101·4	16·5	12·1	201·4	127·1	113·0	—
Hajdu	103·6	5·8	8·0	158·2	127·1	118·2	—
Somogy	99·2	1·8	6·2	149·4	134·4	122·8	—
Szabolcs	99·9	3·9	4·6	164·4	126·9	129·9	—
Szolnok	98·6	9·1	7·8	176·8	125·1	116·4	—
Tolna	94·7	3·5	4·1	158·9	125·0	146·6	—
Vas	98·0	4·9	7·5	165·9	131·6	129·3	—
Zala	99·7	6·0	3·8	176·6	120·2	155·0	—
Underdeveloped counties, total	98·6	65·8	75·5	172·1	128·8	123·3	343·0
Developed counties, total	118·5	178·0	70·2	198·1	116·2		
Budapest and Pest county	122·6	301·0	52·0	199·2	107·9	111·9	292·0
of which: Budapest	122·4	285·7	0·4	184·5	100·1		
Hungary, total	110·5	544·8	197·7	192·3	114·7	117·7	313·0

approved between 1957 and 1959 to tackle the problem, and in the period of the second five-year plan (1961–5) efforts were to be seen to develop the backward areas.

Conditions favourable to a more balanced development were in part created by the industrial plants already established in those areas. In part the fact of the comparatively large manpower reserve in the agricultural areas – at the time of increasing exhaustion of national reserves of manpower – became more and more an attractive factor in industrial development. Finally, these areas possessed various favourable economic and geographical endowments (water resources, agricultural raw material supplies, a local market for goods, recently discovered new sources of energy, a favourable position on import–export routes).

In the last analysis, in spite of the emphasis on the reconstruction aspect of development, considerable results were achieved in this period in raising

LE SIX

ANGES IN INDUSTRIAL STRUCTURE IN THE UNDERDEVELOPED
UNTIES OF HUNGARY, 1953–65

:al of all industry in each year = 100)

| | 1953 | | | | | 1965 | | | | |
| | Heavy | Engin- | of which: Chemi- | Light | Food | Heavy | Engin- | of which: Chemi- | Light | Food |
Counties	Industry	eering	cals	Industry	Industry	Industry	eering	cals	Industry	Industry
s-Kiskun	32·1	25·7	—	11·0	56·9	28·9	22·7	2·7	46·8	24·3
és	24·8	6·4	—	32·1	43·1	25·1	10·4	0·6	51·3	23·6
ngrád	19·9	10·2	—	60·2	19·9	22·3	16·0	2·0	63·7	14·0
du	45·0	31·7	3·3	25·8	29·2	48·6	33·3	6·0	35·9	15·5
ogy	15·6	1·6	—	40·6	43·8	28·0	12·9	—	47·1	24·9
olcs	32·7	20·0	7·3	16·4	50·9	28·6	10·6	6·0	38·7	32·7
nok	49·1	36·6	2·7	25·0	25·9	43·4	28·0	3·0	42·6	14·0
na	48·6	8·3	—	30·6	20·8	27·8	16·0	0·5	54·1	18·1
	31·6	21·9	—	47·4	21·0	30·7	23·6	2·4	56·1	13·2
	60·5	13·2	2·6	26·3	13·2	52·6	12·6	2·8	33·9	13·5
lerdeveloped unties, total	34·6	18·2	1·3	34·6	30·8	32·8	19·5	2·6	48·5	18·7
eloped unties, total	83·1	13·9	2·4	8·7	8·2	75·1	16·9	5·5	16·8	8·1
apest and est county	64·7	50·7	4·5	27·1	8·2	60·2	42·8	7·2	33·1	6·7
of which: Budapest	64·8	50·6	4·8	27·5	7·7	60·4	42·7	7·7	33·4	6·2
ungary, total	66·8	33·9	3·4	21·9	11·3	59·3	29·4	5·7	31·0	9·7

the general and economic levels of the backward areas, and in their industrialisation, as may be seen from the tables and charts referred to above.

The industries and individual plants earlier established in these areas were expanded by the addition of new lines of production and the industrialisation of further towns was started. An improvement began in the industrial structure of the areas; as against the earlier dependence on the food and light industries, additional branches of industry began to play an increased role, for example the chemical, engineering and building material industries. The pace of industrialisation also gathered momentum. As against a national average growth of industrial employment by 15 per cent, it increased in the counties concerned by 33 per cent, while the increase was 15 per cent in the developed rural areas and 7 per cent in the capital. In this period 40 per cent of the increment of employment was represented by jobs in backward areas.

Some progress occurred also in adapting agricultural development to resource endowments. Substantial vineyards and fruit plantations were established in the underdeveloped counties and there was also an expansion of irrigated farming. A considerable concentration of farms took place (they decreased in number by one-third) and the profitability of agriculture also rose considerably in these areas.

The process of urbanisation having been invigorated, the population of towns increased in five years by 280,000 and at the same time, the concentration of the population of certain parts of the country was diminished. In certain counties, however, the emigration still exceeded the natural increase and an absolute decrease of population followed mainly in respect of the young, productive age groups. There was some progress also in raising the level of infrastructure in these areas. As in the case of industry, this kind of development occurred mainly in the county capitals, but gradually extended to the other towns in the countryside and even to the villages.[1]

3 EXPERIENCE GAINED IN THE DEVELOPMENT OF BACKWARD AREAS [2]

The regional development policies of the past two decades and the major experiences gained in the course of the location and planning work aimed at the levelling out of backwardness in the underdeveloped areas may be summed up as follows:

(1) In the industrial development of backward areas a decisive role is played by investment and particularly by the carefully considered location of new projects. Though new projects provided in the relevant period only a comparatively small part (15–25 per cent) of the increment of employment measures on a national scale, in the backward areas – precisely because of the backwardness of industry – they were a decisive factor in industrial development. Their importance reaches far beyond the direct effect of increase in employment.

They mean above all that an industrial basis has been created in the given area and – depending on the character of the industry in question – they provide favourable conditions for fairly intensive further industrial development in the forms of a skilled labour force, reserves of capacity,

---

[1] A detailed analysis of regional development is contained in: *Major Tendencies in the Regional Development of Productive Forces in 1961–65* (in Hungarian: study by the Institute of Planning, Regional Section, May 1966) and *Major Trends in Regional Development of the Economy in the Second Five Year Plan*, Central Statistical Office, Regional Department (under publication).

[2] See also Z. Tatai, 'Topical Problems of Industrial Location' (in Hungarian), *Közgazdasági Szemle*, no. 3 (1967).

opportunities to co-operate with other undertakings, an expansive consumer market, a basis of technology and other respects. They induce directly or indirectly a development also of such associated activities as transport, warehousing, trade, public utilities, energy supplies and the like. This again contributes to the general technico-economic opening up of the area in question. In this way a major industrial project may start a kind of 'self-sustained growth' in the industrial and general development of a given area. Beside the many positive examples of this there are also many negative examples to be drawn from the experience of the past two decades.

Even in the early stages of the socialist industrialisation policies, but particularly since the end of the fifties, efforts have been made to locate new investment projects in increasing numbers in areas which need to be developed industrially for the first time, since both the individual enterprises and the ministries concerned have mostly tended to choose the already developed areas in the capital of the country towns to benefit from the advantages due to industrial facilities and the general level of economic development. This has been partly due also to the fact that the interests of the national economy and a dynamic approach to economic and social efficiency have not been sufficiently emphasised either in planning or in the methodology of investment efficiency computation. The actual location of a project has often been decided on the basis of the investment costs and operational expenditures demanded by the given enterprise or industry from the investment fund, and on the basis of expected profits without regard to possibly considerable additional investment and other costs which might arise indirectly, and perhaps at a later stage, on the national level if another location, possibly in a backward area, were not chosen. This explains why certain plants which might have effectively promoted the industrialisation of underdeveloped areas have not in the end been located in such regions.

The experience gained and the conditions to be satisfied in this field can be formulated as follows. If the basic conditions of operation of an important industrial project, in terms of raw materials, energy, co-operative institutions, consumer market, labour can be realistically and efficiently secured in a given situation in some suitable backward region, this location alternative should be preferred. The additional investment and even additional temporary operation costs on the national economic level must be borne. Since they are due to the momentary underdeveloped character of the area, the additional costs will be repaid in the long run. They will be amply repaid within the given investment project itself, or in further associated investments and their operation, or in promoting some objectives of economic and social policy which cannot always be expressed in terms of money but are still substantial. This principle must not be applied, however, to imposing locations which are wholly irrational and inconsistent with the actual location requirements of the industry in question.

(2) If only in order to mitigate and offset as far as possible the disadvantages of lack of development in the backward areas and those of high capital intensity and slow returns in technical development, it is very important to apply in such areas the principle of concentration of development.

This means that the investment projects to be undertaken in these areas should be deliberately concentrated into relatively few places possessing favourable resource endowments from the point of view of industrial and general development. In the process of location, efforts should be made to develop an industry in vertical stages, to be a suitable establishment of wider technological interrelations in the area. Advantages may be secured also by locating together in a single concentration technologically unconnected plants in cases in which a common location offers favourable conditions for the individual plants, for example by joint development of the area, the establishment of public utilities, connection to the transport and energy network, or through useful sharing of a labour force for example by males in one plant and female labour in another.

How many places can be simultaneously developed on such a concentrated basis depends principally on the development resources available and the new industrial projects to be started as well as on the industrial distribution of development and such relevant factors as the general manpower situation. One of the most delicate problems of development and planning is the correct location of this concentration and of the system of individual centres to be developed.

To take an example, in the period of the first five-year plan, seventy-four places were earmarked for industrial development. In practice, considerable industrial development was achieved in about thirty-five settlements and the lag behind the targets set was greatest in the most underdeveloped areas. In the period after 1957, an immensely greater concentration was enforced. In the underdeveloped areas, industrialisation efforts were concentrated in two major towns, Szeged and Debrecen, and, in addition development took place in ten or twelve county capitals and other major towns. In this case there was considerably more success.

In the current third five-year plan period a substantial part of industrial development is concentrated mainly on the same limited number of places in the underdeveloped regions. In addition, however, there is to be a gradual expansion of industrial development to a somewhat larger number of places favourably situated from the point of view of resource endowments, in order to reduce the movements of population.

Over a longer perspective it seems that about 110–30 places out of a total of about 3,200, are suited to become the bases of a locally concentrated but nationally decentralised industrial development. About half of them fall in the underdeveloped areas.

(3) Experience has shown that it is generally advisable to operate in certain stages in the industrialisation of underdeveloped areas. This means that – in view of the lack of a background of skilled labour and technology – it is often expedient to locate first in these areas rather simple types of production and develop gradually on this basis, and to rely for the more exigent branches of production on the existing resources of technology and skilled labour.

A gradual process may help also in the sense that a development of local industry of a handicraft type can serve as a preparatory stage to more comprehensive industrial development. Development of such a limited character may be achieved fairly rapidly, within the limits of local conditions, without any major technical preparations and development, mostly on the basis of local initiative, and possibly with rather smaller investment. In addition, they make possible the employment of large numbers of workers with a relatively small investment, and this is important in an underdeveloped area. At the same time, the local industrial plants will gradually create a local labour force for the industry in question and in this way also considerably facilitate further development, as has often happened in the past, for example in the plastics industry, the rubber industry, electrical appliances, the textiles and clothing industries, wood processing and other cases.

In this way the local authorities or councils can make progress within the framework of their own limited development resources, and, by using central resources to a smaller extent, overcome the initial difficulties of local industrial development and establish favourable conditions for a much larger industrial development at some later date.

Such development by stages cannot, of course, be practicably pursued in all industries. On the other hand, this kind of progressive industrialisation and the establishment of up-to-date large-scale industrial plants are two elements of industrialising the backward areas which are not mutually exclusive but are complementary to each other.

(4) It is only essentially another aspect of this that experience shows that it is of greater advantage to the areas to be developed if large nation-wide enterprises establish branches in the given area than if independent enterprises are brought into being. Technical difficulties are smaller, the problems of technical managerial staff and experts can be solved by the enterprise by internal pre-arrangements and by temporary transfers and the enterprise can help its daughter company with continuing technical assistance.

(5) Between 1958 and 1962 a series of government decisions restricted industrial development in Budapest and the surrounding sixty-four places and required that new industrial projects should be established only by a

special permit from the Government. They also required the transfer of certain industrial plants from Budapest to the countryside. This helped in diverting choices of location, which tended towards the capital, to the rural areas and in some cases even to the backward areas. In this sense government decisions became an important factor in the industrialisation of the underdeveloped area.

The obstacles mentioned under (1) above limited the effects of these decrees. In spite of this, the tendency to concentration somewhat weakened and up to the time of writing more than thirty plants employing about 6,000–7,000 people have been transferred to the rural areas and mainly to industrially underdeveloped areas. These include some important plants.

The transfer of plants was facilitated by the creation of a special fund for this purpose. Though not a substantial sum (about Ft 150 million between 1961–5), it was used efficiently and proved a useful way of encouraging the industrial development of underdeveloped areas by supplementing the allocations to ministries, initiating smaller projects, securing and reconstructing buildings for industrial use, and the like.

To make the Budapest restrictions effective and reduce the migration to Budapest, certain administrative measures had also to be introduced. For example a system of licences and limitations was introduced controlling the right to settle in the capital, to build flats or to purchase durables. A maximum level of employment was fixed for individual industries; in 1965, for example, it had to be no higher than the preceding year. Judging from experience, such measures can have only temporary and limited results.

There were also a number of other measures to encourage industrialisation in the rural areas and the transfer of Budapest plants to the country. For example, a special allowance was given to experts intending to live near the new plants established, the training of workers was organised, these areas enjoyed preference in the allocation of housing investment and so on.

(6)   There is a good deal of evidence to show that infrastructure improvement, removing the backwardness which exists in this respect, is an important factor in the industrial development of underdeveloped areas. In selecting a place for the location of an undertaking, the technical and general cultural standard of a given area is weighed more and more, and this particularly holds for some industries. The chances of industrialisation of underdeveloped areas have increased because in the larger towns of the rural areas a number of secondary and higher technical schools, technical and architectural colleges have been built, thus promoting the growth of a 'local' technical and other intellectual stratum. A rising level of education (eight forms are compulsory and the extent of education beyond that is considerable) means that the underdeveloped areas have not

simply labour reserves but that they possess a reserve of young labour representing a higher stage of education and with corresponding technical abilities.

Development of the transport facilities in the underdeveloped areas, and the improvement of their communal, housing, health and cultural services, makes them more attractive to industry. Thus quite apart from the importance of achieving a certain general minimum level of development, it is important also that the resources available for infrastructure development – generally insufficient to meet the demands – shall be utilised to a large extent on a principle of concentration of effort, in the places which have the most favourable conditions for development. The scope of development should be expanded progressively in this field also.

In the longer run it seems, for example, advisable to concentrate infrastructure development both on the national level and in the underdeveloped areas to about one-third of all settlements, putting at the same time emphasis on the 110–30 settlements which show the prospective capacities for industrialisation.

Between industrialisation and infrastructure development there exists also a reverse relation: substantial industrial development leads to infrastructure development – transport facilities, public utilities, communication, and the like – and to the concentration of population and the process of urbanisation. It is therefore advisable to couple as far as possible industrial development with the development of the local services and particularly the modernisation and development of towns. In the opposite sense, if industry is not developed in existing towns, new towns will have to be built at substantial cost but at the same time improvements of the infrastructure of existing towns and other settlements will be necessary.

(7) Modernisation of agriculture has an important role to play in solving the problems of underdeveloped areas. This particularly holds for countries – including Hungary – in which agriculture is of equal importance with industry in the total national economy.

The introduction of more intensive forms of agriculture, such as grapes, fruit, vegetables, in the backward areas on a massive scale, improvement of the irrigation system, amelioration of poor soils, mechanisation, a gradual establishment of the framework and conditions for more up-to-date large-scale farming have all considerably contributed to reducing the economic and cultural backwardness of these areas as compared with other regions in the country.

In general, the modernisation of agriculture reduces the demand for labour. But if modernisation includes greater intensification of farming, the release of manpower will be moderate and an additional demand for manpower may arise. On the other hand, modernisation of agriculture releases mainly the older generations, those already beyond the age of retirement, and requires at the same time a considerable number of new

L 2

younger workers with technical skills. This will provide an opportunity to prevent an exaggerated migration of younger people, and the demographic erosion characteristic of backward areas, since a modernised agriculture can earn a higher and more stable income and can raise the technical and general cultural level of the countryside. At the same time, greater employment of the younger generation in the villages may become itself a decisive factor in raising the cultural and technical standards of the countryside and of agriculture in general.

(8) I mentioned earlier that the migration of great masses of population from the backward areas is one of the major consequences of regional inequalities. But since some of these areas have the highest natural increases in the country, the manpower reserves found in them cannot be absorbed by the areas themselves. Thus encouraging the regional redistribution of the surplus population and manpower may itself prove to be a necessary measure for raising the relative economic standard of these areas. The measures to be employed may be: reduced fares, special supplementary payments for those not living with their families, hostels for workers with reduced rates, organised manpower recruitment and training or retraining.

(9) An important factor in the economic or industrial development of backward areas may be a rational participation in the international division of labour. In the past two decades one of the factors in developing the eastern and southern underdeveloped regions of Hungary has been that they lie on the export–import routes to neighbouring countries, and that useful co-operation could be established with the adjacent regions of these countries. Advantage will continue to be taken of this in the future also.

(10) Since in some countries this is an important factor, it is worthwhile mentioning that in Hungary there are no problems of nationalities, of racial or religious minorities in particular regions, such as would affect – either favourably or unfavourably – policies designed for the spatial development of the economy and the development of underdeveloped areas.

(11) Last but not least it must be mentioned that, in the light of experience, it is an important precondition of developing the backward areas that the country should have a comprehensive regional development and location programme consistent with the development objectives of the national economy.[1] This programme should outline for a longer period and plan in more detail for shorter (say, five-year) periods the strategy and tactics of industrial, agricultural and infrastructure development of these regions, taking into account the natural, demographic and economic endowments of the area and also the general trends of the national economy, its rate of growth structure and material resources. In the absence

[1] See L. Köszegi, 'The Role of Regional Planning in National Economic Planning'. Paper submitted to the Conference of Senior Economic Advisers, Geneva, 1964.

of such a comprehensive programme, improvisations and ill-considered decisions are likely to predominate, and that would have an adverse effect on the development of backward areas. It is equally important to draw up so-called physical (land use) plans consistent with this programme especially in relation to the planned technical development of selected areas by such means as industrial estates.

4 FUTURE TASKS AND PROBLEMS

The major problems to be solved in the future are indicated in Tables 1–4. There are still important differences in economic development levels and considerable disparities in the spatial distribution of the economy. Their gradual elimination is a fundamental task of the future.

A basic precondition, and at the same time a contribution to the solution of this problem, is to formulate the policy of comprehensive development mentioned above. Most of its elements have already been discussed, but – as regards the problem as a whole – it is the task of the next few years to formulate such a comprehensive policy for a period of about fourteen years, consistently with the national development objectives and the expected trends of the national economy.

A whole series of new and quite novel problems and difficulties will arise in connection with the introduction on 1 January 1968 of a new system of economic management in Hungary. As a result of this reform, the independence of economic units – particularly in respect of simple pro-duction – will increase, but at the same time a considerable range of de-velopment projects will be affected. It is an important feature of the new mechanism that, in most cases, actual economic forces will have a greater role in regulating economic processes. From the point of view of regional development this means that, for enterprises interested in maximising their profits, the advantages from co-operation, from agglomeration, and in some industries the advantages due to location near the raw material sources, will have increased weight and this will, in many cases, tend towards further development of the areas already industrialised. In itself, this is a realistic tendency if market relations transmit to enterprises at the same time the disadvantages on the national level of this trend.

The problem, therefore, consists in establishing such a system of regula-tors as will realistically balance out at the national economic level the one-sided influences and secure a suitable regional trend and development. According to present ideas, its major elements would be the following:

The main element in, and the main means of carrying out, the regional development policies formulated will continue to be investment financed from the central budget and central determination of locations. This pro-cedure essentially determines the fundamental regional relations and structure (these individual projects, relatively few in number, represent about 40–50 per cent of the value of industrial investment over a five-year period).

Another important instrument is an allocation among county councils of the financial funds to provide infrastructure investments differentiated so as to take into account the development requirements consequent on major investment projects as well as those necessary to enable the under-developed areas to catch up with others.

One essential measure to promote the right regional trends will be bank credits, to be granted on terms differentiated according to the government preferences in respect of areas to be developed or restricted. Subsidies may also be considered for enterprises which plan development in the selected areas with their own funds or borrowings.

The rate of the non-deductible wage tax may also be reduced in selected areas from the average 15 per cent to 5 per cent where a proposed development conforms to general objectives and is desirable from the point of view of the local resources endowments.

The rate of the land rent – the price or rent of plots of land and a form of tax – will be considerably higher in Budapest than in the country towns, and in the latter it will be differentiated again according to the size of the town. In addition, the councils may encourage enterprises proposing to locate in the underdeveloped areas by granting other facilities also.

It may be hoped that these measures will offset the advantages from location in already developed areas. How these hopes will be justified in practice can be judged, of course, only from future experience, and the system of regional planning and regulation will need to be improved progressively in the light of this.

17 The Transformation of one of the Most Backward Regions of Central Asia into an Advanced Industrial Republic: The Case of the Uzbek Republic

N. Plotnikov

CORRESPONDING MEMBER OF THE U.S.S.R. ACADEMY OF SCIENCES

1 INTRODUCTORY

The history of humanity covers a great number of great events but none which produced so great an influence on the course of world development as did the October Socialist Revolution of 1917. This revolution radically changed society's entire political and economic set-up. The experience of the Soviet State has shown that only after the October Revolution were the necessary conditions created in the Soviet Union for the transformation of the country's backward regions into progressive industrial regions with highly developed industry and agriculture, science and culture. One of the republics of the Soviet Union, the Uzbek Republic (or Uzbekistan) can serve as an illustration of this.

Thanks to a progressive national policy, the peoples of Uzbekistan, with the generous help of the Russian people and other peoples of the U.S.S.R., have succeeded in liquidating their economic and cultural backwardness and have progressed from the pre-capitalist forms of economy to the socialist economy. The growth of the economy of the Uzbek Republic is based on socialist relations of production. Today, in its level of economic development, its structure of productive forces and its technology, the Uzbek Republic holds one of the first places in the economy of the U.S.S.R. It is a rapidly developing industrial region of the U.S.S.R., a centre of mechanised and irrigated agriculture, and the Soviet Union's principal producer of cotton, silk and karakul. In a short period of time Uzbekistan, formerly a backward region of Tsarist Russia, has become a prosperous socialist republic.

2 THE ECONOMY OF PRE-REVOLUTIONARY UZBEKISTAN

Before 1917, Uzbekistan was an agrarian appendage of Russia. The Tsarist government set obstacles in the way of the industrial development in this region, assigning to it the role of supplier of agricultural raw materials, to be processed in central Russia. In Uzbekistan only agriculture

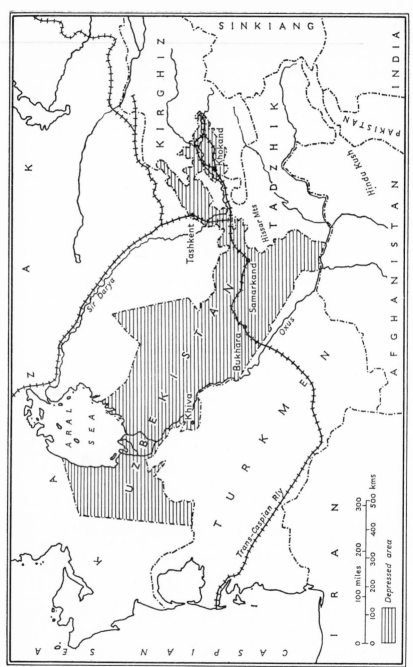

THE FORMERLY BACKWARD REPUBLIC OF UZBEKISTAN

was encouraged. Russian capitalists wished to create there their own source of cotton supply for their textile industry. This attitude was to be explained by the rapid growth of the Russian textile industry, which was becoming more and more active in foreign markets. Cotton production was growing. It was stimulated by the raising of tariffs on imported cotton and by the construction of the two railway lines connecting Central Asia and Russia (the Trans-Caspian railway built in 1888 and the Tashkent–Orenburg railway built in 1905). In the years preceding World War I over 50 per cent of the Russian textile industry's demand was satisfied by home-produced cotton, the greater part of which was grown in Uzbekistan.

Though the Russian bourgeoisie was interested in the development of some of its branches, Uzbekistan's agriculture as a whole remained extremely backward and primitive. The Uzbek peasants lived in misery and want. The manufacturing industries of Uzbekistan developed very slowly as a result of Tsarist colonial policy, and were essentially unbalanced. In 1913 the industries processing agricultural produce (cotton processing and seed oil production) accounted for over 80 per cent of the industrial output, while the heavy industries accounted for only 2 per cent. The food (apart from oil seed production), leather and other industries accounted for the rest of the output. Uzbekistan, which was the main producer of cotton and raw silk, had not a single cotton or silk mill. Fabrics, ready-made clothing, foot-wear, metal goods, fuel and many other consumer goods were supplied by the capitalists of Russia, who thus made enormous profits. The secondary industries of Uzbekistan were technically backward and of a semi-domestic character. Employers had a ready supply of cheap labour and were not interested in raising the technical level of production or in using modern equipment.

The main form of industrial production in pre-revolutionary Uzbekistan was domestic production. About 100,000 handicraftsmen were engaged in the production of silk fabrics, clothing, earthenware, agricultural implements, metal goods, footwear. The pauperisation of peasants and the ruin of handicraftsmen and artisans led to the growth of unemployment. The capitalists took advantage of this by imposing very low wages on workers. Women were paid 40–50 per cent less than men; young people still less. The cultural level of the population was extremely low. There was only 2·9 per cent literacy among the Uzbeks. There were few specialists with higher and secondary education.

3 THE DEVELOPMENT OF THE INDUSTRY IN THE YEARS OF SOVIET POWER

During World War I, the industries of Uzbekistan fell into decay. By the time the Uzbek Republic was formed the production of the secondary industries had diminished sharply and in 1924–5 was only 40·7 per cent of the pre-war level. Thus Uzbekistan, like the other republics of the Soviet Union, embarked on peacetime reconstruction in the difficult conditions of post-war ruin.

The Soviet government undertook a vast task of reorganisation designed to restore the country's economy and develop its productive resources. It provided extensive economic aid to Uzbekistan. The Russian Republic (R.S.F.S.R.) supplied the necessary equipment for textile and paper mills, leather-making and soap-manufacturing plants, repair shops and other enterprises. As a result of the generous aid of the Russian working class, the process of the economic restoration of Uzbekistan proceeded rapidly. By 1924, about one-half of the industrial enterprises of Uzbekistan had been reconstructed. In this period great attention was also devoted to the establishment of new industrial enterprises.

By 1928 Uzbekistan had not only recovered the pre-war level of industrial production (on a new technical basis) but had created new industries and, what is most important, had ousted private capital from industry.

The reconstruction of the economy of the Soviet Union enabled the Soviet people to take a further step towards the industrialisation of the country and the socialist reconstruction of agriculture. Acting on the assumption that only a highly developed heavy industry would be capable of ensuring a radical technical reconstruction of all branches of the economy and creating the material and technical basis of socialism, the Soviet Government adopted industrialisation as its general policy. This policy of socialist industrialisation was of especial importance to such economically and culturally backward national republics as Uzbekistan where industrial employment was small. Industrialisation meant that a basis was created for the uplift of the whole economy, the growth of the working class and the exchange of goods between manufacturing industry and agriculture. This, in turn, created the necessary conditions for the strengthening of the union between the working class and peasants, the strengthening of the leading role of the working class in the framework of the socialist system, and the participation of the broad masses of the population of the national republics in socialist reconstruction.

The Soviet State overcame great difficulties and successfully solved the problem of finding sources within the country for the finance of socialist industrialisation and the development of the economy. As no loans from capitalist countries could be expected, the main source was the profits made by the socialist industrial enterprises. The economy and culture of Uzbekistan grew on the basis of the unified plan for the development of the economy of the U.S.S.R. This took account of the advantages of division of labour throughout the country and of the common interests of the Uzbek republic and all other republics of the Soviet Union.

Taking account of the natural resources of Uzbekistan and the already existing economic links, the republic was developed as the main cotton supplier of the Soviet Union. At the same time attention was paid to the development of the republic's manufacturing industries. The rate of economic growth in Uzbekistan was as high as everywhere in the Soviet Union. The Uzbek people are proud of the achievements of their republic in the years of Soviet power – achievements which resulted in the creation of the republic's powerful socialist economy.

As a result of the consistent policy of socialist industrialisation and the high rate of growth of secondary industries, the total industrial output of the Uzbek republic was by 1963 24 times greater than in 1913 (that in cotton-ginning increasing 6·2-fold, and in the rest of the industry 7·9-fold). A radical change occurred in the structure of the secondary industries in Uzbekistan. In 1913 cotton-ginning accounted for 80 per cent of industrial production; after the revolution, because of the rapid growth of the heavy, light, food and other industries, this imbalance was eliminated.

The heavy industries which form a basis for the growth of all other branches of economy were developed very rapidly. In Uzbekistan there were introduced the machine-building industry, ferrous and non-ferrous metallurgical industries, natural gas, oil and coal production, the chemical industry, the building materials and building industry, and power production. At the same time light industry and food processing also developed rapidly.

In the process of this industrialisation, new industrial centres sprang up in Uzbekistan. At present the republic holds a leading place in the production of a number of important industrial goods. It holds the first place in the U.S.S.R. in the production of machinery for cotton growing, equipment for the cotton industry, and in the production of cotton and raw silk; it stands second in the production of machinery for the textile industry and in the production of cotton fabrics; it stands third in the production of chemical machinery, cables, excavators, cranes, seed oil and fertilisers; it stands fourth in the production of natural gas and coal; it stands fifth in the production of crude oil.

In the years of Soviet power great attention has been paid to the increase of electricity supply. The big Chirchik–Bozsui hydro-electric project which consists of sixteen hydro-electric power stations with a total capacity of 319,000 kW. has been built. The construction of these stations has increased not only electricity generation but also the supply of water to the irrigation system of the Chirchik valley. Immediately before World War II the Farkhad hydro-electric power station, of 126 mw., at the time the largest in Soviet Central Asia, was completed. The construction of this station gave a tremendous boost to secondary industries and agriculture. In 1963 Uzbekistan produced 4 times as much electricity as did the whole of Tsarist Russia in 1913. Electricity production in Uzbekistan by 1958 had reached 4·68 billion kWh.; by 1963, 8 billion kWh.; and by

1965, 11 billion kWh. The *per capita* production of electricity in Uzbekistan in 1965 was 1,080 kWh. (in 1958 it was 585 kWh.). The building of power lines has enabled almost all regions of the republic to enjoy electric power supply from the central system. Energy supplies have also been successfully developed. In pre-revolutionary Uzbekistan they were practically non-existent save for some very primitive and small-scale oil production and refining. The growth of energy supplies was absolutely indispensable for the development of the republic's resources. Geological prospecting was crowned with success. It was established that the republic had considerable coal deposits (about 3·5 billion tons). Since Soviet power, oil production and oil-processing have also been established in the Uzbek republic. Large oil fields were discovered in the Fergana Valley and the Surkhan–Darya region. These oil fields have contributed greatly to the growth of crude oil production. At the oil wells new techniques of automation and tele-control are widely used. In 1964–5 the oil-refining industry produced a wide range of new products including white paraffin and 72-octane gasoline. In the very near future the Uzbek republic will be able to satisfy all its own needs for oil products and lubricants.

The discovery of huge deposits of natural gas in Uzbekistan has radically changed the whole fuel balance of the republic. It has also become possible to supply other important industrial regions of the Soviet Union with this cheap raw material and fuel. The natural gas deposits of Uzbekistan are the largest in Soviet Central Asia and among the largest in the U.S.S.R. The main natural gas deposits of the republic are found in the Bukhara–Khiva region, which is rapidly becoming one of the most important centres of the Soviet natural gas and chemical industries.

Of great importance also is the chemical industry of Uzbekistan. The republic's large plants produce nitric and phosphorous fertilisers, sulphuric acid, paints, rubber, pharmaceutical and other chemical goods. The Chirchik electrochemical plant is one of the largest in the Soviet Union.

The ferrous and non-ferrous metallurgical industries are among the principal achievements of Uzbek industrialisation. The first large industrial enterprise built was the Uzbek metallurgical plant. Geologists have discovered in Uzbekistan rich deposits of non-ferrous and rare metal ores (copper, lead, tungsten, molybdenum, gold, etc.) and on this basis the non-ferrous metallurgy is being rapidly developed. Of extreme importance is the Angren–Almalyk mining region. It is rich in non-ferrous and rare metals, bauxite, building materials, coal, etc. The copper and lead-zinc deposits of this region are among the best in the U.S.S.R. In this region the large Altyntopkan non-ferrous industrial complex, comprising mines, lead-zinc and copper-producing plants and other industrial enterprises, has been constructed.

Since Soviet power the machine-building industry has been introduced into Uzbekistan. This most important industry contributes greatly to the technical re-equipment of the republic's economy. New and efficient machinery is being designed and produced; old models are discarded. The introduction of new machinery contributes greatly to the further development of the economy. The light industry of the republic has also developed rapidly. While the light industry of pre-revolutionary Uzbekistan merely processed agricultural raw materials sufficiently to make them transportable to Russia proper, the republic now has a well-developed light industry, able to satisfy consumer demand for fabrics, clothing, footwear, and the like.

The following figures illustrate the growth of light industry in Uzbekistan:

TABLE ONE
LIGHT INDUSTRY IN UZBEKISTAN 1913–65

Products	1913	1940	1950	1955	1958	1963	1964	1965
Cotton (000 tons)	179	538	670	997	989	1,012	1,219	1,165
Raw silk (tons)	—	693	762	762	803	960	993	1,000
Cotton fabrics (m. metres)	—	107	161	212	220	247	258	264
Silk fabrics (m. metres)	—	4·5	8·7	17·5	21·2	31·4	35·9	39·6
Unwoven fabrics (m. metres)	—	—	—	—	—	1,457	2,700	4,000
Hosiery (m. pairs)	—	8·6	7·8	11·6	13·9	24·0	27·6	29·0
Knitted goods (m. pieces)	—	1·0	0·6	0·9	1·3	2·6	4·1	4·9
Knitted underwear (m. pieces)	—	2·5	8·4	8·6	8·5	11·7	13·8	16·8
Leather footwear (m. pairs)	—	3·8	4·4	6·6	9·1	13·2	13·7	14·1

After the October Revolution the Uzbek cotton-ginning industry was radically transformed. Small and primitive factories have been superseded by a modern industry with advanced technique.

The food processing industry of the republic has undergone a similar transformation. It cannot now be compared to that of pre-revolutionary Uzbekistan. Its importance in the exchange of products within the Soviet Union has grown considerably. Uzbekistan holds a prominent place in the country's production of seed oil, canned food, dried fruit and wine.

The food industries of the Uzbek republic have increased their production to the extent shown in Table 2:

TABLE TWO
FOOD PROCESSING INDUSTRIES OF UZBEKISTAN 1913–65

	1913	1940	1945	1958	1963	1964	1965
Meat (000 tons)	—	26·7	13·1	50·1	76·5	83·0	86·0
Seed oil (000 tons)	36·5	142	41	218	281	320	312
Butter (000 tons)	—	0·95	0·83	6·1	6·4	6·8	6·9
Canned food (m. cans)	0·19	39·3	27·8	146·5	239·1	236·0	246
Confectionery (000 tons)	—	13·0	4·9	40·3	48·1	53·1	66·8
Wine (m. decalitres)	0·5	1·9	0·6	2·65	3·66	3·8	4·1

As the industry of Uzbekistan has developed, its economic ties with the rest of the Soviet Union have expanded. At present Uzbekistan sends to other republics of the Soviet Union not only agricultural produce (cotton, raw silk, seed oil, etc.) but also cotton and silk fabrics, natural gas and coal, gasoline, diesel fuel and other oil products, fertilisers, non-ferrous metals, cement, agricultural machinery and implements, textile machinery, earth-moving machines, diesel engines, pumps, and compressors, electric machinery, cables and other machines and equipment.

4 THE EXPANSION OF EXTERNAL ECONOMIC TIES

From year to year Uzbekistan exports more and more goods. Uzbek produce is exported to nearly sixty countries – to the socialist countries, to many countries of Asia, Africa and Latin America, to the U.S.A., the Scandinavian countries, Britain, France, West Germany, Italy and to other countries of Europe. Uzbek goods have become known and valued on world markets for their quality. In the past ten years the value of the Uzbek exports has increased more than 6-fold. Among the republics of the U.S.S.R., Uzbekistan is one of the main exporters. Not only has the number of countries to which Uzbekistan exports grown but the composition of its exports has also undergone a complete change. Formerly Uzbekistan mainly exported agricultural products (cotton, silk, karakul) and those of light industry. In recent years the chief place in its exports has come to be held by the products of such heavy industries as machine-building, electrical engineering, light engineering, oil-refining and the like. The republic supplies the world markets with over 200 types of industrial products. It exports cotton, raw silk, cotton and silk fabrics, karakul, wool, wine and different produce of the light and food industries as well as seed-drills, cultivators, cotton combines, sprinklers and other agricultural machines, diesels, cranes, electric machines, excavators, pumps, compressors, textile machinery, cotton-cleaning and chemical machinery, cables and electrical appliances, film-projectors and equipment, cement, lacquers, oil-products, etc. Machinery and equipment produced in Uzbekistan is exported to all corners of the globe. Goods, destined for export to the countries of Asia, Africa and Latin America, are produced specially for tropical conditions. The republic exports machinery and equipment for complete industrial enterprises. Many cotton-cleaning plants and spinning-mills in Bulgaria, textile mills in Poland, Czechoslovakia and Hungary, cotton-ginning plants in the Korean People's Democratic Republic are equipped with machinery produced in Uzbekistan.

Uzbekistan has actively contributed to the economic aid provided by the U.S.S.R. to new independent states of Asia and Africa for the development and strengthening of their national economies. It has supplied these countries with machinery and equipment, and technicians are sent to install the machinery and to help local technicians in building and running industrial enterprises. It has participated in the construction of machine-building and mining equipment plants in India, in oil-prospecting and the building of the water pipelines in Syria, in the building of the Bagdad–Basra railway and of the educational centre in Iraq, in the construction of the Aswan dam and of industrial enterprises in the U.A.R. and in the building of large industrial enterprises in Afghanistan and other countries which have attained national independence. Many specialists from Uzbekistan have gone to India, the U.A.R., Syria, Sudan, Mali, Guinea, Afghanistan, the Democratic Republic of Vietnam, Cuba, Poland, Hungary, Czechoslovakia and other countries to share their know-how and to give technical help in prospecting, in building canals, factories and plants, and in installing machinery and equipment. Their designers have prepared projects for industrial enterprises, irrigation schemes, and the like to be built in many countries. And Uzbekistan has helped in the training of specialists: many students from Vietnam, Afghanistan, India, Cuba, Pakistan, the Mongolian People's Republic, Congo, the U.A.R., Nepal, Yemen, Nigeria and other countries have studied in the Uzbek institutions of higher learning.

5 THE GROWTH OF CULTURE AND WELL-BEING OF THE UZBEK PEOPLE

The training of a great number of skilled workers and specialists for all branches of the economy, and for the secondary industries in particular, is one of the principal achievements of Soviet power in Uzbekistan. In 1913 the secondary industries of Uzbekistan employed only 26,400 workers. The rapid development of the economy resulted in a tremendous increase in the number of workers and of technical and office personnel. In 1962 there were 1,892,000 workers and other employees employed in the economy of Uzbekistan – 17 times the number before the Revolution. Of this number 431,000 were employed in manufacturing industries.

The working class of Uzbekistan has acquired new skills: before the Revolution only 16–18 per cent of all workers were skilled workers. According to the census of 1959, 80 per cent of all workers in the republic were skilled; in the chemical industry as many as 98·8 per cent; in engineering and metals, 92·8 per cent; in the metallurgical industries, 87·4 per cent; in electricity supply, 88·3 per cent; in food processing, 94 per cent; in the textile industries, 87 per cent. From 1959, considerable progress has been made in eliminating unskilled manual labour and in raising the technical and cultural level of workers.

Before the Revolution there was 2·9 per cent literacy among the Uzbeks. Today Uzbekistan is a republic of complete literacy. 477 persons per

1,000 persons employed in the economy have higher and secondary education. The republic has trained specialists for all branches of its economy. Pre-revolutionary Uzbekistan had only one technical school; by 1963 there were eighty-six technical schools with 79,300 students. Before the Revolution Uzbekistan had no institutions of higher learning; by 1963 139,200 students studied in twenty-nine such institutions. In recent years over 14,000 students graduate annually from the institutions of higher learning, and 14,700 from technical schools. The successes of Uzbekistan in the field of education can be gauged from the fact that the republic has 142 students per every 10,000 of the population; the corresponding figures are: for the U.S.A., 120; for Britain, 41; for France, 50; for Japan, 67; for Turkey, 22; for Iran, 10. We have seen a tremendous development of science in the republic. An Academy of Sciences and a number of research institutions have been set up.

Uzbekistan's great achievement in the socio-economic sphere has been the reduction of working hours to 6–7 per day and the general raising of wages. Houses are being constructed in large numbers in the towns and villages. The development of the economy has been accompanied by a radical improvement of the health system, the building of hospitals, and other services. The population of Uzbekistan no longer suffers from such diseases as plague, cholera, small-pox, malaria, which in the past used to kill thousands. And the improvement in the conditions of life and work and the raising of the cultural level has more than doubled the expectation of life.

6 FURTHER DEVELOPMENT OF THE RESOURCES OF UZBEKISTAN

The further development of the productive resources of the Uzbek republic will, as before, be based on cotton production. But the mineral riches of Uzbekistan will also ensure the rapid development of the natural gas industry and non-ferrous metallurgy. The fact that the republic possesses large resources of raw materials will serve as a stimulus to the still more rapid development of the chemical industry which is certain to become of all-Union importance.

One of the immediate tasks confronting Uzbekistan is to increase the production of fertilisers to satisfy fully the needs of cotton growing and other branches of agriculture and at the same time to improve their quality. It is planned to increase considerably the production of defoliants and of other chemical products. For this purpose, it is planned to put into operation the second stage of the Ferghana nitric fertilisers plant, the Navin chemical plant, the Samarkand nitric plant and to raise the capacity of the Chirchik electrochemical plant.

Large plants producing synthetic fibres, synthetic resin and plastics, will be built on the basis of a complex utilisation of natural gas and other mineral resources. The production of rubber and chemical consumer goods will be further expanded. The resulting chemical products will be widely used not only in agriculture but also in all other branches of the economy. This will contribute to a growth of national product and to an increased output of better and cheaper capital and consumer goods. Thus in the very near future Uzbekistan will have a highly developed and diversified chemical industry.

The natural gas industry will be developed on a large scale. Preliminary calculations show that production will reach 37–42 billion cubic metres (in 1965 it was 16·3 billion). Over one-half of this gas will be transported to the industrial regions of the Urals over the Bukhara–Urals pipe-line. The neighbouring republics of Kazakhstan, Kirghizstan and Turkmenistan will also get large quantities of this gas. There will be a considerable increase in the use of gas in Uzbekistan itself for technological purposes, for power generation, and for domestic and other purposes. The growth of the natural gas output will create favourable conditions for the rapid development of the whole complex of the productive forces of the republic and the improvement of living standards. The energy balance will be radically improved; the share in it of the economically efficient source of energy represented by gas will increase. Uzbekistan will become one of the most important centres of the Soviet natural gas industry.

At the same time, the oil industry will be developed. It is planned to increase crude oil production by over 20 per cent and to double the output of the oil-refining industry. The coal-mining industry will also increase its output. Much attention will be paid to further development of electricity supply. New high-voltage lines are to provide practically all industrial enterprises, collective farms and state farms, town and villages of the republic with electricity supply from a central system.

It will thus be seen that Uzbekistan has all the necessary conditions for the full utilisation of its natural resources. This will make possible the use of the most modern and efficient production processes. To take an example, sulphuric acid obtained from metallurgical gases produced in the copper and zinc works at Almalyk will be used for the production of nitric and phosphorous fertilisers.

During the next few years the output of copper ore, copper concentrates and refined copper are planned to rise. The capacity of the copper-smelting plant will be increased and the necessity will thus be eliminated of shipping copper concentrates to other regions of the Soviet Union. It is planned also to raise the output of lead-zinc ores by increasing the capacity of the existing mines and developing new ones. It is planned to build a zinc plant to process zinc concentrates. The production of tungsten and molybdenum is also to increase. Rich gold deposits have lately been discovered in Uzbekistan. Huge sulphate-sodium-magnesium deposits (in the Karakalpak Autonomous Republic) make possible large-scale production of sodium, magnesium and chlorine. The extraction of rare and dispersed metals will increase.

Despite the rapid growth of the engineering industry of Uzbekistan it is at present still unable to satisfy fully the needs of the republic. In three years' time the mechanisation of cotton-growing will be completed. For that reason it is planned to increase the production of agricultural machinery – cotton-combines, tractors, cultivators, drills and other machinery and implements. Further electrification of the economy will stimulate the development of the electric machine-building industry. The production of transformers, electric motors, cables, welding equipment, electric equipment, home electric appliances, etc., is to be increased considerably.

To be able to fulfil the giant construction plans involved in all of this, it will be necessary to use industrial methods of construction. The plans provide for the rapid growth of the building materials industry. Modern building materials are to be produced. At the same time, the rate of growth of the light industries and food processing will be higher than before. The rapid development of the chemical industry and agricultural production will ensure for them a steady supply of raw materials. In addition, it is planned to increase the production of cotton and silk fabrics with a view of satisfying the home and export demands. In 1963 the textile mills of the republic turned out 31·4 million metres of silk fabrics; by 1970 they will produce 3 to 4 times more. It is also planned to increase the production of non-woven fabrics, clothing, footwear, knitting goods and hosiery. The textile and knitted goods factories will by 1970 use 10 times more synthetic fibres (capron, lavsan and others) than now. This will enable them to improve the quality of their goods.

The main task of the Uzbek food processing industries during the coming years will be to satisfy the needs of the population of the republic for food and to increase the shipments of vegetable oils, wines, fruit and vegetables to other republics of the Soviet Union. It is planned to raise the production of meat and meat products, dairy produce, butter, cheese, canned foods, bread, confectionery, and the like.

The progress of the Uzbek Soviet Socialist Republic in terms both of its economy and its culture shows the great advantages of the socialist planned economy and its policy of industrialisation. Soviet Uzbekistan in the course of its development has progressed from feudalism to a most advanced socialist society, from national disunity and inequality to the creation of a socialist state based on real democracy, from age-old economic and cultural backwardness to a highly developed economy and an advanced culture, national in form and socialist in content. Since Soviet power all the necessary conditions have been created in Uzbekistan for the further growth of its productive resources, the further development of its economy, its science, its culture and the growth of its prosperity. The only conclusion must be that the socialist system opens before the peoples liberated from capitalist exploitation new and grand vistas of economic, political, social and cultural development. Nor must it be forgotten that the Soviet people achieved their successes despite the fact that for a number of years all their efforts were concentrated on repulsing imperialist aggression and that enormous material resources had to be diverted to purposes of defence.

18 The Industrial Development of the Backward Region of Armenia

A. Arakelyan

ACADEMICIAN OF THE ACADEMY OF SCIENCES OF
THE ARMENIAN S. S. R.

1 THE ARMENIAN ECONOMY BEFORE INDUSTRIALISATION

In Tsarist Russia, Armenia was an underdeveloped region, supplying only raw materials and agricultural products. In 1913, 89·5 per cent of the population lived in villages and only 10·5 per cent was urban. The Armenian demand for industrial commodities was met mainly by import. There was virtually no industry. Large-scale industry was represented by two branches only – the copper and wine-cognac industries. The former was in the hands of French capitalists; cognac production was in the hands of Russian capitalists. The greater part of the output was produced by small domestic enterprises; these were responsible for 68·7 per cent of all output. Such industry as existed in Armenia was based on backward techniques, with hard manual labour predominating.

The First World War which broke out in 1914 brought the country to ruin. It exhausted in large degree its material and human resources. The whole of west Armenia was devastated and plundered and the greater part of the population was slaughtered by the army of Osmanni Turkey. A small fraction of the Armenian population, which had escaped from genocide, migrated to the present territory of Armenia. The number of unemployed and homeless people was greatly increased.

The adventurous domestic and foreign policies of the bourgeois-nationalist government of dashnacks which held power from 1918 to 1920 damaged Armenia still further. During these years devastation reached its highest level. In 1920 the output of industrial production was less than one-tenth of its volume in 1913. Agriculture, transport, the communication system had been almost ruined. Armenia was brought to almost complete collapse. It became a land of refugees and of suffering; there was an army of orphans numbering 100,000. Starvation and disease were rampant throughout the country.

The proclamation of the Armenian Soviet Socialist Republic on 29 November 1920 was the turning point in the history of Armenia, the starting point of the construction of Socialism. In 1921 the reconstruction of the national economy including that of the Armenian republic was begun on the basis of the new economic policy (N.E.P.). It proceeded despite the resistance of the displaced capitalists, of bourgeois-nationalist forces, and the support of the imperialist countries. But these were not the only difficulties of the time. The reconstruction of the national economy faced special difficulties. The most important was the wide prevalence of economic breakdown. This necessitated relatively high capital investment; unusually large capital construction was required for the starting of an enterprise. There was not a single branch of industry (or even an enterprise) reconstruction of which could be carried out quickly in order to get profits which might be used for the reconstruction of other branches of the economy.

A considerable proportion of the population of towns and villages had, moreover, been lost as the result of war, starvation and epidemics. Those workers who survived moved to the villages or to other regions in search of work to support their families. There were hardly any technical specialists left in the republic.

The State nationalised the big enterprises and began the reconstruction of the national economy, In general, during the period 1921–8 the industrial enterprises were restored and the level of output was brought back to that of 1913. The funds available for production and the number of workers had been restored during this period to their pre-war levels. The period 1921–8 was mainly directed to the reconstruction of the pre-war economy. This was particularly true of the years 1926–8. For example, during the reconstruction period new power stations were built and along with the reconstructed ones gave 4 times more electrical energy than in 1913. During this period the first textile mill was built in Leninakan and the basis of the textile industry of the republic was created. It is necessary to stress that by the end of the reconstruction period Armenian industry differed essentially from the pre-Soviet condition in its social nature: it was socialised.

Thus before the beginning of industrialisation in Armenia, its damaged industry had been restored and had undergone the basic social reconstruction – it had become common socialist property.

2 SOCIALIST INDUSTRIALISATION IN ARMENIA

The restoration of the national economy was only the first step along the path of socialist construction. The Communist Party and the people faced a very complex task: it was necessary to carry out the socialist industrialisation of the country in order to give security to the victory of socialism. From an economic point of view, socialist industrialisation means not only – and not so much – the quantitative increase of the extent of industry, and not only the transformation of agrarian countries which have followed the socialist path of development into the advanced industrial countries, but essentially the creation of the material basis of socialism. Such a basis takes the form of socialist large-scale industrial production in all branches of the national economy and in all republics and economic regions. It provides the steady and planned growth of productivity of labour and for the raising of the people's well-being, the increase of the country's defensive capacity and the development of socialist productive relations.

The industrialisation of Armenia, carried out under the pre-war five-year plans, was not proceeding as an isolated process but as a component of the integrated process of the industrialisation of the U.S.S.R. as a whole. The economy of Soviet Armenia was and is an integral and organic part of the U.S.S.R. economy. This fact predetermined two important factors in the transformation of the Armenian economy to the basis of socialist large-scale modern technical production.

Firstly, the industrialisation of Armenia was taking place within a balanced division of labour among the various economic regions and republics of the U.S.S.R., all of which shared the same economic and political system. To make efficient use of the natural and labour resources of the country, Armenia during the process of industrialisation developed its production after taking into consideration its advantages in respect of economic and natural conditions, its traditions and experience, its industrial resources, the demands of other regions. The republic was developing its economy as a whole, taking into account this need for specialisation. Along these lines of development Armenia, like other Soviet republics, secured the best utilisation of its resources, economising capital investment and current expenditure and rapidly raising the welfare of its population. Considerable advantages and benefits were derived from the specialisation. As a member of the Union of Soviet Socialist Republics, Armenia was able to develop those branches of production in which it was most efficient, on the basis of the national plan as a whole and to enjoy multilateral exchange with other Soviet republics. Armenia has become an industrially developed republic in the full modern sense of the word through the planned introduction of those branches of industry which can be most advantageously developed, taking account of the advantages of economic and natural resources, and which can thus make possible a rapid growth of the whole economy and culture of the republic, and at the same time contribute to the economic growth of the Soviet Union and raise its defence potential.

Secondly, industrialisation in Armenia has been achieved with the help of all the republics and economic regions of the U.S.S.R. It has taken place under conditions in which there has been no exploitation or national oppression, when and in which there have been no conflicts between the centre and the outlying districts. Considerable divergence between the level of economic development of Armenia and of Russia as a whole has been gradually eliminated thanks to socialist methods of development. Within the process of the general development of the industrial potential of the U.S.S.R., the industrialisation of Armenia has been more intensive in character. If pre-Soviet Armenia was becoming more backward as compared to Tsarist Russia as a whole (the gap between them was widening, the discrepancies were becoming greater) the socialist industrialisation has been mainly directed to the equalisation of their levels of economic development.

This is an absolutely new type of the social and territorial division of labour – a result of the victory of the great October Revolution. Armenia as a member of the U.S.S.R. is developing its economy much faster than it could do under other conditions.

While during the period 1929–37 the annual increase of the capital formation was 25·7 per cent in Armenia, and 24·4 per cent in the U.S.S.R., it was only 5·4 per cent in England and in some countries a fall in capital formation was to be found. During this period, the annual decrease of capital formation in the U.S.A. was 8 per cent, in France 8 per cent, in Italy 5 per cent and in Germany 3·7 per cent. During the pre-war decade many large enterprises were constructed in Armenia. A number of power stations were built: the Yerevan power station, the Leninakan power station, the Dzoragess power station, the Kanaker power station and others. The Yerevan hydro-electric power station (put on stream in 1932) was the first automatic station in the history of Armenia, and of the U.S.S.R. also. In 1937, the forty-eight power stations of the republic generated 258·3 million kilowatt-hours, as compared with 5·1 million kilowatt-hours generated by ten hydro-electric power stations in 1913. In 1940 the bulk electric energy generated in the republic reached 395·3 million kilowatt-hours. Apart from the construction of power stations, the building of the Kirovokan chemical enterprise, the Yerevan synthetic rubber plant named after Kirov, the complete technical reconstruction (virtually a new construction) of the plants of the copper industries in Kafan and Alaverdy provide the most brilliant pages in the history of Armenian industrialisation.

Apart from these giant state industrial enterprises, constructed in the pre-war period, many medium- and small-size enterprises were also constructed. At the same time many enterprises were wholly reconstructed and equipped with modern technology, so that as a result the enterprises became virtually new.

During this pre-war decade of socialist industrialisation, Armenia introduced and developed many new branches of industry unknown hitherto. New branches of the engineering industry were established to produce modern technical equipment and new types of machinery. At the same time new branches of industry were introduced, including the production of construction materials, chemical, textile, knitting-goods industries.

Parallel with the growth of the material requirements of industry there was an increase in the number of available workers. Many thousands were drawn into industrial production. During the pre-war decade the number of industrial productive personnel increased from 11,000 to 44,000. By 1940 the number of employees in the national economy of the Armenian U.S.S.R. was 156,000 people. At the same time there had been radical changes in the qualifications of the available staff. Manual labour was replaced by very efficient processes, requiring manpower with a very different level of technical knowledge. Equipment and the number of workers did not increase at the same rate: the volume of equipment outstripped the increase in the number of workers. A considerable rise in the technical level of work and in the available energy per worker was the result of this process.

During this pre-war decade an expert production personnel had been built up on the basis of the preferential development of heavy industry. With the help of this personnel, Soviet workers considerably increased their productivity.

During this period of peacetime socialist expansion (1921–40) the growth of industrial production was approximately 20 per cent a year. In contrast to the continuous growth of Soviet industry three world crises took place in the capitalist world during the period 1920–40: in 1920–1, in 1929–33, and in 1937–8. These crises greatly retarded the growth of production in the capitalist countries.

The process of socialist industrialisation brought radical changes in the pattern of the national economy of Armenia. In 1928, industrial production in Armenia represented 28·3 per cent of the total of gross industrial and agricultural output. It reached 80 per cent in 1940, as a result of the fulfilment of the pre-war five-year plans.

Great changes took place also in the structure of industry itself. The Soviet State achieved a high rate of growth of the branches of Group 'A' (the production of means of production) involving a new relationship of the different constituents of the social product. In 1940 the production of all the industry of the republic exceeded the 1913 level 8·7 times, the production of heavy industry (Group 'A') exceeded the 1913 level 11·4 times, and that of light industry (Group 'B') 6·9 times.

The heavy industry provided the equipment of labour in all branches of the national economy; it was the basis of technical progress, the growth of labour productivity and the re-equipment of the whole of the national economy. Socialist industrialisation provided the technical basis for the socialist development of productive relations in all branches of the economy. It played a decisive role in the victory of socialism over capitalism and in carrying out the collectivisation of agriculture and the creation and development of co-operative kolkhoz property.

Socialist industrialisation thus turned out to be the prerequisite for the elimination of economic and cultural backwardness in the undeveloped districts and republics. The most intensive industrialisation was taking place in the formerly backward districts with an unbalanced and un-diversified structure of production. Thanks to the help of the more advanced industrial regions of central Russia, considerable industrial development took place in the Caucasian, Central-Asian and other formerly undeveloped republics. In these republics new branches of industry were established. The construction of large plants, factories, mines, power stations in the formerly undeveloped regions promoted the upsurge of the economy, the training of specialists from the local population, the raising of the political and cultural level of the peoples of the national republics.

These facts played a vital role in the strengthening of the friendly relations between people of different nationality, in the development of fraternal collaboration within the country as a whole, and in the political equality of the peoples of the U.S.S.R., cemented by the equality of their economic and cultural life.

The socialist industrialisation of the country demanded a titanic labour from the Soviet people. It was carried through thanks to the conscience, energy, enthusiasm, initiative and creative efforts of the vast masses of the working people. The history of industrialisation in our country was rich in the devoted labours and the heroic struggles of the working masses. The Soviet people had to overcome countless obstacles and many difficulties; they suffered much, for they were the first to follow the road to socialism. This deep and fundamental change had started under conditions of poverty and destruction, under shortages of material and financial resources, under lack of skilled labour, without any help from abroad, under the aggressive activity of a capitalist encirclement and of exploiting elements within the country.

3 POST-WAR GROWTH OF INDUSTRY IN THE ARMENIAN S.S.R.

The modern industry created in the republic in co-operation with other republics, was designed to contribute to the development of all branches of the national economy (agriculture, construction, transport, communication, trade, communal services) and to secure a further large rise of the material and cultural level of the people. The achievement of this task was interrupted by the 1941–5 war. The economy underwent immense changes resulting from conditions created by the war. As a consequence of the war and because masses of workers had been called to the forces, industrial production was reduced and in 1945 amounted to only 93 per cent of that of 1940. The next stage was to restore the economy to the peacetime path of development as quickly as possible after the war. The industry turned over to peacetime operation had been expanded continuously with a high rate of growth and a degree of specialisation consistent with modern technical progress. The further growth and modernisation of industry, based on advanced techniques, required large capital investments. Average annual rates of growth of capital investment in industry exceed 3 to 4 times the rate of investments in the industrially developed capitalist countries.

One of the features of such a highly industrialised economy as the Armenian S.S.R. is that it makes a larger advance in its productive resources each year as compared with earlier periods when it was necessary to spend several decades to achieve similar results. For example, today the total annual capital investment is larger than that of the whole of the first twenty years after the establishment of the Soviet Republic (1921–1945). The largest volumes and anticipations of capital investments are to be seen in some branches of the engineering industry, in the chemical industry and in non-ferrous metallurgy. As a result of this there has been an increase of the income of their main funds and a rapid improvement of the technical equipment and of the horse-power per head of the labour force, as well as a wide introduction of science into production – a decisive factor in making work less onerous and increasing its productivity.

The chief branches of heavy industry, which account for its leading place in the distribution of labour, are the non-ferrous metallurgy industry developed on the basis of a complex exploitation of copper-molybdenum deposits, the chemical industry which makes use of local raw materials and the waste products of non-ferrous metallurgy, the engineering industry (mainly machine-tool construction), the electrotechnical industry, the instrument-making industry. A direct link is established between the enterprises of non-ferrous metallurgy and the rapidly developing electrotechnical industry in the republic, the instrument-making industry and other branches of the engineering industry. The main direction of the specialisation of the engineering industry of Armenia is in the production of electrical machines and apparatus. This production forms more than 60 per cent of the total output of the engineering industry; this may perhaps be explained by the presence of highly skilled workers in the republic and the production of non-ferrous metals. The Armenian Republic holds the third place in the U.S.S.R. (after the Russian Federation and the Ukrainian S.S.R.) in production of electrotechnical manufacturing articles. In 1965 Armenia produced 9,159 metal-cutting lathes, 5 times more than the whole of Tsarist Russia in 1913. Thanks to the creative abilities of its industrial workers, Soviet Armenia produces electronic computers, machine-tools and compressors, electric appliances and high-capacity generators, mobile electric-power stations, accurate measuring instruments and other apparatus.

A variety of products of organic chemistry are now being produced in the republic. The production of electric energy is rapidly increasing. In 1965 electric energy generation was equal to 1,320 kWh. *per capita* against

295 kWh. in 1940 (a growth of 4·5 times). A building materials industry has been introduced and is successfully developing.

Many branches of light industry and the food industry have been created. Thanks to this, many consumer goods which were formerly imported or made in domestic conditions are now produced by industrial methods in the republic. Part of the production is exported to the other regions of the U.S.S.R. – cotton fabrics, knitted fabrics, hosiery, soap, tanning goods among others.

The Armenian S.S.R. occupies 0·13 per cent of the territory of the U.S.S.R. and its population represents 0·9 per cent of the U.S.S.R. population. In spite of this, the republic has a large share in some forms of production of the total output of the U.S.S.R. A considerable part of the national output of molybdenum products, blue vitrol, calcium carbide, acetic acid, synthetic rubber, automobile tyres is produced in the republic, as well as 23 per cent of mobile electric-power stations, 7 per cent of power transformers, 8 per cent of a.c. electric motors of over 100 kW. capacity, 13 per cent of centrifugal pumps, 5 per cent of metal-cutting lathes, 6 per cent of wine, 4·8 per cent of the knitted wear of the U.S.S.R.

It can thus be seen that the pre-Soviet Armenia which possessed no industry has been completely transformed. The copper that was mined and the agricultural raw materials produced then received no processing in the republic but were shipped to the central districts of Tsarist Russia from which many of the products of processing industry came back. Today the Armenian S.S.R. is a republic with a clearly defined industrial image. In 1966 two-thirds of the social product was the share of industry. The urban population is now 55·1 per cent of the total population, as against 10·5 per cent in 1913.

Thanks to full employment, the absence of exploitation and the steady growth of labour productivity, the industrial output rises continuously and rapidly. Before the establishment of Soviet Armenia the republic did not differ much from its neighbours in the level of development of its productive resources. The almost complete absence of industry was a characteristic of Armenia as well as of Turkey and Iran. The economic development of Armenia during the past forty-six years in comparison with that of Turkey and Iran is a brilliant example of the rapid development possible in an advanced socialist country. The Armenian S.S.R. generates approximately 8·5 times more electric energy *per capita* than Turkey and 22 times more than Iran. It is notable that almost all the population of Armenia enjoy the use of electric energy in the home while approximately 70 per cent of Turkey's population and the vast majority of Iranians are deprived of such a possibility.

Turkey and Iran lag very far behind Soviet Armenia in industrial output, especially in the engineering industry, not only per head of population but also in absolute volumes. For example, the Armenian

M

republic produces 40 times more electric instruments and 10 times more electric bulbs than Turkey in spite of the fact that the territory of the Armenian S.S.R. is no more than one-twenty-fifth and the population one-fifteenth of that of Turkey. Armenia produces several thousand times more of a variety of chemical goods per head than Turkey and Iran. This lag is very obvious when one compares the production volumes of certain products. For example, in 1963 Armenian S.S.R. produced 43,000 thousand tons of sulphuric acid and Turkey 22,000 tons; of caustic soda they produced 35,000 and 2,000 tons respectively.

With the rapid growth of the republic's economy the volume of production has considerably increased and the composition of production has radically changed. In the past Armenian exports mainly consisted of the products of light industry and the food processing industries, in addition to agricultural raw materials; today Armenia mainly exports a variety of industrial engineering products as well as products of other branches of industry. It exports more than 150 items of different commodities to seventy foreign countries. A great variety of goods are exported to England, France, Japan, Czechoslovakia, India, Argentina, Chile, Uruguay and others. England buys hydro-pumps, electro-measuring apparatus, watches, carpets; Italy buys electric engines, hydro-panels, radial drilling tools, perlite. The Federal Republic of Germany imports from Armenia benzene monochloride, cognac, watches; France buys sodium acetate, precision instruments, hydro-valves. Austria buys metal-pressing equipment, tools, electro-technical articles; Belgium and Finland import chemical products, power pressing machines. The products of the industrial engineering, electrotechnical, instrument making industries are exported to the United Arab Republic, Syria, Guinea, Iraq, Somalia, and other countries. Armenia is a general contractor in the construction of the biggest Iraq enterprise – the Baghdad electric equipment plant. The staff of the electric engine building plant named after Lenin has prepared the technical designs for the production of many components. Ninety articles of non-standard equipment were sent to Baghdad ahead of time. Armenian specialists have provided assistance during the period of construction of the enterprise and are training specialists for this enterprise.

Soviet Armenia has given aid to a number of other developing countries by providing power plants, technical designs and staff. The republic is assisting in the construction of the Aswan complex in the United Arab Republic, in the construction of the hydro-electric power station on the Black Volta river in Ghana, in the construction of one of the world's largest hydro-electric power stations at Naglu in Afghanistan. It is aiding Somalia in the construction of hospitals, schools, radio-stations and other projects.

This great industrial growth and the creation of a huge complex of widely diversified industry has resulted in the elimination of the one-sided colonial allocation of productive forces.   As a result a number of new towns and industrial centres have come into existence.   The continuing development of Armenian industry is now characterised by higher rates of growth of production than in the U.S.S.R. as a whole.   Another peculiarity of the larger-term outlook for Armenian economic development is abnormally high rates of growth in industrial engineering and its more highly specialised branches – electrotechnical, radio-technical, instrument-making, the organisation of those types of modern heavy industry which demand large numbers of highly skilled workers.   While in many branches of Armenian industry the average volume of production is to increase 1·7–1·8 times during the current five years, the enterprises of electro-technology and radio-electronics are to increase their output 9–10 times.

   These two peculiarities of the Armenian economic development – that the rate of industrial growth in the republic exceeds the average of growth in the U.S.S.R. and the exceptional growth of heavy industry – are closely connected with a demographic factor.   In 1920 the population in Armenia was 780,000; by the beginning of 1966 it has risen to 2,200,000.   During the period 1939–64 the population of the U.S.S.R. has increased by 18 per cent and of the Armenian S.S.R. by 6·1 per cent.   Population density and its rates of growth is higher in Armenia than in the U.S.S.R. on average.   In addition the immigration of population has to be taken into considera-tion.   During the years of Soviet power, about 200,000 Armenians have moved back to their homeland.   The provision of full employment for all able to work has been one of the most important assumptions in the determination of the rates and the patterns of Armenian industrial development.

4   ADVANCED INDUSTRY AS THE BASIS FOR PROSPERITY

The creation and expansion of advanced industry is not an aim in itself. It is subordinate to the objective of achieving a continuous increase of the material welfare and culture of the people.   Unemployment was eliminated in the republic during the process of industrialisation.   The working day has been shortened to 6–7 hours a day.   Wages have increased, especially for the low paid.   The reduction of taxes has started.   Social funds for consumption in Armenia total at present some 350 million roubles.   This alone implies that the individual income of a working family is increased by one-quarter.

   Housing construction has been expanded considerably.   Living space in the Armenian S.S.R. had increased from 0·35 million square metres in 1921 to 7·9 million square metres by the end of 1965.   In comparing these figures, one must bear in mind that most of the old houses have been pulled down (they were not fit for habitation) and new houses with modern conveniences have been erected.   Today much more living space is made available annually in the towns of Armenia than all the living space the republic possessed according to the 1926 census. Soviet Armenia holds one of the first places in housing construction per 1,000 inhabitants.

During the years of Soviet power the appearance of the countryside has also been radically changed. In pre-revolution Armenia, a considerable proportion of the rural population lived in mud-huts. Today the villages have a quite different appearance. The countrymen live in well-built houses. In no more than seven years (1959–65) the collective farmers have built 49,000 new houses. And during the period 1958–65 almost one million people – half of the population of the republic – have moved into new flats or have improved their living conditions. This tremendous volume of housing construction has been associated with an increase in public services in the towns and villages.

During the years of Soviet power a real cultural revolution has taken place, involving all aspects of the spiritual life of the people. The steady and rapid development of the national economy has made it possible to allocate immense sums of money for public education and for other measures to raise the cultural level. Armenia has become a republic of complete literacy, where every fourth inhabitant is a student at some educational institution. According to the 1963 figures in Armenia 2,207 children per ten thousand of total population were attending school. In England the figure was 1,595 children per ten thousand, in France 1,677 per ten thousand, in the German Federal Republic 1,323, in Italy 1,247 children per ten thousand population.

Before the revolution Armenia did not have a single institution of higher education. Today Armenia has eleven institutes with 39,000 students. Now Yerevan has as many students as it possessed population in 1913. In 1965 the number of students per 10,000 population was 177 in Armenia. The number of students in Armenia is 2·5–3 times higher per 10,000 of population than in the U.S.A., England, France, West Germany, Italy or any other developed capitalist country. As compared with the neighbouring capitalist countries, the difference is even greater. If one takes 1962 figures, there were 133 students in Armenia per 10,000 of population, twenty-five in Turkey and eleven in Iran.

Science has greatly developed in Armenia. The Academy of Sciences has been organised with a big network of scientific research institutes. Side by side with the Academy of Sciences there exist a number of other scientific institutions and laboratories which contribute greatly to the growth of the economy. In 1965, scientific research institutes numbered 102. The number of scientific research workers in the Armenian S.S.R. amounted to 7,773, according to the 1965 figures. There were 254 doctors of science and 2,039 post-graduate students in science.

This wide network of larger scientific and cultural institutions in the republic is the fruit of the socialist revolution and the highly developed industry serves as its material basis. During many centuries Armenia had had no real scientific or cultural centres in its territory, as a consequence of its lack of political independence, of the double oppression of foreign domination and domestic exploitation, and of having a backward economy. Such centres were established outside Armenia and the talented members of the nation were forced to wander to many countries of the world. Now scientific and culture are prospering in an industrially-developed Armenia.

The balanced development of the national economy was accompanied by a radical improvement of public health. In 1913 there were 57 physicians in Armenia; by 1965 the number had increased to 5,977. The number of physicians per 10,000 men in the republic averages 27·2. It is 1·5 times more than in the U.S.A., twice more than in England, France and Japan. In 1965 there were 81 hospital beds per 10,000 of population. This is approximately 6 times more than in Turkey, Iran and Pakistan. Such dangerous diseases as the plague, cholera, small-pox, typhus, malaria, which in former years brought terrible disaster to the population, have been wholly eliminated. Poliomyelitis and diphtheria are on the way to liquidation also.

In conclusion one may say that during the forty-six years, 1921 to 1966, Armenia has achieved such success in its economic and cultural development that it has left far behind its foreign neighbours and many capitalist countries in Europe also. Thanks to the fraternal help of other republics of the U.S.S.R. and due to the creative efforts of the working masses of the republic, under the leadership of the Communist Party, Armenia, a former backward outlying region of Tsarist Russia, has now become a prosperous socialist republic with a highly developed industry, mechanised agriculture, advanced science and culture.

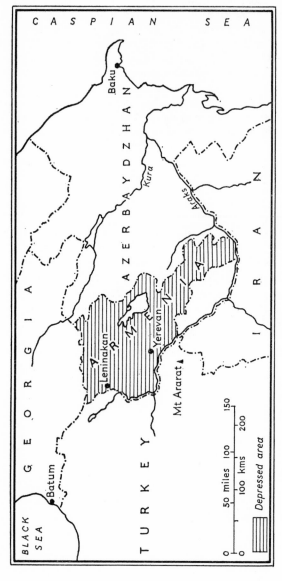

THE FORMERLY BACKWARD REPUBLIC OF ARMENIA

Part 4 The Issues in Backward Area Policy

19 Some Old and New Issues in Regional Development

Edgar M. Hoover

UNIVERSITY OF PITTSBURGH, U.S.A.

1 INTRODUCTORY

I am only too painfully aware of being probably the only participant in this conference who is innocent of any experience in actually diagnosing and prescribing for the problem of a backward area in an advanced country. Under the circumstances, it seems most fitting that I try to contribute by offering the impressions of an interested observer on some of the controversy on relevant development theory and policy in recent years. I shall attempt, then, to put into focus what seem to me the most important issues at stake, and to relate them to each other. Little if any of this will be news to members of the conference, but I may succeed in making some sufficiently provocative statements to provide a basis for constructive discussion by the real experts. I shall also have occasion, towards the end of this paper, to propose some fruitful lines of further inquiry.

2 WHY THIS RAPID DEVELOPMENT OF NEW IDEAS?

First, we might ask ourselves why interest and public concern about regional development and policy have mushroomed so impressively in the last couple of decades after having lain dormant so long. What prompted all these new ideas and controversies? And in particular, how has there come to be an important concern at the national policy level for the development of specific regions within the country? In answering these questions I shall have to refer primarily to American experience, but I think most of what I shall say is more generally applicable.

As recently as 1948 it was possible to write, without being challenged, that: 'Although governments have a large stake in the results of locational development, great power to influence that development, and a correspondingly heavy responsibility for influencing it in socially desirable directions, few governments have ever followed any coherent policy in regard to location.'[1] The 'few governments' referred to certainly did not include the United States.

But a radical change in thinking was already brewing. In Britain even before World War II, it had become clear that the depressed economic

[1] E. M. Hoover, *The Location of Economic Activity* (McGraw-Hill, N.Y., 1948) p. 242.

M 2

position of the northern and Welsh industrial areas presented an intract-
able problem, and controversy was rife on what national policies might or
might not work. Since the 1950s, we have been observing with some
frustration that the so-called 'developing countries' do not seem to catch
up with the more advanced ones automatically, or even with continued and
massive international assistance of various types. And economic sta-
tisticians and historians who have been investigating the phenomenon of
interregional disparities of income within the United States have found
that what had been taken for granted as a trend towards convergence was
really just a change that had occurred at certain periods in onr history (for
example, 1880–1920 and 1930–50); while other periods (for example,
1840–80 and 1920–30) have been characterised by *widening* disparities
in income levels, and it is difficult to establish whether we are presently
in a period of convergence or divergence. The equalisation of wage and
income levels between North and South and between small towns and
metropolitan areas has been repeatedly heralded as imminent by a long line
of prophets, but appears to have been at least retarded if not arrested.

One definite basis of interest and search for better understanding and
policies, then, was a realisation that regional stagnation or depression can
be quite resistant to cure.

Another basis for increasing concern stems from urbanisation and the
declining relative importance of agriculture. Unemployment in urban
areas is more visible and more unsettling for both the individual and the
community than its equivalent in rural underemployment. In the United
States the rapid shift of Negro population from rural to urban slums [1] has
intensified this change; and along with a complex of other problems of
urban adjustment, has vastly enlarged the number of local areas calling for
external economic aid.

Still another factor contributing to the search for better understanding
and policies for regional development has been disillusionment with the
effects and the objectives of at least the more naïve forms of local and
regional self-promotion. As everybody gets into the act, a greater
proportion of such effort is recognised as simply cancelling out (that is,
each community has to do it in self-defence just because the others are
doing it). And more and more the question is raised about whether
growth *per se* is a sensible standard of community interest and objective
of public action at the local level.

Next, it appears that there has been a significant shift in the attitude of
the general public, as well as most economists, towards population growth
on a local, regional, national, or world basis. Less than a generation ago,
the American credo of the beneficence of population growth was un-
questioned, and Alvin Hansen and others were pointing with alarm to the
perils of economic stagnation that would beset us if we did not get busy

[1] The non-white population is now more urban than the white population.

breeding more young consumers. Malthus' gloomy nineteenth-century warnings were dismissed as a discredited fantasy.

This attitude has vastly changed in a mere twenty years. In part this is the result of frustration from seeing hard-won output gains in so many of the underdeveloped countries cancelled out by mushrooming population growth. And meanwhile at home, the post-war baby boom, the all-too-evident pressures of population growth in urban and outdoor-recreation areas, the generally inflationary bent of the economy, and the relatively high fertility of people low on the economic and education ladder, have all helped to undermine the tradition that the nation and each community will be better off the more people they have. Thinking and policy today are accordingly much more directed towards welfare objectives such as fuller employment and higher income, rather than to the misleading standard of aggregate growth.

Still another contributing factor in the shift towards more enlightened approaches to regional promotion is what might be called the dilution of provincialism. Much more than ever before, we now find it normal that an individual makes his home in several different communities and regions during his lifetime. This more varied exposure is conducive to more objective feelings about programmes that may benefit one region at the expense of another.

Let me wind up this section of my remarks by mentioning some important changes in the make-up of the forces that determine the location choices of producers and consumers. These changes, arising mainly from changes in technology and increased income and leisure, really underlie a good many of the developments already mentioned, and have certainly played a significant part in the re-thinking on regional development.

These changes in location determinants have been spelled out so often in recent years that they scarcely need emphasis. For present purposes, I suggest that the most relevant changes include the following:

(1) In terms of linkages between industries and their sources of materials and markets, the costs of physical transport of heavy and bulky goods are less important, and increased importance attaches to the speedy and flexible transportation of high-value goods and above all to communication – that is, the transmission of intangible services and information.

(2) Access to markets has increased in importance for most industries relative to access to sources of raw materials and energy sources.

(3) Amenity is more and more important. This means good climate, housing and community facilities, and access to recreational and cultural opportunities. This change reflects rising standards of income and leisure, the increased importance of white-collar employment, and the fact that industries in a dynamic growth stage

require a high proportion of well-trained and educated people who are in short supply and so can afford to be choosy about where they will live and work.

(4) There seems to be an increasing degree of dependence of particular industries on various services locally supplied by other industries, institutions, and public bodies. Thus we hear more of the 'external economies' of a location well supplied with such services and facilities. We hear more of the importance of an adequate regional or community 'infrastructure' supplying such things as local utility services, police and fire protection, schools, hospitals, reference libraries, and the like as a necessary basis for development of profitable enterprises producing goods and services for outside markets.

3 SOME BASIC CURRENT ISSUES

Up to this point I have been giving my impressions about the technical, social, and political changes that have stirred up so much new interest in regional development policy in the period since the War. I have suggested also some ways in which our approaches to the problem have become more sophisticated.

I certainly do not want to give the impression that I think the subject has been mastered. Trying to understand and improve the workings of a regional economy is at least as complicated as trying to understand and improve the workings of the human body. The biologists and doctors have been working on this latter problem for a much longer period, and with much larger research budgets and facilities for experimentation. Yet, I am told, it was not until a few decades ago that medical knowledge and practice had developed to the point where there was as much as a 50 per cent probability that a visit to a doctor would significantly benefit the patient. And in our field, one may also observe, a good many quacks of assorted types are doing a flourishing business.

Perhaps our greatest gain is that certain key issues have come clearly into view, around which research and controversy and experimentation can constructively focus. The rest of this paper is in the form of a series of basic policy questions. I think we are now at least asking more of the right questions, even though we do not have by any means all of the answers.

(I) WHAT IS THE RELATION BETWEEN NATIONAL AND
       REGIONAL WELFARE?

Experience has taught us that we cannot expect any satisfactory solution to the problem of regional unemployment or arrested development except in the context of a prosperous national economy. In a depression period, businesses are doing relatively little capacity expansion, and have little difficulty in finding at their existing locations the necessary labour and services and space for such expansion as they do want to undertake. Their investment is more likely to take the form of cost-cutting improvements in existing plants, and this may well involve closing down some branch facilities at the more marginal locations. Moreover, in slack times the surplus manpower in any area has literally no place to go and less resources to go anywhere, so that we cannot look to labour migration for any significantly useful adjustment.

We have found also that the national monetary and fiscal authorities jointly have great powers to increase the nation's money supply and disposable income, and thus to stimulate spending and investment in the aggregate. This can provide the necessary buoyant climate in which constructive regional adjustments by people and industries can occur.

Some have argued that that is where the national interest and responsibility ends in regard to regional economic welfare. To me it seems that we can and should go a step further on the basis of the existence of what is called 'structural unemployment'.

In a prosperous economy, inflation is always just around the corner if not banging on the door, and keeping an economy prosperous is truly an art of brinkmanship. In the United States for example it does not seem to be possible to push the economy hard enough to provide jobs for more than about 95 or 96 per cent of the labour force without getting warning symptoms of inflation. Why is this? Largely because there are such wide disparities in the employability of different groups in our labour force. There is a poor matching – perhaps even increasingly poor – between the kinds of labour that are in demand and those that are available, and not enough mobility and interchangeability within the labour force. This makes it inevitable that we run into shortages, rising costs, and consequently inflation while millions of the less-employable are still out of work.

Obviously, any policies that will reduce these wide disparities and make manpower more mobile and interchangeable will have the good effect of shifting the inflationary brink closer to the ideal of full employment.

We can, then, add to our list of legitimate public programmes such things as education and worker training and re-training, plus more direct aids to spatial and occupational mobility: for example, improved information about job opportunities, assistance to migrants, and removal of racial and other discrimination in employment. It is clear also that such efforts ought to focus on upgrading the least advantaged types of workers and reducing their competitive handicaps.

But, just about here, we pass from consensus into controversy. It is tempting to argue that if public policy should specifically help the less advantaged classes of workers to find jobs, then it should by the same token seek to underwrite the prosperity and growth of all regions and communities.

This inference is a dangerous one indeed. Probably the most costly mistake our regional development policies can make is to take as an ultimate objective the welfare of *areas* (what Louis Winnick in a recent book [1] calls 'Place Prosperity') in lieu of their only legitimate ultimate objective, which is 'People Prosperity'. I am going to raise some more specific issues on how these two kinds of objectives are related.

(II) WHO NEEDS GROWTH?

First, it is in order to raise the question of Place Prosperity *v.* People Prosperity at the local level. It has long been gospel in most communities that growth (meaning both more people and more jobs) benefits everybody. The local government and all the residents and taxpayers ought to be glad to devote money and effort to promoting growth. If the community's growth is less than the national or state average rate, something is wrong and should be corrected. If there is a net outward migration of people, something is wrong; and an actual loss of population is an unmitigated disaster.

My impression is that this cult of Place Prosperity, which I have just stated in extreme terms, is particularly prevalent in North America; but that it does seem to be losing some ground there. But it is also beginning to be realised that even if an area does succeed in growing rapidly, it has obtained a mixed blessing at best. Is a place that grows in population and jobs at the rate of 10 per cent per annum necessarily a better place to live and work than an area that grows at 2 per cent, or zero per cent? This is a question on which we admittedly need a lot more fact-finding and hard knowledge, and less superstition. But the answer clearly depends on what kind of growth it is and whose benefits and costs we are talking about.

Some benefits from local growth are quite obvious. The established retailers, utilities, banks, real property owners and realtors are all in a position to translate community growth into profits. They are quite correctly motivated to co-operate and contribute time and money to anything that will make the community expand, and they have no reason to worry about whether the growth is at the expense of some other community.

But these are purely business and personal interests of some members of the community. Large elements of the population are not particularly affected one way or the other by the rate of growth. Still others may suffer varying degrees of economic injury or inconvenience. What shall we say of the long-time resident who is pushed out of his pleasant and familiar

---

[1] Louis Winnick, 'Place Prosperity *v.* People Prosperity: Welfare Consideration in the Geographic Distribution of Economic Activity', in *Essays in Urban Land Economics* (in honour of the 65th birthday of Leo Grebler), Real Estate Research Program, University of California at Los Angeles, 1966.

neighbourhood by the bulldozer or by urban blight as the city expands? What of the established industrial firm to which community growth brings mainly higher wage costs, higher taxes, traffic congestion and water and air pollution? Should we count as part of the community's gain the new jobs that are filled by newcomers, or the new business opportunities that are taken up by new firms from outside?

No one to my knowledge has ever really set out to measure what is gained and lost in a community by its expansion – but quite clearly it is a mistake to count some people's gain, ignore others' losses, and use the result to rationalise *public* policies aimed at underwriting the growth of areas as such.

(III) SHOULD PEOPLE MOVE TO JOBS, OR JOBS TO PEOPLE?

If manpower is scarce in some areas while jobs of similar types are scarce in other areas, the situation can presumably be improved either by moving some jobs or moving some people or both. Both kinds of adjustment do take place spontaneously, though not by any means to the extent that would be necessary to eliminate regional structural unemployment. Both can be assisted or impeded to some extent by public policies. The question of which policy should be emphasised is a perennial one, and was debated with particular heat a generation and more ago when the British Government was trying to decide what to do about certain depressed industrial areas.

Worshippers of the false god of Place Prosperity are of course convinced that jobs should always be moved to people rather than the other way round. But no one else has seriously suggested that either policy should be followed to the exclusion of the other. It is in fact hard to think of any sound and effective attack on regionalised unemployment that does not stimulate both people and jobs to move to one another.

I have already stated the view that any such effective attack must involve special assistance to the less-employable groups, mainly in terms of education and vocational training. Such programmes will make them more employable, either in their own areas and previous occupations or in other areas and occupations; and by the same token, will make them more of a manpower asset that may help to attract and expand employment in their areas. Another eminently appropriate policy aimed at making more effective use of our manpower resources in all regions is the development of better employment survey and exchange information: that is, telling people in depressed areas about job openings in more other places, and telling employers and industry locators in labour-shortage areas about available workers in other places. Obviously this line of effort does involve making both labour and industry more mobile in their searches for one another.

The danger is that this benefit may be thrown away by misguided efforts to curb migration – for example, by training people only for the kinds of jobs that occur in their home areas, or by pension plans and employment agreements that discriminate against newcomers.

(IV) AREAS OF NEED, OR AREAS OF PROMISE?

Although, as I have suggested, the only legitimate final aim of public policy is to improve the welfare of people rather than that of areas as such, many programmes will continue to involve policy decisions about where and how to focus assistance for maximum effectiveness. Some basis for selection becomes more and more essential since the promotional interests in practically every community and region quite understandably want to be in on the distribution of any kind of public subsidy.

The first question that arises here is, to put it baldly, whether external aid to lagging regions is to be regarded as charity or as investment. Should the degree of distress (i.e., low income and unemployment) be the test for eligibility, or should we try to allocate the assistance wherever it will best pay off in terms of new added jobs per dollar of assistance?

I invite attention here to an interesting shift in the use of terms to describe areas to which national public development-assistance programmes are directed. The British used to refer in the 1920s and 1930s to their 'depressed areas'. Later these same objects of solicitude were re-christened under the curiously neutral terms of 'special areas'. Still more recently they have come to be referred to as 'development areas'. In our own country, we used to refer similarly to 'problem areas', or 'stranded areas' in the 1930s; later, to 'redevelopment areas', and now to 'development areas', and to 'growth centres' within them. As to our less fortunate brethren across the seas, we used to refer to them as simply 'poor' or 'backward', or 'low-income' countries. Later they became 'undeveloped' and then 'under-developed'. Nowadays it is considered more tactful to speak of the 'less-developed' or the 'developing' countries.

What conclusion can we draw from all this re-christening? Insofar as it reflects a more positive emphasis on growth potential rather than on sheer relief, it is all to the good. If, on the other hand, we should reflect on the fact that much the same old areas seem to bear the new names, this could reflect just an effort to make allocation on the basis of distress seem more respectable, and to *conceal* the important distinction that I have been stressing between the criterion of distress and that of growth potential.

(V) THE ROLE OF GROWTH CENTRES IN DEVELOPMENT POLICY

In some quarters at least, we have an emerging awareness that though it is proper to help *people* according to their needs, areas should be helped to develop on the criterion of their growth potential. This has led in turn to the concept of 'growth centres' or 'growth poles' for a region. The rest of this paper treats some important questions of development theory and strategy that have arisen in connection with this concept.

I merely mention in passing the question whether growth-centre strategy should be expected to play the same role in an advanced country as in a country in earlier stages of development. More directly relevant to the scope of the present conference is the question of a distinction between two kinds of areas to which assistance is given within advanced countries. On the one hand, there are the relatively backward regions which have never experienced real industrialisation (such as Appalachia or the Canadian Maritimes or the Mezzogiorno); on the other hand there are distressed industrial areas (for example Clydeside or south-eastern New England or Pittsburgh) where the trouble is arrested growth and the threat of regression. There has been a tendency to lump the backward and the distressed-industrial areas indiscriminately together in major programmes for regional assistance, and this may or may not be justifiable. I suggest that at least we need to keep the distinction in mind; and the 'growth centre' aspect of regional growth is the one where the distinction comes most clearly into focus.

The backward and the distressed-industrial types of region, of course, have common symptoms of maladjustment. Both suffer, essentially, from obsolescence of the bases for their former economic viability; both need help in making a structural shift to a new base in response to changes that have occurred in demand, resources availability, and competition from other areas. For both, a successful transition calls for modernising human and capital resources and infrastructure, and attitudes, so that they can effectively grasp new opportunities provided by technological and economic change and thus become more resilient, self-reliant, and generative.

But just about there, the similarity ends. In respect to needs for education, the two kinds of areas are likely to differ substantially. The population of a distressed industrial area may show no particular deficiencies in all-round literacy and capability for productive industrial or tertiary employment. Internal and external transport and communication facilities in such an area, also, are likely to be adequate or better. There are substantial local resources of capital and at least some relevant industrial know-how. The basic elements of a growth centre are already there, and the problem is essentially one of modernisation – reorienting the local labour force, business community, infrastructure and public sector towards the opportunities of today and tomorrow rather than those of yesterday.

In the truly backward areas, by contrast, the necessity of finding or creating specific growth centres is of major concern. We no longer believe as Henry Ford and many others did a generation ago, or as the planners in India did till much more recently, that there is any point in trying to bring industry to every village or small town. We are realising that the only reasonable hope for improvement for people in most parts of an area like Appalachia lies in commuting or migrating to some place where there is enough concentration of the necessary supporting services and facilities, both private and public, to support a sustained development of industry.

Let me take note, next, of an important distinction between two elements in the rationale for the growth-centre approach to regional development. The first of these ideas is a rather limited, almost negative one. It stresses urban size and availability of infrastructure as prerequisites for industrialisation, and thus justifies concentration of effort at growth centres on the ground that they are the *only* locations where such effort will really take hold. 'Unto every one which hath shall be given', as the Bible says. There is of course abundant historical evidence of the cumulative interaction of industrial concentration and urban growth, one of the most interesting recent contributions being Pred's study of the growth of American cities prior to World War I.[1] If the external economies of urban agglomeration are indeed so fundamental as such historical evidence suggests, a strategy of focussing growth-assistance at the places which have already grown the most seems to commend itself. I shall have occasion later, however, to raise some question as to whether the cumulative growth advantages of established centres are quite as compelling now and in future as they were under the technological conditions of such earlier periods as the one analysed by Professor Pred.

Generally, however, there is also a second argument implicit in the growth-centre rationale. This is the idea that economic improvement initiated in the growth centres will spread to their less-urbanised hinterlands; so that the best way to help those hinterlands in the long run is not by direct assistance but indirectly, by fostering the progress of nearby growth centres. This is an argument sometimes difficult to put across politically, but still somewhat more hopeful and acceptable than the negative one previously mentioned. It is important that its validity be assessed.

Actually, we do not yet know much, particularly in quantitative terms, of the way in which a favourable economic effect is propagated from an urban growth centre to the surrounding territory, or the range and speed of the various impacts. Most of our quantitative knowledge of the process refers (1) to the 'multiplier' effect of local purchases of goods and services, as traced via a regional input-output table, and (2) to the improvement of the regional employment situation through commuting and migration from the surrounding territory to the growth centre.

The multiplier effect through local purchases does not seem to furnish any real rationale for the strategy of concentrating stimuli in growth centres. Indeed, it would seem just as reasonable to invoke this effect in advocating that growth ought to be initiated in the hinterland – whereupon the purchases of the hinterland from the major distribution and supply centre

[1] Allan R. Pred, *The Spatial Dynamics of U.S. Urban-Industrial Growth, 1800–1914* (Cambridge, Mass. and London: The M.I.T. Press, 1966).

of the region would automatically create at the centre additional income and employment in the whole range of 'central-place' distributing and service activities.

Conversely, growth initiated in the main urban centre would yield additional income and employment in the surrounding area to the extent that this urban centre is a purchaser and collector of goods and services produced in the hinterland. But there is no reason to assume in general that the latter type of impact is more important than the former. On the contrary, one might expect that the dependence of a city on its hinterland for markets is somewhat greater than the dependence of the hinterland upon its city for markets – if only because the city supplies a higher proportion of the kinds of goods and services that move relatively short distances and go directly into final consumption.

Consequently, the case for the growth centre strategy has to rest on grounds other than the secondary and induced impact of local purchases, or what has been called 'backward linkage'.

This limits the direct relevance and usefulness of regional input-output tables in their present form, which are primarily adapted to the simulation of backward linkages but do not come to grips with forward linkages, scale and external economies, or shifts of production factors. There is a recognised need for more adequate techniques for evaluating these other important impacts, which are the keys to the crucial role of growth centres in regional development.

It is difficult in principle to make a meaningful distinction between the 'forward linkage' and the 'external economies' effects of growth centre development, since in both cases an activity initially established in the centre provides cheaper and more accessible inputs which make possible the establishment or expansion, in the development area, of other activities dependent on access to such inputs. Generally, we seem to prefer to speak of 'external economies' when the initially-established activity is of a so-called 'threshold' type normally associated (because of scale economies) with a certain minimum size of urban or industrial concentration, and when it provides products or service inputs to a wide variety of other activities in the same locality. We are more likely to refer simply to 'forward linkage' when those conditions do not hold, and when the initially-established activity supplies inputs to just one or a few activities which are locationally oriented primarily to sources of that input. But both cases involve a similar principle of input orientation or 'forward linkage'.

As I have already noted, this kind of effect eludes the otherwise highly useful techniques of the input-output model, and requires specific location studies of industries or industry complexes. I have only one suggestion to offer by way of possible advancement of our analytical capability in this regard. We might consider trying to fill in empirically the cells of an inter-industry table in which the direct link between activity i and activity j is stated not in terms of the value of sales of i to j, but in terms of the cost per mile of transferring whatever it is that i supplies to j – firstly per unit of j's output, and secondly per unit of i's output. The two resulting matrices of coefficients would measure, respectively, the transfer-cost incentive of any activity j to locate near its various suppliers i, and the transfer-cost incentive of any activity i to locate near the various activities j to which it sells. Such a construction would represent an effort to express inter-industry relationships in locationally relevant terms, and might develop into a powerful tool for the evaluation of both backward and forward linkage effects. At the least, it would provide an integrated framework into which could be fitted otherwise unrelated individual analyses of industry location. The definition of transfer costs might be progressively broadened to cover more and more elements in addition to bare freight costs. The problem of non-linearity of transfer costs with respect to distance might be attacked in somewhat the same way as orthodox input-output analysis has attacked the similar problem of the dependence of technical input coefficients upon scale of output.

What can be said about the transmission of benefits from a growth centre to the surrounding area through movements of labour? In so far as this refers to daily commuting of workers, the impact is a very short-distance one, and tells us merely that in the placement of development assistance, it is appropriate to consider areas at least as large as individual labour markets. But in practice, growth centres are regarded as fewer and farther between than labour markets, and a stepped-up migration of people into the growth centre's labour market area is assumed.

An important hypothesis implicit in the growth centre strategy, then, is that people in backward regions will migrate much more rapidly to relatively nearby urban centres than they will to more remote ones. In other words, *distance is assumed to be a principal determinant of migration flow.*

On the face of it, that hypothesis seems quite reasonable, and a considerable number of empirical studies have supported Ravenstein's 'Law' [1] which makes the migration flow between two points an inverse function of the distance between these points.

Some recent studies of mobility and migration, however, seem to cast serious doubt on the importance of the distance factor; particularly where migrants out of extensive distressed or underdeveloped areas are concerned and in countries with well-developed transport and communication systems. For example, Lowry [2] found that distance is a factor of relatively little significance in explaining statistically the migration flows among major American labour markets in the 1950s. And in regard to migration

---

[1] Cf. Everett S. Lee, 'A Theory of Migration', *Demography*, vol. 3, (1966) no. 1, pp. 47-57.

[2] Ira S. Lowry, *Migration and Metropolitan Growth: Two Analytical Models* (Chandler Publishing Co., San Francisco, 1966).

from the largest and best-known underdeveloped area in the United States let me quote a recent statement by Ralph R. Widner,[1] the Executive Director of the Appalachian Regional Commission:

> Recently, I visited a neighborhood of 40,000 Appalachians in Chicago – Appalachians who had come there to find work. There are similar neighborhoods in Cleveland and Cincinnati and a number of other cities.
>
> But there are no Appalachian neighborhoods in Pittsburgh despite the fact that it is the only major metropolis in the area.

Mr Widner goes on to explain this phenomenon in terms of the special economic structure, skill requirements, and wage structure of the Pittsburgh labour market area. The important finding, for our purposes, is that migrants from Appalachia have preferred to move in large numbers to employment centres hundreds of miles away. Distance, we may conclude, has not been a significant deterrent once the decision to move has been made. We may surmise that in future, with continued improvement of spatial mobility from easier transport and communication, education and basic industrial training, and more adequate employment information and placement services, distance will be an even less significant impediment to migration that it is now. If that is so, it would suggest that an optimum set of policies for the benefit of the people in the backward areas would put more and more emphasis on measures to increase mobility and employ-ability and less emphasis on building employment in growth centres within the region itself.

Another recent statement that lends support to this view is the following: '. . . a good part of Appalachia's development effort should be concentrated outside the region, and . . . the region itself should be restructured and, as it were, apportioned among the metropolitan regions on its perimeter.'[2]

4 SOME CONCLUSIONS

In closing, I have one more observation suggested by consideration of the role of growth centres. It is clear that the most basic attribute of such centres is sufficient size: the economies of agglomeration in general, and more specifically the external economies of urban concentration, are fundamental to the whole concept. Among the various strands of locational and regional economic theory, the theory of central places and urban hierarchy is involved here. The approaches associated with Christaller, Lösch and von Thünen are more directly involved than those associated with Alfred Weber.

[1] Ralph R. Widner, 'Experiment in Appalachia', *Pittsburgh Business Review*, vol. 37 no. 3 (Mar 1967) p. 14.
[2] John Friedmann, 'Poor Regions and Poor Nations: Perspectives on the Problem of Appalachia', *Southern Economic Journal*, vol. xxxii, no. 4 (Apr 1966) p. 472.

It is interesting to speculate on whether this current direction of thought may reflect in part economic and social changes which lend increasing relevance and importance to the hierarchical in contrast to the simply spatial dimensions of locational patterns and development. I can think of several good reasons why both private and public locational preferences and decisions these days may be giving more attention to size of place (level in the urban hierarchy) and less attention to choice of region.

One reason is the increasing non-linearity of costs of transfer with respect to distance – resulting from the relatively greater speed of long-distance transport and communication and the increasing importance of time as an element in costs of transfer for goods, people, services, and information. In respect to communication, personal travel, and shipment of an increasing range of goods, the added time required for an additional several hundred miles is often less than the time required for the first ten miles.

Another powerful factor is the increasing importance of amenities (and more elaborate and urbane *kinds* of amenities) in our choices of places to live and work, which follows largely from rising standards of income, culture, and leisure.

Still another is the increasing importance of specialisation and linkage among activities arising from elaboration of products and processes and the increased importance of tertiary activities. This increases the scope of local external economies.

As a result of these trends and probably others, I suggest that in advanced countries at least, we have a tendency of diminishing differentiation in economic and social structure and locational advantage as among broad regions, and at the same time towards more differentiation in these respects as among large and small centres, i.e., different levels of the urban hierarchy. If true, this would imply that economic activities may be expected to be increasingly footloose between major regions or parts of a country and less footloose in regard to size of community; and consequently, that public policy may operate with increased lee-way (but perhaps diminished urgency) in interregional terms and with increased constraint (but perhaps increased urgency) in terms of the choice between different sizes of urban centre. Perhaps it will become more and more important to know just how big a viable growth centre needs to be, but less important to choose among centres of a given size in different parts of a developing region or in different regions.

These last remarks are of course hardly more than speculative conjectures. But if we want to try to substitute knowledge for conjecture, here are two lines of inquiry that might help.

One of these would be an attempt to find out whether there really has been a trend in the direction I have hypothesised, i.e., towards less differentiation among regions and more differentiation between sizes of place.

We might appropriately focus first on differentiation in terms of economic structure or mix of activities. Some techniques are available for measuring the divergence among the industrial structures, for example, of a set of areas for which data are available. In any given country, it should be possible to apply such a measure first among regions or states as the areas compared, and then among urban size classes. If such comparison were to be made for the most recent date possible and for one or more earlier dates, such a trend as I have hypothesised might or might not be in evidence.

A second line of inquiry would involve development of a variety of types of regional and interregional accounts (inter-industry tables, income and product accounts, statements of stocks and flows) with the 'regions' being defined not in the usual areal sense but as urban hierarchy levels.

And here I shall stop. I have put before you few if any new answers; but many questions, some of which may be new and provocative.

Part 5 Summary Record of Discussions

D. C. Hague

Location Theory, Regional Economics and Backward Areas

Discussion of Paper by Professor E. A. G. Robinson

Professor Hoover said that Professor Robinson's paper set up excellently the essential frame of reference for these complex problems. He would simply make a few observations, picking out points which would lead to fruitful discussion.

First, Professor Robinson tried to identify the most appropriate kind of economic theory to use. He set it out in terms of three distinctions, but Professor Hoover thought one could put these distinctions more clearly. First, should one use micro- or macro-theory? Here we were mainly interested in macro-economic theory. Second, there was the kind of competition to assume. Should we use pure- or monopolistic-competition theory? Here, the latter was usually more appropriate. Third, should we use general or partial equilibrium analysis? Both Professor Robinson and he would like to use a partial equilibrium approach.

Then there was central-place theory. Professor Robinson's simple model – of local, regional and national markets – had shown its value in a number of empirical studies. Professor Hoover was troubled that this 'model' depicted a world with only two locational forces. One was economies of scale, the other was access to markets. The scheme ignored transport costs on inputs. It also ignored the supply of factors of production – land, labour etc. It seemed illogical to organise location theory wholly around markets. Why not emphasise access to inputs instead?

Professor Robinson's paper then pointed to the need for a dynamic theory. He illustrated his points from the U.K., stressing the apparent inertia of her population in response to such changes. In the U.S.A. there did not seem to be the same inertia. The withering away of small centres of population in agricultural areas was striking. The urban centres had changed out of all recognition within the last twenty years.

Professor Hoover suggested further that in many countries regional adjustments of population would be more rapid were it not for differentials in birth-rates. He thought migration was always quick to respond to changed economic conditions and wondered how far, in other countries, differences in birth-rates among regions were lessening, as they were in the U.S.A.

Professor Robinson anticipated further growth in urban areas and looked to the need to restrain it. One should distinguish two separate points. First, there were the external diseconomies of high urban concentration. Distinct from this was the danger of social capital lying idle in backward areas. This latter problem could be tackled by ensuring that prices reflected low marginal costs in backward areas. This pricing problem, especially for labour, warranted our attention. Should the preferred solution allow wages to be lower in backward areas? This seemed better than either allowing unemployment or encouraging subsidisation.

Professor Robinson finally discussed the problem in terms of the regional balance of payments. Thinking on this topic had developed rapidly in recent years. Professor Robinson had not only set out his alternative adjustments open to us, but which were most important in which situations. He thought one needed a fuller analysis of this.

As for his policy prescriptions, a passage in Section 4 of the paper puzzled him. Why should it be desirable to reduce the ratio of outward to inward transports costs? This seemed equivalent to saying that every region would benefit from the imposition of tariffs.

Finally, we were always reluctant to write off a backward area, but perhaps we should face the problem of how to abandon or reduce such a region.

Professor Samuelson commented on the distinction between micro- and macro-economics. He had recently had a letter from Dr Nourse, the first Chairman of the Council of Economic Advisers in 1946. The latter had asked Alvin Hansen for the origin of the term macro-economics. Hansen had suggested that he (Samuelson) had invented it. This was not true, but he did not know where it came from. It was not in the first edition of his textbook, published in 1949. He had wondered whether the term had been invented by Ragnar Frisch in the 1930s, since articles on the subject had appeared in *Econometrica* as early as 1935. It turned out that early writers had used the term macro-dynamics. The first use of the word macro-economics had been in the 1940s, and then in only one of its two present meanings. Perhaps we needed to distinguish these two meanings in the conference.

First, macro-economics was concerned with the kind of theory put forward in Keynes's *General Theory* in 1936. This had to do with effective demand, with aggregates. But it was not the sense in which the word was first used in the 1940s, when it was used to describe simplified general equilibrium theory. In the early 1900s, J. S. Clark had produced a kind of macro-economic model with marginal productivity determining factor shares, and with a production function. It was a very different model from Marshall's partial equilibrium analysis, but also from Walras' general equilibrium analysis. Therefore, one of the first macro-economists, in this sense, was Ricardo and not Malthus, despite the latter's emphasis on deficient effective demand. Professor Samuelson said he saw, as he read this paper, that Professor Robinson had both meanings in mind.

In looking at partial versus general equilibrium, Professors Hoover and Robinson were both on the same side. If general equilibrium analysis was so general that it was vacuous, then he joined them. But much of the dissatisfaction with spatial analysis was that all writers saw their immediate predecessors as too partial in their approach. Professor Samuelson would argue, and perhaps he had Marshall on his side, for a more eclectic approach. In particular, we must not take a worm's eye view, because what was taken for granted in partial equilibrium analysis often turned out to be an unresolved issue at a higher level of theory.

Professor James made two comments. In Section 2 of his paper, Professor Robinson spoke of the twentieth-century agricultural revolution. It was right to emphasise that this had meant increases in productivity. The emphasis was right in principle, and the figures were right both for cereals and for all agriculture. If one looked at France, the emphasis was right for cereals and fruits, but it was striking that in the centre of France the price of land dedicated to cereals had risen much faster than that of pasture. The agricultural revolution of the twentieth century had been much more one for cereals and fruits than for animal raising. He wondered if this was true outside France. For example, did one need artificial feeding? He thought that in France there had been no changes in methods of animal feeding similar to those in other types of agriculture. There had been changes in poultry feeding, but not for other livestock.

Professor James said his second point was more important. As we were concerned with underdeveloped areas in developed regions, perhaps we should make a distinction between two very different situations. First, there was the region growing more slowly than the whole country, for example, Languedoc; second, there was the region in actual decline. Economic theory never studied a declining area. At the national level, one had few examples of a decline like that in the Roman Empire. But decline did happen regionally. He thought that the reasons why regions declined were essentially different from the reasons why regions grew at less than the national rate. Introducing new capital was not enough. One needed completely new techniques. Economists needed to study the reasons for outright decline.

Professor Vito made two brief comments. Concerning Section 3 of Professor Robinson's paper, all agreed there was a conflict between private and public advantage. It was true that private entrepreneurs might choose to produce in overcrowded areas because of economics external to the plant, but internal to the industry. They were not likely to take account of external diseconomies. Could one not put the same problem more positively? What kind of diseconomies were we considering; those internal to the plant or to the industry, or external diseconomies in general? Could one speak of private *versus* social costs? Then, one could argue that in overcrowded areas private costs were low but social costs high. In underdeveloped areas the reverse was true. Where one had a balance or an imbalance between the sum of private and social costs in overcrowded areas, and that seen in underdeveloped areas, there would be a clear indication of the national solution to location problems.

Professor Vito did not think Professor Robinson ignored declining areas. His idea of a negative multiplier took them into account. But the distinction was important. The benefits to a backward area were not the same whether it was declining or simply slow-growing. In the first case, the area was already industrialised and had social capital; a slow-growing area might have no infrastructure at all. It might well be easier to redevelop a declining area than to speed up the growth of a slowly-growing one.

Professor von Böventer suggested how to distinguish between the use of macro- and micro-economics. If one wanted to judge a situation, one needed to know how one had got there, and where one wanted to go. To analyse a situation, one needed aggregate data and relationships between aggregates. But one also needed knowledge on the structure of the aggregates, including input-output analyses and information on the spatial structure in question. In practice, one then left macro-economics and turned to micro-economic relationships and to partial-equilibrium analyses. If one wanted to draw conclusions in order to make policy suggestions, one had to pull the results of partial-equilibrium analyses together. It would be impossible to say, even for a particular problem, that one or other approach was right; one must often move constructively from one to the other and back again. We did not know enough about spatial relationships, in particular what determined the economies of large agglomerations and the conditions under which agglomerations occurred. We needed such knowledge not only for production but also for consumption. Among other things, this raised the problem of when and why people were willing to move to an agglomeration.

He thought that central-place theory, which dealt with these problems, was itself still underdeveloped. For example, economists like Lösch had had to throw out economies of agglomeration in their *exact* formulations of spatial models. It was important to know to what extent development was possible without a raw material base; or how cities could exist in a region with no natural resources. To answer such questions one needed aggregate relationships as well as micro-economic relationships, costs of infrastructure, and so on. As an important policy question, he mentioned this: in her backward regions, should West Germany bring in industry or let people move out? The problem of declining areas, like that of declining sectors, was not new. Economists had already studied the problems of the declining sectors of an economy, and one should try to draw on their analyses.

Professor Delivanis said that Professor Robinson had stressed many points which were often forgotten not only by governments but by economists too. First, there was the importance of considering personal preference, quite independent of the cost involved, whenever the site of a new investment was chosen. This was often noticed when decisions were taken without regard to cost, for example, in some investments in the U.K. in the 1930s, despite the advantages to be expected in the depressed areas. He fully agreed that investment in infrastructure alone was not enough to secure development if other investments did not follow. The latter could not be carried through if raw materials and labour were not available in the appropriate quantities and qualities. He would add that of course Professor Robinson was right when he stressed that in areas with no satisfactory infrastructure, wage costs had to be lower than in the nation as a whole. As low wages were unacceptable to the workers involved, the only solution was to subsidise employers from public funds in order to induce them to operate in the area. He thought that from a human point of view, this would be best, but would like to hear Professor Robinson's reactions, in view of his great experience with such problems in general, and particularly in the U.K.

Professor Robertson said that there was always a superficial attraction in the idea that if a region was backward, one should move people out quickly and painlessly. This did not happen in practice. Where there was a prospect for development in the backward area, it was desirable to encourage it. Since moving people out was hard and slow, the economy suffered from unemployed resources in the backward region, which had an above-average rate of unemployment. Another line of policy suggested that if people would not move, they must be paid a lower wage reflecting lower efficiency (which might or might not mean lower real wages). In the U.K., money wages were alleged to be the same in all regions, but in fact were not. To some extent, therefore, the labour market appeared to carry out the policy being suggested. It was also true, however, that low wages in a backward region inhibited development, not just because they reduced the size of the market, but because they reduced the number of richer, innovating consumers. This prevented the rapid introduction of refrigerators, central heating and, especially, the automobile. Statistics on car ownership in the U.K. bore this out. It was therefore important to raise efficiency and money wages. Training opportunities were not sufficiently stressed in Professor Robinson's paper. Usually there was (1) a shortage of one or two occupational groups, or (2) an overdevelopment of particular skills, and a need for training people to possess other skills. One did not necessarily need an absolute increase in training outlay, but a complex process of changing the pattern of training. The real cost of training was therefore easy to exaggerate.

Professor Groenman noted that, in cattle rearing, the Netherlands had (1) electric milking, stimulated by a shortage of labour; (2) scientific cattle-raising, with artificial insemination; (3) systematic grazing. One could see little effect on the price of land. He was not sure that in Holland there was a strong relationship between the price of land and the level of milk production. Fodder imports allowed up to 4 times as many cattle per acre as the land itself would support, part of the cattle-rearer's land lying at la Plata!

Professor Robinson commented on the discussion thus far. What Professor James had said really bore out what he himself had said. He was trying to explain why, in the twentieth century, a big increase in population and in income per head had caused a fairly big increase in food consumption; yet in the U.K. the pressure on the soil had fallen. Output of agriculture per hectare had risen more than that of agriculture as a whole; for cereals alone, output had risen rather more than output per hectare; it could be inferred that for other products output per hectare had risen somewhat faster than that for cereals. In the 1930s there had been big improvements in grasslands, raising yields dramatically. This would lead one to expect Professor James's phenomenon. Yet the pressure on land was not great. At the margin, the price of pasture land had risen little, though the price of intramarginal land had risen greatly.

On types of theory, he was reminded of his experience in the I.E.A. conference in Lisbon in 1957 on the Economic Consequence of the Size of Nations, when many participants had been surprised to find so little previous work in the field concerned. He had found difficulty in using existing theoretical structures, because spatial economics had not been adequately assimilated into general economics. For example, in the U.K., elementary economics courses said virtually nothing about spatial economics. He asked himself why there was, as he thought, a bigger inertia in population redistribution in Europe. He had only taken the U.K. as an example; he thought its experience was repeated in Italy, France and other European countries. Was it true that changes in the pattern of demand in the U.S.A. were more quickly reflected in population redistribution?

He especially agreed with Professor Vito on the difference between redeveloping a declining area with both an existing infrastructure and a tradition of skilled work, and developing an area never developed before. The latter was very similar to an underdeveloped country – the climate of thought into which one was bringing new industrial development became important.

Professor Robinson wanted to clarify what he had said about wages. He was only trying to explain the problem. When looking at a problem, he tended first to ask how the classical system would solve it. It would here assume that a backward area would have low wages and so attract business. If one interfered, should one make the wages policy reflect the classical system, or, having interfered, did one replace the classical by a different process? He preferred action through subsidy to wages.

As regards Professor Hoover's question as to why he wished to see a reduction of the ratio of outward to inward transport costs, he would remind him that at that point he was discussing remedies for a disequilibrium situation.

Professor Lajugie suggested that the problem could not be looked at as macro-economics in the broadest sense. On the analytical plane, he thought one needed to distinguish between ordinary development and decline – as Professor James had done. He would stress the importance of the market forces which brought about growth; the role of external economies and the way factors of production were drawn to an agglomeration or spread around the country. If one looked at the problem in terms of the most pure economics, there was no problem. Factors would be distributed in line with their marginal productivities. The existence of underdeveloped areas was an intolerable strain. The problem was not to develop the region in its own interest, but in that of the nation.

All agreed that an active policy was needed to reduce disparities in development between regions. Such a policy would prevent partial, micro-economic solutions. In France there had been a subsidised policy for the distribution of labour, partly for political reasons. He thought the solution could not be found only through wages. It was a bad thing to base policy on low wages in under-developed regions. For low wages were themselves a brake on development.

Obviously one needed to choose places to develop and activities to develop these. Not only techniques but demand had to be considered, including forecast demand. We had to avoid both economic and technical isolation, which led to the idea of 'growth points' (poles de developpement). All this was not done by waving a magic wand but by using the most up-to-date analysis, including multiplier analysis.

Replying to Professor Robinson, *Mr Petrella-Tirone* said that three studies by geographers showed that recently there had been some fluidity in the structure of population in Italy. One could not speak of inertia. Especially in the South, there had been not only the well-known emigration to Western Europe and Northern Italy, but also a marked interregional movement from the country and small towns to provincial and regional 'capitals'.

On more general issues, it seemed to Mr Petrella-Tirone that any analysis of regional problems required, above all, an adequate theoretical apparatus for studying spatial economics. Existing analyses of the spatial distribution of economic and residential activity had not yet reached the level of a true general theory of space economy. Was this because we still had no adequate formalisation of concepts and theories for studying spatial problems? Or did it raise again the existing difficulty in co-ordinating analyses of the rules upon which the spatial aspects of economics were based?

The theory of location had the merit of having introduced important conceptual tools into economic analysis, like transport costs and the economies of agglomeration. Perhaps there should be an effort on the lines of the theories of Lösch and Christaller to look into the existing relations between territorial structure and the distribution of economic activity. Today, the tendency seemed to be to pay great attention to particular problems rather than to that of spatial equilibrium in the economic system.

Mr Petrella-Tirone went on to argue that a weakness of the distinction between backward and declining regions was that it seemed to depend on the time period in question. Could one really say that a backward region was one which had never attempted economic development, when, for instance, 100 years ago old forms of industrialisation had flourished in Southern as well as in Northern Italy? Would it not be better to introduce the concept of 'structure' in the sense of the existence or non-existence of a system of relationships for the organisation of economic space? If so, one could argue in terms of structured and non-structured space. One could study structured space as being more or less articulated on the basis of the nature, type and intensity of existing economic relationships, and so on. He thought the structural criterion could lead to interesting theoretical analyses which would also provide effective operational solutions.

Finally, given that, as Professor Robinson had pointed out, the distinction between local and regional activities was destined to lose its true meaning, could one not hope for a two-fold classification? One could distinguish (1) products of regional specialisation (playing a role in developing the region, having an interregional market and being of interest to the whole economy), and (2) products giving local satisfaction. This would allow one to study the region and the economy in the light of links between the various types of product.

Professor Patinkin thought that a lot of what seemed to be inertia in society depended on people's tastes – on preferences for a given area. This might explain the differences between Europe and the U.S.A. In spite of its size, cultural and language homogeneity were greater in the U.S.A. It was then difficult for an economist to object to apparent inertia.

Professor Patinkin said one might find mobility masked by natural population increase. We must be careful what we used as an index; it must be some kind of flow relatively to the total population. If we used wage rates, taxes would enter in. We also needed to look at wage movements over time. The data might exaggerate wage differences because of a need to look at productivity as well. If there was labour of different qualities, determined by education, differences in wages could be a reflection of these different qualities of labour. If minimum wage legislation covered a whole nation, then backward areas would have higher wages relatively to the efficiency of labour. One useful policy measure might be to raise the level of education in backward regions. Perhaps this was not so significant, for example, in Italy, where labour could move from the South to the North. We needed to hear from the experts on this. But there were other problems too. For instance, one needed managerial talent and the problem might be to persuade managers to move to backward regions.

One question Professor Patinkin wanted to ask was whether encouraging the establishment of nation-wide firms might be one way to deal with this problem. In a large firm, one could shift managerial talent within the firm to a backward region for a few years and then back to more popular areas.

Professor James said Professor Samuelson had spoken of macro-economics.

N

His own problem was, how could one simultaneously use partial and macro-analysis. It was not impossible. Walras had constantly discussed poles of general equilibrium, though his method was always a micro- method. At the same time, Professor Patinkin's work often moved from micro- to macro-analysis.

He thought the difference between macro- and micro-economics was a question of the method rather than the field of study. Macro-economic theory was concerned with groups or with individual firms of unequal strength. Was it not possible to look at partial equilibrium policies and at the same time use the macro- method? When we looked at regions these were not whole economies, and so we had partial equilibrium problems.

Dr Marsan said, with Italy in mind, that inertia meant resistance in starting movement, as well as in stopping it once started. The more enterprising part of the population moved, leaving behind the less enterprising. This bleeding of a region might jeopardise its future, so he saw inertia in terms of too much mobility which could not be stopped – a drain from the weak region. It required an urgent all-out effort to save the region.

Professor Samuelson recalled that Professor Robinson had said there was too little work on regional economics. There could be two reasons for this; (1) there might be good theory but it might be neglected; (2) we might really lack such theory. On balance, he thought the latter was true. But he would throw no stones because he saw very big difficulties in providing this kind of theory.

In the history of the application of mathematics to real-world problems there were two types of application. First, there was the continuum and the calculus, which were very successful in physics. Second, there were problems concerned with discreteness. For example, there was the right-angled triangle with sides of 3, 4 and 5. We had whole numbers as distinct from Pythagoras, whose theorem applied to any right-angled triangle. Unfortunately, many spatial problems were discrete in this way.

The simplest example was where one had two kinds of land. Each was homogeneous and used homogeneous labour. This was a simple problem, and Ricardo saw the answer. One applied labour to one grade of land and drew the (continuous) marginal productivity curve. One then did the same for the second grade of land. Then one found where a horizontal line cut both curves and allocated all labour on this basis between the two types of land.

Later, Haberler had used a concave (from below) production possibility frontier and obtained the same answer. But where one had increasing returns, one could not proceed by small steps. In Marxian language, a problem of quantity became one of quality. This could be seen in terms of programming. The theory of linear programming, which used concave (from below) programming, worked out simply. But if one had convex functions, then there was a big problem of scale. If one had twenty different cities and forty products, to solve the resulting allocation problem defied the capacity of the biggest computer. He suggested that this was one reason why spatial economics remained unconsidered by sophisticated theorists.

Professor von Böventer agreed that this was important, but it did not justify the neglect of spatial theory in economic textbooks. When comparing spatial economic relationships with economic relationships in a world without spatial dimensions, one had to consider three additional phenomena. (1) The location of products was important; identical products became different products when at different locations. In principle, this was the same as with products at different points of time or in different stages of production. (2) Spatial competition was similar to heterogeneous competition. (3) There were external economies and diseconomies; and agglomeration economies were but a special kind of such external economies.

The geographical co-ordinates of points in space corresponded to just two dimensions of the 'quality co-ordinates' of a point in a 'quality space' hetero-geneous products; in either case, the numerical determination of an optimal point was difficult. If one looked at general economic theory and considered heterogeneous products in one big market, for example television sets, one found the same lack of conclusive results as one often found in spatial analyses.

If one extended the analysis, either in spatial or in one-point models, by con-sidering external economies, the same kinds of difficulty emerged again. There-fore spatial economics and general economics suffered from similar difficulties, and it was mostly owing to the difficulty of reaching general conclusions that these problems were not dealt with in ordinary textbooks.

Professor Robinson concluded the discussion, saying that when he had asked for a full discussion of the macro-economics of the subject, he did not want to exclude micro-economics. He agreed with Professor James that we needed to operate at both levels at once. He was impressed by what Professor Samuelson had said regarding the complexity of these problems as seen from a mathematical point of view. But we needed sometimes to persuade the mathematicians of the importance of tackling the full complexity of real-world problems.

He agreed with Professor Patinkin that we needed always to look at population changes. So often our problems were those of an area where there was high population growth but a slow rise in demand for the main product of the area and a rapid rise in productivity in it. One found examples of this in the U.K. where there were areas of increasing productivity and a declining demand for labour, but where the population was growing. So the demand for labour lagged behind the supply of labour in the region.

Professor Robinson was glad that, in discussing Professor Groenman's paper, the conference would be emphasising the importance of social and political factors, and so moving away from pure economics.

SECOND SESSION

Social Aspects of Backwardness in Developed Countries

Discussion of Paper by Professor S. Groenman

Professor Marchal said that in looking at human problems in regional de-velopment Professor Groenman went back to underdeveloped countries. He distinguished two kinds of obstacle – cultural and structural, especially family and social structure. To this he added problems of communication between the backward regions and the outside world.

On culture, Professor Groenman said that cultural obstacles were still important in backward areas in developed countries. They flowed from value systems. In backward areas, the population was opposed to any activity that meant risk-taking and to the introduction of new industries like electronics. Professor Groenman saw a tendency for the educational system to develop arts rather than science or business subjects. He said that if these obstacles had always existed one would not overstress them. Their origins would be far enough back to have little influence on current events. The strength of these obstacles kept in power an élite group which held common values and whose economic, social and political position would be threatened by development. Professor Groenman made the interesting distinction between poverty and backwardness. Backwardness was a relative concept. The population came to know it was backward only when communications with richer countries developed. Up till that point, it was merely poor. Here we came to the problem of communication to which he would return later.

Professor Marchal pointed out that Professor Groenman said that structural factors were less important than cultural ones in underdevelopment. Professor Marchal thought one could make three points on structure. First, in backward areas, wealth and power were concentrated in the class concerned with maintaining the *status quo*. Second, the power of this class was not threatened by political democracy. The rest of the population kept out of political life. The élite maintained political power and operated as a screen between the central government and the people of its own region. Third, in these conditions, the social hierarchy was rigid. The population centred its aspirations on the family and the village. Rapid population increase worsened the economic situation. Married women refused paid work. Entrepreneurs emphasised their independence from the State.

Professor Marchal wondered if these arguments were more relevant for underdeveloped areas than for backward areas in developed countries. For example, in France, there were clearly some very backward areas in the Massif Central. Could one really say that a small élite class was sustained by the remainder of the population in the Massif Central and not threatened by democracy. Nor did he think that there was an élite which acted as a buffer between the government and the people of the region.

The system of patronage was characteristic of Spain or Brazil. Could one say the same of advanced countries? The pressure of representatives from backward areas on the public authorities helped development, but Professor Marchal suggested that the process was a special one and did not represent a point at which the theories of underdeveloped areas and of backward areas in advanced countries coincided.

On the improvement of communications, there were two main questions. First, did improved communications help development, or did they simply lead to increased differences between rich and poor? According to Professor Groenman, the former was a reasonable thesis, but only if market forces operated freely. With state intervention, the backward areas were included in national plans for development. If a region wanted the latest technology it might well find this easier to obtain if it was a backward area than if it was an under-developed one. Professor Groenman rejected the idea of bringing intermediate techniques into a backward area. He also accepted that improved communications were desirable rather than undesirable.

Keeping to social aspects, Professor Marchal said that he accepted Professor Groenman's position that the spread of education would increase the desire for economic development in backward areas. Then Professor Groenman went on to more disputable ground, arguing that backward areas were far from the centre of countries. Was this true? First, it seemed to be true only of land areas: maritime frontiers did not seem to hold back development. Second, the facts did not fit this thesis. The Massif Central was far from the frontier, but was backward. Yet some of Germany's frontier areas were very advanced. The problem was whether countries were powerful enough to develop those regions which were on their frontiers.

Professor Vito argued that communication was crucial, but for the rest, it was hard to generalise especially about social and human factors. In his paper, Professor Groenman spoke of an unwillingness to leave the soil (pp. 24-5). Professor Vito did not think that one could accept this statement in an unqualified way. In the late nineteenth and early twentieth century, there had been much migration from the Mediterranean to the New World. In one single year, about one million people had left Italy. Only in 1917 and 1921, as a consequence of legal action in the U.S.A., did emigration stop. From then on, population pressure had meant that marginal land had to be brought into cultivation, and this aggravated the European agricultural crisis. Professor Vito said that he was offering no judgement but only presenting facts. Once the demand for labour in Europe rose, there was again emigration from the South, and also migration from Southern to Northern Italy.

Professor Vito suggested that a model of a dual economy would be Brazil. Some economists also thought that one could apply this model to Italy, but he did not share this view. This model had been introduced at the beginning of this century when studying colonial economies. There, one had an island of western economic institutions and organisation which was surrounded by an archaic and primitive type of society. But there was a barrier to inter-penetration, and the phenomenon was self-perpetuating. It was not similar to what happened in Italy where there was no such barrier because of the existence of only one culture.

Professor Vito wondered whether improved communication had made the rich richer and the poor poorer. Theoretically this might be true. It would have happened in the Common Market except for the safeguards intended to protect weaker economies. Progress in economic thinking taught one how to prevent this happening.

Finally, resistance to change was a common feature of all communities who lived in isolation – intellectual and not necessarily material isolation. It was not different from the position which inspired the Luddite movement in Britain. The Luddites did not have the intellectual information required to enable them to see the value of the change associated with mechanisation. Professor Vito therefore accepted that the human factor came into economic development mainly as a limiting one.

Dr Schmidt-Lüders said that Professor Marchal had doubted whether distance from the centre was important for a backward area. Professor Groenman had said that many backward areas were far from the centre – not all of them. When the Massif Central was mentioned one should not take this too literally. Geographically, the Massif Central might be in the middle of France, but Paris was the real centre.

Dr Schmidt-Lüders said that one major point of principle in the discussion on regional development had been the difficulty of coming to terms with criteria. People had asked what was backwardness. The O.E.C.D. had made a synopsis of the standards which member countries applied in working out whether a region was backward or not. There was not the slightest agreement, but a great variety of standards which differed even within the country over time – and with governments. This was where cultural and political aspects came in, because decisions as to what regions needed assistance were made by political bodies, reflecting the cultural and political pattern of a country. The economists' criteria were used as advice of an auxiliary nature, but were not decisive.

Professor von Böventer suggested that improved road systems would help market forces to become more effective. Whether the results would be good or bad – stabilising or destabilising – depended on the relevant production functions. To obtain general results we should have to know these production functions and other behaviour functions.

Professor Groenman commented on the discussion so far. If one wrote this kind of paper it was bound to be too all-embracing. Also, in sociology, people were reluctant nowadays to formulate 'laws'. Many qualifications were made. If one took his own paper, he hoped that no such general rules were suggested, though he might have failed to live up to his intentions. Because of this, he had not formulated a 'law' about backward areas being on frontiers. As Dr Schmidt-Lüders had said, he had only said that there were many such areas. Again, if he had emphasised the position of the ruling hierarchy, his view might not be universally true. He was again offering no all-embracing law. However, many examples were given in his paper. In the Netherlands, one had striking examples of such a hierarchy in various parts of the country. If one had several political parties, the élite joined all of them and was still voted into power.

He agreed with Professor Vito that it might be necessary to qualify what he had said about migration. One could find other examples to support Professor Vito, but he thought his own point was basically right. He agreed that a dual economy was less important in Europe. As for whether communication increased or decreased differences between areas and countries, he thought it might be true that communication had worsened the position in Italy. But he thought that in the long run increased communication would reduce income differences between countries.

On resistance to change, he thought it was hard to say what tradition meant in a backward area. The situation in most countries was not static, and the situation in a traditional country could therefore develop satisfactorily if the country was static. The movement of migrants was a sort of inertia. What we called traditional behaviour was only perhaps a different way of speaking of a laziness in taking decisions. For example, he noted that everyone in the I.E.A. Round Table chose to sit in the same seats in the conference room. He had simply tried to reach some conclusions about why people behaved in 'traditional' ways.

Professor Groenman said he had been careful to say that the social drawbacks in a backward area and an underdeveloped area were sometimes different in degree. Since he was coming to a meeting of economists it had seemed fair to quote Myrdal, because he was the economist. However, he agreed it was dangerous to mix what one said about underdeveloped and backward areas.

Professor Delivanis wanted to be allowed to say that the paper applied more to underdeveloped countries than to backward areas in developed countries. If we accepted this, we would then agree that frontiers constituted barriers and prevented development, while within developed countries, particularly with the reciprocal extension of social services, this was not so. He wanted to add that limited entrepreneurial initiatives in backward areas were not dictated by political considerations but by the inability or the difficulty of mastering complicated problems, particularly when decentralisation was not excessive. Emigration from Mediterranean countries had been intensified, during the decade up to 1965, by overemployment in Western Europe which made people reluctant to go outside Europe or even to leave for other countries within Europe.

Professor Delivanis wanted to add that it was correct to distinguish the influence of communication on development according to whether one was concerned with activities of the government or private firms. It would give us the chance to think over the implications.

Professor Turčan said Professor Groenman had brought us back to human factors. He thought many regionalists shared the opinion that one could not distinguish between backward and developed areas. Though there was a large range of factors which lay behind this distinction, it was mainly the human factor which characterised it. The paper by Professor Groenman showed the importance of determining carefully how to develop backward areas. This was not a distinction depending on laws in certain countries, because the administrative or legal aspect of the problem depended on the economic policy of the country. We had to look at the social-economic aspects of problems. How advanced a country was; how big the region was; the type of population it had; all these led to differences. Professor James had distinguished between backward and declining areas. This was important when the human factor was taken into consideration because the type of area helped to determine the degree to which the human factor affected mobility. It affected the extent to which unemployed labour was willing to migrate. The potential for migration was limited because a region was concerned only with the natives of one country. He wanted to point out that with backward areas in very advanced countries, to assure dynamic and stable development required concentration on techniques of production of a very advanced type.

But this assumed an ability to absorb investment, so that one came back to the human factor. He knew that there was a lot of writing about Southern Italy but he thought that it had ignored the intellectual infrastructure. In very advanced countries one must be certain of getting qualified men from local sources because this helped to solve the problem of dualism. Bringing men into a factory from outside could make it harder to develop a growing enterprise.

Professor Valarché said that Professor Groenman's table about the élite was basically correct. But he had reservations about how generally it would apply. It would probably be correct for Fribourg and Brittany, but less true elsewhere. Professor Valarché was worried about the content of the social model. The problem of origin should be split off from continuing backwardness. For example, Fribourg had held back industrialisation because this would have altered the social structure; it had held it back for fifty years. Now the problem was how to eliminate backwardness.

Professor Robinson wanted to get Professor Groenman to act more as an advisor to a group of civil servants. One often found that in a backward area there were those who wanted to preserve its isolation but who also used the political system to demand economic change when they voted. In Wales, Northern Ireland, and perhaps Scotland, there were strong pressures for economic growth. But how did one change the psychological atmosphere sufficiently to get those in the region to accept the growth which, in fact, they wanted?

Professor Groenman said that one should give opportunity, and change would come. *Professor Robinson* suggested that there were some examples in the U.K. where this had happened. For example there was South Wales in the 1890s where agricultural workers moved into coal-mining. A similar situation had existed in Northumberland and Durham. It was noteworthy that in both areas the feudal nobility had pushed ahead the economic development of the area. But this was not general. So how did we persuade people to become psychologically attuned to accepting change? Could Professor Groenman step outside his strict role as a scientist to give this opinion.

Professor Robertson said that essentially we were concerned with the will to develop. He had distinguished the Highlands, a decayed peasant society, with landlords opposed to development and little desire for development in the rest of the population. In the Lowlands, the gentry had assisted development, but the mid-twentieth century industrial gentry was not so much opposed to development as not enthusiastic about it. In other words perhaps there was a weakness in the managerial class.

Professor Robertson said he wanted to go on considering Scotland but would try not to be parochial. On social mobility, he would stress the distinction between those educated in the humanities, including law and the church, and those educated in technical and managerial subjects or those which led to management. One could have a big educational system with a high technical content but too little interest in entrepreneurship. This was a good description of the Scottish system. It had moved from emphasis on the humanities to include pure science and engineering but had exported trained men. If they had gone into management, many would have remained. Yet, for example, Scotland trained more than twice as many doctors as she needed. One wanted two things. First, a proper balance of the technologies in education. Second, emphasis on education leading into management. For example, Scotland exported economists as well as large numbers of accountants, because the Scottish accounting education gave a professional rather than a management slant. Within the managerial sector one needed to emphasise motivation.

Professor Robertson was bothered because Professor Groenman wanted more movement while Professor Vito and Professor Marchal said there was already too much. He thought one should distinguish a peasant society from a backward area in a developed country. Scotland had needed to move people out in the nineteenth century, both abroad where they could be with relations and to England where there was a more direct economic reason for movement. But this was enough mobility. Unless one intended an area to disappear, one could have too much movement. One already had the type of community that Professor Groenman wanted.

It was important to distinguish movement between regions from movement within one region. A Scotsman would go abroad, but he would not move ten miles down the road. One should also distinguish between salaried men and wage-earners. A salaried man would move in both directions; a wage-earner moved away and stayed away. One needed to look at gross and net flows. Scotland had high gross emigration but too little gross immigration. It was perhaps harder to reduce gross emigration – which was the result of habit – than to improve gross immigration, and so lead to a net inflow of population. One must attract back those who had left, or attract those who moved to the region for the first time. The discussion had focused on the need to emphasise the advantages offered by an area as somewhere to move into, either as a new area or as one where a person had previously lived.

Professor James returned to the problem of frontier regions. He wanted to reconcile what Professors Groenman and Marchal had said. He thought one should distinguish political and economic frontiers. What Professor Marchal had said was true of political frontiers but more so for economic ones. In an economic sense, the Massif Central was on the frontier. He would ask Professor Vito if there was not an economic frontier between Palermo and Rome. The Common Market was changing economic frontiers, and this led to the kind of problem we were discussing.

Professor Lajugie wanted to see how Professor Groenman's factors had worked out in South-West France. He thought the problem there was largely psychological – the role of men in development. The role of men was fundamental, because it had either a breaking or a driving influence. The need was to overcome the breaking force in South-West France to start take-off.

Some managers there were ignorant of the problems of an underdeveloped region. In the past they had had high standards of living but they were now dreaming of past splendour. The political objection to change led to an economic argument about avoiding great changes of structure. There was a fear of expansion and the rest of the population became used to the existing situation. There was therefore no demand for development – indeed a brake on development.

This had to be overcome by continuing efforts at spreading information and giving training. It was strange that the most receptive medium in the South-West had not been the industrialist but the agricultural manager. Young farmers had seen the need for change – to alter market structures and techniques. Experience showed that one big factor was imitation. One therefore had to make an effort at creating an infrastructure which would attract business. When one international firm decided to set up near Bordeaux, others followed, having confidence in the first firm's decision that this was a good location. One could see the importance of the psychological threshold to development which was hard to cross, but which must be crossed if take-off was to occur.

N 2

Professor Sovani said that he had nothing against the opening quotation in Professor Groenman's paper from Kusum Nair's book on India, but would merely like to remark that the book should not be taken as giving a representative picture of the Indian rural scene.

Reference had been made in the paper and by other participants to the concept of a dual economy in backward areas. The concept had been developed by Dutch social scientists particularly for Indonesia. It was initially associated with colonial economies but was later found to be realistic for non-colonial areas as well. He felt, however, that the concept was not very realistic and its analytical value was questionable. In practice, it was very difficult, if not impossible, to demarcate the two or more socio-economic sectors which were supposed to characterise dual economies either geographically or in terms of market or population. As such, the 'dual economy' remained a theoretical construct of doubtful usefulness.

Professor Groenman's paper made a distinction between backward areas in developed countries on the one hand, and backwardness in developing countries on the other, and emphasised that the problems in the two, though sometimes appearing superficially similar, were quite different. Professor Sovani thought that the distinction was vital because backwardness had a different texture in economic growth (backward areas in developed countries) or in the absence of it (developing countries). If the problem was stated in these terms rather than in terms of developed and developing countries, it gave more meaning to the role of the human element in backwardness that Professor Groenman had underlined. The example of Libya was perhaps interesting in this connexion. In the early fifties an expert group made a report on the possibilities of economic development in Libya. It noted that there were no entrepreneurs, etc., and that most of the preconditions for development were absent. It was generally very pessimistic about the possibilities. After some years oil was discovered and the whole situation changed dramatically. With the economic impetus from the development of the oil industry, mostly by foreign capital and technicians, indigenous entrepreneurs in other lines began to appear round every corner ! The expert group, when it revisited the country at this juncture, spent its days there laughing at its own earlier report !

While the role of the human element in economic development was important sometimes too much was made of it. Some writers overstressed the role of social factors in growth, such as education. There was a strong international lobby pushing education. In some developing countries, however, a very large proportion of the newly educated remained unemployed. Social and economic factors played parallel roles in development and one could not succeed without the other. They were complementary.

Professor Patinkin said that if we knew the answer to Professor Robinson's question we should know a great deal. He did not think one could state the issue in this way. But Professor Groenman's paper suggested two alternatives. If there were structural forces holding back development, then this meant that a power élite was at work. If this force saw its own interests correctly it would prevent development unless a revolution threw it out. Or it might learn that it could join the bandwagon and own the enterprises in the new types of development. If one had a traditional situation, then everything depended on education, information, etc. Again there was no hard and fast distinction. In modern society, a traditional framework accepted an élite. If education led to a change of structure, the élite could not sustain its position if either there was a revolution or long, heavy emigration. Sociologists rarely mentioned economic factors and Professor Groenman's paper was one example of this. On page 24, he talked of the power élite preferring investment in real estate, etc. Professor Patinkin suggested that the alternative rate of return on real estate might be high and investing in real estate therefore the best thing to do if one really was interested in the most profitable investment.

Professor Vito said that the answer to Professor James's question was both No and Yes. It was No if one took the frontier in the sense of an obstacle to the flow of goods and capital. It was Yes if one meant by a frontier that there was a real difference between the two communities.

Professor Groenman replied to the discussion. He said he would take up a few of the points made. He wanted to return again to the question whether backward areas were likely to be found on frontiers. Professor James had suggested a reconciliation and he accepted this possibility. But in his paper he had meant political frontiers. He was sorry he had not had the other papers before he wrote his own. He would especially have liked to have the paper by Professor Davin. But he accepted the point about the frontier. Professor James had suggested that in the Common Market frontiers were disappearing, as at Mont Blanc. But at the moment there was depression in the coal industry in the Netherlands, Belgium and Germany. The Netherlands was making its own plans to deal with the problem, and so were the other countries. There was no co-ordination; in other words the frontier was effective. This was what he meant. The frontier was important. Professor Marchal had mentioned maritime frontiers. The sea clearly prevented opportunities as well as encouraging them, but he agreed that there was no general rule about what effect a sea frontier would have.

On Professor Robinson's invitation to advise, Professor Groenman said he was grateful for Professor Patinkin's distinction between culture and structure. As a sociologist, he nevertheless gave priority to economic necessity. So economics came first. What a sociologist could do was to give guidance and education. This was very vague and made him conscious of his own position. To influence thinking through press articles, conferences, reports, etc., might take a long time. However, Rotterdam had the idea of developing the Rhine delta. This was a kind of self-fulfilling prophecy. The physical conditions did not justify the development; but prophecy made things happen. Professor Groenman was also convinced, with Professor Lajugie, that imitation was important. There was a big task for the State here, in persuading big firms to settle in backward areas. Perhaps one needed support for increased education. He agreed with Professor Turčan that there was a need for human infrastructure. He agreed that there were other structural factors that he had not mentioned, but did not think that the ones Professor Sovani had mentioned were critical.

To Professor Patinkin, he said that if the structure of a country hampered the development of its backward areas one did not want a real revolution. But one might have a peaceful revolution. He did not think the members of the élite in a country were chosen for their ability as risk-taking entrepreneurs, but to maintain the *status quo*. What they did might be the best things for themselves, but for the region it would be better if they chose risk-taking. Only in this way could one develop a backward area.

Regional Problems and Policies in the United Kingdom and the United States

Discussion of the Papers by Messrs Robertson, MacLennan and Chinitz

Professor Samuelson said that this was a straightforward paper. On the descriptive side, it was a familiar story. The U.K. was an unusually urban area. The recent physiocratic doctrine of Professor Kaldor was that one needed a farm problem; if one had one, there was a reservoir of labour. According to the new doctrine, the transfer from this to manufacturing was the key of rapid progress. It was like the tight shoe theory of comfort.

The U.K. was urbanised. The London complex had 15 per cent of the population. The regional problem was a dual one, with backward areas in the North and West, and rapid growth in the South. This interaction was important. The problem areas had a nineteenth-century industrial pattern. As in Veblen's thesis, the U.K. came early to the industrial revolution, and became frozen and fossilised too early. Ships, coal and cotton textiles had lost dynamism relatively to consumer good industries. It was a common pattern, with low wages and an older, less dynamic occupational pattern. Unemployment was above the national average. Emigration led to a skewed distribution of manpower. Social capital remained but was out of date.

Policy had developed in three stages. In the 1940s and 1950s there had been a social welfare objective. There had been transfer payments, with more automatically going to the problem areas. With only transfer payments used, one needed repeated doses to obtain the welfare effect. So, in the 1960s, a more positive policy had emerged, linking regional growth to national development as a whole. The regional aspect was emphasised both by the N.E.D.C. and in the National Plan. The growth areas faced problems of urban development, especially the planning of new cities. The backward areas often needed redevelopment too. How could we relate regional to national growth?

Robertson and MacLennan used several arguments. First, there was a waste of resources in backward areas because one could increase full-employment output by using them. He suspected some double counting in the paper. For this paper also said that when the balance of payments was difficult and there was a cyclical upswing, the regions added to total national resources and kept down the inflationary gap. This, to his mind, was the same point. If the other point was not valid, he doubted this one. Was it valid? Did backward areas hinder or help growth? Should we build on strength or weakness? It was undesirable to help only the best areas in a pluralistic society. Helping backward areas could mean throwing resources down the drain. Were not some subsidies to the region holding it back and not contributing to growth? It had been argued in a Swedish conference he had attended that forced investment in North Sweden led to a sentimental distortion of the production pattern. He would be surprised if there were no such conflict of interest in the U.K.

Second, Robertson and MacLennan argued that regional policy made labour more mobile; men moved from low productivity jobs to high. This was a gain to the nation. But it left stranded complementary but immobile factors, for example, workers too old to want – or be forced – to move, and capital with a useful remaining life. He thought he could construct a model where this did happen, but he could build others where it did not, and where the best thing would be to equate marginal productivity in every case. This was a good principle even where complementary factors were involved. Was this a utopian view of prices and costs in backward areas?

The British methods for solving the problem were direct controls, with industrial development certificates generously given in backward areas. There were also capital subsidies. The Regional Employment Premium (R.E.P.) gave a $7\frac{1}{2}$ per cent rebate on labour costs for seven years, and helped in the initial period. This implied that factor prices were high. Wages were low but perhaps not when compared with productivity. The American view was that the power to tax was the power to destroy. The power to tax differentially was the power to create. In the U.S.A., economists took a poor view of all erosion of the tax base, for whatever reason. If one had a useful social purpose, one should look at its costs and spend it openly. The argument for the R.E.P. was like the infant industry argument for protective tariffs. The infants would grow and then go on alone. Had research been done to see if this was the case?

In Puerto Rico, some firms stayed for the period of the tax relief and then left for Hong Kong. Footloose firms would follow a subsidy. The social scientist rarely checked up, later, on the effect of government policy. He wondered if the discussion could help.

Professor Samuelson reminded the conference that regions were not autonomous. As with Karl Marx's tombstone, the point was not to discover production coefficients, but to transform them. How would regional planners do this? He saw an analogy with the centre of a city and its suburbs. There was a backward region in the old centre of many American cities. The centre had too many old people. Should industry move to these people or vice versa? In the U.S.A. there was also the Negro problem. This was not regional because the bulk of the Negroes were now urban and they carried about the problems of backward areas. One of Professor Samuelson's neighbours would have liked to employ more Negroes, but they would not come ten miles into the suburbs, and bad public transport made it difficult. Negroes had few cars. Brazilian scholars had suggested moving the plant into the city, but there one could have riots. Would manufacturers move into cities and then face higher insurance rates?

In all regional planning there was a conflict of interest. Either policy was initially in the hands of special pleaders, or they were made so by the job. The problem was not one of an old (feudal) élite but of one created by the process itself. Those representing the region in Congress had reasons for not wanting it to develop.

Professor Lundberg introduced the paper by Professor Chinitz. He wondered if California really was a backward area according to accepted criteria. It had high unemployment but also relatively high income per head. One aspect that was neglected in Professor Chinitz's paper was the dependence of unemployment in backward areas on the level and growth of total demand. The concept of structural unemployment, and even more its actual size, should be a function of total demand pressure, measured by the average rate of unemployment. But there were plenty of people who liked to see the backward area issue completely as a structural problem that could not be helped at all by policies for general expansion. Now that total unemployment had been brought down from 6 per cent to below 4 per cent, unemployment in distressed areas must also have gone down. Professor Chinitz did not go into this question deeply. He said that the number of high unemployment areas had been going up. But how much had the rapid expansion of the U.S. economy since 1961 helped to bring down the degree of distress, and how much further could one go in this way?

Professor Lundberg illustrated the point from Swedish experience. Sweden had had potential distress in textiles after the Korean War. But full employment generally and a special shortage of manpower in engineering had attracted branch factories to the textile areas, so that the potential unemployment never became actual. If there were full employment and good training facilities, this would not eliminate backward area problems, but it would help a great deal. When a country like the U.S.A. got a more expansionist policy, then the problems of some of the distressed areas were reduced, especially with a more mobile labour force. To attain lower unemployment, support was needed from geographical and occupational mobility. If an efficient mobility policy existed, the expansionist policy could be more courageous without higher risk of inflation.

He did not think the U.S.A. wanted a policy of much movement of labour, but rather of more growth in the backward areas. But within wide margins there was no conflict between these policy aspects. One could work at the same time for more general expansion and more mobility combined with a selective policy for areas in distress.

He understood from Professor Chinitz that the U.S.A. needed various policy measures for different areas. He mentioned tax policy measures briefly. Could Mr Cameron, who was representing Professor Chinitz, give more details? In his second category of backward area, Professor Chinitz asked for technical assistance, long-term cheap funds, etc. He said these policies should be effective; but would they? For categories 3 and 4, Professor Chinitz asked for development distress, growth points, etc. He again said these were likely to be effective, but gave no empirical evidence in support. Was there any?

Also, what about the ghetto? There was room here for sociologists to comment. For economists with their methods of analysis, it was not easy to understand the problem. Professor Chinitz said there was sharp disagreement over the right strategy for ghettos. Should one work with or against market forces? A lot of the trouble came because Negroes were living in slums and in rented homes with absentee (perhaps white) owners. Would people not care more for property and become more active if they owned their houses even if kept in the present slum districts?

Professor Hoover said that Professor Chinitz had discussed the programmes of just one governmental agency. He pointed frankly to two indefensible aspects of the programme which no responsible person could defend. For example, there must be at least one area assisted in each of the states. Under another criterion, it was mandatory to give aid to the unemployed in Southern California. Both were perhaps necessary evils in the programme. On California, the Southern Californians were perhaps the most mobile people in the world. They were quite able to return or go elsewhere without undue distress. This was not an area of national concern. Professor Hoover felt that Professor Chinitz did not do justice to the regional effort as a whole, because he ignored manpower training and retraining. Probably in the long run this would be more effective than the measures he did talk of. Professor Hoover underlined the peculiar character of 'Appalachia'. This was not a region in an operational sense. It was too big, and had no centre and little intercommunication. The appropriate policy for the Appalachian region was to break it up. Each part was amenable to improvement by attachment to a growth point outside the region.

Professor Robinson had been reflecting on the challenging point made by Professor Samuelson, asking how valid was the argument that one was misusing capital if one applied it to the development of backward areas rather than to leading points of growth. He took this point, but felt one had to look more critically at the argument that if one concentrated on growth points, one was going to maximise the productivity of capital. Thinking in terms of the U.K., he wanted to go back to Professor Robertson's point that by concentrating the capital investment in this way, one lost the chance of giving employment to some people. One left behind in the regions not only males with jobs, but also the females with them. In nearly all less-developed parts of the U.K., participation rates for women were low. Movement out of the region left considerable numbers of people unemployed. Would we get more from a better use of capital than we thus lost from fewer at work? What happened to the total effect of our use of capital if we concentrated on growth areas? This meant mainly the London area and the Birmingham area. London was already bursting, and we were devoting much capital to building overspill towns to move people from London to the rest of the South-East. One not only had the capital costs of houses and social services; one also needed new road systems. He thought that while it might be a valid point that the productivity of capital in plant was higher at growth points, when one included social capital the aggregate return to capital might be lower than if one accepted lower productivity in the industrial sector but had less need to invest in infrastructure.

Professor Robinson did not believe that one could abstract from all the wider aspects of political economy. We needed to be ready to ask the question: Should we accept the ghetto problem and create a system where a manufacturer was not prepared to start a new plant where people lived? The ghetto was largely a question of the over-concentration of people in existing growth points. In the long run, we should try to develop more growth points.

In his own paper, Professor Robinson said that he had tried to make the point that it was right to think in terms of the infant industry argument. Professor

Samuelson said one should look and see what results there had been ten years on. There had been a careful study by the N.I.E.S.R. in the early 1950s of the problems of setting up plants in South Wales and other regions. What came out was that the learning period was longer in South Wales than if one built a factory in, for example, Birmingham. In the long run, these plants had survived and were now an essential part of the mother industry. In this case, an infant industry had thrived in the long run.

Professor Patinkin found Professor Robinson's analogy interesting. A uniform tax policy exacerbated these problems. Decentralising the tax levy for road construction would get some reflection of social costs. Differential subsidies might lead to the same results but they were not tied down to specific social costs.

Professor Penouil wondered about regional and cyclical policy. One could not ignore the effect of the cycle on regional development. In a period of expansion – inflation – the backward areas would experience exaggerated development, as, for example, in Pittsburgh. In a depression, backward areas were hit hard. One therefore got an amplification of movements. Depressions were often both more severe and more lengthy in backward areas.

A cycle for the nation had structural effects at the regional level. Depression led to difficulties throughout the economy, but especially in the underdeveloped regions. Some plans in backward areas might fail, with severe effects on the region. This was because national policies often ignored effects on the regions. So, when one stimulated demand, this only aided growth areas and did not help backward regions equally. This emphasised the need for greater co-ordination of national and regional policies.

Professor Samuelson, replying to Professor Robinson, said he would speak as Devil's Advocate. Every conference needed someone from Chicago to remind it of the value of the pricing system. Professor Robinson had said there were low participation rates for women in backward areas. If female labour really was available, why did this not show in its price? In the anthracite areas of the U.S.A., firms had moved in to employ the wives of miners. Were we back to the effect of national minimum wages? These were introduced for charitable reasons, but helped least those one most wanted to help in backward areas. Was a labour surplus being wasted?

In Sweden there was the same concern as in London about congestion. He saw the point about London. Again, there was a problem of the centre versus the suburbs. He would make the point that in city centres, one often wasted police, sewer pipes, etc.

Why, again, were there not low tax rates? In fact, tax rates in cities were high. One reason was that the transfer costs of welfare had to be borne. In a national economy with local taxes, people could move out of the city for tax purposes, but still use all its resources. This viewpoint gave a case for a return to the old view of the 1940s that one should meet stress where it was, by transfer payments. If one moved this burden, perhaps low tax rates would reflect the cost of capital in cities. In any case, was outworn social capital really all that useful? Perhaps we should put welfare costs on bigger rather than smaller units.

Professor Robertson said that Britain was a broader example of the Pittsburgh case – perhaps six Pittsburgh cases linked together. The other Chinitz categories had little relevance to Britain, though some might want to classify the Scottish

Highlands as corresponding to certain of Chinitz's categories. Professor Robinson had mentioned labour. It was clear that in the U.K. labour was perhaps the key factor in growth. The labour force would not grow at all, so we needed all possible growth in productivity. New developments would need and deserve labour. The country's reserves of labour depended on its pattern of employment as well as on participation rates. To raise productivity often meant structural change, moving labour from low-productivity sectors to high-productivity sectors. Given that the regional problem was largely a structural one, we were trying, in a sense, to obtain a new labour supply. We were trying to 'kill off' some industries as fast as possible. The change from lower to higher labour efficiency would take time. However, one could hope to reverse the change whereby former high-productivity areas had become low-productivity ones. He would advocate changing the regions as fast as possible, because this was the way to get self-sustaining growth in the long run.

Did we know the results? It was true that a number of industries in the regions were now declining. However, Scotland was, for example, now a centre of office machinery, earth-moving equipment and electronics production.

All areas in the U.K. were small. The standard American reaction to British problems was surprise about how worried we were about our regional problems, although Americans could see a source of worry in our labour supply. The point about the effect of a national minimum wage might be valid in the U.S.A. but not in the U.K. Higher minimum wages might hit small manufacturing industries but would not have a particularly strong effect on the regions. Higher minimum wages would hit the service trades, especially catering, which were found everywhere. There was a tendency for wages in backward areas to be higher than they should be. But should one push them down, given the ultimate objective of a national minimum wage brought about by greater efficiency? Or should we offset over-high wages in the short run? If so, this was a reason to support the R.E.P. We should not only look at backward areas in discussing regional problems in Britain, but at London and Birmingham too. The long-run choice was not whether to let labour move to London or Birmingham. Rather it was where the third agglomeration should be. Many conurbations were in backward areas. Where should the overspill go? Should it be 150, 200 or 400 miles from London? Taking any of these would leave one reasonably near a conurbation. But some policies would increase the population of Southern England, and others would shift the emphasis to conurbations that needed redevelopment, and to industries that needed structural change. On another point, the problem was not over the return on old social capital but over where to put some new. Professor Robinson was right that the overall return from capital might be higher if one went farther north and west.

Professor Plotnikov had found both reports very informative and interesting. He had two questions. (1) He would like more information on the effect of the policy of nationalisation in the U.K. on the development of backward areas. (2) A passage in the Robertson-MacLennan report referred to the R.E.P. How was the rate of the R.E.P. calculated?

Mr MacLennan said he would begin by discussing some aspects of Professor Samuelson's criticism of regional policy. As Professor Robertson had explained, the British regions were very much Chinitz, Model 2. They needed redevelopment rather than development. The problem was not so serious in terms of unemployment rates, or migration or participation rates, as in many other countries. The aim was to incorporate regional development into national policies aimed at raising the rate of growth of national output. Regional development could help by (*a*) bringing into production unused or underused resources at an opportunity cost of zero; (*b*) by making the demand for labour more uniform over the whole U.K. and so preventing the creation of excess demand in the South and Midlands while demand was still inadequate in other regions. Not only could extra output be got from existing resources but there would be an improvement in the balance of payments, removing its constraint on investment and so on growth; (*c*) the development of the regions would raise output in areas where the amounts that had to be deducted from it to allow for the necessary social costs (i.e. infrastructure) were less than in prosperous areas where such costs were higher. In the U.K., calculations on these points suggested that there was a case for regional development. The return to the nation as well as to the region from outlay on regional development was likely to be positive. This argument justified giving incentives to the less-developed regions.

Professor Samuelson had asked about infant industries. It was very important to remember that many backward areas were the growth areas of the previous century, with a history of good productivity. They would be easier to develop than, for example, South-West France or the Scottish Highlands. The labour subsidy given by the R.E.P. was very important since a learning period was inevitable before productivity rose to the same level in the backward as in the other regions. Incentives in the past had always been directed towards lowering initial capital costs. The R.E.P. was intended to reduce operating costs for a period. This was not a deliberate effort to alter relative factor prices; its aim was to offset the learning period. Second, where the problem of development was that of a backward region with clusters of productive industry, one needed to help those firms already there. R.E.P. could be regarded as a regional devaluation that would make the backward regions more competitive. The backward areas contained some efficient firms within declining industries. They could benefit from the R.E.P. and become the core of a reduced and rationalised industry. With Britain's balance of payments constraint, there was a need to exploit any way of getting extra output where it would not cause inflation. The argument for the R.E.P. was that it would cause little leakage of demand from the regions, but stimulate increased output and bigger sales to the more prosperous regions, with a consequent fall in the pressure of demand there. One would then have export-led regional growth as the result of a regional policy which developed the regions in a way that reduced the loss of national production and helped to remove the balance of payments constraint.

Mr Cameron wanted to steer the discussion towards the U.S. case. Both Professor Robertson and Mr MacLennan had said these were difficult and rather different problems. He would try to clarify the position. Professor Chinitz had five categories of area. First, there were areas, mainly in California, that were prosperous growing regions with high median incomes, immigration, high growth and high demand for labour. Some had a narrow (perhaps defence) base and were hit by demand changes. Some had a broad base but a tremendous population inflow. Between 1950 and 1960 some had population increases of

100 per cent.   The growth in labour demand was not yet fast enough to take this up.   Some had highly productive agriculture, especially large-scale vegetable production.   They were areas that would not be regarded as backward if one were not looking for a national strategy.

The second group of areas was found in New England, Pittsburgh, the Alleghenies, etc.   These were of two kinds.   The first were centres with a hinterland to supply, like Pittsburgh.   The second were small manufacturing or mining towns that grew up in the shadow of Boston and so had small tertiary sectors.

Third, one had the rural areas, with a lot of labour in agriculture and a rough balance between immigration and emigration.   Natural resources were inadequate and one had the problem of adapting to a new economic base.

Fourth, one had poor, depressed counties.   These were mainly in the South-East of the U.S.A., for example, the coastal area of North Carolina.   There was a low median income, high outward migration, a slow growth of jobs, but a rapid natural population increase.

Fifth, there were areas like Tennessee, Kentucky and Arkansas.   These had low median incomes, rapid natural population increase and high unemployment, even rates of 25 or 30 per cent.   In terms of unemployment, the problems were most severe in categories 4 and 5.   Birth-rates were high, the problem long term, and there had been little benefit from the expansion of the U.S. economy since 1964.   Other areas had been brought closer to equilibrium.

Taking the 1,387 areas of the U.S.A., category 1 accounted for only 38; category 2 only 37; category 3, 492; category 4, 441, and category 5, 242.   The problem areas were thus mainly rural areas needing development rather than renovation.

Professor Winiarski stressed certain common points in the theoretical approach to the problems of backward areas in the United Kingdom and in Poland.   First, there was a similarity in definitions.   Backward areas were characterised by incomplete use of natural resources, manpower and (in certain cases) existing fixed assets.   The development policy was to lead to better use of those resources.   Second, the backward areas were characterised by a lower standard of living, the raising of which was the social aim of development policy.   The need to concentrate on developing chosen regions stressed by Professor Robertson and Mr MacLennan therefore seemed very important.   There was a need to rationalise economic policy by choosing such backward areas, where economic activity would be most effective.   This required an approach which would take account of general national economic policy, considering spatial aspects in a developing process.   In order to base policy on economic theory, it was essential to link classical location theory with modern growth theory.   The integration of those theories represented a promising field of research.

Professor Groenman discussed ghettos.   The fact that people lived in ghettos did not make them a regional problem.   A backward area was not a social group, though it was a social system, with strong relations between the surroundings and the people.   We tried to develop a region, living together.   The ghetto similarly displayed concentration, but the basis of the system was largely a social one.   Instead of classifying it as a region, there was a better case for putting the ghetto in the same class as old-age pensioners or war veterans.

Dealing with a ghetto meant dealing with a particular social category. We must look first at its position in society.

Professor Nussbaumer wondered if one needed to consider Professor Chinitz's category 1 a case for development. Only insufficient income and too little employment for old residents should properly be regarded as criteria of under-development; otherwise a circular argument would result. Areas incorrectly regarded as offering exceptional opportunities and attracting population would have to be granted aid until they came near to offering the opportunities immigrants were looking for. The only case for aid therefore was if the area had a narrow economic base, which made it more a member of category 2. He also commented on the question of how much area development should be carried out. He thought the problem was not whether or not to do it, but how much was needed.

The Round Table had scarcely mentioned the question of how detailed regional plans should be. First, should one not distinguish sectors of the economy? Was not a general R.E.P. too global? Should it not specify sectors? Second, should not particular smaller areas within a backward area be given special treatment? We needed a well laid out pattern of growth points in each backward area.

Dr Marsan wondered about the difficulties of the American South. Were these now problems of minor areas, or of the South as a whole?

Professor Vito commented that a national minimum wage was said to hinder the development of backward areas. One could exaggerate its importance. It was not so much the uniformity of the wage level that was the problem, as the fact that this level was higher than labour productivity. Yet it was hard to conceive of a variable minimum wage. Especially in backward areas, too low wages would reduce demand. In practice, the wage structure in any country was differentiated. Some areas had strong trade unions and wages much above the minimum wage. What was the significance for the whole economy of a wage higher than productivity in growing areas? This problem was much more important than the minimum wage. Professor Vito wondered if the R.E.P. was not a compensation for minimum wages being higher than marginal productivity.

Professor Lajugie noted that in their paper (p. 46) Professor Robertson and Mr MacLennan wrote on the relation between regional and national planning. He was especially interested in what they said at the end of page 47, where it was suggested that a regional plan must be effective. It must not be just a set of measures but a coherent statement, for example, an input-output table.

Professor James was grateful that Professor Chinitz had produced several categories of backward area and that Mr MacLennan had spoken with the accent of the Sorbonne !

In their paper (p. 40), Robertson and MacLennan said 'A further argument for regional development which is particularly important in the British context is the opportunity which the underemployed regions offer for running the economy at a higher level of capacity utilisation without creating inflationary pressures'. He did not understand this because he did not see how one could thereby prevent inflation. He thought development was necessarily inflationary. As a region developed, the rate of wages must rise. He saw that in the early stages there might be no inflation because of underemployment. But was underemployment a worse evil than full employment?

The discussion of the R.E.P. seemed to be based on Professor Kaldor's ideas. Did Messrs Robertson and Maclennan share these views?

Professor Robertson began the reply to the discussion. To Professor James he said that no Scotsman ever said anything he would not stand by himself! His general attitude was that regional policy was not worthwhile unless it was concerned directly and purposefully to contribute to the growth and development of the whole economy. The social function of regional policy in the past was not now relevant, so one must link regional policy to the productivity and efficiency of industry in the region. Policy must therefore (*a*) alter the industrial structure, killing old industries as fast as possible; (*b*) be linked to growth area policy; (*c*) aim to raise private investment in the region; (*d*) use resources which would not otherwise be used, or would actually be misused.

One must also integrate regional policy with a policy to get the best return from public investment, especially in transport. In his view, it was not possible to develop as good a regional policy as Britain had without much public control. He did not defend the details of the policy, but thought it was better than it used to be and perhaps better than in the U.S.A. The public investment required was partly in social capital, like roads, partly in road and rail transport; it partly reflected the fact that Britain had social control over housing, health, and educational investment. In the U.K. it was necessary to look at the details of locational policy and come to terms with the physical planner.

Mr MacLennan argued that the justification for regional policy in the U.K., and especially for the R.E.P., could be set out in terms of increasing the output of the national economy. If the R.E.P., as was hoped, halved the difference in unemployment between the less prosperous regions, and the national average, raised participation rates and slowed down migration from the declining regions, then it could be shown that there was a positive real return to the policy. Should the R.E.P. be more selective? There were problems here. How would one select? How long would it take to decide each case? If it were not selective, might not infant industries remain infant? How would an employment subsidy aid firms? If one assumed monopolistic competition, the fall in the cost curve would raise output to an extent depending on the elasticity of the demand curve and the degree of competition. If there were oligopoly and the R.E.P. lowered cost curves, but within the gap in the marginal revenue curve associated with the 'kinked' demand curve, then one must turn to the idea of industry being encouraged by higher profit margins. In the long run this would create expansion, which would further lower costs. Would firms leave development areas when the R.E.P. ended? One had to remember that there were still important capital subsidies available in development areas and constraints on setting up firms in the prosperous areas. A firm might well be better off in a backward area.

He thought that one could demonstrate that the R.E.P. would be an important additional factor in increasing regional output and exports, evening up the pressure of demand over the whole economy.

Mr Cameron thought that Professor Samuelson had caught the philosophical mood of American economists and that this was right. The basic problem was one of high unemployment often associated with low incomes. Professor Samuelson had noted the risks of investing in such areas, where it was tempting for each to claim federal funds.

Positive returns, except under careful definition, were not likely to be great. Agricultural areas had low production and low motivation. There was very limited social capital in these predominantly rural areas. One must examine the correct strategy. Conceptual justification in the U.K. case (raising full-employment output, lessening inflation, etc.) was not relevant in the U.S.A. Two things were being tried. First, more power was being given to the regions with problems. The Appalachians showed how states could work with federal involvement and good results. This scheme emanated from the states, and before any legislation there was a two-year study of relevant problems. In the rest of the U.S.A. there was a scattered policy, concentrating investment in the worst areas first. This, he thought, would compound problems.

On the ghetto, there was as yet no clear understanding that the solutions to rural depopulation and to the ghetto problem were related. Often Negroes moved from rural areas. Because political and social issues came in, it was not easy for the economist to measure costs and benefits. An effective policy for raising aggregate demand within the U.S.A. would be better. Increasing wages in depressed areas merely increased their problems.

FOURTH SESSION

An Appraisal of Regional Development Policy in the Aquitaine Region

Discussion of Paper by Professor M. Penouil

Professor Groenman said that this paper gave a descriptive and critical account of regional policy over a period of time. It was concerned with Aquitaine, near the Spanish frontier in the South-West of France. The discovery of gas there gave a chance to test the theory of growth points or areas. Apart from oil and gas, however, there was no growing sector.

Professor Groenman asked a number of questions. (1) Why was there relative stagnation and permanent backwardness in Aquitaine? (2) Was the Lacq development the creation of growth poles? (3) Had the coming of new gas-using industries already failed to occur? (4) Was the growth pole policy therefore a failure? Professor Penouil was pessimistic but there was no reason to reject the growth pole theory.

Professor Groenman said he would begin from Professor Penouil's important distinction between a growth point and a growth point focus. For him, this was a distinction between developing the whole region and only a part of it. The difference suggested that a growth point should have strong links with other areas, and also social and human elements. In defining what might be growth points, interpretation was important. A growth point and a development point (growth point focus) might be similar in their effects, but the latter was much less integrated.

Professor Penouil distinguished three features of growth. First, one had new, dynamic activities within an economic and human environment. This could provide technical staff and equipment. Second, a growth point was not market oriented, but had local raw materials. Third, the more a growth point used local manpower, the bigger were the multiplier effects. Was Lacq a real growth point? Professor Penouil's answer was negative. The impact on the local economy was small. The product was not processed locally and labour costs were only a small component in the total cost structure. The effect on the regional balance of payments was not favourable. Thus, this was only a development point (growth point focus) and no more. The great hopes raised by Lacq gas were idle. But was ten to twelve years long enough to justify so definite an answer?

Why was Aquitaine still backward? The influence on its structure had been too small, said Professor Penouil, to reorganise production. The same was true of the aerospace industry. There were other reasons. There had been state support, for example, of oil refining and aerospace. With such grants, the region got support for bridges, roads, hospitals etc. Tourism had been stimulated, but Professor Penouil doubted if the stimulus could ever be effective because of its seasonal character.

Aquitaine had been privileged in its government grants, but only relatively to the rest of France. Public assistance had been largely symbolic. The State had too many commitments elsewhere, not excluding its efforts in integrating France with the rest of Europe. There was a tendency towards a dual economy, because secondary industries had already developed outside the region. It was easier to carry out a development policy in the nation than in a region. The conclusion was that growth point activities could be combined with 'scatterisation'. Only if state intervention was in line with development plans for the region would it help.

Reverting to his questions, Professor Groenman said that on (1) he wondered if the time was too short for Professor Penouil's pessimism. In the Netherlands, the Philips complex at Eindhoven was a real growth point. It had taken more than twenty years to develop.

On question (2), was Professor Penouil right that the growth point idea had not been tested? Were there other real examples of growth points to evaluate their effects?

Third, if there were such regions, were they planned growth points or did we merely speak of them *post factum*.

Fourth, if we wanted growth points, what could the State do to encourage them, especially in Western Europe?

Fifth, was not Professor Penouil's distinction strange? It seemed to have been invented afterwards and was descriptive only. It needed bringing closer to action. Suppose one had a regional development policy, wanted growth points, and had the means to introduce them. One then tried to evaluate their success. One was disappointed if the region was not revolutionised and thought the policy a failure. Did one say 'Sorry, but we made a development point and not a growth point.' This was not a satisfactory distinction, and his advice was to forget it. Let us simply evaluate why growth points did or did not lead to the results we wanted.

Professor Robinson said that when Professor Turčan and he had planned the programme, they had wanted to raise particular types of problem in relation to

particular countries.   In France they had thought it important to raise the issue
of growth points.   This term was naturally associated with François Perroux.
They had also thought France a country which was very highly polarised around
Paris, and lagged in having fewer growth points than, for example, the U.S.A.
Could we therefore concentrate the discussion on growth points, and bring in the
experience of other countries?   Was the apparent failure of Lacq a condemnation
of the whole theory of growth points?

Professor Fauvel wanted only to try to help situate Aquitaine, which included
Guyenne, the former British possession, in the French economy.   If one looked
at the industrial development of France, there had originally been coal and steel
industry in the North-East and various developments in the Paris area.   There
was also industrialisation around Lyons and Annecy, and in a small area round
Marseilles, though not as much as around Genoa.   Instead of development
linking Paris and Alsace-Lorraine, more recently the Seine basin between Paris
and Rouen had developed, and the Rhône valley.   But it remained harder to
integrate the rest of France into the E.E.C., especially the Massif Central and
Brittany.   Also there were no cheap transportation facilities and not much trade
or business linking Switzerland and the Atlantic coast.   The region south of
Bordeaux was in similar difficulties.   This was a simplified introduction, but he
hoped a useful one.

Professor Lajugie wanted to show the precise place of the region.   Professor
Fauvel was right that development had first been strong in the North-East.   At
school one had been taught that there were two parts of the French economy.
There were the industrial areas north and the agricultural region south of the
Loire.   The line now went from the mouth of the Seine to the mouth of the
Rhône.   The area to the east was industrial and that to the west was rural.
Aquitaine was in this western region and its position was worsened by its
distance from the centre of the country.   The notion of the Aquitaine region was
not widely accepted.   Professor Fauvel had complained that this had an historical
origin in being a British possession.   When administrative divisions in France
had been created to help regional development, France had been divided into
twenty-one regions.   Aquitaine was a region based on Bordeaux with five
departments.

Mr Petrella-Tirone thought it useful that Professor Penouil's definition of a
growth point was central to the notion of a complex of activity.   It seemed to Mr
Petrella-Tirone that an indispensible condition for ensuring that such a growth
point had the expected effects, and through it the success of a 'big push' policy,
was the simultaneous creation of a coherent complex of activity.   This was,
moreover, one of the conclusions of the group of E.E.C. experts which had studied
the conditions for establishing a growth pole in the Bari-Taranto area of Italy.

Mr Petrella-Tirone wondered if Professor Penouil was right that it was almost
impossible to create a development pole in a very poor area.   Could one not
envisage the possibility of regional action by the creation in such an area of a
series of secondary, supporting poles linked to the most important, or the nearest,
development poles?   A practical conception of development should be based on
the idea of axes and networks of development, not simply on growth poles.   This
would provide a coherent and rational solution to the conflict over the concentration or dispersion of investment.

This emphasised the need to know who should set about creating development poles, what criteria should decide the geographical and spatial distribution of different growth points, and what, apart from industrial investment, was required for the success of such a policy. In this field, it would require a change of view, especially in countries where regional policy had been strongly empirical.

On the first point, Professor Penouil thought the role of the State in creating growth poles was limited. Mr Petrella-Tirone thought it would be hard for a poor region in an industrialised country to make real progress without massive state intervention.

Professor Samuelson wondered, on growth points, if one should not accept Carlyle's distinction between the role of the great man in history and the gradual accumulation of known forces. Was the growth point theory of Carlylian character? He would give an example of an apparently successful effort in New Hampshire and Vermont, an old area. Professor James had distinguished slowly-growing areas from ones in actual decline. Vermont's population had been declining from 1860 to recent years. The reason had been the opening of the railroad and of the prairies. This had ruined Vermont as a farming area. Abandoned farms were everywhere, occupied by professors as summer homes at low prices.

Every state in the U.S.A. shared in aid. In 1961 it had been found that three states did not qualify for aid on existing criteria – Vermont, New Hampshire and Iowa. It had been hard to provide for Vermont and New Hampshire. This was old textile territory, like Pittsburgh, and the North-West in the U.K. Textiles had gone south. One possible western growth point was Manchester, New Hampshire. There, a huge textile mill was broken up and fifty small companies occupied parts of the mill. There had been a shift in comparative advantage. Wages were low and firms took advantage of them; it was like setting up the South in the North! Firms produced machine tools and paper products. This was small industry, and it had worked. So now Vermont grew. The situation was similar in Massachusetts. The town of Laurence had been distressed, but was now an electronics centre. To keep things in balance, one must remember Maine. This was nearer the border and was at a disadvantage in transport and electric power. It was still a low-income area, but was making the best of its opportunities, though it found it hard to qualify for federal aid.

Professor James noted Professor Penouil's definition of a growth point and of a development point, which were both interesting. A growth point involved a short time period and a limited area. A development point covered a larger area and a longer period, changing the structure of the region. So in Professor Penouil's paper there was some interesting thinking on growth points. Why was Lacq not a real growth point? Perhaps a good growth point had to have a product that was hard to move, for example, coal. Electricity and textiles were too easy to transport, and gas too. So Aquitaine was not a good region for a growth point.

Professor James had liked Professor Chinitz's list of categories of backward area. This supported his point in the discussion of Professor Robinson's paper, on the difference between slow-growing and declining areas. The Chinitz distinctions were more subtle. Professor James said that a region in outright decline was the Lozère. In Aquitaine one had positive growth, though slow.

The Lozère département had lost 50 per cent of its population in fifty years. What could one do in such a region? No one would think of making it a growth point. Several efforts had failed. This kind of region was hard to develop because there was the wrong cultural situation. He thought that with such long-run and structural decline, one needed a quite new kind of activity. Perhaps tourism, or woodwork, would help; there had been American help in attempting to establish these. But all initiative seemed to be from outside, the young people having left. The Lozère was clearly not the whole French economy, but its problems illustrated an important point.

Professor von Böventer listed factors essential for the growth of a new centre, factors which to a large extent were substitutes for one another – and hence were neither necessary nor sufficient. First, there must be other raw material sources that could attract additional firms; this way certain agglomeration economies might arise. Second, if the first firm or firms were big enough and had important inter-industry links, other firms might find it profitable to settle close to, or on, them. Third, one needed satisfactory transport and communications facilities; this would be a way to develop hinterlands and to connect the whole area with the rest of the national economy. Fourth, one had to have administrative functions to attract other people. Fifth, one needed a big enough hinterland, with a population that was sectorally mobile but not too mobile regionally. Then people would move into growth sectors but not out of the region. Unless the combined effect of all these factors was strong enough, satisfactory growth would not occur.

Professor Robinson wanted to pursue this line of thought. Could one consider Lacq and generalise from its experience? In Italy, in 1954, when he had worked on the Vanoni Plan, the philosophy had been that such a plan would first create a set of expectations in the whole nation. In the South, there would first be an investment in infrastructure, giving local multiplier effects, with the incomes spent in the region. Things had worked out less well in practice, perhaps because there had been large leaks of expenditure. Much investment expenditure had gone to the rest of Italy or the rest of the world. Incomes were often spent on the products of other parts of Italy, so that the Plan did not raise incomes in the region as far as had been hoped. It might have been better to concentrate on potential growth points, like Naples or Bari, hoping that these would let smaller leaks of expenditure out of the region, and that the local multiplier would spread.

If one looked at Lacq, this was a growth point only in a limited way. Local investment expenditure was low; wages expenditure in Lacq was a small part of total income from Lacq. So the multiplier was small and leaks were large. If one was trying to work by creating new growth points, what were the essential things? First, one needed potential growth points as efficient centres of operation. One should not try to create a growth point in remote Highlands or in North Michigan, because one wanted to reduce unemployment in these areas. One needed a real comparative advantage for the future. Second, one needed to establish activities with a high proportion of local inputs. Third, it was very desirable indeed that a large proportion of the products established in growth points should sell outside the region one was trying to develop, so as to finance necessary imports of inputs and of consumer goods for the region. Finally, the building of a local infrastructure should be used as initial investment to develop further activities. He kept returning to the discontinuities mentioned by Professor Samuelson in the first session. One needed a minimum scale of activity for a local subsidiary or for a new firm in each activity. Small, hesitant expenditures were almost useless. Larger expenditure might, in the end, pay off better. But there was almost certainly a minimum critical size.

Professor Vito congratulated Professor Penouil on his report, and agreed with Professor Robinson on the experience of the Vanoni Plan. Two types of structure could be called growth points. One, like Lacq, with natural gas and oil resources. The other type of growth point was where investment concentrated in an underdeveloped area, with a major industrial complex built up under public ownership, like Taranto. These two types were both growth points in respect of the hopes placed in them, the expected polarisation of much activity and the stimulation of a whole region. One could not say the experiments had failed, but they had not lived up to expectation. Natural gas had been found both in less-developed and in highly developed areas. In the latter case, Northern Italy, one did see multiplier and other effects occurring. In Sicily, which was underdeveloped, the same effects did not occur when natural gas was found; there was no polarisation of economic activity.

What lessons could one draw from this theory of growth points? The theory did not yet exist, but had been derived from history and experience, for example, the history of coal and steel in Northern Europe. Coal had a polarising effect of considerable importance. One could interpret the French situation as a case where several centres were built up but concentrated in the North and East. No doubt, one could envisage a theory of growth points on the basis of past experience. One could make a further step by saying that the essential need for a successful growth point was to choose a point with high development potential. One could try to foresee where the multiplier effects of an increase in incomes would be greatest, and where integration effects would have most influence both up- and down-stream of the growth point.

To Professor James, Professor Vito repeated that the chances of success were greater if the necessary infrastructure already existed in declining regions. Critical regions with no infrastructure were hopeless, but areas like Liège had a favourable situation where the multiplier effect could be felt. As for the discovery of gas, did the planner have any choice? The planner came after the event. Could we expect the same effect from natural phenomena as from considered planning decisions? Lack of results from discoveries like that of natural gas should not lead us to disregard the idea of growth points. The time scale was significant. In a Liège-type area, one got results quickly, but in a totally undeveloped region, it took much longer.

Dr Marsan thought that Italy had probably made more mistakes than Professor Robinson had suggested. A growth point was usually a large firm, in the beginning. Large firms were more mobile. Most large enterprises in Italy, both I.R.I. and private, had set up plants in the South. But a large firm with mainly forward linkages – like gas – had least potential to begin growth. Nor could the multiplier effect in the case of a product like gas be very important. One needed manufacturing firms with backward linkages. There was still little experience of this in the Italian South. Smaller firms, even if specialised, would not move automatically. This introduced problems of incentives and how to use them.

But some things, like management training and research, while lacking, could hardly be compensated for. So even if one did not dismiss the balanced growth concept, reading the textbooks did not help much.

Professor Penouil replied to this first part of the discussion. His aim had been to begin from a concrete example and find in what circumstances one could transform the structure of an economy and start growth. Not every attempt at industrial expansion, of whatever kind, led to growth. Professor James had underlined the distinction between growth points and development points. He wanted to note that the economic mechanisms were a little different. With growth points, there was emphasis on the activity created. Lacq was a growth point. It had considerably raised local production. It was not a development point because some mechanisms were missing. Development points were based especially on multiplier effects and these would not work if there were too many leakages. The gas industry was not one which could help the region in which it was based to any great extent. So he thought there was a marked difference between the two concepts – a difference between economic mechanisms.

On the problem of time, Professor Penouil said that in the case of Lacq one could make a judgement, despite the short time period. The product went to the most developed parts of the whole economy. So, if there was going to be polar-isation in the region, there had been an opportunity for it to occur. With gas, once the industrial infrastructure was created, there was a fall in investment.

Professor Penouil thought that one of the most important problems of growth points was the relation between the activity created and the climate in which it occurred. He had looked at a number of characteristics, for example, size. He thought this was not an essential feature. He rather saw a link between size and climate. A large firm could play the role of a growth point, but the importance of an industry could be out of proportion to the size of the region, and its activity could therefore fail to fit into the local climate. So we should ask whether the essential thing was to have close links between the industries or activities in the area. The growth point would play this role if it was established in a receptive environment. If not, multiplier effects would not occur. Professor Penouil gave the African example of Abijan, in the Ivory Coast. He was struck by the fact that no large industry had developed there, but a multitude of small private firms, with close relationships. This had created the kind of climate where growth could occur, and that had not happened in some neighbouring economies. So perhaps one should seek to create both the economic and human climate needed to make a growth point develop.

There were four points *Professor Delivanis* wanted to raise.

(1) How dangerous it was to reach conclusions on the basis of incomplete data. We did not face this danger with Professor Penouil, who provided a lot and added the appropriate comments. Professor Delivanis disagreed, however, on the concentration of firms as a mark of development. Very often big firms had smaller profit rates than small ones, as was shown by a recent investigation in the U.K. In those cases, businessmen were right in avoiding too-big firms as they might not be able to master their problems. On the other hand, the percentages of increased turnover in various French harbours, with Bordeaux coming low in the list, might be due to the fact that turnover in the basic period was already high in Bordeaux.

(2) An unfavourable geographical position and unsatisfactory transport possibilities were a handicap to economic development. This was the case with Aquitaine, which was also in the less-developed part of the French economy. The Common Market connection aggravated this disadvantage, as had been mentioned by Professors Fauvel and Lajugie.

(3) The creation of a pole of development simply by starting a big exploitation of a single sector was very difficult. In order to secure this, it was necessary that within the area concerned the product involved underwent numerous treatments, that much employment was given, that the plants involved were not too complicated so that local manpower might be used, that spare parts, raw material and machinery could be produced on the spot; and lastly, that there were no income leaks on a scale worth mentioning. It was difficult to secure all these conditions in a developing area. This explained why so often development plans based on one sector failed. We could conclude, as had Dr Marsan and Professor Penouil, that development plans had more chances of being successful when based on the concept of balanced growth in as many sectors as possible. Of course everything became more difficult, particularly when the government indulged in nationalisation, or even did not prevent the fear of it. Success became more probable when the development sectors were able to export from the area.

(4) His last point was on the greater difficulties of regional take-off as compared with national. This was stressed by Professor Penouil, and more could be said by our Italian colleagues, who had experience of it during their successful efforts to develop the South.

Mr MacLennan wanted to pick up some of Professor Penouil's gloomy conclusions. He wanted to concentrate on size, because this was the crucial aspect of growth point theory. Professor Robinson had introduced the idea of critical sizes. He would suggest some reasons why such discontinuities were important. First, there was the question of how many more jobs were needed in a region, in a given period of time, to prevent emigration. He thought that to deal successfully with the problems of a backward area, perhaps one or two large firms were necessary in order to give a sizeable initial boost to the number of new jobs.

Second, infrastructure was always emphasised as an attractive factor, but to get maximum benefits from it required planned concentration. This was closely related to the minimum size of community required in a certain region if it were to act as a focus of growth in that region.

Third, there was size of plant. This had to be big enough to give the economies of scale required to compete in markets outside the region – to export. One needed adequate scale to get the inter-industry effects of size; to allow backward linkages in particular. Furthermore, to get high incomes in a given region, one probably needed to depart from the example of Vermont or New Hampshire. One might have problems, if one let small firms develop, in getting firms that could pay high wages.

Still on scale, one had to look at the size of plants in component firms. If these were on an adequate scale elsewhere, the firms would not be induced to move to serve new plants in a region unless transport costs were high, or unless the size of the client firms in the region were such as to permit economies of scale to be obtained by new component plants in the region.

Professor Robertson said we had discussed three versions of declining areas, those in outright decline, agricultural areas in need of development, and industrial areas. In the U.K. examples of outright decline were the North-West Highlands and perhaps Mid-Wales. They had no economies of scale or reasons for development. There was no case for developing them unnaturally, since they lacked one essential ingredient – people. In the North-West Highlands, there was no area where one could bring together a labour force for work. Should we not, therefore, forget this area? Even oil or natural gas would not help. The second type of area was agricultural. Such areas had some economies of scale, but one needed a good case for expanding outside existing market-places like Plymouth in South-West England, or Inverness in the North-East Highlands. The third type of declining area was industrial. In this type of area, it was essential to select a growth point, and it mattered little where one chose so long as one kept to one's choice. In the centre of Scotland one had an industrial centre of two million people (the Glasgow conurbation) and in the east an administrative centre of about half a million people. The first need for economic development was labour. The main centres for development might therefore lie between Glasgow and Edinburgh. The labour must also have the right characteristics. This meant training. It was desirable to allow a diversity of occupations to develop, including non-manufacturing occupations, and to create an environment that would supply, over the years, enough managerial labour. One therefore needed to bring in hospitals, universities, etc. These had to be of a minimum size, but their location was also under governmental control. One needed a communication system, as one had between Edinburgh and Glasgow. One needed to co-ordinate administration so that all decisions could be taken for the benefit of the region as a whole. Administrative services would give to growth points those things that most areas had even without having industry. Many towns had employment without any industry. How big had towns to be to give employment on a sufficient scale to get the necessary diversity of occupation?

Professor Davin said there were three essential factors for a growth point; two – time and functional integration – had been much discussed. The third was the need for a centre of decision. Only rarely did one see the three factors considered together. Integration was not just a physical matter, but required an intellectual framework. Many problems were partly human. Professor Penouil was right that a growth point was above all a complex of activities which led to the polarisation of incomes. Whereas Professor Robinson stressed the value of labour-intensive growth points, he would say that capital-intensive plant could help the region because of the income flows they brought to it. They made possible economies of scale and of specialisation. We needed to know how to get this functional integration. Introducing banal activities was useless. If firms were so specialised that they sold to a large area, one had in the long run a complex of activity which could develop.

As for the centre of decision, if this was not in the region, there was a danger of multiplying decisions. Decisions would also be taken, perhaps, in pursuit of objectives other than those of the region itself. With all three factors considered, growth point policy could succeed.

Professor Mihailović said we naturally asked where the idea of growth points originated. The influence of Marxist thought was evident. Terms like 'structure' and 'contradictions' had been borrowed from Marxism. The growth point might be conditionally used as synonym for the dominant element with the greatest formative force in the structure.

One could look at both theoretical and practical reasons for having confidence in growth points, but on condition that these were interpreted as the key elements in changing structure. Structure was the basis both for theory and for practical measures. It was necessary to make new efforts to develop the concept of structure.

In changing structure, where did one start? An important activity would contribute a great deal to changing structure if it were appropriate to regional conditions. Professor Penouil's paper found no broader local influence from the discovery of gas. But, perhaps, gas would start a growth point if one could base industries on it.

Professor Nussbaumer said that the rapid development of the area around Linz in Austria in the last thirty years was a good example of successful development policy and showed the conditions which had to be fulfilled. The region had been a prosperous agricultural area, favourably located, with a government centre and some medium-sized industries. However, it needed a heavy industrial base and firms to take up labour released by agriculture. Development of the big-push type came with German industrialisation of some focal points of the area, efforts which were continued after the Second World War and favoured by the fact that the area, situated in the American occupation zone, was eligible for Marshall Aid. Large and steady investment over many years had made the area one of the most prosperous in Austria, rivalling even Vienna. The area also proved large enough to provide advantages of regional concentration and for a take-off into self-sustained growth.

Professor Fauvel said that the discussion had not concentrated much on Aquitaine. This was the region of the Gironde, and the Garonne valley, that of the Universities of Bordeaux and Toulouse, and no one had ever imagined that the population of Bordeaux or Toulouse would move more than a hundred miles to the South. Lacq was an important source of power, but in a mountainous, sparsely populated agricultural region, somewhat isolated in the Pyrenees. These issues, i.e. the development of the urban areas around Bordeaux, Toulouse and even Bayonne, were more important than the possible development of Lacq and its gas.

Professor Penouil, replying to Professor Delivanis's point on the size of enterprise, said he could understand that small enterprises earned above-average profits. In Aquitaine, small firms were not dynamic, and the profit margin was low. Most of them were suffering from the recession at the moment. This penalised Aquitaine because of the small markets of these firms; bigger firms might have done better. The region suffered from its isolation. It was a region badly linked to the rest of France, and to Europe. So one might ask if the E.E.C. had not penalised this part of France. If one wanted more than a growth point, it was better to concentrate on areas with good links with the more developed parts of France. As for the port of Bordeaux, he agreed that it was in decline. What was serious was the comparison of the growth of the traffic of Bordeaux with that of other parts. Development had had little effect on

Bordeaux's trade, except for oil products. Bordeaux could perhaps not hope for a big export trade.

There had been general agreement in the debate on a number of points. First, economic development, which created a number of complementary activities, would be the most successful. Second, the provision of good communications was one of the first needs for economic development. Geographically isolated growth points could not succeed. Third, economic development implied state intervention. Professor Davin had insisted not only on the role of the State, but also of public and private decision centres. He thought that often the State had to work under enormous constraints. This was clear in the French economy. When the State decided to act, it could do so only in sectors where it had unusual control. These sectors were not necessarily important or relevant to the region. For example, there was aerospace industry near Bordeaux. But it was too early to use the aerospace industry to establish a growth point. The labour needed was of a specialised kind and had to be well-trained. So, while the role of the State was vital, it could not always operate as it would ideally wish.

Finally, there was the problem of markets. For development, local firms clearly needed markets. Now, with the development of the E.E.C., when new demands appeared they were quickly satisfied by dynamic firms in the North of France, Belgium, Germany or Italy. The development of the E.E.C. had therefore tended to make it progressively harder for the local firm in a backward area to develop. It had to make bigger and bigger efforts, and even then, might well not succeed.

FIFTH SESSION

Two Case-Studies: The Walloon Area of Belgium and the Fribourg Area of Switzerland

Discussion of Papers by Professors L. E. Davin and J. Valarché

Professor James introduced Professor Davin's paper. He said that his problem was serious. The Walloon area was not a small part of a country that was a backward area, but half of the country. He would not discuss Professor Davin's figures, and would avoid political problems. He thought one should say that in the paper there were two things, an analysis of the problem and a suggested solution. He thought it was best to look at solutions rather than diagnosis. In what category was the Walloon area? Its position was less good than that of Aquitaine – less good because the latter's rate of growth was reasonable. This was a region where the two main industries were in decline – coal and metallurgy. This was not a cyclic recession, but a structural one. Thus, the Walloon area was in a situation between that of Aquitaine and an area in outright decline.

Professor Davin's analysis was again in terms of growth points. His definition was interesting and took us back to what Professor Robinson had said on the first day. Professor James wondered whether a growth point could begin from one big industry or several smaller ones. If one could base a growth point on several smaller industries, could one then guarantee growth without co-ordination between these industries? And would the market alone do this, or would one need some kind of planning? Professor Davin's solutions seemed valid for other regions. Some of his ideas were for institutional changes. Since 1966, sub-ventions had given quite good results. Thinking of bigger areas, not just mining ones, it was necessary to make a new start. One had to attract new, expanding industries. This raised problems of technical choice. For example, Professor Davin spoke of introducing metal fabrication. In the Walloon area, this needed metal workers, well trained. He agreed that it was a growing sector, but one would need agreement with other countries in the E.E.C. Professor Davin also spoke of bringing in the electrical industry. This was also expanding, but Belgium would face competition from big Dutch producers. Electronics and nuclear power were also mentioned. He was hesitant about these because in Europe there was a lot of discussion of nuclear power; but again its development needed European consultation.

Professor Davin emphasised the need to seek industries with external econ-omies, and he agreed that the Walloon area needed industries like those in Northern France, Germany, etc. So she needed joint plans for industrialisation, quite apart from the removal of tariff barriers, which would be achieved by the E.E.C.

Development also needed transport. The Walloon region must be linked with some of its neighbours. It needed an axis of development, which passed through it, perhaps from Lille to Cologne, but not from Rotterdam to Paris. Was it feasible to put the area on such an axis?

Professor James wondered if Professor Davin looked to European industrial planning to save the Walloon area.

Professor Šik said the paper was interesting not only because Belgium had regional problems similar to those of Czechoslovakia, but similar solutions too. The basis of the regional problem was structural. In earlier days it had been seen as a simple problem of the relation between agriculture and industry. This was how the retarded development of Slovakia, with insufficiently developed industry, had been considered. Czechoslovakia had tried to solve this problem by the rapid industrialisation of Slovakia. This had happened in a way that was linked with the earlier planning system, using state subsidies. It was a system in which efficiency had been entirely neglected. Professor Šik said he did not want to go into further details but simply to say that economic equality between Slovakia and the Czech lands had not been achieved by the earlier planning methods.

Czechoslovakia had now moved to economic management and this made it clear that the problems were far more complicated than the relation between agriculture and industry. Though industrial production in Slovakia had risen, productivity was not as high as it was in the older industries of the Czech area. The problem of efficiency also arose in other sectors and regions of the economy. Earlier, heavy industry had developed where coal and iron ore were found. Now,

O

when the criteria for efficiency were enforced in both the industrial and regional allocation of investment, the danger was that incomes and welfare might lag in some areas. This might be because of an insufficiently complex industrial development like that in Slovakia. Or it might result from a one-sided emphasis on heavy industry like that in some old, traditional industrial regions (Kladno and Ostrava).

Incomes and the standard of living had risen fastest in the regions with modern industries like chemicals, electrical engineering and electronics. This was because old, traditional industries needed, on average, less-qualified labour than the newer ones which were no longer tied to particular areas. These industries moved especially to where they found infrastructure available – such as well-qualified labour, colleges, universities, research institutes and cultural attractions for their executives. Enterprises in the new industries were, therefore, reluctant to go to Slovakia or other areas lacking such infrastructure.

Should one rely on spontaneous development or induce new industries to move into the less-developed regions? Prof. Šik thought it would not be economic if Czechoslovakia were not interested in faster industrial growth in these areas, especially since this growth had a bearing on the development of agriculture. As soon as the industrially-backward areas began to be neglected, agricultural activities in these regions also declined. It would also be unfortunate not to use existing social capital like housing and infrastructure. Nor would it be economic to concentrate the whole of economic development into a few great industrial areas.

This was why Czechoslovakia was trying to solve these problems in a planned way and by using financial measures similar to those mentioned in Professor Davin's paper. Besides moving modern industry into backward Slovak areas with an unbalanced industrial structure, Czechoslovakia wished to encourage new complexes which would supply services to agriculture and process agricultural products.

In order to interest the management of enterprises in investment in the backward areas it was first necessary to speed up the development of infrastructure and to extend the education of qualified labour. The development of cultural activities in these regions was necessary as well. Moreover, the Government had to make these areas attractive to firms by making possible lower rents and cheaper land. It was possible to use a payroll tax with different rates according to regions so that labour would be made cheaper where development should be encouraged. There would be investment credits with both lower rates of interest and slower repayment. These were new problems that the conference should help to solve. As soon as they were expressed quantitatively, Professor Šik thought it could be seen how little we knew about these problems even today.

Professor Hoover was troubled by one point in Professor Davin's paper. On pages 127–8 it was said that unemployment in the Walloon area was high, (about 30 per cent higher than in Flanders) and that it would be higher still were there not substantial emigration. So he was surprised (on p. 125) by the strong recommendation for an increase in the Walloon birth-rate and the encouragement of immigration, especially since foreign workers tended to move straight to the mines. Population growth was a symptom of the problem, not a cure.

Professor Lajugie made two points. First, he thought it was because it was a frontier region that the Walloon area looked for different solutions. Second,

Professor Davin said the solution must be to bring in new industries (pp. 137–8), but this could not happen autonomously. This was similar to the problem in the U.K. where it was argued that there was a link between local and national development. Here we had European planning too. Would there not be difficult problems in reconciling these various levels of planning? So far, it seemed that the E.E.C.'s efforts were inadequate. Was it likely that there would be European co-operation on investment?

Mr Cameron discussed how to select prime-moving industries. (1) They should meet regional, or national, demand. (2) They should produce goods with high income-elasticity of demand. (3) The net value added should be high. (4) There should be strong backward linkages. (5) They should suit the labour supply. (6) There should be a marked spill-over to the general efficiency of the region.

Professor Davin assumed that one should bring in large industrial groups. He would himself appeal for greater flexibility. He would accept the value of large industrial groups but would be more flexible on the scale of plant. There were several reasons. First, in the U.S.A. the fastest-growing industries often had small or medium plants. Second, in industries like electronics, learning costs were high, and production required a good deal of research. Skilled white collar workers liked working in metropolitan centres. Firms learned from their competitors in major metropolitan centres which had active entrepreneurs. Perhaps in electronics, when firms had found a standardised process, they could then set up smaller units in backward areas. There was some evidence that in some industries, at some scale of production, external economies were internalised. For example, this happened in accountancy, management services and business equipment. Major groups had a small backward linkage effect in the region though a big one in the economy.

Third, management was important. In big industrial groups, managers often regarded the regional plant as a sub-optimal unit for non-economic reasons. Managers saw being sent there as a kind of penalty, or as a test to be taken. Mr Cameron asked for much more flexibility in thinking about the prime-moving industry. Both large and small groupings were needed. The unit did not have to be large.

Professor Robinson also wondered about the types of industry to attract. He agreed with Mr Cameron that these areas did not want to become too specialised. First they needed to represent big enough aggregates to get the relevant external economies. These were external either to the unit or to the industry or to the whole group of firms. His impression was that external economies were becoming more mobile and available to firms outside a given area. But in many respects the external economies of the town were becoming more important. What one wanted was an economic aggregate at the growth point, big enough to begin growth, but also with the right mixture of occupations. One wanted a centre that would use labour from agricultural areas, and with high female participation rates. In the U.K. it had proved hardest to revitalise decayed mining towns. One often had to start afresh.

He was surprised that no one had referred to industrial estates and new towns. Industrial estates had been started in the 1930s at Slough, in South Wales and in Durham. Later there were a number of new towns. Initially the aim was to establish towns of not less than 100,000 people. Now there were three in the South-East, at Stevenage, Crawley and Harlow. All were approaching that size and all had a wide variety of industry. The important thing was to think not of one industry but of a total complex of the right aggregate size.

Professor Arakelyan said that the problems being discussed were serious and complicated. He had been interested in the different approaches. Basing himself on Russian experience, he thought the best approach to regional and national development was a 'complex' approach. He shared the opinion that one had to develop backward areas as complexes, with a variety of industries represented. He wanted to outline the approach of the U.S.S.R. where an economic region was taken as a basis for planning. We were speaking not of backward areas but of regions.

First, there were national industries. Firms in these industries were large enough to use mass-production methods. Then there was the medium range of industries, supplying these national industries with what they needed. Third, there was the lowest range of the industrial structure – industries producing for local consumers. These included enterprises in the food industry, in ready-made clothing and so on. The right kind and degree of co-operation between the three groups of industries allowed the U.S.S.R. to approach the development of a given region by setting up industrial 'complexes'. Ensuring the proper correlation between these groups of industries and enterprises was a major task for planners and for economists in the U.S.S.R. He did not want to hide the fact that there was some inefficiency in such planning, but on this basis the U.S.S.R. had achieved success in developing all its regions, including the leading and backward ones. He thought this approach – the 'complex' approach – was bound to succeed.

Professor Vito had read with satisfaction of the breakdown of areas into depressed and less-developed areas. Naturally the distinction implied different treatment. Professor Penouil had said that it was not necessary to encourage small- and medium-sized enterprises, and said that he preferred leading enterprises. Professor Vito thought that where there were external economies, even small and medium plants could develop and have an influence on the area. He did not understand why anyone should be discouraged by the need to train management, so that producers could be managers.

Professor Vito agreed that the most appropriate sectors were where value-added was highest, but he wondered why it was necessary to appeal for the co-operation of the State. Was it to ensure markets of sufficient size?

Professor von Böventer saw some similarities between the Walloon region and the Ruhr. One was that in both cases the mining firms had been hesitant to work out genuine solutions to their problems; and solutions had now become harder. In the Ruhr one had neither established new towns nor systematically revitalised old ones. Actually, the cities at the fringes of the area had grown faster and had drawn on the labour at the centre in the unemployment area. The best example was Cologne. Had similar developments occurred in the Walloon area?

Professor Davin replied to the discussion. The first basic issue, whether to concentrate on the poorer areas, the richer, or both, was an old controversy. The solution must vary according to the size of the region, and whether the region was an integrated one. The answer depended basically on the degree of functional and intersectoral links within the region and with other regions.

On the problem of employment, he accepted that Professor Hoover had found an apparent conflict in his paper. But one must separate cyclic and structural issues. The problem of employment in steel was cyclic, but in coal it was structural. The structure of production and the system of education and training could be more easily changed with a younger population structure.

Third, one needed to alter a declining economy; but with which industries? He thought this was a problem which depended on the present speed and acceleration of technical progress. One needed to find which of the entirely new industries one could bring in to reanimate the region. One must operate on the psychological plane. So one had to ask again about size of region.

Fourth, how could one revitalise the region? He had no magic solution for Belgium, which was one-quarter of the area of France. Could one set up a nuclear, a space or an oil industry in its underdeveloped region? No. He must call for flexibility. The region needed new industries, but also to benefit from built-in stabilisers. This must be done in a bigger area, a bigger political unit.

On this, he thought that where finance was concerned, one should look less for subventions to solve the problem than to new markets and a changed structure of competition. How did one get international competition?

The problem of the Walloon area was that of ageing industry, an ageing population, and psychological ageing too. In face of this, local policy makers were overwhelmed. There was no plan, method or philosophy. In this small region, renewal was possible only by collaboration with France, the Netherlands and West Germany. One could make a national effort to reach a common policy. First, Belgium had tried to get France and Belgium together, but this had been a failure. The only result had been discussion and debates. The only lesson learned was that problems were easier to solve if there was co-ordination. Smaller problems had arisen in discussions between Belgium, the Netherlands and West Germany over coal, and these might well turn out to be equally unsuccessful. In France and Germany, their peripheral regions were concerned with exports. In the Walloon region, we were concerned with a unified region in Europe. There was this difference between regions in a small and in a large country. So he was pessimistic on natural agreements. The more hopeful line was through E.E.C. The answer was gradually to wear the problem down. Changing structures was like starting a revolution. The efforts of intellectual pressure groups might in the end lead to a radical solution to the problem.

In opening the Discussion of the Paper on the problems of Switzerland by Professor Valarché, *Professor Delivanis* said it turned out that Professor Valarché had in fact written two papers, one on the backwardness of the canton of Fribourg and the other on the role of the teritiary sector in Switzerland. He intended first to deal with the first paper, raising points on which he disagreed with the author, and stressing the main points on which there should be discussion. He would then go on to question certain points in Professor Valarché's second paper.

The points of disagreement were (*a*) the astonishment of the author that, despite Switzerland's small size, there were regional differences; (*b*) the attribution of Switzerland's slow development to its liberal policy; and (c) the attribution of Fribourg's delayed development to its rich neighbours.

He believed that regional differences were to be found in every country in the world, even if they were smaller than in Switzerland. The differences there were intensified by the mountains, and by historical developments of the past when certain Swiss cantons had been incorporated into foreign countries.

Professor Delivanis wanted to stress that planning could secure faster development only if one could accept that planners were infallible, and could apply the economic principle within the framework of the national economy. Since planners made mistakes, just as private entrepreneurs did, a liberal policy could not be the problem. Being close to rich neighbours as a rule accelerated economic activity, as orders were given to the poor neighbour, and increased employment made available to its inhabitants. Certain shops and professions might suffer a setback, but this could not affect the development of the whole area.

Professor Delivanis then drew attention to the context of Professor Valarché's first paper. Fribourg was not underdeveloped, but simply below the Swiss average, somewhere near the quite favourable Austrian level. The inferiority of the development of the canton of Fribourg was proved, according to Professor Valarché, by differences in the following, all going against Fribourg canton:

(a) income per head as shown by the proceeds of the federal defence tax, and the turnover of post office remittances, according to estimates by Dr Rosen of Basel;

(b) employment in the primary sector, which employed 10 per cent of the active population in the whole country, and 30 per cent in Fribourg;

(c) the quality of houses;

(d) the ratio of health services to inhabitants;

(e) the ratio of cars to inhabitants;

(f) the expansion of the tertiary sector;

(g) the number of girls attending high school and university.

Industrial decisions were, as a rule, made outside the canton, even if the plants were there.

Professor Valarché explained that regional development was carried out in Switzerland first, through federal government subsidies for road construction and maintenance, in negative relation to the cantons' financial strength, and to aid the population of mountain areas; second, by the canton itself; third, by municipalities; fourth, by individuals who got responsible jobs and were able to show initiative in the private sector. The canton of Fribourg attracted firms because manpower and natural resources were available, often helping firms to reduce costs, to rationalise and to reduce fluctuations in employment. Professor Valarché believed that the relative absence of external economies and of investable funds both in the private and in the public sector, contributed to regional stagnation. He added the attractions of neighbouring areas and cities. This certainly applied to trade in expensive items like luxury services.

As far as the second paper of Professor Valarché was concerned, Professor Delivanis disagreed on three counts: (a) that the secondary sector was more important than the tertiary in Switzerland; (b) that the tertiary sector was concentrated; and (c) that the latter was not sufficiently developed.

He did not think he could share the author's opinion about the extraordinary importance of industrial exports for Switzerland's prosperity. Services were very important, and investments financed in part by foreign capital, despite the efforts of the central bank, even more so. There was no doubt that Swiss banks and insurance companies were concentrated, but this did not apply to hotels, trade, the liberal professions and, beyond a certain degree, even the co-operatives.

The author believed that the tertiary sector was not sufficiently developed in Switzerland, as 40 per cent of those employed worked there, while the percentage in the U.K. was 50 per cent. This was no proof. He also considered that Swiss education was not satisfactory without proving it. Professor Delivanis felt that Professor Valarché should prove his assertions, which he could certainly do, given his extended knowledge of the Swiss economy.

Professor Valarché commenting on the first of his two papers said that what was important was to justify the choice of such a small region as Fribourg for his topic. It really was a region, with political and economic unity. All parts of the canton had an agricultural population with low incomes. The neighbouring cantons had less agriculture, more tertiary activity and higher incomes. Fribourg was not a declining area, but a slower-growing region. It was not like Southern Italy. It had a high proportion of farmers and farm workers in its population, and an income per head like that of Switzerland thirty years ago. Compared with South-West France, Fribourg was more industrialised. Also, in his sense, it had no support zone. Bordeaux was a bigger town than Fribourg, and there was more planning in France.

Professor Lajugie asked questions on the financial system. Professor Valarché said in Section 3 that federal institutions were rare. It was mainly the canton and communes which had to finance industry. Yet, in Section 5, the paper underlined that the canton suffered loss of private capital. It seemed to him that firms already in the canton financed development as well as activities in the rest of Switzerland. Was it possible to measure the size of financial flows to and from the canton of Fribourg?

Second, on methods of regional development in Switzerland, Professor Valarché said one-fiftieth was financed by cantons, but that they were allowed to act on a private basis, with no programme for co-ordinating decisions. There seemed to be no co-ordination of policy. This 'market' system determined the sectoral distribution of activity. Was it possible to accelerate these movements?

Professor Penouil returned to the problem of the frontier. One needed to look for its influence on the region and accept the diversity of situations. The Ruhr was on a frontier, as was Fribourg. So were the French regions of the Nord, Grenoble and Aquitaine. Each had a regional problem with three basic causes. First, there was the place of the region in the national economy. When a frontier region was important, the national plan would make use of its resources. If it was a backward area, it was penalised. Second, there was the level of development of the region on the other side of the frontier. This might be very developed. Third, there was the opening of the economy to others, via institutions like the E.E.C. In the E.E.C., developed regions would benefit more than backward areas. It was a matter of conquering markets. Underdeveloped regions risked a disruption of their trade.

However, one could modify regions by tourism. In this sense a frontier region often benefited. Switzerland as a whole was an important and interesting example of this. Did tourism help it to develop growth points?

Dr Marsan understood that Switzerland did not co-ordinate the regions centrally. This kind of lack of co-ordination in development policies had led to problems in Italy and in U.S.A. The shortage of labour in Switzerland had been relieved especially because it was near the frontier of an overpopulated country (Italy).

Professor Robinson was puzzled by a phrase in Professor Valarché's paper (p. 157). This dealt with the absence of external economies. He was surprised that proximity was a problem. He thought of the way complementary industries to the Birmingham motor works spread right out into South Wales, to Swindon and other towns at considerable distance and were only too willing to do this. Similarly, British printers were always looking for cheap labour in small towns. Again, the wool textile trade was centred in Bradford, but later established plants in the North-East of England where there was female labour available. He was puzzled why surplus labour could not be mopped up if economic policy in Switzerland was expansionary enough.

Professor von Böventer wondered why Switzerland imported so much foreign labour when there was underemployment in agriculture.

Professor Vito said there had been a comparison of Fribourg with Southern Italy. Fribourg was not declining and the level of income per head was not very high. The level of underdevelopment was not to be seen in absolute terms but relatively to the rest of the country. The solution might be the same for Fribourg and Southern Italy.

Professor Valarché wound up the discussion. He pointed out that Fribourg was part of the Swiss plateau, with no mountain barrier. Although there was much movement of labour, Fribourg still had a lower income per head than neighbouring cantons. This had tended to mean that the service sector was drawn away. There was an exodus of qualified labour, perhaps for social or cultural reasons.

Professor Delivanis had asked if the tertiary sector helped development. Tourism accounted for only 10 per cent of the receipts of the Swiss balance of payments. In Austria it accounted for 30 per cent. It was not a major influence. The best period for Switzerland had been 1945–55, when it had exported a large amount of manufactured goods, especially mechanical engineering products and chemicals.

The tertiary sector was not very concentrated, though in Fribourg there was some concentration on shoe shops. As for whether the tertiary sector was too small, Professor Valarché said that Switzerland was the second country in the world for income per head, but had a smaller proportion of the population in the tertiary sector than the U.K.

Professor Valarché said there were no figures on the flow of profits from Fribourg. However, Fribourg received funds from the centre for investment in roads.

Professor Penouil had asked about the influence of frontiers and the place of the region in the national hierarchy. One did not always find the poorer regions on the frontier. Fribourg had a bad reputation for its economic base. However, he did agree with Professor Penouil that tourism was a factor that was able to accelerate economic growth.

Dr Marsan had asked about the lack of planning. The difference in income per head between rich and poor cantons was in the ratio 1 to $3\frac{1}{2}$.

Professor Robinson had asked about the role of external economies. Fribourg did have big factories, but they were very isolated. One only got external economies if one produced goods for sale outside the region.

Professor von Böventer had asked about foreign labour. Peasants from mountain villages found it hard to integrate themselves into large towns, so they remained in agriculture, while foreign labour worked in industry.

Professor Valarché agreed with Professor Vito that backwardness was relative. He saw three kinds of backward region. (1) Declining regions like the Walloon area. (2) Underdeveloped areas which had not yet taken off. (3) Slow growers, like Fribourg. In fact, Fribourg was growing as fast as the rest of Switzerland, but it was thirty years behind.

So far as the role of the tertiary sector in accelerating growth was concerned, in Fribourg the tertiary sector was growing slower than the secondary. The tertiary sector depended on state intervention. In the period of rapid growth, 1955–1965, the number of employees had risen 50 per cent in the secondary sector and only 20 per cent in the tertiary.

Professor Valarché distinguished three kinds of tertiary establishment. First, one had independent ones, like the Church. Second, there were those that accompanied industrialisation, like commerce, transport, etc. The third promoted growth, as did banking and insurance. Fribourg was too small to have a reasonably big tertiary sector. The State had intervened, for example, in developing education. Differences in average incomes between Fribourg and the rest of Switzerland ranged from 50 per cent to 100 per cent; transfer payments reduced these differences to between 5 per cent and 10 per cent.

SIXTH SESSION

Regional Economic Problems and Policies in West Germany and Sweden

The Discussion of the Papers by Professor E. von Böventer and Professor E. Bylund

The papers were discussed together, but were introduced separately. *Professor Nussbaumer* introduced the paper by Professor von Böventer. The point about backward areas often lying on frontiers seemed to be proved by the German case, with only one backward region not located at a border. However, even this exception was interesting because it showed that the influence of centres of

o 2

agglomeration was important only over relatively short distances. Besides, one could not easily speak of absolute underdevelopment in Germany, and differences between regions were often small. Border problems also were emphasised by West Germany being a federal state.

The measures taken by the political authorities were similar to those elsewhere. Infrastructure was improved, cheap credit was given, the Government placed orders in the relatively underdeveloped regions, etc. An interesting aspect was the respective roles of federal and local government.

Professor Nussbaumer was interested by the fact that there were two reasons for underdevelopment in West Germany. The first was the historical one that this was an agricultural area with too little industry. The second was an outside shock – the Second World War. There had been a large population inflow since 1945, and a new border between East and West Germany. The new frontier had broken many economic ties, disorganised industries and changed good locations into bad ones and vice versa. Conditions had also been relatively favourable to widespread economic development since 1945. If one looked at Germany in 1950, the population was evenly distributed, partly because of the war. Also the high mobility of the population had aided economic development. With the loss of Berlin as the capital, there was no dominant centre of agglomeration, in the political sense; Germany was the only country with this degree of decentralisation.

Professor von Böventer went on to discuss several examples of development. First, there was that of the comparatively well-to-do agricultural area Schleswig-Holstein, which lacked industry. Second, there was a comparatively poor agricultural and forest area, East Bavaria and the Upper Palatinate. The third was an area close to the zonal border, North Hessen. There were small farms, poor agriculture, the post-1945 population inflow, and the new border as a symbol. There was consequently a shortage of transport routes. The effect of the new border was obvious and serious.

Professor von Böventer used North Hessen to discuss some principles. He argued that it was not so much raw materials that made for growth as a well-balanced industrial structure. A high dependence on agriculture might even help by providing for reserves of labour. This conclusion was important whatever industry set up there. He argued that the development of towns depended largely on accessibility – a transport problem.

Professor Nussbaumer thought the influence of frontiers was sometimes exaggerated, and was decreasing with the development of the E.E.C. Professor von Böventer showed that the effects of a border were obvious for only about twenty kilometres. He also showed that in Germany, the optimal size of a town was 100,000 or more. The growth chances were better for a town of more than 100,000. Having an administrative centre increased the attraction of the region. Professor von Böventer thought forty to eighty kilometres was a good distance between cities. But was this a useful point? Professor Nussbaumer thought that perhaps half an hour by private transport, or three-quarters of an hour by public transport, was a better criterion, since this was a distance easily tolerated by commuters, and since time was often better suited to express economic distance than mileage.

Professor von Böventer talked of the main reasons for development and growth, and asked how far one could split up an aggregation to find what was the minimum economic size.

Finally, Professor von Böventer provided a model for regional development in West Germany. This was perhaps more relevant to his country than to others because it was relatively homogeneous. He constructed a model like those of Lösch and Isard for studying the spatial pattern of a region. Professor von Böventer's general conclusion was that there were no really serious regional problems in West Germany, and only slight backwardness.

Two questions remained. First, what was the optimum size of an agglomeration in a less rigid (politically) country? Second, how could one use resources in agricultural areas more efficiently? His solution was: improved communications and a more helpful political context.

Professor Turčan said that Professor Bylund gave an interesting discussion of the problems of Norrland, a backward and underpopulated region which was predominantly engaged in agriculture and forestry. Especially during the 1920s and 1930s, the Swedish Government had encouraged immigration into the region. The combination of agriculture and forestry with timber and mining industries guaranteed a prosperous life for a long period. With a rapid growth of a widely dispersed population, labour surpluses appeared. The development of agriculture in Southern Sweden, with the industrial specialisation and the rationalisation of forestry, made economic development harder in a region like Norrland which depended on its primary sector. The growing surplus of labour had led to emigration to the South, with its high level of activity and its shortage of labour in its population centres since 1950. This emigration had been selective, and, with the fall in population, had led to an ageing of the population, and to economic and social problems.

From an economic point of view, it was important to make sure of enough labour for forestry, which was important for the whole Swedish economy. The social problems sprang from the current and expected fall in the population in the interior of the region. This increased the dispersion of the population so much that even essential services were no longer assured. Professor Bylund held that a village where the population fell below 3,000 lost the economic base needed for schools, sanitation and service trades. With transport equally unprofitable, contacts between the people of the region diminished.

To halt this process, the Government had chosen a policy of economic and political intervention. Over five years it would spend 800 million kroner to give credit and subsidies to industrial firms which expanded or began activities in Norrland.

Even ignoring its modest scale, Professor Bylund showed that this policy led to two kinds of problem. First, in a period when the aim was to make the Swedish economy more efficient, the Government was using some of its resources to help an industry which, from a national point of view, was of only marginal importance. This slowed down the rational process of moving population from the North towards the industrial centres of the South where labour was always needed. Second, the policy of governmental support went outside the region that needed it. Credit and subsidies had to be asked for by the firms that wanted them. With firms concentrated on the coast, 80 per cent of aid went to exactly those areas which were growing quickly without it; only 40 per cent went to the needy central area. This policy had slowed down emigration from the North as a whole, but did not solve the problem of the interior of the country.

Sweden had developed an efficient economy. In the South there was a dynamic, specialised industry and an agriculture which supplied many of the primary products needed by the population. In the North, the coastal towns had modern infrastructure, and industries based on the natural wealth of the region, especially timber. The agricultural areas in the interior of Norrland had old-fashioned characteristics and lost their ability to move into new lines of activity. Forestry, which was of prime importance for the region, had experienced a period of rapid rationalisation and increased its output while using less labour. In these conditions, emigration simply reflected the interests of the population, especially the young, in leaving agriculture in the interior of Norrland and moving to where they had a bigger range of jobs to choose from, more opportunities for training, and better cultural and leisure activities.

Professor Turčan did not see how small towns could survive in Norrland. Migration to the South and within it would strengthen its industrial centres, and the coastal towns of the North would develop quickly. There might well be widely-separated larger towns in the interior of the North, but they must be big enough to support an efficient and profitable service sector. Perhaps the problems of forestry, which were mainly social, would become purely technical ones.

Professor Oelssner compared the development of the German Democratic Republic (G.D.R.). This was a fairly small country with a population of 17 million in a territory of 108,000 square kilometres. But it was one of the world's first ten industrialised countries. After 1945 the most backward areas of Germany were in the G.D.R. – the provinces of Mecklenburg and Brandenburg. The former's people, said Bismarck, were always 100 years out of date. But Brandenburg was even further behind. The Junker landlords ruled completely until 1918, with a residue of feudalism. Even under the Weimar Republic, there was no development. The Junkers wanted government subsidies. After 1945 the main task of the G.D.R. was not to develop backward areas but to overcome the consequences of the war. The fact that nevertheless the G.D.R. overcame the backwardness of Mecklenburg and Brandenburg had two causes. First, the development of a socialist society made it possible to concentrate on the most important tasks. Second, regional and general policies coincided. Administrative reform in 1952 sub-divided the two provinces into six smaller areas.

Development in the G.D.R. was influenced by the division of Germany. The engineering industry in the G.D.R. was cut off from old markets. Indeed, part of the industry had to be recreated in the G.D.R. Many of these new plants were in Mecklenburg and Brandenburg. A new steel complex was created near Frankfort-on-the-Oder with a new town. In Rostock there were new shipyards, with engineering and fishing and fish processing. Cottbus was a most important energy area in the G.D.R. with soft-coal mines and four electrical plants. There was a high-temperature coke plant. Potsdam was now a metal-producing centre of 40,000 people with three steel mills. To give a general indication of how things had worked out since 1945, industrial production in Rostock was up 175 per cent, in Brandenburg 159 per cent, in Potsdam 143 per cent. Rostock had a large deep-sea harbour. Agricultural output developed largely by concentration on small farming in co-operative units. So the number of cattle per 100 hectares of land was up in the Rostock area from 49 to 71; Schwerin 52 to 68; Brandenburg from 43 to 65, and so on.

Professor Oelssner noted that favourable conditions existed because the leading property-owning class in Germany had been eliminated. By land reform, estates of more than 100 hectares were distributed to peasants. The general state of the nation's health, especially the provision of doctors, was improved. There was a very impressive development of education. The 'one-class' school for 7–14-year-olds had dominated pre-war Germany, but was eliminated in the G.D.R. The reasons for this were that the socialist State concentrated funds on education. This was done partly at the expense of light industry.

A few years ago the G.D.R. had introduced a new system of planning and directing the national economy. One result was the decentralisation of economic activity. Factories could re-invest accumulated funds. Would a new regional imbalance be created thereby? He thought this danger could be overcome. Planning was not diminished but concentrated on a plan for five years. Here structural development was decided.

Integration within COMECON could lead to change. For example, the spread of synthetic fibres had hit traditional textiles. Labour in textiles was often in small towns and immobile. So the problem had been solved by introducing a dynamic electrical and electronic industry in these areas. Labour had been retrained (and paid). The skills needed were easily acquired because production needed only semi-skilled labour. Perhaps private industry would have shied away from the task of retraining. New factories were not needed. It was clear that a backward area had been developed only because of social changes in the G.D.R. Backwardness could be overcome only if (1) the most important means of production and exchange were in the hands of society and the basis of private property vanished; (2) the socialist State had power to integrate regional development for the whole economy, and the planned and balanced evolution of the whole socialist State guaranteed development of economic and cultural activity in all regions.

Professor Davin said that Professor von Böventer had looked at the problems of the Eifel. This was near the Ardennes, and the problems of both were similar. He would ask how far the initiatives in the Eifel took account of needs on the other side of the frontier.

Second, on planning, how far was economic policy in West Germany able to accept planning, which seemed essential to balanced economic growth in North-Western Europe? We all spoke of regional economic policy, but behind this concept were there not sharp distinctions? Was not regional economic policy in West Germany exclusively a matter of infrastructure? Other countries also chose which regions to develop. So, in the Netherlands, there was regional improvement, but a choice of which regions to improve, and sectoral choice too. Was this not a big obstacle to bringing regional policies in these countries into line?

Professor Delivanis said that Professor von Böventer was perfectly right in saying that West Germany had no backward areas but only regional problems. These existed in low-income agricultural areas with overpopulation, backward agricultural areas with small farms, special problem areas caused by the

East–West frontier, and new problem areas with inflexible and backward industrial structures. The two first types of problem were cured by prosperity and over-employment, combined with a mobile labour force, and in some cases, e.g. the Black Forest, by bringing in new industries. The third group had to be tackled by planning, supported by private initiative. The last clearly needed planning, and he wished the paper writer would give more information on what the German authorities and those who were directly affected had in mind.

Professor Bylund's paper implied that the Swedish policy of subsidisation had pushed those living inland in the Norrland to settlements near the coast, aggravating the problem inland. Did not Professor Bylund exaggerate this danger, as well as the fear of excessively big cities developing, and of amenities for the old being inadequate? In view of all Sweden's achievements, he would be interested in hearing more about differences in income per head between the coastal and inland areas.

Professor Winiarski asked Professor Bylund what kind of links there were between regional planning and Swedish Government policy aiming at reducing spatial disparities. He also asked, what range of co-operation there was between regional planning institutions, the Government and private firms to help regional development.

Professor Groenman had heard that Sweden was to begin research into the viability of villages. In Professor Bylund's paper, the minimum number of inhabitants was put at 3,000. In Professor von Böventer's paper, one found mention of villages of 1,000. Was this because of differences in population density in the two areas? And what about the viability of villages under economic planning?

Professor Robertson also wanted to talk about size. For industrial societies, he agreed with what Professor Robinson had said on Professor Davin's paper, that in the U.K. the new town experiment had been relevant and interesting. Now we had moved to the view that a new town needed a population of at least 100,000. If this held in all areas, then the Norrland area was on the way to extinction.

He agreed with Professor Turčan that the real hope was for larger coastal communities. He did not see why agriculture could not get higher labour productivity. Forestry gave a long lived crop, and so cycles of employment. It could not give steady jobs without considerable industrial backing. In the U.K., forestry was attractive for the Highlands, but these did not give regular, small-scale employment, or work for relatively immobile female workers. Tourism was also seasonal and so unsatisfactory. He saw little hope for Norrland, and while attracted by villages of 3,000 thought them unlikely to succeed. One would end up with market towns bolstered by service employment, but even this would need a concentration of population. He could not see the answer for such an area. In an industrial area, he thought the figure of 3,000 about right.

Professor Robertson said he was surprised by the East German steel town of 40,000. This was an industry with mostly male employment. He thought 40,000 a difficult number. There would not be enough services so that the town would lack the fastest-growing employment sector. Why was it less than the

100,000 which Britain had in its new towns? This gave a labour force of around 50,000. If two big employers took 12,000, this would still leave 38,000. One did not want only one employer, or one would lose balance. With the 38,000 one could have a big service sector, and a total population of 100,000 allowed the town a reasonable shopping and office centre. One might have, say, 16,000 employed there, leaving around 20,000 for other industry. Of the 100,000, one might have 16,000 women at work, out of which 8,000 might work in the services. One wanted not less than 100,000 to get a reasonable railway and airport system. Similarly, 100,000 allowed good hospitals and education, as well as facilities for training and retraining. But above all, this was the sort of community which grew automatically in Britain. It was the big towns that grew, and were developed. To develop small towns would be uneconomic. One could argue over whether 100,000 was right, but he thought one would have to go up rather than down from this number.

Professor Robinson asked Professor von Böventer two questions. First, he was interested by the comments of Professor Lajugie on Professor Penouil's paper. Professor Lajugie saw the possibility that the E.E.C. would increase rather than ease the problems of outlying areas. He wondered what Professor von Böventer would have to say about West Germany. On the face of it, one would expect the E.E.C. to lead to centralisation and to larger-scale production; he would expect fewer but stronger growth points. Was this what those in the E.E.C. expected, and was it happening? Was development going to become harder for the less-strong growth points and the non-growth points?

Second, the I.E.A. had, two years before, held a conference on the agricultural policies of advanced countries. On that occasion, German agricultural policy had posed something of a problem. In many European countries, agricultural policy was part of a more general backward area policy. But it had seemed then that German agricultural policy was hard to interpret. It appeared to support the kinds of less-efficient agriculture to which Professor von Böventer referred. Germany was mainly agricultural, and was to some extent drawing people out of peasant agriculture into industry and into service occupations. But with high levels of agricultural activity and employment, it was very largely drawing labour from Sweden, Italy, Greece and so on, into industrial activity. This seemed a paradoxical policy. Looking again at German agriculture in 1967, this time from the viewpoint of backward areas in advanced countries, he was still puzzled about the apparent antagonism between agricultural policy and the need to improve backward areas.

Professor Lundberg pointed out, as a complement to the paper by Professor Bylund, that problems of location policy were linked with the non-optimal sectoral division of the Swedish economy. Sweden had a higher income per head than the rest of Europe, but a rather bad spatial distribution of activity, and perhaps a bad sectoral one too. Other European countries must be still further away from the optimum in other ways for Sweden to perform relatively so well. There was now a squeeze in the Swedish economy, with too large wage increases hitting industry and trade. The evidence becomes clear that the number of plants in most industries was too high; there were too many inefficient small firms located in areas where regional problems were appearing. The number of failures and successes has been growing rapidly, creating employment problems in various parts of the country. The rapid structural reorganisation of the various branches of industry and trade was a necessary condition for an increased standard of living.

If one looked more broadly, all in Sweden had agreed that high mobility of labour from declining to expanding activities was basic rapid growth. Some 1–2 per cent of the labour force was continuously under training organised by the Labour Market Board. The geographical movement in Sweden must be considered from these perspectives. The development of Southern Sweden was important for growth, so there was a need to move labour from the North to the South. This policy had been especially easy as long as there was overemployment and inflation. Firms were tempted to locations where there was surplus labour. This development could not go on, however, because there had been too much wage inflation. Sweden must now keep down employment and demand pressure in order to dampen the rate of wage increase. This meant a need for an *active* mobility policy. We were back to the problem of whether – or rather in what relative degree – to move jobs to the workers, or vice-versa. The problem was complicated because there were, as already mentioned, too many small firms. For example, Sweden has steel works producing less than 50,000 tons per annum and probably needed to re-locate steel firms – a tremendous problem. He thought Sweden was in danger of putting too much of its localisation policy subsidies into small plants and areas of too low a population, which might well be making Sweden's industry less efficient.

Professor Bylund answered some of the questions Professor Delivanis had asked about income differences due to migration to the coast. There were income differences but not very big ones, so one could not use these as a good way of identifying backward areas in Sweden. But the migration caused some increase in differences in income, which were higher in the coastal area.

So far as the Lapps were concerned, one found a small population of 2,500–3,000 with much lower incomes than the rest of the inhabitants in Norrland. But they might decline in number as a result of the structural and economic rationalisation of raising reindeer.

On old people, it was not always a question of comfort or of material help but a question above all of how they could get enough contact with other people. In Sweden there was a tendency to create a sort of comfortable 'ghetto' for the old. This was the main problem, and this contact problem was often bigger in major cities than in rural areas.

To Professor Winiarski, Professor Bylund said that co-ordination between planning in the various sectors was not good. Sweden was beginning to create a new organisation, with strong links between the governmental and county level, as well as communal level, with links between economic and administrative planning. One now had county councils dealing with investment in firms asking for subsidies. These councils had members from the different industrial sectors, so he hoped for integration of both the sectors and the regions of the economy in planning.

Professor Lundberg had answered Professor Robertson's question showing the dilemma in Sweden, and it was hard to say much more. But he would talk about the size of villages in Central Norrland. It was clear there was no future for agriculture, but forestry must be continued as it was a major export industry for Sweden. There would be fewer working in forestry, and therefore small populations on which to base satisfactory service facilities. He could now say that a village of about 3,000 was the lowest level to give satisfactory services to the consumer. In future, this would be too small. In five to seven years it would have to go up to 8,000 to 12,000 inhabitants, yet the number of forestry workers would fall. This would lead to a serious problem in providing adequate services, and one that must be faced because forestry had to go on, and satisfactory services needed to be guaranteed.

Professor von Böventer said that West Germany's agricultural policy puzzled everyone because it was not primarily based on economic but rather on political and human considerations, and depended largely on the lobbying power of agricultural organisations. The problem was how to get a different distribution of government funds going to agriculture. Too little had been spent on reform and too much on pure subsidies.

On the new border with East Germany, he would stress that the bigger a city a given distance from the border, the greater the detrimental influence of the border. The observation that the influence of the border was felt for twenty kilometres was true only for small cities. The city of Hamburg, though located farther away, had been hit hard by the coming of the border, and the same was true of cities east of the border. Göttingen and Kassel were exceptions because of good north–south communications.

Writing his paper, he had concentrated on structural changes in the economy. A structural change that had helped economic growth was that the percentage of the population in agriculture had fallen because of the population inflow from the East. Most of the migrants had not moved into agriculture even if they had been in agriculture before. The whole population had become more mobile, and this had helped to modernise the whole economy.

Second, since cities and factories had been destroyed during the war, a new structure had emerged that was better adapted to the needs of the 1950s and 1960s. The scattering of population also meant that a large part of the population became footloose and this had helped to ease structural changes. Mobility had probably declined rapidly since the middle 1950s, though this remained to be seen.

Professor von Böventer was very interested in the layout of cities, but thought it hard to give definite answers on the quantitative relationships between cities. In general, small villages had not grown very fast, but he had found that towns with a population of 1,000 had grown at least as fast as big cities. There seemed to be certain thresholds. Cities with administrative responsibilities and population figures of about 20,000, of 100,000–200,000 and above 500,000 tended to grow faster than cities with sizes between these figures. Also, the bigger its hinterland, the easier it had been for a city to develop. This was seen quite clearly in North Hesse.

The optimal sizes of cities depended on the economies of scale that they give rise to. This led to the question: to what extent did firms need contacts with other firms at the same location? What bearing had contact with people or firms one kilometre away as compared with those twenty kilometres away? His own small town had four relatively big firms. One had moved away because of the limitations of its particular site in a small valley, but the others would stay.

One therefore had to ask the question: how far were such small cities integrated with bigger centres? Particularly important was the question: did small centres share the bigger centres' labour markets?

What had to be investigated was, in particular, the cost of infrastructure in relation to the demand for the use of that infrastructure. Costs alone were unimportant; it was the willingness to pay in relation to cost that counted (which, anyhow, was taken for granted in general economic theory). Therefore one had the important question: at (different) *given profit levels*, what would a certain firm be willing to pay for a 'representative bale of urban services' (land and infrastructure use) as a function of the number of other firms at the same location, given the demand functions for the firm's products and its cost function (with regard to *private* costs)? 'Other firms' to be considered were competing firms as well as firms that were supplementary in their functions. There were also firms with which there were no direct economic links and that were competitors only for land and labour.

This way one would obtain functions relating the *number of other firms* at a given location with *hypothetical prices for urban services* that would yield the same profits to the firm. It would be interesting to see for which numbers of firms these iso-profit curves (or price-indifference curves) for 'urban services' reached extreme values. These hypothetical prices should be compared with the supply prices (land rents plus infrastructure costs). Then an optimum could be determined.

Professor von Böventer said he would not go into more detail, save to say that the relevant cost was the marginal cost of infrastructure. He wanted to emphasise that a system would come closer to optimum if taxation and subsidies were based on marginal costs, in particular if falling or rising marginal costs were taken into account. We also needed to investigate the dynamic problems of moving and how dynamic policy prescriptions differed from those based on static analyses.

Dr Schmidt-Lüders said that the von Böventer paper supported Professor Groenman's paper on the importance of historical and cultural forces. As to West Germany, it had been in cultural equilibrium because in its past so many dynasties had provided centres of education and culture – in the case of Munich, even of industry. The post-war development of West Germany was a good example of industrial activity spilling over into marginal (rather than backward) areas. In Germany, it was not yet clear if the marginal areas would feel the impact of the present recession faster than others, especially since, so far, the recession was a mild one.

Professor Vito had the impression that West Germany was very different from Italy. Was there really a problem of backward areas at all in Germany? The problems appeared to be more those of general development than of regional policy. The latter had proved too difficult for much to be achieved.

Professor von Böventer had said that agricultural policy had failed, mainly because of the interests of pressure groups which wanted subsidies to aid subsistence farming. While it was an understandable policy, this meant that the Federal Government had compensated lower productivity with price subsidies. This might be a reasonable social price to pay, but he doubted if such a state of affairs could go on for long within the E.E.C. In fact, he thought the transfer of labour would be eased because industrial development was scattered across West Germany.

Professor von Böventer thought agglomerations were necessary because they usually meant diversification and high external economies. They also stimulated industrial zones and connected agglomerated zones with each other – they behaved 'rationally'. But what was the optimum size of an agglomeration? Probably the answer was in terms of a balance between external economies and external diseconomies. But external economies were for the firm, while external diseconomies reflected social costs. Could this problem be solved?

Professor Lajugie turned to the methods of regional policy. The papers showed two different situations. In West Germany, there was a national scheme for the selection of a number of regional centres for development. In Sweden, the movement was towards industrial decentralisation, with a number of firms sent to the regions. He thought both countries rejected partial measures as inadequate. So he wanted to know if all measures for a regional policy did not prove inadequate without coherent and compatible regional plans. Could one elaborate regional plans in Sweden and West Germany, and would that be acceptable in the near future?

Professor Nussbaumer noted that Professor von Böventer suggested that for the Eifel the alternatives open were industrial development or tourism. Was tourism an alternative or simply a subsidiary source of income? For Saturday-Sunday tourism, the kind one might expect in the Eifel, was an unsatisfactory source of income.

To Professor Bylund, Professor Nussbaumer suggested that uniform aid to backward areas would cause development at the margins of underdevelopment. What we wanted was a way of equalising marginal productivity plus aid, as the sources of regional income. Since at the edges of an area one would have less difference in marginal productivity, development would concentrate at the margin. So one probably needed differential aid, which raised the question of how much differentiation was politically and economically acceptable in a market economy.

Professor James noted that, unlike the underdeveloped areas of Germany, the Ruhr was threatened with outright decline. What precautions had West Germany taken to prevent decline in the Ruhr, and what further measures were planned?

Mr Cameron pointed out that in the U.S.A. there had been two studies on city size. One had projected the demand for labour to 1975 and showed that communities of less than 50,000 people had a high chance of a rate of growth below the national average, but those between 50,000 and 500,000 had a good chance of an above-average growth rate. Those of over 500,000 were likely to have a below-average growth. This was a very complex issue. It was hard to explain, but research using the shift-share technique could show greater-than-expected gains in cities as compared with their structure. Work had been done for both cities and regions, and very sophisticated independent variables were now being used. This was a method whose use might be looked at in greater detail. It would supplement Professor von Böventer's interesting paper.

Professor Oelssner commented on the new steel town of Eisenhüttenstadt. Professor Robertson has claimed that this was too small to make use of all the female labour it would have. In fact, the opposite was true. Female labour was widely used in the steel combine, not only in administration, which was not very big. Women also worked on the shop floor, although not on heavy manual jobs. The women employed were mainly those with considerable technical training. Creating such a new town also meant a need for services and infrastructure, and women were employed there. So the problem was not to find jobs for women but how to get women, especially married women, to work and to become trained. There was a general labour shortage in the G.D.R.

Professor Oelssner noted that the creation of a large industrial complex in a backward area created the necessary conditions for the diversified development of a region.

Professor von Böventer replied to the discussion of his paper. He said that a major problem concerning agglomerations was the practical one of whether to allow (and induce) existing cities to grow (say Hamburg or Lübeck) or to set up new industrial regions (say a new triangular industrial region in the centre of Schleswig-Holstein). Was a distance of eighty kilometres from existing centres (Hamburg–Lübeck) too much and if not, should the new industrial region be complementary or different in character? The same issues arose in Bavaria and the Eifel region. As to the Eifel, Professor Nussbauer was right that it was hard to see what to do. Tourism by itself was unlikely to allow the region to develop sufficiently, and there were only small industrial centres.

Co-ordination, this was clearly desirable, but he thought that efforts in this direction had to be stepped up considerably. Also one had to develop more clear-cut concepts about the function of the various regions and of smaller areas.

If new centres were being planned, it was necessary to try to get cost to the firm as close as possible to marginal social cost. In a theoretical model covering a whole area or an entire nation, taxes (and/or subsidies) should be used so as to equalise private costs and marginal social costs, after social costs had been multiplied by a factor which ensured that actual total costs were covered in cases where marginal costs were falling. One would come closer to this goal if taxes were based on the *use of certain inputs* so as to reflect marginal social cost.

In West Germany, no detailed and useable policy concept had been developed in the past; except that some attempts had been made to give the country a moderate degree of decentralisation in line with the federal structure. Planning had largely been piecemeal. In the past, whatever the Government did, economic forces working through the pull of the agglomerations had been stronger than the effect of government policies. This was particularly true up to the later 1950s, but less so now. In the Ruhr, on balance not much had been achieved through policy actions, partly because often individual actions had been neutralised one another. Subsidies to coal had served to perpetuate the existing structure.

On whether overall regional policy was good or feasible, he thought more of it was needed, but based on much more research. Before concluding that this would probably not happen, one should note that the climate of opinion on the merits of planning had changed greatly in West Germany in the last year.

Professor Bylund closed the session by discussing the question of distance. Often in Sweden this was spoken of as a key issue. That was true, but distance was not basically a question of transport costs, which represented a diminishing part of total costs. One should measure distance in terms of contours showing the loss of time for each point on the map. In these terms, the interior of Norrland must lag in the future. Such a concept of distance could be used, at least in Sweden.

Problems of Underdeveloped Regions of Italy

Discussion of Papers by Professors F. Vito and P. Saraceno

Mr MacLennan introduced the paper by Professor Vito. He said that the two papers together provided a very important case study in regional development. Professor Vito's paper was especially provoking and challenged a number of accepted theses about the Italian problem.

The problem in the South was that of an underdeveloped rather than a formerly developed, but now backward area, like Scotland. Professor Vito stressed the point that the union of Italy 100 years ago had not benefited and had perhaps even harmed the South. He went on to say that Southern Italy as a region had to be developed if emigration was to be halted. Increased productivity in agriculture could not alone solve the problem fast enough, so industrialisation was necessary. There was also a need to create, not replace, infrastructure, especially in communications and power.

Apart from the scale of the problem, the institutional instruments used to deal with it were interesting, especially public investment and the spending of controlled funds in the South. It was puzzling that Professor Vito favoured gradualism rather than the 'big push'. Mr MacLennan was not clear on precisely what Professor Vito had in mind here. If gradualism meant that the infrastructure, the labour force, etc., must be developed before one could have a 'push' toward industrial development, then he agreed. But if Professor Vito meant that the development of the South must be undertaken within the limits of the existing economic structure, then he was surely on the wrong track.

Professor Vito next went on to discuss the aims of policy. He said that an economic and social policy was needed for the whole of Italy. Economists should consider how to develop the South at minimum opportunity cost. Whether the loss of output for the nation as a whole would be too great was a matter for concern.

Finally, Professor Vito believed that growth poles must be the basis of development in the South. However, he was doubtful about the possibility of successful development while there was the vastly more competitive economy to the north.

Mr MacLennan said he would suggest a point for discussion. In Southern

Italy, one had an economy which suffered from competition with the more-developed North. Did the South therefore run the risk of even more damage as the E.E.C. developed? He was not sure what evidence there was on this. It was clear that once it lost tariff protection with the coming of the union, and with no possibility of devaluation, improved economic communications opened the way to drain resources from the South. The industrial structure in the South was such that it could not compete on equal terms with the northern economy, with its economies of scale and external economies. A situation arose which kept capital from leaving the North, and attracted labour from south to north. Given this, attempts to stimulate expenditure in the South merely meant that it would leak back via the multiplier process. The effect of the E.E.C. on the development of the South seemed, at first sight likely (*a*) to increase competition from the North; (*b*) to increase the importance of the North's economies of scale and external economies; and (*c*) to open further opportunities for emigration. In practice, capital might not be much easier to acquire for southern development because of the deficiencies of the South. If the Government tried to draw capital into the South by limiting investment in the North, it might simply go outside Italy altogether.

What effect did the E.E.C. have on the North? It forced the North to be more competitive. The scope for sending capital to the South must thus be reduced. To get higher productivity in the North, competition in the labour market must cause the North to seek labour in the South, worsening the problem there. The consequence was therefore that if the E.E.C. did not take steps to lessen the damage, the South might have to achieve the results of devaluation by something like the British R.E.P. If this were not done, Italy might be forced to live permanently with the South getting poorer and poorer, and finding it harder and harder to develop, so putting the North under ever greater pressure to be efficient in order to sustain transfers of welfare payments to the South.

Although it might sound cruel, Italy needed a ruthless regional policy aimed not at propping up the South but at making it efficient.

Dr McCrone introduced the paper by Professor Saraceno. He said that the Italian problem, like the French, was primarily a problem of underdeveloped areas. But unlike most of the French problem regions, Southern Italy was very densely populated. Thus its present condition was more serious than that of any part of France because of its greater poverty. But paradoxically the size of its population might help its development in the long run, since a sparse population could provide neither the market nor the labour essential for industrial growth.

The Italian problem showed itself in large income differences between north and south, in unemployment, underemployment and migration. Unemployment figures, however, greatly understated the problem owing partly to the huge size of the agricultural sector and partly because many of those available for work found little purpose in registering as unemployed.

Italian policy was conducted largely by the Cassa per il Mezzogiorno, a body unique in Western Europe. This was a public department, presided over by a committee of ministers, whose purpose was to develop the South and to co-ordinate the activities of other government departments in the region. In the early stages the emphasis was primarily on agriculture and infrastructure. Agriculture had been greatly helped by the elimination of malaria and by the reclamation and irrigation of the plains which this made possible; but it could not solve the employment problem since its need was to shed labour rather than absorb it. Substantial investment had gone into infrastructure. Indeed there were now better motorway links between the north and south of Italy than between Glasgow and London. But as a stimulus to development this had so far proved disappointing.

Direct encouragement of industrialisation did not come till 1957, and here the most interesting aspect of Italian policy had been the role assigned to public holding companies. E.N.I. and I.R.I. had been used to provide the spearhead of development. Among other projects the I.R.I. had been responsible for the steelworks at Taranto, while E.N.I. had played a large part in stimulating petrochemicals in Sicily.

The results of policy in the South were disappointing if judged against the targets of the Vanoni plan. Although Italy fulfilled those targets, the North made faster and the South slower progress than anticipated. The gap between North and South had not widened, but it had not been reduced either. The figures showed that, as measured at constant prices, southern growth rates had fallen slightly below the North; but at current prices, owing to a movement in the terms of trade in favour of the South, the South accounted for a slightly increasing share of Italian G.N.P. At a time when northern growth rates had reached unprecedented levels, it was probably unrealistic to imagine that the South could have caught up; that it had been able to maintain its position *vis-à-vis* the North was something of an achievement.

Dr McCrone asked a number of questions. The growth pole idea had been much discussed, but how did one start a growth pole in Italy and what were the steps to be followed? Professor Saraceno estimated that the assistance given to the South was equivalent to a tariff protection of 5 per cent. Had Italy been still two countries the South could have used both devaluation and tariffs. Within a unitary state such measures had to be ruled out, but much more could be done to give regional protection by fiscal means. For example, had the Italians given any thought to a payroll tax such as the Regional Employment Premium now used in Britain or to the possibility of applying the value-added tax on a regional basis?

Professor Vito wanted to clarify his position on the effects of the political unification of Italy. He did not dispute the need for political unification. It was simply that at the time of unification, prevailing economic thought believed that a bigger joint market assisted both richer and poorer countries, whatever their respective degrees of development. It was now accepted that this was not always true.

Professor Davin said that Professor Vito had shown the technical and economic limits to the use of infrastructure as a source of development. He wondered if the spontaneous creation of infrastructure was not also important.

Another limitation was the extent to which the north and south of Italy were integrated. If there were a serious slump in the North, would this not cause a similar collapse in investment in the South? Perhaps the best thing would be to push ahead with development in the North but at the same time to develop north-south links which helped the South.

Professor Davin said he had not quite grasped the point about 'gradualism'.

At one point in his paper, Professor Vito supported special action of the kind implied by the 'big push'.

Professor Davin regarded industrialisation as the way to raise the standard of living in backward areas. But what kind of industry? Why steel in Taranto? For at the time when Taranto was built the Dutch had held back development at Rosenburg because of the difficult future foreseen for the whole international steel industry.

Professor Groenman thought the problem of the South was a European problem. It was also a political rather than economic problem. Political problems were socio-economic ones. Perhaps at the level of decision taking, we should say there was political activity dealing with economic-social forces. Politics was based on the need for choice. Once the choice was made, it must be made effective to achieve what was wanted. Professor Vito was not always clear on this. If one were concerned that these were political problems, could one be more ruthless, with more investment, even given the scarcity of resources of production? The principal decision was to accept wholeheartedly that because this was a difficult problem one needed more state intervention and enterprise to start growth points. Professor Vito did not want growth points, because he had doubts about the absorption capacity of human beings, but people could accept change, as at Taranto. Could one not have a 'big push' going to the root of the matter – investing to improve infrastructure in the broadest sense, and creating the conditions for state-owned enterprise? It appeared that in Italy there was more reason than ever for calling this a political problem.

Professor Mihailović thought this had been a useful conference for those interested in the south of both Yugoslavia and Italy. He was himself especially interested in egalitarian problems. Illusion or not, egalitarianism helped in developing backward areas. Egalitarianism was not a utopian idea, but a value which had existed for more than 2,000 years. Did such a value help or hinder economic development?

Professor Perroux had suggested a different approach to mass production and mass consumption, taking the needs of the whole population into account. Mass production was needed for a bigger market and vice versa. Perhaps it could solve the problems of a backward area in a developed country.

Professor Vito had mentioned the obstacles to growth in the South, stressing the absorptive capacity of the region. In his own country, it was often said that absorptive capacity was lacking, but at the same time Yugoslavian enterprises worked efficiently, building up factories in Czechoslovakia, hydro-electric stations in Canada or raising living standards in India.

What kind of social conditions did one need to produce entrepreneurs? Was it really necessary to teach anyone or was it, perhaps, better to give the chance to teachers? One could not hope that big owners of capital would come in today, apart from existing companies and the State.

The choice between gradualism and the 'big push' had been posed in the Hungarian paper, where Dr Köszegi had been led to advocate handicrafts and small industry. Was gradual growth more appropriate for small firms, and big firms for the big push?

Professor Mihailović had no solution to suggest for the population problem in Southern Italy. One needed to think of the costs of high population, and the long-run consequences if one did not hold back population growth in backward areas. The existence of excess population growth showed how we had failed to solve the problem of regions.

Professor Robinson thought that, of all Western economies, Italy was much the most interesting case study. He had worked as an O.E.C.D. representative with Professor Saraceno and Dr Marsan on the Vanoni Plan. He noted a tendency to treat the Vanoni Plan as if it were a plan for the South. It was, in fact, a plan for Italy. If one looked at Table 3 in Professor Vito's paper, it showed that unemployment in the whole of Italy in 1952 was over 2 million, with $1\frac{1}{4}$ million of this in the North. The figure for the South was misleading because it under-stated effective unemployment at that date. It took account only of those registered for work; many who did not register in agricultural areas would have liked to move, but saw no prospect of a job. One therefore had to look at the total problem. In 1953 Italy had been near economic and political collapse, and expansion was needed in Italy as a whole, north and south. So the Vanoni Plan was only partly aimed at improving conditions in the South.

Experience in the U.K. suggested that it was easier to tackle the problems of backward areas if one had full employment in the country as a whole. Italy had needed first to get the North near to full employment, so that big firms would be prepared to open branches in the South and thus contribute to development. In the last twelve years there had been a miracle in Italy. There had been un-precedentedly fast growth of the whole economy, though not uniformly spread. This made the effort of helping the South possible. The health of the North, as Professor Davin had said, was important to the South.

Professor Robinson supported Professor Mihailović in stressing the impor-tance, not only of large, but also of small-scale enterprise wherever it was easy for it to meet demand both from within the backward area and in the whole country. He wondered if effective ways had been found of bringing small enterprises in. In the mid-1950s he had been anxious to get Italy to accept the idea of industrial estates, and even new towns, as a way of providing the necessary infrastructure, not only for public but for private enterprise. He had been similarly anxious to give opportunities to hire as well as buy machinery. It was clear that there was entrepreneurial ability in the South which could not grasp opportunities because it lacked capital. At that time, Italy was reluctant to accept what were seen as fascist ideas, making the 'big push' difficult then. But he regarded these as promising ideas, and wondered how far they had now gone.

Professor Nussbaumer asked for amplification of some points. Professor Vito argued that the role of agriculture could not be ignored because the South was not self-sufficient and needed further development. But what methods would be used? It seemed to him that land reform might provide some advantages like better-sized farms and more individual initiative.

He also wondered how far costs to the public and external benefits for industry in the same area could be compared, in an attempt to measure the efficiency of indirect development aid.

Third, on the conflict between the 'big push' and gradualism, there was reason to believe that in Southern Italy a big push would be better. The paper argued that one needed social and human development, but those who emigrated did well. External economies depended on the size of the agglomeration. The problem was how big the big push would need to be, and when it should be given. If one wanted co-ordinated development one certainly could not ignore heavy industry altogether. But to what extent was it needed and when should medium-sized firms be encouraged? There might be antagonism in the South from relatively small local communities towards the large growth points needed if the big push method was to be applied.

Professor Valarché was interested in the effect of unemployment in the South, and the influence of the E.E.C. If there was slow growth in the South in the nineteenth century, this was not because of tariffs but because of a large public debt. This public debt was mainly held in the North, and perhaps the South paid too much of the interest on it. As for the E.E.C., he thought the situation was very different because there were measures to counteract the effects of economic fluctuations on such areas, and specific arrangements for buying agricultural production from the South by other European countries.

In his paper (p. 232), Professor Saraceno wrote of the richer regions accepting measures to help the backward areas as the price of social peace. Professor Valarché thought it dangerous to think that any region could live on charity from others. For example, if there were no investment in the South, one would have congestion costs in Northern Italy. One should not talk of charity to help the South.

Both papers seemed a little pessimistic and spoke of deception. But there had been some rise in the relative standard of living of the South, and some examples of good agricultural practice there. What 'deception' had there been? Had the population risen unexpectedly fast? Or was there an inability to absorb aid? Perhaps there was an unwillingness to operate the economy efficiently. Or was there political resistance to government action?

Professor von Böventer thought the situation in Italy was in one respect similar to that in relations between East and West Germany. He meant in the problem of destabilising factor (labour) movements. All this would lead him into politics, but he would nevertheless try to concentrate on economic aspects. Up to 1945 there had been little difference in the level of economic development in East and West Germany; they had been part of the same national economy. For a number of (mainly political) reasons, subsequent experiences had differed. First, West Germany had received Marshall Aid, but East Germany had not; second, East Germany had paid reparations while West Germany had not. This alone would have caused a significant difference in the level of welfare in the two parts of the country.

Within a national economy, there were usually three ways of adjustment: labour movement in one direction, capital movements and transfer payments in the other. In the case of Germany, there had been large labour movements from East to West (similar to some movements within West Germany – for example, from Schleswig-Holstein to the Ruhr). The economic situation in West and East would have led to such a drain, quite apart from political factors. But within West Germany, there had been transfer payments and capital movements into Schleswig-Holstein. Labour movements, capital movements and transfer payments had led to full employment throughout West Germany. But there had been no offsetting capital movements to the East and no transfer payments. To reduce the labour movement to high-income regions, there had to be substantial capital movements and transfer payments. Since in the case of East Germany these were ruled out on political grounds, the only solution had been to introduce barriers to labour movements. This was done in 1961. This was a radical measure, and meant cutting down freedom of choice, but after this, the economic position and the growth rate were higher in East Germany than if such measures had not been taken.

Professor Robertson suggested that participants might ask what would have happened if they had been called in by the Kingdom of Naples as economic advisers. They would have to abandon two views often expressed. First, they could not have told all the inhabitants to leave, as American economists were too ready to do. Second, they could not have suggested that it was improper to accept aid. One would first study labour resources and would see the low wages in the area as favourable to development. One would increase education and training. One would note potential growth points, but accept that if Naples grew too fast, one would have a single-city country. One would want to introduce general measures to develop agriculture throughout the country, but probably industry as well in the growth areas. One might have a good balance of payments, with few exports to buy foreign consumer goods but a large volume of emigrant funds coming from abroad.

What of the disadvantages of such an economic policy? He would say the desire for social well-being led to the danger of funds being spent over too wide an area. One must not lose manpower for ever. One must also remember that the advisers would change frequently. One would know the economies of scale available, and so would want wider development but, as advisers, would accept the 'ruthless' policy with its emphasis on growth points. At present, he doubted if Southern Italy would accept a 'ruthless' policy.

Mr Petrella-Tirone said that beyond the measures of the E.E.C., with their institutional and financial limits, it was interesting to know what strategies dominated the geographical spread of investment in the Common Market. There was a clear tendency for investment to be concentrated in the 'strong' zone of the E.E.C. – the Amsterdam–Paris–Strasbourg triangle. For instance, in the mechanical industries, 92 per cent of new E.E.C. investment in 1964 was in the developed regions. Only 3·4 per cent was in underdeveloped areas. Of American investment in the Common Market in the same year, about 57 per cent was in large towns in or near the triangle. In total, 94 per cent of American investment went to the developed regions and only 1·3 per cent to underdeveloped ones.

On the other hand, a second European 'strong' zone seemed to be developing between Milan, Genoa, Marseilles and Lyons. This development was popular with planners in Northern Italy, who saw the long-term risk of being far from the dominant centre of the European development.

In the face of this situation, what place should be attributed to the European marginal and underdeveloped areas like Southern Italy and Southern France? What would be the policy on the location of investment in these areas to counterbalance the spontaneous tendencies described above?

Professor Delivanis wanted to say how much he agreed with Professor Vito on the desirability of choosing gradual progress. Like Professor Vito, he was against calling attention to the dualistic character of the Italian economy. He saw the danger which foreign competition posed for industries of a new type; for example, electronics firms which developed in underdeveloped areas. Professor Delivanis was also in full agreement on the need to industrialise Southern Italy, not only for the benefit of the South but also to avoid having to build the new infrastructure in the North which would be needed if industry there were to expand further. However, he wondered if these new industries developed with the taxpayer's money would not represent a danger to private industry. They would not be restricted by a credit squeeze or a rise in interest rates.

Both papers mentioned that Southern Italy was like Greece. Professor Robinson had asked him to say a few words on the repercussions of the latter's association with the Common Market on its backward areas. For the time being, Greek investment had not fallen, despite various changes in the economic climate, and despite the gradual reduction of customs duties on Common Market goods coming into Greece. Of course Greek manufacturers argued in favour of subsidies and the maintenance of customs duties. Greece suffered from excessive centralisation, both economic and administrative. Her association with the Common Market, by eliminating customs duties and quotas, would lead to a more liberal policy, and to the avoidance of unprofitable projects. Both would contribute to the development of private initiative even in backward areas. Very few industries were operated by the State, and loans from the European Fund were earmarked only for infrastructure. Perhaps later Greece would face the same problems as Southern Italy with its need for industrialisation.

Professor Oelssner replied to Professor von Böventer. He would not agree that the starting point of development in the two parts of Germany was the same in 1945. German industry (including heavy industry) had been concentrated on the Ruhr and the Rhine, where there was coal and iron. Foreign trade passed mainly through West German ports. There were industrial centres in parts of the G.D.R. but they depended on natural resources in the Ruhr. There was also more destruction in East Germany during the war. The G.D.R. had inherited the most backward parts of the country.

After 1947, development had been different. West Germany had received Marshall Aid. East Germany had paid reparations for the whole of Germany, so that heavy industry had been wholly dismantled and reparations paid from current production. As Professor von Böventer had said, the migration of the labour force, especially skilled and educated men, had hampered the development of the G.D.R.

Turning to the issue of the 'big push', Professor Oelssner said that, given this situation in which the G.D.R. had few industrial centres, it had concentrated development on these. The whole economy had thereby been 'dragged' forward.

Professor Vito accepted that the problem of Southern Italy was essentially a political one. What was the role of economics in dealing with a political problem? He had not tried to deal with this issue in detail, but had mentioned attempts to reconcile the economic, political and social aspects. If one emphasised economic aspects, one tended not to give much importance to regional problems, but emphasised the need to use economic resources in the most productive way. Since carrying out new investment in existing industrial areas produced external economies and other advantages, there was a case for shifting resources to these regions. If one emphasised social and political aspects, one would pay less attention to economic issues. How could all these factors be reconciled? One could distinguish long-run and short-run problems. In a long-run approach, economic forces would be most important. To accelerate development in the short run, one would need to accept non-optimal development. One could not overcome backwardness in an area quickly. But how long was the long-run? This was hard to say.

Economic problems were concerned with allocating scarce means between alternative ends. One could not accept purely economic solutions in a country where some parts of the population did not have a standard of living compatible with human dignity.

Mr MacLennan had not been clear what gradualism meant. Professor Vito suggested that there were three elements. First, if one was industrialising, one was interested first in the infrastructure. Second, one must have higher incomes if one was to make use of the increased stock of capital. Third, human factors like entrepreneurial and technical ability were needed. Even where one had invested in infrastructure, one would not have these conditions fulfilled.

Professor Vito said one could easily show that some investment in the South had wasted resources. For example, special medium-term financial institutions had been created, but who should get cheaper credit from them? There was a big difference between the number of projects accepted and rejected. Nor had all the projects accepted been carried out.

Professor Vito saw no contradiction between advocating concentration of investment, and rejecting the big push. The latter was the Rosenstein-Rodan idea for the very poor countries. He was concerned with the location of investment; Rosenstein-Rodan with the scale of that investment.

So far as growth points were concerned, big direct investment not only determined the area in which investment could have an effect; it also gave forward and backward linkages. Professor Vito did not question the theory, only its application to underdeveloped countries.

Professor Vito said he had followed with interest the idea of industrial estates, but he did not think Southern Italy had the human resources needed to take advantage of such estates.

As for steel at Taranto, this was an '*industrie motrice*' that would help to meet the rising future demand for steel. Taranto had been chosen in the hope of creating a growth point.

To Mr Petrella-Tirone, he suggested that sooner or later the E.E.C.'s policy would concern itself with the development of industry in all parts of the area. He did not know if each government would accept this in what could not be a supernational unit – or the U.K. would never have applied to join. The role of industrialisation in the E.E.C. was the same as in a country. How much investment was needed in a region to ensure development? The interests of different regions must also be reconciled.

Professor Vito agreed with Professor Robinson about the employment figures. He also agreed that the policy of the Vanoni Plan had been to encourage small-scale enterprises, but perhaps Dr Marsan could give more information on this.

Land reform was a purely political device. The *Latifundia* had had to be abolished quickly, allowing little time to calculate the optimum size of farm. He did not think the change had contributed much to agricultural development in the South.

To Professor Valarché, he would say he was not a pessimist.

Dr Marsan said that, in replying to the discussion, he would try to be as faithful as possible to Professor Saraceno's line of thought.

One big question raised by Mr MacLennan was that of the impact of E.E.C. on the South. In this connection Dr Marsan recalled that Italy had started by joining the European Coal and Steel Community in 1953. Its steel industry had traditionally been weak and highly protected. About 40–50 per cent of the industry – including all ore-based plants – was at the time under a State-controlled management corporation (the I.R.I.). As the demand for steel had grown fast in the post-war period, this gave the I.R.I. the opportunity of locating in the South, at Taranto, a large plant with a capacity of three millions tons, capable of competing successfully in an integrated European market. As a result the South now had 30 per cent of Italian steel capacity, as against 11 per cent in 1953. Nor had the Taranto project held back development in the rest of Italy. The northern plants had indeed been increased to a more efficient scale, while the new plant was being built in the South.

Dr Marsan thought it important to follow Professor Saraceno in regarding public enterprise as a type of incentive, because it would accept, if only temporarily, lower returns than private industry and by its moving into the South could pave the way for additional private investment. It was probably significant, too, that since the E.E.C. had been set up, there had been a good deal of foreign investment in the South, here again in a number of cases through joint ventures with public enterprises.

Dr Marsan explained to Dr McCrone that if output were expanded in the South, this would certainly prevent manpower from moving to the North. Would this have inflationary effects? This brought him to the important point that, whatever happened, the South apparently stood to lose. Real or imaginary fears were always a good reason for development in the South to be held back. He thought that if one did not want inflation, one should not agree that in order to prevent it one should sacrifice the objective of developing the South.

For years the North had had an inflow of manpower comparable only to that into West Germany since 1945. Could this go on for ever, disregarding the costs to other regions as well as the growing congestion of the North? True enough, investment alone could not solve the problems of the South. But saying so did not solve the problem. Either one got results in the early 1970s, or one would seriously impair the future possibilities of self-sustaining growth of the South.

There had been some disappointment in steel as a growth industry. Notwithstanding the large size of the plant, it imported its raw materials by sea and could export most of its output; so one would get some benefits, but nothing like what Professor Perroux's theory suggested.

Dr Marsan said that the Bari–Taranto study contained the valuable new idea that economies of agglomeration could not be derived simply by looking at input-output relationships in a closed system. A large number of inputs might come from considerable distances. But having created an attractive model did not mean mean that it was easy to choose which bunch of industries to develop. Moreover, when the report came out, economic conditions were rather stagnant and this made it hard to get industry to co-operate. Some suggested that the first firms to move into the area should necessarily be public. This neglected the fact that large groups such as the I.R.I. could do little with small-sized enterprises. The Taranto–Bari study proposed nineteen plants with some 10,000 employees in total. Small firms needed more flexible management than could be achieved within a large and complex organisation. However, the study contained some really original ideas.

Recent studies showed what the existing fiscal and financial inducements in favour of the South were worth, as a percentage of a firm's total costs (or sales). The order of magnitude turned out to be 5 per cent. In the case of public enterprises one should allow for the fact that they might wait longer for a return than private industry; but it could not be assumed that this would add more than one or two percentage points to this figure of 5 per cent; even an I.R.I. enterprise, which through transitory financial backing from the State could give up a normal return for the first four or five years, could offset no more than 6–7 per cent of total costs in the South, as compared to a northern location. This was why he felt not enough had been done to attract industry to the South.

To Professor Mihailović, Dr Marsan said the rate of population growth in the South was still higher than in the North, but it was falling. The vital question was when the labour reserves would be exhausted. Of course, the return of Italian emigrants would be welcome.

Replying to Professor Robinson, he argued that, although the Vanoni Plan was mainly aimed at the South, it was indeed a national plan. But it never became a plan in the sense of being adopted as a guiding rule by any government. The fact that the Vanoni Plan had used a 5 per cent growth rate was important. Actual growth had been 6 per cent. This left too many people satisfied, and made the problem of the South seem less acute. By now one had a situation where the fact that the North was richer in a sense made things easier. Of course one did not want a 'dole' for the South but jobs. With the present new plan the north-south problem had been brought at once to the fore. In future, no policy or programme by any government department or agency should be able, as had happened more than once in the past, to ignore the need to solve the problems of the South.

Dr Marsan thought that the 'big push' essentially required one to choose the scale of industrial location. The advantage of Southern Italy was that it was a large area with a number of old-established towns.

So far as Mr Petrella-Tirone's 'zones of strength' were concerned, one wanted to choose industries for the South effectively. The South had been up to a certain point disappointed by industries like steel and chemicals. This was why incentives should be flexible. His own view was that the inducements given to certain firms were perhaps too big, while in other cases they were clearly insufficient. One really wanted to give equal conditions as between south and north, not to give excess profits in the South. The argument was that the disadvantages of being in the South were real but temporary. Any form of flat-rate payment gave 'rent' to intramarginal firms.

So one needed a flexible policy, with temporary, and probably diminishing, incentives. This flexibility was hard to obtain. In engineering especially, with mass production, there were very big external economies, and such firms could develop many peripheral activities. It was hard to calculate, as one should, what incentives to offer.

The hardest problem remained the small- or medium-sized firm, and it was here that the shortage of managerial skill was serious. If there had been a failure in policy for the South, it was a failure to recognise how serious this problem was. A management-training centre had now been set up in the South jointly by the Cassa and the I.R.I. Professor Saraceno did not reject the idea of a major contribution from the small firms. The problem was to get the right people to accept State policy. Good firms did not want aid, but bad ones saddled the public sector with a burden.

Dr Marsan explained that there had been industrial estates even before 1939, and one near Venice had been a success. But this was still a small, restricted area. What we wanted now was to link a number of towns, with their industries. However, in 1955 a new law had been adopted to extend incentives to all poor towns of less than 10,000 people. Ninety-five per cent of these were now accepted as depressed areas, including no less than one-third of the population of the North. How could one expect small- or medium-sized firms to go to the South?

To conclude, an essential issue of development strategy was whether growth would be accompanied by large migratory flows. Or would one accept from the beginning the constraint that we must avoid big and upsetting movements of population between a country's regions.

EIGHTH SESSION

The Development of Backward Areas in Czechoslovakia and Yugoslavia

Discussion of Papers by Professor P. Turčan and Professor K. Mihailović

Professor Robinson wished to say something as Chairman of the Programme Committee. The Round Table had finished all of its discussions on backward areas in what we called capitalist countries, though really most were 'mixed' economies. We were going on to discuss socialist countries. He would like to say a few things. All countries tried to learn from both their successes and their failures. Here we all wanted to learn from both success and failure. In capitalist countries we had both, and nearly all of us could give a list of failures in our own country. For the socialist countries, we wanted to learn both of the successes (of which we knew a lot) and of the mistakes and the way these had changed methods of planning. Might we be frank about failures?

Second, he wanted to make the general point that all of us in western countries were trying to understand better the new economic policies which most socialist countries were introducing. We wanted to know especially if the policies of decentralisation, of greater use of the market, and of greater emphasis on economic efficiency, could make it harder to develop backward areas.

Third, we had studied in great detail the problems of a number of countries. This was fascinating, and, he thought, necessary for a general understanding. In our discussions it was tempting to ask for more detail. Interesting and valuable though this was, he thought, for this conference, it was better to concentrate on the major issues, and try to understand policies and ways of looking at problems. Perhaps he could suggest what had emerged in the discussions of capitalist countries.

First, there was the problem of how to identify an area for special action – by the level of unemployment, income per head and other criteria. Second, and he thought this most interesting, we had to decide how to deal with unemployment and redundancy in the more remote areas, like some agricultural areas of the U.S.A., the Scottish Highlands, or Sweden. Did we agree that not all areas could be modified and developed? Did we agree that one therefore needed a new focal point, near enough to draw on such sources of labour, and in the same cultural area, but that the right way to provide opportunities for modern development might be in a new place? Here again, he wanted to draw on the experience of socialist countries. Yugoslavia especially had similar problems.

Third, did we agree that if development was to be tried, this was best done where a useful infrastructure could be built up? If so, how large should the urban units be? Should they contain 10,000 or 100,000, or indeed 200,000 people? Fourth, we had met the issue of how best to deal with underused reserves of female labour. Usually women were well employed in an agricultural area. Outside agriculture, one often found them unused. How could one best choose development areas so as to take advantage of this? Finally, were these problems short-term ones, needing immediate action but later solving themselves so that new centres of economic efficiency developed? Or did trying to deal with a backward area mean one was building a long-run problem because one was attempting to establish firms in a relatively inefficient location?

Professor Sovani asked some questions about Professor Turčan's paper. He thought that his questions might sound quite naïve because the sense of the original paper might have been lost in translation and because he was not very knowledgeable about conditions in Czechoslovakia. He wanted to apologise in advance if he had misunderstood Professor Turčan.

Professor Sovani thought Professor Turčan felt that the present industrial structure in Slovakia was weak because it was in many ways complementary to that in the Czech area. Professor Sovani felt this a rather puzzling observation. Was not Professor Turčan overdoing this point? He seemed to suggest that a backward area like this should have a self-sustaining development and its own industrial links. Could one legitimately suggest that an area should have a self-sufficient industrial structure with no economic links with other parts of the country? Were we applying the analysis for a whole nation to a part of it? If this was what Professor Turčan was suggesting, the other facts in his paper seemed still more puzzling. During the period 1948–64, the two big industrial complexes that had been developed in Slovakia were for iron and steel and petrochemicals; both were dependent upon imports of raw materials from the U.S.S.R. Were not these industries complementary to the raw materials in the

P

U.S.S.R? Why, then, did Professor Turčan not feel obliged to correct these complementarities but insist on correcting those between industries in Slovakia and in the Czech area? Or did different considerations apply to raw material and industrial complementarities?

Professor Sovani also found Professor Turčan puzzling on agriculture. The latter attributed the lack of progress in agriculture in Slovakia to the transfer of labour from agriculture and to the remaining labour force being more 'aged' (p. 248). Yet further on in his paper (p. 250) he seemed to regard the encouragement of emigration from rural to industrial centres as essential for a long-term plan. This seemed a little contradictory. He also observed (on pp. 247–8) that agriculture was neglected in the development phase between 1948 and 1964. The evidence did not convincingly show this. Agricultural productivity had increased both per acre and per worker. The fact that it was lower than in the Czech provinces surely could not be regarded as sufficient evidence for the neglect of agriculture.

On page 255, the paper noted a lack of psychological motivation, particularly among the agricultural population of the area and the need for its elimination. Yet from the previous account, the population seemed to be willing to migrate, quit agriculture; the young, in particular, seemed to be deserting it anyway. Agricultural yields had increased and there had been technological improvement in agricultural production. This did not seem to indicate a lack of psychological motivation, and possibly in the long run everything would be all right.

Finally, Professor Sovani felt that the drift of Professor Turčan's remarks led in the direction of recommending a self-sustaining, self-sufficient industrial economy for Slovakia, not dependent in any way on the Czech provinces. Did this not ignore all natural and technical advantages that might lie in complementarities, regional links and so on? Surely this went much beyond a proper policy for a backward region. Was this particular orientation due to the fact that Professor Turčan considered Slovakia not a backward area but a backward 'nation' within a country?

Professor Lajugie introduced the paper by Professor Mihailović. He said Yugoslavia was a particular, and important, type of economy. This was a federal country, and also a socialist country, but one of an unusual kind.

The paper was in three parts. The first considered the geography of Yugoslavia. The second looked at the aims and results of its policy towards backward areas. The third considered a number of theoretical issues suggested by this policy. The first part of the paper went into the reasons for the backwardness of the underdeveloped parts of Yugoslavia. These were two wars and the operation of a free market. There were big differences between the richest and poorest regions, but the whole country was underdeveloped, both in terms of income per head and of the percentage of population in agriculture. So the first problem was whether it was better to attack the problem of backward areas at once, or to wait until average income per head was higher. For both economic and human reasons it was essential to take the former view. The problem was made harder by the multiplicity of languages, religions and so on, making it an unusual one. The influence of Marxism was to lead to far greater solidarity between regions.

On the institutional aspects, Professor Mihailović recalled that Yugoslavia had six republics and two autonomous regions. The fact that each had its own legislative and executive authority aggravated the problem. Several curious things should be noted. First, four of these regions were classified as underdeveloped, but what did this mean, and what results did it have? Second, having the federal government was seen as an advantage, enabling it to bring out the gravity of regional problems. But Professor Mihailović said that frontiers between the regions held back the mobility of labour, and therefore integrated development.

Finally, the paper looked at the methods used for backward areas. Detailed planning had been abandoned to get greater decentralisation of decisions. Planning was largely indicative. This raised interesting questions. Had the revival of market forces had serious effects on the backward areas? Since 1956, when the new policy was introduced, the development of backward areas had been much more rapid. This suggested that the move towards greater use of market forces had not had bad effects on the backward areas. Of course, there was now a higher rate of planned growth for them, and the central government could also use its expenditure to assist the regions. The period of centralised planning had coincided with the establishment of heavy industry, especially in the backward areas. The period of more flexible planning had coincided with the growth of lighter industry.

The main policy objective had been rapid growth in all areas, with a higher rate of growth for the backward areas. The paper gave a good deal of information, especially in Section 3, though Professor Mihailović said that the tables in this Section needed careful interpretation because of apparent contradictions. These figures also allowed Professor Mihailović to point to differences between the various backward areas. For example, income per head was higher than the national average in two areas, and lower in two others. Professor Mihailović saw this as the result of three factors: the rate of population growth, the level of investment in each region, and the nature and distribution of this investment.

Professor Lajugie found some lack of clarity in some of the tables, for example, those on social welfare payments and fixed funds per head (p. 264). Did this latter concept cover all investment or only funds especially devoted to backward areas?

In the third part of the paper, the links between regional and sectoral development were considered. Professor Mihailović thought that investment had been lower in the backward areas. This was partly because of a shortage of skilled labour, and partly because of a lack of external economies. But, above all, it was because the distribution of investment depended on the sectoral structure of the region. Professor Mihailović looked at the effects of structural differences on the growth of backward areas (pp. 267–8). For example, Montenegro had had a lot of investment in its main sectors; in Macedonia the emphasis was on primary industry and agriculture. So Macedonia had grown more slowly than Montenegro. It was also shown (p. 268), that there were probably the same differences between other regions, including the developed ones.

Another idea emphasised by Professor Mihailović was that there was a clear division of labour between regions. The backward areas were mostly primary producers; the others emphasised manufacturing industry. This led to unfavourable terms of trade for the backward areas. Could Professor Mihailović expand on this?

Professor Lajugie found some lack of clarity in the final part of the paper. This discussed active and passive regions and sectors. What was the interdependence here?

An issue flowing from all this was that Professor Mihailović gave great emphasis to differences in regional structure during periods of development. Had attempts been made to look at the precise effects of regional structure? This must require input-output tables and regional accounts, as well as figures for manpower distribution. Professor Lajugie realised how hard it was to construct regional accounts, as French experience showed, and especially to identify regional flows of goods and money. But in a country with a federal structure, this might be easier. He wondered what was being done.

Professor Fauvel said that Bohemia and Slovakia seemed similar, in their natural resources and climate. How was it that one found pessimism over the last twenty years in Slovakia? Was Professor Turčan exaggerating the slowness of growth? In Czechoslovakia there was solidarity in the economic development of the country; Slovakia possessed 30 per cent of the Czechoslovak population and 30 per cent of its investment. There had clearly been considerable central government support for Slovakia. We were back to 'scatterisation'. Villages would be modernised in existing locations, and factories spread around the region every few kilometres. The agricultural population had fallen, and there had been a trebling in output per man. So, on the basis of what had been done, and with a good deal of agricultural education, would not things improve greatly? One could say that in industry things had not gone so well. Perhaps there was too little technical 'know-how' and managerial ability. But again, the basis for growth had been laid. With time, the benefits of education would show.

Professor Davin asked some questions, directed generally to socialist economists. The first was on functional integration and motivation. In all countries in Europe these were two essential elements for regional economic development. On the first, he agreed with Professor Sovani, and wanted to ask Professor Turčan whether he regarded the lack of functional integration between Slovakia and the Czech area as important. Would he have preferred autonomous development in Slovakia?

The second question led from the first, and was about motivation. Why did one have a regional economic policy? Was it to help the whole country, or the regions? The absolute level of welfare might not rise if one developed the regions without functional integration, national and international. Regional policy in socialist countries had to take account of the new role of the market. The new policies obviously applied outside the backward areas. Now wider, even world, markets would affect the backward regions. Would not these changes require a radical revision of regional economic policy?

Finally, in socialist countries, the co-ordination of national and regional plans ought to be much easier, but did things work out so well in practice?

Professor Turčan wanted to correct a possible misunderstanding. He was sorry if Professor Sovani imagined that he was pleading for the autonomous development of a region. One could develop a region in an industrial country only if it had close links with the rest of the economy, and indeed, over a wide area. Professor Davin had emphasised the need for functional integration with the outside world. All integration must have a clear context. Integration must be such that if Slovakia had a big petrochemical complex, with partly-refined products going to the rest of the region, there was a high value-added in the region. The multiplier effect of investment depended on technical factors. For instance, if aluminium was produced, but all of it was processed outside the region, this was functional integration but not of the kind one wanted in order to develop a particular region.

Professor Turčan thanked Professor Fauvel for his interest in Slovakia, but said that the new economic system would reveal weaknesses in the Slovak economy.

Professor Mihailović said that in Yugoslavia it was not hard to find differences between regions because of the dual structure, which was the consequence of the Austro-Hungarian and Turkish occupation. When defining a developed region, we could not rely on one criterion only, say, income per head. It was necessary to look at the development of the whole structure, analysing its components: income and the value of fixed funds per inhabitant, the development of the infrastructure, the share of industry, agriculture and other activities in income formation, the structure of the population, the degree of employment, the living standard, etc.

He did not have time to say much about investment. By fixed funds he meant the real value of realised and current investment. According to the plan, throughout the next five years, 820 milliard dinars would be invested from Federal fixed funds in backward regions. This fund was financed by taxes, amounting to 1·85 per cent of the national product of the social sector of the economy.

Professor Oelssner said he would take up an earlier point of Professor Robertson's and discuss the optimum size of a new industrial town. There was no one criterion. The optimum size depended on the size of the country, its population, on the existing infrastructure, on the nature of the economy of the region, and other things. One could take as an example the U.S.S.R. with new industrial towns like Magnitogorsk. In the G.D.R. there were no such large new towns. Historically East Germany had more small to medium-sized centres. At present there were only eleven towns with more than 100,000 inhabitants. There were ninety-five towns with 25,000 to 100,000 people. Some of the smaller towns were very important industrial centres like the Zeiss plant, or the large metal complex in Brandenburg. At present, the G.D.R. planned the creation mainly of new towns and centres with populations of 30,000–40,000, including a town to produce soft coal. They were thinking there of a population of 140,000. Elsewhere there would be a large petrochemical complex, with an oil pipe-line from the U.S.S.R. There would be some small towns of only 25,000 people but with plans to go up to 40,000. This was the present picture, so he saw no clear criterion for the size of urban centres.

On the efficiency of capital in backward areas, he would look again at the G.D.R. A low efficiency of capital applied to new branches of industry too. When building a large new industrial plant, it took time for this to become profitable. If one considered the metal combine in the G.D.R. mentioned earlier, this was built on a greenfield site near the River Oder, with no coal or ore, and used imported materials. It was not very profitable. Was building it a mistake? He did not think so, because there was no alternative way of getting steel. After giving the plant large subsidies, efforts were now being made to reduce its losses. The size of the plant was being increased, to give economies of scale, and rolling mills were being introduced as well as furnaces. Once this was done, the losses would fall, and indeed, the plant would soon begin to make profits. The investment would then be worth while.

Professor Šik thought it would be unfortunate if the impression were given that economists in socialist countries were more concerned with propaganda than with economic science. It sometimes seemed that there was nothing but progress in socialist countries, that everything was proceeding well and that the solution of regional problems was easy. This was not so. Despite progress with industrialisation, new and difficult problems had to be solved. Overall development had required much more effort than it often seemed to do. Today, in most socialist countries, there were economists who carefully investigated economic problems. There had been a period, perhaps, when rapid industrialisation, especially the development of heavy industry, had been necessary at whatever cost. A relatively large industrial foundation was needed, and it was possible to build this quite rapidly because of surplus labour in rural areas. With rising costs, however, this policy had to be reconsidered.

For a period, socialist countries had created more and more heavy industry. Initially this rapid fulfilment of the plans was welcome. Later, economists saw that the productivity of marginal investment was falling rapidly. In 1952, Czechoslovakia had a marginal capital-output ratio of 1·3. In 1960, it was 2·4; yet in 1963 it was 18·2 ! This deterioration was the result of continued investment in some industries, regardless of costs. Effectiveness was not calculated at all and an administered price policy made these calculations entirely impossible. It was true that overall growth had, in the earlier stages, probably required a rise in the capital-output ratio. In Czechoslovakia, labour productivity was rising only slowly and inputs of raw materials were increasing fast. Total investment also increased rapidly, so that there were no economies in production costs to offset rising capital costs. Over a time period, rising investment meant increasing total costs at a time when the output did not rise equally fast. Also, Czechoslovakia had both to produce more capital goods herself and to import more.

There was production for the sake of production, and increased production could always be shown to be necessary. This was a self-justifying process. Quantitative plans were always completely fulfilled. Yet the progressively slower rise in the G.N.P., and the impossibility of increasing the home output and imports of consumer goods meant a slower rise in the standard of living. Since 1960, wages in Czechoslovakia had risen more slowly than in any other country, and there were balance of payments difficulties. Something had to be done. The policy of industrialisation at all costs had to be ended.

This was why, in Czechoslovakia, what was needed was a combination of the modern market mechanism and socialist macro-economic planning. In future, industrial enterprises would have to meet all expenditure from their earnings and face domestic as well as foreign competition. From the point of view of the regions, this would mean allowing themselves to be guided by rational investment decision-making in the enterprise and, at the same time, carrying out regional planning centrally, guiding the decisions of enterprises by financial tools. The objective would no longer be to industrialise at any cost, but to develop industry in such a way as to achieve the most rapid growth of incomes that was possible and to make production competitive both at home and abroad.

Professor Šik thought Czechoslovakia needed an economic policy with clear long-run goals, sophisticated tools of economic analysis and co-ordination of national and regional economic policy. It was no longer a question of maintaining investment and production in real terms. There should be plans giving enterprises targets to meet and using more and more financial incentives. This would mean that economic policy in Czechoslovakia would be similar to that in the West, except that the enterprises were socialist and that there was a macro-economic policy for the whole economy. The Government should use income and fiscal policy to achieve this. New kinds of regional economic policy would have to be developed which would play a larger role in future. The problem of how to use advanced analytical methods in regional planning had been neglected.

Professor Valarché was interested in the nature of the stimulants used. In Slovakia there had been a large industrial investment, not simply of money, but of entrepreneurship and of labour. Yet this was an agricultural area with no skilled industrial labour or enterprise. What had happened? Had labour been imported, and why? Were wages increased, or were other measures used? And what about entrepreneurs? Was there administrative pressure on them, or were higher incomes offered?

Professor Delivanis thought the papers showed that the two countries had tried hard to reduce regional differences for both economic and political reasons. Despite their efforts, and despite the sacrifices of the more-developed areas in favour of the less-developed, differences in incomes per head had not lessened. In some cases they had even increased, despite improvements in absolute terms. So far as increase per head was concerned, percentage changes depended on the point of departure. He wondered what developments in productivity there were in Slovakia, and was eager to know if the improvement of industry took account of the disappearance of craftsmanship in Czechoslovakia.

He ended by stressing the explanation given by Professor Mihailović of the way more-developed areas had helped less-developed ones, namely, the unfavourable prices paid by the authorities for agricultural commodities and for raw materials.

Professor Nussbaumer suggested that one thing to be learned from Professor Mihailović's paper was the importance of both national borders and those of planning areas. Whenever regional development areas were chosen, we should seek therefore to separate out real economic regions.

Second, both papers showed the extreme importance of the regional terms of trade. A backward area needed products with high value added and good price prospects. This could not be too strongly stressed. Professor Mihailović especially had shown the serious effects of keeping agricultural prices relatively low.

Professor Robertson said that Professor Turčan had stressed the need to go back to agricultural improvement, but emphasised the need to push on also with industrial development. In earlier sessions, the Round Table had associated agricultural development essentially with remote areas. The agricultural issue here was similar to that of any other industry. It needed new techniques, a new labour force, and better training facilities. It also needed markets, so that one had the same kind of needs in agriculture as in industry. In all this, the work of the physical planner would be important, and the same kind of analysis was appropriate to both the industrial and the agricultural case.

Mr MacLennan wondered whether, in the era of central planning, there had been too much dispersion of investment. Was this due to an attempt to spread industry evenly on social rather than economic grounds?

On price reform, he wondered how far there was a desire to go back to using the market, accompanied by better methods of planning public expenditure in backward areas.

Mr Petrella-Tirone said that the differences in the problems of regional development between East and West Europe seemed to be caused by the efforts of the former to introduce a new medium into the economy. Professor Mihailović stressed that economic and social equality were the motivating force in the Yugoslav economy, and Professor Winiarski also stressed the central role of equality.

Two questions arose. First, was equality unrealisable? If so, what could be the idea motivating a regional policy to replace that of equalisation? Could it be rising living standards, or the optimal spatial distribution of economic activity, or something else?

Second, taking the conclusions of papers by western economists into account, could one say that the search for a new economic policy in Eastern Europe had not yet given the expected results?

Professor Mihailović's paper touched on another problem, largely ignored in the meetings: the link between economic and administrative regions. Was it not reasonable to say that an essential basis for the State's regional policy was to base the national economic plan on true spatial economic units? Unfortunately we were far from knowing how such regionalisation could be achieved. Space still seemed to be absent when development plans were built. Only economic regionalisation could lead to more interest being shown in spatial factors.

Professor Penouil wondered whether studies had been made to see whether the previous price system had helped or hindered backward areas. On the whole it seemed to have helped. Under the old system, were the prices of individual products based on national or local factors? What effect would the new system have in industrialisation in Slovakia?

Professor Turčan returned to the fundamental question raised by Professor Sovani, who had reproached him for seeking to bring about equality between the regions. He agreed, but one must distinguish regions. If one took a micro-region, a district of Slovakia, this was very different from the whole of Slovakia. He thought it was necessary to bring Slovakia up to the level of the whole country. But there would still be differences within Slovakia.

To Mr Petrella-Tirone, he would say only that an emphasis on raising the standard of living could not be achieved simply by subsidies to social consumption. A rise in the standard of living depended on raising the performance of the whole economy.

On agriculture, it was true that there had been some success, but in Slovakia they had not taken advantage of the possibility of using agriculture as the basis for the development of the whole area. It was because agricultural development would not lead to balance of payments problems, because it used local resources, that he put so much emphasis on agriculture. There was a great similarity here between agriculture and industry. It was not just a matter of mechanisation. Young, dynamic labour left agriculture, so that the region could not use even the capital assets which agriculture already had.

This brought him back to the prices of agricultural products and the need to raise the profitability of farming. Professor Fauvel had spoken of 'scatterisation'. Professor Turčan thought he had been right to emphasise this because the big investment in Slovakia had led to exaggerated development. It was now necessary to create a better-integrated system in order to make use of these investments. The whole national economy needed a big rise in productivity per head. He would stress that it was the economic reforms which had shown the weaknesses of Slovakia.

Professor Penouil had asked about prices under the old system. Prices had played no important part, so there was really nothing to say about their role in regional development. In the new system all the weaknesses of firms and of the industrial structure would be revealed clearly. This was why they were worried in Czechoslovakia about the effects of introducing a more active market, and the decision to fix the correct prices for backward areas.

Professor Mihailović was grateful for the way Professor Lajugie had entered into the spirit of his paper. He would just take up the issue of integration. This could be looked at in many ways. What was happening in Yugoslavia was the integration of industry on an interregional basis. However, this sort of integration was not enough. One had first to develop the economy of underdeveloped regions as a precondition for fuller integration. One could have a common aim for the whole economy. What was to be the basis of integration? It should be the distribution of labour between the regions.

On price reform, the role of the market could increase regional problems. The way it was intended to help backward areas was not only to give investment funds, but to provide compensation for unfavourable terms of trade.

To Professor Penouil, he would say that prices had a big role in socialist countries. There had been big differences in prices. As a rule, they were low for primary goods and high in manufacturing. The pricing system had been especially important in its effects on the agricultural regions in Yugoslavia. With the reform of prices, regions producing agricultural and other primary products had gained greatly. So far as the role of prices was concerned, he thought agricultural prices played little role in backward areas. In Yugoslavia it was the northern regions which were in a difficult position. But where they had industry, the backward areas had benefited.

What seemed important was that there was a compromise between national and regional interests in the distribution of income. As for centralisation versus dispersion, one could use a centralised system to eliminate regional differences. But regional influences obviously lay behind even a centralised system.

P 2

NINTH SESSION

The Development of Backward Areas in Poland and Hungary

Discussion of Paper by Professor B. Winiarski and D. L. Kőszegi

Professor Robinson said that unfortunately Dr. Kőszegi could not be present. It was also unfortunate that Professor Vajda, who was an expert on the Hungarian economy, would be ready to assist us to understand the development of the Hungarian economy, yet though he would not necessarily want to defend the paper in detail.

Professor Peronöü introduced Professor Winiarski's paper, which he referred to a number of these that had been considered already. First, there was the role of historical and human factors. Second, there was the influence of the time factor or development policy. Third, there were the problems of integrating regional and national policy. He wanted to draw out a number of points from the paper. There were two kinds of preoccupation. The first was to define regions and their subdivisions. The second was to show how economic policy could help to redevelop such regions.

This paper had a three fold approach. First, there was an historical and causal approach to explain political and economic decisions by historical factors; for example, the effects of nineteenth century politics, as in Yugoslavia. Second, there were the results of the inter-war period, and of World War II, with new frontiers, and which changes in the distribution and organisation of the population.

The second approach was to distinguish types of region. Professor Winiarski gave a spatial typology. First he distinguished the regions in the West of considerable development. Second, there were the reconstructed regions. They were important but the infrastructure had to be rebuilt after the war. Third, there were weakly developed regions.

The third approach in the paper was perhaps the most interesting. Here Professor Winiarski asked what were the criteria of regional underdevelopment. Two of these related to the state of employment and two others to the standard of living. Unless a region had a number of these attributes, it was a backward area.

The triple approach was completed by a study of development policy. The organisation of planning was dealt with in detail, especially the problems of planning. He would concentrate on problems of planning, especially the three-coordination of national and regional planning. There was a choice of policies. One could draw up pure regional plans, or the coordination could start at the national level. An administrative structure was not enough to think national and regional planning.

Professor Peronöü first questioned how was the significance of this analysis. Was a retarded economy conditioned by analysis by historical factors? Behind them there were more essential factors like geography and natural resources.

The ideal of statistical data uses ... of full analysis is. How would one make these historical effects more precise?

A second series of questions was as to the criteria of defining backward areas. For Professor Péter Enyedi, the four criteria given were not enough. One needed more emphasis on the level of income and on the individual standard of living. Nor did the criteria given seem significant. Agricultural output per head here was as a very specialised idea. It could hardly provide the criterion of the development of backward area.

Professor Péter Enyedi found Professor Wiesel's paper interesting on the organisation of planning, but he wanted to know how location decisions were taken. How, and by whom, were current prices calculated? What about the availability of regional plans? It seemed to him that authorities had little power to direct investment or the use of factors of production. Perhaps the position could be made clearer. The plans seemed to depend more on wishes than on the planners' activities.

The Polish example was important because it raised the question of the time scale of planning. It showed how initial actions could lead to others. Economic development had occurred, based on new links between old land use in industries. If the plan had not predicted this well, could not economic development have been held back? There were so interesting problems of adaptation here.

Professor Mihailović introduced Dr Kőszegi's paper. He said it showed how a small country like Hungary suffered from some original imbalance. It was clear that the industrialisation of the backward areas depended most on the growth of Budapest. The paper showed how great the concentration there was. One could see how the issues related to it, might just be regional ones.

In the early period, the need to develop the whole economy had overshadowed regional problems. Investment in agriculture had been neglected. The paper showed on pages 30-2 that after firms were determining ... which region to go to or from the point of view of the various costs. Why were not macroeconomic criteria developed? The diversion of industry from Budapest was mentioned. Why was this necessary already in 1956 if developed regions offered a favourable location? There also seemed to have been an underdeveloped infrastructure in the underdeveloped regions.

An outsider perhaps with a superficial view, would feel that one could have a bigger number of centres than the paper suggested. Were not the effects of inadequate infrastructure overestimated? Hungary was not short of infrastructure, or of skilled labour. This impression was strengthened by experience in the period 1965-5, when there was a further concentration and rapid growth in the backward areas. Such rapid industrial development could not take place if there had been no infrastructure. Labour reserves in backward regions had become an attractive factor. What, then, was the appraisal of the potential of the whole economy or of emigration from backward areas. Hungary had a rather slow increase in population. This was a doubtless useful in aiding the backward areas.

There were clearly doubts in Hungary about the best policy to follow. There was agreement on the important role of agriculture because of Hungary's natural resources, but also because of its ... effect. Hungary was not the only socialist country which needed to develop agriculture if it were not to develop its backward areas. The role of agriculture depended on the changes in the structure of the economy which it could cause in some historical contexts.

Dr Köszegi advocated development of the infrastructure in order to improve the whole of the backward areas. It was not quite clear what Dr Köszegi's view was on the concentration of population. There were clearly problems here. The size and functions of towns had not been stated clearly enough in the paper. There was the statement that there were only five towns of more than 100,000 and that it would be desirable to have more.

Professor Mihailović suggested that the role of big and small enterprises needed to be clarified. Many thought that handicrafts and small-scale industries had a lot to contribute. He doubted whether some of these ideas were good: they were close to the German historical school.

On manpower training, the paper repeated some views that had largely been disproved in practice. Managerial staff was clearly important, and there was the idea that big enterprises could co-operate with small units in backward areas, having more experience of technical progress. Entrepreneurs in backward areas were only executives; while the planning of research, etc., was carried out in big centres. This might perpetuate the economic dominance of big cities.

The intention to introduce a new system of economic management at the beginning of 1968 reminded us of the problem of how to prevent this damaging the backward areas. There would be finance from the central government and easier credit from banks. Would such measures, indirect as they were, work with existing price differences?

Professor Winiarski thanked Professor Penouil for his introduction which raised some interesting but complicated problems. He said he would like to add to his paper on relations between national and regional planning.

Regional growth policy should be considered an integral part of national planning for economic growth. The political and economic aims were included in the national plan. In Poland there were perspective long-term plans and plans for shorter periods.

Regional planning was a part of perspective planning which covered a period of twenty years. One well-known method for elaborating a perspective plan was that of Professor Kalecki, presented at the Conference in Geneva in 1963. According to Kalecki perspective planning began by setting the overall growth rate which it would be possible to achieve within those twenty years. Next, the amount of investment required was defined by the formula:

$$r = \frac{1}{m} \cdot \frac{I}{Y} - a + u$$

where

$r =$ annual rate of growth of national income;

$m =$ the capital coefficient (the number of units of investment required to raise the national income by one unit);

$\frac{I}{Y} =$ the investment ratio, i.e. the share of investment in national income;

$a =$ the amortisation coefficient; and

$u =$ the improvement coefficient, i.e. the rise in national income with zero net investment, by better use of fixed assets, improved organisation, and so on.

With the given figure of the national income at the end of the perspective plan and its division into investment and consumption, one could calculate consumption per head. Different regions would show deviations from the mean value at the start of the plan. Regional development policy aimed to eliminate the existing disparities and to reach, in each region, a level similar to the average national level at the end of the plan.

In order to reach the general growth rate fixed in the plan there must be an appropriate structure of the economy and of investment. That structure was influenced by the growth rate. The structure could be fixed using input-output tables. The sector and branch structure of the economy defined the kinds of investment and resources to be exploited during the twenty years. The resources were located in various regions; so, the particular investments must also be located in those regions. However, the sector branch growth structure and that of investment might not be adjusted to the structure of regions. It might require investment in natural resources, and so could be carried out only in regions rich in natural resources. It would then be difficult to speed up the growth of regions where there were no suitable resources. It would also be hard to raise consumption there to the planned national average. These contradictions between regional conditions and the requirements of the sector branch structure were well known in Poland. It explained why speeding up of growth in the eastern regions poor in natural resources had been very hard to achieve.

More could be done in modern branches of industry which required fewer natural resources: for example, the chemical industry.

The international division of labour also contributed to the process of adjusting the regional and the sector branch structure. Individual countries could supplement their resources by specialising in branches whose development would be adjusted to regional conditions. For example, the U.S.S.R. supplied crude oil for Poland. The building of the oil pipeline provided the structure of production needed in Poland and also opened up new possibilities for developing the eastern regions. On the basis of crude oil and natural gas, new centres had been established in Plock and Pulawy – regions poor in natural resources. Similarly, co-operation with G.D.R. and Czechoslovakia had made it possible to use the brown coal resources in South-West Poland. In this case, the electricity is sold to Czechoslovakia and the G.D.R.

The co-ordination of regional development plans with national plans was thus a matter of assuring harmony in the resources of different regions; raising their performance, and improving the sector/branch structure of production and of investment; taking into consideration the possibilities for international co-operation and the modernisation of economy. To attain the given growth rate in particular regions those branches of activity should be chosen which were best adjusted to regional conditions. Deviation from this rule was possible only in so far as social aims were put before economic objectives.

Professor Vajda said that to be able to speak of backward areas in Hungary at all was a sign of progress. Twenty years earlier, the whole of Hungary had been backward. He still thought Hungary's problems were national rather than regional. Hungarian poets had said that the country had three million beggars – the peasants. The first need was to end this state of affairs, and it was not surprising that in an effort to end unemployment and underemployment, a wave of industrialisation had started as in Czechoslovakia, jay with the concern for costs. This was awkward the egg as extensive in industrialisation. It would have been foolish to introduce labour-saving techniques. But it is proved to be a vicious circle, leading to a pattern of investments which was a matter of competitiveness on the world market. Dr Kösege said with all twenty years of a planned economy all had big effects on the backwardness of regions. He did not wholly agree. It was more in the sense of backwardness that people had become aware of. The review of village life as the only lively life. One could quote a number of Hungarian intellectuals who looked on freeing about the backwardness of village life, but rather implied that the greater cities, especially Budapest, were centres of office.

This is the backward almost historical approach, but not to go on to look at the last twenty years. The tendency to aggregate in the Budapest area continued in spite of great efforts to the papal it. The period was characterised by big shift to industrialisation. But what papa of it? It was a clear and generally accepted that agriculture had contributed to the costs of industrialisation. Stagnation in agricultural techniques and had social conditions in the country-side, in the side of the past, continued with relatively slow progress — even though progress was marked by superior to that of former periods near that it had to overcome costs. These twenty years had dominated the problem of the general backwardness of agriculture and the gap between rural and urban living standards.

The tendency towards stagnation was reinforced by extensive migration from the villages to the towns. It was a migration of young people who could be remaining in the countryside. This a shift in the demographic pattern of the rural population which was detrimental to technical progress and to the introduction of new production techniques. Migration from rural areas also had been caused by economic factors only especially in the last 5 years there had been shortage that an abundance of labour especially at harvest time. The pattern of life for young people from villages then community of urban life was largely responsible.

A second area of stagnation was that as in Czechoslovakia, there was a protectionism paralleled in economic history with the concern for its costs. This was bound to lead to technical stagnation to a state where quick progress was possible in large parts of the country especially agricultural areas.

Professor V said was sure that industrialisation in Hungary was a necessity and on the whole successful. But it did not mean that its failings contradictions could should be corrected. A recent calculation of the so-called aggregate productivity showed that with 1000 of industrial productivity in Hungary the corresponding figure in Czechoslovakia was 1600. And Czechoslovakia itself was not satisfied with its own productivity.

Hungary was a small country poor in natural resources. It was second only to Denmark in Europe. So to raise the level of the economy and the standard of living Hungary had to concentrate on adding value. The international division of labour was of decisive importance. More than 53 per cent of the GNP was from foreign trade. There again Dr Kösege's paper showed that the whole so the eastern part of the country was a backward undeveloped. There was no population within the of the neighbouring countries. The backward areas were on the periphery. The important elements of Hungary are in the

North, and the best of form of co-operation would be to look plants in Czechoslovakia and Poland with them. He would have liked to see visible progress on these lines, but it succeeded to be unrealistic so long as the bureaucracy had a monopoly in negotiating international contacts. He expected fundamental changes from national following direct links between Hungaria and other, including western enterprises. The most important changes were likely to be at the national level.

Professor Dürr in changing the regional policy was as above all an open policy, and the successes of regional economics were also open. Mr Achberman and Professor Winarski said that the predisected about an interdisciplinary regional policy in their own countries, policies based on great collaboration. But that failed to explain in how an interdisciplinary collaboration was possible.

Mr Commenos asked a question. He had been fascinated by Professor Winarski's exposition. It was logical that one should want to maximise national growth over a period, given the capital-output ratio. Yet some regions had a poor or development possibilities. If their aim was a high maximisation of the G.N.P., then some regions would find their position diminished — either by private decisions or by national direction. He wanted to know if this had been thought about in Poland, and if the State had been actively engaged.

Professor Turean commented that Professor Penouli had mentioned that it was hard to look only at Poland. He wanted to say that in both socialist and other countries, one must distinguish between regional policy to be carried out at the regional level, and regional strategy to be carried out mainly at the centre. The central one could carry out either regional policy or sectoral policy, and the regional point of view would be represented at the centre.

Professor Bönten noted that Professor Penouli had said that an historical approach was probably not appropriate. He thought that in this situation one kind of historical approach was appropriate. One needed to know the role and speed of development which was known in the past. To establish quantitative relationships of the present one always had to go into the past.

Second, there was a point arising from Professor Ayada's remarks. How was the conflict between balanced growth and balanced regional growth to be solved? One might have a conflict between maximal growth and regional justice. A neglected region for a period of time might be better off after ten years if the region had higher growth rates and could then help it. How far had such problems played a part?

Mr Peall Hitano responded to the paper about an interdisciplinary approach to the problems of the Ruhr Valley by drawing attention to page 13 of Professor Köszeg's paper where he had advocated linking industrial development with that of the settlement network, particularly the need in situation and development of towns.

When Professor Robinson asked for studies of the problems of new towns, and when Professor Dürr or wanted regional policy to be based on the diversification of economic activity in different branch centres, this seemed to go to the root of the problem, the link between industrialisation and urbanisation.

A town was not simply a collection of residential and communal activities, but of economic, cultural and other activities too. The town had an important function in organising the spatial environment. One could perhaps speak of villages matrices and of urban axes of development.

One reason for the backwardness of Southern Italy was the absence of some real urban centres. Apart from Naples and Bari, the South simply had 'human dormitories'. While in the North a town like Como, with 100,000 people, had an integrating role for its area, one like Reggio Calabria in the South was far from doing so.

The solution of problems of urban structure was central to any regional policy. How to do this, and by what criteria to link together policies for industrialisation and for urban reorganisation, remained to be shown.

Mr MacLennan spoke about the question of concentrated development mentioned in Dr Köszegi's paper. First, on page 311, it was said that one third of all settlements in Hungary would be chosen for development. This sounded a very high proportion. One could hardly 'concentrate' on so many units. Infrastructure was expensive, and so had to be concentrated if it were to yield maximum benefit. Again, if there was surplus labour, this might have to be attracted into a few sizeable labour market areas.

A second point concerned stages of development. On the one hand, one had a suggestion of concentrated development; on the other, one had to respect certain stages. On the one hand, one had unbalanced growth, and on the other balanced. Perhaps there could not be too long a period between stages if one wanted to concentrate development.

Finally, the idea of restricting the growth of Budapest was interesting because many European countries were wanting similarly to restrain development around large cities. In the London area, for example, the British Government could restrain growth by preventing firms from doing what they wanted to do. Given that it had been decided to restrict Budapest, and given the existence of national planning in Hungary, had anyone worked out at the national level a land-use plan for the settlement pattern implied by such restrictions? Where could firms from Budapest develop?

Professor Vito stressed that to understand underdevelopment, it was often useful to know the history. Behind any discussion of regional policy lay economic and social history. It was certainly vital to an understanding of the situation in Italy.

He was impressed by what Professor Vajda said about there being a national rather than a regional problem in Hungary, but what was the point of reference? Other parts of Hungary, or other countries? Must it not be a reference point within the country?

He could see danger in concentrating investment where productivity was highest – in an advanced region. One would not then be getting balanced growth.

Professor Robertson said that both the countries discussed had planned systems allowing movement in decision-taking from the centre to the periphery and back. With land-use planning one wanted to look at the infrastructure to see how much might be needed, in the way of changed facilities, to make a given population expansion feasible or desirable. As economists, if we thought a city was needed, we tended to imply that one would arrive. If land-use planners studied various locations, they would rule out some on the ground that they lacked the land or easily extensible facilities. So one would have a better indication of which existing centres to develop. A negative answer would strengthen the case for outward movement.

Professor Hoover noted that in Professor Winiarski's paper, at the end, it was recalled that one could not locate investment efficiently and still take care of all backward areas. But Professor Winiarski went on to argue that this problem was eased because services were becoming more important. This implied that services were footloose enough to help. We usually thought of services as not footloose. Was this what Professor Winiarski meant? If so, what kind of services could one use in this way?

Professor Groenman had been challenged by Professor Davin's comment. One might wonder if the proceedings of the Round Table were interesting enough for a sociologist. At first the papers had seemed to reflect only economic considerations. Not only were they interesting, but sociological elements were present, if only by implication. Their apparent absence was largely a question of language, and of the type of problem they chose to analyse. He was happy with Professor Davin's explicit study of sociological problems in Belgium, and also what was said in the papers by Professors Turčan and Mihailović. The role of political forces showed clearly. He did not himself draw a clear line between political science and sociology. What had been heard in this session showed that ideological and sociological factors could be effective in not putting regional development on a strict economic basis.

Replying to Professor Davin, Professor Groenman said he saw no great difficulty in collaboration between economists and sociologists. The problems were not so much between the disciplines as such, but in institutions. In the Netherlands, each province had three development institutes. One was concerned with economics, one with physical planning and one with community organisation. When one looked at them, one found all three employing the same kinds of people. He had himself advised all three types of organisation. The problem was the desire for institutional independence. It was a problem of public administration, of how to persuade these bodies to collaborate.

Professor Robinson said that in reading these papers, he had asked himself whether, if it were simply a matter of economics with no political or cultural issues, we should be here at all. Should one be prepared to say: 'Here is a country; let us behave as though there are no prejudices about where to develop'? In the U.K., should one have a location policy allowing Scotland, Wales and Northern Ireland to keep together their existing communities? Or should one assume that there was a need to break these up for the benefit of Britain (others would say England !). This really was a problem of political economy. Ought we to be simple-minded followers of classical economics, assisting solutions to work themselves out as they would? Ought an economist to impose his own view of the priority of economic considerations on others? He himself was interested in the cultural unity of these areas, and wanted to find the best economic solution consistent with them. Did we know enough about the relative costs of solving these problems with and without constraints imposed on the locations of points of growth?

Dr Marsan felt that at present the main preoccupation in Eastern Europe was clearly dissatisfaction with the system, which it was hoped would be reduced by allowing greater decentralisation. One should not, however, mistake the inefficiencies of the economic system for the handicaps of location If one did, this could have bad consequences for the backward areas. Moreover, one saw

... all half-hearted arguments in favour of unbalanced or rapid growth. If one talked in terms of regions, the stress should be that if one was a late in developing a backward area the risks was that at a late in making migration would deal with the point in a damaging permanently by the human resources, including the changed distribution of the region. We must be ready to stick to the objective of a more balanced regional growth through the necessary subsidies and other effective measures.

Professor von Böventer said he would go on one step further. There was a tendency to assume the same cultural conditions everywhere. It was so in societies using substances whether one wanted to keep certain cultural areas at a higher rate of growth. These two points should be distinguished clearly. One might so societies support a particular region for purely cultural reasons.

Professor Robinson suggested that, even so, one needed to know the cost.

Professor von Böventer argued, but one conceded that one should not define the cost in economic terms what one could not be defined that way.

Professor Ladjusing had been interested in what Professor Winiarski had said about regional plans. He was very interested in planning methods in a socialist and western economies. He thought that regional plans were elaborated by the same authorities in Poland as were concerned with national planning. Was the central administration to be concerned with regional and national plans?

Professor Winiarski replied to the debate. To Professor Ladjusing he said that the elaboration of regional plans in Poland was the task of regional institutions, i.e. of specialised planning offices existing in all parts of the country. In their studies they took into consideration not only local interests, but the lines of central planning. There was a constant dialogue between regional and central planning bodies about the directions and size of a task being set in the plans. Recently the method of iteration had been widely used to obtain optimal solutions on a regional and national scale. Each region elaborated several alternative propositions aimed at accelerating the rate of growth and to reducing the deviations from the average national rate. These propositions were analysed and compared centrally where a solution was chosen which corresponded to the aims of general policy and, at the same time, assured its effectiveness.

This problem was connected with Professor Penouil's question about the responsibility of regional bodies. The choice of regions to develop was made centrally. The central body also defined the rate and direction of growth of individual regions. Here the central body decisions were based on the plans and opinions of regional authorities as well as on the results of analyses made by regional bodies and compared centrally. The choice which the region for shaping infrastructure and services belonged to the regional authorities.

The problems of backward regions in Poland were complicated, because the administrative division of the country did not reflect the division based on economic disparities. Within administrative regions there were both developed and undeveloped areas. That fact created difficulties in comparing statistical indices. The indices used by the Central Office of Statistics were not sufficient, but there were more exact statistical data about the districts of the first years after the war. Now broader aspects could be taken into consideration.

Professor Odd closed the discussion. He said he was far from suggesting a general rule on the relation between national and regional policy. He simply felt that, at present, in Hungary, national policy had a priority. Only this would on a feat on over to tackle regional problems. Which countries like Italy, where agriculture was an area of ... by a backward, one could not generalise in such a way.

To Professor von Böventer, he said that the ... should not ... but it had just ... to be done to people and to regions. The right to justice was an emphasised debate because for a long time the organisation of the economy was itself felt to be unjust. If producers had to sell their production at less than production costs, and if, later, they were given credits which they could not repay and which therefore had to be cancelled, one could not accept this as fair. These producers had the right to restore the propositions. Of course, they always used state aid in balance. The aim of policy now was to eliminate it.

On Budapest as a will to ... Professor Vajda did not think that statistics were fully satisfactory. In industry had been very unevenly spread. But Budapest demonstrated the greatest strength of manufacturing, and the statistics did not always show this. When planning began in Hungary an initial aim was to reduce the dominance of Budapest. Despite the figures given in Dr Köszegi's paper, he doubted whether much progress had been made. It was hard to stop such an agglomeration growing. The whole agglomeration was a fact, and for the present, no solutions seemed to be in sight.

Mr Mácha had said that the number of selected centres selected for development was too big. There were, however, pressure groups in this system too. This showed one result of the pressure.

TENTH SESSION

The Industrial Development of Backward Regions of the USSR.

Discussion of Papers by Professors A. A. Adamyan and N. N. Rotkikov

Professor Vito introduced the papers. He felt he should apologise for having accepted this task because he is not directed knowledge of the U.S.S.R. was inadequate and because he did not speak Russian. However, he had learned many things on his visits to the universities of Moscow and Leningrad.

The papers referred to the Armenian and Uzbek republics. Both had been backward areas, but were now advanced industrial countries. Professor Vito outlined the main points of the papers, explaining how both the regions had developed in the period since 1917. One paper emphasised the favourable performance of Armenia as compared with that in the remainder of the U.S.S.R. and in Iran and Turkey. As for Uzbekistan, it held a leading position in several kinds of production, especially cotton, power, natural gas, and a number of other areas. It was a major contributor to the exports of the U.S.S.R.

He would suggest the general proposition that perhaps we found it hard to compare industrialisation in these two republics with regions we knew better. If one took 1917, he thought we were not looking at a backward area but at an underdeveloped country, rather like post-war Hungary. He wondered if others shared this view.

He had a number of other points. First, we were told the U.S.S.R. used the division of labour and location policy, but we did not know how far this applied to the whole U.S.S.R. One could not make comparisons without such knowledge.

Second, it was hard to tell if there had been a programme for increasing the infrastructure. He would not be surprised at a negative answer to this question. In a largely closed economy with much underdevelopment, like the U.S.S.R. was in 1917, the country had to begin without an infrastructure and with no direct competition.

Third, what methods were used to move workers from rural to urban areas? Were wage differentials used?

Fourth, how was industry financed? We were told that Armenia was helped by all the other republics and that finance in Uzbekistan came from the profits of socialist enterprises. Did this mean enterprises within Armenia or outside it?

Fifth, the improvement in social conditions, housing, health, education, etc., was shown to be the result of development. Were these not considered an important element in infrastructure, and a pre-condition for raising the efficiency of labour? He would expect such investment to be needed early in development.

Sixth, there was the now familiar question of how far the economic system in the socialist countries was now being altered.

Professor Mihailović said Russia had produced interesting theoretical works on planning soon after the revolution that had kept their freshness. The U.S.S.R. also had a regional approach to its problems.

He wanted to ask some questions of interest to both the U.S.S.R. and us all. The first was on the agglomeration around Moscow. He understood that efforts were being made to reduce concentration there. Why was this? And what methods were being used?

As for smaller towns, all countries had problems of underemployment in these. Should one look at the relationship between large and small towns more closely?

Third, we all knew that the U.S.S.R. had problems of stimulating activity in an enormous territory, and thus of building new towns. Much had been heard of other countries' new towns. Perhaps the U.S.S.R. had something to teach us here?

Professor Robinson wanted to recall a discussion which Professor Groenman and he had had with Professor Arzumanian and Professor Kollontai when they were first planning the work of the Vienna centre. His memory of the account they were given of the U.S.S.R. was vivid, but was it right? He was told that when first confronting a backward area, the U.S.S.R. sent a team of geologists, to discover all that could be known about its resource base. He was therefore fascinated by Professor Plotnikov's description of the astonishing resource base of Uzbekistan. Here it was the geologists who gave the first impulse to development. His memory was that economists and technicians were then brought in to look at alternative uses for the resources thus disclosed. They looked for the comparative advantages of the region. Then there was a construction period, but he had been told this was used for an educational programme angled towards the needs implied by the future pattern of the region. Simultaneously, experts looked at the transport facilities and began the task of building the transport system.

So, his first question was this. Both papers spoke of development as part of the planned division of labour. What exactly did they mean? We all knew the general Marxist principle that one began from heavy industry and then worked forward to other activities. In Uzbekistan one now found much heavy industrial development and machine-building. He was too ignorant of the geographical basis of this development to be sure whether it was based on rich iron-ore deposits not mentioned in the paper. Nor did he know whether Uzbekistan had coking coal which could be used for steel production. But the issue he wished to pursue was whether they really worked in such cases of regional development on the Marxist principle of starting with heavy industry and moving to light. Or was this only true at the national level, and not for each region? And what about the relevance of this principle in other socialist countries? Or did each region pursue its own comparative advantages whatever this implied for the balance between heavy and light industry?

One could not but be impressed by the vigour of development in these two areas. But were these problem areas in the same way as the other areas considered in the Round Table? If resources like those of Uzbekistan had been found in capitalist countries, one would have expected very vigorous development. And what if this had been a poor area for resources in the U.S.S.R.? Would funds still have been poured into the region, or would population have been withdrawn?

Professor Robinson had found it hard to see what were the policy problems in the papers. Economic policy problems were usually issues of the alternative uses of limited resources. Was he right in thinking that the major problem in Uzbekistan was whether to diversify as much as they had, or to embark on more specific development? He got the impression from Professor Plotnikov's paper that he would himself have argued for more specific development than there actually was on activities in which Uzbekistan clearly had a comparative advantage. Again, in developing these two areas, how far was development spread widely, and how far was the aim to create growth points, in the sense in which we had been using this term in the Round Table?

Finally, on a point close to that of Professor Mihailović, suppose it had been decided to build a new plant in a backward area, and the resource base was small, so that costs were higher than in more favoured regions. How were these costs covered? Were there higher prices for the products of these particular plants? How far were costs spread by averaging them into the price of all steel in the U.S.S.R.? Or if total costs were high in given plants, were the wages paid by them reduced to counteract this?

Professor Delivanis said that Soviet economic policy aimed to improve the lot of people in backward areas, and to reduce the gap between living conditions in these areas and those in the western republics. The means available for doing this were, of course, the technical and material help of the latter, and also the forced savings and increased labour of the inhabitants of the backward areas. The two papers agreed that results in Armenia and Uzbekistan had been satisfactory but it would be very interesting to have figures before or at half of the development policy of income per head at constant prices, first of the Soviet Union, second of Armenia, and third of Uzbekistan. As far as Armenia was concerned, Professor Arkadya stressed the great importance of foreign trade without mentioning figures. This was at the establishing in view of the small importance of foreign trade in the Soviet Union. Professor Arkadya further mentioned the rationalisation of big firms, whereas several although that there were no given the backwardness of Armenia before the Communists took over. He further concluded that there was no waste of labour in Armenia. What was the standard of university and highlighted school education, considering the large number of students studying. Usually, with more students, standards of achievement fell.

Professor Tinbergen said in the paper on emphasis the success of development in the regions. He thought that in the U.S.S.R. regional problems existed at several levels. First there were interregional differences between republics, between economic regions. Second, there was the problem of the relationship between the areas as a whole west of the Urals. There was a greater part of the U.S.S.R. was well industrialised relatively to the eastern zone. There was also an advantage of the western part of USSR as using up its natural factors of development while the eastern areas still had unexploited resources. One view of the big effort of the Government of the U.S.S.R. to speed the development of Siberia.

Could Professor Arkadya and Plotnikov explain in what way was the view of regional economists in the U.S.S.R. on several points. First, why what was the mechanism which enabled the U.S.S.R. to arrive at a policy measures to achieve balanced growth between the two main parts of the country? He was not interested in aims which were well known but in the mechanism by which such results would be achieved. The problem seemed similar to the one in Canada.

Second, do economists want to put more emphasis on development in the East relatively to the West in the twenty-year perspective plan?

Professor Hoover thought that the paper gave an impressive array of aggregate information on such factors as production and investment for whole regions. But he had some questions. There was the problem of population distribution. He assumed that in both areas the most valuable being high population shifts. How were people moved? For example, what was the role of housing? Second, what determines the minimum feasible size of settlements? Third, in this aggregation distribution, were some parts of the regions ignored for some or all of the population? What problems did this cause? Were there problems linked to those already mentioned in our discussions of the Scottish Highlands or of the Swede?

Professor Genenov recalled that in Professor Arkadya's paper (p. 338) there was information about educational development. He too concluded this was assessed. What were children in this context? At which what was an academy by systems at'? In Professor Arkadya's paper it was said (p. 338) that Armenia had 42.3 times more students per head of population than in the U.S.A., England, France, etc. However, Professor Plotnikov showed much smaller disparity.

In Professor Arkadya's paper (p. 333) we found the statement that while during the period of 1929–37 the annual increase of the capital formation was 25.5 per cent in Armenia, and 24 per cent in the U.S.S.R. it was only 4 per cent in England and in some countries such as Italy capital formation was to be of mind. This is a sort of progress, but perhaps is of doubtful use too. To illustrate this, if there were a small initial level of investment, one could quite easily have a big increase in investment. Later the rise in investment would be smaller; then the marginal level even be an absolute decrease. For example, in the Netherlands there had been a big advantage to housing. Figures of... showed that, in 1946, 2,000 houses were rebuilt. In 1947, 6,000 might have been rebuilt - a rise of 400 per cent. In 1948, 20,000 houses might have been rebuilt - a rise of about 25 per cent. The last one year would still have shown an absolute increase, but falling in percentage rise. The number of houses rebuilt might then be higher than ever, but the percentage rise would have decreased. Indeed, once the housing shortage was over, the marginal fall in houses building, and this would be a sign of progress.

Professor Roberts said it was very much to be doubted whether a large number of questions on which we have are totally unfamiliar situation to most of us. He would first suggest that it was useful to take account on our minds of the type of case we were discussing. When we talked of Bukhara or the areas in advanced countries, one problem political authorities in the West would say we simply mean that poorer area. This was a case of a very useful field for economists. A Bukhara or a region must mean that its resources were potentially available in the region and could not be transferred to other regions, but could be developed to general advantage. The two papers dealt with studies where the resources available were natural resources. In other areas the resources were usually labour. The important thing about natural resources was that they had to be used where they were found. With labour, there was a choice of leaving them where they were, or moving them.

Since these were studies of the development of Bukhara areas with underdeveloped natural resources, the choice of development there was, in a sense, forced. But what would happen in the U.S.S.R. if they had big labour resources in a region and no very clear comparative advantage in any one line of activity in the present location?

Professor Roberts said that anyone coming from the U.K. had to get the scale right. He was always talking of small regions. To many Britons, both Armenia and Uzbekistan were countries. They were big places with much room, and with small labour in Bukhara areas within them. Surely some of these smaller Bukhara areas did have perhaps significant natural labour—a labour available, but not natural resources. How did it handle these Bukhara areas? He recognised the increasing concern of the U.S.S.R. with agricultural improvement. One general issue was if large resources could be moved to exist, or what was the optimum size for growth concerns in such an area?

In any region, the labour force needed training and education. It was a danger to increase the skills available in an area simply by bringing in elements into the labour force. Probably many North or Italians in the South would prefer to go home, as would Scottish or English men in the North. These in the regions wanted the best jobs, but needed experience as well as education. So there had to be an immigrant group. What tends did in these two areas of the U.S.S.R. by immigration? Did in bring in senior management, middle management, or foremen? Search, how well was the immigrant group assimilated?

Professor Boserup said that, if he remembered his geography, Uzbekistan consisted of a rich valley with a narrow strip of land connecting it to barren steppe. In what sense was Uzbekistan an economic region? He deduced from its geography that an integration of regional policy in Uzbekistan with that in other regions must be essential. How did economic planning take this apparently unusual geographic situation into account?

Professor Plotnikov said he would concentrate on the issues of most general interest. First, he wanted to say why Professor Arakelyan and he had chosen Uzbekistan and Armenia for their papers. Uzbekistan was typical of all the republics in the Central Asian region. Armenia was typical of the Caucasian area.

On the criterion of backwardness, he would say there was economic backwardness in Armenia, an absence of manufacturing industry, or the presence of backward manufacturing plants. There was backwardness in agriculture, with serious hidden unemployment. There was also cultural backwardness, and even lack of civilisation in the European sense of the word.

How were these problems solved? He would say that when there was planned development, plans were based on several principles. First, they took natural resources into account. Second, from the very beginning great hopes had been pinned on specialisation. In Uzbekistan, for example, development had been based on cotton growing. In Azerbaijan development was based on using its oil. So the proper use of existing natural resources was the basis for 'take off'.

The U.S.S.R. did its best to differentiate its approach even within these big regions. In some smaller areas, they had developed industries requiring a good deal of electric power where it was available. Elsewhere, where there was ample labour, they had tried to develop the labour-intensive branches of industry. Transport costs for finished goods were taken into account, but in the early stages they had faced a serious problem – the lack of skilled workers among the indigenous population. This was, indeed, the biggest obstacle to development. The approach had been to bring skilled labour from the more central areas of the U.S.S.R., as well as training the indigenous population. He wanted to emphasise the importance of this migration from outside the region. These workers could also act as a nucleus for an efficient labour force. The process resulted in a great change in the national composition of the population of the backward regions.

How was this movement stimulated? Here one had an advantage of a planned economy. The employment of specialists was planned. So, for example, engineering graduates from technical institutes were sent to regions needing their particular skills. He did not want to conceal the fact that some such specialists did not want to go. It had not been possible, especially in the early period, to persuade everyone to want to go to these regions. Compulsion was a relative notion, but one had to remember that in the U.S.S.R. students studied free of charge in higher technical institutions. So they had a moral duty to go where the planners wanted for the first three years after they graduated. Then human factors came in. Once they went to the region, they often became attracted to it, or married and so were prepared to stay. At the beginning of this process, the whole country was too poor to use material stimuli, but now that the U.S.S.R. was richer, it was easier to offer material incentives to move to the regions.

Most of this related to the period before World War II, which had led to evacuation of plants to regions like this, greatly benefiting them. Many of these plants remained after 1945. Moscow, Leningrad and other towns established new plants. There were therefore some historical peculiarities and legacies in Russian development that one could not overlook. The larger Soviet passenger aircraft, for example, were being produced in Uzbekistan.

As for the finance of development, Professor Plotnikov was an expert in this field. When industrialisation began, the problem of finance was very difficult. There were no loans from abroad; but the problems had been solved. The U.S.S.R. had to rely on ploughing back the profits of nationalised enterprises, and on loans from the population. These funds were distributed among the regions of the U.S.S.R. but when industrialisation was financed in Uzbekistan, it took no account of the fact that Uzbekistan could finance very little of this development. At present 50 per cent of all resources for financing economic development came from central budget funds, and 50 per cent from local planning bodies. The latter knew the needs of their own regions.

Professor Mihailović had asked about urbanisation and whether there were attempts to control the growth of towns like Moscow. The authorities were trying to stabilise the size of Moscow at its present size. But the growth of Moscow after 1917 had been very rapid. It was now 3 times the 1917 size. The U.S.S.R. intended to prevent the population of Moscow going beyond seven million. It was not intended to allow the urban region to attract new plants, but to create a number of satellite towns some 50 to 100 kilometres from Moscow. Holding back the growth of large urban aggregations was a difficult problem. Towns with a population of not more than 50,000 were regarded as small. Despite the benefits of Russia's planned system, industry tended to develop in the large towns. So, unfortunately, one did not get the harmonised development of both large and small towns. One of the tasks in the current five-year plan was somehow to bring this about, but it was hard even now to see what the solution was.

Professor Turčan had asked about the harmonisation of the growth of the East and West of the country. Nature had decided that the bulk of Russia's national resources would be in the East, but 85 per cent of the population was at present in the West. It was very difficult to populate the East. One problem was climate. Everyone had heard of the Siberian winter, though the stories were often exaggerated. The current 5-year plan paid great attention to the development of the eastern part of the U.S.S.R., but skilled labour was short. It was now possible to use material incentives to persuade people to go east. The U.S.S.R. was now a different, richer country. In perspective-planning over twenty years, attention was now concentrated on the East. To give examples, the U.S.S.R. was creating one economic centre on the newly-discovered rich oil deposits of Siberia. In a climatically difficult part of Siberia, Russia was developing a large industrial complex based on diamond mining. The discussion of Lacq had shown how hard it was to base development on an easily-transported raw material. So the opportunities offered by central planning were taken. Few workers were needed for diamond mining, but one needed a sizeable town to make life tolerable for the workers; so more industry was being planned which could use other resources, in this case, timber.

Professor Plotnikov said they accepted what Professor Groenman had said about it being easy to have a high rate of growth if one began from great backwardness. Perhaps they should have elaborated this point more fully. But it was the final results of development that one should consider in reaching a judgement about growth in Uzbekistan and Armenia. Professor Plotnikov liked Goethe's remark that if a poet liked his poems too much, he should stop writing poetry. Similarly, had Russian economists liked their economic development simply because no problem remained, they would have stopped being economists. They wanted to be equally self-critical. This was why there were so many discussions of economic policy in Eastern Europe. The main task of economic science in the U.S.S.R. at the moment was to base planning in the future on a much more scientific understanding of the planning process. At present there were about fifty economic research institutes in Russia, with 20,000 economists trying to solve these problems. Special attention was being given to the role of mathematical methods in planning.

Professor Vito accepted the answer to the question on the movement of labour from rural to urban centres. Professor Plotnikov had said this was done by planning, and explained how one could transfer trained men. It was a way to repay the benefits they had been given through higher education. Did this mean there had been no use of wage differentials, even when the proportion of unskilled labour had been very high?

Professor Plotnikov had also said that 50 per cent of the finance of development came from the central planning body and 50 per cent from local allocations. Did this mean that a republic which could put more into development received more from the central department too?

Professor Arakelyan said he was grateful for the stimulating approach of the Round Table to these two papers.

He had been asked why Armenia had nationalised enterprises but no manufacturing. The nationalisation of industry occurred in Armenia in 1921. In his paper, he had said that large-scale industries were nationalised. He meant by this, copper mines, firms making wine and brandy, the railway system and the banks.

He had also been asked about the sources of aid to Armenia. Was it from the central area of the U.S.S.R.? He wanted to stress that originally it had to come from the more developed central area. However, the local population did not simply wait for aid, but contributed to economic growth itself. The economic development of Armenia was based on a degree of specialisation because industries which could use local resources were developed first. He emphasised that Armenia now accounted for only 0·13 per cent of the territory of the U.S.S.R. but for 9 per cent of its population. To give an idea of the kind of specialisation, he would explain that Armenia produced up to 25 per cent of the total output of some products made in the U.S.S.R. He was proud of the fact that Armenia could now sell its products to other parts of the U.S.S.R. and, indeed, could export goods like machinery.

On the question about children, he said that the definition was that schoolchildren were those from 8 to 16 years of age. Education was compulsory in the U.S.S.R. during this period. The figures on the number of students related only to institutions of higher learning – of university level. There were many postgraduate students.

The demographic upsurge in Armenia had been strengthened by immigration, especially after 1945. To create jobs for the population, various methods were used to stimulate economic growth, and this explained why the rate of growth in Armenia was so much higher than in the U.S.S.R. as a whole.

Professor Plotnikov, in answer to Professor Vito, explained that, in 1913, 67 per cent of the population of the U.S.S.R. lived in the country. There were now 77 per cent in towns. This migration was encouraged by the better material conditions found in the towns, the higher cultural levels, and differences in wages between town and country.

It had been pointed out that even in Australia it was agreed that planning would be needed to develop the Northern Territories. So it seemed that some planning was needed in all countries, whatever their political system.

ELEVENTH SESSION

Some Old and New Issues in Regional Development

Discussion of Paper by Professor E. M. Hoover

Professor Robertson said he would look not only at Professor Hoover's paper, but at the work of the conference as a whole, in an attempt to draw together the work of the Round Table.

Professor Hoover could not possibly have known when he wrote the paper what would be the main points to emerge from the discussions. It was a tribute to him that, despite this, his paper went a long way towards summing up the work of the conference.

The paper itself, Professor Robertson said, first asked why we had suddenly become so interested in regional policy, giving a number of reasons. He would himself have added other reasons. For example, he would have put more emphasis on problems of congestion. He would also mention the fact that countries had become disillusioned with grandiose plans that were not based on detailed information. It was therefore necessary to add a regional dimension to national planning. The Round Table had shown that there were common problems here for western and socialist economies. In the eastern countries, there was a broad plan, formulated at the centre, giving weight to what would be required by what we should call market forces.

Professor Hoover went on to discuss national and regional welfare, making the point that national growth required one to use fiscal as well as monetary measures, and that structural unemployment could co-exist with inflation. This led back to problems of the labour force, and especially of training, which might lead, in turn, to regional policy. Here Professor Hoover became sceptical, stressing that not all regions needed help. Professor Hoover pointed out that not all relevant areas benefited from growth. Professor Robertson said he would simply say that all suffered from decline. On whether to move jobs to people or people to jobs, Professor Hoover stated the differences between place-prosperity and people-prosperity, favouring the latter. Professor Robertson agreed that more mobility was desirable if accompanied by more training, but that the solution was not necessarily to move the worker to the work. Fair as ever, Professor Hoover favoured a little of each.

Professor Hoover went on to ask if regional policy was charity or investment. He did not seem certain of the answer. He said that it was necessary to try to increase human welfare, but Professor Robertson would argue later that this was an ambiguous term.

The next major issue in the paper was growth poles. The paper pointed out that these differed in poor and rich countries; in agricultural and rural areas. The paper suggested that there should be more growth points in the U.S.A. in rural areas. The contribution of larger rather than smaller growth points was to solve regional problems by creating a link with developing regions. They also benefited the 'foreign trade' of the region. There might be leakages from the multiplier effects of the initial investment in small growth areas because of a lack of service trades on which to spend.

Professor Hoover went on to consider whether intraregional migration was easier than wider migration. He said it was not, but the evidence was American and related especially to Pittsburgh and the Apallachian region.

Finally, the paper turned to the size of urban centres and its effect on growth and regional policy. Perhaps, in future, the issue would not be a matter of size but of the relationship between centres of different sizes.

Professor Robertson said he had concentrated on criticisms of Professor Hoover's paper. He would now comment on what he thought had been the most important issues during the Round Table meeting.

What were these issues? What was the problem? It had become clear that there were differences in the scale of the problem of backwardness, and between the problems in developed and backward-rural regions. There were also differences in economic and social systems between countries. But one could quite easily set down a fairly comprehensive list of the indicators of distress in a region. Almost all the stress here had been on low income, unemployment, disguised unemployment and heavy outward migration.

But all this was perhaps descriptive. Was not the issue how to use the resources of the region, whether natural resources or labour? Backward areas in advanced countries always had labour resources, though they might also have underused natural resources, as explained in the papers about the U.S.S.R. Where there were good natural resources, the problem was not so much a regional, as a development, problem.

The basic problem of backward areas was therefore how to tap the labour potential for development. The classical answer would be that people would move. The labour surplus would lead to low wages, and labour would move out to earn more. One could not advocate this as a policy, although it might be a possible answer. It might even be the right answer for some areas. But one could not wish away the whole of large regions and communities. A continuing tendency to the under-use of resources, on the other hand, would bring some tendency for people to leave. So regional policy stated that, despite emigration, and despite some particular places being abandoned, one needed to choose priorities for the development of backward areas in order to steer industrial development and infrastructure towards them, and asked for a commitment by the Government to do so.

If one accepted, as Professor Hoover had, the objective of improving social welfare, this was a topic that was dealt with in very long books, and there was in any case the question of whose welfare. Professor Hoover had not discussed what were the units whose welfare one was improving. To some extent the answer for regional policy was simply the inhabitants of backward areas, but one could not stop there. Even without any regional policy, there was already a commitment to the social welfare of those in backward areas. It was national policy to pay benefits to the unemployed, the sick, etc. So one wanted some return on these social payments. One might take the growth of national output as the policy objective, but the question then was: where? There was always some choice of where to concentrate at any moment. Professor Robertson believed there were always limitations on one's objectives, but the precise limitations on regional policy had to be looked at individually in each particular case with an eye to the returns as well as the costs of the priorities selected.

Everyone had agreed that one must select, and then appraise, the potential of the region before doing so. This implied some evaluation of a social character and some physical planning too. Then came the question of the degree of commitment to the various regions. One might look at (*a*) the increase in national output if a given region was developed; (*b*) how far the use of resources in a region was costless because they would not otherwise be used; (*c*) the extent to which the country was already committed to create an infrastructure so that, again, there were no opportunity costs in using such infrastructure effectively within the region. Having tentatively accepted a given policy one was therefore required to carry out some kind of at least rudimentary arithmetic to calculate the return on it.

Professor Robertson was worried by the increasing tendency in the West to measure the return on investment with discounting techniques which seemed to overlook the fact that both decline and growth were very long-run processes. He suspected there would have been no growth at all in some countries if some contemporary decision techniques had been applied. There would have to be some general policies for regional development, for example, for education and training. Some general policies for industry were equally useful for regions. The provision of general advice was also a policy. Here, however, he would emphasise the need for selective policies on providing infrastructure. Infrastructure had advantages if concentrated in particular areas. First, it created employment and income. Second, it conferred external economies of scale and minimised leakages. As for the location of a growth point, this did not have to be a completely new location, but it had to be one to which there was a special commitment. There must be some potential for growth. It must not be a very large urban area, because one then got problems of congestion, and when economists associated growth centres with new areas, this was often because the existing centre was too big to be safely increased in size. Whether new or old, there must be a clear choice and commitment.

Countries had limited resources, and one could not get economies of aggregation everywhere. He did not necessarily think that agricultural areas had to have smaller growth centres than industrial areas, though this would usually happen. He had concluded from the discussions that the minimum size of a growth centre should be about 100,000. It was interesting that one got this figure both in the U.S.A. and in the U.S.S.R.

Professor Robertson did not think the conference had paid enough attention to the fact that an effective regional policy required administrative coherence. Whatever else it did, regional policy had to consider all aspects of a region and it was difficult to get government departments always to hold the same views, or even to discover from them what current government policy was. Agencies to co-ordinate regional policy were therefore essential. The Round Table had shown that even where regional policy was coherent, one still had to work out the right machinery.

Professor Hague said he would like to comment on the pleas for more interdisciplinary work in the field covered by the Round Table. He felt certain that work on a behavioural theory of the firm by men like Cyert and March would turn out to be a major contribution to economics in the next decade. One major contribution of this work was to show that the aims of the firm were multiple and somewhat inconsistent. While this might make it difficult to explain what went on in the firm, he believed it could help those who actually ran firms. It helped them to see that the conflicting objectives and untidy organisation of firms was something that could be analysed and understood.

He thought the same help could be given to civil servants and politicians trying to work out policies for backward areas of developed (or, indeed, under-developed) countries. They had to face the same complexity and inconsistency in objectives. This not only meant that a new field for interdisciplinary analysis of the firm was opening up; it also meant that different parts of economics were beginning to be linked together in new ways.

Professor Hague briefly mentioned four other points. First, as a citizen of Manchester, he was surprised that the weather had not been mentioned as a factor determining where people wanted to live. Once a country became affluent, people were bound to feel more and more free to live in places that attracted them, often well away from the older industrial centres.

Second, he thought that one of Europe's problems was the way in which people were much more tied to existing social capital – especially buildings – than was true in the U.S.A. He doubted whether the social capital in the North of England and in Scotland was as valuable as some participants had suggested. He wondered, with Professor Samuelson, if we did not exaggerate the cost of abandoning older conurbations and setting up new industrial centres in more attractive and economic locations.

Third, and in some ways linked to this, he wondered if there was not some special pleading in the scepticism of Professor Robertson about the use of discounted cash flow techniques in investment decision taking. He had taught large numbers of both businessmen and civil servants who wanted to stop using D.C.F. whenever it failed to give the answer they had decided on in advance. It was vital that we should all be scrupulously honest in the way we took this kind of investment decision, and D.C.F. was one way of checking on ourselves.

Finally, Professor Hague wanted to point to the role of universities as what a Frenchman might call 'institutions motrices'. He thought especially of the 'Research Triangle' in North Carolina, with Duke University, the University of North Carolina and the State College of Raleigh at its vertices. This had attracted the research departments of a number of firms. No doubt, links between university and industrial research were easier to foster in the U.S.A. than in other countries, but the role of universities in fostering economic development was easily overlooked. He had felt for some time that in the U.K. new universities should be established only near growth points in development areas, where they could provide direct employment to the service trades as well as perhaps helping to attract research-minded firms.

Professor Davin made three points. On the population problem, he thought it correct that one could have doubts about a policy that ignored the population explosion, though population pressure was not the same everywhere. Perhaps one should compare India and some developed countries. He did not think the problem was too serious in holding back development. There was not a population explosion, but ageing. One did not have to condemn a policy that accepted an increase in population. And even if there was excess population, one could solve the problem by emigration or an appropriate investment policy.

Second, mobility of labour was therefore the way to eliminate an excess of population. Mobility depended on the particular region and on whether the emigrants were made welcome elsewhere. In advanced countries, trade unions often put a brake on emigration. Finally, accessibility to markets could be a stimulating element.

Professor Winiarski said that Professor Hoover was well known in Poland as an exponent of the classical theory of spatial economics. What he would like to know was what Professor Hoover meant by the effect of the development of regional science on the general theory of economics. How could one link the theory of regional economics with the theory of economic growth?

Professor Groenman said Professor Hoover had a good deal to say about the contribution of the false gods: place-prosperity and people-prosperity. We knew all about the bad effects of emigration. However, he was not quite satisfied about what was said on population and jobs. He agreed that a growth of population was not a blessing in itself. In the Netherlands, if a town reached a population of 100,000 they hung out flags – but why? Was not income per head more important than numbers of persons or numbers of jobs?

Professor von Böventer said he had been giving thought to some theoretical questions during the Round Table, and especially to the relation between aggregates and structures.

If one were in a very simple world (with very simple functional relationships), one would split regional problems into two separate kinds. First, one would have the problem of mobilising resources – a regional approach. Then one could consider the development of industry via a sectoral approach. The real situation was not so simple. The complexity of the theoretical relationships ruled out these approaches.

If *all* the relevant initial conditions and functional relationships as well as the goals of individuals and of society as a whole could be stated in a sufficiently clear and exact manner, and if mathematics was able to solve this optimising problem, then the macro- and micro-economic approaches would merge. Nor would it make any difference whether, on the one hand, one solved the problem as a micro-economic problem with the macro-economic relations as side conditions or whether, on the other hand, the micro-economic relationships were treated as the side conditions of a macro-economic optimising problem.

Because – owing to the lack of information and the complexity of the functional relationships – this was impossible, we had to start where we felt reasonably certain. One could start from a micro-economic approach, from partial approaches to particular problems and then proceed to something broader, taking account of important macro-economic restrictions. One would have to fit together all partial solutions, trying to remove contradictions. One could determine the optimum of the system by a process of iteration.

To illustrate the difficulties encountered in the determination of an optimal location, he returned to an example with no spatial dimensions, but with the two dimensions of size and quality of a commodity in a highly heterogeneous market. What were the optimum values for these two dimensions that a producer should choose? If one did not have more specific information, one would have an infinite number of degrees of freedom. To derive everything from scratch, as it were, one would have to postulate the supply and demand functions for each quality of product and for all individuals, assume some kind of utility maximisation, and then solve the whole system for any number of different kinds of heterogeneous products. This was too complex, partly because one must allow for the fact that utility functions themselves depended on the industrial structure. It would therefore be impossible to solve the problem in this way.

How, then, should one proceed to reduce the degrees of freedom? In location problems (with two spatial dimensions), raw material sites could serve as guideposts for finding locational optima. In the model of a heterogeneous market, an analogy to this could be found: predetermined *sizes* of inputs that the firm uses. Input sizes and qualities could therefore be treated as data in the two-dimensional quality space, just as the raw materials concentrated at particular points in space were treated as data in locational problems. In this way, the number of degrees of freedom was somewhat reduced, but not enough to yield satisfactory solutions. Keeping in mind that in reality optimal sizes and qualities of, say, television sets to produce were also not derived within theoretical economic models, one should not be surprised that optimal locational patterns also had to be determined by trial and error, or by iterative procedures.

Professor von Böventer suggested that we should tackle the problem on three levels. First, one could start from the given resources of the economy, and especially from the available production techniques. One could derive from comparative advantage and from empirical inter-industry relations an optimum sectoral structure for the economy. This should simultaneously determine optimal output quantities, optimal input coefficients, and the optimal size of enterprise. Having determined all this, one could go on, secondly, to ask what was the optimum spatial layout. This would be a function of the locations of the immobile resources of the economy. Their locations would reduce the number of degrees of freedom substantially.

For the empirical study of spatial relationships, one did not simply have to determine input-output relations, but the structure of a much wider range of economic relationships than the usual input-output relationships. One needed to know which other enterprises each firm found it necessary to be close to, and what were the costs of being farther away from other economic agents – not just in terms of transportation costs for inputs. Optimal locations and sizes of industrial complexes would have to be chosen in such a way as to maximise the number of the internal locational relationships of the complexes and to minimise the relationships that meant high transport or information costs. So one would go on to supplement the first analysis with spatial relationships.

The third approach required an analysis of agglomeration economies for the service factor. On the one hand, there was a kind of hierarchical Christaller system of supply sites for services. On the other hand, for other services, one had a certain degree of specialisation between different service centres. This analysis had to include a consideration of the sizes and input coefficients of service enterprises and of their spatial relationships. The effects of the spatial layout of administrative centres or offices had also to be brought in.

Finally, what preferences did the population have as to where it wanted to live, as distinct from where to work and where to do its shopping? Community size was relevant; this had to be seen more and more as a sociological problem.

These four different approaches did not necessarily all produce the same answer. So one needed to determine an optimum for all four aspects simultaneously. At the same time, one had to study the effect of the traffic and communications system on the optimal spatial structure. One could see how hard it was to get a satisfactory result. The solution always meant breaking up the problem and using an iterative procedure by which one gradually approached the optimum.

Mr MacLennan thought one point neglected in the discussion was regional planning. A good deal of work was being done on this in many countries. For example, Professor Penouil had mentioned the work in France, and a lot of skilled manpower and time was being devoted to regional planning in the U.K. To justify regional policy in national terms meant that regional and national plans must fit together. The first need was thus for a national policy for the regions, with some consideration of points like those made by Professor von Böventer. For instance, if a lot of old social capital in certain areas had to be replaced, there would be interregional effects, for example, in roads. The development of backward areas took time, and unless one based national development on a certain pattern of regional development, one would be half-hearted about it. The rate of growth would then be optimal, neither for the regions nor the whole economy.

Second, regional planning was being practised in the U.K., but the question of what regional planners should do was still in debate. Would Professor Hoover advocate concentrating on problems of technique and measurement on a large scale? This was a costly option and carried with it the implication of control over the location of private industry in accordance with static models. There were important issues here. Was there an alternative function of regional planners? Should they concentrate instead on certain deficiencies of regions, like the lack of adequate and planned infrastructure and suitable labour?

Professor Vito said that Professor Hoover had asked whether growth points did not have the same role in both advanced and backward regions. Of course

Q

they did not, but there were doubts on what one would suggest for backward areas. Professor Hoover said the population must migrate or commute. He would add, for Italy, the need for investment in infrastructure to develop the regions. Professor Vito thought that information was always important in advanced countries, but better information could also help underdeveloped and declining areas.

Finally, there was the big problem of place-prosperity versus people-prosperity. All agreed that in principle one wanted the latter. But regional growth was a mixed blessing because not all benefited from it. One needed more details of industrial measures and tasks, and on the precise objectives of regional policies. To distinguish between people- and place-prosperity was not enough. One needed to look at the problem in more detail.

Dr McCrone emphasised the need for better statistical data. At present far too little was known about the development of many problem regions and this was why there was so much disagreement on what should be done. For example, the Scottish Plan had contained growth targets; yet there were no official estimates of the Scottish gross domestic product even for current years. There were few European regions in a better position.

He thought it was essential first of all to have regional income and output figures if the circumstances of the regional economy were to be properly understood. Too often policy was based on unemployment percentages and thereby tended to become a social rather than an economic policy. But to have proper statistics, it was necessary to define regions. In the U.K. definitions had changed many times and some government departments used different classifications from others. This was an unnecessary addition to the problems that had to be faced.

Second, a clearer understanding of costs was essential to policy decisions. For example, a rational decision on whether to move work to the workers or vice versa in a particular case should be based on a full appreciation of the costs involved, both economic and social. This type of cost/benefit analysis was quite impossible with present information. It was necessary to have some idea of the effect on industrial costs of operating in different locations and the effect on costs borne by the community of a concentrated or dispersed pattern of economic activity.

Professor Mihailović returned to migration. How did one distinguish this? Should territorial or social groupings be considered? Although it was important to make all factors mobile, one needed to look at mobility in its historical context and in different countries and conditions. In Yugoslavia, there was migration pressure from rural to urban areas. But they did not know the costs of inter-regional migration. The migration was not just a question of people looking for jobs, but of the whole population. What did it mean if one said a region must die? What were the psychological consequences? Even in a dying region, social and economic attitudes were an important barrier to change. Many problems had to be tackled in regions, such as education, for instance.

Professor Robertson said he did not agree with Professor Hague on D.C.F. He would not want to throw it away, but nevertheless doubted how successful it would be for taking decisions at the regional level because of interrelations between investments and the importance of economic and social factors. One so often had to deal with a series of investments that were linked in both space and time, like roads or airports.

So far as tastes were concerned, people often wanted to live in places they were used to. Migrants usually moved to jobs or houses linked with higher incomes. Only quite marginal changes might be needed, since what mattered was net migration, allowing for both inflows and outflows.

To Dr McCrone, he would simply say that the British statistics were nothing like so bad as he suggested.

Professor Hoover replied to the discussion of his paper and made some comments on the Round Table as a whole.

In his paper he had suggested that various attitudes about population growth and the effects of static or declining population were held mainly in the U.S.A. He now saw that this was wrong, and that there were similar tendencies in Europe, including some irrational views. Indeed, he saw greater reason for Europeans to hold narrow, even parochial, views on the growth of population in a region.

So far as Professor Robertson's introduction was concerned, the suggestion appeared to be that the paper contained more sins of omission than of commission. He suspected he would later become aware, however, of a few Scottish time bombs !

Early in the paper he had said that one had a choice between giving charity to regions or investing in them. His view was that one would need both. One gave charity to people, but people in need of charity were concentrated particularly in backward and distressed regions. One could do three things. First, one could move these people to where there were better opportunities. Second, one could subsidise or redevelop the region. Third, one could put people on the dole – make transfer payments to them. The third solution represented pure charity, though there might be elements of charity in subsidies to development. In the end, perhaps one might decide that the best way to help the people in a region was to do so by developing the existing region, even though one might get better returns from development elsewhere.

He had suggested that the establishment of growth points raised special problems for rural areas with no industry. This might be a particularly American attitude, but surely it must be a valid view in every context. One did not need to worry about creating growth centres as such where there was a complex of large cities supplying an urban focus for development.

Turning to the distance factor in migration, Professor Hoover said he had been trying to qualify the traditional view that it was easier to promote migration over shorter rather than longer distances. This was essential to the idea that one had to create growth poles. He agreed that the evidence he had given in his paper was about a particular case and was not to be taken generally. But he would argue that the declining importance of constraints on mobility was part of a real trend for the future. He had suggested in his paper that the time and money costs of travelling longer distances were progressively declining relatively to the cost of travelling shorter distances. So, with improved communication, regions were becoming more alike. He thought the influence of distance as a factor holding back migration was progressively diminishing.

Professor Hoover said that Professor Vito had pointed to a passage in his paper (p. 355) where he argued that for people like those in the Appalachians the only hope was to move, or to commute to the growing centres. Professor Vito had interpreted this to mean that they must leave the Appalachians. He had actually said they must either migrate or commute, which allowed them to live at home but travel to work, so he had given alternatives. He had merely pointed out the implications of a falling population for the economic development of an area. Professor Robertson had argued that a decline in the population of an area was bad because it meant underutilisation of resources. He could not accept this. What was underutilisation of resources? What indeed were resources? Professor Robertson presumably meant that if resources were committed to a location, they should not be moved, and these resources might or might not be people.

As Professor Hague had said, one could reasonably doubt the value of much old social infrastructure. This was often worse than valueless because one would actually have to demolish it. Industries as well as regions declined, and economists did not always think of the obsolescence of industrial capital as bad. If a particular new location seemed ideal, one would not have a cost for infrastructure simply because one was building there.

He was afraid that members of the Round Table had exaggerated on some points, and fallen into using clichés. A lot had been said about the bad effects of emigration and its effect on the quality of the remaining population in an area, especially its occupational and age structure, which might destroy the possibility of progress. He would, on the contrary, assert that emigration could make the future development of an area easier. Were participants not confusing the total depopulation of an area with its scaling down? He did not think the total depopulation of an area was a likely issue. A worked-out oilfield on the Persian Gulf might present a case for total depopulation, as there had been in some mining areas in North America. But such cases were very rare.

Professor Samuelson had mentioned Vermont, where there had been a drastic reduction of population because the area could no longer support so big a population. This was the logical result. Similarly, the population of Manhattan Island had been falling since 1910, and everyone welcomed it because it reflected relief of extreme congestion in slum areas.

We should remember that when we thought of emigration depleting the labour reserves of an area, we were thinking of really valuable resources. We looked on emigration as taking away those with skills, and so actively creating a labour shortage in the midst of high unemployment. This was a paradoxical idea, but perhaps, in general, it was a potential shortage of skills, not an active one. If skilled workers really were scarce, they would be likely to stay. What it came to was that there were none to spare, and any expansion would mean a shortage of skilled labour. Participants had said a lot about the selective character of migration, but what did we really know? Could we be as sure as we should be about its nature and effects without much more serious studies of it? He would, however, point out that probably migration from the American South-East did not follow this pattern. It was concentrated not on the most, but the least, productive and educated part of the population, with a big emigration of Negroes, contradicting the idea that it was the most able and educated that left.

Even if one granted that emigration was selective and that the area lost those of most use to it, this did not necessarily mean that one should curb emigration. There was an alternative. One could make emigration less selective, taking a more balanced cross-section of the population. Most aids to mobility, like education or information, would make emigration much less selective and so less damaging.

Professor Hague had spoken of the role of universities as growth centres, and had quoted the case of North Carolina. There were similar concentrations in Boston and California. In Pittsburgh there had been discussions on whether there might not be great possibilities there for the encouragement of local industrial growth *via* research. It had turned out that, despite the large amount of research carried out in Pittsburgh, this was not quite the attractive force one might have expected. First, it was confined mainly to the internal laboratories of large corporations, for their own benefit, and with consequent barriers to communication. It was less of a community asset than if carried out in universities or small firms, where it could more easily become common property. Second, there was a narrow field of industrial specialisation, with most units engaged in ferrous metallurgy, glass, and a few other fields. A broader base would have been more attractive. Third, the area lacked other factors, like amenities. It was not generally considered to be quite as desirable as Southern California or North Carolina. Most of the areas of the U.S.A. where there had been a research boom were ones which were notably pleasant for scientists to live in as well as to work in.

Professor Hoover recalled that he had suggested that a simultaneous and equal increase in the size of population and the number of jobs was not necessarily beneficial. He accepted Professor Groenman's alternative criterion of income as a measure of benefit. But again a doubling of income accompanied by a simultaneous doubling of population was not necessarily beneficial either.

Professor Winiarski had asked a question to which a good book on location theory would be an answer, and Professor von Böventer had provided a better answer than he would have done himself. Yet even Professor von Böventer did not go into the dynamic aspects of the problem, though he did suggest that iteration was an appropriate technique to use. Professor Hoover was glad that Professor von Böventer saw prospects for using a matrix of inter-industry attraction, since he had suggested it in his paper.

Mr MacLennan had asked what regional planners should do. He did not feel qualified to decide, but thought Mr MacLennan was right in what he had said. He would argue that problems of techniques and of measurement were more fruitfully tackled on a wide scale. In the U.S.A., more and more thinking was being done on these matters in Washington on the national scale. For example, input-output tables were being worked out, not just for one region at a time, but also on an increasingly comprehensive multi-region basis.

Professor Robinson finally attempted to sum up some of the general results of the Conference, following the lines printed as an introduction to this volume.

Index

Entries in Black Type under the Names of Participants in the Conference indicate their Papers or Discussions of their Papers. Entries in Italics indicate Contributions by Participants to the Discussions.